T0296279

Artificial Intelligence for Healthcare Applications and Management

Artificial Intelligence for Healthcare Applications and Management

Boris Galitsky
Oracle Corporation, Redwood City, CA, United States

Saveli Goldberg
Division of Radiation Oncology, Massachusetts General Hospital, Boston, MA, United States

Academic Press is an imprint of Elsevier
125 London Wall, London EC2Y 5AS, United Kingdom
525 B Street, Suite 1650, San Diego, CA 92101, United States
50 Hampshire Street, 5th Floor, Cambridge, MA 02139, United States
The Boulevard, Langford Lane, Kidlington, Oxford OX5 1GB, United Kingdom

Library of Congress Cataloging-in-Publication Data
A catalog record for this book is available from the Library of Congress

British Library Cataloguing-in-Publication Data
A catalogue record for this book is available from the British Library

ISBN: 978-0-12-824521-7

For information on all Academic Press publications
visit our website at https://www.elsevier.com/books-and-journals

Publisher: Mara Conner
Editorial Project Manager: Chiara Giglio
Production Project Manager: Swapna Srinivasan
Cover Designer: Christian J. Bilbow

Typeset by STRAIVE, India

Contents

Contributors

Stanislav Belyaev
Critical Care, Eastern New Mexico Medical Center, Roswell, NM, United States

Boris Galitsky
Oracle Corporation, Redwood City, CA, United States

Saveli Goldberg
Division of Radiation Oncology, Massachusetts General Hospital, Boston, MA, United States

Dmitry Ilvovsky
Computer Science, HSE University, Moscow, Russia

Mark Prutkin
NICU, Regional Children Hospital, Ekaterinburg, Russia

CHAPTER

Introduction

1

Boris Galitsky

Oracle Corporation, Redwood City, CA, United States

...the day will come when, if we feel ill without knowing why, we will go to a physicist, who without asking us anything will draw blood into a syringe, derive certain data, multiply these, and the, havingconsulted a table of logarithms, cure us with a pill. For the moment, nevertheless, if I fell sick I would still go to an old country doctor, who would look me up and down, pat my stomach, put handkerchief over my chest and listen awhile, then cough, fill his pipe, and, stoking his chin, smile at me in order to cure me... I admire science, but I also admire wisdom.

de Saint-Exupery, A., 1982. Wartime Writings 1939-1944. Harcourt Brace Jovanovich, p. 9.

In recent years, advances in artificial intelligence (AI) technology have led to the rapid clinical implementation of devices with AI technology in the medical field. More than 60 AI-equipped medical devices have already been approved by the US Food and Drug Administration (FDA) in the United States, and the active introduction of AI technology is considered to be an inevitable trend in the future of medicine. AI applications are broadly used in pathology, radiology, dermatology, ophthalmology, oncology, and many other medical fields.

There are many factors driving the adoption of virtual health, including dramatic improvements in technology, increases in patient demand, restructuring of healthcare systems, accommodations in state and national health policies, and major improvements in health insurance coverage for virtual visits (Rutledge and Wood, 2020). Virtual health augmented with AI is expected to increase physicians' diagnostic accuracy, improves access to care, reduce costs, and alleviate provider shortages. AI in combination with virtual health creates a number of opportunities for unique interactions between physicians, patients, and technology.

Most AI in health applications today is in the field of **image analysis**. No matter how time-consuming and complex the tasks of medical image analysis are, the machine and the physician are in relatively equal conditions. Both have the same information for making a decision. One would hope that the reliability of the result obtained when testing the AI system would be preserved during its operation in the real-world hospital environment. A similar situation occurs when the actions of AI are based on objective laboratory and/or functional parameters of the organism. However, in medicine, the patient often stands between the state of the body and the physician with his or her assessment of the patient's condition. The physician must understand the real picture relying on this assessment. An AI system should do the same thing, but the task is more complicated now as the subjectivity and uncertainty of the doctor, who provides information to the AI, is added to the patient's subjectivity and uncertainty. Chapters 4, 5, 12, and 13 tackle these conditions.

Artificial Intelligence for Healthcare Applications and Management. https://doi.org/10.1016/B978-0-12-824521-7.00009-0

Search is a central application of AI in medicine, combining:

1. a hybrid semantic-keyword retriever, which takes an input query and returns a sorted list of most relevant documents, and
2. a re-ranker, which further orders the documents by relevance. The retriever is composed of a deep learning model that encodes query-level meaning, along with two keyword-based models (such as BM25, TF-IDF) that emphasize the most important words of a query. The re-ranker assigns a relevance score to each document, computed from the outputs of a question-answer module that gauges how much each document answers the query.

To account for the relatively limited dataset, a text augmentation technique is required. This splits the documents into pairs of paragraphs and the citations contained in them, creating millions of (citation title, paragraph) tuples for training the retriever. We focus on search applications in Chapter 7.

Improving **prediction** is one of the key challenges the medical industry faces in advancing patient care. Enhancing diagnosis, individualizing treatments, and understanding disease progression are all matters of prediction, an area where machine learning (ML) and AI excel. Reading this book, one can discover the impact AI innovations can have in medicine on both traditional healthcare systems and decision-making approaches. Through health industry case studies, the reader will better understand AI's applications and limitations, examine the challenges AI can help overcome, and explore how AI has already been deployed successfully in the sector.

Today, most patients do not encounter AI-supported medical treatment decisions on a regular basis, even in the most advanced healthcare service environments. We analyze why this is the case, provide historical insights on successful AI decision support (Chapter 5), and propose a number of techniques to make decision support more robust, natural, and usable for physicians' offices and hospitals.

AI has a key role in making a diagnosis, a deep understanding of what a patient is experiencing (Chapters 2–6, and 8).

A man walks into a doctor's office. He has a cucumber up his nose, a carrot in his left ear, and a banana in his right ear. "What's the matter with me?" he asks the doctor. The doctor replies, "You're not eating properly." (Fig. 1, Travelingboy, 2020).

The **COVID-19** global pandemic has resulted in international efforts to understand, track, and mitigate the disease, yielding a significant corpus of COVID-19-related publications across scientific disciplines. Throughout 2020, more than half a million COVID-19-related publications were collected through the COVID-19 Open Research Dataset. The dataset requires a semantic, multi-stage search engine designed to handle complex queries over the medical literature, potentially aiding overburdened health workers in finding scientific answers and avoiding misinformation during a time of crisis. We devote Chapters 7, 8, 11, and 14 to the semantic analysis of health texts.

The evolution of the SARS-CoV-2 virus, with its unique balance of virulence and contagiousness, led to the COVID-19 pandemic. Since December 2019, the disease has spread across our society exponentially, catalyzed by a modern air and road transportation system, along with dense urban centers where close contact amongst people yielded hubs of viral spread. We propose a technique to track people's contacts and reasons about their behavior, combining all kinds of data in a unified discourse pattern in Chapter 14.

A global effort has been made to stop the spread of the virus. Governments have shut down entire economic sectors, enforcing stay-at-home orders for many people. Hospitals have restructured themselves to cope with an unprecedented influx of intensive care unit patients, sometimes growing

FIG. 1

Making a diagnosis.

organically to increase their number of beds. Institutions have adjusted their practices to support efforts, repurposing assembly lines to build mechanical ventilators, delaying delivery of non-COVID-19-related shipments, and creating contact-tracing mobile apps and "digital swabs" to track symptoms and potential spread. Pharmaceutical enterprises and academic institutions have invested significantly in developing vaccines and therapeutics while deeply studying COVID-19. In Chapter 2, we explore possibilities to discover accompanying disorders from textual descriptions and patient records. Chapter 15 is devoted to content generation: how to substitute a doctor in writing personalized treatment plans at scale.

The health impacts of this crisis have been matched only by the economic backlash to society. Hundreds of thousands of small businesses have shut down, entire industrial sectors have been negatively impacted, and tens of millions of workers have been laid off. Even after our global society succeeds at controlling the virus' spread, we will be faced with many challenges, including re-opening our societies, lifting stay-at-home orders, deploying better testing, developing vaccines and therapeutics, aiding the unemployed, and more. One of the things that will assist recovery is openness and access to information facilitated by a dialogue system, such as the one described in Chapter 9.

The global response to COVID-19 has yielded a growing corpus of scientific publications about coronaviruses and related topics, increasing at a rate of ten thousand per month. Healthcare practitioners, policymakers, medical researchers, and others fighting the disease require specialized tools to keep up with the literature. This book presents a series of linguistic technologies supporting this fight. The persistence of the personnel fighting the disease can only be matched by the persistence of the chatbot presented in Chapter 10.

As COVID-19 continues to spread across the globe, companies and researchers are looking to use AI as a way of addressing the challenges of the virus. A number of research projects are using AI to identify drugs developed to fight other diseases but that could now be repurposed to take on coronavirus. BenevolentAI's knowledge graph can digest large volumes of scientific literature and biomedical research to find links between the genetic and biological properties of diseases and the composition and action of drugs (Richardson, 2020). We focus on building a knowledge graph in Chapter 11.

While a large body of biomedical research has built up around chronic diseases over decades, COVID-19 only has a few months' worth of studies attached to it. However, researchers can use the information they have to track down other viruses with similar elements, see how they function, and then work out which drugs could be used to inhibit the virus. The COVID-19 Open Research Dataset Challenge (CORD-19) is an initiative supported by the US White House and other prominent institutions. Chapter 11 addresses the handling of a large corpus of texts for data mining in medicine.

The COVID-19 virus binds to a particular protein on the surface of ACE2 cells. The knowledge graph helps to look at broader processes surrounding that entry of the virus and its replication, instead of focusing on anything specific in COVID-19 itself. Having assigned knowledge graph nodes to specific studies, scientists can look back at the literature that concerns different coronaviruses, including SARS, and all of the kinds of biological processes occurring while viruses are being taken in cells (Best, 2020). In Chapter 2, we focus on the linguistic support for multi-case-based reasoning, and in Chapter 11, we focus on knowledge graphs and ontologies.

The potential of AI **to transform health care** through the work of both organizational leaders and medical professionals is increasingly evident as more real-world clinical applications emerge. As patient datasets become larger, manual analysis is becoming less feasible. AI has the power to process data efficiently far beyond our own capacity, and has already enabled innovation in areas including chemotherapy regimens, patient care, breast cancer risk, and even ICU death prediction (Fig. 2). In Chapter 3, we explore ways to support diagnosis relying on linguistic technologies.

AI prediction systems were capable of forecasting the coronavirus outbreak, stating that it could become a global pandemic. This was done at the beginning of winter 2019/2020, back when COVID-19 was still localized to the Chinese city of Wuhan (O'Brien and Larson, 2020). The earliest signs of the outbreak were identified by mining in Chinese language local news media such as WeChat and Weibo to highlight the fact that you could use these tools to uncover what is happening in a population. The information retrieval system identified the growing cluster of unexplained pneumonia cases before human researchers did it manually, although it only ranked the outbreak's seriousness as "medium."

In this book, the reader will develop a thorough understanding of AI's growing role in health care. The reader will also explore how AI strategies have already been successfully deployed in health care, and learn to ask the right questions when evaluating an ML technique for potential use within a specific environment. The book provides an overview of discourse analysis technology before delving into its practical adoption in language-related tasks, in both hospital processes and resource management.

The reader will examine the use of AI in diagnosis and patient monitoring and care and explore how it can be applied to enhance healthcare data management. The book develops a framework to assess the viability of using AI within a medical context.

1. The issues of ML in medicine this book is solving

- **Errors in train and test datasets.** As more ML systems are being developed and deployed in healthcare establishments, the accuracy of ML systems exceeds an average accuracy of decisions of physicians, according to ML professionals. However, ML accuracy is determined by the golden set

FIG. 2

Learn AI for health!

for train and test parts: the model obtained from the train set is assessed on a test set. The golden set frequently contains errors and these are not always random. These errors distort both the model and its accuracy estimates, and thus the performance of ML systems (Chapter 4).

- **ML methods are inadequate for a given medical problem**. Attempts to achieve 100% accuracy are inconsistent with the nature of a given medical problem. This is particularly true for the task of predicting the recovery process of a disease. Long-term recovery is frequently affected by the model features that cannot be considered in patient medical records at the stages of diagnosis and treatment. COVID-19 is an example of such a disease. Frequently, it is hard to make a correct diagnosis; sometimes, multiple simultaneous diagnoses are possible. Moreover, the accuracy of the diagnoses themselves is questionable (Chapter 5).

- **ML applications are limited with respect to locations and dates.** Health databases describe patients being treated at a specific location and at a specific time. However, the application of our conclusions is assumed not only in a given place and not in the past, but in the future. The problem of the representativeness of the training sets is a standard, well-known problem of ML; however, in medicine it is even harder and more significant as illnesses occur and evolve in space and time (Chapter 5).
- **Discrepancies in terminology and understanding of medical terms** and the level of reliability of medical indicators between the place of application of the ML and the place of development. This general ML problem is well known, but in medicine it is increased by discrepancies in the understanding of medical terms, symptoms, and diagnoses as well as the reliability of medical equipment, even in different hospitals, not to mention different countries (Chapter 5).
- **Cognitive bias in physician-provided information to ML systems.** In the practice of using ML, the doctor provides a description of the patient to obtain the ML decision and its explanation. In this case, a manifestation of the physician's subjectivity in the choice and assessment of disease parameters is possible. The doctor observes and pays attention to the features that correspond to his, perhaps unconscious, initial hypothesis about the diagnosis but does not notice the features that contradict it. Thus, the doctor who is not sure of his hypothesis, but nevertheless subconsciously selects the facts confirming it, receives the same decision from ML based on these facts. Now the physician is confident in their decision that is possibly erroneous (Chapter 5, Fig. 3).
- **AI's estrangement from real medical practice.** The doctor usually has to make a sequence of decisions. Relying on ML decisions in one step of this sequence, without a clear understanding of

FIG. 3

Machine vs human learning.

this decision, can negatively affect subsequent decisions and destroy the entire chain. The loss of physician's time because of this may be more significant than the benefit of the AI (Chapter 5).

- **A lack of understanding of AI solutions.** The need to explain AI decisions is becoming such an important element of AI that it is now necessary for implementing AI (Chapter 12).
- **A loss of physician responsibility for clinical decision and a loss of qualifications.** The growing credibility of AI solutions inevitably diminishes a physician's sense of responsibility for decisions and results. By reducing the need for doctor experience, the use of such systems can gradually lead to the loss of human competence as well as the accuracy of future decisions. It is well known that a reduction in the accuracy of the ML system is caused by the evolution of the domain, when the training occurred based on the original, and old patient records and current patient records, which may deviate significantly. The evolution rate in health informatics can be much faster than that of the self-learning ability of ML (Chapter 12).
- **Legal, psychological, emotional, and ethical** problems in the relationship between the doctor and the AI system, as well as strengthening and stimulating intellectual activity of physicians. Chapter 13 discusses the use of AI to create game situations, psychological stimulus, and context-based visual presentation of information to enhance the intellectual activity of physicians in problem solving.
- **Recommending questions to ask.** With a high load on the physician, it is hard to remember which questions a patient has been asked and which they have not. There is a need for a decision support technique that automatically suggests questions a patient should ask a doctor, as well as questions a doctor should ask a patient. This facilitates proper diagnosis as well as proper understanding of the treatment by the patient (Chapter 6).
- **Most available AI systems lack necessary knowledge.** There is a need **to acquire knowledge from text relying on ontologies**, and discourse analysis helps to identify portions of text to extract ontology entries from (Chapter 11).
- **Medical knowledge is represented in both text and numerical values.** In particular, health records combine textual descriptions with features expressed in strings and numbers. How to unify data processing algorithms over texts and numerical data? How to conduct health management that relies on a wide variety of data modalities such as phone calls, web logs, driving trajectories, and text messages? We propose a unified approach to discourse that covers various forms of data in Chapter 14 (Fig. 4).
- **Personalized medical content** tailored to the needs of an individual patient (Chapter 15).

Fig. 5 shows the popularity of various ML algorithms as assessed through searching within health care on PubMed. In this book, we apply SVM in Chapter 14, Neural Networks in Chapters 6–8 and 15, Nearest Neighbor in Chapters 2, 3, and 11, and Decision Tree in Chapter 2.

2. AI for diagnosis and treatment

Despite AI breakthroughs for diagnosing and curing particular diseases, there is a long way to go until patients feel that AI supports their illness as outpatients or while they are in the hospital. Therefore, AI for **health management** is a bottleneck on the path toward a fully integrated intelligent environment for patients, which is the topic of the current book.

FIG. 4

Computers handle multimodal data.

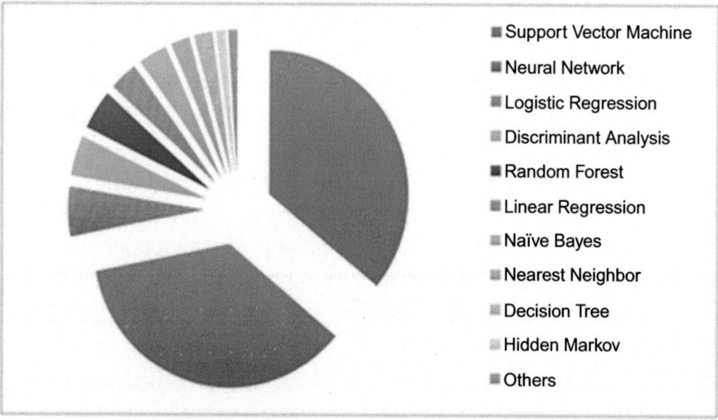

FIG. 5

ML methods in health and their popularity (Jiang et al., 2017).

We enumerate examples of great AI deployments in various classes of diseases (Fig. 6).

Oncology: Somashekhar et al. (2016) showed that the IBM Watson for oncology would be a reliable AI system for assisting the diagnosis of cancer through a double-blinded validation study. Esteva et al. (2017) analyzed clinical images to identify skin cancer subtypes.

Neurology: Bouton et al. (2016) designed an AI system to restore the control of movement in patients with quadriplegia. Farina et al. (2017) tested the power of an offline man/machine interface that uses the discharge timings of spinal motor neurons to control upper-limb prostheses.

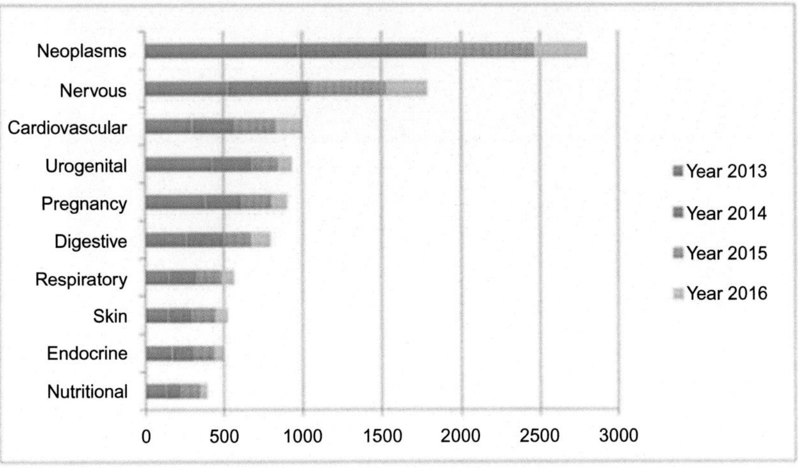

FIG. 6

AI research per disease class (Jiang et al., 2017).

Cardiology: Dilsizian and Siegel (2014) introduced the potential application of intelligent systems to diagnose heart disease through cardiac imaging. Arterys (2017) received clearance from the FDA to market its Arterys Cardio DL application, which uses deep learning to provide automated, editable ventricle segmentations based on conventional cardiac MRI images.

Radiology is one of the areas where AI technology has been maximally adopted. Interestingly, most of the intelligent medical devices approved by the FDA related to oncology are in the field of radiology.

Although a majority of recent successful intelligent systems for medicine rely on unexplainable deep learning, patients demand full explainability from doctors (Fig. 7).

3. Health discourse

Most work in applications of computational linguistics in health relies on syntax and semantics of language. Syntax is important for information extraction, drug matching, processing electronic health records, and other tasks. Semantic analysis is essential for health recommenders, medical decision support, and to solve other problems requiring intelligence. Although semantic analysis builds and handles a logical representation of text, discourse analysis performs this task at a higher level of abstraction. As discourse analysis represents how doctors organize their thoughts on making diagnoses and suggesting treatment, these representations are essential for automated diagnoses and automated support of patients. Health discourse forms a skeleton of this book, providing underlying techniques for supported decision trees, matching multi-cases, dialogue management, multi-model representation, and content generation (Chapters 2, 3, 6–11, 14, and 15 and Fig. 8).

FIG. 7

Patients need doctors to explain the diagnosis and treatment.

FIG. 8

The main theme of this book.

Acknowledgments

The second author is grateful to E. Tsibulkin, D. Kazakov, M. Sklyar, V. Lomovskikch, and A. Makhanek, without whose participation there would be no DINAR2 (Chapter 5); D. Savelyev who programmed SAG (Chapter 13); M. Ancukiewicz, A. Turchin, and A. Niemerko, who took part in the analysis and prevention project of errors in databases (Chapter 4); D. Meshalkin for participation in the development of the concept to Dr. Watson-type systems (Chapter 13); and E. Pinsky, B. Weisburd, and A. Temkin for their participation in the development of the Meta-Agent concept (Chapter 12). We are grateful to M. Shifrin, N. Shklovsky-Kordi, Y. Metelitsa, and I. Novikov for fruitful discussions on all aspects of AI in medicine. Separately, I would like to thank V. Sluchak, J. Weisburd, B. Goldberg, and G. Steblovsky for editing this manuscript.

The first author is grateful to Dmitri Ilvovsky, Tatyana Machalova, Saveli Goldberg, Sergey O. Kuznetsov, Dina Pisarevskaya, and other collaborators for fruitful discussions on the topics of this book.

The first author appreciates the help of his colleagues from the Digital Assistant team at Oracle Corp.: Gautam Singaraju, Vishal Vishnoi, Anfernee Xu, Stephen McRitchie, Saba Teserra, Jay Taylor, Sri Gadde, Sundararaman Shenbagam, and Sanga Viswanathan.

The first author acknowledges substantial contribution of the legal team at Oracle to make this book more readable, thorough, and comprehensive. Kim Kanzaki, Stephen Due, Mark Mathison, and Cindy Rickett worked on the patents described in this book and stimulated a lot of ideas that found implementation in this book.

Supplementary data sets

Please visit https://github.com/bgalitsky/relevance-based-on-parse-trees to access all supplementary data sets.

References

Arterys, 2017. Arterys Cardio DL Cloud MRI Analytics Software Receives FDA Clearance. https://www.dicardiology.com/product/arterys-cardio-dl-cloud-mri-analytics-software-receives-fda-clearance.

Best, J., 2020. AI and the Coronavirus Fight: How Artificial Intelligence is Taking on COVID-19. https://www.zdnet.com/article/ai-and-the-coronavirus-fight-how-artificial-intelligence-is-taking-on-covid-19/.

Bouton, C.E., Shaikhouni, A., Annetta, N.V., Bockbrader, M.A., Friedenberg, D.A., Nielson, D.M., Sharma, G., Sederberg, P.B., Glenn, B.C., Mysiw, W.J., Morgan, A.G., Deogaonkar, M., Rezai, A.R., 2016. Restoring cortical control of functional movement in a human with quadriplegia. Nature 533, 247–250. https://doi.org/10.1038/nature17435.

Dilsizian, S.E., Siegel, E.L., 2014. Artificial intelligence in medicine and cardiac imaging: harnessing big data and advanced computing to provide personalized medical diagnosis and treatment. Curr. Cardiol. Rep. 16, 441.

Esteva, A., Kuprel, B., Novoa, R.A., Ko, J., Swetter, S.M., Blau, H.M., Thrun, S., 2017. Dermatologist-level classification of skin cancer with deep neural networks. Nature 542, 115–118.

Farina, D., Vujaklija, I., Sartori, M., Kapelner, T., Negro, F., Jiang, N., Bergmeister, K., Andalib, A., Principe, J., Aszmann, O.C., 2017. Man/machine interface based on the discharge timings of spinal motor neurons after targeted muscle reinnervation. Nat. Biomed. Eng. 1, 0025.

Jiang, F., Jiang, Y., Zhi, H., Dong, Y., Li, H., Ma, S., Wang, Y., Dong, Q., Shen, H., Wang, Y., 2017. Artificial intelligence in healthcare: past, present and future. Introduction. BMJ J. 2 (4), 230–243.

O'Brien, M., Larson, C., 2020. Can AI Flag Disease Outbreaks Faster than Humans? Not Quite. https://apnews.com/article/100fbb228c958f98d4c755b133112582.

Richardson, P., 2020. How AI Is Changing Pharmaceuticals. https://qeprize.org/news/how-ai-is-changing-healthcare.

Rutledge, G.W., Wood, J.C., Lawless, W.F., 2020. Virtual health and artificial intelligence: using technology to improve healthcare delivery. In: Mittu, R., Sofge, D.A. (Eds.), Human-Machine Shared Contexts. Academic Press, pp. 169–175.

Somashekhar, S.P., Kumarc, R., Rauthan, A., Arun, K.R., Patil, P., Ramya, Y.E., 2016. Double blinded validation study to assess performance of IBM artificial intelligence platform, Watson for oncology in comparison with Manipal multidisciplinary tumour board. Cancer Res. 77 (4), 382–386.

Travelingboy, 2020. http://travelingboy.com/archive-travel-raoul-healthwarning.html.

CHAPTER

Multi-case-based reasoning by syntactic-semantic alignment and discourse analysis

2

Boris Galitsky

Oracle Corporation, Redwood City, CA, United States

1. Introduction

Medical diagnosis is the procedure of identifying the cause of a patient's illness or condition by investigating information acquired from various sources including physical examination, patient interview, lab tests, patient medical records, and existing medical knowledge of the cause of observed signs and symptoms (Balogh et al., 2015). Obtaining a correct diagnosis is the most crucial step in determining the best treatment for a patient's condition. It is a complicated, time-consuming process that requires much effort. Because of the complex nature of this process, it is subject to various errors (Chapter 4) and misdiagnosis is very common. According to the World Health Organization (WHO), every twentieth patient was misdiagnosed in 2015. This is disturbing, especially when people's lives are at stake.

While Natural Language Processing (NLP) has been leveraged in many fields and industries, its deployment in medicine is essential. Nowadays, there is an increasing use of online medical records, which has led to much more clinical information being stored in a well-organized and structured way. However, there is still a high volume of clinical information that is stored in an unstructured way, in plain text. It is obtained via dictation, typing, voice recognition, and writing. While this unstructured plain text contains valuable information for the person who reads it, any essential data contained within it cannot be automatically analyzed and used by a decision support system until it has been organized and structured. Hence, within the medical field, the use of NLP allows free text information that has been entered into the patient record to be turned into potentially useful data interpretable by a decision support system.

In this chapter, we build a text-based Symptom Checker Engine that takes a textual description of a patient problem and tries to find symptom descriptions and/or labeled cases to identify the disease. There is a special focus on diagnosing multiple diseases by splitting the textual description into fragments and finding symptom descriptions and/or labeled cases for each fragment such that:

(1) If multiple sources are matched with a fragment, they all must agree to confirm the diagnosis for individual disease.

(2) When multiple sources are identified for multiple fragments, the relations between these sources must agree with the relations between the fragments the patient description is split into.

Artificial Intelligence for Healthcare Applications and Management. https://doi.org/10.1016/B978-0-12-824521-7.00008-9

The input of the Symptom Checker Engine is an electronic health record (EHR). As the original resources for medical management, EHRs are the best summary of clinical experiences and a valuable source for knowledge accumulation. EHR-based innovations can improve the productivity of health personnel. With the rapid development of information technology and its in-depth application in hospitals, EHR processing tends to be increasingly intelligent. Different artificial intelligence (AI) methods, such as ontology (Galitsky et al., 2011), semantic analysis (Sheth et al., 2006), NLP (Takemura and Ashida, 2002), and fuzzy logic (Supekar et al., 2002) are applied to medical record processing. An electronic medical record system, the medical record interface, diagnosis-specific visualizations of electronic medical records, and medical record validation are beneficial in many medical fields such as cardiology (Sharony et al., 1989). The relevant computer-aided systems are also applied in dental fields (Gu et al., 2010).

A diagnosis of a disease or a condition relies on the information that contains factors that make getting it correct challenging. These factors include ambiguity, uncertainty, and conflicts as well as resource and organizational constraints. Many symptoms are nonspecific and variable, depending on the person. Many diagnostic tests are expensive, not regularly done, and often do not give a *yes/no* answer. Furthermore, physicians are usually prone to cognitive bias and incorrect applications of heuristics during the diagnosis stage (Chapter 4). They are more biased toward diseases or conditions that they have diagnosed in the past. They often trust the initial diagnostic impression, even though further information might not support that initial assumption. The Symptom Checker Engine is intended to mitigate these issues.

Recent developments in AI allow technology and healthcare scientists and engineers to create intelligent systems for optimizing and enhancing current diagnostic processes. Machine learning (ML) and NLP have been applied in a variety of areas within the healthcare industry such as diagnosis, personalized treatment, drug discovery, clinical trial research, radiology and radiotherapy, smart EHRs, and epidemic outbreak prediction. In medical diagnosis, ML, data mining, decision-making, and decision support are particularly useful. They can quickly capture unforeseen linguistic patterns in large databases of health records. With unbiased and balanced datasets, ML algorithms can mitigate the aforementioned cognitive bias problem and produce greater accuracy.

Case-based reasoning (CBR) is a methodology for reasoning in which a computer attempts to imitate the behavior of a human expert and learn from the experience of past cases. Medical reasoning involves processes that can be analyzed systematically, as well as those characterized as implicit and not easily interpretable. In medicine, experts not only use rules to diagnose a problem but they also use a mixture of textbook knowledge and experience. The experience consists of cases, both typical and exceptional, and the physicians consider them for reasoning. Therefore CBR methods should be very efficient in the domain of medical diagnosis, mainly because reasoning with cases corresponds with the typical decision-making process of physicians. In addition, incorporating new cases means automatically updating parts of the changeable knowledge (Schmidt et al., 2001). However, CBR is not always as successful in the medical domain as it is in other fields for building intelligent systems. More precise text-based similarity computing is needed.

CBR is defined as a model of reasoning that integrates problem solving, understanding, and learning, and incorporates all of them with memory processes. It involves adapting earlier solutions to meet new demands, using old cases to explain or justify new solutions, and reasoning from past events to interpret a new situation. In CBR terminology, a case usually denotes a problem situation (Aamodt and Plaza, 1994). CBR is a form of analogical reasoning since the basic principle that is implicitly assumed to be applied in problem-solving methodology is that similar problems have similar solutions (Choudhury and Begum, 2016).

2. Multi-case-based reasoning in the medical field

In this chapter, we combine CBR with syntax and semantics for text matching. CBR turned out to be adequate for unstructured domains and is therefore appropriate for the development of diagnostic support systems in multidisciplinary medical services.

In recognizing medical records, it is frequently necessary to establish a match between the different parts of these records with various cases, that is, a set of other records rather than a single record. In recognizing a text of a case, we need to split it into fragments to match with texts of known, assigned cases. Hence we need an efficient way to split a text into fragments for matching. To do that, discourse analysis helps to identify logically connected fragments and represent the way the whole text, such as a medical record, is organized.

We refer to matching with multiple cases via text as *multi-CBR* (Fig. 1). A seed (unassigned) case to be recognized is split into text fragments and relationships between these fragments are established. Then, for each fragment, we find the known (labeled, assigned) cases (Fig. 1, right). These cases are candidates; they can be accepted only once a set of relationships between them is established (shown in orange) and the set is determined to correspond well to the relationship between the fragments on the left (shown in green).

We formulate a multi-CBR strategy by:

(1) splitting a case to be recognized (a seed) into subcases for matching;
(2) establishing relations between the subcases;
(3) establishing a match into a known case for each subcase;
(4) identifying relations between known cases;
(5) establishing and approving a correspondence between the relations for the unknown subcases and the relations between the known cases; and
(6) recognizing an unknown case (assigning it a class).

We focus on specific multi-CBR scenarios where cases are texts:

- Relations between the portions of text are rhetorical relations of discourse analysis (Galitsky, 2020c)
- Relations between cases are ones such as case hierarchy or ontology-based (Galitsky, 2019b) that can be mapped into rhetorical relations

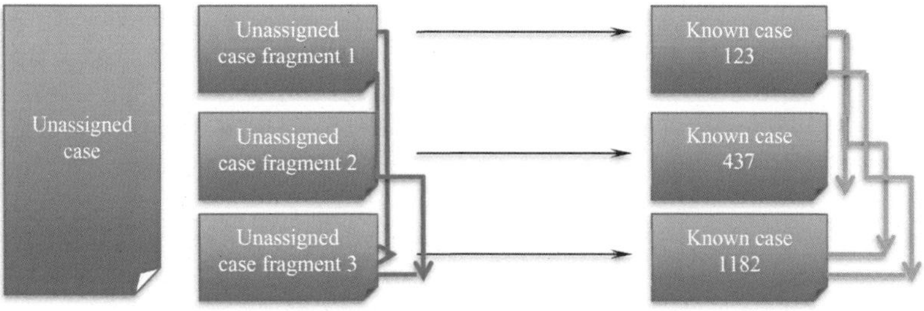

FIG. 1

A high-level view on multi-CBR methodology.

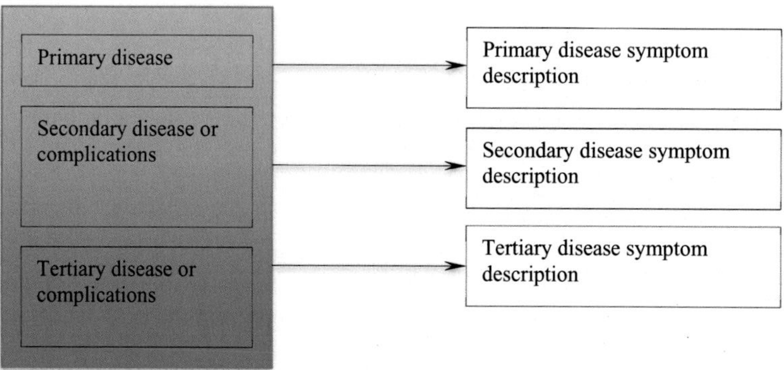

FIG. 2

Text fragments in a medical text description may correspond to primary, secondary, or tertiary diseases.

Finally, in the medical application domain, unknown cases are patient records with complaints that usually contain multiple illnesses. The assigned cases are instructions on illness diagnoses and sample disease descriptions (Fig. 2).

In terms of search engineering, there is a major difference between a conventional search and a multi-CBR search. In the conventional search, results (documents) are obtained and ranked, and no search constraints are associated with relationships or links between ranked search results. Conversely, under multi-CBR, search results come as a structured set of documents with certain relations between them.

We have the following description of a patient problem:

I experience fatigue and hunger because I do not acquire enough energy from the meals I eat. I urinate and feel thirsty fairly frequently. I lack a sharpness of vision resulting in the inability to see fine detail.

Later I started feel tingling in the hands and feet. After that, I feel numbness, pain and burning sensations starting in the toes and fingers then continuing up the legs or arms. I lost loss of muscle tone in my hands and feet, as well as a loss of balance.

As a result, I started feeling fatigue, pale skin, chest pain and irregular heartbeat. I noticed blood in urine, which is now dark, a drop in mental alertness and itchy skin.

We use a discourse representation such as a discourse tree (DT), which shows a high-level view of how a patient describes their problems. We will explore DTs in detail in Section 2.5. Fig. 3 shows a DT with the indentation denoting the levels of hierarchy. To find a split in the patient's description, we select a higher-level rhetorical relation (here, *Elaboration*) such that in each fragment there is a non-default rhetorical relation of *Explanation*, *Enablement*, *Cause*, or another one. Hence we identified three text fragments (shown highlighted).

We proceed to an example of syntactic similarity assessment implemented as finding a map between corresponding (synonymous) entities and phrases (Fig. 4). We perform a generalization of two short paragraphs to find a commonality between them (Galitsky, 2016). This commonality is a key to learning as well as a measure of similarity between these texts. Instead of just counting common

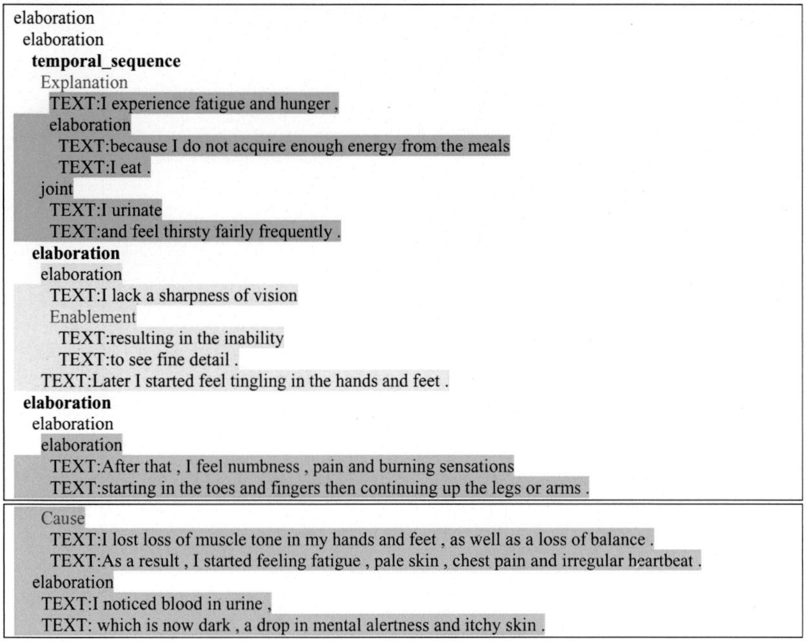

```
elaboration
 elaboration
  temporal_sequence
   Explanation
    TEXT:I experience fatigue and hunger ,
    elaboration
     TEXT:because I do not acquire enough energy from the meals
     TEXT:I eat .
   joint
    TEXT:I urinate
    TEXT:and feel thirsty fairly frequently .
  elaboration
   elaboration
    TEXT:I lack a sharpness of vision
    Enablement
     TEXT:resulting in the inability
     TEXT:to see fine detail .
   TEXT:Later I started feel tingling in the hands and feet .
 elaboration
  elaboration
   elaboration
    TEXT:After that , I feel numbness , pain and burning sensations
    TEXT:starting in the toes and fingers then continuing up the legs or arms .
```

```
   Cause
    TEXT:I lost loss of muscle tone in my hands and feet , as well as a loss of balance .
    TEXT:As a result , I started feeling fatigue , pale skin , chest pain and irregular heartbeat .
  elaboration
   TEXT:I noticed blood in urine ,
   TEXT: which is now dark , a drop in mental alertness and itchy skin .
```

FIG. 3

A discourse tree (DT) of the patient's complaint split into three fragments according to the top-level rhetorical relations.

keywords, we apply a much more sensitive measure of similarity approaching the semantic level by building a map between the structural (syntactic) representations of texts. The generalization operation is denoted by "^."

Symptoms of diabetes included increased thirst, frequent urination, extreme hunger and unexplained weight loss. There is a presence of ketones in the urine, a drop in mental alertness and itchy skin.

^

I experience fatigue and hunger, because I do not acquire enough energy from the meals I eat. I urinate and feel thirsty fairly frequently. I lack a sharpness of vision resulting in the inability to see fine detail.

The result of generalization expressed in a simple first-order representation is: *urination(frequent), hunger(high), thirst(frequent)*.

Rhetorical relations between blocks are extracted from the patient's text (Fig. 5, left). The patient's text is split into blocks accordingly. For a medical complaint, top-level relations hold between the main disease and accompanying diseases or between complications. "Official" or labeled descriptions of symptoms are shown on the right of Fig. 5. For a proper diagnosis, the blocks of text on the left should correspond to the official descriptions of symptoms, combined with the help of the relations corresponding to the ones on the left. If a match of individual text blocks is broken, or a relation mapping is not a bijection, then the diagnosis cannot be made. *Temporal_sequence* is mapped into

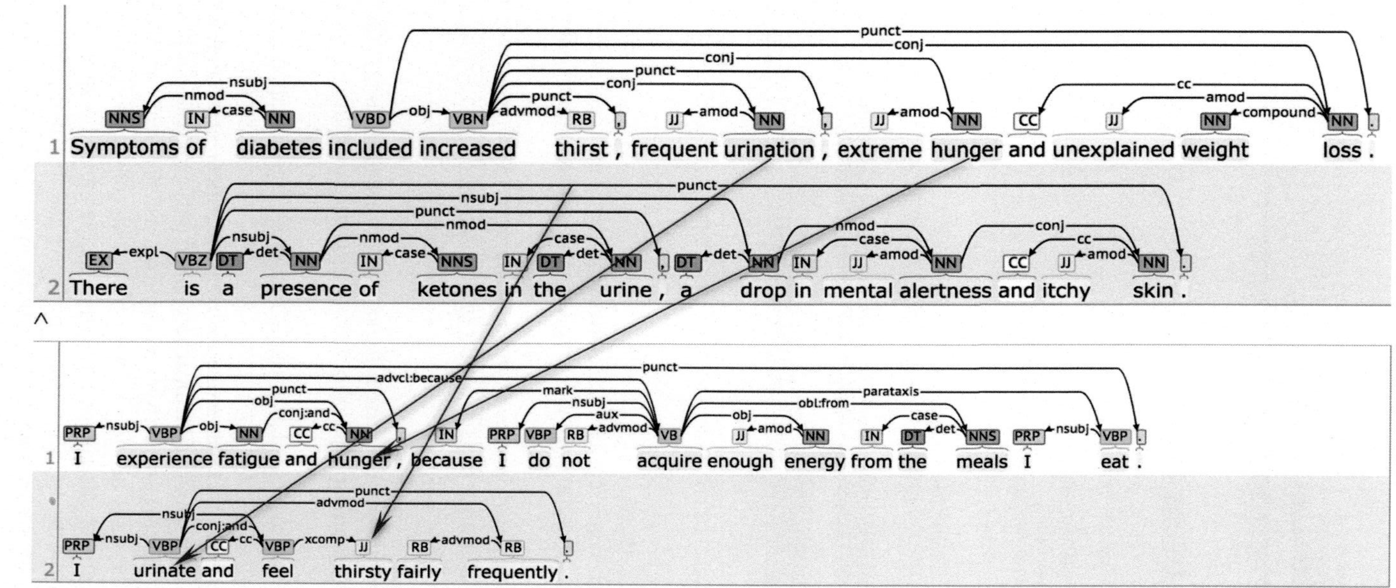

FIG. 4

Syntactic generalization between a seed case text and its matched labeled case text.

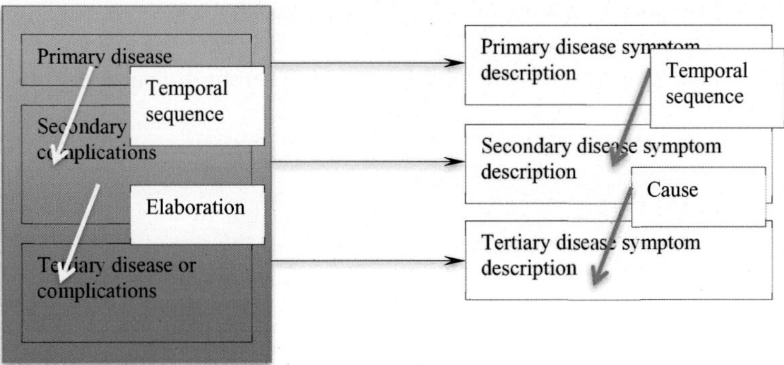

FIG. 5

The relationships between fragments in the patient's complaint are mapped into the relationships between the assigned matched cases.

Temporal_sequence, and *Elaboration* is mapped into *Cause*. The second mapping is acceptable since in the patient's description, the two diseases might not necessarily be connected, but in the official part, the fact that one disease causes another is specified. The opposite mapping *Cause* → *Elaboration* should not be accepted because if the patient believes one disease causes another, this should be addressed in the labeled cases.

2.1 Mixed illness description

We show a medical record in the form of abbreviated physician notes where discourse analysis is hardly applicable (Fig. 6).

Sometimes, a complaint contains a mixed description of symptoms for two illnesses. We show in green and pink the symptoms and the diagnosis. However, when a patient describes their complaints in

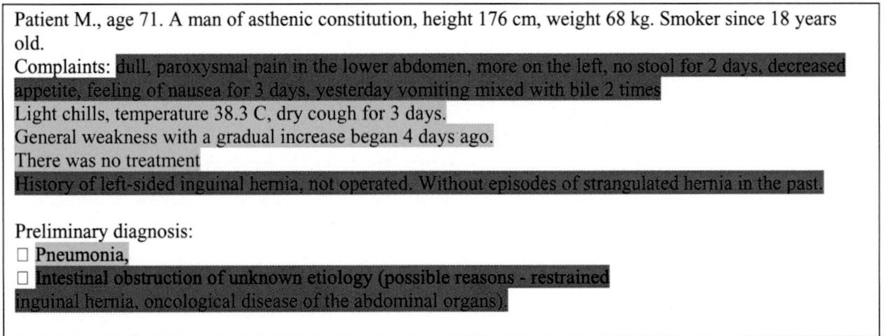
Patient M., age 71. A man of asthenic constitution, height 176 cm, weight 68 kg. Smoker since 18 years old.
Complaints: dull, paroxysmal pain in the lower abdomen, more on the left, no stool for 2 days, decreased appetite, feeling of nausea for 3 days, yesterday vomiting mixed with bile 2 times
Light chills, temperature 38.3 C, dry cough for 3 days.
General weakness with a gradual increase began 4 days ago.
There was no treatment
History of left-sided inguinal hernia, not operated. Without episodes of strangulated hernia in the past.

Preliminary diagnosis:
□ Pneumonia,
□ Intestinal obstruction of unknown etiology (possible reasons - restrained inguinal hernia, oncological disease of the abdominal organs).

FIG. 6

A medical record in the form of abbreviated physician notes.

plain words, we would expect a smoother text that can be naturally subject to discourse processing. A patient would formulate a complaint to cause compassion and reflect her perception of the illness as well as express their expectation for treatment and recovery. Therefore, a patient complaint is expected to be rich with discourse markers.

I had pain in the lower abdomen, more on the left, no stool for 2 days, decreased appetite, feeling of nausea for 3 days. Moreover, yesterday I had vomiting mixed with bile 2 times. ***At the same time,*** *I felt light chills, temperature 38.3 C, dry cough for 3 days, and a general weakness with a gradual increase began 4 days ago. However, there was no treatment.*

Fig. 7 (top) shows a sample patient complaint that corresponds to the physician's notes. The DT that splits the complaint into two fragments is shown on the bottom. The Symptom Checker Engine can rely on the top-level *Parallel* relation to infer that the patient is expressing two sets of symptoms at the same time, so the text can be split accordingly. Identified symptom descriptions are shown in rectangles at the bottom of Fig. 7. The rhetorical relation *Parallel* in the patient's complaint corresponds to taxonomic relation *independent-diseases* between the descriptions of illness symptoms. If the rhetorical relation were *Cause*, then the pair of identified diseases would be expected to have certain dependence information.

Multiple cases are navigated in the course of a medical consultation dialogue (Fig. 8).

The patient reported some health issues and the doctor asked questions to obtain more specific information, switching from the case associated with bellyache to the case associated with indigestion. Finally, the doctor made a diagnosis and gave medical advice based on both the collected information and clinical experience.

We will focus on dialogue management in Chapters 9 and 10.

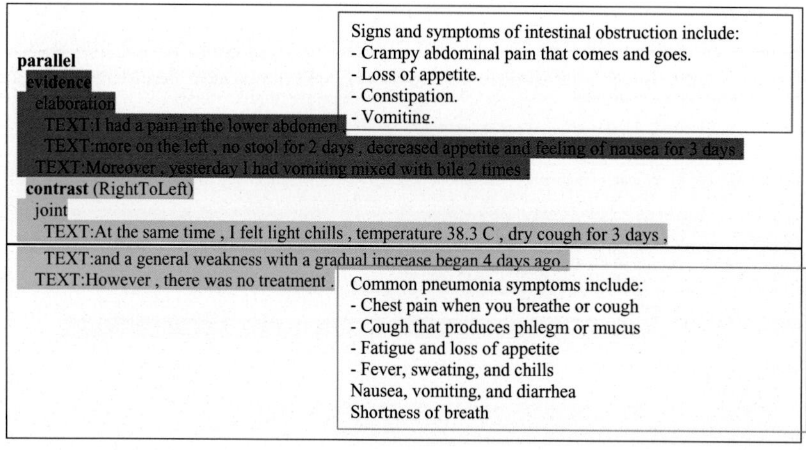

FIG. 7

A discourse tree (DT) for a patient complaint and mapping of sections into the symptom descriptions.

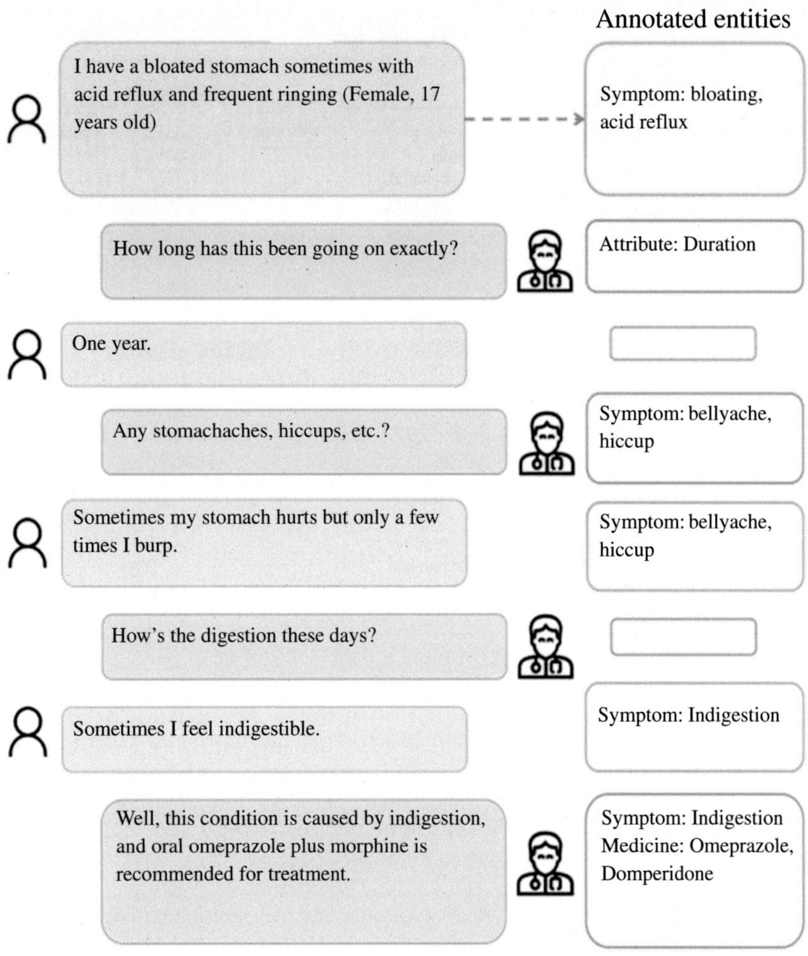

Annotated entities
I have a bloated stomach sometimes with acid reflux and frequent ringing (Female, 17 years old)
Symptom: bloating, acid reflux
How long has this been going on exactly?
Attribute: Duration
One year.
Any stomachaches, hiccups, etc.?
Symptom: bellyache, hiccup
Sometimes my stomach hurts but only a few times I burp.
Symptom: bellyache, hiccup
How's the digestion these days?
Sometimes I feel indigestible.
Symptom: Indigestion
Well, this condition is caused by indigestion, and oral omeprazole plus morphine is recommended for treatment.
Symptom: Indigestion
Medicine: Omeprazole, Domperidone

FIG. 8

A medical consultation dialogue between a patient *(orange)* and a doctor *(blue)* with corresponding annotated entities.

2.2 Probabilistic ontology

When receiving patients' self-reports, doctors first grasp a general understanding of the patients with several possible candidate diseases. Subsequently, by asking for significant symptoms of these candidate diseases, doctors exclude other candidate diseases until they can confirm a diagnosis. The doctor's thought process can be formalized probabilistically.

Fig. 9 shows the conditional probabilities between diseases and symptoms as directed medical knowledge-routed graph weights, in which there are two types of nodes (diseases and symptoms).

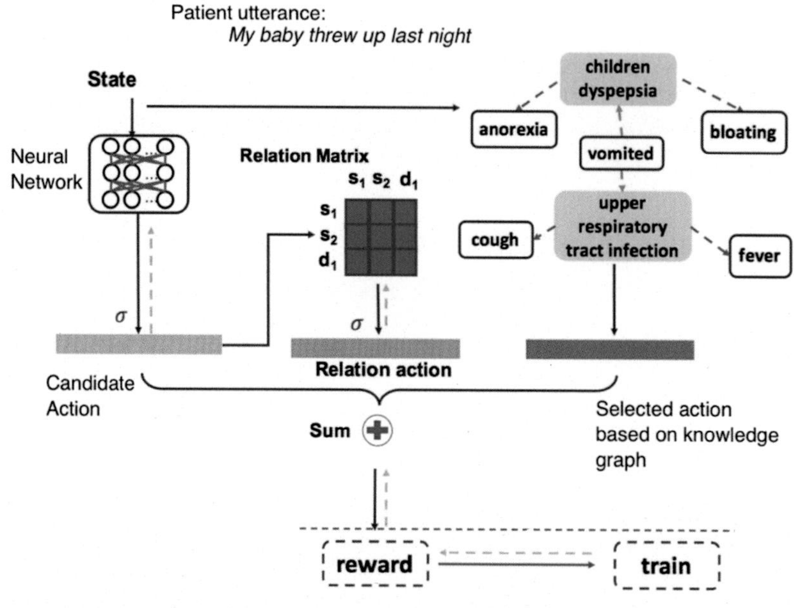

FIG. 9

The architecture of a knowledge-routed neural network for making diagnoses.

Edges only exist between a disease and a symptom. Each edge is assigned two weights (M is the number of diseases, N is the number of symptoms):

(1) conditional probabilities from diseases to symptoms $P(dis \mid symp) \in R^{MxN}$
(2) conditional probabilities from symptoms to diseases $P(symp \mid dis) \in R^{MxN}$

During communication with patients, doctors may identify several candidate diseases. A candidate disease probability is a disease probability corresponding to observed symptoms. Symptom prior probabilities $P_{prior}(sym) \in R^N$ are calculated through the following rules. For the mentioned symptoms, positive symptoms are set to 1, while negative symptoms are set to -1 to discourage related diseases. Other symptom (not sure or not mentioned) probabilities are set to the prior probabilities, which are calculated from the dataset. Then, these symptom probabilities $P_{prior}(sym)$ are multiplied by the conditional probabilities $P(dis|sym)$ to obtain disease probability $P(dis)$, which is formulated as:

$$P(dis) = P(dis \mid sym) \cdot P_{prior}(sym)$$

Considering candidate diseases, doctors often inquire about some notable symptoms to confirm diagnoses according to their medical knowledge. Likewise, with disease probabilities $P(dis)$, symptom probabilities $P(sym)$ are obtained by matrix multiplication between disease probabilities $P(dis)$ and the conditional probabilities matrix $P(sym|dis)$:

$$P(sym) = P(sym \mid dis) \cdot P(dis)$$

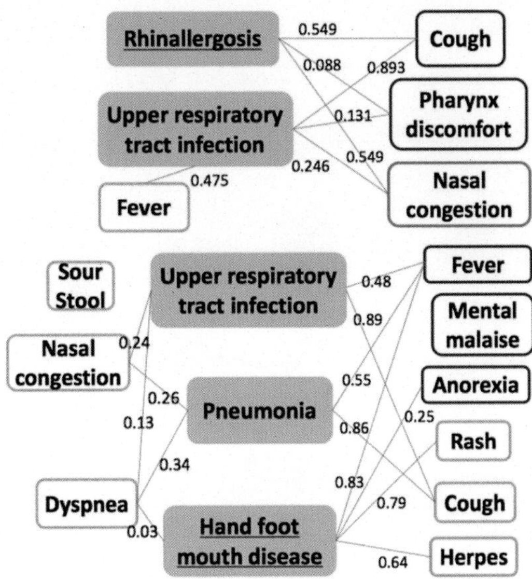

FIG. 10

Associations between symptoms and diseases.

Fig. 9 shows the architecture of involving a prior medical knowledge and modeling relations between treatment actions. The basic branch generates a rough recovery plan. The relational branch encodes relations among actions to refine the results. The knowledge-routed graph branch induces medical knowledge for graph reasoning and conducts a rule-based decision to enhance the recovery plan. The three branches can be trained jointly by means of reinforcement learning (Xu et al., 2019). Fig. 9 shows the disease nodes in a solid color and the symptom nodes in frames.

Fig. 10 shows associations between symptoms and diseases obtained from a fragment of our evaluation dataset. Red-framed boxes are used for symptoms from self-report, green boxes are used for *true* symptoms, and gray boxes are used for *false* and *unconfirmed* symptoms. The solid-blue rectangles denote diagnosed diseases.

Fig. 11 presents the results of mining for disease-symptom relationships from the PubMed bibliographic literature database. The associations between symptoms and diseases are based on their co-occurrence in the MeSH metadata fields of PubMed (Zhou et al., 2014). A disease network is constructed with nodes representing diseases and arcs representing symptom similarities between diseases. The authors extracted more than 7 million PubMed bibliographic records with one or more disease/symptom terms, deriving a total of 4000 disease terms and 300 symptom terms. To quantify the relationship between a symptom and a disease, a TF*IDF measure was applied. This research covers most disease categories, including broad categories like cancer as well as specific conditions like cerebral cavernoma. The two most frequent diseases in PubMed are breast cancer and hypertension, which reflects the available cumulative corpus of study rather than the epidemical ratios of diseases. The authors observed highly clustered regions of diseases that belong to the same broad disease category.

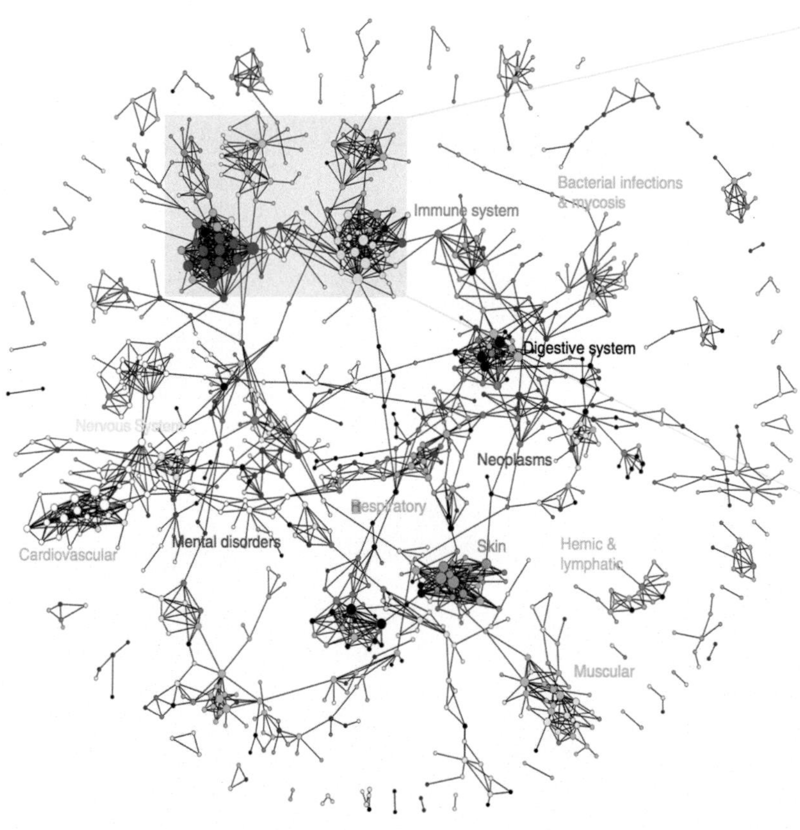

FIG. 11

A fragment of a symptom-disease association network (on the top).

2.3 Mapping a patient record to identified cases

A medical case is a remedial record in forms of literal records, images, and videos, like patients' information, symptoms, check-up results, diagnoses, and treatment. It is a combination of doctors' experience and wisdom, which can be expressed as follows:

DCH = DCH {CASE-ID, CASE-TYPE, CASE-GENERAL, CASE-PERSONAL-SPECIALITY, CASE-MEDICAL, HISTORY-SPECIALITY, CASE-SYMPTOM-SPECIALITY, CASE-EXAMINATION-SPECIALITY, CASE-OTHERSSPECIALITY, CASE-CONTENT}

This is our first example of an ontology fragment. Now we describe a dentistry case by Backus-Naur form (BNF), as shown in Table 1.

Ontologies are used to associate words in patient records with words in official illness descriptions. Other kinds of ontologies, such as the *International Classification of Diseases* (ICD, 2020), help to relate one disease with another. The ICD, which is supported by the WHO, is a widely used resource and diagnostic means for health management and clinical purposes. Originally designed as a healthcare classification system, the ICD contains diagnostic codes for classifying illnesses, including nuanced classifications of a wide variety of signs, symptoms, abnormal findings, complaints, social

Table 1 A dentistry case described by Backus-Naur form Meta BNF description.

CASE-ID CASE-ID::=;

CASE-DENTAL-ILLNESS-TYPE CASE_ENTERPRISE_TYPE:: = {< Periodontal Treatment >|< Orthodontic Treatment >| < Dental_Prosthetics >|< Endodontic_Diseaset >|< Tooth_Extraction >|};

CASE-GENERAL CASE_ GENERAL::={< Chief_Complaints >};

CASE-PERSONAL-SPECIALITY CASE-PERSONAL-SPECIALITY::={< Sufferer_Sex >};

CASE-MEDICAL-HISTORY-SPECIALITY CASE-MEDICAL-HISTORY-SPECIALITY::={< Passed_ History > < Family_ History > < Today _ History >};

CASE-SYMPTOM-SPECIALITY CASE-SYMPTOM-SPECIALITY::={< Color >< Ache >< Inflammation >};

CASE-EXAMINATION-SPECIALITY CASE-EXAMINATION-SPECIALITY::={};

CASE-OTHERS-SPECIALITY FEATURE-LIST::=< Diagnosis_ Speciality _Set >< Therapies _ Speciality _ Set >;

CASE-CONTENT CASE-CONTENT::={Sufferer_Basis_ Information >< Chief_Complaints > < Illness_ History > < Diagnosis_ Information > < Therapy_Program >< First_Treatment_Record >}

circumstances, and external causes of injury or disease. The ICD is designed to map health conditions to corresponding generic categories together with specific variations, assigning these a designated code that is up to six characters long. Thus, major categories are designed to include a set of similar diseases.

For example, we have the following classes and codes of diseases:

- BA00–BE2Z circulatory system
- CA00–CB7Z respiratory system
- DA00–DE2Z digestive system

Fig. 12 shows an abbreviated entry in the ICD.

We proceed to an example of a medical record (Fig. 13). We show the structured data that is not the focus of the current chapter in a smaller font (See Chapter 11 for structured data and ontologies). We depict the textual parts that can potentially be split into fragments in frames with the thumbnail charts on the right.

In Fig. 13, we provide an example of a medical record and show the sections that can be mapped into the disease descriptions by the Symptom Checker Engine. We use the medical record dataset (Natarajan, 2020) to match the *notes* fields with disease description. To do the entity matching, an ontology such as the ICD and its derivations can be used. In our examples, disease entities are expressed in different words (Fig. 14). Cases are shown with grayed backgrounds.

Description
This is a group of conditions characterized as being in or associated with the nervous system.
Exclusions
Endocrine, nutritional or metabolic diseases (5A00-5D46)
Complications of pregnancy, childbirth and the puerperium (JA00-JB6Z)
Certain conditions originating in the perinatal period (KA00-KD5Z)
Injury, poisoning or certain other consequences of external causes (NA00-NF2Z)
Coded Elsewhere
Injuries of the nervous system ()
Neoplasms of the nervous system ()
Structural developmental anomalies of the nervous system (LA00-LA0Z)

FIG. 12

An entry to class 08 of diseases.

We proceed to an example of a medical record (Fig. 13). We show the structured data which is not the focus of current chapter in a smaller font (See Chap. 11 for structured data and ontologies). We depict the textual parts that can potentially be split into fragments in frames with the thumbnail charts on the right.

Name: Adam Pie	**Home Phone:** 888-888-8888
Address: 1111 Donut Road Fast Food, California	**Office Phone:**
Patient ID: 0000-88888	**Fax:**
Birth Date: 08/08/1948	**Status:** Active
Gender: Male	**Marital Status:** Married
Contact By: Phone	**Race:** White
Soc Sec No: 111-11-1111	**Language:** English
Resp Prov: Carl Savem	**MRN:** MR-111-1111
Referred by:	**Emp. Status:** Full-time
Email:	**Sens Chart:** No
Home LOC: WeServeEveryone	**External ID:** MR-111-1111

Problems

DIABETES MELLITUS (ICD-250.)
HYPERTENSION, BENIGN ESSENTIAL (ICD-401.1)
DEPRESSION (ICD-311)
RETINOPATHY, DIABETIC (ICD-362.0)
POLYNEUROPATHY IN DIABETES (ICD-357. 2)

Medications
HYTRIN CAP 5MG (TERAZOSIN HCL) 1 po qd
Last Refill: #30 x 0 : Carl Savem (10/27/2020)
PRINIVIL TABS 20 MG (LISINOPRIL) 1 po qd
Last Refill: #30 x 2 : Carl Savem MD (10/27/2020)
HUMULIN INJ 70/30 (INSULIN REG & ISOPHANE (HUMAN)) 20 units ac breakfast
Last Refill: #600 u x 0 : Carl Savem MD (10/27/2010)
PROZAC CAPS 10 MG (FLUOXETINE HCL) 1 po qd
Last Refill: #30 x 2 : Carl Savem MD (10/27/2020)
Services Due
HEMOCCULT or SIGMOID, BP DIASTOLIC, BP SYSTOLIC, FLU VAX, PNEUMOVAX, MICROALB URN, FLU VAX, BP DIASTOLIC, BP SYSTOLIC, FUNDUSCOPY, DIAB FOOT CK, ALBUMIN URIN, TSH, CHOLESTEROL, HGBA1C, CREATININE.

OFFICE VISIT
History of Present Illness
Reason for visit: Routine follow up to review medications Chief Complaint: No complaints
Social History: His wife Marzipan died 5 years ago this month and he is more introspective.
Diabetes Management
Hyperglycemic Symptoms
Polyuria: no
Polydipsia: no
Blurred vision: no
Sympathomimetic Symptoms
Diaphoresis: no
Agitation: no
Tremor: no
Palpitations: no
Insomnia: no

Review of Systems
General: denies fatigue, malaise, fever, weight loss
Eyes: denies blurring, diplopia, irritation, discharge
Ear/Nose/Throat: denies ear pain or discharge, nasal obstruction or discharge, sore throat
Cardiovascular: denies chest pain, palpitations, paroxysmal nocturnal dyspnea, orthopnea, edema
Respiratory: denies coughing, wheezing, dyspnea, hemoptysis
Gastrointestinal: denies abdominal pain, dysphagia, nausea, vomiting, diarrhea, constipation

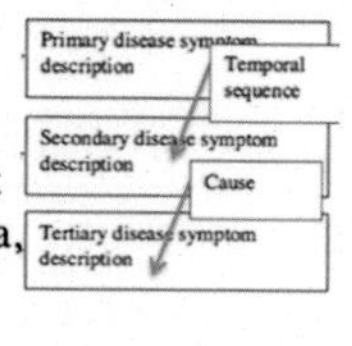

FIG. 13, CONT'D

Genitourinary: denies hematuria, frequency, urgency, dysuria, discharge, impotence, incontinence
Musculoskeletal: denies back pain, joint swelling, joint stiffness, joint pain
Skin: denies rashes, itching, lumps, sores, lesions, color change
Neurologic: denies syncope, seizures, transient paralysis, weakness, paresthesias
Psychiatric: denies depression, anxiety, mental disturbance, difficulty sleeping, suicidal ideation, hallucinations, paranoia
Endocrine: denies polyuria, polydipsia, polyphagia, weight change, heat or cold intolerance
Heme/Lymphatic: denies easy or excessive bruising, history of blood transfusions, anemia, bleeding disorders, adenopathy, chills, sweats
Allergic/Immunologic: denies urticaria, hay fever, frequent UTIs; denies HIV high risk behaviors

Physical Exam
General Appearance: well developed, well nourished, no acute distress
Eyes: conjunctiva and lids normal, PERRLA, EOMI, fundi WNL
Ears, Nose, Mouth, Throat: TM clear, nares clear, oral exam WNL
Respiratory: clear to auscultation and percussion, respiratory effort normal
Cardiovascular: regular rate and rhythm, S1-S2, no murmur, rub or gallop, no bruits, peripheral pulses normal and symmetric, no cyanosis, clubbing, edema or varicosities
Skin: clear, good turgor, color WNL, no rashes, lesions, or ulcerations

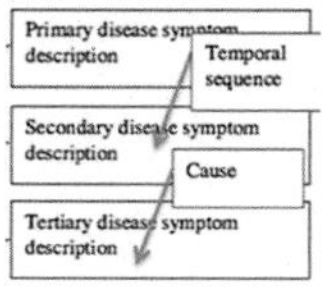

Primary disease symptom description
Temporal sequence
Secondary disease symptom description
Cause
Tertiary disease symptom description

Assessment
Problems (including changes): Adam is voiding better since increasing Hytrin to 5 mg/day.
Blood pressure is lower. He is following his diet, by his account. He has not had any hypoglycemic episodes, no night sweats. Feet are inspected and there are no callouses, no compromised skin. No vision complaints.

Impression: Sub optimal sugar, control with retinopathy and neuropathy, high glucometer readings.
He will work harder on diet. Will increase insulin by 2 units. BP and symptoms of prostatism are better.

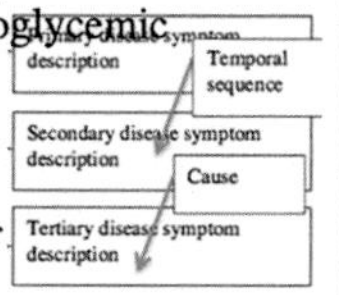

description
Temporal sequence
Secondary disease symptom description
Cause
Tertiary disease symptom description

Home Glucose Monitoring:
AC breakfast 110 to 220
AC breakfast mean 142
AC dinner 100 to 250
AC dinner mean 120

Plan
Medications:
HUMULIN INJ 70/30 20 u ac breakfast
PRINIVIL TABS 20 MG 1 qd
HYTRIN CAP 5MG 1 qd
PROZAC CAPS 10 MG 1 qd

Fig. 13. A Sample Medical Record (AHRQ 2020)

We provide an example of a medical record and show the sections which can be mapped into the disease descriptions by the Symptom Checker Engine. We use the medical record dataset (Natarajan 2020) to match the *notes* fields with disease description. To do the entity matching, an ontology such as International Classification of Diseases (version 11, ICD 2020) and its derivations can be used. In our examples, disease entities are expressed in different words (Fig. 14). Cases are shown with grayed background.

FIG. 13

A sample medical record (Agency for Healthcare Research and Quality, 2020).

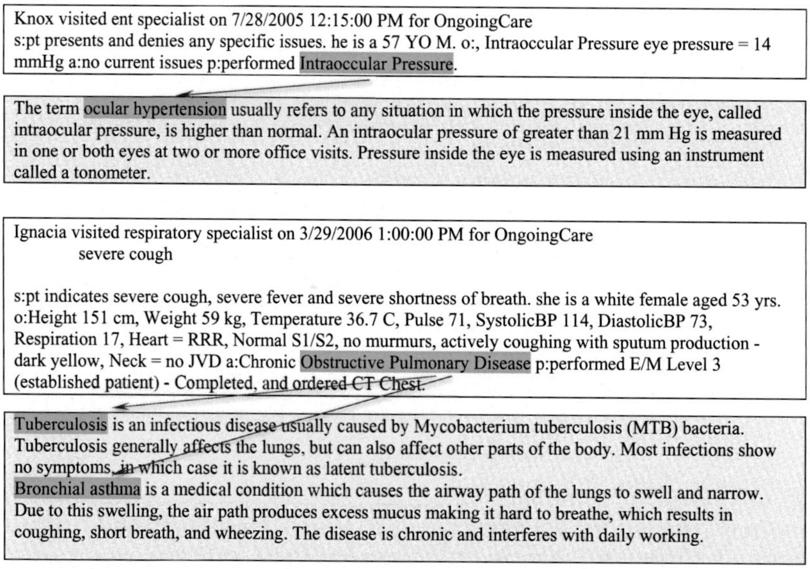

Knox visited ent specialist on 7/28/2005 12:15:00 PM for OngoingCare
s:pt presents and denies any specific issues. he is a 57 YO M. o:, Intraoccular Pressure eye pressure = 14 mmHg a:no current issues p:performed Intraoccular Pressure.

The term ocular hypertension usually refers to any situation in which the pressure inside the eye, called intraocular pressure, is higher than normal. An intraocular pressure of greater than 21 mm Hg is measured in one or both eyes at two or more office visits. Pressure inside the eye is measured using an instrument called a tonometer.

Ignacia visited respiratory specialist on 3/29/2006 1:00:00 PM for OngoingCare
severe cough

s:pt indicates severe cough, severe fever and severe shortness of breath. she is a white female aged 53 yrs. o:Height 151 cm, Weight 59 kg, Temperature 36.7 C, Pulse 71, SystolicBP 114, DiastolicBP 73, Respiration 17, Heart = RRR, Normal S1/S2, no murmurs, actively coughing with sputum production - dark yellow, Neck = no JVD a:Chronic Obstructive Pulmonary Disease p:performed E/M Level 3 (established patient) - Completed, and ordered CT Chest.

Tuberculosis is an infectious disease usually caused by Mycobacterium tuberculosis (MTB) bacteria. Tuberculosis generally affects the lungs, but can also affect other parts of the body. Most infections show no symptoms, in which case it is known as latent tuberculosis.
Bronchial asthma is a medical condition which causes the airway path of the lungs to swell and narrow. Due to this swelling, the air path produces excess mucus making it hard to breathe, which results in coughing, short breath, and wheezing. The disease is chronic and interferes with daily working.

FIG. 14

A mapping between a reference to a disease in a patient note and an official definition and description.

2.4 Learning semantic similarity

One of the subtasks of the Symptom Checker Engine is to compute a similarity between a patient record and a labeled, known case. The trick is to effectively combine distributed word embeddings with a keyword frequency measure into a single sentence representation that contains most of its semantic information. Some studies average or maximize across the embeddings in a text (Weston et al., 2014) or combine them through a multi-layer perceptron (Godin et al., 2014) by clustering or by trimming the text to a fixed length. The Paragraph Vector algorithm finds suitable vector representations for sentences, paragraphs, and documents of variable length, attempting to find embeddings for separate words and paragraphs at the same time for a collection of paragraphs known in advance. De Boom et al. (2015) proposed the idea of combining both TF*IDF and word-embedding information.

It is obviously worth leveraging knowledge from both TF*IDF and words themselves. Relying purely on the words with the highest IDF component of all words improves the overall similarity assessment quality. Naturally, low-IDF words have no clear-cut semantic meaning in a domain such as health, and since these words are present in many sentences, there is more coincidental overlap between non-related sentences. Removing these words from a text representation naturally succeeds in separating the average similarity between pairs and between non-pairs.

The learning procedure is implemented as follows. For every couple $c = \{c^1, c^2\}$ in the training set, the words are sorted in both texts (c^1) and (c^2) according to their document frequency (i.e., the word with the lowest document frequency comes first). This way, we arrive at ($c^{1'}$) and ($c^{2'}$). After that, the word-embedding vector of each word $w_j^{1'}$ and $w_j^{2'}$ are multiplied by an importance factor i_j; these

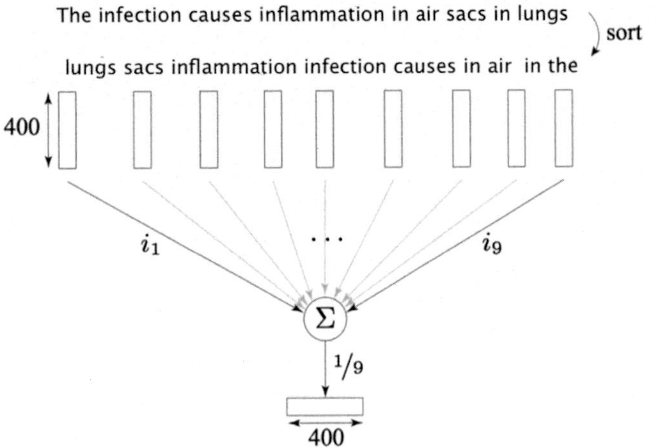

FIG. 15

An importance factor approach.

importance factors are global weights that are the subjects of learning. Finally, the mean of these weighed embeddings is considered to yield a fixed-length vector o^1 for (c^1) and o^2 for (c^2):

$$\forall \ell \in \{1, 2\} : \mathbf{o}^\ell = \frac{1}{n_c} \sum_{j=1}^{n_c} i_j \cdot \mathbf{w}_j^\ell.$$

Fig. 15 depicts the learning procedure. Initially, the words in the sentence are sorted according to their IDF component. Then, their 400-dimensional word-embedding vectors are multiplied by importance factors, and finally the mean is taken.

To learn the importance factors, De Boom et al. (2015) define a loss function as a function of any couple c that minimizes the distance between the vectors of a pair and maximizes the distance between the vectors of a non-pair. A squared Euclidean distance function is used.

$$f(c) \triangleq \begin{cases} d(\mathrm{o}^1, \mathrm{o}^2) & \text{if } c \text{ is a pair} \\ -d(\mathrm{o}^1, \mathrm{o}^2) & \text{if } c \text{ is a non} - \text{pair} \end{cases}$$

with $d(\cdot)$ a distance function of choice. Then the following objective is optimized as a function of the importance factors. A stochastic gradient descent with batches of 100 couples is used (Fig. 16).

$$J(i_1, \ldots, i_{n_c}) = \frac{1}{|D|} \sum_{c \in D} f(c) + \lambda \sum_{j=1}^{n_c} i_j^2.$$

Fig. 16 shows a plot of the importance factors that were learned through the previously described optimization procedure. We clearly notice that the importance factors steadily decrease in magnitude; words with a low document frequency therefore have much greater weight in comparison with words with a high document frequency. The factors at the end are approaching zero.

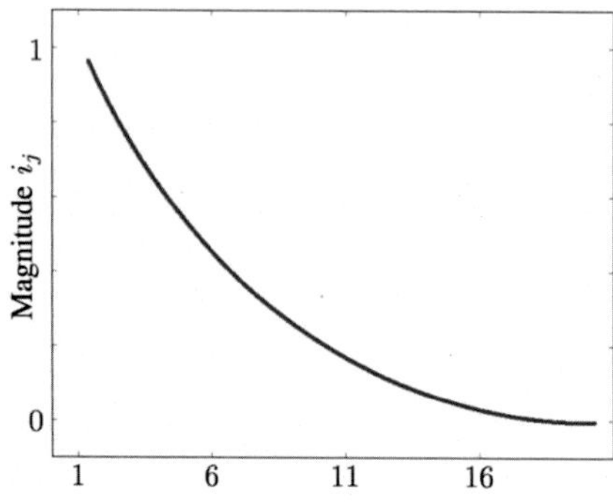

FIG. 16

The importance factor magnitudes curve.

2.5 Discourse analysis and discourse trees

Discourse analysis of text and communicative discourse trees (CDTs) are designed to combine rhetorical information with speech act structures. CDTs are DTs with arcs labeled with expressions for communicative actions (Galitsky, 2017a). These expressions are logic predicates expressing the agents involved in the respective speech acts and their subjects. The arguments of logical predicates are formed in accordance to respective semantic roles, as proposed by a framework such as VerbNet (Kipper et al., 2008). The purpose of adding these labels is to incorporate the speech act-specific information into DTs so that their learning occurs over a richer set of features than just rhetorical relations and syntax of elementary discourse units (EDUs). We intend to cover by these features how author thoughts are organized and communicated irrespectively of the subjects of these thoughts (Galitsky, 2017b).

The main classes of discourse connections between sentences are:

(1) Anaphora. If two areas of keyword occurrences are connected with an anaphoric relation, the answer is most likely relevant.

(2) Communicative actions. If a text contains a dialogue, and some question keywords are in a doctor's question and others are in the patient's reply, then these keywords are connected and the link between the doctor's question/explanation text and the patient's text is relevant and can be used for multi-CBR. To identify such situations, one needs to find a pair of communicative actions and to confirm that this pair is of question-answer or request-reply type (Galitsky and Kuznetsov, 2008; Galitsky, 2019a).

(3) Rhetorical relations. These indicate the coherence structure of a text (Mann and Thompson, 1988). Rhetorical relations for text can be represented by a DT, which is a labeled tree in which the leaves of the tree correspond to contiguous units for clauses (EDUs). Adjacent EDUs, as well as higher-level (larger) discourse units, are organized in a hierarchy by rhetorical relation (e.g., *Background, Attribution*). An anti-symmetric relation involves a pair of EDUs: nuclei, which are core parts of the relation, and satellites, which are the supportive parts of the rhetorical relation.

The most important class of discourse connection between sentences that we focus on in this book is *rhetorical*. Once an answer text is split into EDUs and rhetorical relations are established between them, it is possible to establish rules for whether query keywords occurring in the text are connected by rhetorical relations (and therefore this answer is likely relevant) or not connected (and this answer is most likely irrelevant). Hence, we use the DT so that certain sets of nodes in the DT correspond to questions where this text is a valid answer and certain sets of nodes correspond to an invalid answer.

Discourse parsing required to obtain DTs from text is a hard, multifaceted problem (Joty et al., 2019; Afantenos et al., 2015) that needs "understanding" and modeling of various semantic and pragmatic features as well as revealing the structural properties that a DT can have. Most current theories and computational models formulate an extremely simplified version of discourse structure. One of the most widely cited theories, Rhetorical Structure Theory (RST, Mann and Thompson, 1988; Taboada and Mann, 2006), requires that only *adjacent* EDUs be connected with a rhetorical relation. RST represents how a text author organizes their thoughts. RST structure outlines which entities are primary and being introduced first and which other entities and their attributes would follow.

Another popular discourse model, the Penn Discourse Treebank (PDTB, Prasad et al., 2008), addresses the issue of the discourse connectives that label the attachment of potentially arbitrary text spans but does not introduce any constraint for the overall discourse structure of the resulting annotation. Computational models of the PDTB take the attachments of text spans as given in discourse parsers. In both cases, the attachment problem, finding which discourse units are attached to which, is vastly simplified; however, it is sufficient for a broad range of NLP tasks.

There is a substantial corpus of research characterizing texts in terms of domain-independent rhetorical elements, such as schema items (McKeown, 1985) or rhetorical relations (Mann and Thompson, 1988; Marcu, 1997). Conversely, Barzilay and Lee (2004) focus on content-based, domain-dependent dimension of the structure of text. They present an effective knowledge-lean method for learning content models from un-annotated documents, utilizing a novel adaptation of algorithms for hidden Markov models.

Whereas DTs are a static representation of discourse, Discourse Representation Theory (Kamp, 1981) treats interpretation of NL dynamically. An NL discourse as a sequence of utterances is viewed from the standpoint of representation structure, such as a parse thicket in this study. Discourse Representation Theory interprets indefinite noun phrases via an introduction of discourse referents for the entities that are the focus of a given EDU. From the standpoint of logic, these discourse referents are free variables; hence indefinite noun phrases are represented without a use of existential quantifiers, whereas the quantification is formed by a larger context. This larger context will then determine if an indefinite noun phrase gets an existential interpretation or not (van Eijck and Kamp, 1997).

One of the goals of this book is to intrigue the reader with the diversity and depth of various applications of discourse analysis. Each chapter will have its own application, and in this chapter we learn how to establish links between documents for individual diseases for a multi-case CBR. Although there has been a substantial advancement in document-level RST parsing, including the rich linguistic features-based of parsing models (Joty et al., 2013), document-level discourse analysis has not found a broad range of applications. The most valuable information from DT includes global discourse features and long-range structural dependencies between DT constituents.

DTs and their extensions are a very promising subject of study for logical AI. Logical AI studies subjects such as logic forms and logic programs that are very limited in quantity in the real world. However, logical AI tries to make sense of them; DTs are fairly interpretable structures. Statistical/deep ML has big text data available at its disposal but does not really make sense of it from the perspective of logical AI. Communicative DTs can be obtained in a large quantity on one hand, and they are adequate logical AI subjects on the other hand. That is why DTs and their extensions are such an important subject of study for AI in domains such as health.

3. Alignment of linguistic graphs

In our previous studies, we computed linguistic similarity as the maximal common subtree of syntactic parse trees (Galitsky et al., 2012). We approximated finding the maximal common subtree via phrase-level alignment (Galitsky et al., 2013; Galitsky, 2013). To thoroughly track the phrase structure at various linguistic levels (phrase, sentence, paragraph), in this chapter we apply a full-scale graph alignment approach to avoid losing potentially important linguistic features. These features might play important roles in finding correspondence between how patients describe their symptoms and how they are described by physicians in symptom-checking instructions.

Alignment is an essential operation for matching a patient's record with a labeled case, performed at the levels of distributional semantics (Section 2.4; Galitsky, 2020b) along with syntactic and semantic match to be presented in this section. We first introduce an abstract graph-alignment algorithm inspired by biological applications. One of its implementations targets the task of code similarity assessment (Dayanand, 2018).

3.1 Abstract meaning representation

Abstract Meaning Representation (AMR, Banarescu et al., 2013) was proposed as a general-purpose meaning representation language for broad-coverage text, and work is ongoing to study its use for a variety of applications such as machine translation and summarization. An AMR bank provides a large new corpus that enables computational linguists to study the problem of grammar induction for broad-coverage semantic parsing (Artzi et al., 2015). However, it also presents significant challenges for existing algorithms, including much longer sentences, more complex syntactic phenomena (Eremeev and Vorontsov, 2019), and increased use of non-compositional semantics, such as within-sentence coreference.

AMR aims to abstract away from various syntactic phrasings. The motivation is to assign the same AMR to sentences phrased differently that have the same basic meaning. AMR has a tree representation format as rooted, directed, edge-labeled, and leaf-labeled trees.

Fig. 17 shows a graph representation. A conventional AMR representation is

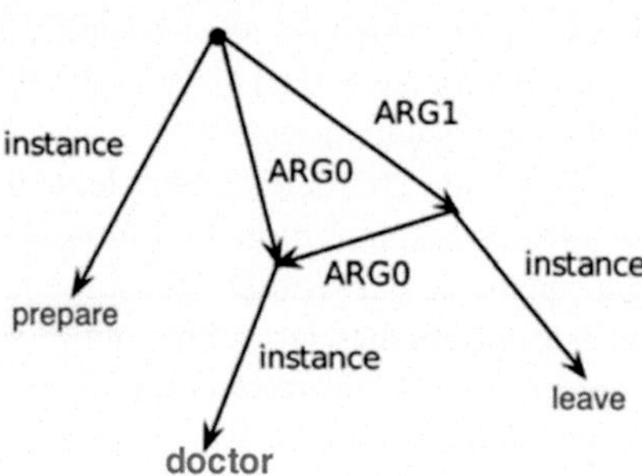

FIG. 17

An AMR-directed graph representing the meaning of *"The doctor prepares to leave."*

(w / prepare
:arg0 (b / doctor)
:arg1 (g / leave
:arg0 b))

For the logical representations, we differentiate between semantic types and the instances. In our further examples, we skip the instance notation where it does not introduce an ambiguity. As a logical form, this reads as:

$$\exists\, w, b, g: instance(w, prepare) \wedge instance(g, leave) \wedge instance(b, doctor) \wedge arg0(w, b) \wedge arg1(w, g) \wedge arg0(g, b)$$

AMR relies on PropBank framesets to abstract away from English syntax. For example, the frameset *associate-01* has three pre-defined slots:
:arg0 is the agent doing association,
:arg1 is the thing being associated with, and
:arg2 is an association thing.

(associate-01
:arg0 (teacher)
:arg1 (m2 / apple)
:arg2 (d / ball))

AMR has multiple syntactic relations: "*The physician spoke to the patient as she walked in from the street.*"

(speak
:arg0 (physician)
:beneficiary (patient)
:time (walk
:arg0 (patient)
:source (street)))

This structure covers various phrasings: "*While the patient was walking in from the street, a doctor spoke to her. The patient walked in, and had the physician spoke to her. As the patient walk in, there was a physician speaking to her. She was walking in from the street; the doctor was speaking to her.*"

AMR authors separate annotations for named entities, co-references, semantic relations, discourse connectives, temporal entities, and so on. Each annotation is evaluated separately, and training data is split across many resources. Since there is a lack of a simple readable semantic bank of English sentences paired with their whole-sentence, logical meanings, an extensive semantic bank promises a new work in natural language understanding, resulting in semantic parsers that are as ubiquitous as syntactic ones.

The motivations for AMR are that it is:

(1) represented as rooted, labeled graphs rather than trees that can be subject to traversal;
(2) expresses an abstraction away from syntactic idiosyncrasies. The same AMR are assigned to sentences that have the identical meaning;

(3) heavily relies on PropBank Framesets;
(4) agnostic about how we might want to derive meanings from lexical units or the other way around. In translating sentences to AMR, we do not dictate a particular sequence of rule applications or provide alignments that reflect such rule sequences. This makes semantic banking very fast, and it allows researchers to explore their own ideas about how strings are related to meanings; and
(5) heavily biased toward English.

AMR has gained substantial popularity in computational linguistics. This is due to the simple tree structure of AMRs, showing the connections between concepts and events, making them easy to read. Also, because AMRs can simply be expressed as directed acyclic graphs, machine-generated output can be evaluated in a standard way by computing precision and recall on triples of gold-standard AMRs (Cai and Knight, 2013). Moreover, AMRs are arguably easier to produce manually than traditional formal meaning representations, and, as a result, there are now corpora with gold-standard AMRs available (Banarescu et al., 2015).

Here we describe the graph alignment algorithm that is a foundation for multiple text alignment under CBR. The purpose of alignment is twofold:

(1) to combine structural information about a text (such as a question); and
(2) to assess its similarity of meaning to another text, such as a labeled case.

A syntactic, semantic, or joined graph alignment problem is formulated as follows (Galitsky, 2020a). We denote the two graphs that we are aligning by $G_1 = (V_1, E_1)$ and $G_2 = (V_2, E_2)$, where V_i is the set of nodes and E_i is the set of edges in graph G_i. We assume that $|V_1| \leq |V_2|$. We build an injective mapping (that does not map two nodes into one) to align each node in G_1 to exactly one node in G_2 with a similar topological neighborhood (syntactic and/or semantic properties). Formally, *topological similarity* of nodes is defined by using the notion of 73-dimensional "graphlet degree signatures" and the "signature similarity" measure specified below. This approach produces a global network alignment, since our node mapping is defined for all nodes in V_{G1}. Thus, we do not allow "gaps" (i.e., nodes without a match) in G_1, but we do allow them in the larger network, G_2.

We first define a query graph that can be straightforwardly mapped to a logical form in λ-calculus and is semantically closely related to λ-dependency-based compositional semantics (DCS, Liang, 2013). For expression "*citizens who live in Boston*" the regular λ-calculus gives $\lambda x.\exists e.PlacesLive(x, e) \wedge Location(e, Boston)$ and λ-DCS gives *PlacesLive.Location.Boston*. Hence, DCS attempts to remove explicit use of variables; it makes it similar in flavor to dependency-based compositional semantics.

Matching semantic parse for Q against that for A is formulated as query graph generation in the form of a state transition from a seed alignment toward a full alignment. Each state is a candidate mapping between parses such as $AMR(Q) \rightarrow AMR(A)$ in the query graph representation and each action defines a way to grow the alignment. The representation power of the alignment of a pair of semantic parses is thus controlled by the set of allowed alignment actions applicable to each state. In particular, the actions are split into three main steps: (1) locating the topic entity in the question, (2) finding the main relationship between the answer and the topic entity, and (3) expanding the query graph with additional constraints that describe properties the answer needs to have, or relationships between the answer and other entities in the question.

When aligning an $AMR(V,E)$ against a syntactic dependency parse tree $T(U,F)$ or another AMR graph, we first compute the costs of aligning each node v in AMR with each node n in T. The cost of aligning two nodes takes into account the *graphlet degree signature similarity* between them, modified to reduce the cost as the degrees of both nodes increase, since higher-degree nodes with similar signatures provide a tighter constraint than correspondingly similar low-degree nodes. In this way, we align the densest parts of the AMR graph first.

Let us define graphlets as *small, connected non-isomorphic induced subgraphs* of a large graph such as an AMR graph. We now introduce *graphlet degree vectors* (signatures) and signature similarities to support the graph alignment procedure. This measure generalizes the degree of a node, which counts the number of edges that the node touches, into the vector of graphlet degrees or graphlet degree signature, counting the number of graphlets that the node touches at a particular orbit, for all graphlets on two to five nodes.

Graphlets, introduced in Pržulj et al. (2004) are small, connected non-isomorphic induced subgraphs of a large network. An induced subgraph must contain all edges between its nodes that are present in the large network, whereas a partial subgraph may contain only some of these edges. Moreover, graphlets do not need to be over-represented in the data when compared with randomized networks. Graphlets are used as a basis for designing three highly sensitive measures of network local structural similarities: (1) the relative graphlet frequency distance, (2) the graphlet degree distribution agreement, and (3) a network topological similarity measure that generalizes the degree of a node in the network to its graphlet degree vector or graphlet degree signature (Pržulj, 2007).

The resulting vector of 73 coordinates is the signature of a node that describes the topology of the node's neighborhood and captures its interconnectivities out to a distance of 4 (see Milenkovic and Pržulj, 2008 for details). The graphlet degree signature of a node provides a highly constraining measure of local topology in its vicinity and comparing the signatures of two nodes provides a highly constraining measure of local topological similarity between them (Fig. 18).

The *signature (graphlet) similarity* is computed as follows. For a node u in graph G, u_i denotes the ith coordinate of its signature vector (i.e., u_i is the number of times node u is touched by an orbit i in G). The distance $D_i(u,v)$ between the ith orbits of nodes u and v is defined as:

$$D_i(u, v) = w_i \times \frac{|\log(u_i + 1) - \log(v_i + 1)|}{\log(\max\{u_i, v_i\} + 2)},$$

where w_i is the weight of orbit i that accounts for dependencies between orbits. The total distance $D(u,v)$ between nodes u and v is defined as:

$$D(u, v) = \frac{\sum_{i=0}^{72} D_i}{\sum_{i=0}^{72} w_i}.$$

The distance $D(u,v)$ is in [0,1), where distance 0 means that signatures of nodes u and v are identical. Finally, the signature similarity, $S(u,v)$, between nodes u and v is:

$$S(u, v) = 1 - D(u, v)$$

Clearly, a greater signature similarity between two nodes corresponds to a greater topological similarity between their extended neighborhoods up to the distance of 4. The number 4 corresponds to a typical maximum number of arguments of a verb node of an AMR graph.

Let $deg(v)$ be the degree of a node v in AMR, let $max_{deg(AMR)}$ be the maximum degree of nodes in AMR, let $S(v, u)$ be the graphlet degree signature similarity of nodes v and u, and let α be a parameter in [0,1] that controls the contribution of the node signature similarity to the cost function (that is, $1 - \alpha$ is

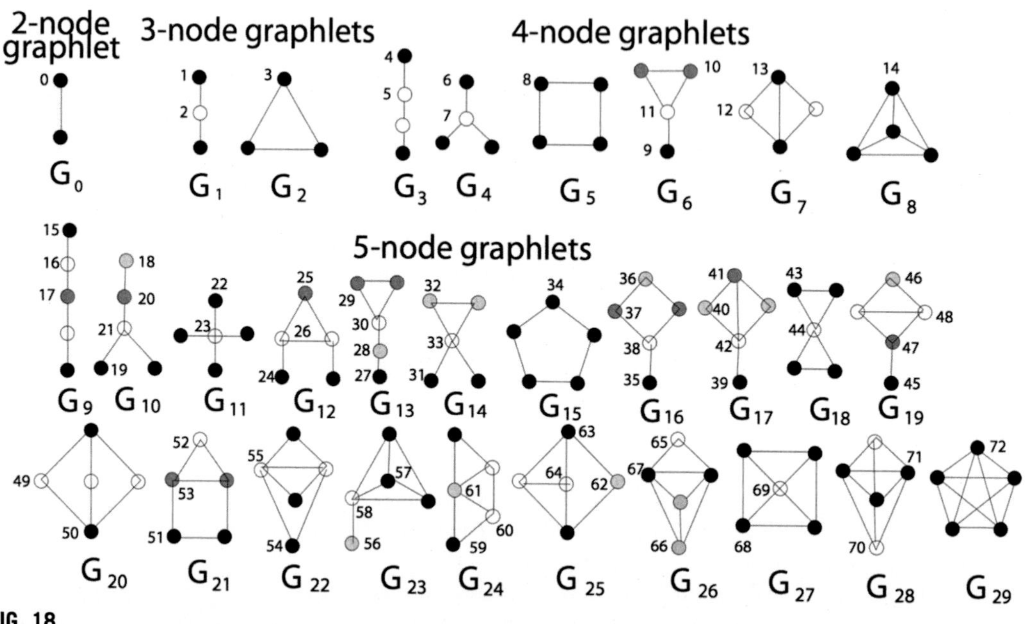

FIG. 18

Thirty 2-, 3-, 4-, and 5-node graphlets $G_0, G_1, \ldots, G_{29}$ and their automorphism orbits 0, 1, 2, ..., 72. In a graphlet $G_{i}, i \in \{0, 1, \ldots, 29\}$, nodes belonging to the same orbit are of the same shade.

the parameter that controls the contribution of node degrees to the cost function). Then, the cost of aligning nodes v and u is computed as:

$$C(v,u) = 2 - \left((1-\alpha) \times \frac{deg(v) + deg(u)}{max\_deg(G) + max\_deg(H)} + \alpha \times S(v,u) \right).$$

A cost of 0 corresponds to a pair of topologically identical nodes v and u, while a cost close to 2 corresponds to a pair of topologically different nodes.

The graph alignment algorithm chooses (as the initial seed) a pair of nodes v and u from *AMR* and *T*, which have the smallest cost. Ties are broken randomly. Once the seed is found, we build the spheres of all possible radii around nodes v and u. A sphere of radius r around node v is the set of nodes $S_{AMR}(v, r) = \{x \in AMR: d(v,x) = r\}$ that are at distance r from v, where the distance $d(v, x)$ is the length of the shortest path from v to x. Spheres of the same radius in two networks are then greedily aligned by searching for the pairs (v', u'): $v' \in S_{AMR}(v, r)$ and $u' \in S_T(u, r)$ that are not already aligned and that can be aligned with minimal cost.

When all spheres around the initial seed (v, u) have been aligned, other nodes in both *AMR* and *T* are still unaligned. We repeat the same algorithm on a pair of graphs (AMR^p, T^p) for $p = 1 \ldots 3$ and attempt to identify a new seed again, if necessary. The graph AMR^p is defined as a new *graph* $AMR^p = (V, E^p)$ having the same set of nodes as *AMR* and having $(v,x) \in E^p$ if and only if the distance between nodes v and x in *AMR* is less than or equal to p. In other words $d_{AMR}(v, x) \leq p$. $AMR^1 = AMR$. Using AMR^p $(p > 1)$ lets us align a path of length p in one graph to a single edge in another graph, which is analogous to allowing "insertions" or "deletions" in a sequence alignment. We stop the alignment procedure when each node from *AMR* is aligned to exactly one node in *T*.

The described graph alignment algorithm is used to evaluate the fit of various network models to real-world networks and to discover a new, well-fitting, geometric random graph model for protein-protein interaction networks (Pržulj et al., 2004; Pržulj, 2007).

A random geometric graph is an undirected graph constructed by randomly placing *N* nodes in some metric space (according to a specified probability distribution) and connecting two nodes by a link if and only if their distance is in a given range (e.g., smaller than a certain neighborhood radius, *r*). The graph alignment algorithm can also be applied to other types of biological networks, such as protein structure networks, which are also called residue interaction graphs (Milenković et al., 2009).

3.2 Aligning AMR

The *abstraction* feature of AMR parsing is associated with alignment between words and their semantic representations (not a graph alignment). This feature is closely related to how we extract concepts from AMR and build mappings between a word's surface form and its semantic meaning. Wang and Xue (2017) tackled this issue with a novel graph-based aligner designed specifically for word-to-concept scenario. They showed that a better alignment result could improve an AMR parsing result. Building the alignment between a word and an AMR concept is often conducted as a preprocessing step. As a result, accurate concept identification crucially depends on the word-to-AMR-concept alignment. Since there is no manual alignment in AMR annotation, typically either a rule-based or an unsupervised aligner is applied to the training data to extract the mapping between words and concepts. This mapping will then be used as reference data to train concept identification models. The JAMR aligner (Flanigan et al., 2014) greedily aligns a span of words to a graph fragment using a set of heuristic rules. While it can easily incorporate information from additional linguistic sources such as WordNet, it is not adaptable to other domains. Unsupervised aligners borrow techniques from Machine Translation and treat the sentence-to-AMR alignment as a word-alignment problem between a source sentence and its linearized AMR graph (Pourdamghani et al., 2014). Wang and Xue (2017) proposed a hidden Markov model (HMM)-based sentence-to-AMR alignment method with a graph distance distortion model to leverage the structural information in AMR.

Fig. 19 illustrates the need for alignment distortion. The concept *we* in an AMR list of tokens is mapped into the English word *our*, and the AMR concept of *current* is mapped into *Currently*. Hence, the alignment is essentially non-monotonic.

Fig. 20 shows the joint syntactic and semantic alignment between sentences. Red vertical lines between the words in the syntactic parsing (on the bottom) give a hint to the semantic level (on the top) which words and phrases need to be attempted to be mapped into each other.

For example, we map *VBD-stopped* into *VB-develop*, taking into account *RB-not* at the syntactic level. In the semantic level, this map induces (shown by the indigo vertical arcs) mapping between {*not, develop-02*} and {*stop-01, progress-01*}. Syntactic mapping gives the semantic level a hint on which phrases to check with respect to similarity; *not-develop* turns out to be synonymous to *stop-progressing*, but for other syntactic mapping it might not be the case. Hence the syntactic mapping provides the semantic layer with the hypotheses on which semantic mapping might be plausible. Since the similarity on semantic level is not necessarily grounded in syntactic mapping, it can also induce some insightful syntactic level maps, which cannot be derived by the syntactic information alone.

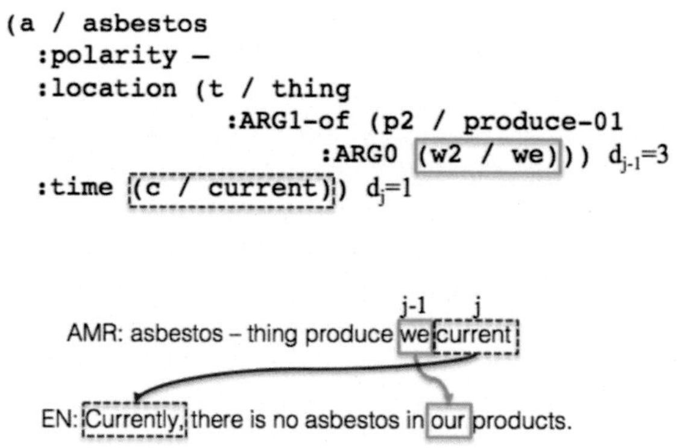

```
(a / asbestos
  :polarity -
  :location (t / thing
                 :ARG1-of (p2 / produce-01
                             :ARG0 (w2 / we))) d_{j-1}=3
  :time (c / current)) d_j=1
```

j-1 j

AMR: asbestos – thing produce we current

EN: Currently, there is no asbestos in our products.

FIG. 19

Alignment between a sentence and its AMR representation.

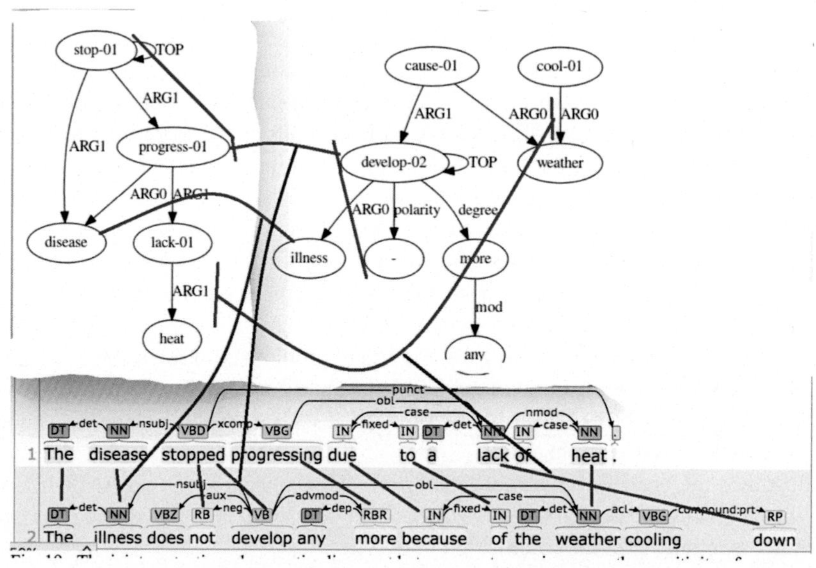

FIG. 20

The joint syntactic and semantic alignment between sentences improves the sensitivity of similarity assessment.

3.3 Alignment algorithm

Fig. 21 presents the chart for the alignment algorithm. Unit *findSeed*(G_1, G_2) takes as an input two graphs and identifies the best alignment seed, which is a pair of nodes (u, v) such that $C(u, v)$ is minimal. Ties between nodes are broken uniformly at random. Unit *makeSphere*(u, *radius*, G) returns a set of nodes from graph G, which form $S(u, radius)$ in G. Procedure *alignSpheres*(S_1, S_2) takes two sets of nodes S_1 and S_2 from graphs G_1 and G_2, respectively, and performs alignment of the two sets in

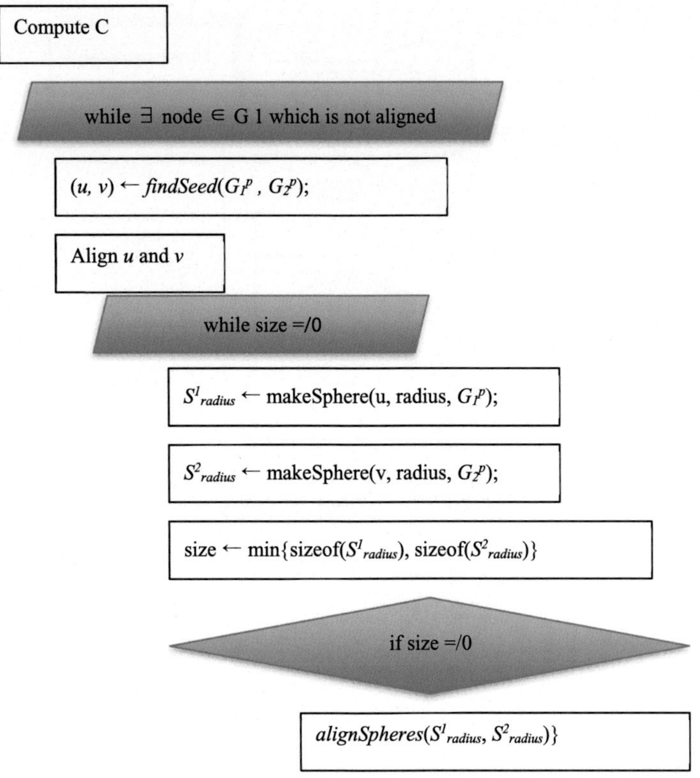

FIG. 21

The chart for the alignment algorithm.

the greedy way by identifying node pairs (u, v): $u \in S_1, v \in S_2$ with minimal cost $C(u, v)$. Ties are broken uniformly at random. S_1 and S_2 are not necessarily of the same size. If, for example $sizeof(S_1) > sizeof(S_2)$, then $sizeof(S_2) - sizeof(S_1)$ will not be subject to alignment. Note that in each iteration, after the seed was identified, spheres S^1_{radius} and S^2_{radius} can be aligned in parallel for all values of *radius* because their alignments are independent of each other.

4. Case-based reasoning in health

The key value of CBR in health is an automatic formation of a facility-adapted ontology (Schmidt et al., 1999), which is a very important aspect in medical decision-making. In addition, the constantly changing nature of medical ontologies, presence of multiple solutions, and complexity in simulation also make CBR deployment in the medical domain valuable (Holt et al., 2005). The observation that the methodology of CBR systems closely resembles the reasoning pattern of a physician also suggests an effective use of CBR.

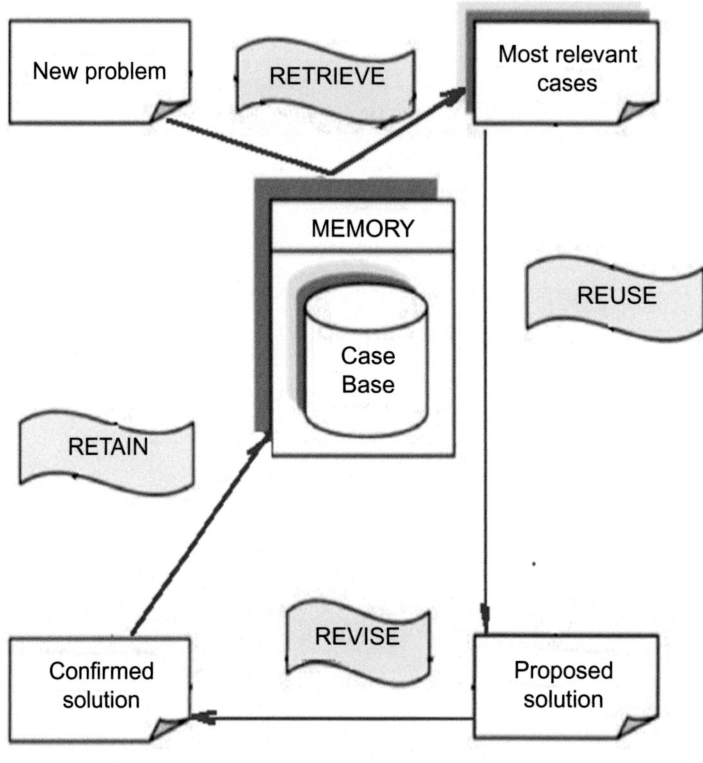

FIG. 22

R4 model for CBR.

Various CBR models have been proposed in the literature. The most widely used model with the highest level of abstraction is the R4 model. The processes involved in this model are (Fig. 22):

(1) retrieve the most similar cases to the seed one;
(2) reuse the data and knowledge from retrieved cases to solve the problem;
(3) review the proposed solution and update if necessary; and
(4) retain the recognized case of this solution for future use.

The most commonly used retrieval techniques include nearest neighbor retrieval (as we do in this chapter with text; also Galitsky et al., 2009), inductive learning approaches, knowledge-guided approaches, validated retrieval, and Discretized Highest Similarity with Pattern Solution *Re*-use algorithm (Patterson et al., 2003).

Fig. 22 shows a more detailed representation of the R4 model adjusted for the health domain. We now proceed to more CBR architectures in health.

Reasoning is the cornerstone and the core of CBR. The knowledge reuse process of abstract cases includes the following five phases:

(1) Input a new inquiry for writing a new case history;
(2) Retrieve similar cases from the case-base;

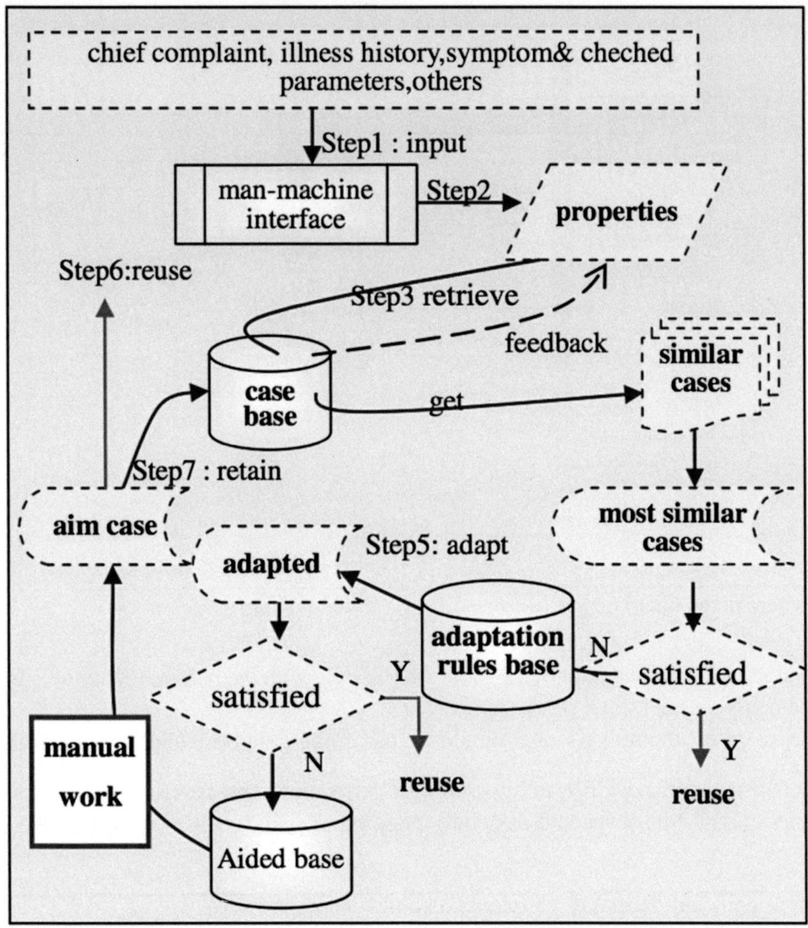

FIG. 23

An architecture for CBR in health.

(3) Adapt the most similar case;
(4) Reuse the adapted case; and
(5) Retain the new case into the case-base after reuse.

In Fig. 23, the case representation, case retrieval, and adaptation are three key links. The reasoning process includes the following steps:

- Step 1: Input the seed case
- Step 2: Retrieve from a knowledge base or an ontology and identify some similar cases; if case founded can be used to solve the above case, go to step 3, otherwise go to step 4
- Step 3: Case reuse
- Step 4: Select the most similar case, adopt some methods to revise and optimize it. If it meets the requirements, go to step 5, otherwise go to step 6

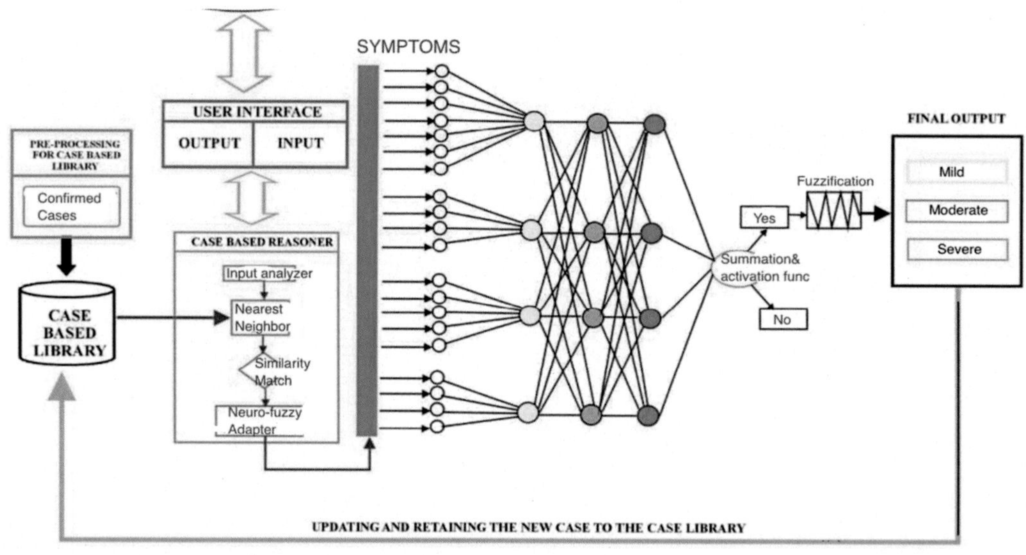

FIG. 24

System architecture of the neuro-fuzzy CBR model.

- Step 5: Produce a further revision of the most similar case with the help of the knowledge base until the requirements are met, then go to step 6
- Step 6: Reuse cases; the revised case should be put in the case base and case study is finished

Fig. 24 depicts the neuro-fuzzy CBR architecture that performs the processes to detect a suspected disease and further classify the suspected case into a degree of severity. We enumerate the steps of the algorithm:

- Step 1: Input personal observed symptoms as a new case
- Step 2: Submit the input symptoms for diagnoses
- Step 3: Activate the Euclidean distance as a nearest neighbor algorithm
- Step 4: Compare the new case with all the sets of past confirmed positive and negative cases stored in the CBR library for a measure of similarity match using the Euclidean distance model in a numerical feature space or textual similarity
- Step 5: Determine which labeled case the new case resembles the most
- Step 6: Continue processing IF a measure of similarity match is found, otherwise go to step 9
- Step 7 Re-use that solution of the most similar past case
- Step 8: Adapt the past case solution to obtain a solution for the new case using the a neural network model
- Step 9: Activate the neural network model
- Step 10: Compute $X=\sum_{i=1}^{n} x_i * w_j$
- Step 11: Compute $Y=\{\text{Yes if } x>0 \text{ and No otherwise}\}$
- Step 12: Activation of the fuzzy logic model
- Step 13: Compute the degree of severity $Y=\sum_{i=1}^{n} L_3(x_i)$

- Step 14: Generate classified output {mild, moderate, severe}
- Step 15: Retain the new case and its solution into the case-based library for reference purpose in solving future cases
- Step 16: Update the CBR library

4.1 Mining cases from health forum threads

Online forums provide a convenient channel for people to share their experiences and exchange ideas. As they attract more and more users, these forums become valuable resources for extracting useful knowledge through the forum search, question answering, and expert finding. A typical forum thread consists of a sequence of posts ordered according to the time when the post is submitted. Thread data can be a useful source to match an unknown case.

Logically, a thread can be represented by a tree structure, where each post has one parent to which it replies, except the first post, which is the root of the tree.

One post can be replied to by multiple posts (i.e., it can have many children). Fig. 25 shows an example of a forum thread in tree representation. The tree structure of forum threads can boost the performance of automated forum information extraction (Duan and Zhai, 2011; Liu and Chen, 2013). In addition, reconstructed thread links can save users time and effort to track and get involved in the discussion and help them to understand the interaction among forum users, such as who is following whom or who is the receiver of a suggestion.

An important research question is how to reconstruct complete thread structures (Liu et al., 2019; Aumayr et al., 2011; Wang et al., 2011a). Most of the online forums do not have complete thread structures available, which means the parents of some posts are unknown. Many forum authors just use the default mode to reply without explicitly indicating to which posts they reply or citing existing posts. There is a corpus of research for learning forum structure, such as thread conditional random fields, proposed by Wang et al. (2011b).

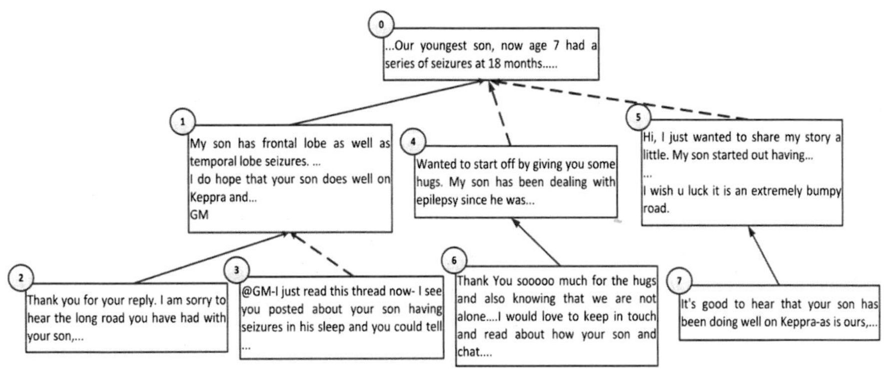

FIG. 25

An example of a thread. *Solid lines* indicate request-response relationship; *dotted line relations* need to be inferred.

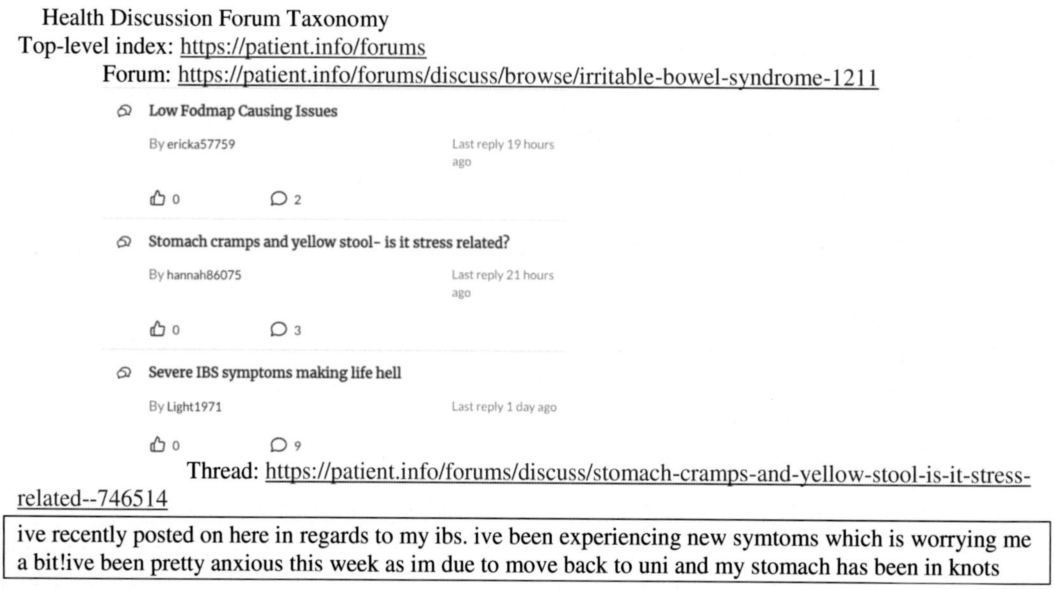

Health Discussion Forum Taxonomy
Top-level index: https://patient.info/forums
Forum: https://patient.info/forums/discuss/browse/irritable-bowel-syndrome-1211

Low Fodmap Causing Issues
By ericka57759 Last reply 19 hours ago
0 2

Stomach cramps and yellow stool- is it stress related?
By hannah86075 Last reply 21 hours ago
0 3

Severe IBS symptoms making life hell
By Light1971 Last reply 1 day ago
0 9

Thread: https://patient.info/forums/discuss/stomach-cramps-and-yellow-stool-is-it-stress-related--746514

ive recently posted on here in regards to my ibs. ive been experiencing new symtoms which is worrying me a bit!ive been pretty anxious this week as im due to move back to uni and my stomach has been in knots

FIG. 26

A health discussion forum taxonomy.

They typically require training data that have complete thread structures, which is not always available and sometimes obtained through labor-intensive manual labeling. We observe two properties in online health forums that we would like to leverage to learn thread structures in a scalable way without manually labeled training data. One is the prevalently available partially labeled thread structures in online forums, and the other is the key role that person references play in person-centric forums.

Usually, health forum users introduce problems and make comments in a subjective way, describing personal experience and giving feedback to other users (Fig. 26). In other words, a thread has a collection of user cases raised by some forum users and commented on by others. Since a post often refers to other persons mentioned either in this post or in the parent or ancestor post, identifying the correct thread structure in person-centric forums is important to understand the context.

The discourse structure of the thread is represented as a rooted, directed acyclic graph with speech act labels associated with each edge of the graph. In this example, user A initiates the thread with a question (speech act = *Question-Question*) in the first post, by asking how to create an interactive input box on a webpage. In response, users B and C give independent answers (speech act = *Answer-Answer*). After that, A responds to C to confirm the parameters of the solution (speech act = *Answer-Confirmation*), and at the same time, adds extra information to their original question (speech act = *Question-Add*), that is, this one post has two distinct dependency links associated with it. Finally, D gives a different solution again to the original question.

The dialogue-oriented speech act includes five categories: Question, Answer, Resolution (confirmation of the question being resolved), Reproduction (external confirmation of a proposed solution working), and Other. Each question category contains four sub-categories: *Question*, *Add*, *Confirmation*, and *Correction*. In addition, the Answer category contains five sub-categories: *Answer*, *Add*,

Confirmation, *Correction*, and *Objection*. For example, the label Question-Add belongs to the *Question* category and *Add* sub-category, meaning "addition of extra information to a question" (Chapter 10).

4.2 Discourse disentanglement

Discourse disentanglement (such as classification of links between portions of texts or documents) and dialogue/speech/communicative act tagging have been extensively studied (Wang et al., 2011b). Discourse disentanglement is the task of splitting a conversation (Elsner and Charniak, 2008) or documents (Wolf and Gibson, 2005) into a sequence of distinct portions of text (sub-discourses). The disentangled discourse is modeled via a tree structure (Grosz and Sidner, 1986; Seo et al., 2009), an acyclic graph structure (Rose et al., 1995; Elsner and Charniak, 2008), or a cyclic chain graph structure (Wolf and Gibson, 2005). Speech acts are used to describe the function or role of an utterance in a discourse, similarly to our CDT representation, and have been employed for the analysis of communication means including conversational speech, instant messaging, security analysis of documents (Galitsky and Makowski, 2017), online forums (Kim et al., 2010; Galitsky et al., 2007), and chats (Galitsky and Ilvovsky, 2017). Automated answer scoring benefits from semantic and discourse analyses as well (Wanas et al., 2008). For a more complete review of models for discourse disentanglement and speech act tagging, we refer the reader to Kim et al. (2010).

Wang et al. (2013) presented the task of parsing user forum threads to determine the labeled dependencies between posts. Three methods, including a dependency parsing approach, are proposed to jointly classify the links (relationships) between posts and the dialogue act (type) of each link. The authors predicted not only the links between posts but also showed the type of each link, in the form of the discourse structure of the thread. A richer visualization of thread structure (e.g., highlighting the key posts that appear to have led to a successful resolution to a problem), and more sensitive weighting of posts in threads can be beneficial for indexing for search.

5. Building a repository of labeled cases and diagnoses

In this section we explore the possibility of applying discourse analysis not just at the level of short text but also at the level of documents, such as patient cases and treatment manuals. We extend the notion of a DT and set rhetorical relations between the documents and their sections to match with multi-case descriptions of patient illnesses.

5.1 An example of navigating an extended discourse tree for three documents

We now present an example of a content exploration scenario based on an extended discourse tree (EDT) covering three documents (Fig. 27). These documents in our example are related to "Faceted search," which plays an important role in medical applications.

For instance, a search across healthcare policies would require facets on diseases, symptoms, and treatments, and additional resources. Determining the top categories can take some time so that these categories reflect common shared knowledge and vocabulary. The top facets do not have to be less than five, but they do need to contain what is needed by the application and users to organize the content.

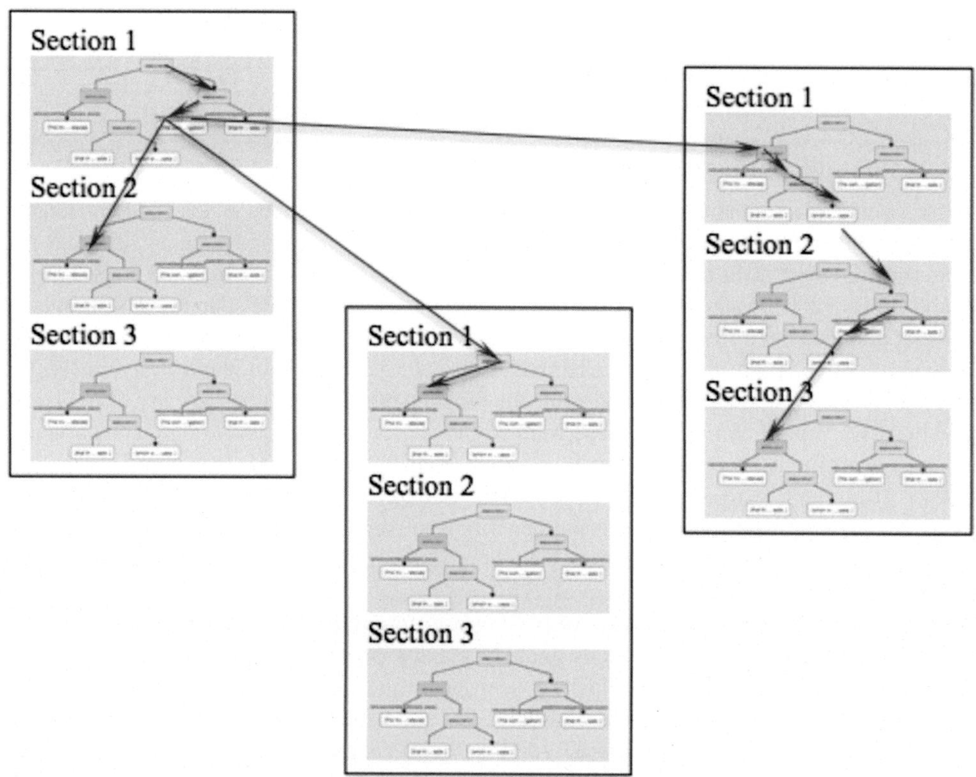

FIG. 27

Illustration for the idea of extended discourse tree (DT): intra-paragraph rhetorical relations are combined with inter-document links also labeled as rhetorical relations.

Faceted Search

Facets correspond to properties of the information elements. They are often derived by analyzing the text of an item using entity extraction techniques or from pre-existing fields in a database such as author, descriptor, language, and format. Thus, existing web pages, product descriptions, or online collections of articles can be augmented with navigational facets.

Within the academic community, faceted search has attracted interest primarily among library and information science researchers, but there is also some from computer science researchers specializing in information retrieval.

Entity Extraction

Entity extraction, also known as entity name extraction or named entity recognition, is an information retrieval technique that refers to the process of identifying and classifying key elements from text into pre-defined categories.

Information Retrieval

...

Documents that are not linked by the multi-CBR Symptom Checker Engine need to be subject to EDT analysis. EDT analysis can help to associate entities by a human explorer (Fig. 28). Let a user ask a

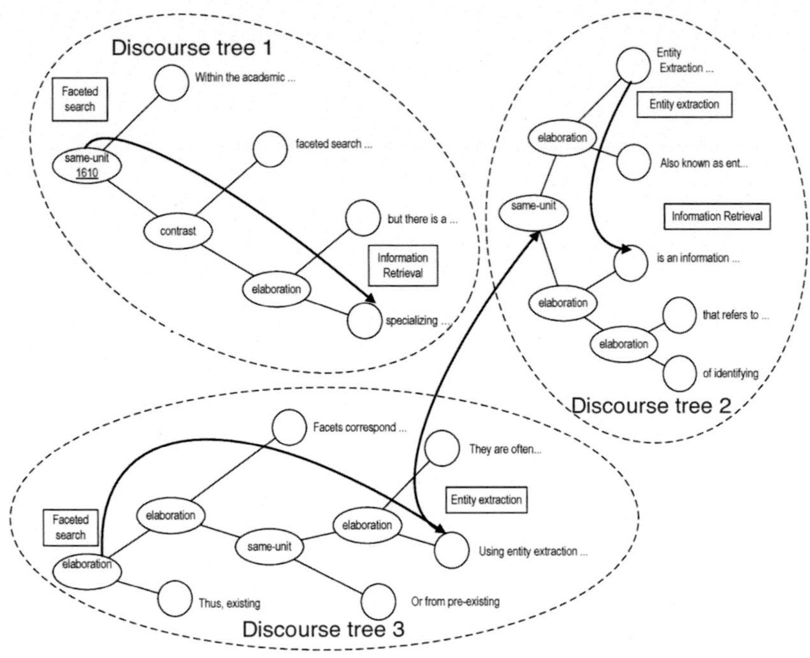

FIG. 28

Another way to represent an extended discourse tree (EDT) connecting documents.

question "What is a faceted search?" To understand how the faceted search works, it is necessary to become fluent with other concepts associated with faceted search. A search engine component within multi-CBR provides further content exploration or search options based on satellite EDUs in the DT of the document "*Faceted search*" (Fig. 28, top left). It built multiple DTs (one for each paragraph; two are shown) and formed the following items for content exploration:

- "entity extraction"
- "information retrieval"
- pre-existing fields in a database
- augmented with navigational facets

The user can either follow the link to land on a single piece of information or run a new search to get multiple search results to choose from. If a user choses "entity extraction," they are led to the respective document (Fig. 28, top right). The Symptom Checker Engine proceeds to the next iteration, discovering the phrases from satellites of the DT node corresponding to "entity extraction":

- "entity recognition"
- "information retrieval"

If a user now selects the second option, they would navigate to the "information retrieval" document.

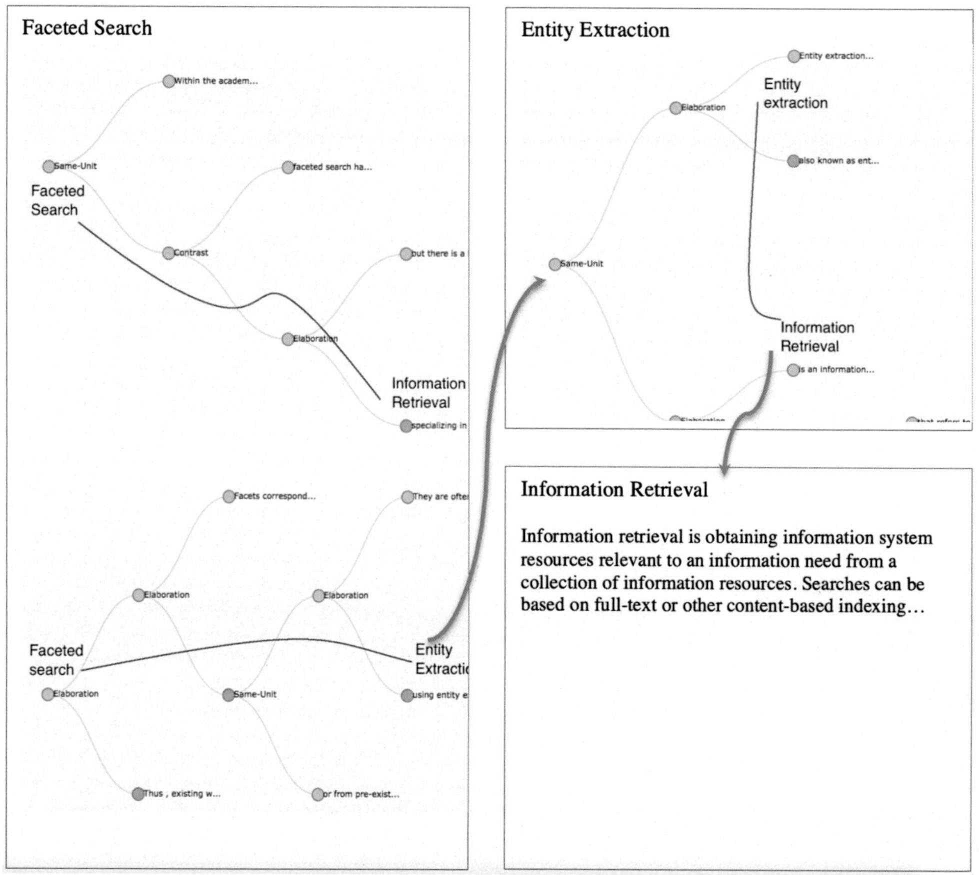

FIG. 29

Extended discourse tree (EDT) for a set of documents used to navigate to a desired document or its portion.

Whereas a DT of a sentence, paragraph or a document is a well-explored area, algorithms for building a discourse-level representation of a collection of documents in various formats and styles from different sources has not been explored well. Irrespectively of the document granularity level, the same relationships such as *Elaboration*, *Contrast*, and *Attribution* may hold between the certain portions of text across documents (Fig. 29).

5.2 Constructing extended DTs

To construct EDTs, the focus is building rhetorical links between text fragments in different paragraphs or documents. The main difficulty here is identifying a relationship between mentions similar to how it is done in coreference analysis. The other difficulty is to label an inter-document rhetorical relation. To address this, we form a fictitious text fragment from the respective text fragments of the original paragraph and perform coreference analysis and discourse parsing.

The input of the EDT algorithm is a set of documents, and an output is an EDT that is encoded as a regular DT with the labels of document identification for each node. The processing flow is as follows:

(1) Build a set of all DTs for each paragraph in each document *DTA*
(2) Iterate through all pairs of DT_i and $DT_j \in DTA$
(3) Identify noun phrases and named entities in DT_i and DT_j
(4) Compute overlap and identify common entities E_{ij} between DT_i and DT_j
(5) Establish relationships between occurrences of entities in $E_{i\ j}$ such as *equals*, *sub-entity*, and *part-of*
(6) Confirm these relationships by forming text fragment merging EDU(E_i) and EDU(E_j) and applying coreference resolution
(7) Form inter-paragraph rhetorical links R(E_{ij}) for each entity pair occurrence in E_{ij}
(8) Classify the rhetorical relation for each rhetorical link by forming a text fragment merging EDU(E_i) and EDU(E_j), building its DT and using a recognized relation label for this rhetorical link

To construct conventional DTs, we used one of the existing discourse parsers (Joty et al., 2013; Surdeanu et al., 2015; Feng and Hirst, 2014).

Radev (2000) introduced the cross-document structure theory (CST), a paradigm for multi-document analysis. CST takes into account the rhetorical structure of clusters of related textual documents. He specified a taxonomy of relations between documents known as cross-document links. CST is intended as a foundation to summarize a collection of documents initiated by a user as well as to navigate the collection by an abstract information-access machine.

To proceed from RST to CST, one cannot employ the deliberateness of writing style, relying on discourse markers within individual documents. However, it is possible to leverage a logical structure across documents that are systematic, predictable, and useful. CST attempts to attach a certain reasoning flow to an imaginary "collective" author of a set of documents.

One of the first studies of rhetorical relations between documents was presented by Trigg and Weiser (1987) for scientific papers, such as citation, refutation, revision, equivalence, and comparison. These rhetorical relations are grouped into Normal (inter-document relations) and Commentary (deliberate cross-document relations). However, it is hard to see this model's applicability beyond the scientific domain.

One way to represent the multi-document navigation structure is a multi-document cube (Fig. 30, top). It is a three-dimensional structure that represents related documents with dimensions of *time* (ordered), *source* (unordered), and *position within the document* (ordered).

We now proceed from the multi-document cubes toward a way to represent text simultaneously at different levels of granularity (words, phrases, sentences, paragraphs, and documents) via the multi-document graph (Fig. 31). Each graph consists of smaller subgraphs for each individual document, which in turn consists of DTs. Two types of links are employed. The first type represents inheritance relationships among elements within a single document. These links are drawn using thicker lines. The second type represents semantic relationships among textual units. The example illustrates sample links among documents, phrases, and sentences.

Fig. 32 shows the multistep CST-based algorithm for building the navigation graph, given a corpus of documents.

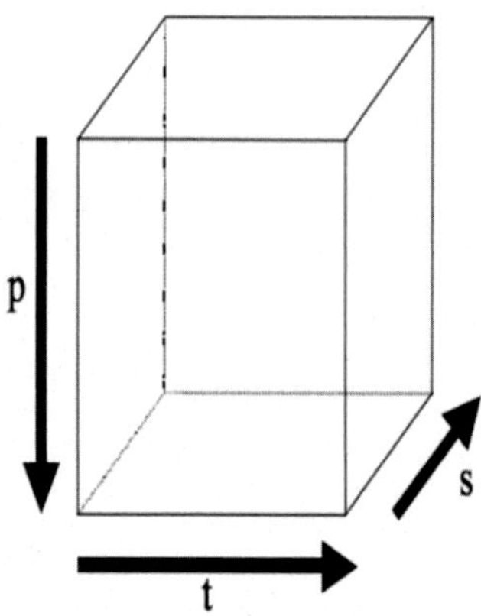

FIG. 30

A multi-document cube.

FIG. 31

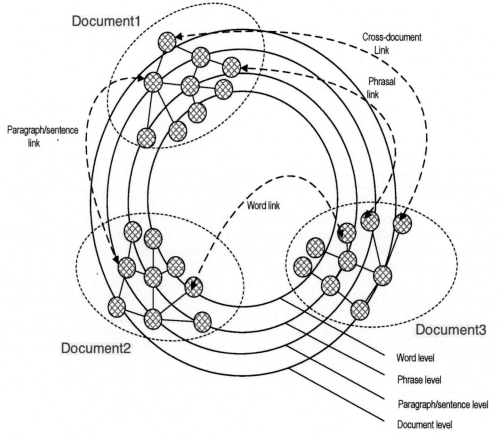

Multi-document cube (top) and navigational graph (bottom).

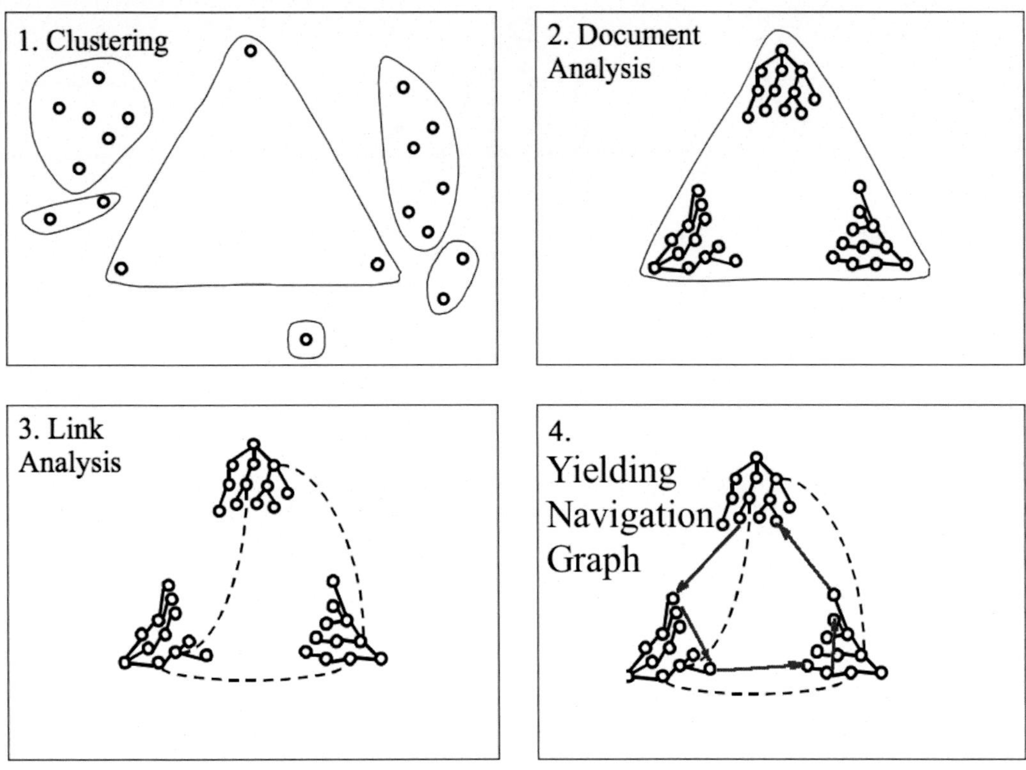

FIG. 32

The steps of building a navigation graph based on extended discourse trees (EDTs).

The first step is clustering, which can be done based on document similarity (Allan, 1996). Another option is to have clusters as the sets of documents returned by a search engine; the results will depend on a user query. The second step, document analysis, includes the generation of document trees representing the sentential and phrasal structure of the document. The third step is an automated building and categorizing of links between textual spans across documents. Here the following family of approaches can be used: lexical distance, lexical chains, information extraction, and linguistic template matching. The lexical distance can use a cosine similarity across pairs of sentences, and lexical chains (Barzilay and Elhadad, 1997) can be more robust leveraging synonymy and hypernymy.

A graph-based operator defines a transformation on a multi-document navigation graph (MDNG) G that preserves some of its properties while reducing the number of nodes. An example of such an operator is the link-preserving graph cover operator (Fig. 33). Its effect is to preserve only these nodes from the source MDG that are associated with the *preferred* cross-document links. In this example, the central circled area represents the summary subgraph G_1 of G that contains all five cross-document links and only these nodes and edges of G that are necessary to preserve the textual structure of G_1.

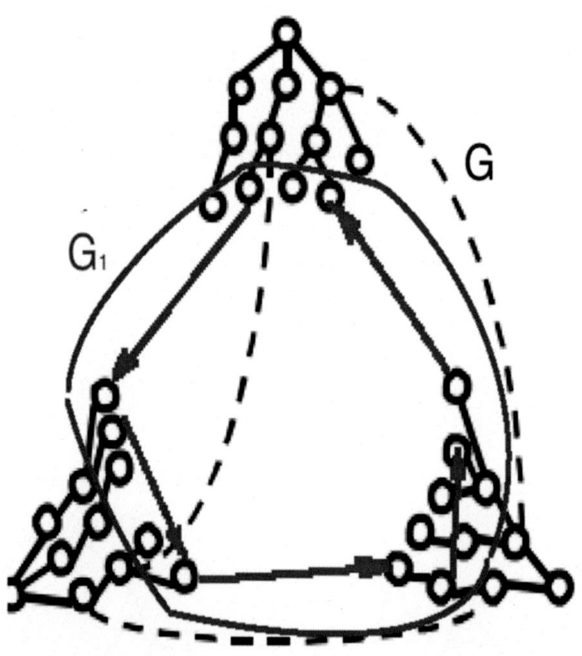

FIG. 33

A multi-document navigation graph—an early alternative to CDT.

6. System architecture

Having considered conventional CBR architectures in the health domain in Section 4, we now focus on the multi-CBR architecture of this chapter. Fig. 34 depicts the Sources for Diagnoses Manager chart. We have five sources, each of which is subject to individual source-specific split into texts for single diseases. Each source has its own way to establish relationships between described symptoms. All sources are then subject to entity extraction (Chapter 11), text indexing, relationship storage, and a special indexing for lookup. The Sources for Diagnoses Manager assures that any text will be matched with multiple sources in a uniform way and search results will be ordered according to search relevance to produce a list of candidate matches with the rhetorical relationship between them, as described in Section 2. The bottom component's implementation is described in Section 5.

Fig. 35 shows the overall architecture of the Symptom Checker Engine. The input to the system, the textual patient complaint, is on the top left. Discourse-level operations are shown on the top right and other lower-level linguistic operations are shown on the left. Section 2.4 describes the semantic similarity assessor and Section 5 describes the *Relationship Agreement* verifier with other DT processing. Section 3 presents the internals of the *Matching Engine* that performs the alignment on both syntactic and semantic levels.

The bottom part of the figure shows iterations for filtering matching candidates. Once a current split of seed text is performed based on the DT, a match with each text fragment occurs. As a set of relationships between labeled cases is established, it is assessed in terms of agreement with the relationships

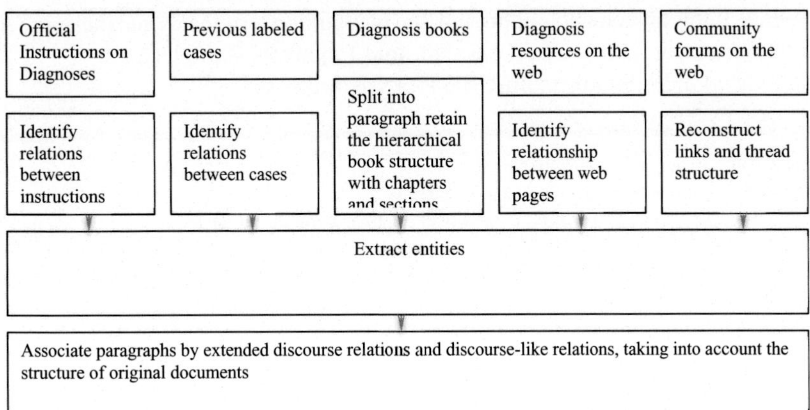

FIG. 34

The sources for diagnoses manager.

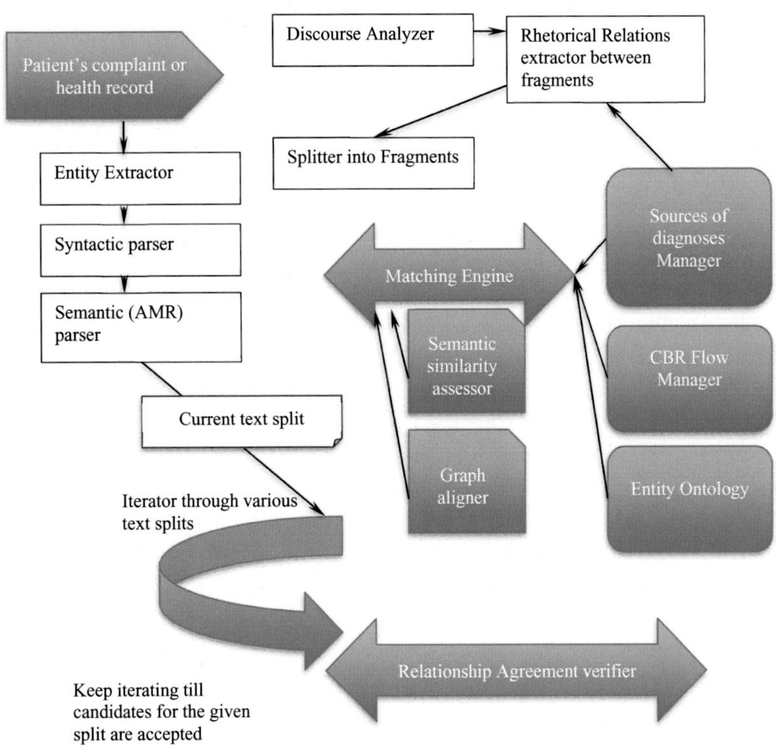

FIG. 35

Overall architecture of the Symptom Checker Engine.

between fragments. If this agreement is approved, the recognition terminates and the approved matched label cases form the output. Otherwise, a new spit into fragments is produced.

Hence a high-level algorithm of multi-CBR looks as follows:

(1) Split text S into fragments such as paragraphs
(2) Further split S into fragments for individual diseases F
(3) Perform discourse parsing and determine rhetorical relations between fragments F
(4) Form a query for each F_i and obtain labeled candidate cases C_i
(5) For each F_i find a set of matching candidates C_i by running the queries
(6) Iterate through the sets of $F_i \rightarrow C_i$
    a. Form a network of rhetorical-like relations between C_i
(7) Find C_i^{best} returning to steps (2) and (6).

7. Evaluation

We evaluate the performance of Symptom Checker Engine in a wide spectrum of health domains, recognizing diseases mentioned in all kinds of medical texts, from patient records to reports to physician notes.

7.1 Datasets

In Table 2 we enumerate our five major sources of patient complaints and disease symptoms. Grayed rows denote both seed patient complaints and labeled cases, and other rows denote only labeled cases. We use Bing Search API (Microsoft Cognitive Services) to access cases online and offline for both matching and scraping. Once we form a query from the seed text, we run both local and web searches to obtain candidates for similar cases. Then the similarity between the seed text and candidates is performed to approve or reject candidates (Sections 2.5 and 3). As multiple candidates with the same disease label are approved, the Symptom Checker Engine makes the decision.

For health forums such as PatientInfo, we scrape at least 20 topics in each category and at least 30 forums for each topic.

Our evaluation heavily relies on ICD. For disease identification instructions, we collect the disease name from ICD and then form the Bing query "*How to diagnose*" + <ICD disease name>. The first pre-prepared answer is scraped and put into the lookup.

7.2 Evaluation of text matching

We define a diagnosis as *correct* if three or more matches (labeled cases) are identified and more than 80% of these cases have the same disease label. If only three or four cases are identified, all of them must agree on the disease label. In the situation with five matches, only one foreign label is allowed.

Table 2 Sources for the Symptom Checker Engine.

Source	Size, # disease descriptions	Characteristics	Web sources	Access for Symptom Checker Engine
Identification instructions	1700	Covers the majority of diseases including rare diseases	https://icd.who.int/browse10/2019/en#/M30	Local
Labeled cases	2450		Kaggle, https://data.world/arvin6/medical-records-10-yrs	Local, multi-hop web searches
Diagnosis books	3200	Free books from public sources	www.medicalbooknew.com www.pdfdrive.com designed robots that use Bing API to get book PDF links, which are then used for download	Google book search, local Amazon search
Diagnosis resources from the Web	12,000	Accessed via Bing API and/or scraped	Web MD www.allthingsmedicine.com	Via web search, WebMD search, search of WebMD via Bing
Health forums	4000	Not curated by medical professionals	Patient Info ehealthforum.com/health/health_forums.html www.healthforum.com/ www.spine-health.com/forum forums.menshealth.com/ www.netdoctor.co.uk/interactive/discussion/index.php www.mentalhealthforum.net/forum/ www.mcmasterhealthforum.org/ www.womens-health.com/boards/forum www.healthyplace.com/forum/ www.healthfulchat.org/health-forums.html https://forums.womenshealthmatters.ca www.topix.com/forum/health able2know.org/forum/health/ www.psychforums.com/ curezone.com/forums/ www.syracuse.com/forums/health/ forums.realhealthmag.com/ forums.psychcentral.com/	

A majority vote algorithm can be applied to classification candidates as well as to classifiers themselves. As we obtain the classification from multiple candidates or multiple classifiers, we select the result obtained by a larger subset of candidate samples (Ruta and Gabrys, 2005; Theodoridis and Koutroumbas, 2009). The majority vote approach "confirms" the classification automatically. However, an additional automated check on the labeled data is needed to estimate the error rate of the majority vote decision, which is estimated to be 5.2%. In more than 5% of cases, the majority vote on candidates gives one result, but the true result is different. This error rate yields the deviation estimates of the accuracy values presented in Tables 3 and 4.

We first evaluate how the text match can deliver relevant cases in a one-to-one case→case setting. We chose a patient's complaint with a *single illness* and searched for a *single illness* identification instruction, case, description, or community blog post as both unknown and labeled cases and experimented with similarity assessment. For text matching evaluation, we only used the seed data (simulating patients complaints), which is labeled with a diagnosis.

Table 3 The Symptom Checker Engine recognizes a *pair* of diseases.

	Any relation between labeled cases		Only proper relation between labeled cases	
Source ***Two diseases***	**%**	**Avg # of matches (OR match)**	**%**	**Avg # of matches (AND match)**
Identification instruction	68.7	8.3	74.3	3.1
Labeled cases	70.4	10.1	75.8	2.9
Diagnosis books	69.3	8.4	74.7	2.0
Diagnosis resources from the Web	67.2	12.0	74.0	2.7
Health forums	66.7	14.2	73.1	4.2

Table 4 The Symptom Checker Engine recognizes a *triad* of diseases.

	Any relation between labeled cases		Only proper relation between labeled cases	
Source ***Three diseases***	**%**	**Avg # of matches (OR match)**	**%**	**Avg # of matches (AND match)**
Identification instruction	47.1	12.2	63.0	2.3
Labeled cases	49.6	14.7	70.5	2.2
Diagnosis books	49.4	15.3	67.0	2.7
Diagnosis resources from the Web	45.2	12.2	68.1	2.4
Health forums	50.8	13.5	65.3	2.2

Table 5 Evaluation of various text-matching techniques.

Source	Keyword/ TF*IDF	Syntactic only	Semantic only	Entity only	Joint entity, syntactic and semantic
Identification instruction	57.1	64.3	71.2	65.3	79.4
Labeled cases	54.2	62.1	70.7	64.1	73.2
Diagnosis books	60.4	65.7	72.4	65.8	76.0
Diagnosis resources from the Web	58.4	62.9	69.5	63.3	75.3
Health forums	55.3	60.4	71.0	66.3	74.8

We experiment with various text-matching techniques and verify which one provides a better single-case match (Table 5). As is fairly natural and confirmed in our previous studies (Galitsky, 2017a), syntactic, semantic, and entity match complement each other in similarity assessment (the rightmost column). The hybrid representation outperforms the keyword baseline by 33%, syntactic matching by 20%, semantic similarity by only 6%, and entity-only matching by 16%.

7.3 Overall assessment of the Symptom Checker engine

We now evaluate the contribution of the main idea of this chapter, the *agreement* between relations between the seed fragments and relations between the labeled multi-case data, to the Symptom Checker Engine. We show the percentages of correct diagnoses computed similarly to the previous section. Grayed columns show the numbers of successfully matched cases, where the majority vote is applied to confirm or reject the diagnosed illness. We show recognition accuracy for *each* identified disease, even though we recognize a pair or a triple of diseases.

We compare recognition accuracy for the complex case where there is a pair of diseases mentioned in the patient's complaint (Table 3):

(1) not enforcing a proper relation between labeled cases (columns 2 and 3)
(2) enforcing a proper relation (columns 4 and 5)

We can observe that enforcing a proper relation improves the recognition accuracy for each disease of a pair by 8.6%, averaging through the sources.

In Table 3, *Avg # of matches* shows the average number of document/case pairs identified. Notice that it is a disease classification (not a document search) problem, so we are not concerned with the recall (the number of documents used to classify the given seed one). The percentages of actual correct classification as a portion of total available correct cases would correspond to search recall.

We observe that enforcing the agreement of rhetorical relations between text fragments yields 5.5%–7% of the disease recognition accuracy for the case of two diseases. Once this agreement is enforced, the number of matched cases naturally drops to about one-third.

For a triple of diseases, one can observe that enforcing the agreement of rhetorical relations between text fragments yields 15%–20% of the disease recognition accuracy. When we ignore this agreement, the accuracy per case is low, approaching 50%. When the agreement is enforced, the number of matched cases naturally drops to about one-sixth.

7.4 Diagnosing forum data

In community forum like PatientInfo, patients share their experiences with each other, and it is sometimes hard to diagnose an illness. We apply the Symptom Checker Engine to the unlabeled forum data and attempt to identify an illness description in an authoritative source on the Web such as WebMD. As the Symptom Checker Engine makes a correct decision most of the time, it would be useful to share its results with the patients and users of community health forums where the illness assignment is not curated by professionals. For evaluating how the Symptom Checker Engine performs on unlabeled community forums, we only use raw seed data (for patients' complaints) that is *not* labeled with a diagnosis. The decision is considered *correct* if the majority vote results produce an agreement among themselves.

Before we proceed to the evaluation, we give another example of the Symptom Checker Engine functionality. An example post (PatientInfo, 2020) is as follows:

I am a 22 year old female and two weeks ago noticed a large lump under my chin. Phoned my GP and he prescribed me an antibiotic as my throat was also a bit achy. I've finished the course of antibiotics now and the lump on my neck has decreased slightly in size but is still there. I was lying on my chest in bed and noticed a pain around my collarbone. I felt around and it seems I have two large lumps on each collarbone with the left slightly painful. I am worried now that it may be something more sinister as last year I had physiotherapy for what was thought to be torn adductors but I am worried now that it may have been a sign of swelling in my groin also. Not long ago I had pain in my lower left abdomen that was so painful I considered going to an emergency room and I have been on/off sick for a few months.

Fig. 36 depicts a DT for this patient complaint. The top-level *Elaboration* relation splits the medical complaint into two parts, each of which needs its own case to identify the illness. The top one is related to *large lump under my chin* and the bottom is related to *large lumps on each collarbone*. Each disease is illustrated by a schematic image on the right.

Red-framed rectangles on the right show the descriptions of the identified labeled cases for each fragment of the patient complaint. We show in blue the relation between these cases, obtained via search query <Entity from labeled case 1> "*causes/leads to/is followed/brings*" <Entity from labeled case 2>. The Google search result is shown in the blue frame, connecting the labeled cases.

Table 6 presents the evaluation results for community forum data. In the left two columns, we enumerate the classes of diseases and the percentages of posts with more than one disease. For example, more than one-third of posts in the *Child Health* class indicate two or more diseases. The third and fourth columns show the single disease accuracy based on the single source and the "fivefold" accuracy based on all five sources, respectively. The former accuracy is estimated to be 10% greater than the latter; this means that if a disease is confirmed by fivefold identification (not a single majority vote), then the confidence is significantly greater.

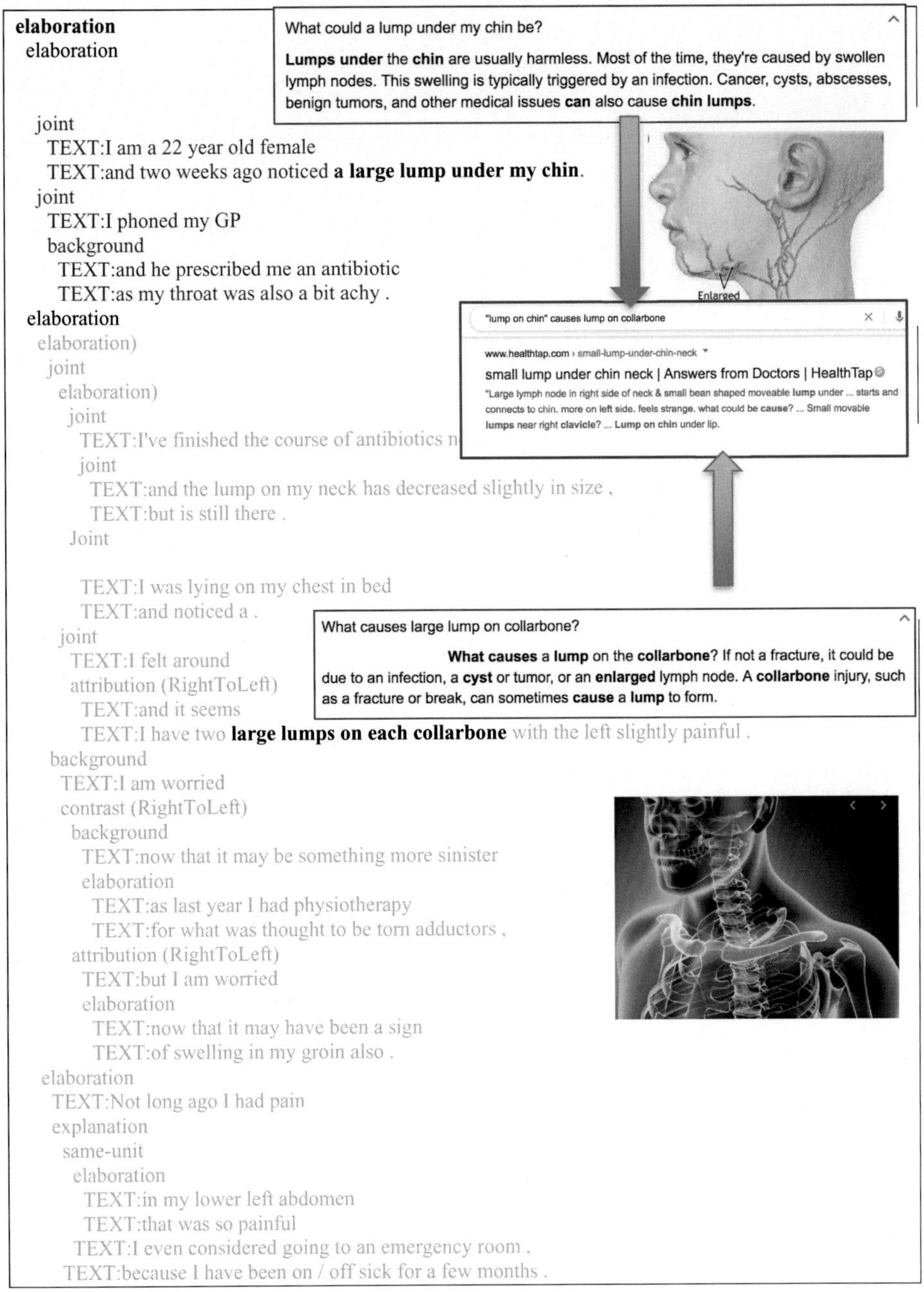

```
elaboration
 elaboration
  joint
   TEXT:I am a 22 year old female
   TEXT:and two weeks ago noticed a large lump under my chin.
  joint
   TEXT:I phoned my GP
   background
    TEXT:and he prescribed me an antibiotic
    TEXT:as my throat was also a bit achy .
 elaboration
  elaboration)
   joint
    elaboration)
     joint
      TEXT:I've finished the course of antibiotics n
      joint
       TEXT:and the lump on my neck has decreased slightly in size ,
       TEXT:but is still there .
     Joint

      TEXT:I was lying on my chest in bed
      TEXT:and noticed a .
    joint
     TEXT:I felt around
     attribution (RightToLeft)
      TEXT:and it seems
      TEXT:I have two large lumps on each collarbone with the left slightly painful .
   background
    TEXT:I am worried
    contrast (RightToLeft)
     background
      TEXT:now that it may be something more sinister
      elaboration
       TEXT:as last year I had physiotherapy
       TEXT:for what was thought to be torn adductors ,
     attribution (RightToLeft)
      TEXT:but I am worried
      elaboration
       TEXT:now that it may have been a sign
       TEXT:of swelling in my groin also .
  elaboration
   TEXT:Not long ago I had pain
   explanation
    same-unit
     elaboration
      TEXT:in my lower left abdomen
      TEXT:that was so painful
     TEXT:I even considered going to an emergency room ,
    TEXT:because I have been on / off sick for a few months .
```


FIG. 36

A discourse tree (DT) for a sample patient complaint from a health forum.

Table 6 Results of the Symptom Checker Engine for community forum data.

		Single disease		Multiple diseases	
Category	Percentages of posts where multiple diseases/ conditions were identified	Disease is identified correctly in one (single) source out if five, %	Disease is identified correctly in all sources out of five, %	Disease is identified correctly for all fragments, %	Relationship between labeled cases is identified correctly, %
Child Health	36	73.2	61.7	43.3	73.2
Heart Health	43	75.4	62.0	39.1	70.4
Men's Health	60	72.0	59.3	37.5	69.0
Mental Health	72	77.2	63.4	46.8	67.3
Pregnancy	17	75.0	64.5	44.0	66.8
Sexual Health	35	70.2	62.7	43.2	65.4
Skin Conditions	40	69.3	63.2	41.4	67.5
Women's Health	57	70.7	64.1	39.5	66.0

The results for a more challenging task that is a target of the Symptom Checker Engine, the multiple disease checker, are shown in columns five and six. The average disease recognition precision for all classes is 43%, and the respective intermediate recognition of the relationships has an average accuracy of 66.6%. This disease recognition accuracy is insufficient for automated decision-making, however, it is reasonably helpful in a decision support setting to assist with or confirm manual diagnoses. The functionality of the Symptom Checker Engine is crucial for the identification of rare diseases or illnesses with implicit, contradictory symptoms that require further confirmation by lab tests.

8. Related work

Despite its explainability, CBR has a strong limitation: its prediction accuracy is usually less than other AI techniques such as deep learning. In order to obtain accurate results from CBR, effective retrieval and matching of useful prior cases for the problem are required. It is still an art rather than computational science to design a good matching and retrieval mechanism for CBR (Galitsky, 2006).

Ahn and Kim (2009) proposed a new method to enhance the prediction performance of CBR, doing a simultaneous optimization of feature weights, instance selection, and the number of neighbors that combine using genetic algorithms. The model improves the prediction performance in three ways:

(1) computing a similarity between cases more accurately by leveraging relative importance of each feature

(2) eliminating useless, erroneous, or noisy cases

(3) combining multiple similar cases that represent significant patterns (similar to the focus of this chapter)

To validate the usefulness of their model, Ahn and Kim (2009) employed it in a real-world environment for evaluating *cytological features* derived directly from a digital scan of breast fine-needle aspirate slides. The experiments demonstrate that the prediction accuracy of conventional CBR may be improved significantly by using the authors' approach. The study also verifies that the model outperforms the other optimized models for CBR using genetic algorithms.

In general, data mining and CBR can be used to extract patterns, illustrate useful properties of existing clinical data, and perform decision support in clinical diagnosis. In *breast cancer* research, the helpful information drawn from different medical datasets is significant for clinical decision-making and treatment. Data can be examined through various parameters by data mining applications. It is possible to find the association among different events, for example, whether breast cancer has an influence on other diseases or has a connection to some clinical features. It is also possible to find similar trends or objects for a specific purpose, for example, whether a group or cluster of breast cancer patients has similar drug sensitivity with the same treatment plan (Gupta et al., 2011). The studies of CBR in health state that there are many opportunities to work in diagnostic support for disabled and elderly (Ocampo et al., 2011; Ting et al., 2011).

Marling et al. (2009) proposed a CBR system for people with *diabetes on insulin pump therapy*. These patients need to control their glucose levels within a certain range. A proper glucose level is required to avoid serious disease development such as blindness or neuropathy. CBR is chosen because of the following:

(1) existing recommendations for managing diabetes are general and must be personalized to individual patient needs
(2) life situations and environmental factors influence blood glucose levels, thus so the cases with patients with similar factors need to be identified
(3) CBR has been applied successfully to the management of other long-term medical conditions

A preliminary clinical study with 20 patients was conducted by Marling et al. (2009) to assess CBR decision support. The researchers collected 50 cases into a case library. A rule-based situation evaluation subsystem was constructed to detect common problems in *blood glucose* level. In addition, information retrieval metrics were proposed to identify the most similar past cases for solving the current seed case.

A mixed-case retrieval approach (Gu et al., 2010) was introduced for the knowledge reuse of *dental records* by employing fuzzy logic that improves a similarity algorithm based on Euclidean Lagrangian distance. The system is used for generating dental cases. The precision of the system, the efficiency of the retrieval method, and the flexibility range are assessed on the built dataset of cases. The system reduces the time of generating health records and improves the overall user impression and quality of making diagnoses and managing of health records.

Ahmed et al. (2012) presented a hybrid clinical decision support system for *stress diagnosis* and treatment based on a family of AI techniques having CBR as a core. By using textual IR with ontology, the system is able to handle a patient's personalized information including life environment and behavioral habits. The fuzzy rule-based classification component bootstraps cases where only a limited number of them are available in the beginning of the deployment. The fuzzy similarity method embedded into the CBR system can handle vagueness and uncertainty inherently existing in clinicians' reasoning.

Das (2019) designed a voice analysis system to detect symptoms of *respiratory problems*. Using a history of the patient, a particular disease or a set of diseases can be predicted when symptoms are known. Using more training data, a forecasting machinery can be extended toward future diseases even before immediate symptoms are known.

Etsimo (2020) proposed an AI-based healthcare platform that enables physicians and *insurance companies* to offer their customers an engaging experience and predictive and preventive care instantly. By combining patient health records with lifestyle data, it is possible to *forecast* the patient's *lifespan* and suggest improvements that can extend the patient's life expectancy and reduce their number of ailing years.

Based on the Apache clinical Text Analysis Knowledge Extraction System (cTAKES), an open-source NLP system (Lin, 2020) constitutes a customized pipeline and processed about 150,000 medical records and notes for a thousand *pediatric pulmonary hypertension* patients for detecting textual mentions and signs/symptoms that may represent *adverse drug* events. The constructed pipeline includes a customized dictionary for interesting term mentions and emphasized term negation, the temporality of events, and proximity among mentions for a refined detection for the co-occurrence of medications and potential drug effects. The evaluation demonstrates that recognizing adverse drug events is up to sevenfold greater in comparison with diagnostic code-based recognition.

Patient notes not only contain patient history and clinical conditions but also are rich in contextual data and are usually more reliable sources of medical information compared to discrete-value EHRs. A medium-sized integrated health system presented by Misra (2020) covers up to 50,000 notes daily. For information extraction on retrospective data, the volume can run into millions of notes depending on the selection criteria. The system annotates notes across the entire spectrum of patient care. Using cTAKES has helped clinicians and stakeholders to extract patient narratives from patient notes using Apache SOLR and Banana.

The Babylon health system provides advice to patients who are ready to see a doctor, primarily a general practitioner. The app employs a model based on 500 million concepts. Patients using the app interact via a dialogue (Chapter 9) that asks about their symptoms. The system contains estimates of the prior probabilities of various diseases and the conditional probabilities of those illnesses given particular symptoms. It uses these probabilities to obtain estimates of the probability of each explanation for a patient's symptoms and recommends to them what kind of help to request. It is hard to imagine building a system on this scale from raw data, as a deep learning system would do. One would think that as collections of data get larger this idea seems more plausible. Nevertheless, it is hard to believe that ignoring the accumulated knowledge of symptoms and diseases would be a meaningful technique.

Although it uses doctors' knowledge, Babylon is not always appreciated by general practitioners who dislike the business model and the fact that it was brought to market without the kind of rigorous evaluation required of new drugs. Many general practitioners share information about its mistakes: a *breast lump* diagnosed as osteoporosis, a 67-year-old smoker with sudden onset chest pain told they have a stomach illness. The system clearly makes errors and it is hard to tell whether the error rate is acceptable.

Recently a Babylon research team published a paper describing a Bayesian network, presumably similar to the one used in its commercial products, which contained information on the conditional probabilities of symptoms given diseases, and of diseases given risk factors (McLachlan et al., 2020). They found that if one enters symptoms that are highly correlated with multiple diseases sharing a common risk factor, this increases the network's estimate of the probability that the risk factor is present, which can lead it to suggest diagnoses that are highly correlated with the risk factor, even when it is an implausible explanation of the symptoms. The system might deduce that a patient with *chest pain* could be obese and then suggest diabetes as a diagnosis. At the same time, using Babylon for counterfactual reasoning (asking, for example, for each possible diagnosis), or inquiring how the array of symptoms would change if the diagnosed condition were successfully treated, significantly improved the accuracy of the diagnoses, especially in cases doctors found difficult. Chapter 5 describes a similar expert system used for child patients.

De Boom et al. (2015) assessed the power of TF*IDF and several word-embedding aggregation methods to relate pairs of very short texts to each other. The authors optimally combined knowledge from both TF*IDF and word embeddings to maximize the separation between pairs and non-pairs. The best performing traditional technique is a concatenation of maximum and minimum vectors. For a large number of words, TF*IDF produces comparable results. The performance of the importance factor approach exceeds that of competitive algorithms.

Wang et al. (2009) presented a recommendation approach that combines semantic Web techniques with CBR-based recommendation techniques to merge both content information and rating information. Instead of using syntactic matching, the authors applied a semantic similarity algorithm to understand and reuse cases stored in distributed case bases. The domain ontologies provide a formal representation that includes semantic descriptions of users and products.

Whereas a number of studies apply syntactic and semantic analyses to improve the performance of CBR, to the best of our knowledge this is the first study that relies on aligned graph-based representation for syntax, semantics, and discourse to assess similarity. Moreover, discourse analysis is used to split a textual case into fragments for individual match of each fragment.

Additionally, the novelty of the technique proposed in this chapter is the new role of discourse analysis in an extended way. Discourse analysis in the broader sense of coordinating relationships between entities and documents is used to verify that the relationships between labeled cases match well with the relationships between the text fragments of the seed case.

Integration of discourse analysis into CBR has been done for dialogue management. Branting et al. (2004) proposed a dialogue management that elicits case facts in a way that reduces overall user efforts with respect to time cost, information cost, and cognitive load. The authors suggested an architecture that integrates CBR with a discourse-oriented dialogue engine. The dialogue engine determines when CBR or other problem-solving techniques are needed to achieve certain dialogue goals. However, we have not identified earlier research that applies discourse analysis to improve CBR itself. We explore dialogue management for chatbots in the health domain in Chapter 9.

Ahmed et al. (2011) outline the following research directions in general CBR:

(1) reducing the search space in case recovery
(2) maintaining knowledge always valid, embedding knowledge in cases to assist in reviewing the conclusions
(3) work adaptation methods that consider allowing local constraints

9. Conclusions

The field of automated medical diagnosis is quite rich with possibilities and advantages such as cost-cutting, early diagnosis, and the potential to save lives. At the same time, it has several limitations such as possible loss of expertise by health professionals (Chapter 5) and privacy. Because of the privacy issues of the patient's sensitive information, extensive data cannot be provided to train ML algorithms. Another limitation is that not many physicians and surgeons are aware of the ML/CBR tools available in the market. Doctors would need to undergo proper training to understand these new technological applications. When it comes to knowledge transfer, it should be noted that technical people working on ML applications and algorithms also need to understand complex medical data and the relationship between patient results and final diagnosis, leveraging all the dependencies.

The Symptom Checker Engine is a tool designed to help a physician make a diagnosis. We expect this tool to be especially valuable for rare diseases, which are usually out of the scope of what physicians suspect to be associated with frequent symptoms like chest pain and cough. Missing these rare illnesses in diagnoses can be dangerous.

The main theme of this chapter is how advanced and abstract-level linguistic analysis can assist in matching symptoms as described by a patient with that of either an official or another patient's labeled description. The main linguistic operation here is alignment of various representations against each other and against representations for different texts (Fig. 37). This alignment is controlled from a higher discourse level by splitting texts into fragments for alignment.

A discourse-level analysis of multi-case-based reasoning cannot be substituted by an end-to-end learning of datasets such as the Medical Consultation Dataset (Liu et al., 2020). Authors' experimental results show that the pre-train language models and other baselines struggle on the automated

FIG. 37

Linguistic alignment assures a high precision in finding the relevant case.

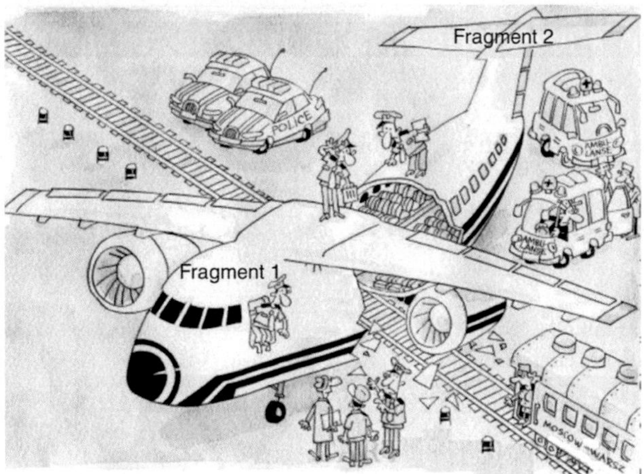

FIG. 38

It is essential to determine how to split a case text into fragments to match with known cases.

consultation dialogue construction task, and the accuracy of constructed utterances can be improved with the help of auxiliary entity information.

It turns out that discourse analysis plays an essential role, coordinating relationships between multiple diseases if they are mentioned in a patient's complaint. For that purpose, discourse analysis had to be extended from the level of a hierarchy of rhetorical relations to broader taxonomic relations between diseases and respective documents presenting the symptoms. The Symptom Checker Engine accepts a patient's textual complaint as an input. Then discourse analysis is used to split this complaint into fragments (Fig. 38) so that each fragment can be associated with an illness description in one of many forms: illness identification instruction, labeled cases, diagnosis book, diagnosis resources from the Web, and community health forums. We maintained a special interest in the case of multiple diseases in a single complaint. In case of multiple diseases, discourse analysis assesses a coordination of the rhetorical relations between the fragments and extended discourse-like relations between the symptom descriptions. These relations can be *Cause*, *Reason*, *Explanation*, *Temporal Sequence*, and *Other*. Matching of texts is performed by means of joint syntactic and semantic representation alignment based on an abstract graph-alignment algorithm. We developed the Symptom Checker Engine within the CBR framework and extend it relying on discourse-level relationships between cases. Our evaluation shows that the proposed technique is adequate for handling complex cases. From the CBR standpoint, we not only identify the most similar cases but we also maintain certain interactions between them that reflect the relationships between the fragments of the case to be recognized.

Supplementary data sets

Please visit https://github.com/bgalitsky/relevance-based-on-parse-trees to access all supplementary data sets.

References

Aamodt, A., Plaza, E., 1994. Case-based reasoning: foundational issues, methodological variations, and system approaches. AI Commun. 7 (1), 39–59.

Afantenos, S., Kow, E., Asher, N., Perret, J., 2015. Discourse parsing for multi-party chat dialogues. In: EMNLP, pp. 928–937.

Agency for Healthcare Research and Quality, 2020. Practice Facilitation Handbook. Sample Medical Record, Adam Pie. https://www.ahrq.gov/ncepcr/tools/pf-handbook/mod8-app-b-adam-pie.html.

Ahmed, M.U., Begum, S., Funk, P., Xiong, N., von Scheele, B., 2011. A multi-module case-based biofeedback system for stress treatment. Artif. Intell. Med. 51 (2), 107–115.

Ahmed, M.U., Begum, S., Funk, P., 2012. A hybrid case-based system in clinical diagnosis and treatment. In: Proceedings of 2012 IEEE-EMBS International Conference on Biomedical and Health Informatics, pp. 699–704.

Ahn, H., Kim, K.-j., 2009. Global optimization of case-based reasoning for breast cytology diagnosis. Expert Syst. Appl. 36, 724–734. https://doi.org/10.1016/j.eswa.2007.10.023.

Allan, J., 1996. Automatic hypertext link typing. In: Hypertext'96, The Seventh ACM Conference on Hypertext, pp. 42–52.

Artzi, Y., Lee, K., Zettlemoyer, L., 2015. Broad-coverage CCG semantic parsing with AMR. In: Empirical Methods in Natural Language Processing. ACL, pp. 1699–1710. Lisbon.

Aumayr, E., Chan, J., Hayes, C., 2011. Reconstruction of threaded conversations in online discussion forums. In: Proceedings of ICWSM. vol. 11, pp. 26–33.

Balogh, E.P., Miller, B.T., Ball, J.R., 2015. Improving Diagnosis in Health Care. Committee on Diagnostic Error in Health Care; Board on Health Care Services; Institute of Medicine; The National Academies of Sciences, Engineering, and Medicine: National Academies Press, Washington, DC.

Banarescu, L., Bonial, C., Cai, S., Georgescu, M., Griffitt, K., Hermjakob, U., Knight, K., Koehn, P., Palmer, M., Schneider, N., 2013. Abstract meaning representation for sembanking. In: Proceedings of the 7th Linguistic Annotation Workshop and Interoperability With Discourse, pp. 178–186.

Banarescu, L., Bonial, C., Cai, S., Georgescu, M., Griffitt, K., Hermjakob, U., Knight, K., Koehn, P., Palmer, M., Schneider, N., 2015. Abstract Meaning Representation (AMR) 1.2.2 Specification. github.com/amrisi/amr-guidelines/blob/master/amr.md.

Barzilay, R., Elhadad, M., 1997. Using lexical chains for text summarization. In: Proceedings of the ACL/EACL'97 Workshop on Intelligent Scalable Text Summarization. Madrid, Spain, July 1997, pp. 10–17.

Barzilay, R., Lee, L., 2004. Catching the Drift: Probabilistic Content Models, With Applications to Generation and Summarization. HLT-NAACL.

Branting, K., Lester, J., Mott, B., 2004. Conversational case-based reasoning. In: Proceedings of the Seventh European Conference on Case-Based Reasoning. Springer, pp. 77–90.

Cai, S., Knight, K., 2013. Smatch: an evaluation metric for semantic feature structures. ACL Short Papers, 748–752.

Choudhury, N., Begum, S.A., 2016. A survey on case-based reasoning in medicine. Int. J. Adv. Comput. Sci. Appl. 7 (8), 2016.

Das, S., 2019. A machine learning model for detecting respiratory problems using voice recognition. In: 2019 IEEE 5th International Conference For Convergence in Technology (I2CT), Bombay, India, 2019, pp. 1–3.

Dayanand, K.K., 2018. GRAph ALigner: Algorithm to Align Two Networks or Graphs. https://github.com/kanthkumar46/GRAAL.

De Boom, C., Van Canneyt, S., Bohez, S., Demeester, T., Dhoedt, B., 2015. Learning Semantic Similarity for Very Short Texts., https://doi.org/10.1109/ICDMW.2015.86.

Duan, H., Zhai, C., 2011. Exploiting thread structures to improve smoothing of language models for forum post retrieval. In: Proceedings of European Conference on Information Retrieval. Springer, Berlin, pp. 350–361.

Elsner, M., Charniak, E., 2008. You talking to me? A corpus and algorithm for conversation disentanglement. In: Proceedings of the 46th Annual Meeting of the ACL: HLT (ACL 2008), Columbus, USA, pp. 834–842.

Eremeev, M., Vorontsov, K.V., 2019. Lexical quantile-based text complexity measure. RANLP.

Etsimo, 2020. https://www.etsimo.com/.

Feng, V.W., Hirst, G., 2014. A linear-time bottom-up discourse parser with constraints and postediting. In: Proceedings of the 52nd Annual Meeting of the Association for Computational Linguistics. ACL, Baltimore.

Flanigan, J., Thomson, S., Carbonell, J., Dyer, C., Smith, N.A., 2014. A Discriminative Graph-Based Parser for the Abstract Meaning Representation. ACL, pp. 1426–1436.

Galitsky, B., 2006. Reasoning about mental attitudes of complaining customers. Knowl.-Based Syst. 19 (7), 592–615.

Galitsky, B., 2013. Machine learning of syntactic parse trees for search and classification of text. Eng. Appl. Artif. Intell. 26 (3), 1072–1091.

Galitsky, B., 2016. Generalization of parse trees for iterative taxonomy learning. Inf. Sci. 329, 125–143.

Galitsky, B., 2017a. Matching parse thickets for open domain question answering. Data Knowl. Eng. 107, 24–50.

Galitsky, B., 2017b. Discovering rhetoric agreement between a request and response. Dialogue Discourse 8 (2), 167–205.

Galitsky, B., 2019a. Learning discourse-level structures for question answering. In: Developing Enterprise Chatbots. Springer, Cham, pp. 177–219.

Galitsky, B., 2019b. Learning chatbot thesaurus. In: Developing Enterprise Chatbots. Springer, Cham, pp. 177–219.

Galitsky, B., 2020a. Employing abstract meaning representation to lay the last-mile toward reading comprehension. In: Artificial Intelligence for Customer Relationship Management: keeping customers informed. Springer, Cham, pp. 57–86.

Galitsky, B., 2020b. Distributional semantics for CRM: making Word2vec models robust by structurizing them. In: Artificial Intelligence for Customer Relationship Management: Keeping Customers Informed. Springer, Cham, pp. 25–56.

Galitsky, B., 2020c. A virtual social promotion Chatbot with persuasion and rhetorical coordination. In: Artificial Intelligence for Customer Relationship Management: Solving Customer Problems. Springer, Cham.

Galitsky, B., Ilvovsky, D., 2017. Chatbot with a discourse structure-driven dialogue management. In: EACL Demo Program.

Galitsky, B., Kuznetsov, S.O., 2008. Learning communicative actions of conflicting human agents. J. Exp. Theor. Artif. Intell. 20 (4), 277–317.

Galitsky, B., Makowski, G., 2017. Document classifier for a data loss prevention system based on learning rhetoric relations. In: CICLing 2017, Budapest, Hungary, April 17–23.

Galitsky, B., Kovalerchuk, B., Kuznetsov, S., 2007. Learning common outcomes of communicative actions represented by labeled graphs. In: Proceedings of the 15th International Conference on Conceptual Structures (ICCS), Sheffield, UK, pp. 387–400.

Galitsky, B., González, M.P., Chesñevar, C.I., 2009. A novel approach for classifying customer complaints through graphs similarities in argumentative dialogues. Decis. Support. Syst. 46 (3), 717–729.

Galitsky, B., Dobrocsi, G., de la Rosa, J.L., Kuznetsov, S.O., 2011. Using generalization of syntactic parse trees for taxonomy capture on the web. In: International Conference on Conceptual Structures, pp. 104–117.

Galitsky, B., De La Rosa, J.L., Dobrocsi, G., 2012. Inferring the semantic properties of sentences by mining syntactic parse trees. Data Knowl. Eng. 81, 21–45.

Galitsky, B., Ilvovsky, D., Kuznetsov, S.O., Strok, F., 2013. Matching sets of parse trees for answering multi-sentence questions. In: Proceedings of the International Conference Recent Advances in NLP, p. 25.

Godin, F., Vandersmissen, B., Jalalvand, A., De Neve, W., Van de Walle, R., 2014. Alleviating manual feature engineering for part-of-speech tagging of twitter microposts using distributed word representations. In: Workshop on Modern Machine Learning and Natural Language Processing, NIPS 2014.

Grosz, B.J., Sidner, C.L., 1986. Attention, intention and the structure of discourse. Comput. Linguist. 12 (3), 175–204.

Gu, D., Liang, C.-y., Li, X.-G., Yang, S.-L., Zhang, P., 2010. Intelligent technique for knowledge reuse of dental medical records based on case-based reasoning. J. Med. Syst. 34, 213–222. https://doi.org/10.1007/s10916-008-9232-y.

Gupta, S., Kumar, D., Sharma, A., 2011. Data mining classification techniques applied for breast cancer diagnosis and prognosis. Indian J. Comput. Sci. Eng. 2 (2), 188–195.

Holt, A., Bichindaritz, I., Schmidt, R., Perner, P., 2005. Medical applications in case-based reasoning. Knowl. Eng. Rev. 20 (03), 289–292.

International Classification of Diseases, 2020. https://icd.who.int/en.

Joty, S.R., Carenini, G., Ng, R.T., Mehdad, Y., 2013. Combining intra-and multi-sentential rhetorical parsing for document-level discourse analysis. In: ACL. vol. 1, pp. 486–496.

Joty, S., Carenini, G., Ng, R.T., Murray, G., 2019. Discourse Analysis and Its Applications. ACL Tutorial Abstracts. ACL, pp. 12–17. Florence, July 28–August 2.

Kamp, H.A., 1981. Theory of truth and semantic representation. In: Groenendijk, J.A.G., Janssen, T.M.V., Stokhof, M.B.J. (Eds.), Formal Methods in the Study of Language. Mathematisch Centrum, Amsterdam.

Kim, S.N., Wang, L.I., Baldwin, T., 2010. Tagging and linking web forum posts. In: Proceedings of the 14th Conference on Computational Natural Language Learning (CoNLL-2010), Uppsala, Sweden, pp. 192–202.

Kipper, K., Korhonen, A., Ryant, N., Palmer, M., 2008. A large-scale classification of English verbs. Lang. Resour. Eval. J. 42, 21–40.

Liang, P., 2013. Lambda dependency-based compositional semantics. arXiv 1309.4408.

Lin, C., 2020. Customize cTAKES for Automated Adverse Drug Event Surveillance in Pediatric Pulmonary Hypertension. ApacheCon. https://apachecon.com/acah2020/tracks/ctakes.html.

Liu, Y., Chen, Y., 2013. Patient-centered information extraction for effective search on healthcare forum. In: Proceedings of the International Conference on Social Computing, Behavioral-Cultural Modeling, and Prediction. Springer, Berlin, pp. 175–183.

Liu, Y., Shi, J., Chen, Y., 2019. Thread structure learning on online health forums with partially labeled data. IEEE Trans. Comput. Soc. Syst., 1–10. https://doi.org/10.1109/TCSS.2019.2946498.

Liu, W., Tang, J., Qin, J., Xu, L., Li, Z., Liang, X., 2020. MedDG: A Large-Scale Medical Consultation Dataset for Building Medical Dialogue System. ArXiv, abs/2010.07497.

Mann, W.C., Thompson, S.A., 1988. Rhetorical structure theory: towards a functional theory of text organization. Text 8 (3), 243–281.

Marcu, D., 1997. The Rhetorical Parsing, Summarization, and Generation of Natural Language Texts (Unpublished Ph.D. dissertation). University of Toronto, Toronto.

Marling, C., Shubrook, J., Schwartz, F., 2009. Toward case-based reasoning for diabetes management: a preliminary clinical study and decision support system prototype. Comput. Intell. 25, 165–179. https://doi.org/10.1111/j.1467-8640.2009.00336.x.

McKeown, K.R., 1985. Text Generation: Using Discourse Strategies and Focus Constraints to Generate Natural Language Text. Cambridge University Press, Cambridge.

McLachlan, S., Dube, K., Hitman, G.A., Fenton, N.E., Kyrimi, E., 2020. Bayesian networks in healthcare: distribution by medical condition. Artif. Intell. Med. 107. https://doi.org/10.1016/j.artmed.2020.101912.

Milenković, T., Filippis, I., Lappe, M., Pržulj, N., 2009. Optimized null model for protein structure networks. PLoS One 4 (6), e5967.

Milenkovic, T., Pržulj, N., 2008. Uncovering biological network function via graphlet degree signatures. Cancer Inform. 6, 257–273.

Misra, D., 2020. Extracting Patient Narrative from Clinical Notes: Implementing Apache Ctakes at Scale Using Apache Spark. ApacheCon. https://apachecon.com/acah2020/tracks/ctakes.html.

Natarajan, A., 2020. Medical Records 10 Yrs Dataset. https://data.world/arvin6/medical-records-10-yrs.

Ocampo, E., MacEiras, M., Herrera, S., Maurente, C., Rodríguez, D., Sicilia, M.A., 2011. Comparing Bayesian inference and case-based reasoning as support techniques in the diagnosis of Acute Bacterial Meningitis. Expert Syst. Appl. 38 (8), 10343–10354.

PatientInfo, 2020. Swollen Lymphs Nodes in Neck and Collarbone. https://patient.info/forums/discuss/swollen-lymphs-nodes-in-neck-and-collarbone-734682.

Patterson, D.W., Rooney, N., Galushka, M., 2003. Efficient retrieval for case-based reasoning. In: Proceedings of FLAIRS Conference, pp. 144–149.

Pourdamghani, N., Gao, Y., Hermjakob, U., Knight, K., 2014. Aligning English strings with abstract meaning representation graphs. In: EMNLP, pp. 425–429.

Prasad, R., Dinesh, N., Lee, A., Miltsakaki, E., Robaldo, L., Joshi, A., Webber, B., 2008. The Penn discourse treebank 2.0. In: Proceedings of the 6th International Conference on Language Resources and Evaluation (LREC), Marrakech, Morocco.

Pržulj, N., 2007. Biological network comparison using graphlet degree distribution. Bioinformatics 23, e177–e183.

Pržulj, N., Corneil, D.G., Jurisica, I., 2004. Modeling interactome, scale-free or geometric? Bioinformatics 20 (18), 3508–3515.

Radev, D.R., 2000. A common theory of information fusion from multiple text sources step one: cross-document structure. In: Proceedings of the 1st SIGDIAL Workshop on Discourse and Dialogue (SIGDIAL) '00, pp. 74–83.

Rose, C.P., Di Eugenio, B., Levin, L.S., Van Ess-Dykema, C., 1995. Discourse processing of dialogues with multiple threads. In: Proceedings of the 33rd Annual Meeting of the Association for Computational Linguistics, Cambridge, USA, pp. 31–38.

Ruta, D., Gabrys, B., 2005. Classifier selection for majority voting. Inf. Fusion 6, 63–81.

Schmidt, R., Pollwein, B., Gierl, L., 1999. Experiences with case-based reasoning methods and prototypes for medical knowledge-based systems. Artif. Intell. Med. 1620, 124–132.

Schmidt, R., Montani, S., Bellazzi, R., Portinale, L., Gierl, L., 2001. Case-based reasoning for medical knowledge-based systems. Int. J. Med. Inform. 64 (2), 355–367.

Seo, J.W., Croft, B., Smith, D.A., 2009. Online community search using thread structure. In: Proceedings of the 18th ACM Conference on Information and Knowledge Management (CIKM 2009), Hong Kong, China, pp. 1907–1910.

Sharony, R., Katz, A., Ovsyschcer, I., 1989. A comprehensive computerized medical record system for the pacemaker cardiologic clinic. Reprod. Toxicol., 297–299. https://doi.org/10.1109/CIC.1989.130548.

Sheth, A., Agrawal, S., Lathem, J., Oldham, N., Wingate, H., Yadav, P., Gallagher, K., 2006. Active semantic electronic medical record. In: Cruz, I., et al. (Eds.), The Semantic Web—ISWC 2006. Springer, Berlin/Heidelberg, pp. 913–926. ISWC 2006, LNCS 4273.

Supekar, K., Marwadi, A., Lee, Y., Medhi, D., 2002. Fuzzy Rule-Based Framework for Medical Record Validation. vol. 2412, pp. 1–27, https://doi.org/10.1007/3–540-45675-9_67.

Surdeanu, M., Hicks, T., Valenzuela-Escarcega, M.A., 2015. Two practical rhetorical structure theory parsers. In: Proceedings of the Conference of the North American Chapter of the Association for Computational Linguistics—Human Language Technologies: Software Demonstrations (NAACL HLT).

Taboada, M., Mann, W.C., 2006. Rhetorical structure theory: looking back and moving ahead. Discourse Stud. 8 (3), 423–459.

Takemura, T., Ashida, N., 2002. A study of the medical record interface to natural language processing. J. Med. Syst. 26 (2), 7984. https://doi.org/10.1023/A:1014866123819.

Theodoridis, S., Koutroumbas, K., 2009. Pattern Recognition. Academic Press Elsevier, The Netherlands.

Ting, S.L., Kwok, S.K., Tsang, A.H.C., Lee, W.B., 2011. A hybrid knowledge-based approach to supporting the medical prescription for general practitioners: real case in a Hong Kong medical center. Knowl.-Based Syst. 24 (3), 444–456.

Trigg, R., Weiser, M., 1987. TEXTNET: a network-based approach to text handling. ACM Trans. Off. Inf. Syst. 4 (1), 1–23.

van Eijck, J., Kamp, H., 1997. Representing discourse in context. In: Handbook of Logic and Language. Elsevier, Amsterdam, pp. 179–237.

Wanas, N., El-Saban, M., Ashour, H., Ammar, W., 2008. Automatic scoring of online discussion posts. In: Proceeding of the 2nd ACM Workshop on Information Credibility on the Web (WICOW'08), Napa Valley, USA, pp. 19–26.

Wang, C., Xue, B., 2017. Getting the most out of AMR parsing. In: EMNLP, pp. 1257–1268.

Wang, H., Nie, G., Chen, D., 2009. Semantic-Enhanced Case-Based Reasoning for Intelligent Recommendation. vol. 5, pp. 697–701.

Wang, L., Lui, M., Kim, S.N., Nivre, J., Baldwin, T., 2011a. Predicting thread discourse structure over technical Web forums. In: Proceedings of the Conference on Empirical Methods in Natural Language Processing, pp. 13–25.

Wang, H., Wang, C., Zhai, C., Han, J., 2011b. Learning online discussion structures by conditional random fields. In: Proceedings of the 34th International ACM SIGIR Conference on Research and Development in Information Retrieval, pp. 435–444.

Wang, L., Kim, S.N., Baldwin, T., 2013. The utility of discourse structure in forum thread retrieval. In: Proceedings of Asia Information Retrieval Symposium. Springer, Berlin, pp. 284–295.

Weston, J., Chopra, S., Adams, K., 2014. #TagSpace: semantic embeddings from hashtags. In: EMNLP.

Wolf, F., Gibson, E., 2005. Representing discourse coherence: a corpus-based study. Comput. Linguist. 31 (2), 249–287.

Xu, L., Zhou, Q., Gong, K., Liang, X., Tang, J., Lin, L., 2019. End-to-end knowledge-routed relational dialogue system for automatic diagnosis. In: Proceedings of the AAAI Conference on Artificial Intelligence. vol. 33, pp. 7346–7353.

Zhou, X., Menche, J., Barabási, A., Sharma, A., 2014. Human symptoms–disease network. Nat. Commun. 5, 4212.

CHAPTER

Obtaining supported decision trees from text for health system applications

3

Boris Galitsky
Oracle Corporation, Redwood City, CA, United States

1. Introduction

Given the tremendous progress in artificial intelligence (AI) in the last several years, the idea of computers taking the role of diagnostic support has become more plausible (Alder et al., 2014). Applications of AI have affected decision processes in clinical procedures, for example, in controlling depth of anesthesia (Schmidt et al., 2008) and detecting drug interactions (McKibbon et al., 2011). Software tools to support physicians in the diagnostic process have been developed in almost every field of medicine. Expert systems (ES) are intended to provide expert-level solutions to complex medical problems.

The main motivation for developing an ES for a particular disease is to compensate for a lack of human experts by helping the physician obtain a correct diagnosis with minimal time and effort. ES serve as educational tools for newly graduated doctors, assisting in their work with their patients and helping in their diagnostic decisions (Mutawa and Alzuwawi, 2019). A user interface of an ES allows physicians (who are not always fluent with computers) to enter symptoms and findings and output diagnostic results. It is frequently difficult to determine the underlying diseases responsible for a given set of symptoms and health problems, especially when the signs and symptoms are unclear. In addition, there are few experts on certain rare diseases, especially in poor and developing countries; therefore, ES are even more valuable in these cases.

For a few decades now, rule-based medical AI systems have been an everyday tool for doctors to validate their assumptions. While assuring a high reliability, these systems do not employ any training data. The other feature of a rule-based AI system, especially the medical rule-based ES is *transparency*, meaning it is easier to interpret results and understand the reasoning from which conclusions are drawn (Galitsky and Goldberg, 2019; Goldberg et al., 2019). In rule-based reasoning, knowledge is expressed by rules (usually in IF… THEN… form). The rules can be newly developed or extracted from decision tables or decision trees (DecTs). In a case-based reasoning approach, the inference engine searches the knowledge base for similar cases (Chapter 2). Knowledge in biochemical or biophysical domains are encoded in an ontology (Chapter 11; Galitsky, 2019b).

DecTs are examples of easily interpretable machine learning (ML) models whose predictive accuracy is usually fairly low. At the same time, DecT ensembles such as random forests demonstrate high predictive accuracy (being unexplainable, black-box models). DecTs often imitate human thinking, so

Artificial Intelligence for Healthcare Applications and Management. https://doi.org/10.1016/B978-0-12-824521-7.00013-2

it is easy to track the results and make reasonable interpretations. DecTs make an AI developer see the logic for the data to interpret (not like black-box algorithms such as support vector machines (SVMs) or deep learning (DL)).

1.1 Supported decision trees for an expert system

Once we have a document or a collection of texts, we can extract a flow of potential recommendations for how an author recommends a reader a pathway to achieve the reader's goal. This flow of recommendations or instructions can be extracted in the form of a discourse tree (DT, Chapter 2; Galitsky, 2017a). Once a set of DTs is obtained, we can combine these trees to form a DecT. When this DecT is available, the system can provide it to users via its visualization as a tree, a web form, or a dialogue. Another option is to incorporate this DecT into an ES. In the latter case, the DecT becomes a structure to perform dialogue management navigating through this DecT such that the questions to the user would provide choices for each node of this DecT (Chapters 9 and 10).

In our first example, the dialogue can be initiated by the question: "Can I reverse/cure/recover from type 2 diabetes?" Then, the user needs to navigate the DecT and specify her parameter from the choices of *diet changes*, *weight loss*, and *remission*. As the user answers *Yes* or *No* for each of these parameters, the DecT system must lead the user to the conclusions of *Yes-Possible* or *No-impossible* by acquiring the DecT from text. To acquire a structure of DecT, the system extracts elementary discourse units (EDUs; Chapter 2) to obtain parameters and rhetorical relations to establish a causal structure for these parameters, that is, *what* causes or probably causes *what*.

Once we form a DecT from text, it can be *refined* when the data for the values of the DecT is available. The default refinement is updating the threshold of values obtained from the dataset rather than from the original text. In the default refinement, the structure of the DecT is retained. Conversely, under substantial refinement, the tree is modified and optimized for the given dataset.

In a regular DecT, obtained from attribute data, only its structure and the values of thresholds retain the information about a decision knowledge domain. Naturally, if attributes are extracted from text and a DecT is built from these attributes, some information from this text is lost. However, when we build a DecT from text where an author expresses his motivations behind the decisions and provides explanations and argumentation, the decision becomes explainable in some cases, in a different sense from the explainability of this DecT itself. Some edges of a DecT provide *additional* information for why this decision is made, on top of a tree structure. This additional information is expressed via rhetorical relations for the respective decision chains, mental states, and actions of mentioned agents attached to these decisions and other semantic and discourse means. Enabling a conventional DT with this additional information to make and back up decisions assures that these decisions are more accurate and personalized to the circumstances of a given subject (Galitsky, 2020). We refer to such enriched DecT as a *supported decision tree* (DecTSup), as the edges are supported by an explanation, argument, rhetorical accent, and other means.

A DecTSup is designed to work in typical as well as atypical, personalized cases. In a typical situation, the averaged optimal decision from the DecT is applied. If an ES determined that a situation is atypical, and is presented via text, some decisions can be made by navigating DecTSup and some by matching the linguistic cue of the case description with the ones attached to DecTSup nodes. An atypical situation presented via attribute values without text is still handled by the DecT.

A DecTSup provides a unified decision framework for various cases of data availability. A DecTSup can be constructed from a single document or from a small number of documents or texts.

If a database or a collection of texts from which attribute values can be extracted is available, the DecTSup will be refined. If only a database and no texts are available, the DecTSup is reduced to a DecT. If a decision case is just a list of attribute values, then the DecT is applied, and if this case includes text, then the full-scale DecTSup is employed.

A DecTSup built from text might not be optimal in terms of order of splitting by an attribute, but it reflects the text author's intuition concerning their experience with making decisions based on attributes mentioned in text. A DecT built from attribute-value associations extracted from text is optimal in terms of which attributes are checked first, second, and last, but they lack the background support for why a given decision is made. A DecT is well suited to decide on an attribute-value case, but cannot accept a textual description of a case. Hence DecTSup is the best of both worlds: attribute-value and semantic representations formed from text. If only tables with valuates are available without any text, there is no need for a DecTSup.

A regular DecT for attributes $a_i \in A$ is defined recursively: for each attribute a we find the feature that best divides the training data such as information gain from splitting on a. Let $\underline{a_{best}}$ be the attribute with the highest normalized information gain. We then form a decision node n that splits on $\underline{a_{best}}$. To proceed, we iterate through the sub-lists obtained by splitting on $\underline{a_{best}}$ and add those nodes as children of node n.

To turn a DecT into a corresponding DecTSup, we label each edge with the information extracted from text for the given decision step:

(1) extracted entity
(2) extracted phrase for the attribute for this entity
(3) rhetorical relation
(4) full nucleus and satellite EDUs

For atypical decision-making cases, we select the edge by matching (1)–(4) from the case description with (1)–(4) of the DecTSup.

2. Obtaining supported decision trees from text

2.1 From a discourse tree to its supported decision tree

A DecT is a tree structure representation of the given decision problem such that each non-leaf node is assigned one of the decision variables, each branch from a non-leaf node is assigned a subset of the values of the corresponding decision variable, and each leaf node is associated with a value of the target (or dependent) variable. For the DecT, the target variable obtains its values from a discrete domain, and for each leaf node, the DecT associates a probability (and in some cases a value) for each class (which is the value of the target variable). The class that is assigned to a given leaf node of the classification tree results from a form of majority voting in which the winning class is the one that provides the largest class probability (even if that probability is less than one-half).

A *decision chain* is a generalization of an *If-Then* statement, an implication or a causal link that can lead a reader to a decision, given a *premise*. This generalization follows along the lines of rhetorical relations between the premise part and a decision part in discourse analysis of text (Galitsky et al., 2010). We want to extract decision chains from texts and then combine individual decisions extracted from various texts on the given topic to form a supported DecT.

elaboration
explanation
contrast (RightToLeft)
TEXT:Although there is no cure for type 2 diabetes ,
attribution (RightToLeft)
TEXT:studies show
enablement
TEXT:it is possible for some people
TEXT:to reverse it .
evaluation
condition (RightToLeft)
TEXT:Through diet changes and weight loss ,
manner-means
TEXT:you may be able to reach and hold normal blood sugar levels
TEXT:without medication .
TEXT:This does not mean you are completely cured .

elaboration
TEXT:Type 2 diabetes is an ongoing disease .
contrast (RightToLeft)
elaboration(RightToLeft)
same-unit
condition
TEXT:Even if you are in remission ,
joint
TEXT:which means you are not taking medication
TEXT:and your blood sugar levels stay in a healthy range ,
TEXT:there is always a chance ,
TEXT:that symptoms will return .
background
TEXT:But it is possible for some people to go years
elaboration
TEXT:without trouble
elaboration
TEXT:controlling their glucose and the health concerns

FIG. 1

A discourse tree (DT) with rhetorical relations connected with decision chains in bold.

We start with an example of two texts, their DTs, and the decisions chains extracted from them (Figs. 1 and 2):

"Although there is no cure for type 2 diabetes, studies show it is possible for some people to reverse it. Through diet changes and weight loss, you may be able to reach and hold normal blood sugar levels without medication. This does not mean you are completely cured. Type 2 diabetes is an ongoing disease. Even if you are in remission, which means you are not taking medication and your blood sugar levels stay in a healthy range, there is always a chance that symptoms will return. But it is possible for some people to go years without trouble controlling their glucose and the health concerns that come with diabetes."

When a text is represented as a DT, it is split into EDUs, denoted by a "TEXT:" tag. EDUs are organized hierarchically according to rhetorical relations between them. For an arbitrary rhetorical relation, and in particular, relation of *Elaboration*, <satellite> elaborates (provides additional information) on <nucleus>. Certain rhetorical relations have an obvious interpretations in terms of what decision <satellite> can be made by means of <nucleus>. For example, *Enablement*(*result*) ⇒ possible to achieve result <nucleus> by the way of <satellite>. Discourse parser (Surdeanu

```
elaboration
 explanation
  attribution (RightToLeft)
   TEXT:Bariatric Surgery helps
   manner-means
    TEXT:you lose weight
    enablement
     TEXT:by changing your stomach and digestive system
     attribution (RightToLeft)
      TEXT:to limit
      TEXT:how much you can eat .
  contrast
   same-unit
    elaboration
     TEXT:Aside from helping
     TEXT:you lose weight ,
    TEXT:it may help reverse diabetes in other ways ,
   TEXT:although scientists do not yet know exactly why .
 elaboration
  elaboration
   enablement
    TEXT:One theory is that it affects the hormones in your gut
    TEXT:to help your body control blood glucose .
   attribution (RightToLeft)
    TEXT:Researchers estimate
     cause
      TEXT:that upwards of three-quarters of people see their diabetes reversed
      TEXT:after bariatric surgery
  comparison
   TEXT:Gastric bypass and gastric sleeve surgery have better long-term results
   TEXT:than gastric banding .
```

FIG. 2

A discourse tree (DT) for the second paragraph of text.

et al., 2015) classified "*Through*" as a hint to the relation of *Condition* and "*without*"—as *Manner-means*:

diet changes and weight loss $\Rightarrow^{condition}$ without medication $\Rightarrow^{manner\text{-}means}$ sugar(normal)
Remission $\Rightarrow^{condition}$ not taking medications & sugar (normal) $\Rightarrow^{elaboration}$ chance◊ symptoms(yes)
OR Remission $\Rightarrow^{contrast}$ control(sugar(normal)) $\Rightarrow^{elaboration}$ symptoms(no)

We denote *sugar(normal)* as a formal representation of target values. Formal representations are in italic and original text is in regular font.

chance◊, *possibility*◊ are the modalities that do not change the configuration of a DecTSup but control the probability of navigation of the given decision chain.

"Bariatric surgery helps you lose weight by changing your stomach and digestive system to limit how much you can eat. Aside from helping you lose weight, it may help reverse diabetes in other ways, although scientists don't yet know exactly why. One theory is that it affects the hormones in your gut to help your body control blood glucose.

Researchers estimate that upwards of three-quarters of people see their diabetes reversed after bariatric surgery. Gastric bypass and gastric sleeve surgery have better long-term results than gastric banding."

A decision chain is defined as a sequence of EDUs with rhetorical relations between sequence elements (Galitsky, 2021). Each element is a whole original EDU or its representation as a logic form that can be obtained as a result of a semantic parsing; it depends whether an entity from this EDU occurs in an available ontology or not (Galitsky, 2019c). For formalized elements of decision chains, it is easier to establish a correspondence or synonymy between entities to form a decision navigation graph.

Elements of a decision chain are connected with $\Rightarrow^{rhetorical\_relation}$ between a premise and a decision. It can be read as "If <premise> then make <decision> according to *rhetorical_relation*." In a decision chain, each consecutive member starting from the second one is a <decision>. Each previous member is a premise (Galitsky, 2019a).

Fig. 3 shows two sections of decision chains extracted from the two texts above. Arrows connect the same (or corresponding) entities (possibly, parameterized diferently) such as *control(sugar(_))→ sugar(normal).*

In the first formalized decision expression *control(sugar(_))*, the outermost predicate is *control(_)* that ranges over control subjects such as *sugar(_)* with an anonymized variable "_."

We call the entities (and the respective EDUs they occur in) in the decision chains *corresponding*, if they are:

(1) formalized and can be successfully unified as logic forms
(2) not formalized, but form a common sub-parse tree which constitutes an entity

To build a decision navigation graph, the nodes of the decision chains with the corresponding entities are merged (Fig. 4, Galitsky et al., 2009). The arcs between the nodes of foreign decision chains are removed as the merge occurs; rhetorical relations in the chains are retained. In the decision navigation graph, $\Rightarrow^{contrast}$ are turned into $\searrow^{contrast}$.

All nodes have the same "importance."

As we form a decision pre-tree, we order nodes of the decision navigation graph according to its importance and form a tree. Nodes for the same entities can be split if it is important for further decision classes (Fig. 5, top). Importance of nodes is determined by the following means:

(1) from the DTs which form the decision navigation graph
(2) from the auxiliary data of the attribute-value format, according to the classical algorithms of DecT formation

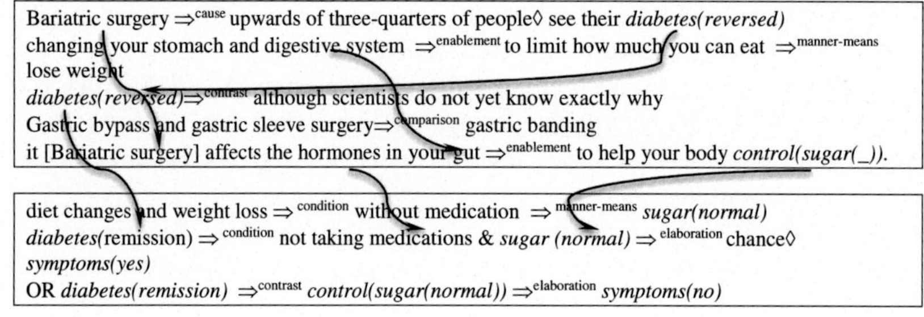

FIG. 3

Two sections of decision chains.

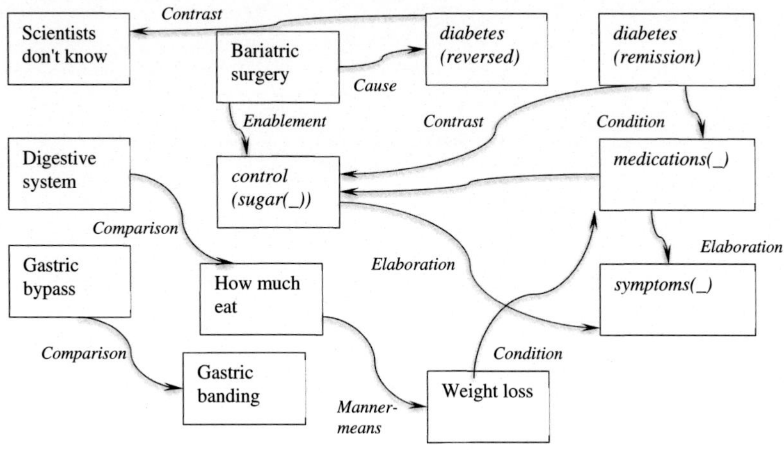

FIG. 4

A decision navigation graph, an intermediate representation between DT and DecTSup.

Each node is also labeled with linguistic information extracted from each EDU such as sentiment, argumentation, explanation chain (Galitsky and Ilvovsky, 2019), and rhetorical relation.

Notice that the decision pre-tree for a given collection of texts is not a complete tree in the sense that some nodes and edges are missing; they are expected to be obtained either from other texts or from attribute-value data. Fig. 6 shows a complete decision pre-tree without missing nodes or links.

Fig. 7 is an exaggeration of the complexity of building a pre-DecTSup from text. It is hard to derive it from a set of decision chains because there are many steps, each of which has its own uncertainty features.

To perform the final step of converting a pre-DecTSup into a final DecTSup, we populate it with an attribute-value dataset updating the threshold values but not the tree structure. The motivation here is that the decision logic from text is more important than data point counts. If such a dataset is not available, we perform the cold start with pre-DecTSup and finalize the DecTSup after some trial-and-error iterations with real-domain decision logs.

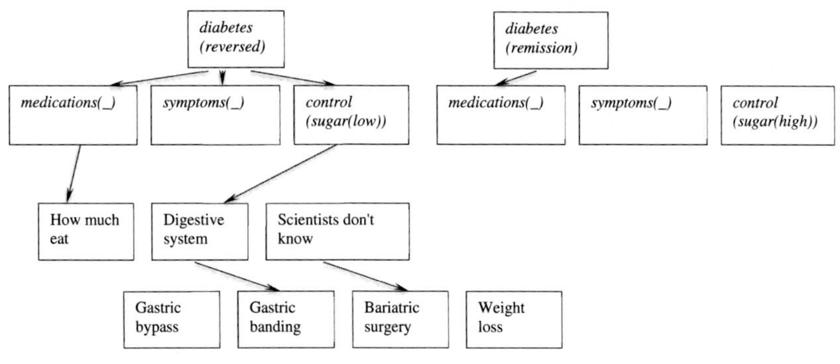

FIG. 5

A fragment of a decision pre-tree obtained from the decision navigation graph.

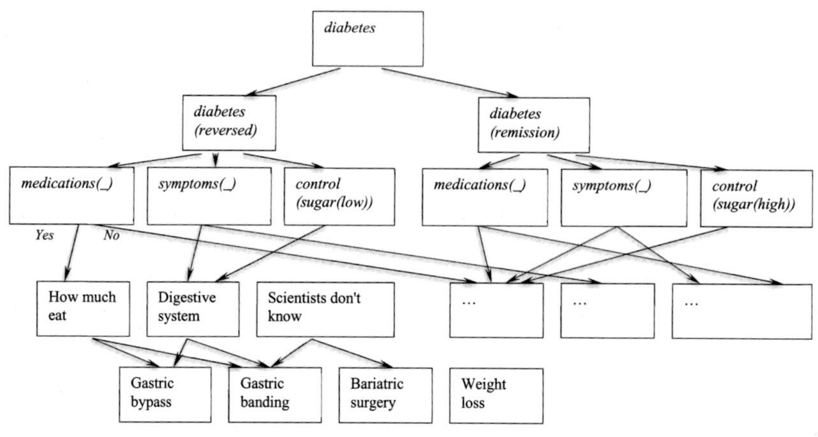

FIG. 6

A complete decision pre-tree obtained from multiple texts.

FIG. 7

A person is getting lost in connecting gasoline pistols. It is hard to coordinate decision chains with each other.

2.2 System architecture of construction of a supported decision tree

We present the system architecture in two charts: construction of a DecTSup fragment for a single text (Fig. 8) and merging multiple DecTSups for a collection (corpus) of texts or documents to form a complete DecTSup for a given domain (Fig. 9).

The top portion of the DecTSup shows the components for building decision chains. For decision chains, it is essential to split a text into shorter EDUs so that each contains a single entity, if possible. Also, it is crucial to identify rhetorical relations associated with decision making, such as *Cause*, *Attribution*, *Explanation*, *Enablement*, *Means*, and other non-default relations. Building a DT is followed by extracting entities from the obtained EDUs. Entity extraction and semantic parsing is supported by a domain-specific ontology.

Once the set of decision chains is constructed, we apply the graph-based transformation and label assignment to proceed to the decision navigation graph and then to the decision pre-tree fragment. Two components on the bottom right provide the *Entity aggregation* and *Assigning Linguistic Information* functionality to produce the DecTSup instead of just the DecT.

Fig. 8 illustrates the construction of the complete DecTSup from fragments by means of alignment. The entity aggregation component is reused, as well as Entity and Linguistic information matching component, to avoid duplication of nodes in the resultant tree. This complete DecTSup contains as many choice nodes as possible given the available data, so it is *complete* in the sense that all information from text is attempted to be leveraged to form decision nodes. Potentially, from more text or more attribute-value data, a super-tree of the constructed DecTSup could be built.

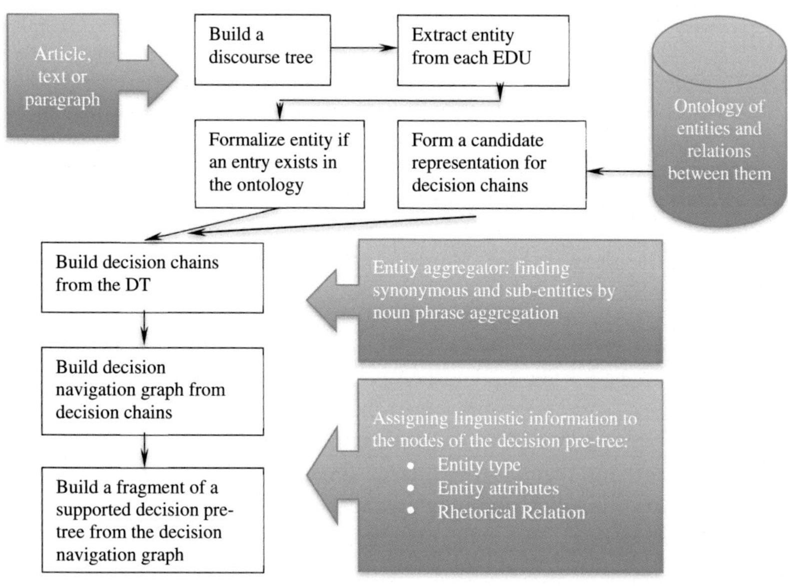

FIG. 8

Building a supported decision tree (DecTSup) fragment from text.

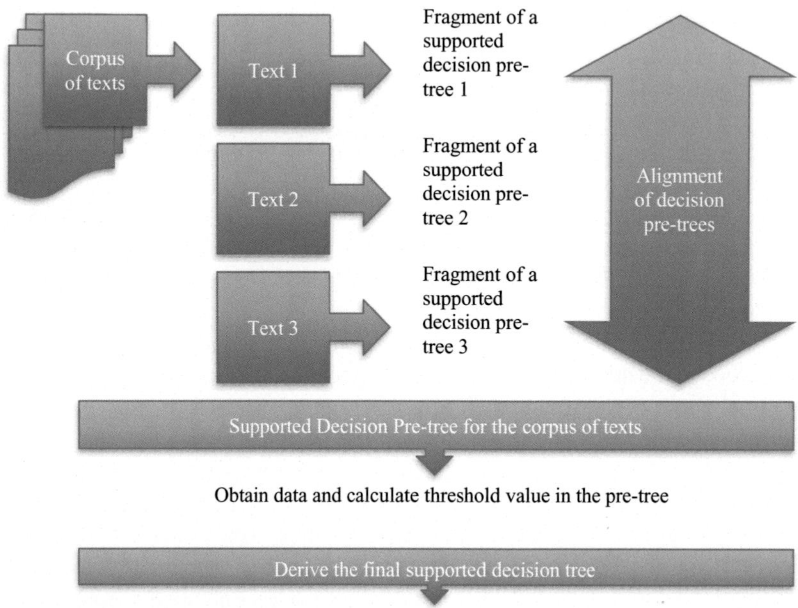

FIG. 9

An architecture for merging supported decision tree (DecTSup) fragments.

3. Evaluation

Generating a DecT involves partitioning the model dataset into at least two parts: a training dataset and a test dataset. There are two major phases of the DecT generation process: the growth phase and the reduction phase (Kim and Koehler, 1995). The growth phase involves:

- deriving a DecT from the training data such that either each leaf node is associated with a single class, or
- further partitioning of the given leaf would result in the number of cases in one or both child nodes being below some specified threshold.

The reduction phase aims to generalize the DecT generated in the growth phase to avoid overfitting (Galitsky, 2017b). Therefore in this phase, the DecT is evaluated against the test (or validation) dataset to obtain a subtree of the DecT generated in the growth phase that has the lowest error rate against the validation dataset. It follows that this DT is not independent of the training dataset or the validation dataset (i.e., commonly called test dataset). For this reason, it is important that the distribution of cases in the validation dataset corresponds to the overall distribution of the cases (Osei-Bryson, 2004).

Many ML tools provide facilities that make obtaining the DecT a relatively easy task. However, in using these tools, a DecT designer has to choose various parameter values such as:

- Minimum number of cases per leaf
- Splitting criterion

- Minimum number of cases for a split
- Maximum number of branches from a node
- Maximum depth of tree

These parameters affect the structure of the yielded DecT. Even in cases where some major objectives of the DecT application are known, such as an accuracy of top events in the first quartile, the choice of parameter values is not trivial. The DecT designer has to experiment with many different sets of parameter values constructing a significant number of different DecTs that must be evaluated. Although the designer may focus on *accuracy*, there are other criteria including *simplicity* and *stability* that are important in determining the most appropriate DecT.

We collect instructions on how to cure diseases from cites like WebMD (2020). We select 10 classes of diseases to diversify the experiments, and track each processing step to identify the performance bottleneck. Fig. 10 shows a sample overview of sinusitis.

To form an extensive attribute-value test dataset, we vary all extracted attribute values through the full range. For example, sugar levels can be *low*, *normal*, *high*, or *overly high*. The test dataset includes exhaustive combinations of all parameter values. Obviously, for most combinations of attribute values, decisions are not specified by the DecTSup, but for those combinations that yield a decision, it can be

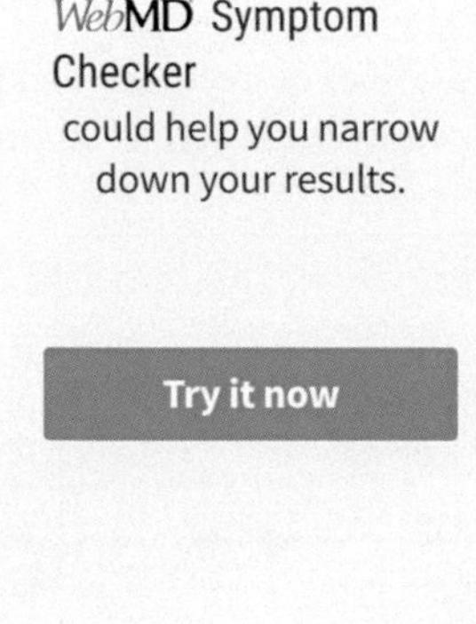

WebMD Symptom Checker
could help you narrow down your results.
Try it now
How Common
About 12% of people will develop sinusitis in a given year.
Overview
Acute sinusitis is an inflammation of the sinuses caused by infection lasting less than 4 weeks. Sinusitis often develops when swelling, inflammation, and mucus from a cold block nasal passages. This makes it easier for bacteria to grow. Organisms can produce gas, and when your sinuses are not draining, pressure can quickly build and cause the infection to spread. Viruses are the most common cause of acute sinusitis, but bacteria, fungi, and allergies may also cause it. Sinus pain and tenderness are common, but severe pain may indicate an abscess or other complication.
Go to the Sinusitis Guide >
Diagnosed By
Doctors diagnose sinusitis by taking your medical history and doing a physical exam. CT scans, X-rays, and MRIs may also be used to pinpoint a sinus infection. Doctors often look up the nose or shine a light into the sinuses to

FIG. 10

A data sample for building a decision tree (DecT) in the domain of curing sinusitis.

compared with the one produced by text. The goal is to have decisions about the treatment produced by text (by a human doctor reading it) identical to those produced by the DecTSup automatically. We used 30 texts for each disease domain in groups of 3–4 to form a complete DecTSup for this group.

Human assessors evaluate DecTSup with respect to:

(1) Local Precision: whether the built DecT fragment yields the same decisions as the original text (Table 1)

(2) Global Precision: whether a corpus of texts/instructions and resultant DecTSup yields the same decisions (Table 1)

(3) Coverage: whether each set of features is covered by text in the same way it is covered by the DecTSup (Table 2, right column)

Table 1 assesses the correctness of the pre-DecTSup. We observe that the error rate of 14.7% for building decision chains increases by 4.5% and then by 4.3% to reach a 21.7% error rate for the correctness of pre-DecTSup. There is a few percent deviation from one disease domain to another.

Table 2 assesses the correctness of building a complete DecTSup.

The difference between the second column in Table 1 and the fourth column in Table 2 is as follows. In Table 1, we show the correctness per text without support. In Table 2, we average through the group of texts to produce a pre DecTSup to be aligned, with the support included. Hence we have a lower correctness percentage.

One can observe that the pre-DecTSup alignment consumes 3.5% of correctness, and the resultant DecTSup produces less than three-quarters of correct decisions on average across all domains. This

Table 1 Constructing decision structures for a portion of text.

Common symptom	Correctness of decision chains	Correctness of decision navigation graph	Correctness of decision pre-tree fragments	Correctness of support data
Bloating	83.4	79.3	**74.0**	81.3
Cough	87.8	83.2	**80.7**	84.2
Diarrhea	88.7	85.9	**81.7**	85.0
Dizziness	84.5	79.0	**76.9**	84.8
Fatigue	86.3	82.1	**78.3**	82.1
Fever	86.1	83.4	**79.6**	83.7
Headache	85.6	82.0	**78.5**	84.0
Muscle cramp	87.2	83.8	**79.0**	87.1
Nausea	80.0	77.2	**75.6**	82.9
Throat irritation	83.5	80.8	**78.5**	84.4
Average	**85.31**	**81.67**	**78.28**	**84.0**
Loss of performance at each step	–	**4.5**	**4.3**	–

The essential correctness values are bolded.

Table 2 Constructing complete decision structures (for a corpus of texts).

Common symptom	Correctness of individual decision pre-tree fragments	Correctness of full decision trees with support	Completeness of DecTSup
Bloating	72.1	70.4	69.8
Cough	80.5	75.8	73.0
Diarrhea	80.1	77.3	66.2
Dizziness	73.6	70.1	69.9
Fatigue	76.0	71.9	71.5
Fever	76.4	71.3	72.7
Headache	75.1	72.1	71.0
Muscle cramp	76.3	73.0	70.6
Nausea	73.0	70.3	68.2
Throat irritation	75.9	71.5	67.7
Average	**75.9**	**72.4**	**70.1**

should not be confused with the number of incorrect DecTSups where at least one node is assigned incorrect decision rules; the proportion of incorrect DecTSups is much higher than one-quarter. Nevertheless, the number of decisions deviating from what should be decided from text is close to one-quarter.

Although the most commonly used performance criterion for a DecT is the predictive accuracy rate or a correct classification rate, in our analysis the goal is to minimize deviation from such abstract rate achieved by a classifier from the original text. For a DecT with binary target variables and a specified target event, various combinations of sensitivity (#true positives/#actual positives) and specificity (#true negatives/#actual negatives) are a conventional measure of accuracy (Bradley, 1997). As noted by Han and Kamber (2001), the accuracy rate is a function of sensitivity and specificity. Simplicity of DecT has also been considered by many researchers. For some, a measure of tree simplicity has been limited to the number of leaves in the DecT, while others have also suggested that the cardinalities of the corresponding rules (a number of conjuncts of decision variables) are also important, particularly when the rules are to be applied by human users rather than computers (Osei-Bryson, 2004). Both of these measures have implications for the interpretability of the DecT.

Accuracy, complexity, and training time have been used to compare the performance of DecT induction algorithms and thus the DecTs that they generated (Garofalakis et al., 2000). Multiple performance measures can be used, making sure to avoid a generation of DecTs that violate performance measure constraints. There is no approach accepted in the industry to select the most efficient combinations of DecT criteria early in the design process; therefore, it is usually necessary to experiment with various combinations of performance measures. Hence the relative measure we rely on in this section, correctness with respect to the given texts where decisions originate, sounds appropriate to us.

4. Decision trees in health

4.1 Defining decision tree as a supervised learning task

DecTs are trees that classify instances by sorting them based on feature values. Each node in a DecT represents a feature in an instance to be classified, and each edge represents a value that the node is assigned with. Instances are classified beginning from the root node and are sorted based on their feature values.

Fig. 11 (top) is an example of a DecT tree for the training set at the bottom of the figure. Using Fig. 11 as an example, the instance $\langle obesity = a1, gender = b2, proper\_diet = a3, blood\ pressure = b4 \rangle$

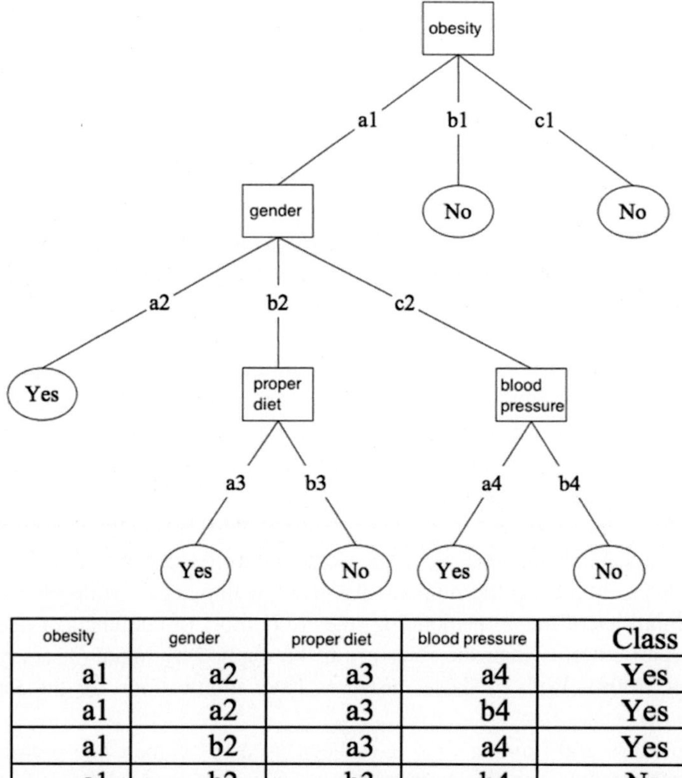

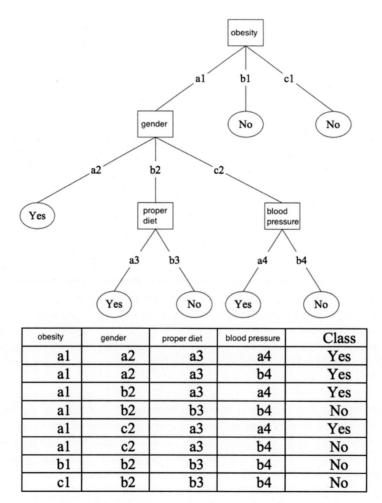

obesity	gender	proper diet	blood pressure	Class
a1	a2	a3	a4	Yes
a1	a2	a3	b4	Yes
a1	b2	a3	a4	Yes
a1	b2	b3	b4	No
a1	c2	a3	a4	Yes
a1	c2	a3	b4	No
b1	b2	b3	b4	No
c1	b2	b3	b4	No

FIG. 11

A decision tree (DecT) for an attribute-value data on decisions related to a diet.

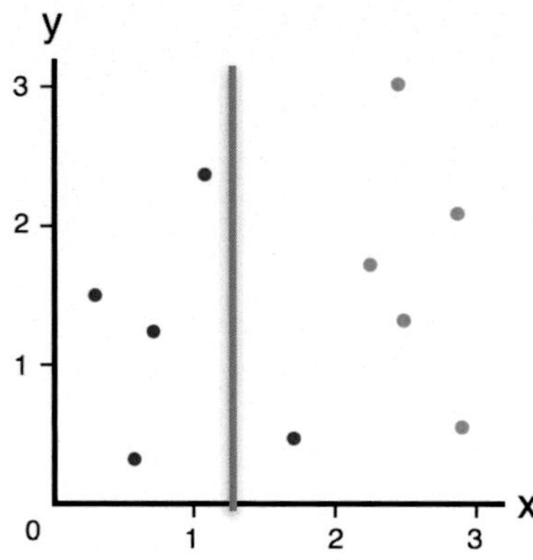

FIG. 12

An imperfect split.

would yield the nodes: *obesity*, *gender*, *proper_diet*, and *blood pressure*, which would classify this instance as being *Yes*. The problem of constructing optimal binary DecTs is an nonpolynomial (NP)-complete problem (Hyafil and Rivest, 1976) and thus the ML researchers have searched for efficient heuristics for constructing near-optimal DecTs.

The feature that best divides the training data would be the root node of the tree. There are numerous methods for finding the feature that best divides the training data such as information gain (Hunt et al., 1966) and Gini index. These metrics measure the quality of a split (Fig. 12). In the context of training a DecT, entropy can be viewed roughly as how much variance the data has. It is measures for C classes as

$$E = -\sum_{i}^{C} p_i \log_2 p_i$$

where p_i is the probability of randomly picking an element of class i (i.e., the proportion of the dataset made up of class i). At the same time, Gini impurity is calculated as

$$G = \sum_{i=1}^{C} p(i)^*(1 - p(i))$$

A Gini impurity of 0 is the lowest and best possible impurity. It can only be achieved when everything is the same class.

A majority of papers on DecT have concluded that there is no single best method. A comparison of individual methods may still be important when deciding which metric should be used in a particular dataset and task in the health domain.

The same procedure is repeated on each partition of the divided data, creating sub-trees until the training data is divided into subsets of the same class (Fig. 13).

Over the last few decades, DecTs have been extensively used both to represent and facilitate decision processes. DecTs can be automatically induced from attribute-value and relational databases using supervised learning algorithms that usually aim at minimizing the size of the tree. When yielding a DecT in a medical setting, the induction process is expected to involve the background knowledge

```
1) compute the entropy for the data set
2) for every attribute/feature:
    a) calculate entropy for all categorical values
    b) take average information entropy for the current attribute
    c) calculate gain for the current attribute
3) pick the highest gain attribute.
4) repeat until we get the tree we desired.
```

FIG. 13

Pseudo-code for building a decision tree (DecT).

used by a physician in the form of health ontology. Physicians rely on this knowledge to form DecTs that are medically and clinically comprehensible and correct.

Comprehensibility assesses the medical coherence and meaningfulness of the sequence of questions represented in a DecT. *Correctness* counts the number of errors in a DecT from a medical or clinical point of view. Some DecT construction methods partially solve these problems by means of alternative objectives such as reducing the economic cost or improving the compliance of the decision process to medical standards. However, from a clinical point of view, none of these criteria is robust when taken in a stand-alone mode, because real medical decisions are taken considering a combination of these criteria, and at the same time other healthcare factors. These merged criteria are not fixed and may vary if the DecT is made for different purposes such as screening, making a diagnosis, forecasting, or treatment prescription. In Section 2, we presented the DecT induction algorithm that uses combinations of healthcare criteria expressed in text and relies on the generated DecTs for screening and diagnosing. The mechanisms to formalize and combine these criteria are also presented.

DecTs control the series of processes that a physician goes through to move a patient from diagnosis to cure. Fig. 14 shows a simple DecT to recognize hepatitis B, C, and B + D (Department of Health and Human Services, 2017).

The knowledge base rules refer to three of the markers involved in these diseases: HBsAg, anti-HDV, and anti-HCV. To create the rules, some logical connectives are used: not ($\neg$), and ($\wedge$), implication ($\Rightarrow$).

The resulting rules are:

$$\text{HBsAg} \wedge \neg\text{anti} - \text{HDV} \Rightarrow \text{Hepatitis B}$$

$$\text{HBsAg} \wedge \text{anti} - \text{HDV} \Rightarrow \text{Hepatitis B} + \text{D}$$

$$\neg\text{HBsAg} \wedge \text{anti} - \text{HCV} \Rightarrow \text{Hepatitis C}$$

The tree that represents these rules (Fig. 15) is a data structure that shows that the system is very simple and clear. The nodes of this graph contain knowledge pieces or logical operators, each node has one or more inputs and a single output (which can be multiplied), and the arcs between nodes carry values of truth.

There are different algorithms to build DecTs. One criterion regarding its dividing features is to be as small as possible. The greedy "divide and conquer" principle requires the most important attribute is tested first. This way, the problem is divided into smaller sub-tasks, which are solved recursively. The first attribute becomes the root node of the tree: HBsAg (Hepatitis B surface antigen is part of the virus).

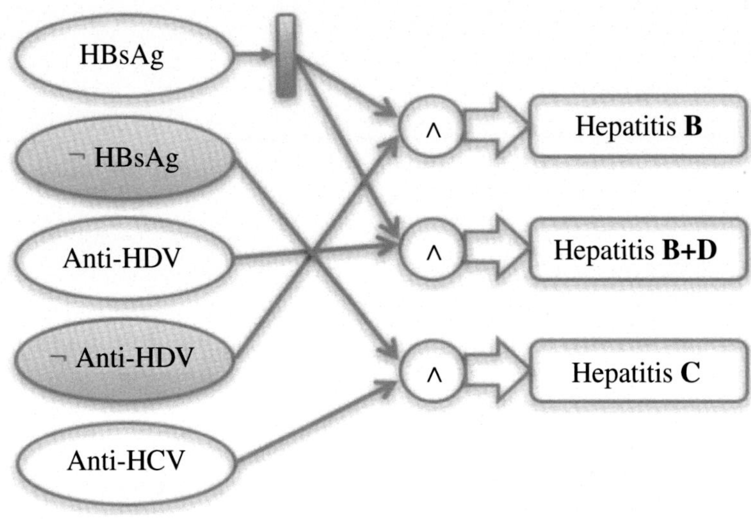

FIG. 14

A simple decision tree (DecT) to recognize hepatitis.

Each node N_i of the tree is associated to an attribute from the input vector. The branches of a node are labeled with the possible values of that attribute.

$$N_i = v_{ik},\ i = 1\ldots n \text{ and } k = 1\ldots m_i$$

where n is the number of nodes and m_i is the number of possible values for a node N_i.

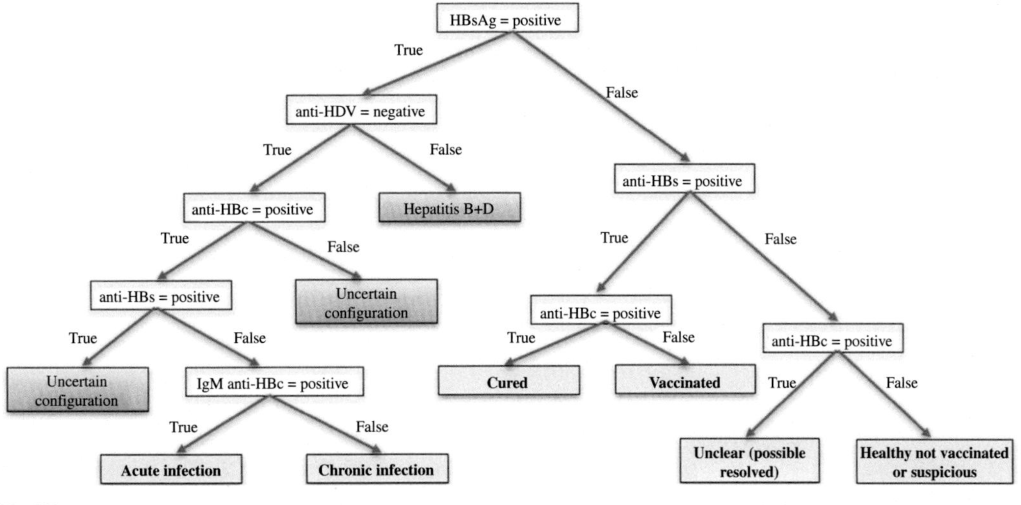

FIG. 15

The decision tree (DecT) to recognize hepatitis B, C, and B + D.

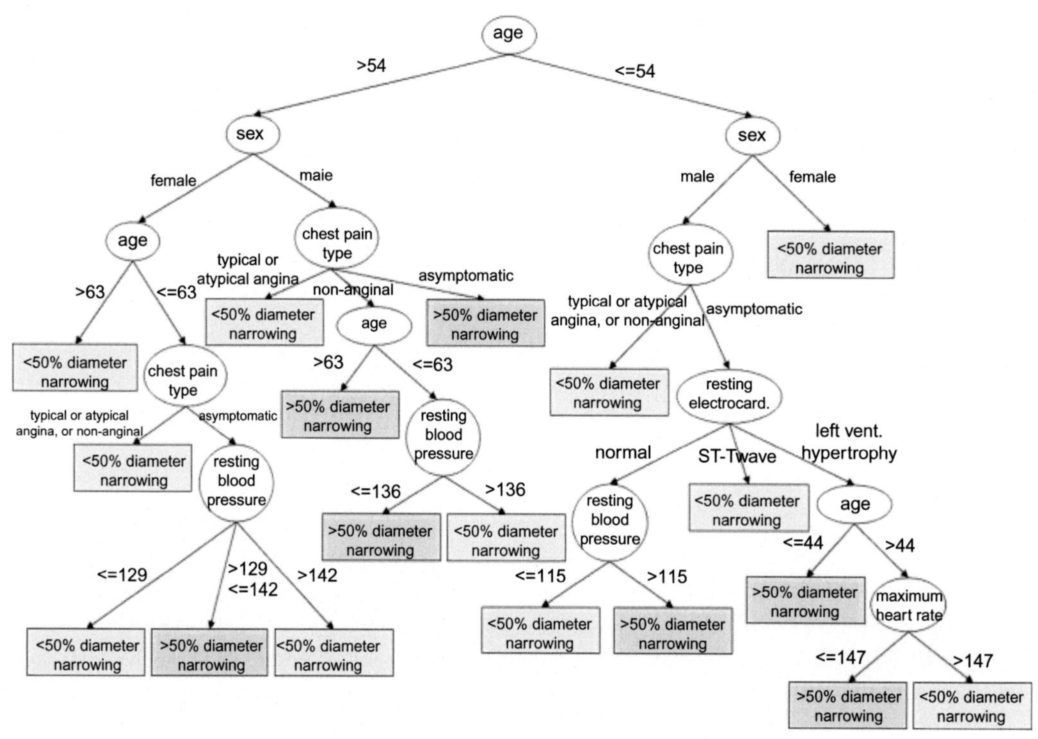

FIG. 16

The decision tree (DecT) for angina.

In developing a decision, the medical analysis must be broken down into a series of events, some of which are probabilistic. That is, a physician performs a treatment and it may or may not help, or it works with some probability. That is a chance node. There are certain decision nodes for events where the physician needs to make a decision. In chance nodes, particularly, in areas of cancer treatment, where the physician might have a very complicated protocol with sophisticated DecTs, there is a high number of chance nodes and decision nodes. Decision nodes might involve questions like, "*Shall I use this particular combination of treatments*?" "*Should I take drugs for 3 days or for a week*?" and so on (Fig. 16).

4.2 Decision trees and COVID-19

(Petrilli et al. (2020) describe characteristic features of more than 4000 patients with lab test-confirmed COVID-19 disease in New York City, 2000 of whom required hospital admission and 650 required intensive care, mechanical ventilation, were discharged to hospice, and/or died. The authors find a fairly strong association of {*older age, obesity, heart failure, chronic kidney disease*} with *hospitalization risk*, with much less influence of {*race, smoking status, chronic pulmonary disease*, and other forms of *heart disease*}. Petrilli et al. (2020) observe the importance of hypoxia in spite of supplemental oxygen and early elevations in inflammatory markers (especially d-dimer and c-reactive (CRP) protein) in differentiating between the patients who would develop critical conditions and those who would not. In the hospitalized population, measures of inflammation turn out to be much more important than demographic characteristics and comorbidities.

Testing was performed for patients taken to the emergency department with any complaint associated with COVID-19, including *fever*, *cough*, *shortness of breath*, *fatigue*, *gastrointestinal complaints*, *syncope*, known exposure to a COVID-19 positive patient, or physician concerns. In addition, ambulatory testing was available by appointment with physician's referral until the end of March 2020, when New York State recommended restricting testing of patients with a mild or moderate illness. Outpatient testing of symptomatic or concerned patients remained available throughout the study period. Repeat testing of negative specimens was done if the physician believed it was necessary. If testing was repeated and a negative test followed by a positive test, the authors took the positive result into account.

The team of authors formed the DecT based on the maximum information gain algorithm (Kotsiantis, 2013; Song and Lu, 2015). DecTs were constructed for both hospital admission (Fig. 17) and severe complications (Fig. 18) to identify the variables that best classified patients into different outcome clusters. For a given dataset, the DecT classification algorithm splits the dataset into two groups using one feature at a time, starting with the feature that maximizes the split between groups relative to the outcome in question. Consecutive splits reconsider each split subgroup for the next best feature. The final dataset in each end node has similar characteristics and outcomes. The authors use the DecT classifier from the Python scikit-learn library employing the maximum information gain algorithm that minimizes entropy for each branch split in the classification tasks. The trees were pruned to prevent overfitting by constraining the maximum depth, a minimum number of samples in a leaf and a minimum sample splits.

Surprisingly, though some studies claimed that high rates of smoking in China led to morbidity in those patients, but Petrilli et al. (2020) did not find smoking to be correlated with an increased risk of

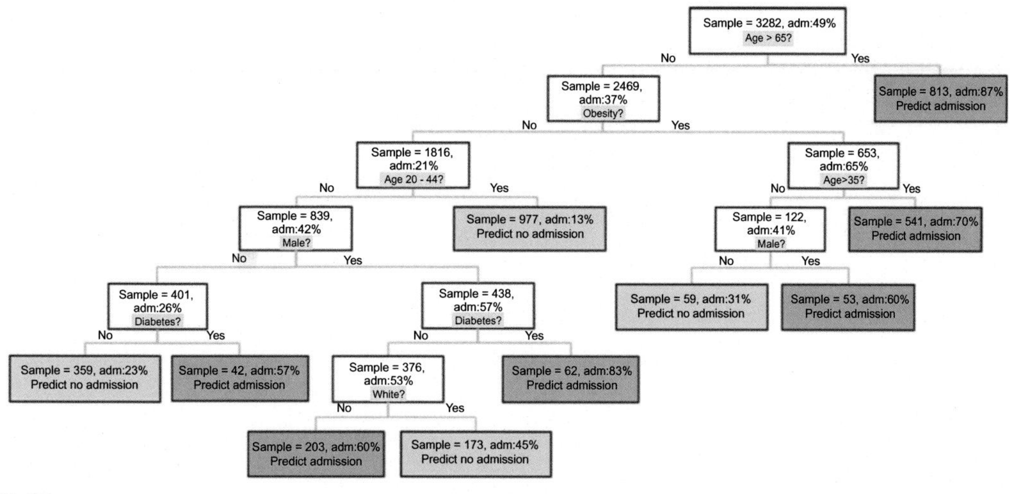

FIG. 17

The decision tree (DecT) for admission/no admission outcome.

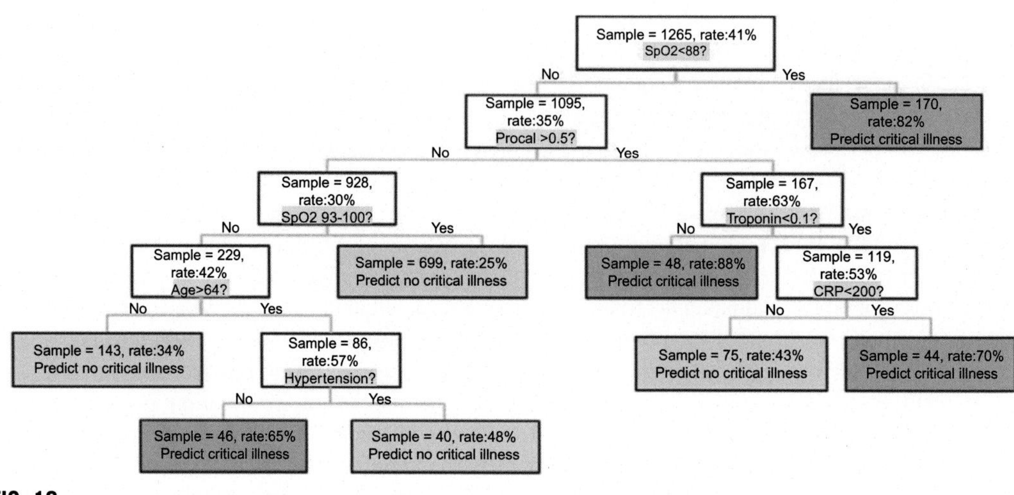

FIG. 18

Decision tree (DecT) for critical COVID-19 illness.

hospitalization or critical conditions. This is consistent with a number of other studies that have shown a lack of correlation between smoking and pneumonia.

There is an importance of inflammatory markers in distinguishing future critical from non-critical conditions. It turns out that early elevations in CRP and d-dimer had the strongest correlation with mechanical ventilation or mortality. The chronic condition with the strongest correlation with critical COVID-19 was obesity, with a substantially higher odds ratio than any cardiovascular or pulmonary disease. Obesity is understood to be a pro-inflammatory condition.
It turns out that the strongest critical illness risks were:

- admission oxygen saturation <88% (OR 6.99, 95% CI 4.5–11.0)
- d-dimer >2500 (OR 6.9, 95% CI, 3.2–15.2)
- ferritin >2500 (OR 6.9, 95% CI, 3.2–15.2)
- c-reactive protein (CRP) >200 (OR 5.78, 95% CI, 2.6–13.8).

In the DecT for admission, the most important features were:

- age >65 years
- obesity

For critical illness, the most important features were:

- SpO_2 <88% (oxygen saturation on presentation)
- *procalcitonin* >0.5
- troponin <0.1 (protective)
- age >64 years
- CRP >200

The authors concluded that *age* and *comorbidities* are powerful predictors of hospitalization; however, admission oxygen impairment and markers of inflammation are most strongly associated with critical illness.

5. Expert system for health management

In this section, we continue our exploration of ES in health, which we started in Chapter 2.

In order to find solutions, a conventional AI system would use well-structured algorithms, data structures, and crisp reasoning strategies. In the face of severe problems with which ES are concerned, it may be more useful to employ heuristics: strategies that often lead to a correct solution but sometimes fail. Conventional ES based on rules use human expertise to solve real-world problems that would typically require human intelligence. Knowledge of experts is often expressed on a computer in the form of rules or data. Based on the problem condition, specific rules and information can be retrieved to solve problems. Rule-based ES have played a significant role in strategic goal setting, planning, development, scheduling, fault control, diagnosis, and so on in modern intelligent systems and their implementations. Today's users can choose from hundreds of commercial software packages with friendly graphical user interfaces with the technological advances made in the last decade.

5.1 Basic expert systems and their values in health domain

Fig. 19 displays the essential components of the ES. All relevant information, details, rules, and relations used by the experts are stored in the knowledge base. The knowledge base may incorporate many human experts' knowledge.

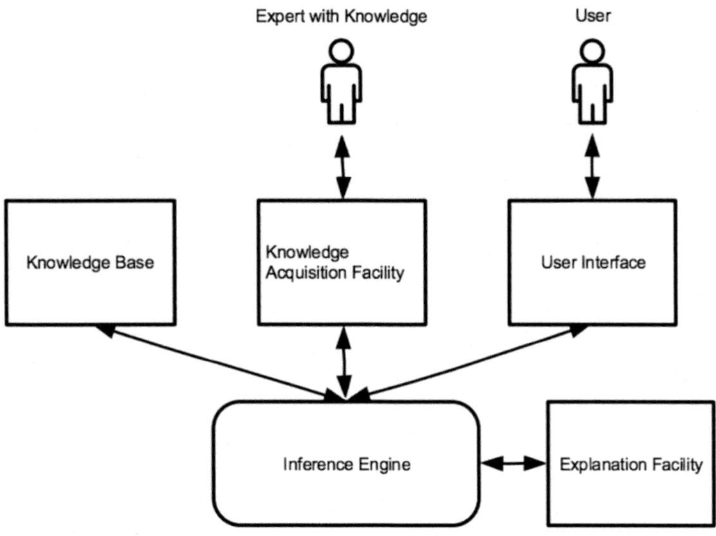

FIG. 19

Main components of an expert system (ES).

There are two significant motivations behind designing and implementing the proposed ES in the spinal anomaly domain (Dashti and Dashti, 2020):

- Helping experts to diagnose spinal anomalies more accurately.
- Determining the potential risk of development of spinal disorders in healthy people.

Even more, since the integrity of knowledge is ensured in the development of the proposed system, it could be used easily by students to learn disorders and related symptoms.

Some of the critical advantages of ES are:

- replication and maintenance of irreplaceable human experience
- ability to deliver a system that is more reliable than human experts in terms of consistency
- minimizing the need for human expert's presence at several locations at the same time (especially in a dangerous environment that is hazardous to human health)
- solutions can be developed much faster when compared to the training procedure of human experts

A *frame* links an item or entity to a set of facts or values. A frame-based representation of knowledge is a well-suited method for object-oriented programming techniques. ES that use frames to store knowledge in the knowledge base are usually referred to as frame-based ES (Sharif, 2004).

The inference engine aims to search for knowledge-based information and relationships and provide answers, predictions, and suggestions in the way a human expert might provide. The inference engine should find and compile the correct facts, definitions, and laws. Two types of inference approaches are widely used: backward chaining and forward chaining. Backward chaining is the practice of beginning with hypotheses and moving backward to the facts that support them (Motlagh et al., 2018).

Forward chaining starts with the initial evidence and propagates to the conclusions. The explainability feature allows a user to comprehend how the ES obtained these outcomes. The purpose of the knowledge acquisition feature is to leverage an effective means to gather and maintain knowledge-based components of the ES. The ES front end is used to model, upgrade, and use it in a regular mode. The purpose of the ES front end is to make ES simpler to use for designers, doctors, and system administrators.

The user interface of an ES plays a key role in its usability. A user interface allows a non-expert to enter symptoms and findings, while the ES outputs the diagnostic output (Buchanan, 1984, Fig. 20). Multiple ways of representation of inference rules, ML models, and cases can be selected. The inference engine examines the knowledge base and produces reasoning (Moens and van der Korst, 1991). The knowledge engineering tool allows for changing or enlarging the knowledge base by adding further rules, cases, models, or explanatory component, which illustrates the diagnostic process. A knowledge-based ES with an empty knowledge base is called a shell. It can be used for the development of other ES by adding a new knowledge base.

Fig. 20 (top) shows the component that handles the linking of data from different sources to a database. The primary functions are the creation, storage, and update of models that enable problem solving inside the ES (Ibrahim, 2018). The model base of the ES integrates various quantitative models, which enables the ES to support clinical decision-making. The ES database contains both qualitative and quantitative data (e.g., problem formulations, model descriptions, data formats for parameters and variables, scenario simulation results, and multi-criteria models). The ES knowledge base contains formal ontologies (Chapter 11) of the different clinical domains, definitions of the roles, relationships, and

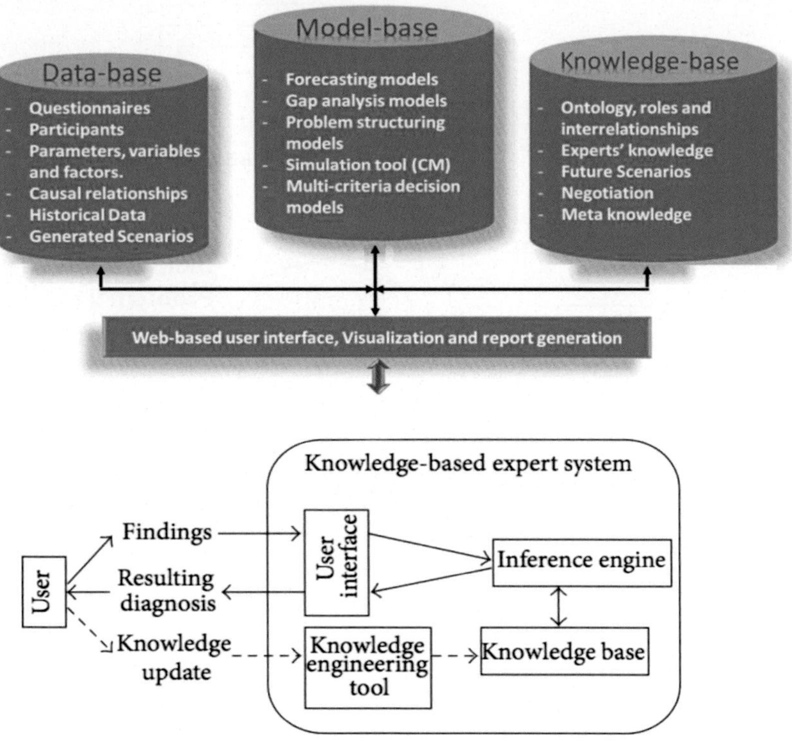

FIG. 20

A typical architecture of a knowledge-based expert system (ES).

interactions among participants (analysts, clinical experts, decision makers and representatives of stakeholder groups), questionnaires, future scenarios, and meta-knowledge (justification and explanation). This structure allows ES users to interact with the databases, quantitative decision models, qualitative knowledge, and other users.

A special case of clinical ES concerns clinical incidents that can be defined as unintended events, no matter how seemingly trivial or commonplace, that could have harmed or did harm a patient during the provision of general practice care (Wong et al., 1999). Fig. 21 (top) shows the architecture of such a system.

The intervention advisory module assists physicians in analyzing incidents and suggests relevant interventions. It lets physicians complete a structured incident report and provides possible interventions derived after an ES-assisted clinical analysis using both a repository of previous incident cases and its acquired generalized knowledge. A new incident report can be automatically updated into an ES's current incident repository.

- The *Explanation* component gives explanation of the suggested treatment based on its collection of domain expert rules and its knowledge of cause–effect relationships between possible underlying symptoms, problems, and interventions.

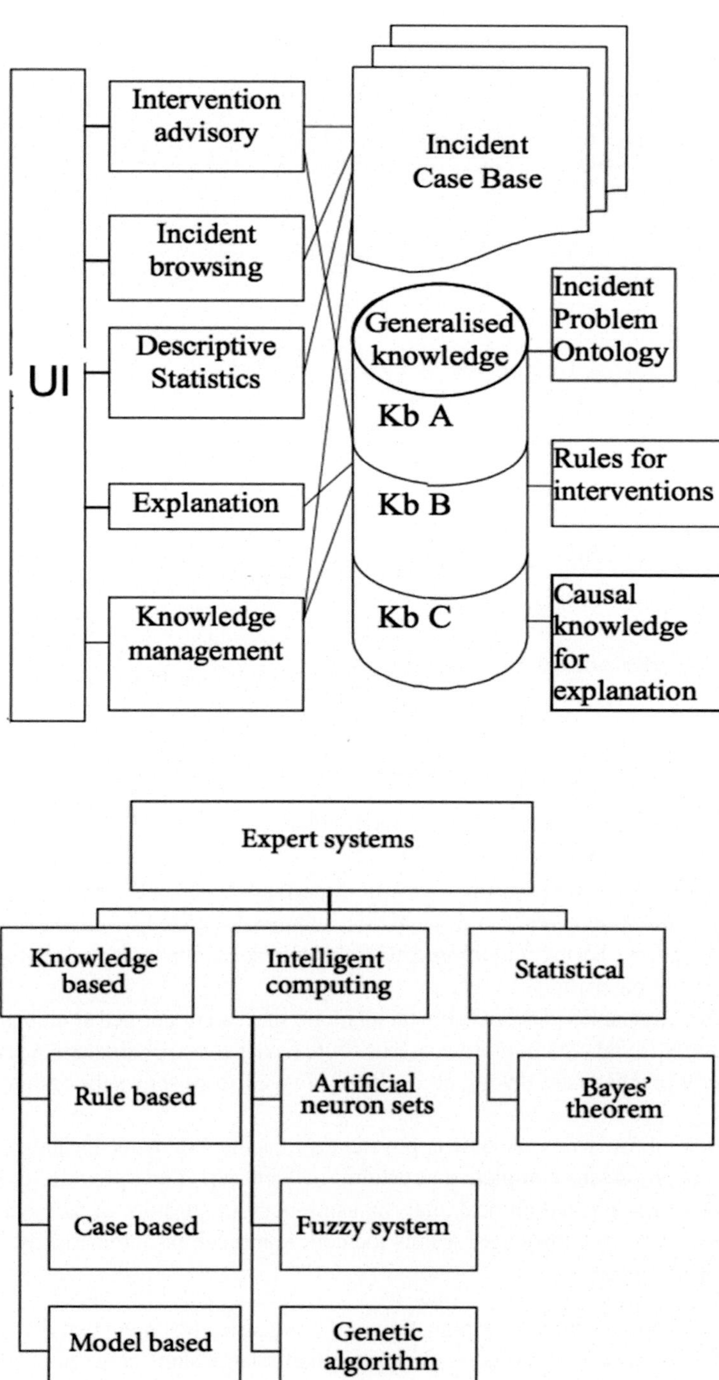

FIG. 21

Components of expert systems (top) and their taxonomy (bottom).

- The *Browser* component allows physicians to browse an ES's incident repository using various queries.
- The *Statistics* component supplies several useful descriptive statistics on clinical incident repository.
- The *Knowledge Management* component allows healthcare domain experts in general practice to moderate, maintain, and update the clinical incident knowledge base with newly reported incidents.

Fig. 21 (bottom) shows the taxonomy of ES, most of which have been deployed in the health domain. The early ES were developed in the 1970s, including MYCIN developed at Stanford University and INTERNIST-1. These were archetypes for the ES that followed, but also demonstrated challenges in the design of intelligent tools. MYCIN was employed for diagnosis and therapy of bacterial infection. INTERNIST-1 was developed at the University of Pittsburgh (Miller et al., 1982) to assist physicians in the diagnosis of complex and multiple diseases in internal medicine. The problems encountered in developing INTERNIST-1 and its successors showed that an effective and extensive knowledge base is required for a correct diagnosis of complex diseases.

5.2 Backward chaining inference

In the case of backward chaining, the primary concern is to align the conclusion of a rule against some known goal. So the "THEN" (consequent) part of the rule is generally not expressed as an action to be taken but rather as a condition, which is valid if the antecedent part(s) is correct. The backward chaining inference is analogous to the validation testing of the hypothesis in human problem-solving. For instance, a healthcare specialist might suspect a patient's problems, which they then try to prove by checking for specific symptoms. This reasoning style is designed by a goal-driven ES quest and is called backward chaining (Al-Ajlan, 2015). It is a theoretical top-down model that starts with a goal or hypothesis and searches for rules to validate the hypothesis. It tries to balance the variables that lead to relevant data facts and shows that the inference moves backward from the intended goal to establish facts that would fulfill the goal. The implementation of backward chaining in a rule-based ES is as follows:

(1) The ES checks the stack memory to see if the target has been added. This step is needed as another knowledge base may have already proven the goal. The algorithm reviews its current set of rules, and if the goal has not been proven before, it continues to look for one or more that contains the goal in its THEN portion. This type of rule is called the goal rule.
(2) The algorithms checks whether the target rule premises are listed in the stack memory. If the premises are not specified yet, new goals or sub-goals are to be recursively checked, and other rules can be used to support them.
(3) The ES keeps iterating in this recursive way until it discovers a primitive premise (not provided by any rule). The algorithm asks the user for details about it when a primitive rule is discovered. This knowledge is then used by the ES to prove both the sub-goals and the original goal.

There are two search algorithms for backward chaining method:

(1) Depth-first search algorithm searches a data in a tree as deep as possible before backtracking.
(2) Breath-first search algorithm searches a data in neighbor nodes before it moves deeper to the bottom of the tree.

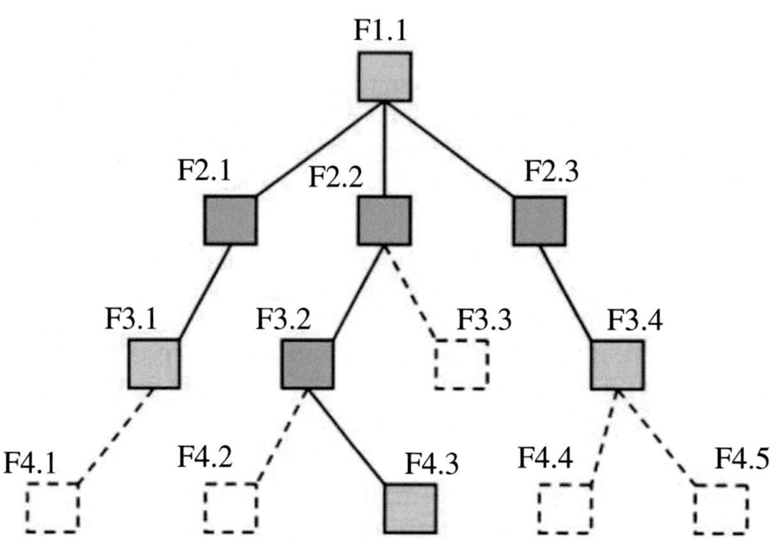

FIG. 22

Backward chaining illustration.

Using depth-first search algorithm, the process of backward chaining can be illustrated as in Fig. 22.

Fig. 22 shows the illustration of backward chaining process of the inference engine of an ES. The known facts are F1.1, F2.1, F3.2, and F3.4 in the beginning of process. The inference process begins from fact F1.1. That fact F1.1 is a *goal*. The inference propagates backward to other facts below the goal. It is a *conditional* part of rule. The inference engine tries to applied fact F2.1, F2.2, F2.3, and so on. The proposed backward chaining uses a depth-first search algorithm.

The following steps describe the inference process of an ES using the backward chaining algorithm as follows (first the left column and then proceeds to the right column).

Goal: F1.1	Fetch: F3.2 → unknown
Fetch: F2.1 → unknown	Fetch: F4.2 → unknown
Fetch: F3.1 → known	Fetch: F4.3 → known
Rule (F3.1, F2.1) → fired	Rule (F4.3, F3.2) → fired
Rule (F2.1, F1.1) → fired	Rule (F3.2, F2.2) → fired
Fetch: F4.1 → unknown	Rule (F2.2, F1.1) → fired ...
Fetch: F2.2 → unknown	

Forward and backward chaining can also be applied to DecTSupp.

5.3 Expert system and health management

The efficient management of health care has become both an economic and political issue. From time to time, a procedure recommended by a physician may not be the most prudent course to follow for a particular patient. Recently, healthcare insurers have become more involved in the decision as to what course of treatment to pursue for a particular medical condition. Such comprehensive case management can result in a more successful outcome for the patient at a lower cost.

In the past, the management of individual patient treatments has been provided on a transactional basis. In other words, each time a patient was diagnosed with a problem, a determination was made as to a recommended course of treatment for that diagnosis. After the treatment was undertaken, any further diagnoses and/or treatments were reviewed individually by the patient's insurer, without a comprehensive review of past diagnoses and treatments for the particular patient. Such a transactional review process can result in a patient undergoing a variety of treatments for the same condition, where an alternative treatment in the first place may have resulted in a better outcome for the patient at a lower cost for the insurer.

To assure a better level of healthcare management, the system of McAndrew et al. (1996) provides an ES for interactively assisting a user in solving problems, such as whether or not to certify a particular medical treatment for a diagnosed medical condition (Fig. 23). The invention can be implemented using a relational database and graphical user interface for data capture and reporting. Dynamic decision support (Goldberg et al., 2021) is a decision concerning whether or not to certify a medical procedure. It provides data and recommendations to case managers, adjusted to the experience level of the case manager, the level of the case manager's authority, and the relevant clinical situation. Policy and clinical guidelines can be authored centrally and used locally by the case managers to ensure consistency in policy- and decision-making.

Significant productivity improvements and operational cost savings are provided by the system. As reviewers (e.g., case managers) move through the workflow, they are supported by the system with information and guidelines tailored to their needs at that time. The information and guidelines are provided on a context-sensitive basis, based on a full awareness of the current medical situation.

The patent (McAndrew et al., 1996) describes a tool for building a knowledge system and running a consultation on a computer. Knowledge systems emulate reasoning tasks by using an "inference engine" to interpret encoded knowledge of human experts stored in a "knowledge base." If the domain of the knowledge base or scope of the problem is sufficiently narrow and a sufficiently large body of information is properly coded in the knowledge base, then performance that matches or exceeds the ability of a human expert can be achieved. In such a case, the knowledge system becomes an ES.

It is advantageous to provide an ES that interactively assists a user in solving problems such as the certification of a particular medical procedure for a given diagnosis, providing a user with all of the information necessary to solve the problem. In the medical context such information would include definitions of medical conditions and treatments, detailed articles from medical journals relating to diagnosis and treatment, policy and clinical guidelines for use in assessing whether a proposed treatment is appropriate for the given diagnosis, and other relevant information such as basic definitions of the diagnosis and treatment. It would also be fruitful to enable a user to selectively obtain full detailed information or a quick synopsis of the relevant information. This feature would allow more experienced users to quickly arrive at a decision without having to plod through a large amount of information that the user may already have knowledge of. An ES should be used by both experienced and inexperienced users. To enable inexperienced users to solve a problem properly, a highly structured approach should be provided to ensure that the user inputs all of the information necessary for the system to make a recommendation. An experienced user, on the other hand, should be able to solve problems properly with only minimal guidance from the system.

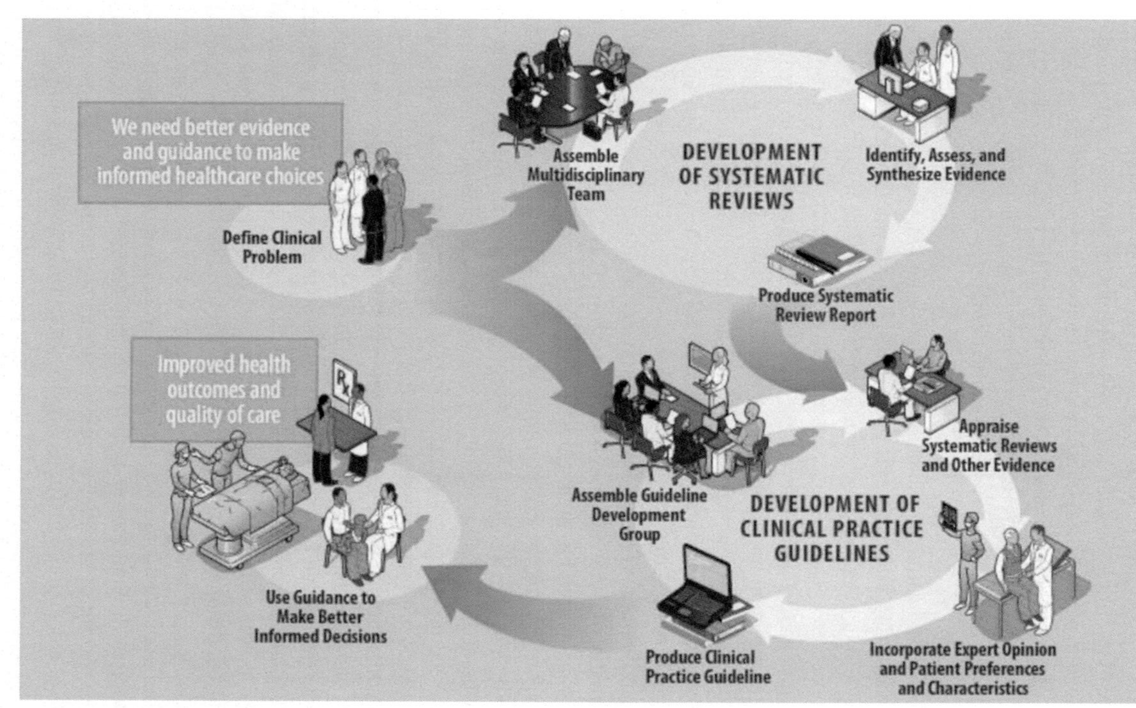

FIG. 23

Medical practice guidelines and decision-making.

The tools provided by McAndrew et al. (1996) help a healthcare professional to screen a case to be accepted (correctly treated) or not, decide if further review is needed by another professional, state policy, negotiate a compromise, and/or make an ultimate decision. The tool included the following models:

(1) The informational model provides reference material, clinical guidelines, and/or clinical policy presented in a manner that supports independent decision-making. It is used to provide up-to-date support to a user, such as a nurse or a doctor, to assist the user in learning about and making an informed decision as to the problem at hand.

(2) The synopsis model is similar to the informational model but provides only a limited amount of information. For example, in the healthcare field, the synopsis model may contain disease- or condition-specific information to provide a general overview on a relevant topic.

(3) The structured and guided models are used to obtain information relating to the problem at hand required by an ES component of the decision-making system. The structured model provides formatted questions with branching logic tables that will lead the physician to a set decision based on the answers to the questions presented.

(4) The guided model provides open-ended questions that elicit information (such as clinical information) and provide the guideline criteria for each question to guide a physician in making decisions (Chapter 6). The guided model is used by experienced doctors, and the structured model is used by lower-level or inexperienced doctors.

The decision-making system places it in the hands of the end user. At the lowest level, the system generates a finite recommendation to the user, through the use of the structured model. At the next level of review, the guided model is used to assist the user by generating a recommendation for a decision. The user has the ability to override the system-generated recommendation in the guided model. At a higher level of decision-making, the system allows for review of information considered during the lower levels, to enable a high-level doctor reviewer to make an independent informed decision. An easy navigation from one topic area to another is provided among the models. Also, easy access is provided to an extensive library of relevant information useful in making a decision via the informational and synopsis models. Each of the models is implemented via software in a user workstation, such as a desktop personal computer coupled to one or more central databases via a local area or wide area network or the like.

Chi et al. (2008) described a new method for constructing an expert system using a hospital referral problem as an example. Many factors, such as institutional characteristics, patient risks, traveling distance, and chances of survival and complications should be included in the hospital-selection decision. Ideally, each patient should be treated individually, with the decision process including not only their condition but also their beliefs about trade-offs among the desired hospital features. An ES can help with this complex decision, especially when numerous factors are to be considered. The researchers method, called the Prediction and Optimization-Based Decision Support System algorithm, constructs an ES without an explicit knowledge base. The algorithm obtains knowledge on its own by building ML classifiers from a collection of labeled cases. In response to a query, the algorithm gives a customized recommendation, using an optimization step to help the patient maximize the probability of achieving a desired outcome. In this case, the recommended hospital is the optimal solution that maximizes the probability of the desired outcome. With proper formulation, this ES can combine multiple factors to give hospital-selection decision support at the individual level.

The most common use of ES is for addressing clinical needs, such as ensuring accurate diagnoses, screening in a timely manner for preventable diseases, or averting adverse drug events. However, expert can also potentially lower costs, improve efficiency, and reduce patient inconvenience. In fact, expert can sometimes address all three of these areas simultaneously, for example, by alerting clinicians to potentially duplicative testing. For more complex cognitive tasks, such as diagnostic decision-making, the aim of expert is to assist, rather than to replace, the clinician, whereas for other tasks (such as presentation of a predefined order set) the expert may relieve the clinician of the burden of reconstructing orders for each encounter. The expert may offer suggestions, but the clinician must filter the information, review the suggestions, and decide whether to take action or what action to take (Winstanley and Courvalin, 2011, Fig. 24).

Adoption of a decision support is challenging when such systems do not have evidence for justifying their recommendations. Decision support systems are broadly used in the medical domain because of the domain's complexity and the high volume of information that makes manual reasoning difficult. Kokciyan et al. (2021) introduced a metalevel argumentation-based decision support system that operates with heterogeneous multimodal data such as measurements, electronic health records (EHRs), and clinical guidelines, while taking into account the preferences of the human target of those

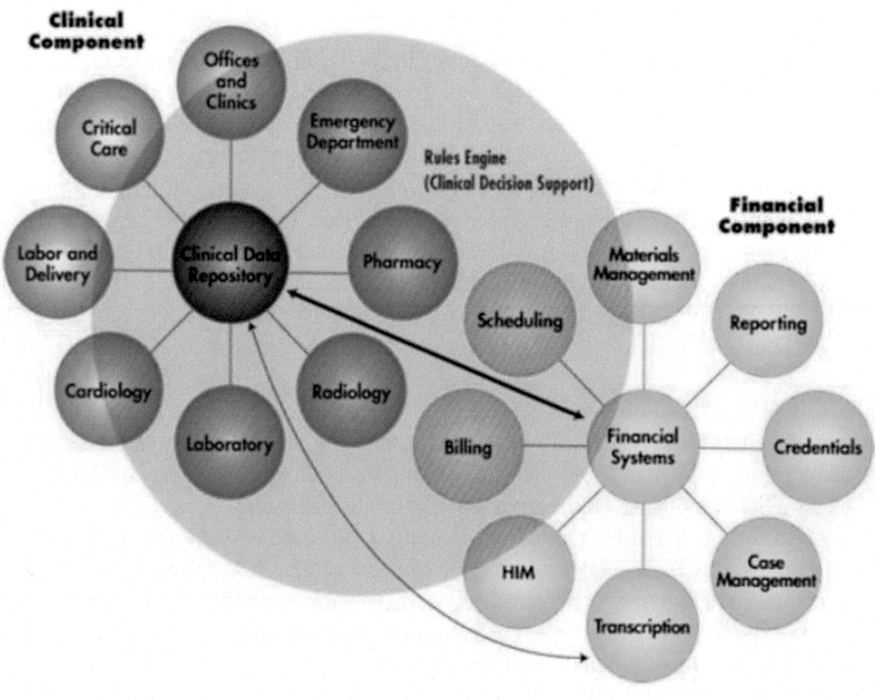

FIG. 24

Clinical and financial components of an expert system (ES).

decisions. Template-based explanations for the system's decisions are generated in the domain of stroke patients.

5.4 Clinical use of expert systems

The following ES features, according to Kawamoto et al. (2005), improve clinical practice:

- the availability at the time and location of decision making
- the integration into clinical workflow
- the provision of recommendations rather than a pure assessment

The wider use of computers in clinical routines, such as the possible use of tablet computers on ward rounds, will facilitate the integration into clinical workflow and enhance the availability at the time and location of decision-making. The need for more detailed documentation for quality assurance may have a positive influence as well. Boegl et al. (1995) described the clinical use of their diagnostic expert system Cadiag-4/Rheuma-Radio.

Kolarz et al. (1999) considered the time required for data input as the most limiting factor. Considering the smaller amount of input data and, as a result, the shorter input time, specialized and restricted ES, like the system that analyzes medical lab results, have an advantage over more comprehensive systems. Kaplan (1991) wrote about an ES with a provisional hypothesis list that updates after every further input. As the data input is limited, risk of a wrong or missed diagnosis exists because of the less thorough questioning. The required time for data input would decrease if the ES were compatible with the hospital information system and consequently could allow direct access to all electronically stored patient data comprising patient history, physical exam, imaging studies, and laboratory analyses. Hence data input and the required time depend on an intuitive user interface, which has the biggest influence on the success of the ES deployment.

The reason for the difficulties in deploying ES in clinical practice has been discussed in detail. Mandl and Kohane (2012) claimed that health information technology in general lags behind other industries. In addition, the authors view the health information technology products as too specific and incompatible with each other. Spreckelsen et al. (2012) evaluated an online survey concerning ES, noting that a lack of acceptance by the medical staff is the main problem in the application of knowledge-based systems in medicine. The different points of view of AI system designers and physicians demonstrate that a better cooperation is necessary. Whereas ES have to be adapted to clinical problems and to clinical workflow, clinicians should become more familiar with the supportive possibilities of ES.

Despite computerized assistance, the user of the ES needs a medical domain-specific knowledge for the detection and the correct description of medical findings. Some ES are developed specifically for the assistance of non-specialists (such as non-rheumatologists). These systems were designed to remind the non-specialist of rare illnesses or to recognize cases that need immediate treatment. Yet, an ES's output is highly dependent on the entry of correct parameters. Therefore, educational parts were added to some of the ES to increase the doctor's diagnostic skills. These educational parts explain certain symptoms or show photographs of findings. In addition, some systems provided a link to literature, such as Medline, for further information.

Ideally, a generally accepted ES covers the needs of general practitioners and specialists offering an easily understandable usage while at the same time not being too basic. The combination of widely accepted diagnostic criteria sets of European League Against Rheumatism (EULAR) into the diagnostic procedure is expected to improve acceptance and credibility of ES (Alder et al., 2014). An ES would also reduce the influence of individual diagnostic strategies of the system designers. The major flaw of diagnostic criteria coming primarily from classification criteria for inclusion in clinical trials, however, is the generally low sensitivity in early disease. This low sensitivity of some criteria forced Leitich et al. (2001) to modify the criteria using fuzzy sets to achieve different, higher levels of sensitivity. The modern upgrade of official diagnostic criteria, which are oriented to the diagnosis in the early stages of a disease, will make the use of low-sensitivity criteria in the ES development more appealing.

In addition, some diagnostic techniques are not well suited to the use of diagnostic criteria, such as statistical or deep learning approaches. These ES acquire their knowledge in the form of implicit rules from patient data, such as symptoms and clinical findings, and the corresponding diagnoses rely on a hopeful correctness of the chosen diagnosis. The diagnostic criteria cannot be leveraged in these ES without merging with another deterministic approach or an adaption of the reasoning process like a manual review of symptom weighing by a specialist.

The progress of fuzzy ES requires great proficiency of domain experts. For this purpose, Safdari et al. (2018) gathered requisite information via interviews with a number of specialist doctors in the field of cancer research including four oncologists and three cancer epidemiologists. Their views concerning input and output variables of the proposed model is very important to pay attention to all risk factors that show an important role in causing gastric cancer. Hence, variables, parameters, and their weighted scores need to be defined. There are 10–15 features that are the basis of the factors leading to gastric cancer. These risk factors are treated as the input parameters of the fuzzy ES with single output that reflect the risk status, which is further divided into "low risk," "moderate risk," "high risk," and "very high risk." The ES of Safdari et al. (2018) includes of a set of fuzzy rules that are constructed given a set of input variables together with their relevance concerning the process of determining the gastric cancer risk, which is presented by clinical experts and can vary somewhat from physician to physician.

5.5 Expert system lifecycle

The creation of a knowledge-based ES requires the construction of an appropriate task list. There must be a task for the ES that justifies the amount of effort and cost necessary to implement it for all stakeholders. As with all software implementations, a formal process must be followed to ensure the requirements for the ES from all levels of an organization are met. Software development methodologies are continually evolving and thus affect how knowledge-based ES are developed (Golabchi, 2008). Modern knowledge-based ES are developed using an iterative development approach (Fig. 25).

The key stakeholders during the development and implementation phases of a knowledge-based ES are an ES product manager, a development staff, an ontology engineer, and the health domain experts. The development staff is a team whose purpose is to construct the components of the ES as designed by

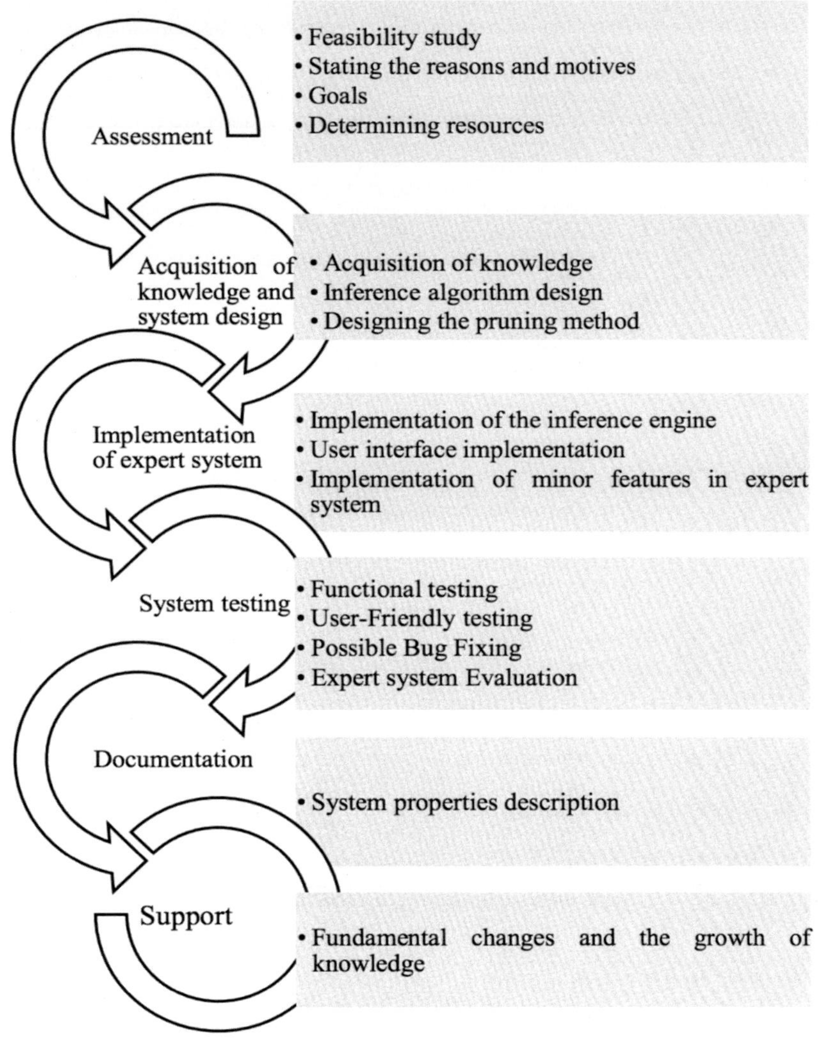

FIG. 25

Expert system (ES) iterative development approach.

the product manager. They will have little problem domain expertise and thus must rely on the ontology engineer to help define the problem domain and associated processes. The ontology engineer maintains domain-specific information from the problem domain experts. The capability of the system is limited by the intelligence and quality of the interviews conducted between the ontology engineer and health domain experts (Millette, 2012).

Fig. 26 depicts a linear model of ES development.

The linear model has been successfully used in a number of expert system projects.
◦ Sequence is repeated until the final system is delivered for routine use.
◦ Each stage consists of tasks. NOT all tasks are necessary
1. Planning Stage
◦ The purpose of this stage is to produce a formal work plan for the expert system development – documents to guide and evaluate the development.
◦ The feasibility assessment is the most important task in the lifecycle
2. Knowledge Definition
The objective of this stage is to define the knowledge requirements of the expert system, which consists of two main tasks:
• Knowledge source identification and selection
• Knowledge acquisition, analysis, and extraction
3. Knowledge Design
The objective is to produce the detailed design for an expert system and involves:
• Knowledge definition
• Detailed design
4. Code and Checkout
This begins the actual code implementation
5. Knowledge Validation
The objective here is to determine the correctness, completeness, and consistency of the system.
• Formal tests
• Test Analysis
6. System Evaluation
This stage is for summarizing what has been learned with recommendations for improvements and corrections.

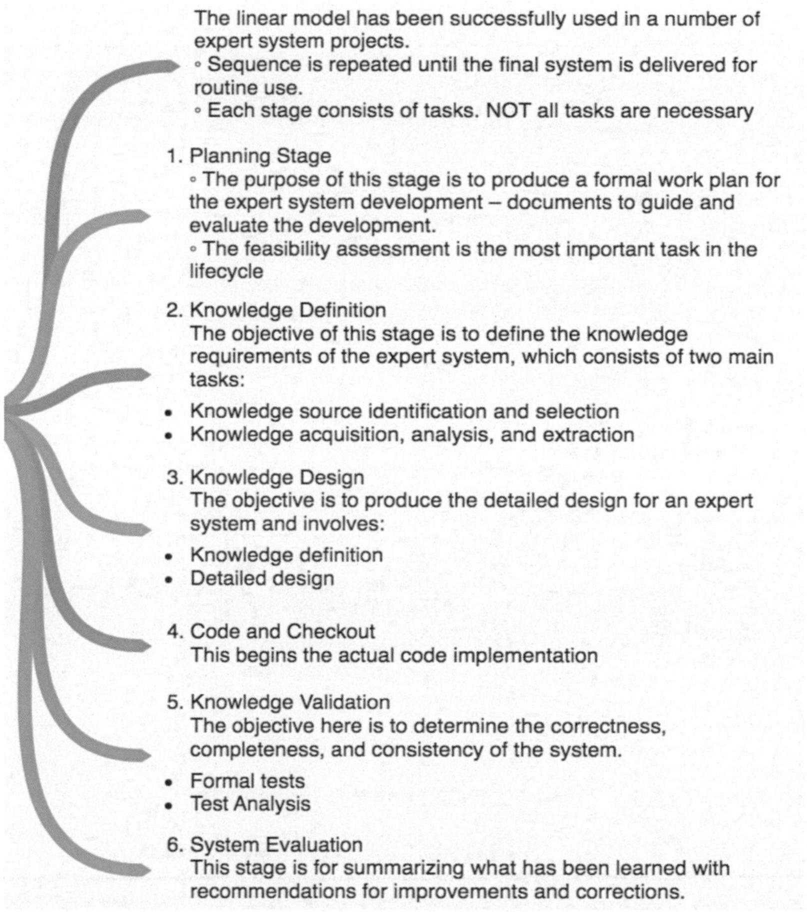

FIG. 26

A linear model of expert system (ES) development.

5.6 Learning ES rules

DecTs can be translated into a set of rules by creating a separate rule for each path from the root to a leaf in the tree. However, rules can also be induced directly from training data using a variety of rule-based algorithms. Furnkranz (1999) wrote an excellent review of existing work in rule-based methods.

Classification rules represent each class by disjunctive normal form. A k-disjunctive normal form expression is of the form: $(X_1 \wedge X_2 \wedge \ldots \wedge X_n) \vee (X_{n+1} \wedge X_{n+2} \wedge \ldots X_{2n}) \vee \ldots \vee (X_{(k-1)n+1} \wedge X_{(k-1)n+2} \wedge \ldots \wedge X_{kn})$, where k is the number of disjunctions, n is the number of conjunctions in each disjunction, and X_n

is defined over the alphabet $X_1, X_2, \ldots, X_j \cup \sim X_1, \sim X_2, \ldots, \sim X_j$. The goal is to construct the smallest rule-set that is consistent with the training data. A large number of learned rules indicates that the learning algorithm is attempting to "memorize" the training set, instead of generalization, which is discovering the assumptions that govern this dataset. This might be an overfitting. A separate-and-conquer algorithm (covering algorithms) searches for a rule that explains a part of its training instances, separates these instances, and recursively conquers the remaining instances by learning more rules, until no instances remain. A general pseudo-code for rule learners is as follows:

Input: the training set with instances

1. Initialize rule set to a default (usually empty, or a rule assigning all objects to the most common class).
2. Initialize instances to either all available examples or all examples not correctly handled by rule set.
3. Repeat
   (a) Find best, the best rule with respect to examples.
   (b) If such a rule can be found
      i. Add best to rule set.
      ii. Set examples to all examples not handled correctly by rule set until no rule best can be found (for instance, because no examples remain).

An ES rule induction system must yield decision rules that have high predictability or reliability. These properties are commonly measured by rule accuracy, which is needed in both the rule induction and classification processes such as J-measure (Smyth and Goodman, 1990). In rule induction, a rule accuracy measure is leveraged as a criterion in the rule specification and/or generalization process. In classification, a rule accuracy value is computed for each rule to address conflicts between multiple rules that are satisfied by the same examples to be classified.

After data acquisition, inference methods and decision-making processes are determined based on the existing data. To reproduce doctors' thinking and to avoid the redundant occurrence of the rules, a hybrid algorithm was formulated by Dashti and Dashti (2020) for the reasoning procedure to achieve high performance in terms of completeness, optimality, time complexity, and space complexity.

In every stage of the decision-making process, an expert can provide the feedback of statistical results by knowing the previous step of queries and answers (Fig. 27). In addition, one could prune the chain through a binary DecT. Because medical ES, including diagnosis systems, are in most cases multi-agent, dynamic, inaccessible, uncertain, and continuous, the system design must be simplified by integrating symptoms into some classes and removing redundant symptoms across the classes. This algorithm frames a "confidence memory," which functions similarly to the human thinking process. The confidence memory sorts the rules in descending order according to the value of their symptoms' confidence effect factor at each moment. The inference process begins when the doctor specifies the type of abnormality they want to diagnose. After that, a query is issued, and the doctor responds to this query by entering a numerical value within a certain range. If the input value is the same or greater than the present confidence value of the symptom in confidence memory, it is inferred that the examined symptom is observed in the patient with a high degree of confidence.

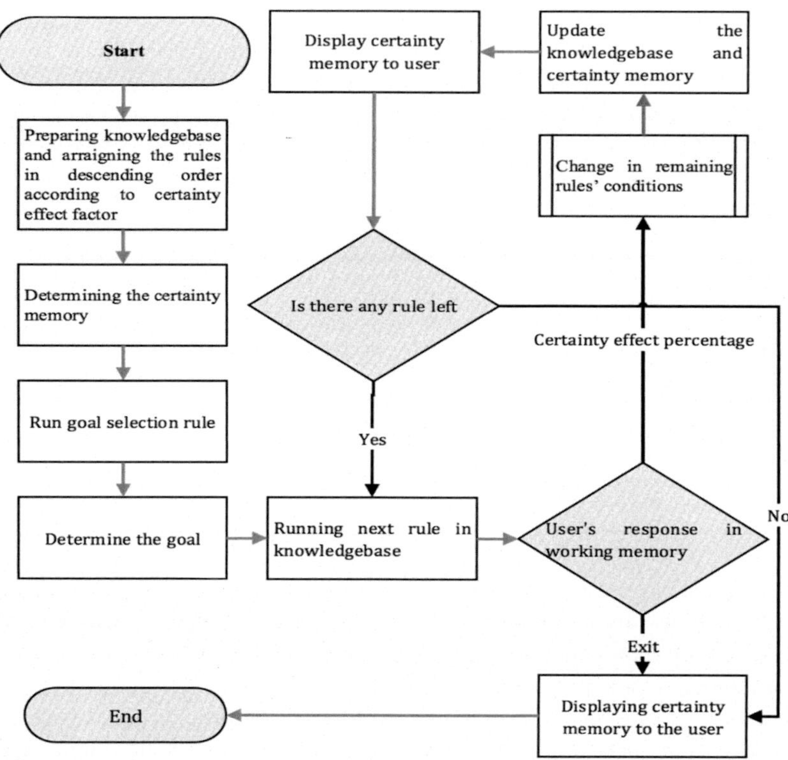

FIG. 27

A rule management architecture for an expert system (ES).

Then, the system will remove the original value of that symptom's confidence value. Next, the user input value of that symptom will be replaced as the new confidence factor while the premise is satisfied. However, if the doctor response is any value smaller than the existing value, the predefined confidence value remains unchanged. That is because of the low chances of observing that symptom in the patient, and as a result, that assumption will not hold.

Finally, all the satisfied assumptions are matched with their antecedents, and goal-related rules are fired. As soon as the rules are fired, the confidence factor of each rule is calculated based on its assumptions. At each stage, when a new rule is fired, the average sum of certainty factor of rules will be calculated as "certainty degree" of the chain of inference. The proposed inference algorithm and approximate responses would require fewer rules than the conventional method of the DecT and explicit responses.

In the proposed algorithm, the user's question-answer process can be stopped at any point while reaching an acceptable answer at any stage of the decision-making process because the events are independent. There is no need to store the path because the certainty memory can compute the relevant statistics at any stage. The possibility to return to previous questions in this algorithm can be accomplished.

5.7 Dynamics of ES usage

We now track how an education of a medical professional evolves and transitions from one to another reasoning pattern (Fig. 28, Bordage, 1994).

We describe the evolution of knowledge structures, outlining the following stages of expertise acquisition:

1. *Reduced.* The physician has little knowledge about disease names and their symptoms and resorts to guessing when problem-solving.
2. *Dispersed.* The physician knows the name of many diseases but few manifestations about each disease. Based on this limited amount of knowledge, the physician attempts to rely on hypothetical deductive reasoning when solving clinical problems.
3. *Elaborated causal.* The physician has a rich knowledge about diseases and their manifestations. Detailed cause-effect links exist in their mind. This doctor uses hypothetical deductive reasoning when solving clinical problems and is more likely to make the correct diagnosis compared to students with limited and non-systematic knowledge.
4. *Scheme induction.* The physician has identified the key points of the clinical presentations in their field of expertise. For each clinical presentation, the doctor organizes the differentials based on common attributes (e.g., anatomy, physiology) into categories, subcategories, disease classes, and short lists of cluster differentials in each class. This structure of acquired knowledge is called a scheme. The learner at this learning step has also managed to reduce a number of key predictors to recognize categories in the scheme.

   Physicians usually reach this stage of deep knowledge understanding and clinical reasoning strategy after a decade of practice. By making the scheme overt and having residents and students use it, there is evidence that their diagnostic skills are enhanced. A trainee physician who has used this scheme inductive reasoning strategy is efficient and would most probably make the correct diagnosis.
5. *Scripted.* From numerous past exposures, the trainee physician has identified the most important differentials of the diseases in the scheme, enabling them to recognize the disease immediately.

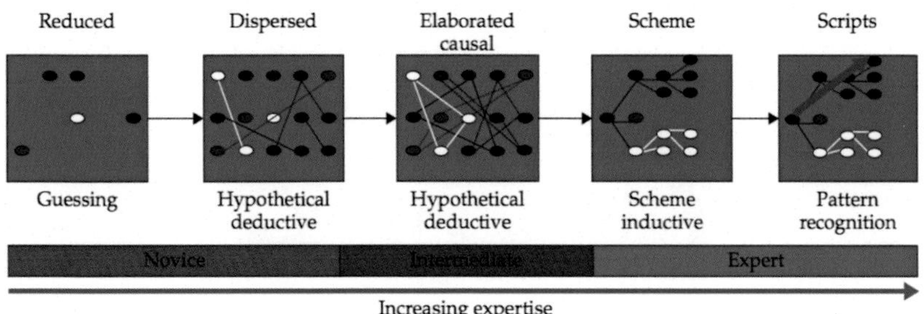

FIG. 28

Evolution of structure from novice to resident to expert.

Extracted from the work by Bordage, G., 1994. Elaborated knowledge: a key to successful diagnostic thinking. Acad. Med. 69, 883–885.

FIG. 29

People and animals make conflicting decisions, each following her own version of a decision tree (DecT).

> Further investigations are primarily confirmatory. This person will use pattern recognition strategy with a high degree of accuracy of obtaining the correct diagnosis.

With advanced reasoning skills, a medical professional can make decisions in a wide spectrum of situations (Figs. 29 and 30).

FIG. 30

Not all decision-makers are necessarily pleasant individuals.

6. Conclusions

In this chapter, we explored a way to build DecTs from text relying on discourse analysis. We discovered a possibility to combine implicit (textual) and attribute-value data to build DTs that are invariant with respect to the nature of available data. An advantage of a supported DecT is that its nodes are labeled with text from where the node rules were extracted; therefore, the supported DecTs provide better explainability compared to regular DecTs. Obtaining DecTs from text, we achieve greater than 72% of the correctness and greater than 70% of the completeness of **full** DecTs with support. The proposed technique allows for building DecTs for textual descriptions of problems solved by humans reflecting the real world, conflicting, not always rational, possibly negative experience (Figs. 29 and 30). In future studies, we will consider building a concept lattice from textual description of data (Galitsky and de la Rosa, 2011), instead of a DecT for authors' instructions on how to do things and make decisions.

Supplementary data sets

Please visit https://github.com/bgalitsky/relevance-based-on-parse-trees to access all supplementary data sets.

References

Al-Ajlan, A., 2015. The comparison between forward and backward chaining. Int. J. Mach. Learn. Comput. 5 (2), 106–113.

Alder, H., Michel, B., Marx, C., Tamborrini, G., Langenegger, T., Brühlmann, P., Steurer, J., Wildi, L., 2014. Computer-based diagnostic expert systems in rheumatology: where do we stand in 2014? Int. J. Rheumatol. 2014, 672714. https://doi.org/10.1155/2014/672714.

Boegl, K., Kainberger, F., Adlassnig, K.P., Kolousek, G., Leitich, H., Kolars, G., Imhov, H., 1995. New approaches to computer-assisted diagnosis of rheumatologic diseases. Radiologe 35 (9), 604–610.

Bordage, G., 1994. Elaborated knowledge: a key to successful diagnostic thinking. Acad. Med. 69, 883–885.

Bradley, A., 1997. The use of area under ROC curve in the evaluation of machine learning algorithms. Pattern Recogn. Lett. 30 (7), 1145–1159.

Buchanan, B.G., 1984. Rule Based Expert Systems: The Mycin Experiments of the Stanford Heuristic Programming Project. Addison Wesley Longman, Reading, MA.

Chi, C.-L., Street, N., Ward, M., 2008. Building a hospital referral expert system with a prediction and optimization-based decision support system algorithm. J. Biomed. Inform. 41, 371–386.

Dashti, S.M.S., Dashti, S.F., 2020. An expert system to diagnose spinal disorders. Open Biochem. J. 13, 57–73.

Department of Health and Human Services, 2017. Interpretation of Hepatitis B Serologic Test Results. Centers for Disease Control and Prevention, Division of Viral Hepatitis. www.cdc.gov/hepatitis.

Furnkranz, J., 1999. Separate-and-conquer rule learning. Artif. Intell. Rev. 13, 3–54.

Galitsky, B., 2017a. Matching parse thickets for open domain question answering. Data Knowl. Eng. 107, 24–50.

Galitsky, B., 2017b. Improving relevance in a content pipeline via syntactic generalization. Eng. Appl. Artif. Intell. 58, 1–26.

Galitsky, B., 2019a. Rhetorical agreement: maintaining cohesive conversations. In: Developing Enterprise Chatbots. Springer, Cham, pp. 327–363.

Galitsky, B., 2019b. Semantic skeleton thesauri for question answering bots. In: Developing Enterprise Chatbots. Springer, Cham, pp. 163–176.

Galitsky, B., 2019c. Building chatbot thesaurus. In: Developing Enterprise Chatbots. Springer, Cham, pp. 221–252.

Galitsky, B., 2020. Navigating Electronic Documents Using Domain Discourse Trees. US Patent 10,853,574.

Galitsky, B., 2021. Managing customer relations in an explainable way. In: Artificial Intelligence for Customer Relationship Management: Solving Customer Problems. Springer, Cham, pp. 221–252.

Galitsky, B., de la Rosa, J.L., 2011. Concept-based learning of human behavior for customer relationship management. Inf. Sci. 181 (10), 2016–2035.

Galitsky, B., Goldberg, S., 2019. Explainable machine learning for chatbots. In: Developing Enterprise Chatbots. Springer, Cham, pp. 53–83.

Galitsky, B., Ilvovsky, D.I., 2019. Validating correctness of textual explanation with complete discourse trees. In: FCA4AI@IJCAI.

Galitsky, B., González, M.P., Chesñevar, C.I., 2009. A novel approach for classifying customer complaints through graphs similarities in argumentative dialogue. Decis. Support. Syst. 46 (3), 717–729.

Galitsky, B., Dobrocsi, G., De La Rosa, J.L., Kuznetsov, S.O., 2010. From generalization of syntactic parse trees to conceptual graphs. In: International conference on conceptual structures, pp. 185–190.

Garofalakis, M., Hyun, D., Rastogi, R., Shim, K., 2000. Efficient algorithms for constructing decision trees with constraints. In: Proceedings of the 6th ACM SIGKDD International Conference on Data Mining and Knowledge Discovery (KDD2000), Boston, MA, pp. 335–339.

Golabchi, M., 2008. A knowledge-based expert system for selection of appropriate structural systems for large spans. Asian J. Civil Eng. 9, 179–191 (Building and Housing).

Goldberg, S., Galitsky, B., Weisburd, B., 2019. Framework for interaction between expert users and machine learning systems. In: AAAI Spring Symposium: Interpretable AI for Well-Being, Stanford, CA.

Goldberg, S., Pinsky, E., Galitsky, B., 2021. A bi-directional adversarial explainability for decision support. Hum. Intell. Syst. Integr. 3 (1), 1–14.

Han, J., Kamber, M., 2001. Data Mining: Concepts and Techniques. Morgan Kaufman, New York, NY.

Hunt, E., Martin, J., Stone, P., 1966. Experiments in Induction. Academic Press, New York.

Hyafil, L., Rivest, R.L., 1976. Constructing optimal binary decision trees is NP-complete. Inf. Process. Lett. 5, 15–17.

Ibrahim, O., 2018. Design and Investigation of a Decision Support System for Public Policy Formulation (PhD thesis). Unib Stockholm. https://www.diva-portal.org/smash/get/diva2:1242925/FULLTEXT10.

Kaplan, R.S., 1991. AI/Consult: a prototype directed history system based upon the AI/Rheum knowledge base. In: Proceedings of the Annual Symposium on Computer Application in Medical Care, pp. 639–643.

Kawamoto, K., Houlihan, C.A., Balas, E.A., Lobach, D.F., 2005. Improving clinical practice using clinical decision support systems: a systematic review of trials to identify features critical to success. BMJ 330 (7494), 765.

Kim, H., Koehler, G., 1995. Theory and practice of decision tree induction. Omega 23 (6), 637–652.

Kokciyan, N., Sassoon, I., Sklar, E., Modgil, S., Parsons, S., 2021. Applying metalevel argumentation frameworks to support medical decision making. IEEE Intell. Syst. 36 (02), 64–71.

Kolarz, G., Adlassnig, K.P., Bogl, K., 1999. RHEUMexpert: a documentation and expert system for rheumatic diseases. Wien. Med. Wochenschr. 149 (19–20), 572–574.

Kotsiantis, S.B., 2013. Decision trees: a recent overview. Artif. Intell. Rev. 39, 261–283.

Leitich, H., Kiener, H.P., Kolarz, G., Schuh, C., Graninger, W., Adlassnig, K.P., 2001. A prospective evaluation of the medical consultation system CADIAG-II/RHEUMA in a rheumatological outpatient clinic. Methods Inf. Med. 40 (3), 213–220.

Mandl, K.D., Kohane, I.S., 2012. Escaping the EHR trap—the future of health IT. N. Engl. J. Med. 366 (24), 2240–2242.

McAndrew, P.D., Potash, D.L., Higgins, B., Wayand, J., Held, K., 1996. Expert System for Providing Interactive Assistance in Solving Problems Such as Health Care Management. US Patent 5517405.

McKibbon, K., Lokker, C., Handler, S., Dolovich, L., Holbrook, A., O'Reilly, D., Tamblyn, R., Hemens, B., Basu, R., Troyan, S., Roshanov, P., 2011. The effectiveness of integrated health information technologies across the phases of medication management: a systematic review of randomized controlled trials. J. Am. Med. Inform. Assoc. 19, 22–30.

Miller, R.A., Pople Jr., H.E., Myers, J.D., 1982. Internist-I, an experimental computer-based diagnostic consultant for general internal medicine. N. Engl. J. Med. 307 (8), 468–476.

Millette, L., 2012. Improving the Knowledge-Based Expert System Lifecycle (Master thesis). University of North Florida. https://core.ac.uk/download/pdf/71998709.pdf.

Moens, H.J.B., van der Korst, J.K., 1991. Computer-assisted diagnosis of rheumatic disorders. Semin. Arthritis Rheum. 21 (3), 156–169.

Motlagh, M.H.A., Minaei Bidgoli, B., Fard, A.A.P., 2018. Design and implementation of a web-based fuzzy expert system for diagnosing depressive disorder. Appl. Intell. 48 (5, SI), 1302–1313.

Mutawa, A.M., Alzuwawi, M.A., 2019. Multilayered rule-based expert system for diagnosing uveitis. Artif. Intell. Med. 99, 101691. https://doi.org/10.1016/j.artmed.2019.06.007.

Osei-Bryson, K.M., 2004. Evaluation of decision trees: a multi-criteria approach. Comput. Oper. Res. 31, 1933–1945.

Petrilli, C.M., Jones, S.A., Yang, J., Rajagopalan, H., O'Donnell, L.F., Chernyak, Y., Tobin, K., Cerfolio, R.J., Francois, F., Horwitz, L.I., 2020. Factors associated with hospitalization and critical illness among 4,103 patients with COVID-19 disease in New York City. BMJ. https://doi.org/10.1136/bmj.m1966.

Safdari, R., Arpanahi, H.K., Langarizadeh, M., Ghazisaiedi, M., Dargahi, H., Zendehdel, K., 2018. Design a fuzzy rule-based expert system to aid earlier diagnosis of gastric cancer. Acta Inform. Med. 26 (1), 19–23.

Schmidt, G.N., Muller, J., Bischoff, P., 2008. Measurement of the depth of anaesthesia. Anaesthesist 57 (1), 9–30.

Sharif, A., 2004. Knowledge Representation Within Information Systems in Manufacturing Environments (PhD thesis). Brunel Univ Dept of CS.

Smyth, P., Goodman, R.M., 1990. Rule induction using information theory. In: Shapiro, G.P., Frawley, W. (Eds.), Knowledge Discovery in Databases. MIT Press.

Song, Y.Y., Lu, Y., 2015. Decision tree methods: applications for classification and prediction. Shanghai Arch. Psychiatry 27 (2), 130–135.

Spreckelsen, C., Spitzer, K., Honekamp, W., 2012. Present situation and prospect of medical knowledge based systems in German-speaking countries. Methods Inf. Med. 51 (4), 281–294.

Surdeanu, M., Hicks, T., Valenzuela-Escarcega, M.A., 2015. Two practical rhetorical structure theory parsers. In: Proceedings of the Conference of the North American Chapter of the Association for Computational Linguistics—Human Language Technologies: Software Demonstrations (NAACL HLT).

WebMD, 2020. Can You Reverse Type 2 Diabetes? https://www.webmd.com/diabetes/can-you-reverse-type-2-diabetes.

Winstanley, T., Courvalin, P., 2011. Expert systems in clinical microbiology. Clin. Microbiol. Rev. 24 (3), 515–556. https://doi.org/10.1128/CMR.00061-10.

Wong, W.Y., Lee, M., Zhang, D.M., 1999. Managing Clinical Incidents in General Practice. AAAI Technical Report WS-99-1.

CHAPTER

Search and prevention of errors in medical databases

4

Saveli Goldberg

Division of Radiation Oncology, Massachusetts General Hospital, Boston, MA, United States

1. Introduction

Corrupted data or missing values can have a serious negative impact on the analysis pipeline. Even ideal machine learning methods cannot find an acceptable solution based on distorted information (Fig. 1). In the last two decades, intensive research has been done to develop algorithms and data cleansing tools. An article from a group of scientists presents an overview of these methods and their successes (Abedjan et al., 2016a,b). However, error detection is a very difficult task due to heterogeneity, simple typos, format errors, legacy data integration, and so on. The quality of data and the effectiveness of data cleansing strategies are highly context-sensitive and dependent on domain, application, and user. In medicine, this manifests itself in specific errors caused by the need for analytical work when entering data and various data types. Errors in data entry are multiplied by errors in initial medical documentation. This chapter describes the medical databases error situation and our experience in avoiding them based on working with health data at Partners HealthCare System, Massachusetts, United States.

2. Data entry errors when transferring information from the initial medical documentation to the studied database

2.1 Analyzed databases

We analyzed the data from several research databases that contained information about treatment and outcomes of oncologic patients who underwent radiation treatment at a single academic medical center. The databases used the MS Access client and PostgreSQL database server. The standard MS Access forms graphical user interface was used for data entry. Trained technicians entered all data in these databases manually, usually by copying from electronic or paper medical records. Constraints by parameter-specific ranges and dynamic constraints based on values in other fields were used to minimize data entry errors. Individuals who entered specific records were not tracked. A typical record contained the patient's demographic information, date of diagnosis of their condition (defined as the date of biopsy), dates of initial and final outpatient radiation treatment visit, date of last follow-up visit (after the radiation treatment course had been completed), and current follow-up status

Artificial Intelligence for Healthcare Applications and Management. https://doi.org/10.1016/B978-0-12-824521-7.00002-8

FIG. 1

"Gold standard" example.

(remission, relapsed, deceased from the treated cancer, deceased from other causes). We have employed two strategies for identifying erroneous entries: highly improbable/internally inconsistent data and data discrepancies between duplicate data entries in different databases (externally inconsistent data).

2.2 Impossible/internally inconsistent data

To evaluate data in research databases for impossible entries and internal inconsistencies, we analyzed two databases (subsequently referred to as "B" and "S") that contained data on treatment and outcomes of oncologic patients (Goldberg et al., 2008). Both databases contained similar data fields. In each of these databases, we evaluated data for the following impossible conditions:

- date of diagnosis on a Sunday (defined as biopsy date, which is not generally conducted on weekends)
- date of the first radiation treatment falls on a Sunday (radiation treatments are usually only administered Monday through Friday and rarely on Saturday)
- date of the last radiation treatment falls on a Sunday
- date of the last follow-up visit falls on a Sunday

We also analyzed the number of date entries that triggered data integrity alarms incorporated into the databases. The alarms were triggered by the following impossible conditions:

- date of diagnosis (database B only): triggered by the date of diagnosis > date of the pathology report, date of diagnosis > date of initiation of chemotherapy, date of diagnosis > date of relapse, date of diagnosis > date of the last follow-up appointment

- date of the first radiation treatment (both databases): triggered if < date of diagnosis, > date of the last follow-up, > date of the last treatment, > 3 months before the date of the last treatment (database "B" only: courses of radiation treatment for patients included in that database cannot be longer than 3 months)
- date of the last follow-up visit: triggered if < date of entry

2.3 Externally inconsistent data

To analyze the data in research databases for external inconsistencies, we analyzed 1006 patient records that were entered incidentally in 2 different databases (subsequently referred to as P1 and P2) at the same time. We analyzed the discrepancies between the records of the same patients in these two databases in the following fields: medical record number (MRN), date of birth (DOB), first and last name, number of treatment sessions, and the date of the last treatment session (Fig. 2). In both databases, demographic information was entered on one screen, and all treatment-related information was entered on another screen.

We see that the discrepancy in different positions ranges from 2.3% to 19.3%. When entering a seven-digit code or possibly a complex name, the number of potential errors is noticeably less than, for example, in the date of the end of radiation therapy. It is speculated that this is because entering the MRN and Name was purely mechanical work, and entering the Radiation Therapy Date required some scrutiny of the medical records. This observation is also confirmed by the coincidence of the number of errors in the same positions in different databases, with a sharp increase in their count in determining the most laborious position, "Radiation Therapy End."

An important result of the analysis is the relationship between the occurrences of errors. The frequency of discrepancies in any field was greater if there was a discrepancy in the same patient record on another field on the same pages. Out of the 21 patients who had a discrepancy in MRN, 5 (23.8%) also had a discrepancy in DOB. On the other hand, out of 67 patients who had a discrepancy in the number of treatment sessions, only 4 (5.97%) also had a discrepancy in DOB ($P = .03$).

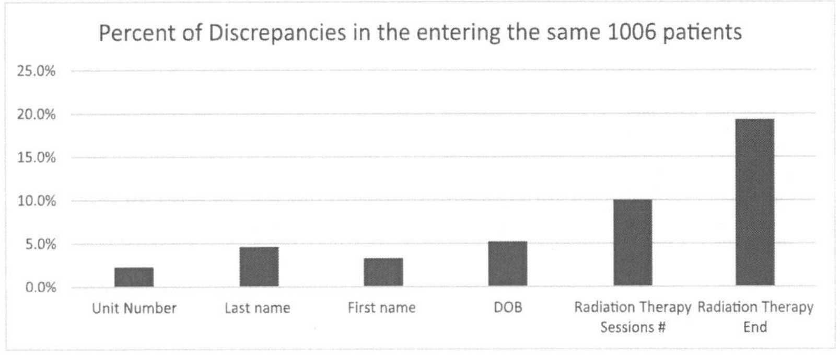

FIG. 2

Results of the discrepancies in P1 and P2 databases on the same patients (*P*-value of homogeneity <.0001).

2.4 Impossible/internally inconsistent data entry in B and S databases

As stated previously, both databases (B and S) had alarm rules to prevent errors at "Radiation Start" and "Follow-up Date." These rules were based on comparison with other dates in databases. The proportion of data records that initially triggered a data integrity alarm ranged from 0.2% of the dates of the last monitoring visit in database B to 1.9% of the dates of the first reception of the radiation service in database S (Fig. 3). There were no significant differences in the frequency of alarms between the two databases. The coincidence of the number of alarms recorded shows the similarity of the results for the data of different entry groups.

The same situation was observed when finding "Sunday" in date fields where events should occur only on weekdays (Fig. 4). The error rates were similar in the same fields in both databases, except for Diagnosis Dates (2.34% vs 0.99%; $P < .0001$). The proportion of Sunday was significantly greater for the dates of the last follow-up visit (>2% for both databases) than for the dates of the first and the last radiation treatment ($P < .001$).

The discrepancy in the date of diagnosis, in our opinion, was associated with the complexity of finding information. Database B mainly contained information about patients who were diagnosed at the same hospital. Database S had a significant proportion of patients who were diagnosed elsewhere and who were subsequently referred for treatment.

2.5 Specific type of the errors "omitted data"

Let us look at survival analysis results based on two datasets of local tumor recurrence for two different projects that two doctors performed independently. They used the same medical records for the same 133 patients (Fig. 5).

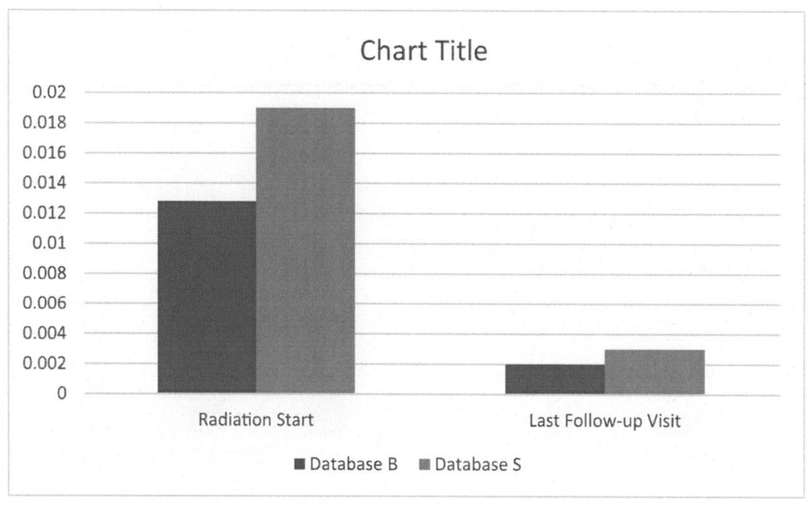

FIG. 3

Internal data integrity alarms.

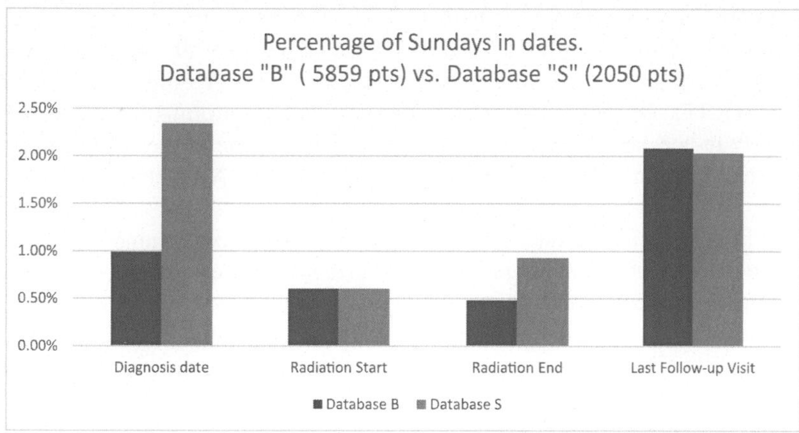

FIG. 4

Sunday in dates (database B and database S).

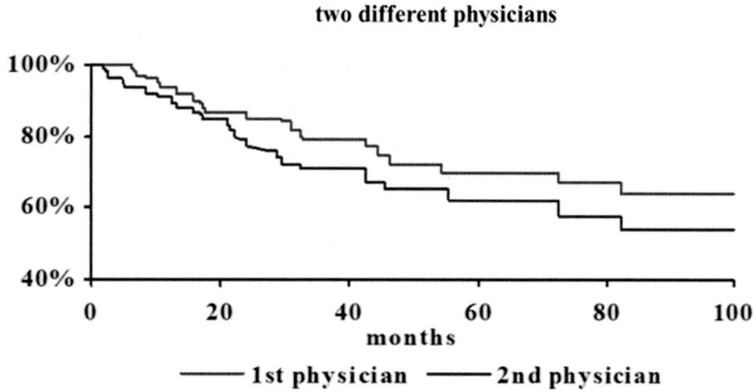

FIG. 5

Results of two studies of the same set of patients.

Only three parameters were used in this analysis: Date of Diagnosis, Date of Follow-up, and Date of Local Failure.

Here is a list of differences in the description of these 133 patients by 2 physicians:

- Different Date of Diagnosis or Date of Follow-up—18 from 133 patients
- Different Date of Local Failure—1 from 33 local failures marked by both physicians
- Mismatch in the failure type (local vs distant) or missed relapse—12 (from real 45 local relapses)

As we can see, the main reason for the different local control results is the omitted local relapses dates.

The absence of the phenomenon that actually took place in the electronic health record (HER) protocol of information is the most dangerous and most challenging type of error to correct.

First, there are many such mistakes. Database S contained 2250 records of patients treated with radiation therapy (XRT). Of these, 344 records did not contain information about XRT start date and were manually re-checked to determine whether documentation of the XRT start date could be found in the patient's records. Manual verification identified the XRT start date for 118 (34.3%) records.

Missing data in other fields (Gender, DOB, Cancer Site) was most common among records with missing XRT start date, which was subsequently found in manual review (at least one of the three fields was missing in 34.7% of the records). Missing data was least common among records (7.6%) where XRT start date was not missing or the missing XRT start date was subsequently identified on manual verification ($P < .0001$). This association remained highly significant for the individual data fields (Table 1).

However, more important than the frequency of such errors is their impact on AI conclusions and the fundamental difficulty of eliminating them. For example, one of the main tasks in treatment is to prevent relapses. Analysis of the vital status data in these databases showed 1161 patients in database B had achieved remission but had the vital status "Deceased from the Treated Cancer". Of these, 98 (8.4%) did not have any information about relapse recorded. Similarly, 62 (10.6%) out of 584 patients in database S who had achieved remission and had the vital status "Deceased from the Treated Cancer" did not have any information about disease relapse recorded as well.

Omitted data constitute a particularly dangerous type of error for data analysis due to its asymmetric manifestation. Omitted data are much more common than erroneously inserted information in the same field. Asymmetric errors are more likely to influence the conclusions of the analysis because their effects do not disappear as in symmetric errors as the number of cases increases.

The "missing data" problem is well illustrated by the error on which we focused our evaluation: omitted date of cancer relapse. This information is not commonly found as a structured field in

Table 1 The relationship between entering XRT date and missing data in some other fields.

	Total	Missing gender, *N* (%, 95% CI)	Missing DOB, *N* (%, 95% CI)	Missing cancer site *N* (%, 95% CI)
Records with XRT Start (no data error)	1906	32 (1.7; 1.15–2.4)	93 (4.9; 4.0–6.0)	24 (1.3; 0.8–1.9)
Record with missing XRT Start not found on manual review (no data error)	226	18 (8.0; 4.8–12.3)	15 (6.6; 3.8–10.7)	20 (8.85; 5.5–13.3)
Records with missing XRT Start found on manual review (data error: omitted XRT start)	118	18 (15.2; 9.3–23.0)	12 (10.2; 5.4–17.1)	24 (20.3; 13.5–28.7)
P-value		<.0001	.031	<.0001

electronic medical record (EMR) systems. Therefore, it has to be manually abstracted from the patient's record by trained personnel through interpretation and cognitive integration of multiple types of narrative documents, including progress notes, operative reports, imaging studies, pathology reports, and so on. Consequently, information about a relapse date would be easy to miss. On the other hand, erroneous entry of a non-existing relapse date is unlikely. Hence, the introduction of wrong data and missing correct data are asymmetric errors. Whereas omitted data in fields containing continuous variables might be successfully dealt with by imputing values based on the other fields in the record, omitted date of relapse would most likely be interpreted as a lack of relapse, potentially altering the conclusions of an automated analysis system.

3. Errors in initial medical information

3.1 Measurement errors "bodyweight" as an indicator of the quality of the initial information

So far, we have looked at errors that arise from difficulties in interpreting or locating data in source documents or from errors in data entry. However, there are errors in the original medical documentation, as explored by (Hsiao et al., 2009; Jha et al., 2006; Ward et al., 2015; Keselman and Smith, 2012; Graber et al., 2019; Hohman, 2019).

We decided to evaluate the volume and sources of errors in the source document using the example of patient weight records in EHRs (Goldberg et al., 2010a). The weights analyzed in this study were obtained from the internally developed certified EMRs at Partners HealthCare System. Partners HealthCare is an integrated healthcare delivery network in eastern Massachusetts that includes founding members Brigham and Women's Hospital and Massachusetts General Hospital as well as several community hospitals and affiliated private practices.

3.2 Algorithm

We developed an algorithm for identifying erroneous weight entries in the EMRs for this project. There are two main business cases for the identification of weight errors in EMR data: (1) alerting the user in real time that the data they have just entered may need to be corrected and (2) retrospective identification of errors in the data for the purpose of data cleaning and/or user feedback. Therefore we designed two versions of the algorithm. The real-time version only considers data that precedes the entry being analyzed, while the retrospective version utilizes all available information (Fig. 6).

Both versions of the algorithm include two main steps:

1. Absolute threshold analysis determines whether the entry value is above or below pre-determined boundaries that define a physiologically possible range of values. The algorithm focused on identification of weight errors in adults and, based on our clinical experience, we selected 50 lbs. and 800 lbs. as the boundaries.
2. Change threshold analysis determines whether the change between the current entry and other entries for the same patient available for analysis is greater than expected. The algorithm takes into account three factors: (1) a relative difference from the entries immediately preceding or following the current entry, (2) a difference from the mean of all entries available for analysis, and (3) time

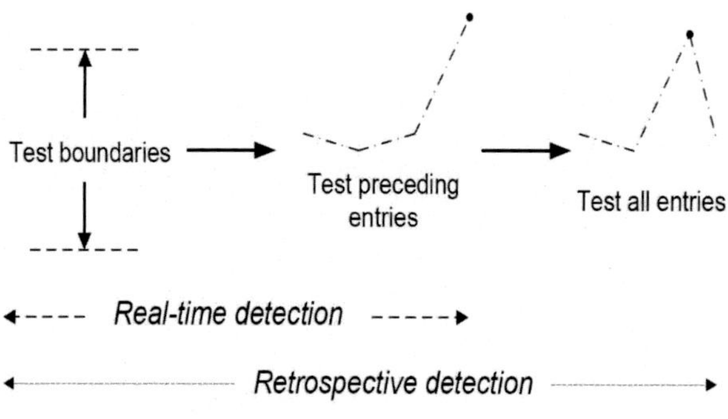

FIG. 6

A diagram of weight errors detection.

elapsed since the last entry. Specific criteria employed in the algorithm were developed empirically based on clinical experience. In the real-time version of the algorithm, the criteria are applied only once from the penultimate entry to the current, whereas in the retrospective version, criteria (1) and (3) are applied twice, from the penultimate entry and from the first subsequent entry. Mean and standard deviation are calculated from the data preceding the value being analyzed for the real-time version of the algorithm and from all data available for the retrospective version of the algorithm.

The overall agreement between the two reviewers of the 186 weight entries used to evaluate the accuracy of the real-time version of the algorithm was 94.1%. The kappa statistic was 0.809 (95% CI: 0.704–0.913), indicating very good agreement.

The positive predictive value (i.e., precision or PPV) of the real-time version of the algorithm was 81.2% (95% CI 74.8%–86.5%). The retrospective version of the algorithm identified 88 out of the original 186 entries selected by the real-time version as erroneous. PPV of the retrospective algorithm was 98.9% (95% CI 93.8%–99.9%). The upper boundary of the sensitivity of the retrospective algorithm was 57.6% (95% CI 49.3%–65.6%).

3.3 Errors in EMR data

We studied the prevalence and characteristics of erroneous weight entries in EMR data on a dataset of 25,000 randomly selected patients. These patients had 420,469 weight entries between 1990 and 2010 entered by 4373 users. The mean weight value was 192.6 lbs., the median 187 lbs., and the interquartile range 159–220 lbs. Of these entries, 645 for 159 unique patients had values less than 50 lbs. or greater than 800 lbs. and were classified as errors during the boundary test phase. Physicians entered 50,343 entries, and non-physicians entered 370,126 entries.

Of the remaining 419,829 EMR weight entries, the real-time algorithm identified 2221 (0.53%) weight records of 1861 unique patients (7.4%) as possible errors. The mean weight value for these entries was 168.6 lbs., the median was 158 lbs., and the interquartile range 125–204.4 lbs. Based on the assessment of the algorithm's PPV, the estimated number of erroneous entries (including boundary failures) in this dataset was therefore 2448 (Fig. 7).

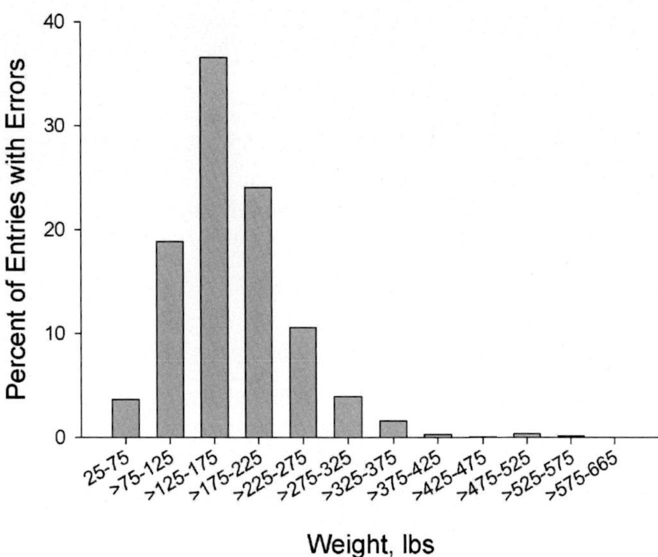

FIG. 7

Distribution of possible weight errors.

Using the same dataset, the retrospective algorithm identified 1107 weight records for 827 patients as erroneous. The mean weight value for these records was 171.8 lbs., the median was 157 lbs., and the interquartile range was 120–209.6 lbs. Based on the high PPV assessed for this version of the algorithm, these entries were used for subsequent analysis of risk factors for errors in EMR weight data.

The average difference between weight records identified as errors and the rest of the weight records for the same patient was 80.1 lbs. (standard deviation 51.2; 45.6% of the non-erroneous weights) for the retrospective version of the algorithm and 62.0 lbs. (standard deviation 46.7; 36.3% of the non-erroneous weights) for the real-time version.

3.4 User history of previous errors

To determine whether user history of erroneous weight entries made subsequent erroneous weight entries more likely, we considered a dataset of 480 users who had entered at least 200 weight records into the EMR. Out of 146 users who had made an erroneous entry among their first 100 entries, 70 (47.9%) also made an erroneous entry among their second 100 entries. On the other hand, out of the 334 users who had not made an error among their first 100 entries, only 92 (27.5%) made an error among their second 100 entries ($P < .001$).

3.5 Physicians vs non-physicians

To determine whether physicians or non-physicians had higher rates of erroneous weight entries, we analyzed a dataset of 766 users who had entered at least 100 weights into the EMR. We limited the analysis to the first 100 entries to mitigate a possible effect of experience entering weight records into the EMR. Of the 105 physicians in this dataset, 27 (24.8%) made an erroneous entry among their first 100 entries, whereas out of the 659 non-physicians, 233 (35.4%) made an error in the first 100 entries (P = .034).

In the analysis that was not limited to the first 100 entries, non-physicians made 1015 errors (0.27%) among 370,126 weight records while physicians made 92 errors (0.18%) among 50,343 records (P < .0001). Physicians were less likely than non-physicians to make errors, possibly because many physicians only enter weight into EMRs when clinically indicated and therefore pay closer attention to the accuracy of the entry.

3.6 Effect of practice location on weight error rates

To determine whether a practice, where the users worked, had an effect on error rates, we analyzed 24 practices with at least 5 non-physician users (practice location was expected to have less influence on physicians than on staff) who had entered at least 100 weight entries each. The Kruskal-Wallis test comparing user error rates by the practice where they worked showed significant differences in rates (P = .034). The significance of the practice effect was even greater for a subset of 19 practices that had at least 10 weight-entering users (P = .015). Practice location of the user had a significant effect on the error rate, possibly reflecting policies and training in place in individual clinics. There is a trend for lower error rates for users with greater experience entering weight into EMRs.

3.7 Error rates over time

To determine whether the rate of weight errors in EMRs has been changing with time, we analyzed data from consecutive years for which there were more than 10,000 weight records available for each year (2001–2009). The fraction of erroneous weight entries decreased gradually from 0.47% in 2001 to 0.15% in 2009 (Fig. 8). A logistic model that adjusted for intra-user clustering showed that the error rates decreased by 9.8% annually (P < .0001).

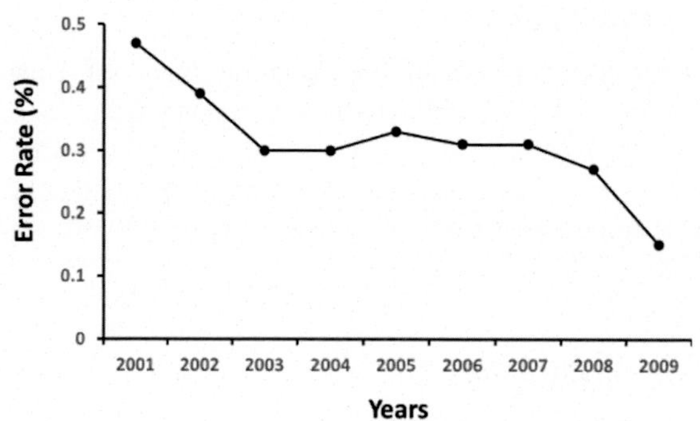

FIG. 8

Errors in weight record over time.

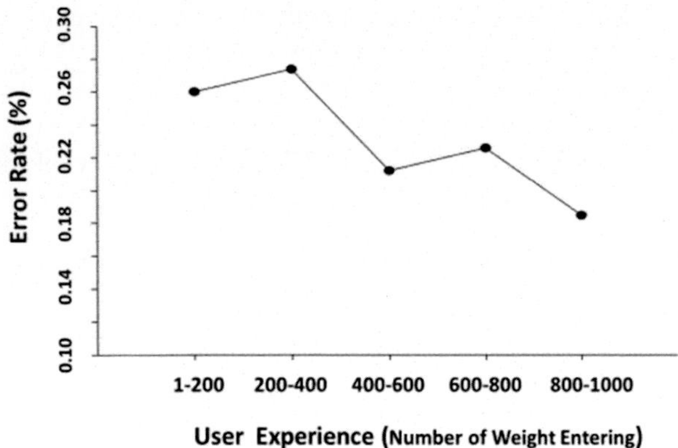

FIG. 9

Error rates and user experience.

3.8 Error rates and user experience

To determine whether user experience entering weight information into EMRs was associated with lower error rates, we analyzed data entered by 763 users who entered at least 100 weights into EMRs. The average error rate for these users was 0.25% in the first 100 weight entries and 0.19% in all subsequent weight entries ($P = .0009$).

Analysis of a subset of 73 users who had entered at least 1000 weights into EMRs showed that the error rate decreased gradually from 0.26% for the first 200 entries to 0.19% for the fifth 200 entries (Fig. 9). There is a trend for lower error rates for users with greater experience entering weight into EMRs. However, in a logistic regression model that adjusted for intra-provider clustering, user experience was not statistically significant. User experience was defined as the number of weight entries the user had made up (specified a random value) to and including the entry for which the error rate was measured.

In this large retrospective study, we developed and utilized a high-precision algorithm for the identification of errors in weight data in EMRs to study their prevalence, characteristics, and risk factors. While the probability that any given weight entry was erroneous was low, most patients had multiple weight entries, and over time the rate of errors per patient accumulated, reaching the overall total as high as 7%.

4. Error reduction

4.1 Detection errors in datasets

Data cleaning tools belong to the following three categories:

1. Rule-based detection algorithms (Haerian et al., 2009; Chu et al., 2013; Fan et al., 2012; Geerts et al., 2014; Wang and Tang, 2014) that can be embedded into frameworks, such as Nadeef

(Khayyat et al., 2015). Rules can vary from a simple rule like constraint "<150 years" to multiparameter dependencies using complicated functions.
2. Pattern enforcement and transformation tools such as OpenRefine, Data Wrangler (Kandel et al., 2011), Katara (Chu et al., 2015), and DataXFormer (Abedjan et al., 2016a,b). These tools discover patterns in the data and use these to detect errors (fields that do not conform to the patterns).
3. Quantitative error detection algorithms (Abedjan et al., 2015; Prokoshyna et al., 2015; Wu and Madden, 2013).

4.2 Alarm system in data entry process

An obvious method for reducing data entry errors would be the minimization of manual data entry by using direct data transfers from EMRs into research databases. However, this is not always possible. Manual data entry remains common in prospective studies where the physician generates data for the research rather than for clinical care (and is therefore not recorded in the EMR). Another common scenario that mandates manual data entry involves collecting retrospective data, which requires cognitive synthesis of the data available in the medical record and/or abstraction of information from narrative medical documents that is not available as an exportable structured data field. Of course, adequate training of the study staff could ameliorate the interpretation of information during the data entry process. In high-value data entry double entry or other techniques, such as read-aloud data entry, could be employed. However, a high level of errors in a simple data entry will not eliminate the presence of errors with double entry, and most importantly, a high expense associated with double-entry implementation may be substantial.

Today, the alarm system is an integral part of the database. Rule-based and/or quantitative methods are used as error detection. Usually, an alarm is presented to the user if there is a very high probability of error ($P < .001$). Our experience shows that even probabilities of error with $P < .05$ are well suited for use in alarm. For example, "Sunday/Saturday was used as a Diagnosis Date" should be an error alarm for B and S databases, although Sunday/Saturday could be a Diagnosis Date in 3% of cases. Strong, but not absolute, suspicions should also lead the user to double-check the suspect entry. More extensive cognitive integration of data fields would likely also lead to a reduction in error rates, in effect imposing dynamic constraints that vary based on the context of the other fields in the record. Usually, heuristic algorithms such as the method for detecting errors in weights from Section 3.2 are used for these purposes, but more and more often, statistical methods are used, for example, regression analysis (Fig. 10).

In this case, you need to go past Scylla (a high alarm threshold, which leaves many errors) and Charybdis (an underestimated alarm threshold, which causes a large number of false alarms).

Our analysis shows that data errors appear to be clustered in accordance with the spatial arrangement of the database fields in the data entry forms. Our evaluation showed that the presence of one data error on the demographic information screen increased the probability of another data error in another field on the same screen several folds, while no association was found between errors in the fields on different screens. One possible explanation could be that a single distracting event may be responsible for both errors on the same data entry screen but does not carry over to another screen.

As shown in Figs. 11 and 12, errors were not uniformly distributed among EMR users. Users who had made an error in the past were more likely to make another one in the future.

$$\text{Alarm if } \mathbf{y}_{\text{entered}} \notin [{}^{-}\mathbf{y}_{\text{predicted}},\ {}^{+}\mathbf{y}_{\text{predicted}}]$$

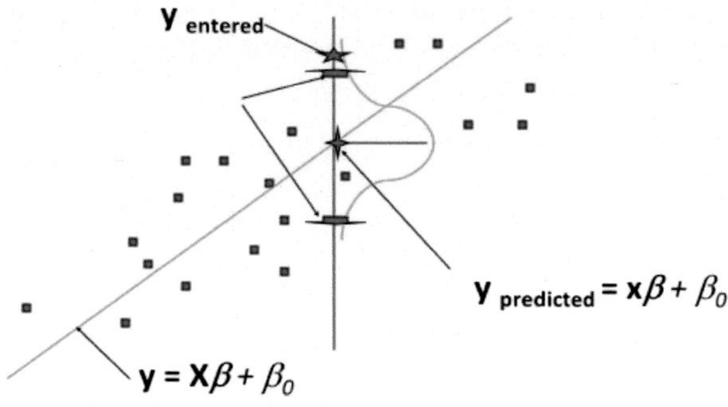

FIG. 10

An alarm rule based on regression analysis.

Example A

TL 5/20/00 (the first set)
8 errors (4 character 4 numeric) in 69 records. 69/8 = 8.6 (70 fields) 4/4=1.00
Average distance between errors 32 fields

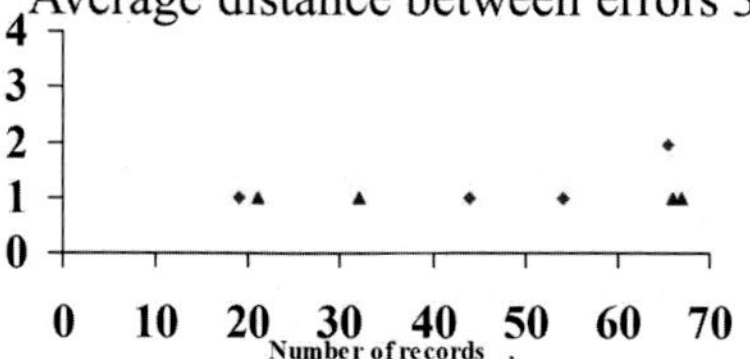

TL 6/10/00 (the second set)
9 errors (5 character 4 numeric) in 66 records. 66/9 = 7.33(59 fields) 5/4=1.25
Average distance between errors 26 fields

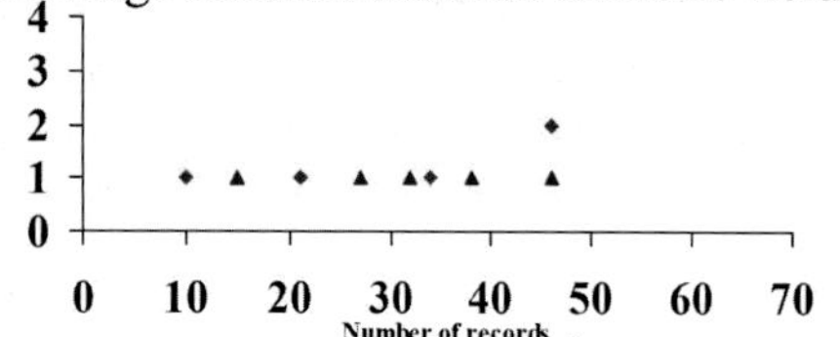

FIG. 11

Volunteer TL.

Example B

DA 5/30/00 (the first set)
12 errors (3 character 9 numeric) in 46 records. 46/12 = 3.8 (30 fields) 3/9=0.33
Average distance between errors 12 fields

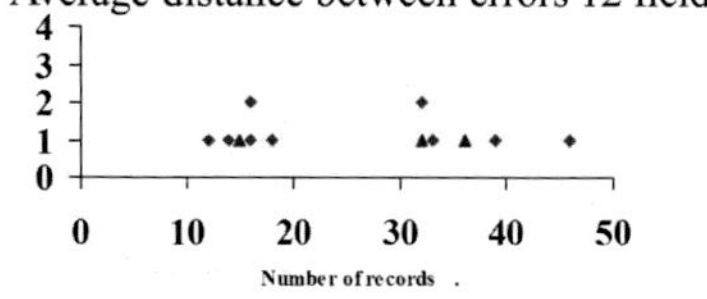

DA 6/23/00 (the second set)
25 errors (7 character 18 numeric) in 70 records. 70/25 = 2.8 (22 fields) 7/18=0.38
Average distance between errors 10 fields

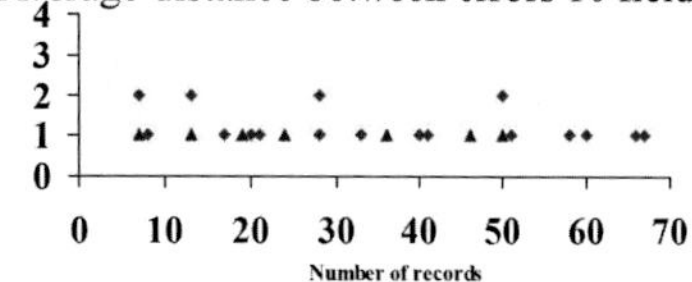

FIG. 12

Volunteer DA.

The specificity of errors for an individual user is also confirmed by our experiments with volunteers:

Testing a data entry person on a pre-prepared template makes it possible to identify such features of this user. Thus, there are a number of additional parameters that characterize the user and the previous history of their errors. All this will help the system to create warning rules for this user (Goldberg et al., 2007). For example, if you take the logistic regression:

$$Alarm\ if\ Pr(error\ in\ records \mid \boldsymbol{x}) > P_0,$$

Where

$$Log\,(Pr/(1-Pr)) = \beta_0 + \beta' \boldsymbol{x}$$

$\boldsymbol{x}$ is a vector of explanatory variables. $\boldsymbol{x}$ includes temporal characteristics of the record, history of the user previous errors, style of the user typing, and str.

4.3 "Follow-up summary" as a method of error prevention

4.3.1 "Follow-up summary" description

It is not always possible to detect an error based on expert rules or numerical methods. This is especially true for the most dangerous errors in the training set, for example, errors in class definitions. It is never possible to formulate rules for these errors; the system must deduce them in the process of ML. However, each error in determining the class in the AI training sample can give rise to a whole neighborhood of errors when using obtained conclusions.

How can such errors be prevented?

Suppose, for example, that our task is to predict the occurrence of metastases in the first 5 years after cancer treatment. It is known that a large tumor is an alarming factor for metastases, but if every time the user introduces a "large tumor," they are asked if they correctly indicated the absence of metastases, it will cause nothing but irritation. In this regard, an attempt was made to indirectly influence the user so that they doubted the consistency of the data and were inclined to double-check it. To this end, many modern electronic data entry systems (for example, online stores or banks) offer the user to review the entered information before completing the transaction. However, a complete view of the data is not possible with clinical trial databases, which typically contain tens, if not hundreds, of fields spanning multiple screens.

The "*Follow-up summary*" is designed to mitigate this problem by applying the following principles:

- focusing on key fields
- the visual combination of information in these fields to facilitate the detection of data inconsistencies
- indication of probable errors

The original name of this method was "*Summary Page*" (Goldberg et al., 2010b); however, it is assumed that "*Follow-up summary*" reflects this idea better.

The screen on which the "*Follow-up summary*" is presented consists of the following main sections:

(1) A verbatim list of selected record fields that represent key demographic and clinical information

The presentation of these fields is organized to show inconsistencies in the data. This is achieved through a menu of items of data, organizing the order in which data is presented, highlighting and changing the font for key parameters. The combinations of parameters that are suspicious of internal incompatibility with each other were obtained in advance based on expert rules and the existing database.

Consider an example of presenting information in section **(1)**.

The analytical algorithm suggests that information about cancer recurrence may have been missed because the patient's record has a large tumor size, a positive margin as a result of surgery, and the second resection was performed relatively late after lumpectomy. The average relapse rate in the first 5 years after diagnosis is about 4%. If the tumor is >2 cm, the positive margin and the distance between the lumpectomy and the second resection is more than 1 month, then the probability of recurrence within a year between the lumpectomy and the second resection increases to 10%. However, an alarm cannot be triggered at 90% false positives.

Regular presentation data without problems should be:

Female 55 years old, T-stage 2, N-stage 0, M stage 0. Tumor size 2.2 cm, CR negative, PR negative, tumor size 2.2 cm. Biopsy 02/28/2009, Lumpectomy 03/04/2009, positive margin. Local relapse 12.06.2009. 2nd Resection 01.07.2009, negative margin. No RT, No Chemotherapy

Case presentation with suspected non-relapse:

*Female 55 years old, **Tumor size 2.2 cm**, T stage 2, N stage 0, M stage 0. Tumor size 2.2 cm, PR negative. 02/28/2009 Biopsy. No RT, No Chemotherapy, 03/04/2009 **lumpectomy with a positive margin. After 8 months, the 2nd resection. No relapses.***

(2) Schematic representation of the chronology of the patient's clinical course

A single view without problems:

_*02/28/2009*___*03/04/2009*__________________*12/06/2009*____*01/07/2009*

Biopsy *Lumpectomy* *Local Recurrence* *2nd Resection*

Case presentation with suspected non-relapse or 2nd Resection date:

_*02/28/2009*___*03/04/2009*___________________________*01/07/2009*

Biopsy *Lumpectomy* *2nd Resection*

(3) "Possible Error" section that lists likely errors based on a set of rules that take into account all fields in the record. Typically, these errors, while likely (>50%), are not fully certain, and therefore do not merit an interruptive alert.

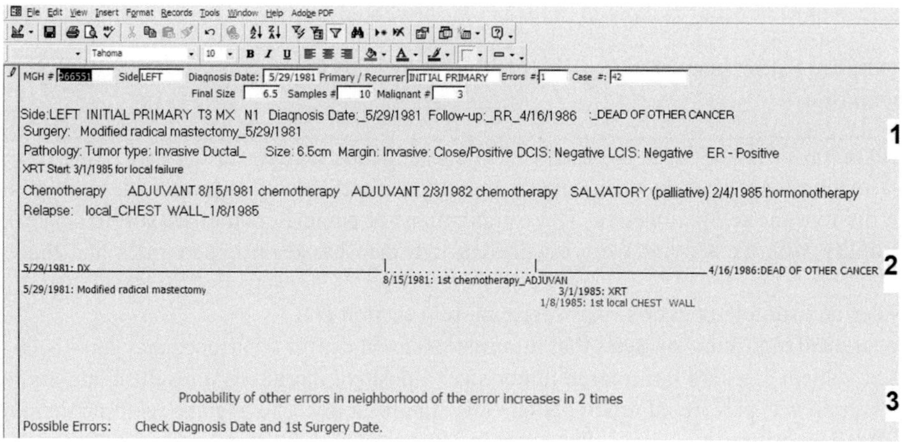

FIG. 13

Example of "*Follow-up summary*" screen.

An example of a possible error that can be identified in the breast cancer database is a new surgical procedure (e.g., modified radical mastectomy after the original lumpectomy) without a documented relapse of cancer (Fig. 13). This is most likely an error where the information about the relapse was omitted. However, the error is not definite since it is also possible that the patient herself requested a more aggressive procedure to be reassured that cancer will not recur. Most of the rules for identifying possible errors involve items of data entered on different screens of the database, so it can be difficult for users to combine them. The "*Follow-up summary*" performs this function.

An additional benefit of using a "*Follow-up summary*" is to view the dangerous part in the data. As shown previously, errors often occur next to each other. A user who finds and corrects one error or omission in a recording may also be more likely to view the remainder of the recording and find other errors.

The "*Follow-up summary*" was implemented as a single screen in a Microsoft Access database that could be accessed from anywhere in the recording. Users could access the "*Follow-up summary*" at any time during the data entry process or ignore the "*Follow-up summary*."

4.3.2 "Follow-up summary" implementation

A working implementation of "*Follow-up summary*" uses a rule system based largely on expert opinion. However, potentially suspicious parameter combinations can also be generated using ML algorithms. In this case, a promising method is "Minimal Antisyndrome" (Goldberg, 1984).

Here is the definition of the "minimal antisyndrome":

Let $\mathbf{x}=(x_1, x_2, .., x_n)$ be a vector of the n input parameters to the algorithm. x_i is categorical (Boolean) variable. Let $\mathbf{X}$ be a set of $\mathbf{x}$.

Minimal "antisyndrome" of class $\mathbf{A} \subset \mathbf{X}$ is the minimum set of parameters, the combination of which is not found in the elements of class **A**. The minimal antisyndrome of class **A** plus any other parameter is an antisyndrome of class **A**, but if we exclude any parameter from the minimal "antisyndrome", then the combination of other remaining parameters is not an antisyndrome for class **A**.

Having a set of minimal antisyndromes, it is possible to construct a recognition rule to determine class **A** versus a class other than **A**, having a training set only from class **A**. Let us now explain this informally, independently of medicine. Usually, syndromes are used to describe an illness: combinations of features determining a given illness. Instead, we use antisyndromes, those combinations of features that do not occur for this illness. We focus on minimal antisyndrome, which stops being antisyndromes once any feature is excluded. A set of all minimal syndromes uniquely identify an illness. For example, of all emergency calls, 35% were for men and 10% for pregnant patients. Combination "*pregnant patient*: Yes + *gender*: Male" will be the minimal antisyndrome of the class of ambulance patients. In our case, the totality of all patients' descriptions is considered as a set of proper combinations of symptoms. The minimal antisyndrome for this totality is a contradictory combination of features. If such antisyndrome occurs in a patient's complaint, one needs to check the correctness of the mentioned features.

Of course, as we have noted a lot in this chapter, there are no perfect descriptions of objects, and in practice, we used a softer definition of antisyndrome. If the probability of occurrence of a set $x_1, .., x_m$, $m \ll n$ provided that the parameters are independent, is $p(x_1, .., x_k) = p(x_1) * \ldots * p(x_m)$ and if in reality in class the frequency of the set $(x_1, \ldots, x_m)$ was much less than $(p(x_1) * \ldots * p(x_m))$ then set of $x_1, x_2, \ldots, x_m$ is candidate to be antisindrome. In recent machine learning development, antisindrome is usually referred to as an "adversarial training dataset" (Tygar, 2011).

4.3.3 "Follow-up summary" *utilization*

"*Follow-up summary*" usage tracings included a date, time, and user ID for each "*Follow-up summary*" access. Database users were not aware that "*Follow-up summary*" access was being monitored.

To determine the utilization of the "*Follow-up summary*," we analyzed all 1356 records (200 new and 1156 updated) that were entered or updated in database B between 07/04/2008 and 03/04/2009. Fig. 14 shows the distribution of "*Follow-up summary*" utilization per record. "*Follow-up summary*" was accessed in slightly less than half (44.2%) of all records. Most commonly, it was accessed only once per record, but in 2.4% of the records, it was accessed three or more times. "*Follow-up*

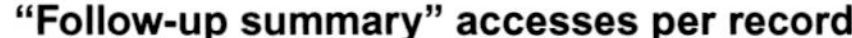

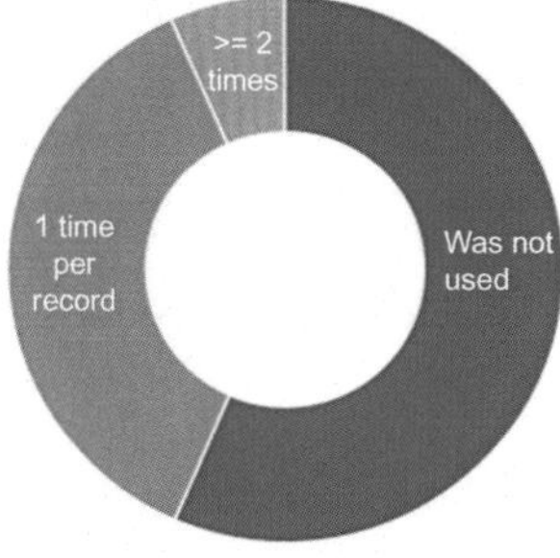

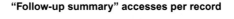

FIG. 14

"*Follow-up summary*" utilization per record.

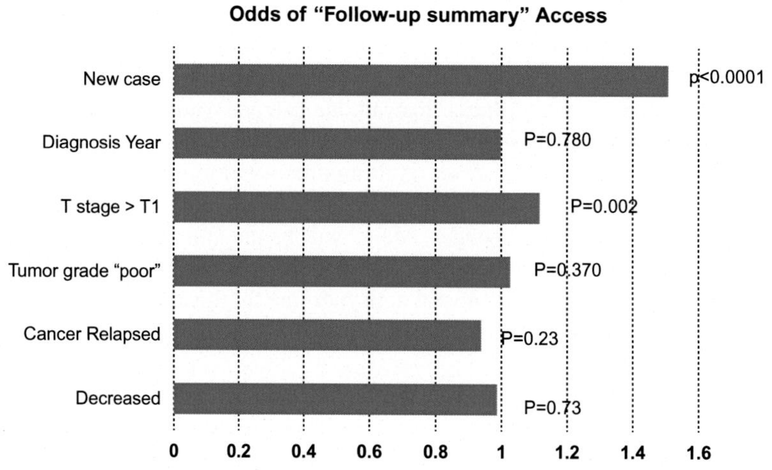

FIG. 15

Predictors of "*Follow-up summary*" access.

summary" was accessed for 69.0% of entries of new records but only for 40.0% of the updates of the records already in the database ($P = .01$). Three data entry technicians worked with the database during this period. Their "*Follow-up summary*" access rates were 84.6%, 47.1%, and 11.8%, respectively ($P < .001$).

In multivariable analysis, the odds of "*Follow-up summary*" access were 12% greater if the patient's cancer had a tumor stage (T-stage) greater than one and more than 50% greater if this was a new record rather than an existing one being updated (Fig. 15). Patients' vital status, tumor grade, whether cancer had relapsed, and the year of diagnosis were not significantly associated with "*Follow-up summary*" access.

4.3.4 "Follow-up summary" *effectiveness*

To evaluate the effectiveness of the "*Follow-up summary*" we analyzed the same 1356 records as we used to test utilization of the "*Follow-up summary*." Among these records, 164 had documented a cancer remission but had the final vital status "Died from Disease," indicating that a cancer relapse had taken place. However, five of these 164 records (3.05%) did not have any information in the relapse date ("Date of Local Failure" or "Date of Distant Failure" fields) recorded. "*Follow-up summary*" was accessed for 86 of the 164 records. None of the records for which "*Follow-up summary*" was accessed had a missing date of relapse. All five missing relapse dates were in 80 records without "Follow-up summary" accessed ($P = .023$).

Among the 1156 records updated during the study period, "*Follow-up summary*" was accessed for 462 records. Relapse information was entered after "*Follow-up summary*" access for 16 (3.5%) of the records where "*Follow-up summary*" was utilized and for 4 (0.6%) of the remaining records ($P = .0003$). The date, time and user ID for each edit of the relapse date fields were recorded. In all 16 records where relapse information was entered after "*Follow-up summary*" access, it was entered

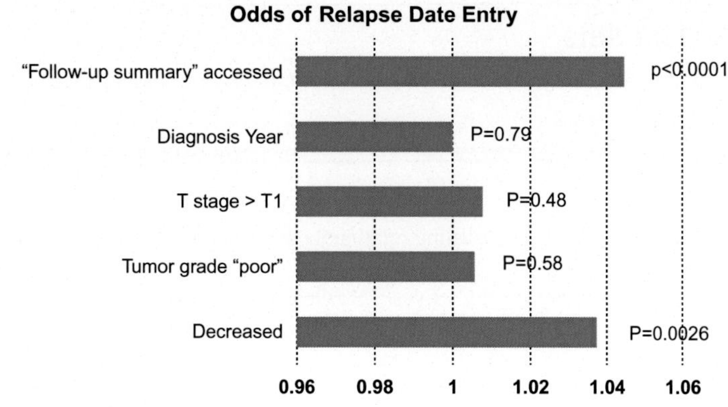

FIG. 16

Predictors of relapse date entry.

within 10min of accessing the "*Follow-up summary*." Similarly, out of the nine records where the date of the very first relapse was entered, it was entered within 10min after "*Follow-up summary*" access for seven records ($P=0.034$). In multivariable analysis, the odds of entry of date of relapse increased by 3.8% if the patient's vital status was "Deceased" and by 4.5% if the "*Follow-up summary*" was accessed during the record update (Fig. 16). Tumor grade, tumor stage, and the year of cancer diagnosis were not significantly associated with the probability of entry of date of relapse. There was no significant difference in the probability of entry of a relapse date between individual data entry technicians.

5. Conclusions

Errors in databases, which are the gold standard of ML, are common and can affect the quality of the rules or generalizations generated by ML. The number of errors varies greatly depending on the database field, and the probability of an error even in one particular field is not evenly distributed. Cleaning learning bases from errors is an important element of the correct operation of ML. The non-randomness of errors, their relationship with each other, and user characteristics can serve as a basis for using AI methods to prevent potential errors in the data entry process. In addition to direct error prevention methods based on expert rules and/or numerical methods, indirect error prevention methods can play an important role here. This is especially important for detecting errors that cannot be detected effectively without a high risk of false alarms. Here, the "*Follow-up summary*" is proposed as such a method. "*Follow-up summary*" based on the entered data forms an integral contextual page describing a medical case. The content of this page is organized in such a way that the doctor himself suspects a possible data error.

However, in addition to the problems with the data used to create AI systems, there is also the problem of the adequate use of AI. We discuss this in Chapter 5.

Supplementary data sets

Please visit https://github.com/bgalitsky/relevance-based-on-parse-trees to access all supplementary data sets.

References

Abedjan, Z., Golab, L., Naumann, F., 2015. Profiling relational data: a survey. VLDB J. 24 (4), 557–581. https://doi.org/10.1007/s00778-015-0389-y.

Abedjan, Z., Chu, X., Deng, D., Fernandez, R.C., Ilyas, I.F., Ouzzani, M., Papotti, P., Stonebraker, M., Tan, N., 2016a. Detecting data errors: where are we and what needs to be done? Proc. VLDB Endow. 9 (12), 993–1004. https://doi.org/10.14778/2994509.2994518.

Abedjan, Z., Morcos, J., Ilyas, I.F., Papotti, P., Ouzzani, M., Stonebraker, M., 2016b. DataXFormer: a robust data transformation system. In: 2016 IEEE 32nd International Conference on Data Engineering (ICDE)., https://doi.org/10.1109/ICDE.2016.7498319.

Chu, X., Ilyas, I.F., Papotti, P., 2013. Holistic data cleaning: putting violations into context. In: IEEE 29th International Conference on Data Engineering (ICDE)., https://doi.org/10.1109/ICDE.2013.6544847.

Chu, X., Morcos, J., Ilyas, I.F., Ouzzani, M., Papotti, P., Tang, N., Katara, Y.Y., 2015. A data cleaning system powered by knowledge bases and crowdsourcing. In: Proceedings of the 2015 ACM SIGMOD International Conference on Management of Data, pp. 1247–1261, https://doi.org/10.1145/2723372.2749431.

Fan, W., Li, J., Ma, S., Tang, N., Yu, W., 2012. Towards certain fixes with editing rules and master data. VLDB J. 21, 213–238.

Geerts, F., Mecca, G., Papotti, P., Santoro, D., 2014. Mapping and cleaning. In: 2014 IEEE 30th International Conference on Data Engineering., https://doi.org/10.1109/ICDE.2014.6816654.

Goldberg, S., 1984. Diagnostics on the basis of the informative space of the antisyndromes. Prob. Control Inf. Theory 13 (6), 401–411.

Goldberg, S., Ancukiewicz, M., Niemierko, A., 2007. Data entry errors in clinical research databases. In: Medinfo 2007: Proceedings of the 12th World Congress on Health (Medical) Informatics; Building Sustainable Health Systems. IOS Press, Amsterdam, p. 2252.

Goldberg, S., Niemierko, A., Turchin, A., 2008. Analysis of data errors in clinical research databases. AMIA Annu. Symp. Proc. 2008, 242–246.

Goldberg, S., Shubina, M., Niemierko, A., Turchin, A., 2010a. A weighty problem: identification, characteristics and risk factors for errors in EMR data. AMIA Annu. Symp. Proc. 2010, 251–255.

Goldberg, S., Niemierko, A., Shubina, M., Turchin, A., 2010b. "Summary Page": a novel tool that reduces omitted data in research databases. BMC Med. Res. Methodol. 10, 91.

Graber, M.L., Siegal, D., Riah, H., Johnston, D., Kenyon, K., 2019. Electronic health record–related events in medical malpractice claims. J. Patient Saf. 15 (2), 77–85.

Haerian, K., McKeeby, J., Dipatrizio, G., Cimino, J., 2009. Use of clinical alerting to improve the collection of clinical research data. AMIA Annu. Symp. Proc. 2009, 218–222.

Hohman, M., Jul. 11, 2019. 3 Most Common Medical Errors Related to EHRs—And 4 Strategies to Prevent Them. Florence Health. https://huddle.florence-health.com/discover/content/article/how-to-prevent-ehr-medical-errors/.

Hsiao, C.J., Beatty, P.C., Hing, E.S., Woodwell, D.A., 2009. Electronic Medical Record/Electronic Health Record Use by Office-Based Physicians: United States, 2008 and Preliminary 2009. National Center for Health Statistics. p. 2009.

Jha, A.K., Ferris, T.G., Donelan, K., et al., 2006. How common are electronic health records in the United States? A summary of the evidence. Health Aff. (Millwood) 25 (6), 496–507. https://doi.org/10.1377/hlthaff.25.w496.

Kandel, S., Paepcke, A., Hellerstein, J., Heer, J., 2011. Wrangler. Interactive visual specification of data transformation scripts. In: Proceedings of the SIGCHI Conference on Human Factors in Computing Systems, May 2011, pp. 3363–3372, https://doi.org/10.1145/1978942.1979444.

Keselman, A., Smith, C.A., 2012. Classification of errors in lay comprehension of medical documents. J. Biomed. Inform. 45 (6), 1151–1163. https://doi.org/10.1016/j.jbi.2012.07.012.

Khayyat, Z., Ilyas, I.F., Jindal, A., Madden, S., Ouzzani, M., Papotti, P., Quiané-Ruiz, J.-A., Tang, N., Bigdansing, S.Y., 2015. A system for big data cleansing. In: SIGMOD, pp. 1215–1230.

Prokoshyna, N., Szlichta, J., Chiang, F., Miller, R.J., Srivastava, D., 2015. Combining quantitative and logical data cleaning. Proc. VLDB Endow. 9 (4), 300–311. https://doi.org/10.14778/2856318.2856325.

Tygar, J.D., 2011. Adversarial machine learning. IEEE Internet Comput. 15 (5), 4–6. https://doi.org/10.1109/MIC.2011.112.

Wang, J., Tang, N., June 2014. Towards dependable data repairing with fixing rules. In: SIGMOD '14: Proceedings of the 2014 ACM SIGMOD International Conference on Management of Data, pp. 457–468, https://doi.org/10.1145/2588555.2610494.

Ward, M.J., Self, W.H., Froehle, C.M., 2015. Effects of common data errors in electronic health records on emergency department operational performance metrics: a Monte Carlo simulation. Acad. Emerg. Med. 22 (9), 1085–1092. https://doi.org/10.1111/acem.12743.

Wu, E., Madden, S.R., 2013. Explaining away outliers in aggregate queries. Proc. VLDB Endow. 6 (8), 553–564.

CHAPTER

5

Overcoming AI applications challenges in health: Decision system DINAR2

Saveli Goldberg[a] and Mark Prutkin[b]

Division of Radiation Oncology, Massachusetts General Hospital, Boston, MA, United States[a]

NICU, Regional Children Hospital, Ekaterinburg, Russia[b]

1. Introduction

A common problem for artificial intelligence (AI) systems is the problem of reconciling AI decision rules with the specifics of the environment, that is, place, time, where these rules are being applied, and the user, for whom these rules apply. In medicine, this problem is especially acute. Differences in the understanding of medical terms, symptoms, and diagnoses can occur not only in different countries but even among different doctors in the same hospital. The subjectivity of the doctor is added to the subjectivity of the patient's description of their condition. Doctors are not always interested in AI help. Even if AI is better at solving problems than an average doctor, that does not mean it is needed by a specific doctor in a specific situation. The cost of the time spent communicating with the AI may seem greater to the doctor than the benefits of such communication.

All of this hinders the use of AI in medicine (Hamamoto et al., 2020; Snapp, 2019). Let's consider these problems in more detail.

2. Problems of introducing medical AI applications

2.1 Domain overfitting

In machine learning and deep learning methods, overfitting refers to a situation where the learning error is small, but the generalization error (the error in determining unknown data) can be large (Fig. 1). Especially it is right in the medical field. It is not only about the limited number of cases versus the large number of fields that are typical for medical datasets. Even more important is the specificity of the place and time of obtaining such data. For example, let the training sample be the patients of the Partners system (a network of some of Boston's hospitals) for 1990–2015. Can an AI system built on such data be used in other counties and regions in 2022? AI models are often fragile, which means they work well with data from one hospital but fail when applied to data in other institutions (Kim, 2021). It is always necessary to evaluate carefully the effectiveness of the generalization of the constructed model. Validation is especially important for the clinical

Artificial Intelligence for Healthcare Applications and Management. https://doi.org/10.1016/B978-0-12-824521-7.00006-5

AI
Based on previous experience,
we will need some palm trees around here.

FIG. 1

Domain overfitting.

implementation of AI medical devices. Their overall performance needs to be confirmed more thoroughly than that of conventional medical devices by clinical trials.

2.2 Terminology problems

Input errors for AI include misunderstanding of clinical concepts, misreporting the objective of a clinical research study and physician's findings during a patient's visit, and confusing and misspelling clinical terms. Medical data description depends on facility characteristics. It has been observed that the accuracy of predicting data from other facilities is significantly reduced when a trainer built by training on data from one facility is used to predict data from another facility. In general, this problem is called the domain shift problem, and it is an important issue that needs to be resolved for the promotion of medical AI (Stacke et al., 2020; Pandey et al., 2020; Bain et al., 2020; Gu et al. 2020). To eliminate confusion in medical terminology, the World Health Organization (WHO) developed the International Classification of Diseases (ICD). The ICD is originally designed as a healthcare classification system, providing a system of diagnostic codes for classifying diseases, including nuanced classifications of a wide variety of signs, symptoms, abnormal findings, complaints, social circumstances, and external causes of injury or disease. However, the ICD is constantly being adjusted. The first version (ICD 6) was published in 1949, and the latest version (ICD 10) was implemented in the United States in 2015. The work is continuing, and a new version is planned for publication in 2022. Moreover, sometimes official medical concepts change even faster

FIG. 2

An example of terminology discrepancies.

than the ICD. For example, the American Joint Cancer Committee (AJCC) released new editions of its cancer staging systems in 1983, 1988, 1992, 1997, 2000, and 2017.

Sometimes doctors use local classifications and definitions. As a result, the AI system and the AI user can use different classifiers (Fig. 2).

Finally, there is a problem with the qualifications of the AI user. Often, AI training is based on verified materials, and highly qualified specialists are involved to create decision rules. We cannot expect this kind of skill and precision from all AI users.

An AI system should include background information and a glossary of medical terms used in the AI system.

2.3 Cognitive bias

Physician cognitive bias can lead to AI errors. Unfortunately, a cognitive bias is typical for humans and physicians in particular. For example, 2230 skin biopsies were performed by 71 residents with a diagnosis confirmed by a panel of expert pathologists. Cognitive biases were associated with diagnostic errors in 51% of 40 case scenarios (versus 16.4% of case scenarios leading to misdiagnosis unrelated to cognitive biases; $P = .029$) (Crowley et al., 2013). Most clinical decision-makers are at risk of bias and this does not correlate with intelligence or other measures of cognitive ability (Hershberger et al., 1994). Not understanding your own bias is common. Physicians who described themselves as "free from bias" subsequently scored even more poorly on formal tests (Klein et al., 2005). These errors can be attributed to inherent biases, social and cultural biases, misunderstandings of statistics and mathematical rationality, or even simple environmental details that distract attention (Stiegler and Tung, 2014) (Fig. 3).

AI
This industrial landscape has its own charm!

FIG. 3

Example of cognitive bias.

The importance of this is so great that we want to cite all types of cognitive biases as presented in O'Sullivan and Schofield (2018):

- **Availability bias**: More recent and readily available answers and solutions are preferentially favored because of ease of recall and incorrectly perceived importance.
  Example: Recent missed pulmonary embolism prompts excessive CT pulmonary angiogram scanning in low-risk patients.
- **Base rate neglect**: This occurs in medicine when the underlying incident rates of conditions or population-based knowledge are ignored as if they do not apply to the patient in question.
  Example: A positive exercise stress test in a young woman prompting an angiogram. The "base rate" is so low in this population that this result is more likely false positive than true positive.
- **Confirmation bias**: Diagnosticians tend to interpret the information gained during a consultation to fit their preconceived diagnosis rather than the converse (Wallsten, 1981; Scherer et al., 2015).
  Example: Suspecting the patient has an infection and the raised white cells proves this, rather than "I wonder why the white cells are raised, what other findings are there?"
- **Conjunction rule**: The incorrect belief that the probability of multiple events being true is greater than a single event. This relates to Occam's razor, a simple and unifying explanation is statistically more likely than multiple unrelated explanations.

Example: A confused patient with hypoxia and deranged renal function is far more likely to have pneumonia than a subdural/pulmonary embolism/obstruction simultaneously.

- **Overconfidence**: An inflated opinion of diagnostic ability leading to subsequent error. The doctor's confidence in their judgments does not align with the accuracy of these judgments (Renner and Renner, 2000).

  Example: A doctor trusting their assessment more than they should, which is particularly problematic with inaccurate examinations, such as auscultation for pneumonia.
- **Representativeness**: Misinterpreting the likelihood of an event considering both the key similarities to its parent population, and the individual characteristics that define that event.

  Example: A man with classic symptoms of a heart attack, but also anxious, and whose breath smelled of alcohol. The latter details have no bearing on the likelihood of a heart attack, nor do they alter the degree to which he is a member of his risk demographic but distract and decrease the diagnostic pick up.
- **Search satisfying**: Ceasing to look for further information or alternative answers when the first plausible solution is found.

  Example: When encountering an acutely dyspneic patient, treating their obvious pneumonia, and stopping investigations at that point, failing to search for and recognize the secondary myocardial infarction.
- **Diagnostic momentum**: Continuing a clinical course of action instigated by previous clinicians without considering the information available and changing the plan if required (particularly if the plan was commenced by a more senior clinician).

  Example: Fixating on a previously assigned label of "possible pulmonary embolism" and organizing CT imaging for a patient who may have subsequent results that suggest otherwise (e.g., positive blood cultures the following day).
- **The framing effects**: Reacting to a particular choice differently depending on how the information is presented to you.

  Example: A pharmaceutical company may present new drug A as having a 95% cure rate, and suggest this is superior to drug B that has a significant 2.5% failure rate.
- **Commission bias**: A tendency towards action rather than inaction. The bias is "omission bias."

  Example: Historical transfusion targets in gastrointestinal bleeds. Traditionally the approach was to aim for higher targets rather than do nothing; "better to be safe than sorry" and to raise the hemoglobin "just in case."

The most powerful sources of AI conclusion problems are confirmation bias, overconfidence, and diagnostic momentum.

2.4 Integration of AI into clinical practice

The physician's interest in AI is a key element of the careful and responsible collection of information for AI, careful and responsible attitude to the result of AI work, and, ultimately, the successful implementation of AI in clinical practice (Fig. 4). AI designers must be aware of the high cost of physician time and sometimes the very high cost of time in making decisions about a patient's condition. The doctor must make a chain of sequential decisions. Making an AI decision at one link in this chain without a clear understanding of this decision can negatively affect subsequent decisions and destroy the

FIG. 4

Example of unnecessary help.

entire chain. This chain of solutions concerns not only purely medical problems but also ethical, legal, and economic problems.

Now we can go to the description of DINAR2 and analyze the causes of its 30-year deployment and effectiveness.

3. Integrated decision support system at the regional consultative Center for Intensive Pediatrics (DINAR2)

3.1 Idea and problems of the regional consultative Center for Intensive Pediatrics

The idea of creating a Consultative Center for Intensive Pediatrics (CIP) at a large regional children's hospital headed by leading doctors was due to the deplorable state of the intensive care service for children in remote or low-income regions of Russia and the former USSR (Tsibulkin et al., 1977). Medical emergencies often occur hundreds of miles from the nearest hospital. Making the wrong decision can lead to wasted time, money, and even a child's life. Without specialized medical knowledge, it can be difficult to determine what is wrong, although the right decision can be surprisingly simple. The creation of the CIP was mainly aimed at providing high-quality medical care at the very beginning of every emergency. The timely referral of a local doctor to a CIP consultant makes it possible to alleviate or even avoid the development of a threatening condition through appropriate treatment. The consultant will provide the local doctor with:

- answers to various medical questions.
- recommendations for treatment using available resources.
- recommendations for transferring the child to the most appropriate hospital.
- organization of transport by the "flying doctor" to the patient for their transfer to a specialized department.

However, the CIP consultant has some specific problems:

- making decisions without looking at the patient, based only on information from the local doctor.
- the local doctor may or may not want the CIP doctor to come and subconsciously distort information about the patient in the direction of a more severe or milder patient's condition.
- problems with the consistency of decision-making from the previous consultant to the current one.
- lack of time for medical and administrative assessment of the case.
- different levels of medical equipment in each location and different skill levels of local staff.

Today, these are classic tasks of telemedicine; however, unlike today's telemedicine, there was no Internet, video communication, or medical indicators that could be transmitted over long distances. At least this was not the case in local hospitals and the percentage of subjective information in the dispatcher's decisions was very high. To solve these tasks and problems, a computerized expert system called DINAR2 was proposed. In the section that follows, we describe the experience of creating and using DINAR2, which was sold by now to 42 regions of the former USSR.

3.2 History of DINAR2 development

Famous in USSR pediatrics, Gubler and Tsibulkin were pioneers of CIP implementation. The first urban CIP was created in Leningrad in 1977 (Tsibulkin et al., 1977). The basis for making a tactical decision was a formalized patient questionnaire completed by a district doctor. Moreover, each physiological parameter in this questionnaire had its own specific gravity in the range from 0 to 9. The sum of the weights of the patient's parameters determined the severity of their condition on the threatening meter scale. A table of 18 clinical signs with weights and thresholds for making tactical decisions (FHD-5.4) was described and used (Gubler and Tsibulkin, 1987). There were several attempts to apply this method in other cities, but they were unsuccessful. Assessment of the patient's condition and making a tactical decision on the provision of care took place without using FHD-5.4 and filling in the fields of the FHD-5.4 table took place after the decision was made. Several computer programs were created that calculated the necessary medical help level based on FHD-5.4 and entered patient data into a database. However, the appearance of the first computer programs supporting CIP activities did not change the situation for the better. CIP-based decision-making

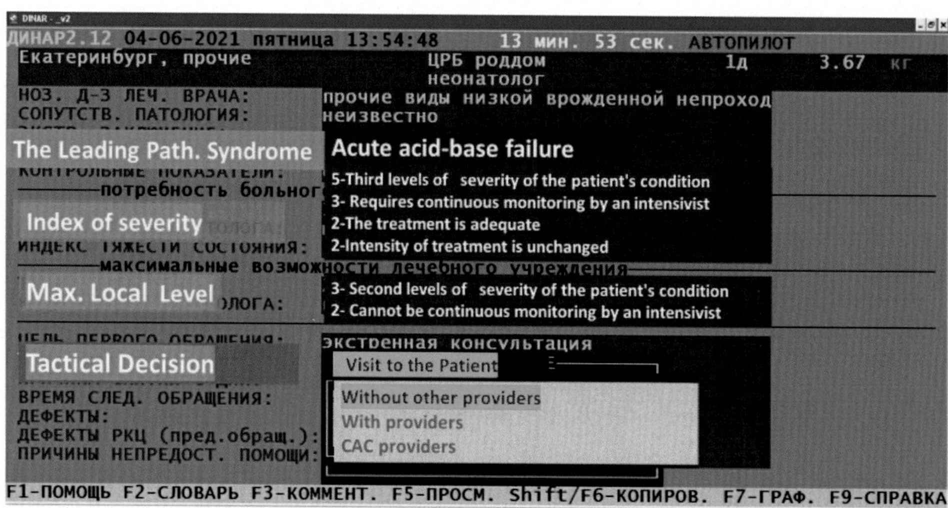

FIG. 5

A screenshot of DINAR2 with a patient's information from a local doctor as recorded by a dispatcher in Russian. DINAR2 conclusions are displayed in English.

was rare. At the same time, the obligatory introduction of data for each patient required additional time and effort of the physician.

CIP was launched in 1985, serving the vast territory of the Sverdlovsk region. In 1987, the operation of the computer program DINAR1 began. The core of this program was the same FHD-5.4 table. The only thing that distinguished DINAR1 from other software based on FHD-5.4 was the presence of the necessary elements of information services: a reference subsystem, subsystem for collecting and analyzing data on CIP activity, and a subsystem for treated patients information and failures in the medical care. The DINAR1 year of work has shown the need to strengthen the decision support system for the CIP consultant. In 1988, it was decided to create a new program, DINAR2. When creating DINAR2 a decision-making model under conditions of direct distortion of information (e.g., because of the subconscious influence of diagnostic hypotheses) was developed. This model was necessary for DINAR2 because most of the information for decision-making is subjective. The differences between the levels of medical care at the local level (in local hospitals) required a special assessment of the severity of the patient's condition for an adequate choice of tactical actions of the CIP and local physician. The initial index of the severity of the patient's condition was developed depending on the required type and volume of therapy (Fig. 5).

From 1988 to 1994, the following functionalities were implemented (Goldberg et al., 1992, 1993) (Fig. 6):

(1) dynamic observation of severely ill children in the region (1988).
(2) optimal dialogue aimed at determining the child's health state and prescribing the necessary treatment (1988, 1990).
(3) determination of the leading pathological syndrome (1988).

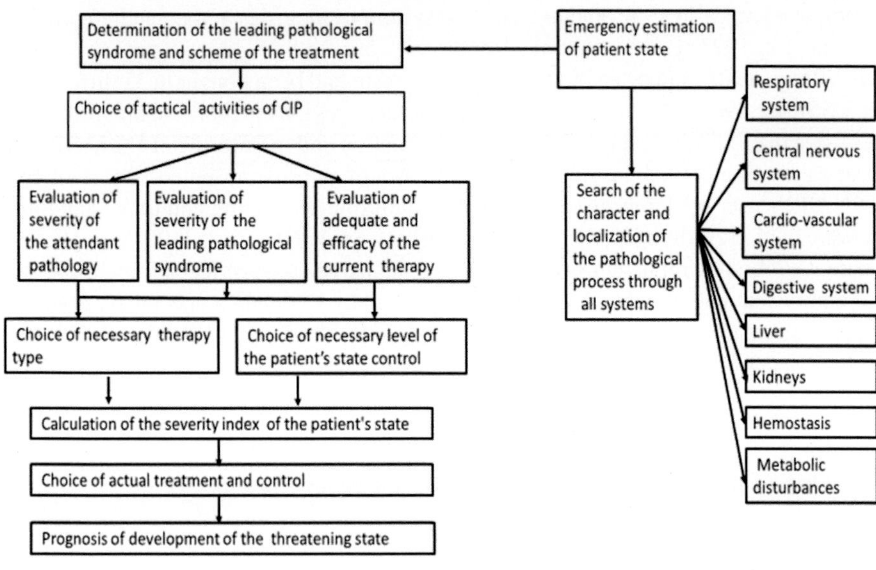

FIG. 6

Block diagram of the expert subsystem operation.

(4) detection of mistakes in the information transferred (1989).
(5) evaluation of the patient's state dynamics (1990).
(6) assistance in prescribing a concrete treatment (1993).
(7) prognosis and estimation of therapy effect (1993).
(8) continuity in the treatment of a patient (1989).
(9) choice of a tactical decision concerning the distribution of the central resources (1988).
(10) visualization of introduced information (1992, 1994).
(11) handing out analytical information on the CIP operation, patients' health condition in the region, defects of the hospitals, and reasons for the emergency aid being unavailable (1988, 1993).
(12) handing out reports on the CIP activity (1989).
(13) supply of physicians with reference information concerning terminology and cognition (1994).
(14) supply of physicians with reference information concerning the capability of hospitals to render assistance in methods of treatment, pharmacology, special methods of treatment, diagnostics, and so on (1989, 1990, 1993).

The most important change in DINAR2 was dividing this system into two separate systems: DINAR2 for children aged 1 month or older and DINAR2 for newborns (<1 month) (1994).

During deployment, CIP got a new important function. CIP became a methodical center of medical children's aid. In conformity with this, an important part of DINAR2 was collecting and analyzing information for regional health chiefs. It is especially connected with discovery and analysis of medical defects. An independent system of children's death-rate analysis was specially created to make impartial decisions (1990). A mathematical statistics subsystem was added in 1991, graphical representations of information were made in 1992, and at last, a subsystem of inquiries at the database of child's mortality was created in 1993 (Goldberg et al., 1993).

The technology of CIP supported by the DINAR2 system had been bought in 35 different regions of the former USSR by 1994. The total population of all these regions is more than 59,000,000, and the total area is more than 11 million km^2. The cost of installation and monitoring of DINAR2 corresponds to the 2-year salary of a skilled physician. The dynamics of sales is presented as certain commercial success. DINAR2's user conferences played an important role in creating and understanding this success. They were held in Arkhyz (1990), Volgograd (1991), Saint Petersburg (1992), and Petropavlovsk (1993). There were both administrators from regional intensive care service and intensive therapy experts from regions that had bought DINAR2 or wanted to buy it. Leading specialists from Russia told the participants about different aspects of intensive pediatrics besides DINAR2 and CIP (most of the discussion time was occupied by clinical problems).

3.3 Methods

3.3.1 Considering data provided by a doctor as input for the operation of DINAR2 as fuzzy sets

DINAR2 faced all the problems discussed at the beginning of the chapter. The general approach to their solution was that the data provided by the local physician was considered by DINAR2 as fuzzy logic. Each presented parameter participated in the DINAR2 analysis along with the neighborhood of its possible errors.

Let $\mathbf{x}=(x_1, x_2, \ldots, x_n)$ be a vector of the n input parameters to the algorithm. x_i can be a continuous (numerical) or categorical (Boolean) variable. Let X be a set of $\mathbf{x}$. Let $\mathbf{v}=(v_1, \ldots, v_n)$ be the particular input values entered by the user. For example, $\mathbf{v}$=(age (62 years), blood pressure (120 mL), headache (moderate), temperature (36.4°C)).

For any parameter of $\mathbf{x}$, its value x_i may have bias or error. This is not only the error of the device measuring but also the errors of the measurement procedure and natural fluctuations in the value of the **i** parameter in the patient's body. So, in our example, the pressure can be 125 mL, the headache is mild, the temperature is 36.2°C, the age is 62.8 years. Therefore, we define $\Omega(x_i)$ as the set of values that are considered within the error bounds for x_i. $G_{yi}(x_i)$ is the probability of y_i when x_i was defined.

Let $\mathbf{D} = \{a_j[SG1]\}, j = 1, \ldots, k$ be the set of k possible decisions or output classes [SG1].

If, within the framework of these errors, the AI makes different decisions, then the AI systems ask clarifying questions to confirm this or that decision.

3.3.2 Construction of diagnostic rules

The decision-making rules were based on expert judgment, rules, and conclusions. This approach is dictated by three reasons:

(1) the need for simplicity in explaining AI solutions, which was the main requirement when creating DINAR2
(2) availability of highly qualified specialists who are ready to collaborate with DINAR2 developers
(3) a lack of representative databases for building mathematical models

To obtain expert rules, the methodology of "diagnostic games" was used (Gelfand et al., 2004; Shifrin et al., 2007), in which the rules of diagnosis and treatment were developed in the process of

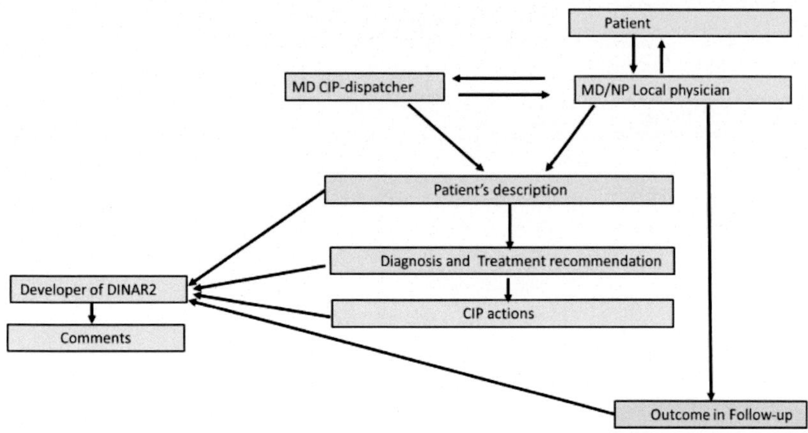

FIG. 7

Communication between CIP dispatcher and a local physician.

interviewing a doctor when discussing real clinical cases. These interviews were conducted in a game-type format. We outline the steps of a diagnostic game in the sections that follow.

Step 1

CIP receives a call from a local doctor about the severity of the medical event. The CIP MD discusses the case with the local physician (LP) and decides on the CIP's actions (Fig. 7).

DINAR1 documents the dialogue between the dispatcher and LP. Information about the patient's condition, diagnosis, recommended therapeutic tactics, and CIP actions is retained. Follow-up patient observations will also be stored in the DINAR1 database. The DINAR2 developer is in the control room and writes down their comments to this contact.

Step 2

The most interesting cases from the developer's point of view formed the basis of the diagnostic game with the participation of two very experienced doctors (experts). Each session of this "game," in which the developer and the expert participated, consisted of a discussion of a specific medical case with known subsequent information (Fig. 8). The expert received the same information as the CIP dispatcher on the first contact with a local physician. Based on this, the specialist made a diagnosis, determined the nature of the treatment, the CIP tactics, and explained all his decisions. In addition, the expert predicted the outcome that would occur if the local physician follows his recommendations as well as the outcome of the patient after the real decisions and actions of the CIP dispatcher. Based on these explanations, the developer created formal rules for the diagnosis and treatment tactics, according to which decisions were made in this particular case. In addition, the developer checked the stability of the rules created in this way by asking the expert additional questions or distorting the reference information about the patient.

Step 3

The same case was played out in the same way with the second expert. The experts did not know at the beginning and never discovered in the future that they were offered the same cases. The expert considered that the developer worked only with him on this case, and the developer's smart

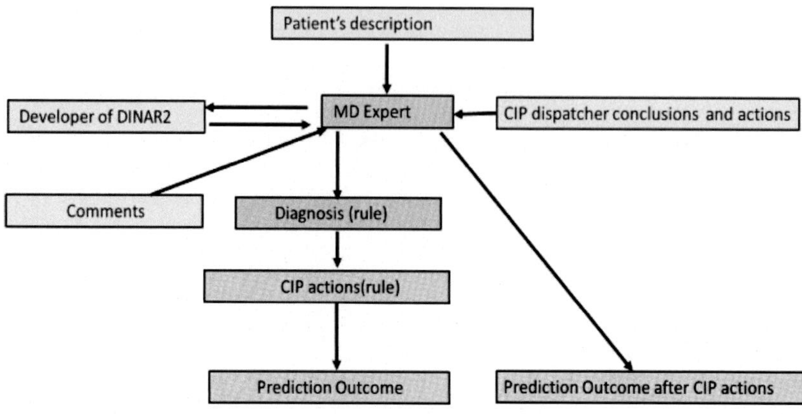

FIG. 8

Communication between DINAR2 developer and an expert.

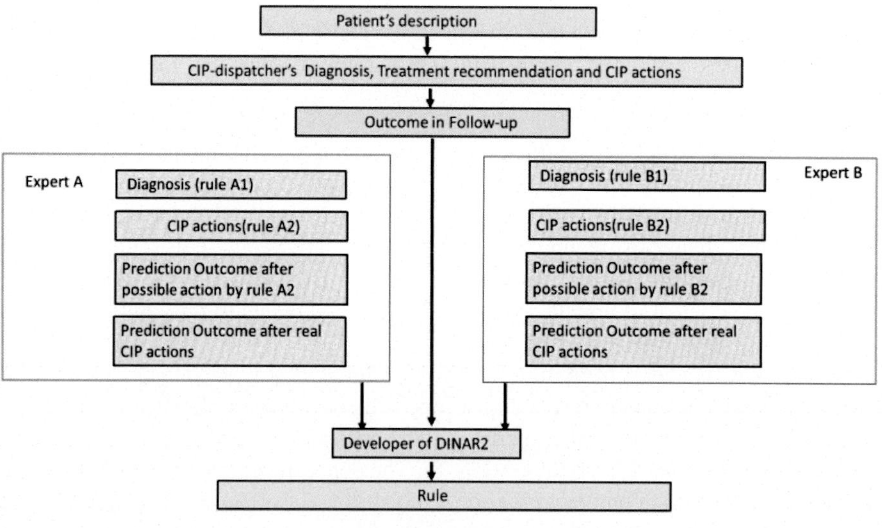

FIG. 9

Rule construction.

questions, if any, were triggered by the developer's presence in the CIP control room when disassembling this situation. If the decisions of different experts differed, then the developer asked, "What would happen if a decision was made that was different from yours?" (Fig. 9).

Based on the analysis of many such protocols, a system of rules was built. An important feature in the construction of such rules was the requirement for their redundancy. Therefore, for example, if a certain set of signs from the point of view of a specialist indicated a diagnosis, it was necessary to indicate accompanying or clarifying signs and symptoms to support the diagnosis.

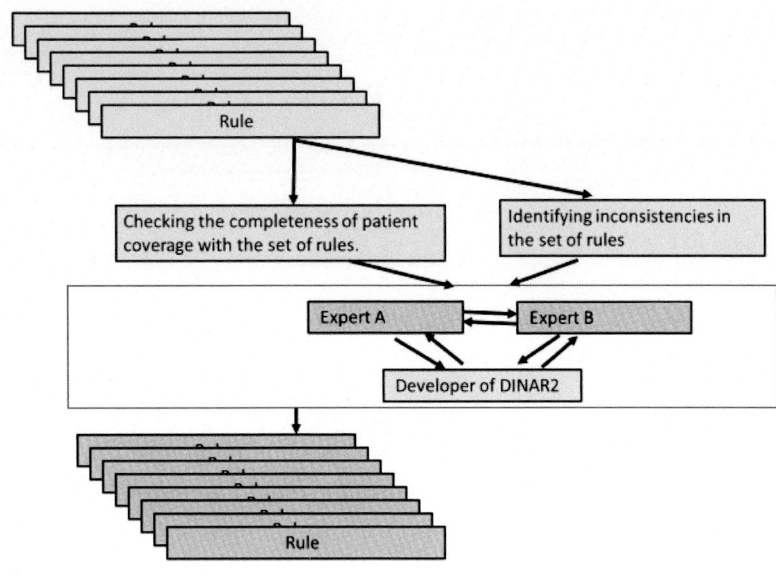

FIG. 10

Checking a set of rules.

Step 4

When compiling a set of rules, the developer checked the set of pavilions for:

(1) Completeness of the ruleset coverage of all patients collected in the DINAR1 database
(2) Consistency of the rules with each other

The obvious problems of the ruleset were discussed with experts and a complete rule set was created (Fig. 10). This set of rules has been constantly revised as DINAR2 works in real life.

3.3.3 An assessment of a patient's state of severity

A key task of a consultant in CIP is to decide tactical actions of CIP:

- consultation by phone.
- hospitalization of a patient at a specialized center.
- CIP experts' expedition to the place of an accident.

The choice of a solution is mainly based on the relation of adequate medical treatment and a level of control over the patient's state to available resources and expertise level of medical staff in the SOS area. Data of a situation in a rural hospital is input into a computer beforehand. That is why the threatening meter scale used in DINAR2 is directly connected with medical treatment necessary to a patient. This contrasts with standard scales, based on the patient's mortality risk. To determine the severity of a patient's state in DINAR2, one should determine the decompensation degree of main systems of the organism (5 degrees), dynamics of applied therapy (4 degrees), and adequacy of applied therapy (3 degrees). Only on the base of these scales can the main threatening meter scale

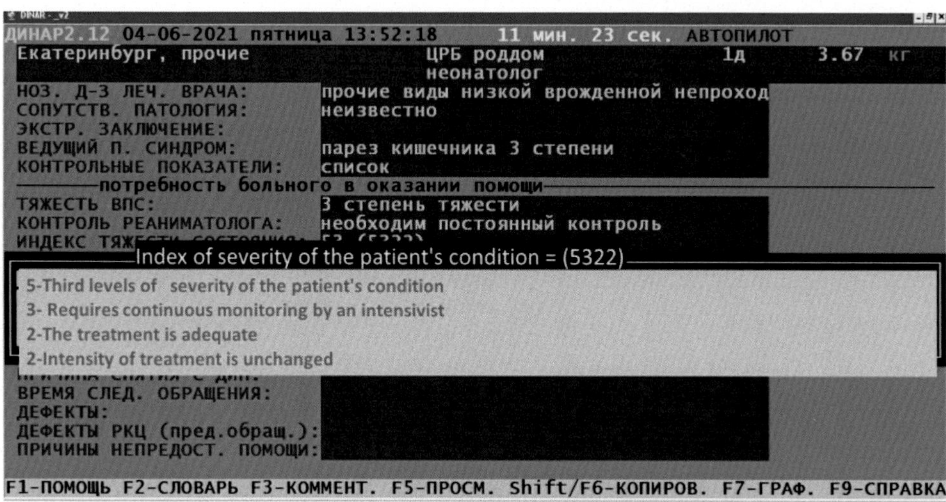

FIG. 11

A screenshot of DINAR2 with a patient's information from a local doctor as recorded by a dispatcher in Russian. The index of severity is displayed in English.

(40 degrees) and required levels of therapy (6 degrees) and control (4 degrees) be defined (Goldberg et al., 1993) (Fig. 11).

3.3.4 A definition of the leading pathological syndrome

In DINAR2 the leading pathological syndrome is regarded as an organo-functional deficiency of an organism requiring urgent medical intervention. The following eight essential systems of an organism are examined: respiratory system, central nervous system, cardio-vascular system, digestive system, metabolic disturbances, liver, kidneys, and homeostasis.

Each of these systems has up to 3–5 degrees of decompensation. The diagnostic process falls into two stages. The first stage deals with formation of basic signs out of symptoms collected by a doctor. Every basic sign presents a logic condition or a calculated formula. Leading pathological syndromes are defined in the second stage. DINAR2 discerns from one to five manifestations of a leading pathological syndrome in an organism.

Each manifestation is made up by a set of basic signs subdivided into five groups: sufficient, obligatory, impossible, specifying, and explanatory. Every sign has a weight according to its group. If the sum of the weights of signs that a patient possesses exceeds the initially given level, the patient is considered to have this syndrome (Fig. 12).

Data about a patient is entered into DINAR2 in the forms of:

- answers to obligatory questions (270 binary tests).
- information input into the computer on the doctor's intention.
- responses to additional questions asked by DINAR2, unless there is enough data for decision-making (out of 200 binary tests).

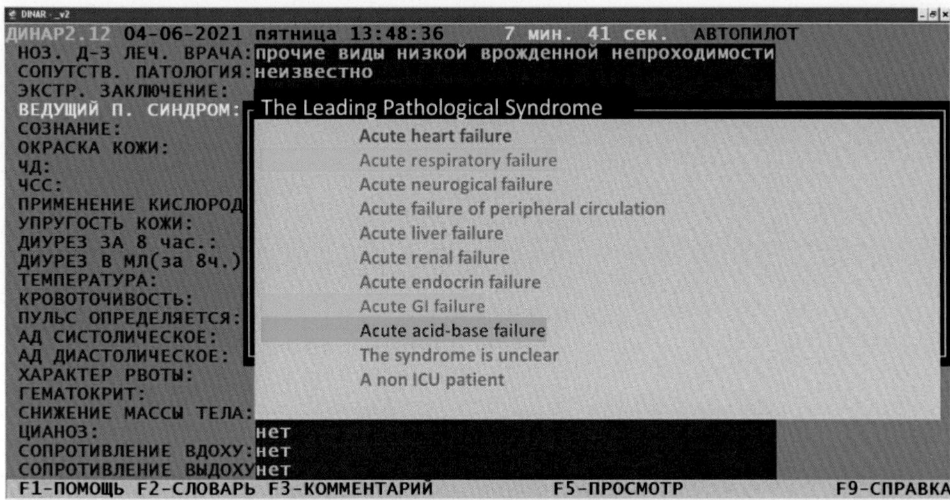

FIG. 12

A screenshot of DINAR2 with a patient's information from a local doctor as recorded by a dispatcher in Russian. The leading pathological syndrome is displayed in English.

A specific character of algorithms of DINAR2 is conditioned by the possibility of heavy distortion of information received by a consultant in CIP. It is supposed that the given distortion may be caused by four reasons:

(1) inattentiveness or incompetence of the local physicians.
(2) divergence of notions and terms between the CIP and LPs.
(3) the desire to present the patient's state as milder or more severe than it really is.
(4) intention to follow one's initially selected hypothesis, that is, the physician sees only what they want to see.

Taking this into account, information about the patient is described as a fuzzy set. Information suspected by DINAR2 as being inaccurate is specified with the help of explanation of terms, that is, breaking up complex notions into more simple ones. According to the data given by a local doctor (including a patient's state and his own conclusions) one may judge a possible distortion of the information influenced by selected diagnostic and tactical hypotheses.

The conclusion algorithm of DINAR2, when removing the distortions, is based on the assumption that true information cannot differ greatly from distorted information, that only those distortions that lead to wrong conclusions are dangerous, and that the causes of such distortions are rather subconscious than intentional. The algorithm idea consists of setting additional questions before receiving information for a stable conclusion. This stability is understood in relation to a purposeful shift of the information to the side contrary to the proposed hypothesis. Value and direction of maximally possible data corruption are changed in the process of the algorithm's work and depend on consistency of the transmitted information (Goldberg et al., 1992).

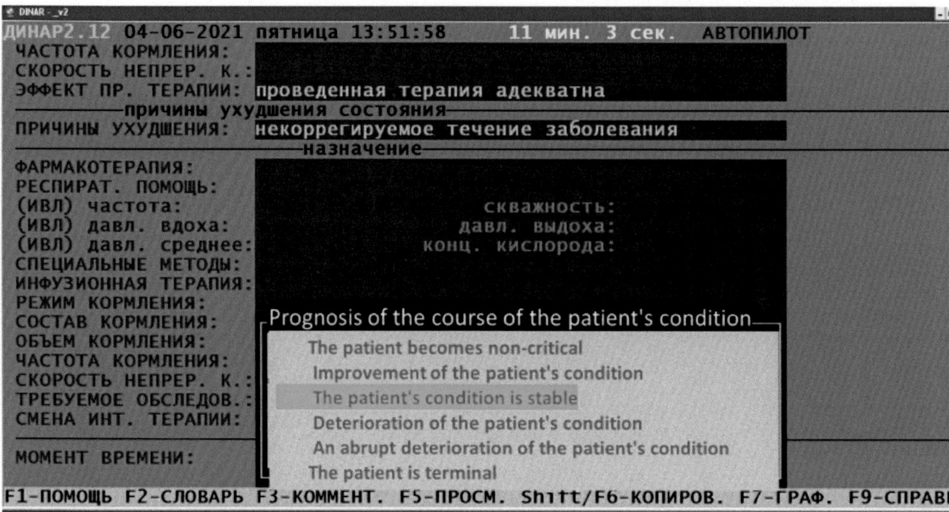

FIG. 13

A screenshot of DINAR2 with a patient's information from a local doctor as recorded by a dispatcher in Russian. The prognosis is displayed in English.

3.3.5 Methods of stimulation of intellectual activity of a CIP consultant

Methods of stimulation of intellectual activity of consultants play an important role in the DINAR2 system. They promote a consultant's feeling of responsibility and critical attitude to his own decisions and help him to exceed standard limits. The following ways and methods were applied to achieve these goals:

- Asking a consultant to predict definite results of a prescribed treatment. The very process of predicting is expected to help make the right choice for an adequate treatment. On the other hand, the discrepancy between a certain prognosis and a real state of things serves as a basis for treatment correction by the same or new consultant (Fig. 13).
- Visualization of information by extensive use of charts and pictograms.
- Contextual reference information.

3.3.6 DINAR2's operation in extreme situations

In 1%–1.5% of life-threatening cases there is a strict time limit for a dialogue with a CIP consultant. The prime task of DINAR2 is to determine time reserves for decision-making. The local doctor gives the address, information about his own qualifications, and evaluates the patient's state as life threatening or extremely severe or just severe. If the patient's state is critical, then the dialogue is limited to three questions:

(1) Does the patient have any reaction to pain?
(2) Does the patient have a pulse in the peripheral vessels?
(3) Does the patient have the existence of cyanosis?

If DINAR2 receives some combinations of "bad" answers, it begins to operate in a hard algorithm on a questionnaire tree principle based on 3–12 questions to an applicant thus defining one of 11 possible reasons that may lead to a child's death within 30 min.

3.3.7 Freedom of a consultant's actions within DINAR2 limits

In DINAR2 the program offers quite a few successive conclusions: assessment of patient's state of severity, state dynamics assessment, therapy effect evaluation, tactics, and so on. At each stage the physician can select their own decision and only this is taken into account in all the following conclusions of the computer. In addition, the physician knows that only their opinions remain in the computer's memory. Besides a relatively short obligatory dialogue with a program, the physician can independently choose the profundity of working out of separate themes, application of those or other additional functions of the system, and the degree of confidence in the information about the patient received from the local doctors and their qualifications.

3.3.8 Organization of a database of local hospitals

The main principles of such a database organization were:

- ease of use
- relevance of information

To this end, all information about the local hospital consisted of only a section on current staff qualifications and a section on current hospital equipment. Both of these sections are displayed on the same screen. The CIP dispatcher, during the consultation process, directly modifies the contents of this single screen (Fig. 14).

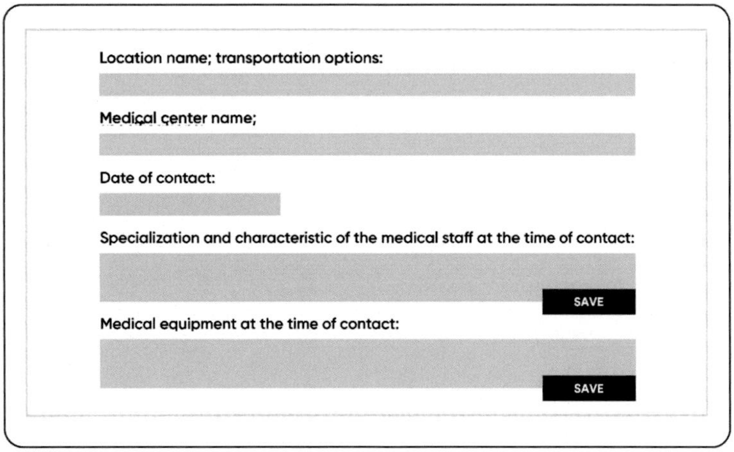

Location name; transportation options:

Medical center name;

Date of contact:

Specialization and characteristic of the medical staff at the time of contact:

SAVE

Medical equipment at the time of contact:

SAVE

FIG. 14

Database screen organization.

3.3.9 Stimulating doctors to improve DINAR2

A fixed bonus was awarded for every bug found and for every recommendation for improvement in DINAR2. The bonus for the proposed DINAR2 improvement was paid regardless of whether the suggestion was used or not.

3.4 DINAR2 efficiency

To assess the effectiveness of CIP+DINAR2, let us consider its work in the Sverdlovsk region of the Russian Federation. The child population (0–14 years old) in this region during the analyzed period ranged from 936,382 to 998,971. The area of the region is the same as in Great Britain: 194,800 km^2 or 75,200 square miles.

Figs. 15 and 16 show the dynamics of CIP activity in the period from 1983 to 1993, which covers four stages of its activity:

(1) 1983. CIP operation without using FHD.
(2) 1984–87. CIP operation using FHD, but without DINAR1.
(3) 1988–89. Implementation of DINAR1 in CIP operations.
(4) 1990–93. Years of implementation of DINAR2 in CIP work from the first components of DINAR2 to the complete set of functions.

At these four stages, the number of patients served on average varied from 312 patients in the first period, 510 in the second, and 807 and 681 in the third and fourth stages, respectively. The percentage of patient visits among all consultations changed from 66.5% during the FHD period to 35.3% during the DINAR2 start period, and the percentage of deaths among all consulted patients changed from 25.6% during the FHD period to 12.5% during the DINAR2 period (1990–93). The percentage of deaths among all consulted patients ranged from 14.8% during the DINAR1 period to 12.5% during the DINAR2 initial period (Goldberg et al., 1992; Kazakov et al., 1996).

Kazakov investigated the effectiveness of the separate work of CIP_Pediatrics + DINAR2_P and CIP_Neonatology + DINAR2_N in the period from 1994 to 2001 (Kazakov et al., 2003). He presents the results of this study in his book on the operation of CIP in large regions (Kazakov 2004).

Figs. 17 and 18 present activity of CIP_Pediatric and CIP_Neonatology in the Sverdlovsk region in the period 1994–2001.

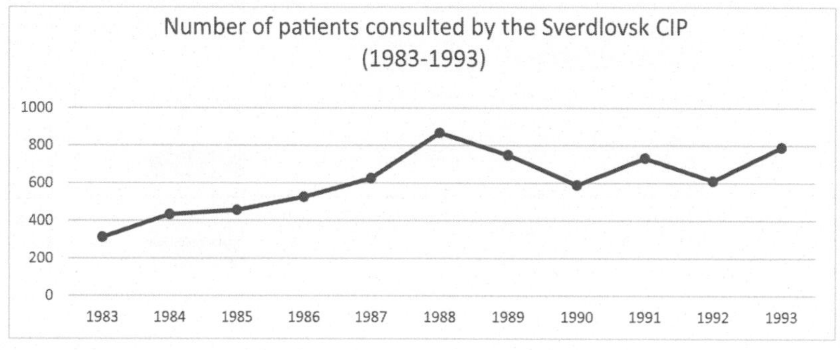

FIG. 15

Dynamics of the number of patients consulted by the CIP.

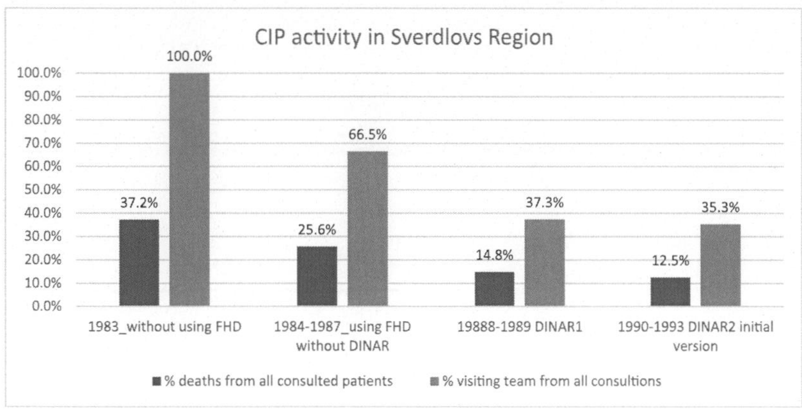

FIG. 16

Rate of mortality and visiting team from all consulted patients.

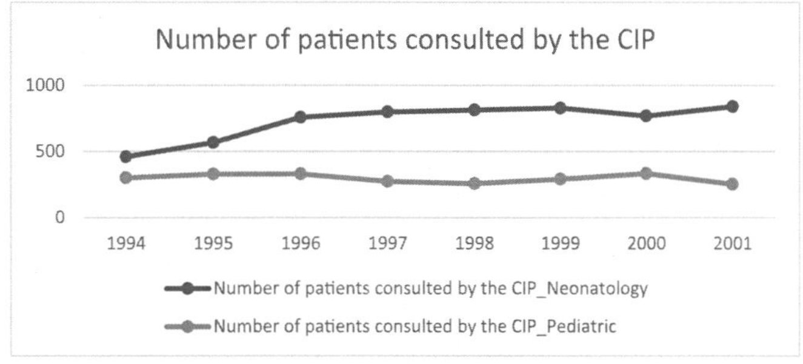

FIG. 17

Number of patients consulted by the CIP_Neonatology and CIP_Pediatric.

The analysis of the effectiveness of CIP_Pediatric and CIP_Neonatology was based on a comparison of two groups located in the Sverdlovsk region (Figs. 19–21).

The study group where the technology of the CIP system was systematically observed: 9 cities and 16 rural areas (57%–59% of children in the region).

The control group in which the technology was not followed or was observed sporadically: 12 cities and 13 rural areas (41%–43% of children in the region).

Of course, all these success numbers are CIP_Pediatric and CIP_Neonatology achievements, not DINAR2's, but CIPs cannot work without DINAR2.

A more complex question concerns the benefits of DINAR's AI functions. In answering this, we relied on a survey of eight doctors in Yekaterinburg (formerly Sverdlovsk) who have worked with DINAR2 for more than 2 years. The main findings of the study are as follows:

- Stability in assessment of some DINAR2 conclusions. Consistently high exactitude in selection of a leading pathological syndrome and a stable satisfactory one in determining a patient's state of severity and determining the CIP tactics.

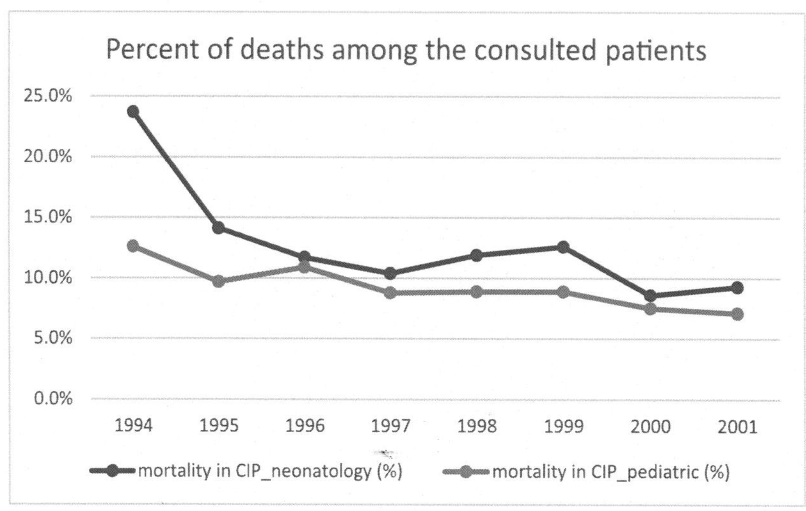

FIG. 18

Mortality (%) among the consulted patients.

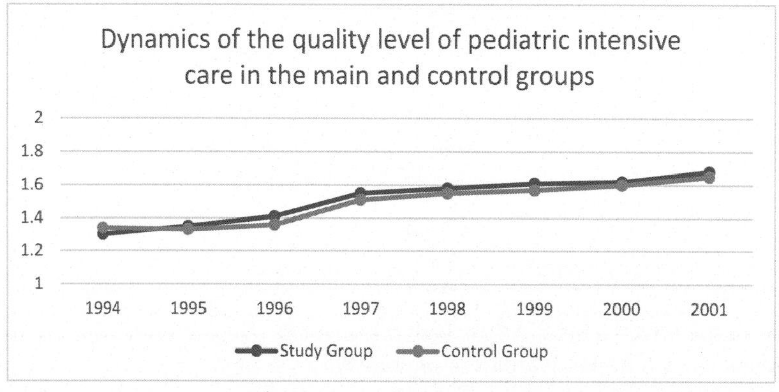

FIG. 19

Dynamics of the quality level of pediatric intensive care in the main and control groups.

- An extremely large difference in assessing the usefulness of individual DINAR2 functions. For example, helping in diagnostically intricate cases was estimated by two physicians as non-realized; by one physician as having no use; by three physicians as producing an insufficient effect; and by two physicians as bringing satisfactory effect.
- Changes in the evaluation of individual features over time. Therefore, help in diagnostically difficult cases was highly appreciated at the beginning of the work of DINAR2. This is currently the lowest rated feature.
- Priority of assistance in solving "dynamic" tasks over "static" ones. For example, assisting in assessing the dynamics of the patient's condition is considered the most valuable function of DINAR2 (six high or satisfactory ratings). This exceeds the degree of assistance in assessing the

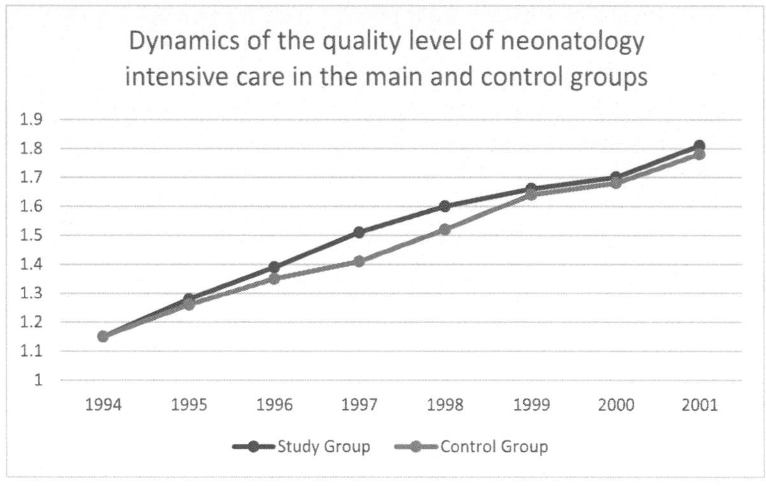

FIG. 20

Dynamics of the quality level of neonatology intensive care in the main and control groups.

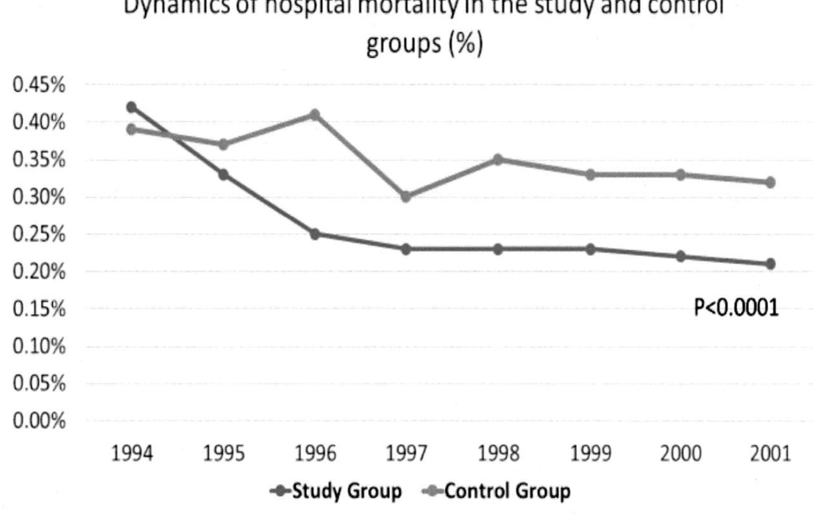

FIG. 21

Dynamics of hospital mortality in the study and control groups (%).

severity of the patient's condition (five high and satisfactory marks), the choice of tactical actions (four high and satisfactory marks), and assistance in relatively simple diagnostic cases (four high and satisfactory marks).

- The most important items for new versions are adequacy assessment and treatment efficacy (eight priority assessments) and a patient's state dynamics assessment (seven priority assessments), unlike treatment selection (four priority assessments) and diagnostics (three priority assessments).

- A certain success of the stimulation method. This could be useful in assessing the dynamics of the patient's condition. This DINAR2 function was rated as successful, but DINAR2 does not provide direct estimates of the dynamics.
- The rest of the functions showed the following results: four doctors highly appreciated the assistance in identifying errors in the transmitted information; three doctors appreciated the assistance in assessing the effectiveness of treatment; and one doctor appreciated the assistance in determining the causes of exacerbation of the condition.

Customer surveys of DINAR2 at a conference dedicated to the analysis of CIP revealed the following moments that prompted them to buy DINAR2:

(1) the need for an integrated computer system for the full functioning of CIP.
(2) ease of incorporating DINAR2 into CIP work.
(3) conditions in the states of the former USSR in 90th years:
  - an increase in the infantile death rate.
  - growing independence of regions along with the former administrative system of government inside the regions.
  - social reconstruction-inducing experiments promote expansion of the adoption.

(4) an active policy of CIP marketing:
  - participation in DINAR2 development, one of the leading specialists in children intensive therapy in the former USSR.
  - an active accompanying the program at the time of its exploitation together with visits of installation places by CIP dispatchers.
  - continuation of DINAR2 development and testing.

(5) The flexibility of DINAR2. The doctor can use only those options that are necessary for him in a particular clinical case.
(6) freedom of consultant's action (user-friendly interface of the DINAR2).
(7) original decisions of concrete questions.

Several more critical than expected points should be noted that were encountered during the sale process:

- necessity of administrative support at the system adoption.
- reluctance to reread the system instructions.
- incorrect use of some functions of the system.
- belief in super possibilities of the system followed by disappointment caused by their actual absence.
- great differences in the tactics of the sale and utilization of DINAR2 in various regions.
- more considerable efforts of ours at the monitoring than they were expected.

The positive effect of utilization in various regions of Byelorussia, Kazakhstan, Uzbekistan, Siberia, and the Far East gives us grounds to think that it is useful and expedient to utilize the DINAR2-CIP system in all territories with low density of specialized medical facilities per square mile.

Table 1 CIP_Neonatology + DINAR2_N activity in 2012–19 years.

	2012	2013	2014	2015	2016	2017	2018	2019
Number of neonatal patients consulted by the Sverdlovsk (CIP_Neonatology + DINAR2_N)	460	520	491	530	565	537	767	769
Number of visiting team to local place among the all consulted patients	338 (73.5%)	366 (70.4%)	369 (75.1%)	387 (73%)	439 (77.7%)	378 (70.4%)	470 (62%)	406 (52.8%)
Number of deaths among the consulted patients	31 (6.74%)	34 (6.54%)	32 (6.5%)	28 (5.28%)	30 (5.3%)	28 (5.21%)	20 (2.6%)	29 (3.77%)

However, the success in the early years of operation and sales of DINAR2 do not explain the 30-year lifespan of this system without significant changes. Table 1 shows the use of DINAR2 to advise neonatal patients from 2012 to 2019 in the Prutkin (2020).

In our opinion, the reasons for this were:

- slow implementation of modern communication systems and computerization in small local hospitals.
- ease of work with DINAR2.
- efficiency of DINAR2.
- habit and conservatism of CIR staff.
- difficulty of transferring DINAR2 to the modern level.
- excessive requirements for the new version of DINAR, the development of which turned out to be too expensive.
- lack of other effective developments besides DINAR to support the work of CIR.
- termination of the DINAR development group after 1995.

4. Conclusions

AI systems developed for medicine may not live up to physician expectations. The field of AI can be overwhelming. The medical approaches and terminology used to create AI may not match those of a particular doctor. In addition, the cognitive base of the data provider can influence the results of the AI. The use of an AI system by a doctor can be successful only when this application is integrated with all other types of professional activities of a doctor and other medical information technologies.

All these problems had to be faced during the development and implementation of the support system for the activities of the Regional Intensive Pediatric Consultative Center (DINAR2). The success of the implementation and operation of DINAR2 is largely explained by the methods of solving these problems, which were used in the development of DINAR2.

It is noted that the performance of AI decision-making systems depends not only on the accuracy of such decisions but also on their compliance with the intellectual needs of the physician. One of the most important of these needs is explaining AI decisions. We devote a separate chapter to this topic.

Supplementary data sets

Please visit https://github.com/bgalitsky/relevance-based-on-parse-trees to access all supplementary data sets.

References

Bain, C., Yuan, C., Wang, J., Li, M., Yang, X., Yu, S., Ma, K., Yuan, J., Zheng, Y., 2020. Uncertainty-aware domain alignment for anatomical structure segmentation. Med. Image Anal. 64, 101732. https://doi.org/10.1016/j.media.2020.101732.

Crowley, R.S., Legowski, E., Medvedeva, O., Reitmeyer, K., Tseytlin, E., Castine, M., Jukic, D., Mello-Thoms, C., 2013. Automated detection of heuristics and biases among pathologists in a computer-based system. Adv. Health Sci. Edu. Theory Pract. 18 (3), 343–363. https://doi.org/10.1007/s10459-012-9374-z.

Gelfand, I., Rosenfeld, B., Shifrin, M., 2004. Essays on Collaboration of Mathematicians and Physicians, second ed. URSS, Moscow (in Russian).

Goldberg, S., Kazakov, D., Lakhova, L., 1992. Information Technology in the Work of the Regional Pediatric Center. Health of the Federation of Russia, pp. 52–59. No. 2.

Goldberg, S.I., Tsibulkin, E.K., Makhanek, A.O., Meshalkin, L.D., 1993. Employment of Dr. Watson type systems (Dr.WTS) in medicine on the example of supporting decision making by a physician of the regional children reanimation consultative centre. In: IOS Press Ebook. Volume 10: Artificial Intelligence in Medicine, pp. 153–156, https://doi.org/10.3233/978-1-60750-854-0-153.

Gu, Y., Ge, Z., Bonnington, C.P., Zhou, J., 2020. Progressive transfer learning and adversarial domain adaptation for cross-domain skin disease classification. IEEE J. Biomed. Health Inform. 24 (5), 1379–1393. https://doi.org/10.1109/JBHI.2019.2942429.

Gubler, E.V., Tsibulkin, E.K., 1987. The use of computers and automated systems in the provision of pediatric ambulance and emergency care. In: Tsibulkin, E.K. (Ed.), Urgent Care in Pediatrics. LMPI, pp. 84–97. 1987 (in Russian).

Hamamoto, R., Suvarna, K., Yamada, M., Kobayashi, K., Shinkai, N., et al., 2020. Application of artificial intelligence technology in oncology: towards the establishment of precision medicine. Cancers 12 (12), 3532. https://doi.org/10.3390/cancers12123532.

Hershberger, P.J., Part, H.M., Markert, R.J., et al., 1994. Development of a test of cognitive bias in medical decision making. Acad. Med. 69 (10), 839–842. https://doi.org/10.1097/00001888-199410000-00014.

Kazakov, D.P., 2004. Emergency Pediatric Care in Large Region. Ykaterinburs, UPSS (in Russian).

Kazakov, D.P., Egorov, V.M., Devaĭkin, E.V., 1996. Organization of resuscitation care of children in a large region. Anesteziol. Reanimatol. (6), 4–6. 9045579. (in Russian).

Kazakov, D.P., Egorov, V.M., Devaĭkin, E.V., Mukhametshin, F.G., 2003. Interhospital transportation of children from paediatric intensive care units within a major region. Anesteziol. Reanimatol. (4), 32–34. 14524015. (in Russian).

Kim, W., 2021. Imaging informatics: fear, hype, hope, and reality—how AI is entering the health care system. Radiol. Today 20 (3), 6.

Klein, J.G., Kahneman, D., Slovic, P., et al., 2005. Five pitfalls in decisions about diagnosis and prescribing. BMJ 330, 781–783. https://doi.org/10.1136/bmj.330.7494.781.

O'Sullivan, E.D., Schofield, S., 2018. Cognitive bias in clinical medicine. J. R. Coll. Physicians Edinb. 48 (3), 225–231. https://doi.org/10.4997/JRCPE.2018.306.

Pandey, P., Ap, P., Kyatham, V., Mishra, D., Dastidar, T.R., 2020. Target-independent domain adaptation for WBC classification using generative latent search. IEEE Trans. Med. Imaging 39 (12), 3979–3991. https://doi.org/10.1109/TMI.2020.3009029.

Prutkin, M.E., 2020. Report Neonatology Department of Sverdlovsk State Children Hospital, Russia. Sverdlovsk State Children Hospital, pp. 43–47.

Renner, C.H., Renner, M.J., 2000. But I thought I knew that: using confi dence estimation as a debiasing technique to improve classroom performance. Appl. Cogn. Psychol. 15 (1), 23–32. https://doi.org/10.1002/1099-0720(200101/02)15:1<23::AID-ACP681>3.0.CO;2-J.

Scherer, L.D., de Vries, M., Zikmund-Fisher, B.J., et al., 2015. Trust in deliberation: the consequences of deliberative decision strategies for medical decisions. APA PsycNet 34 (11), 1090–1099.

Shifrin, M.A., Belousova, O.B., Kasparova, E.I., 2007. Diagnostic games, a tool for clinical experience formalization in interactive "physician—IT-specialist" framework. In: Proceedings of the Twentieth IEEE International Symposium on Computer-Based Medical Systems, pp. 15–20, https://doi.org/10.1109/CBMS.2007.41.

Snapp, S., 2019. How IBM is Distracting from the Watson Failure to Sell More AI. Brightwork Research & Analysis. https://www.brightworkresearch.com/how-ibm-is-distracting-from-the-watson-failure-to-sell-more-ai/.

Stacke, K., Eilertsen, G., Unger, J., Lundstrom, C., 2020. Measuring domain shift for deep learning in histopathology. IEEE J. Biomed. Health Inform. 25 (2), 325–336. https://doi.org/10.1109/JBHI.2020.3032060.

Stiegler, M.P., Tung, A., 2014. Cognitive processes in anesthesiology decision making. Anesthesiology 120, 204–217.

Tsibulkin, E.K., Kukulevich, M.A., Gubler, E.V., 1977. Computational prediction of the outcomes of threatening conditions in acute respiratory viral diseases in young children. Vopr. Okhr. Mat. (in Russian) 22 (12), 45–50.

Wallsten, T.S., 1981. Physician and medical student bias in evaluating diagnostic information. Med. Decis. Making 1 (2), 145–164. https://doi.org/10.1177/0272989X8100100205.

CHAPTER

6 Formulating critical questions to the user in the course of decision-making

Boris Galitsky

Oracle Corporation, Redwood City, CA, United States

1. Introduction

Automatic question-generation (QG) techniques emerged as a solution to the challenges facing test developers in constructing a large number of good quality questions. Automatic QG is concerned with the construction of algorithms for producing questions from knowledge sources, which can be either structured, such as knowledge bases and ontologies, or unstructured, such as plain text. Questions can be generated for validation of knowledge bases, development of conversational agents, and development of question-answering (Q/A) or machine reading comprehension (MRC) systems (Chapter 7).

Learning, understanding, and applying the laws of logic, both classical and non-classical, is necessary to work efficiently in the world of medicine. It allows one to effectively, consistently, and without mistakes perform all the reasoning and prove the hypothesis in a formal way. Deducing important questions that need to be answered and forming conjectures from the obtained answers is an important part of the overall spectrum of reasoning tasks in the healthcare domain.

In education, QG can reduce the cost (in terms of both money and effort) of question construction, which, in turn, enables medical educators to spend more time on other important educational activities. In addition to saving resources, having a large number of good-quality questions enhances the medical teaching process with additional activities such as adaptive testing, which tailors learning to student knowledge and needs, as well as drill and real-world exercises. In addition, a capability to automatically control question characteristics, such as question difficulty and cognitive level, can be leveraged in the construction of good quality tests with specific requirements.

A health case-based questions corpus (Leo et al., 2019) includes more than 400 case-based, auto-generated questions for medical students that follow the following patterns: ("What is the most likely diagnosis?"; "What is the drug of choice?"; "What is the most likely clinical finding?"; and "What is the differential diagnosis?").

The other domains of interest for QG are analytical reasoning, geometry, logic, programming, biology, art, history, relational databases, and science. Simple factoid questions where the answers are short facts that are explicitly mentioned in the input and gap-fill questions (also known as *fill-in-the-blank* or *cloze* questions) are the most popular types of questions for QG (Kurdi et al., 2020; Galitsky et al., 2013). At the same time, our focus in this chapter is on real-life problem solving in medicine

Artificial Intelligence for Healthcare Applications and Management. https://doi.org/10.1016/B978-0-12-824521-7.00007-7

rather than education, so the purpose of the generated question is to actually acquire a required piece of knowledge.

In this chapter, we focus on QG setting where a problem needs to be solved, so the generated questions are expected to be critical for this problem resolution. Instead of generating a question from text, we generate a question for something *outside of* this text that is important. Our focus is a doctor-patient interview, and the goal of the generated question is to make the symptom collection and analysis more efficient for both.

We now present an example of our QG setting. A patient reports that she has "*fever and tiredness and sore throat*." A physician suspects that she might have COVID-19, but what the patient is saying is insufficient to diagnose it. The physician needs more evidence from the patient. Table presents the knowledge base entry for COVID-19.

Most common symptoms	Less common symptoms	Serious symptoms
Fever Dry cough **Tiredness**	Aches and pains **Sore throat** Diarrhea Conjunctivitis	Difficulty breathing or shortness of breath Chest pain or pressure Loss of speech or movement

Bolded features are those reported by the patient. To come up with questions necessary to confirm the diagnosis, the physician needs to *subtract* the set of symptoms the patient is reporting from the set of symptoms in the knowledge base. The set-subtraction result gives questions that are in the knowledge base but have not been mentioned yet by the patient, and thus need to be addressed. The questions derived this way are:

- Do you have dry cough?
- Do you have aches and pains?
- Do you have diarrhea?

Once the patient answers these questions, the diagnosis can be made. COVID-19 is either confirmed or unconfirmed (further investigations are required beyond asking additional questions). In this chapter, we focus on "invention" of questions critical for a diagnosis. The remainder of the diagnostic procedure is outside of the current project.

In this particular case for COVID-19, the symptoms are well structured, so we just needed to do a set-theoretic subtraction (complement operation). However, symptom description can be fussier, in different terms, which requires synonym matching, inference, and other semantic operations with text. A person might say "I don't have enough energy to do things" and the system needs to infer that it means "tiredness" in order to formulate questions. Symptoms are frequently described in more complex sentences, so more processing steps are required to identify what is missing in a patient's description to match a symptom description in the knowledge base entry.
The methods of generating questions fall into five groups (Yao et al., 2012; Alsubait et al., 2012):

(1) syntax-based
(2) semantic-based

(3) template-based
(4) rule-based
(5) schema-based

Syntactic methods deal with the syntactic tree of text to generate questions. Semantic methods rely on a deeper level of text "understanding." Template-based algorithms employ templates including fixed text and some placeholders that are substituted from the input text. The key feature of rule-based approaches is the use of rule-based knowledge sources to generate questions that assess understanding of the important rules of the medical domain. These features require a deep understanding (beyond syntactic level); therefore, we believe that this category falls under the semantic-based category. However, we define the rule-based approach differently, as we show later in the chapter. Regarding the fifth category, schemas are similar to templates but are more abstract, aggregating templates that represent variants of the same problem.

In the current work, since we are inventing questions for knowledge unavailable in the input text, instead of deriving from text, we need to *infer* what is missing rather than modify a sentence to turn it into a question.

QG for MRC is a challenging task because the generation should not only follow the syntactic structure of questions but it should also ask pointed questions, which means obtaining a specified aspect as its answer. Some template-based approaches (Heilman and Smith, 2010) were proposed initially, in which well-designed rules enhanced with manual tweaking are required for declarative-to-interrogative sentence transformation. With the popularity of deep learning (DL) approaches and sequence-to-sequence frameworks, QG is formulated as a sequence-to-sequence problem (Xinya et al., 2017). The question is regarded as the decoding target from the encoded information of its corresponding input sentence. However, in contrast to the existing sequence-to-sequence learning tasks such as machine translation and summarization that could be loosely regarded as learning a one-to-one mapping, for QG, different aspects of the given descriptive sentence can be asked. Hence the generated questions could be significantly different from possible sequence-to-sequence trained results. Several recent projects tried to address this problem by incorporating the answer information to indicate what to ask about, which helps the models generate more accurate questions (Song et al., 2018).

The procedure of QG from a sentence is not a one-to-one mapping because, given a sentence, different questions can be asked from different aspects. In a dataset from Xinya et al. (2017), each sentence corresponds to almost one-and-a-half questions on average and thus the sequence-to-sequence approach may not work well for such ambiguous mapping. Some authors attempted to solve this problem by assuming the aspect was already known when asking a question (Yuan et al., 2017) or could be detected by a third-party pipeline. This assumption makes sense because humans usually first read the sentence to decide which aspect to ask about and then ask questions.

A key element of the medical profession is making numerous decisions. In this process, physicians rely on gained knowledge and experience. However, it seems necessary for them to have the ability to think logically, to use reasoning, to infer, to precisely and clearly express their thoughts, and justify the assertions made. Even when their actions are based on certain algorithms or standards, they have to logically model the situation (Benner et al., 2008). Lack of knowledge concerning the rules of logic can lead to dangerous errors and may result in continuous failures in performance stemming from faulty reasoning processes. Formulating questions to patients is a critical part of this decision-making.

According to deductive inference, true reasons always lead to true, uncontested conclusions. Moreover, schemas and relationships, on which deductive reasoning is based, are logical rules. Narrowly, a deductive inference can be defined as a transition from a general (rule) to a specific (instance). An example of such reasoning may be presented as follows:

All asthmatics are allergic.
Mark has asthma.
Therefore Mark is allergic.

Notice that induction then can be viewed as an inverse process from more specific (instances) to more general ones (generalized rules).

We formulate a critical questions *Qs* problem as follows. We have knowledge *K* and case information *C*.

If K |- C then *Qs* is empty. In many cases, case description is limited, or knowledge is limited, so there is not enough evidence concerning K |- C. Hence there is a need for questions *Qs* such that once they are answered (their variables are instantiated), $K + instantiated(Qs)$ |- C. In other words, once missing information *instantiated(Qs)* is acquired via critical questions, knowledge *K* should be able to cover (explain and provide argument for) *C*. *Qs* is a *minimal* set of formal representation for questions satisfying this condition. For a practical application, we yield questions in natural language, $Q_{NL}s$.

Some examples of *K* and *C* are:

(1) *K* is an IF part of an IF-THEN rule. To make a rule applicable, missing information is acquired by questions.

(2) *K* is how something is expected (how an illness is described in a literature), and *C* is something a patient is describing about how they are experiencing a disease. $Q_{NL}s$ is then a series of questions "*Why is* t_K *is different from* t_C?" for each symptom *t* from the difference between *K* and *C*.

(3) *K* and *C* are two texts. We need to identify the difference between them and convert into questions. If these two texts are associated with two different classes, answering these questions would relate a given situation into either class.

Hence *Qs* is some way of logical subtraction of *K* from *C*; the target of the questions is the part of *C* which is not covered by *K*. Notice the difference with the general QG problem.

We need to set the terminology to handle accurately the logic of the health states of *disorder*, *syndrome*, and *condition*. A *disorder* is a disruption to regular bodily structure and function. *Symptoms* are sensations that the person with the disease can feel but that cannot be seen by others or measured, such as pain or fatigue. A *syndrome* is a collection of signs and symptoms associated with a specific health-related cause. A *disease* is often used in a general sense when referring to conditions affecting a physical system (cardiovascular disease) or a part of the body (foot diseases).

A medical *condition* is an umbrella term for an abnormal state of health that interferes with normal or regular feelings of well-being. Condition is the least specific notion, often denoting states of health considered normal or healthy but nevertheless posing implications for the provision of health care such as pregnancy. The term might also be used to indicate grades of health (e.g., a patient might be described as in a stable, serious, or critical condition).

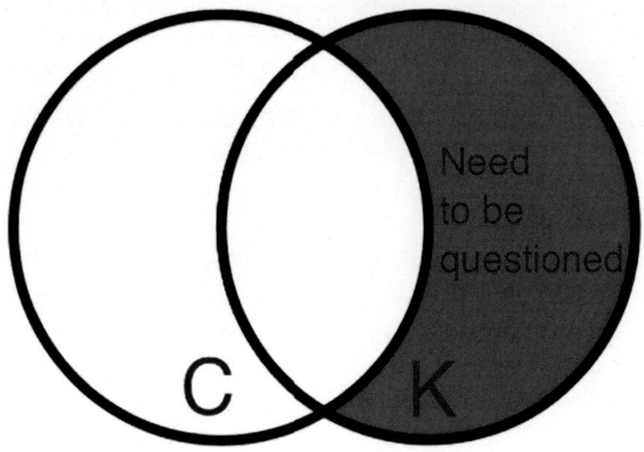

FIG. 1

A chart for identifying *Qs* given *C* and *K*.

Hence a special case of when K = syndrome and C = symptoms deserves special consideration.

Qs can be viewed as information that needs to be added to C to cover K (Fig. 1). To satisfy a condition of a rule from K, which is not included in C before questions Qs are asked, we compute the "topics" of these questions, formulate them, and obtain answers with the goal to fully complement K and apply the rule from K to make a diagnosis.

The essential question builder is important for both fully automated expert systems and decision support systems. For an automated system, it is necessary to clarify symptoms that are not explicitly stated, to make a diagnosis of a certain disease. For a doctor visit, it is fruitful for a patient to prepare their questions for the visit in advance, reflecting on possible issues a doctor might be interested in.

2. Reasoning patterns and formulating critical questions

We start with the entailment rule that is based on the so-called law of detachment (modus ponendo ponens)

$$\frac{\alpha \rightarrow \beta, \alpha}{\beta}$$

Cervical cancer is one of human organ cancers that if detected at an early stage can be 100% cured. In a patient cervical cancer was detected early in the form of the so-called preinvasive cancer (0 degree).
Therefore this cancer will be cured completely.

An example of inference based on hypothetical syllogism rule

$$\frac{\alpha \rightarrow \beta, \beta \rightarrow \gamma}{\alpha \rightarrow \gamma}$$

that is built according to the law of transitivity, may have the following form (Fig. 2):

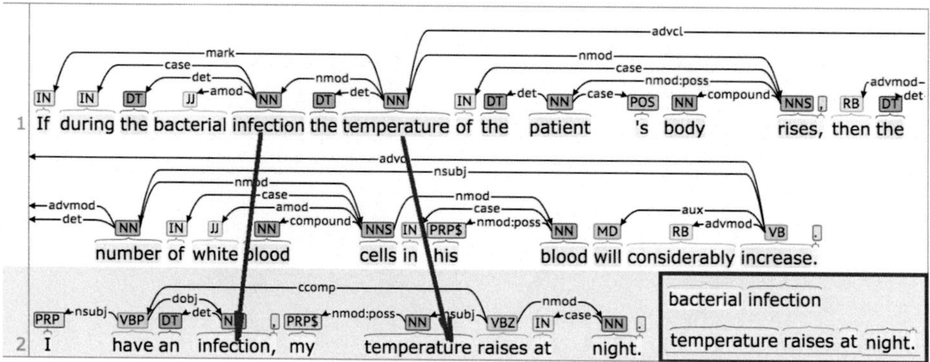

FIG. 2

Mapping of syntactic representations of K into C.

Rule: If during the bacterial infection the temperature of the patient's body rises, then the number of white blood cells in the patient's blood will considerably increase.
Increased leucocyte count causes much faster absorption of bacteria by phagocytosis.
Therefore increased temperature in the course of infection is the immune response of the body and prevention of further development of the disease through phagocytosis.

This rule might have exceptions, for example, the temperature is not necessarily linked with an infection, but we ignore these exceptions for the sake of simplicity of our examples.

In our further examples, we assume that a patient is capable of answering these questions, having lab tests at their disposal.

Case: I have an infection, my temperature raises at night.
Questions:
Case-Rule 1: Is your infection bacterial?
Case-Rule2: Does your temperature raise at night only?

Once both questions are answered positively, we can apply this rule:
As an example the inferences based on modus tollendo tollens rule

$$\frac{\alpha \rightarrow \beta, \neg\beta}{\neg\alpha}$$

that is built on the law of contraposition may be considered $\neg\alpha$ as follows:

If the patient has been infected with varicella virus causing chickenpox, then in the period up to 3 weeks blisters surrounded by red borders will appear on the patient's body.
The doctor suspects that the patient who has not so far suffered from chickenpox may have had contact with a person infected by the varicella virus. The doctor wants to determine whether the patient was infected. After 3 weeks, the rash was not visible on the patient's body.
Therefore the patient was not infected with the chickenpox virus.

We now proceed to the example of reasoning over Abstract Meaning Representation (AMR; Chapter 2).

Case: *Two weeks ago I had blisters with red borders* (Fig. 3).

Each disagreement yields a question "*Why two and not three* [*weeks ago*] *did I have blisters with red border?*" To formulate the critical question, we compute *premise—case* to attempt to reach the state where case covers premise.

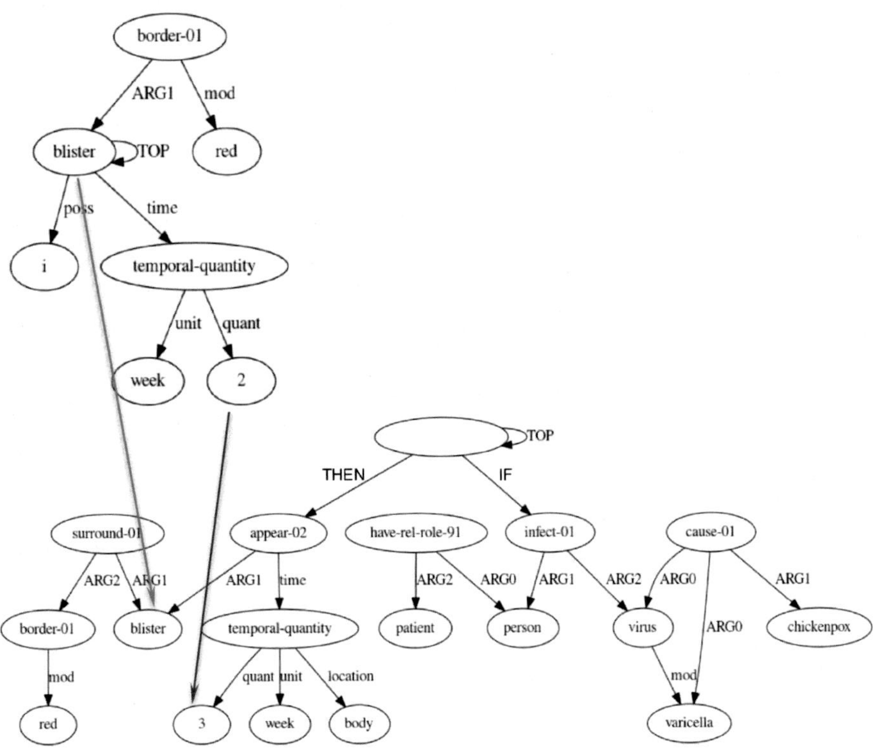

FIG. 3

Mapping of the case into a premise showing the correspondence in *green* and disagreement in *red*.

There are two types of proof: direct proof and proof by contradiction (indirect proof). A direct proof consists of showing a sentence as a thesis from the available, true premises and initial for the logical systems theorems (axioms) using inference rules. A proof by contradiction is known as *ad absurdum* proof, by reduction to an absurd (Antonini and Mariotti, 2008). It is based on contradictions between the assumptions and the negation of the thesis. It allows inferring that if the negation of the thesis is false then that thesis is true. Such reasoning can be performed in two ways: in accordance with the rules of inference or by showing a counterexample. An example of proof by contradiction may take the following form:

Reasoning pattern	**Statement**
What we are proving	If a man with hemophilia A and a healthy woman (who does not have hereditary genetic disorder determined by recessive allele) have a daughter then she is a carrier
Human genetics rule	Healthy woman is always the child of a healthy man
Assumption 1	The patient is daughter of a healthy woman and a man suffering from hemophilia A
We also do a negation of the thesis (Assumption 2)	She is not a carrier
From (Assumption 2) under the human genetics rule we infer that: It contradicts with (Assumption 1)	The patient is the daughter of a healthy man
Conclusion	**Daughter of a man with hemophilia A and a healthy woman is a carrier**

3. Automated building of reasoning chains

AI has long pursued the goal of giving a system explicit knowledge, and having it reason over that knowledge to reach conclusions. (Clark et al. (2020) explore a modern approach to this goal and ask whether transformers can be trained to reason (or emulate reasoning) using rules expressed in language, thus skipping a formal representation. This form of reasoning is capable of supporting question-answering, explainability, correctability, and counterfactual reasoning components and systems.

Reasoning based on rules expressed in language is quite distinct from question-answering as selecting an answer span in a passage, today's prevailing paradigm. Rather, Clark et al. (2020) intend the system to reason over the provided rules to find conclusions that follow. The goal is also distinct from that of inducing rules from examples (e.g., given instances of families which do fairly well). Instead, the authors provide rules explicitly and expect transformers to draw appropriate conclusions. Rather than inducing rules from examples, the authors formulate the task that involves learning to emulate a reasoning algorithm.

Given a set of facts and clauses, the Reasoning Chain Builder applies clauses to facts to derives new facts related to a question (Fig. 4). Rules are linguistic expressions of conjunctive implications condition.

$[\wedge\ condition]^* \rightarrow conclusion$, with the semantics of logic programs with negation (Apt et al., 1988) and the Closed World Assumption (CWA). Reasoning is the deduction of a statement's truth values according to these semantics.

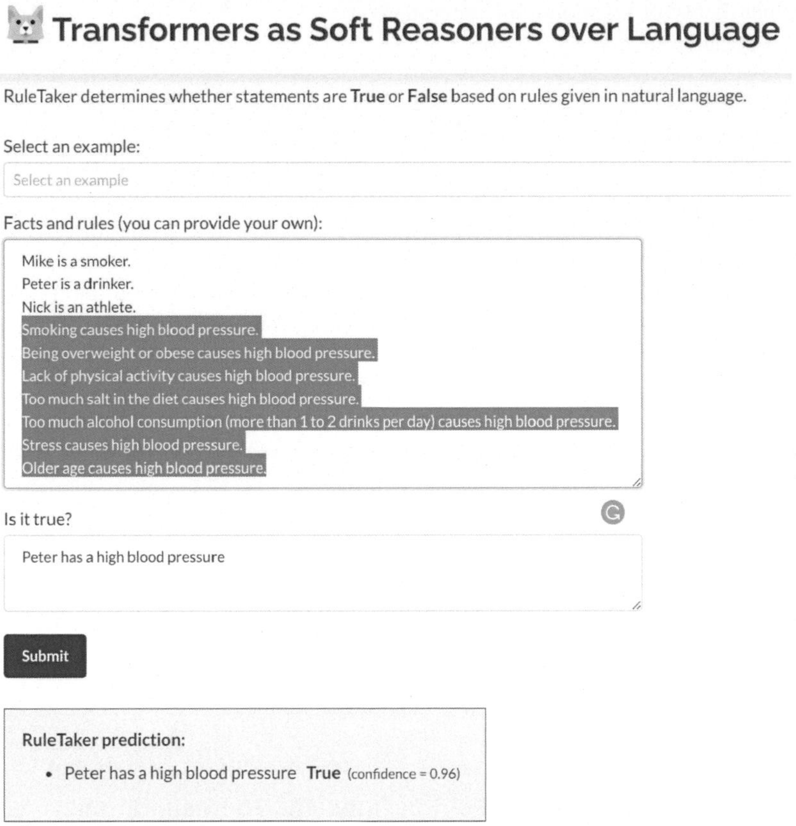

Transformers as Soft Reasoners over Language

RuleTaker determines whether statements are **True** or **False** based on rules given in natural language.

Select an example:

Select an example

Facts and rules (you can provide your own):

Mike is a smoker.
Peter is a drinker.
Nick is an athlete.
Smoking causes high blood pressure.
Being overweight or obese causes high blood pressure.
Lack of physical activity causes high blood pressure.
Too much salt in the diet causes high blood pressure.
Too much alcohol consumption (more than 1 to 2 drinks per day) causes high blood pressure.
Stress causes high blood pressure.
Older age causes high blood pressure.

Is it true?

Peter has a high blood pressure

Submit

RuleTaker prediction:

- Peter has a high blood pressure **True** (confidence = 0.96)

FIG. 4

An example of functionality of the Reasoning Chain Builder (Clark et al., 2020).

One expects that knowledge in an expert system (Chapter 3) should be easy to examine and to change, and that the system should be able to provide explanations of its results. At first sight, the knowledge in a logic program is easy to change, since it consists simply of facts and rules. From the *declarative* point of view, this is indeed the case. However, a common difficulty is that the addition of a rule with an intended declarative meaning has unintended procedural effects when the knowledge is interpreted by a particular inference engine. For example, the rule

("*disease X is associated with disease Y*") if ("*disease Y is associated with disease X*") has an obvious common sense declarative meaning, but it can cause control problems for several well-known inference mechanisms, including that of a logic program.

To address this problem, Apt et al. (1988) proposed a useful class of logic programs with negation, called *stratified programs*, that disallow certain combinations of recursion and negation. Programs in this class have a simple declarative and procedural meaning based, respectively, on model theory and a back-chaining interpreter. The standard model of a stratified program, which gives the program a declarative meaning and is independent of the stratification, is characterized in two ways:

(1) a fixed-point theory of nonmonotonic operators.
(2) an abstract declarative characterization.

CWA is the assumption that what is not known to be true must be false. Reiter (1987) introduced "closed world" assumptions to describe the interpretation of an empty or failed query result on a database as equivalent to a negation of the facts asserted in the query. In a closed world, negation as failure is equivalent to ordinary negation. In other words, the set of facts contained in a database are assumed to be complete descriptions of a given domain. Any proposition that is not either directly stated or indirectly inferable is interpreted to be false.

The Open World Assumption (OWA) is the opposite view. It is the assumption that what is not known to be true is simply unknown. Under OWA, reasoning is monotonic; no new information added to a database can invalidate existing information and the deductive conclusions that can be drawn from it (Sowa, 2000).

Let us consider the following statement: "*Juan has a flu.*" Now, what if we were to ask, "Does Juan have diabetes?" Under a CWA, the answer is "*no.*" Under the OWA, it is "*I don't know.*"

Automated Building of Reasoning Chains component (Fig. 5) is important to dramatically raise the number of questions for the same desired value (such as blood pressure). This is achieved by involving a variety of entities in phrasing to make sure the users are comfortable with at least some ways the questions are formulated. In addition to asking "*What is your blood pressure?*," the component extends the list of associated attributes such as "*Do you have a nosebleed?*" "*Do you experience fatigue or confusion?*"

Hence this component is used to broaden questions, connect them with more entities and more attributes and assure its answering is easy and natural for the user.

3.1 Questions as relative complement of linguistic representations

In this section, we define the representations for desired questions *Qs* via relative complements of *C* and *K* as sets and then as linguistic representation graphs. We provide examples of discourse-level and semantic-level representations for *C* and *K* and show how to derive *Qs* representations from them.

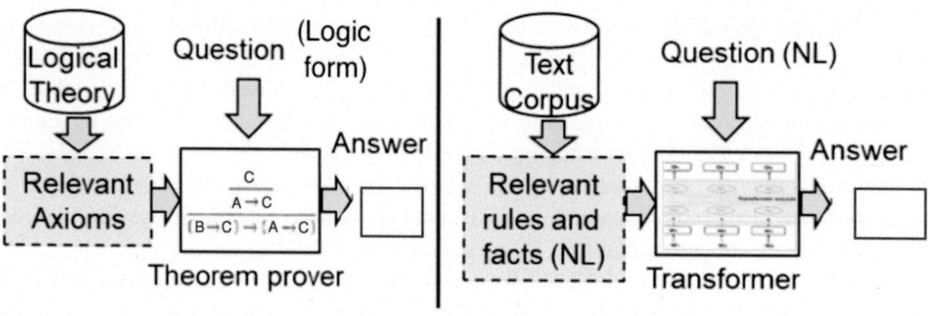

FIG. 5

Traditional formal reasoning applies a theorem prover to axioms to answer a question (left). A transformer serves as a "soft theorem prover" over knowledge expressed linguistically (right).

Below we have a description of a disease we can attempt to consider as a rule to diagnose the condition. The main question is whether we can apply this description to our case.

Symptoms
The most common symptoms of migraine include a dull or severe headache that may be worse on one side of the head, and a throbbing, pulsating, or pounding in the head. Other symptoms may include loss of appetite, nausea and vomiting, sensitivity to sound or light, chills, sweating, numbness or tingling, and increased urination.

Disease Overview
Migraines are a common type of headache that can cause severe pain. They can last for a few hours or a few days and may cause throbbing, sensitivity to sound or light, nausea, or vomiting. Migraines are caused by abnormal brain activity that is triggered by certain foods, stress, or other factors. Some people have an aura before a migraine, which can have symptoms that include temporary vision loss, seeing stars or flashes, or a tingling in an arm or leg. There is no cure for migraines, but medications can help reduce pain or stop migraines from occurring.

Case: A severe headache in frontal area that is pulsating, very low food consumption, vomiting, avoidance of light, with no sweating and with a frequent urination after taking spicy food.

In the case description, the phrases covered by the Rule Condition are shown in green, and phrases not covered by the Rule Condition are shown in red. The uncovered phrases yield questions whose answers are expected to cover them and then use this knowledge in addition to this available rule to handle the case precisely. There is a need for the question "*Does eating salty food* <affect disease>?" so that *Description of a Disease* is hypothetically extended to include "*eating salty food worsens the diabetes*."

Fig. 6 shows a discourse tree (DT) for the *Description of a Condition.*

We show the available part in green and the missing parts of the Rule Condition in red. The questions to be asked should generalize "*Natural therapies such as…*" and put it into the logic form appropriate with respect to the rhetorical relation it occurs within. Since "*natural therapies cannot cure diabetes*" occurs as a satellite of *Contrast*, it must be asked maintaining a negation:

"[Are you aware/'make sure' the patient knows] that *natural therapies cannot cure diabetes?*"

To formulate a question for the missing part, we need to semantically subtract *Case* from *Condition*:

$$Questions = Condition - Case$$

```
contrast
 elaboration
  TEXT:People with elevated blood pressure are at increased risk of diabetes .
  elaboration
   elaboration
    TEXT:The strength of the association declined with increasing body mass index and age .
    TEXT:High blood pressure is associated with stress .
   elaboration
    elaboration
     joint
      TEXT:Natural therapies such as deep abdominal breathing , progressive muscle relaxation , guided imagery ,
      TEXT:and biofeedback can help relieve stress .
     TEXT:And emotional stress affects people ' s blood sugar levels .
    TEXT:So learning to relax is important in managing your diabetes .
 TEXT:However , natural therapies cannot cure diabetes .
```

FIG. 6

A discourse tree (DT) for *K*.

To split the desired but missing part *Questions*, we do this subtraction on the sentence-by-sentence basis.

Description of a Disease*: People with elevated blood pressure are at increased risk of diabetes. The strength of the association declined with increasing body mass index and age. High blood pressure is associated with stress. Natural therapies such as deep abdominal breathing, progressive muscle relaxation, guided imagery, and biofeedback can help relieve stress. And emotional stress affects people's blood sugar levels. So learning to relax is important in managing your diabetes. However, natural therapies cannot cure diabetes.* *Case: I have a high blood pressure, eat salty food, have a low body mass index and an average age of 46. My life is associated with stress. I am worried about a risk of diabetes.*

In Fig. 7, green arrows show the symptoms of the case that are in an agreement with the features of the case. The disagreement between Symptom and Case are shown in red arrows:

Case: *frontal area*, Symptoms: *one side.*

Hence there is a need for a clarification question: around these two entities, taken in the context of the Symptom description, we take the phrase "*severe headache that may be worse on one side of the head*" and form an OR phrase clarifying this disagreement: "*severe headache that may be worse (on one side OR frontal area).*" Finally, we yield the question "*Is [your] severe headache worse on (one side OR frontal area)?*"

Questions are derived from keyword sets of K and C, which are called *relative complements.* If C and K are sets of keywords, then the relative complement of C in K, denoted $C\setminus K$, is the set of elements in K but not in C.

Let us have C, K_1, and K_2 be three sets of keywords for a split knowledge base K_1 and K_2. We have the following set complement expressions:

$$C\setminus(K_1 \cap K_2) = (C\setminus K_1) \cup (C\setminus K_2)$$
$$C\setminus(K_1 \cup K_2) = (C\setminus K_1) \cap (C\setminus K_2)$$

If we need a preferential treatment for K_2 over K_1

$$C\setminus(K_2\setminus K_1) = (C \cap K_1) \cup (C\setminus K_2)$$
$$K_2\setminus K_1 \cap C = K_1 \cap (C\setminus K_1)$$
$$K_2\setminus K_1 \cup C = (K_2 \cup C)\setminus(K_1\setminus C)$$

Now we can proceed to the definition of a complement of two AMR graphs C_{AMR} and K_{AMR}.

In a simple graph G, the *edge complement* of G, denoted G_c, is defined as the graph with the same set of nodes, such that two edges are adjacent in G_c if and only if they are not adjacent in original G (Fig. 8). If H is a subgraph of G, the relative complement $G\setminus H$ is the graph obtained by deleting all the edges of H from G.

Let us denote by M_{AMR} the maximal common sub-graph for C_{AMR} and K_{AMR}. To compute representation for questions Qs, we need to define a *relative complement* $M_{AMR}\setminus K_{AMR}$.

A relative complement of M_{AMR} and K_{AMR}, denoted by $M_{AMR}\setminus K_{AMR}$, is a graph having the same set of nodes as K_{AMR}, with two nodes being adjacent in $M_{AMR}\setminus K_{AMR}$ if the corresponding nodes are adjacent

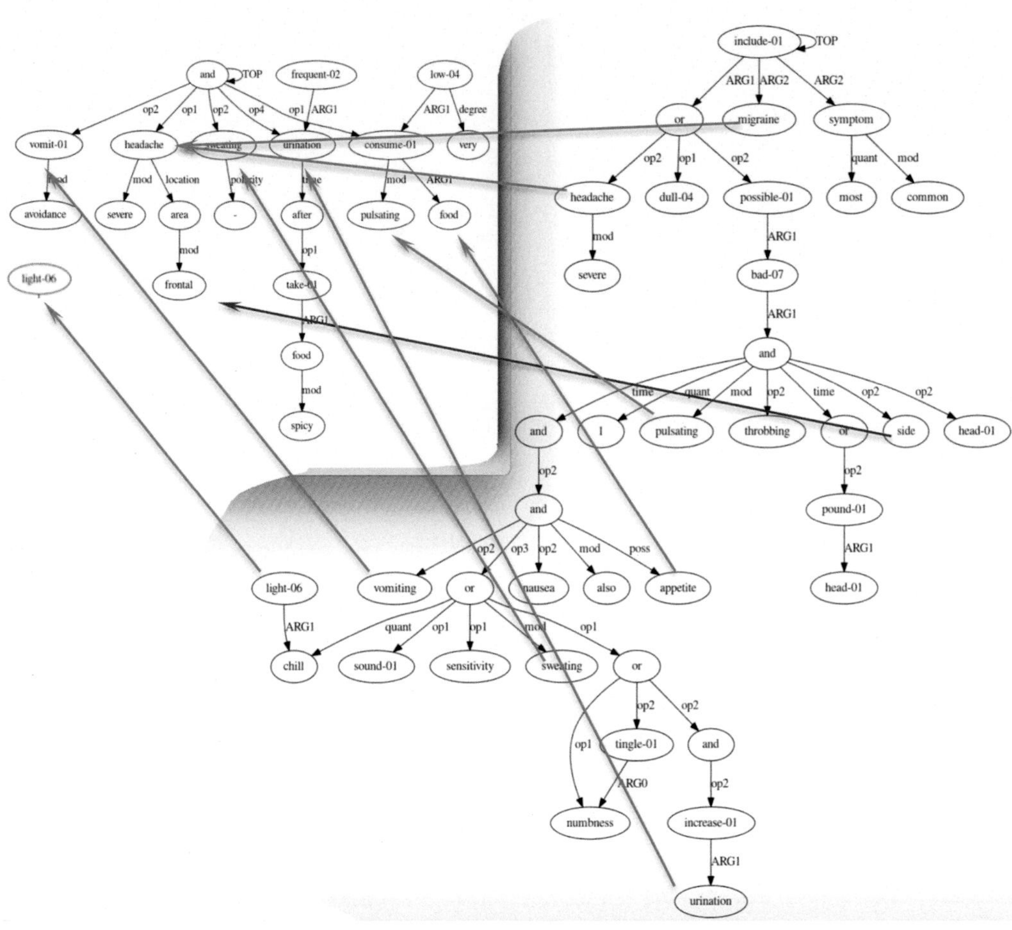

FIG. 7

Mapping between AMR for *K* and AMR for *C*.

in K_{AMR} but not in M_{AMR}. M_{AMR} is a spanning subgraph of K_{AMR} (a subgraph that contains all the vertices of the original graph K_{AMR}).

3.2 Generating text from AMR graph fragment

Wang et al. (2020) utilize graph structure reconstruction for the AMR-to-text generation problem. Link prediction objective and distance prediction objective are proposed for enhancing the capture of the structure information and the semantic relation in the node representations. The authors perform experiments on two English AMR benchmarks and achieve the new state-of-the-art performance.

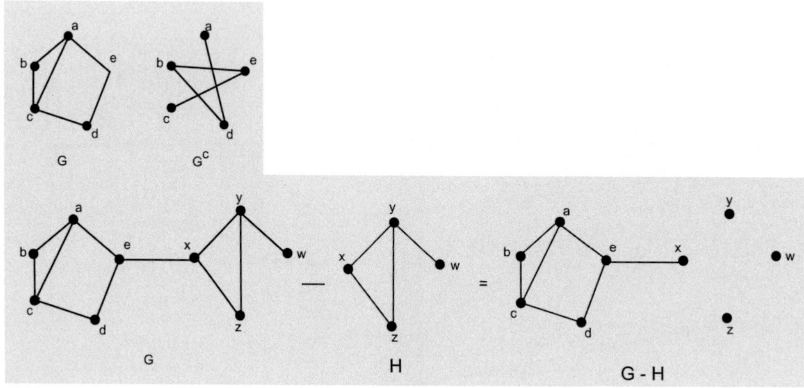

FIG. 8

An edge complement and relative complement examples.

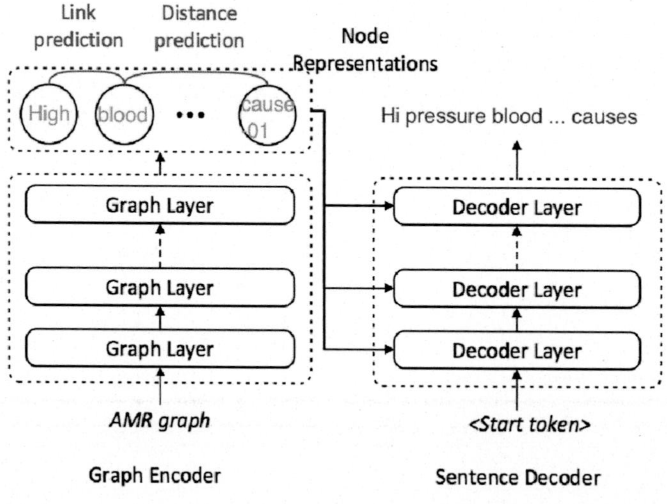

FIG. 9

AMR → *text* architecture.

Link prediction requires the model to predict the relation between two given nodes or predict the target node (or source node) given a source node (or target node) and a labeled edge (Fig. 9). Distance prediction requires the model to predict the distance between two given nodes. All the information to be predicted is explicitly or implicitly provided in the input graph and the model reconstructs the graph structure based on the learned node representations. The former encourages the model to encode the neighbor relation information as much as possible in the node representations, and the latter helps the model to distinguish information from neighboring nodes and distant nodes. The learned node representations with the aid of the two objectives can reduce the errors of a mistranslation of semantic relations and missing information in the output texts.

The capability of generating simple fragments of texts from AMR representation is important once we obtain AMR representations for C and for K and then derive the AMR fragment to form the questions Qs for desired answers. The $AMR \rightarrow text$ component is important to automatically "invent" questions from high-level abstract representations.

3.3 Deriving critical questions via anti-unification

Having described the representation for Qs via sets and graphs, we will now express it as a logical representation. The knowledge that is contained in K but is not covered by C can be computed as a complement in C of a generalization between C and K. More precisely, this generalization needs to be the least general to include as many uncovered chunks of knowledge in C as possible:

$$Q_s = C - \text{anti\_unification}\,(CK)$$

Anti-unification computes generalizations of given abstract objects. Generalization computation is a common task in learning, where an ML system extracts common features from the given concrete examples.

A term r is generalization of a term t if t can be obtained from r by a variable substitution. In logic, the problem is often formulated for two terms. Given s and t, the task is to compute their generalization, a term r such that s and t can be obtained from r by some variable substitutions. The interesting generalizations are those that retain maximal similarities between s and t, and abstract over their differences by fresh variables in a uniform way. Such generalizations are called the least general generalizations (LGG). For instance, the terms $f(a, g(a))$ and $f(b, g(b))$, where a and b are constants, have several generalizations: x, $f(x, y)$, $f(x, g(y))$, and $f(x, g(x))$, but the LGG is single: $f(x, g(x))$. It indicates that the original terms have in common the main binary function symbol f and the unary function symbol g in the second argument, and that the first argument of f and the argument of g are the same.

The problem of finding common generalizations of two or more terms has been formulated as computing an LGG that maximally keep the similarities between the input terms and uniformly abstract over differences in them by new variables (Cerna and Kutsia, 2019). For instance, if the input terms are $t=f(a, a)$ and $s=f(b, b)$, we are interested in their LGG $f(x, x)$. It gives more precise information about the structure of t and s than their other generalizations such as, for example, $f(x, y)$ or just x. Namely, it shows that t and s not only have the same head f, but also that each has its both arguments equal.

Assuming that φ is a given bijection from a pair of terms to variables, LGG can be defined recursively via the function that maps pairs of terms to terms:

$$LGG(f(t_1, \ldots, t_n), f(s_1, \ldots, s_n)) = f(LGG(t_1, s_1), \ldots, LGG(t_n, s_n)), \text{ for any} f$$
$$LGG(t, s) = \varphi(t, s)$$

We continue our example from Section 3.1. We rely on a single predicate *headache()* to formalize both *K and C*.

This predicate *headache()* has the following semantic types of its arguments:

[*strength, location, feeling, associated_symptoms, sensitivity*].

symptom =

headache(strength(severe), location(one_side), feeling([throbbing, pulsating, pounding], [chills(), sweating(), numbness(), tingling()]),
associated_symptoms([appetite(low), nausea(), vomiting(), urination(high)]),
]),
sensitivity([sound(), light()])).

case = headache(strength(severe), location(frontal), feeling([pulsating],
associated_symptoms([appetite(low), urination(high)]),
sensitivity([light(avoidance)])).

LGG(symptom, case) = headache(strength(severe), location(?), feeling([pulsating],
associated_symptoms([appetite(low), urination(high)]),
sensitivity([light(avoidance)])).

One can observe that some absent symptoms disappear from the LGG. They do not prevent this symptom rule from firing. However, the *location(?)* component shows the deviation of the case from symptom, so the *location(?)* needs to be clarified, forming a basis for the question. To obtain the minimal set of necessary questions, we subtract *LGG(symptom, case)* from *case* and obtain *headache(_, location(?),) only. We use* '_' to denote an anonymous variable (any value, unknown value, a result of generalization of two distinct values). '?' is a special case of an anonymous variable where we want to accent our interest in its value.
To derive the maximal set of questions, we subtract *LGG(symptom, case)* from *symptom:*

symptom − LGG(symptom, case) =
headache(location(one_side), feeling([throbbing, pounding], [chills(), sweating(), numbness(), tingling()]),
associated_symptoms([nausea(), vomiting()]),
]).

We now define the operation of relative complement, following Kuper et al. (1988). Imagine that we are given a term t and its m instances $t_1, \ldots, t_m$ of t. $t/t_1 \vee \ldots \vee t_m$ denotes the set G of all ground terms that are instances of t but are not instances of any of the terms $t_1, \ldots, t_m$. The *relative complement* $t_1' \vee \ldots \vee t_k'$ of t with respect to $t_1, \ldots, t_m$ is a minimal explicit representation of G. This means that G is the union of ground instances of the terms $t_1' \vee \ldots \vee t_k'$ and that t_i' and t_j', for $i \neq j$, have no instances in common. Computing the relative complement is useful in ML where a concept can be expressed via a collection of terms along with the exceptions for their values (Michalski, 1983; Lassez and Marriott, 1986).

We proceed to an example of generalization relation on *a set of terms*. A one-to-one generalization introduced previously directly induced from relation $\leq$(... less general than ...) is insufficient to grasp what is required from a correct generalization relation.

We wish to represent men and women with three attributes: *beauty*, *intelligence*, and *size*. What is the negation of term *man(beautiful, intelligent,)*? Intuitively, one single term cannot describe it: a negation could be "*being a woman*," "*being an ugly man*," or "*being a dumb man*." "*Being a dog*" can be discarded by the CWA; this description cannot be obtained by the signature. Thus, to describe the negation, it is necessary to represent all possibilities of incompatible terms (de la Higuera and Daniel-Vatonne, 1996). This can be done through taking the most general of these terms; hence a correct negation could be described through the set of three terms: *{woman(, _, _), man(ugly, _,), man(,dumb, _)}*. But since that forces us to manipulate sets of terms, how does the generalization relation transpose to such sets? Is one-to-one generalization sufficient? Take for instance (for the same signature as above) the set of terms:

$$\mathrm{G} = \{\, man(ugly, , tall), man(\_, dumb, small)\, \}$$

This set generalizes the completely instantiated terms:

$$man(ugly, dumb, tall) \text{ and } man(ugly, dumb, small)$$

by a one-to-one use of relation $\leq$ for the generalization degree. But then, using again the CWA (a man in our signature can only be *tall* or *small*) these are all the possible instances of the term: *man(ugly, dumb, _)*.

Plotkin (1970) proposed an LGG algorithm for clauses, which are disjunctions (or sets) of atomic formulas or their negations. The notion of generalization there differs from the same notion for terms: A clause L is more general than a clause D (written $L \leq D$) iff there exists a substitution ϑ such that $L\vartheta \subseteq D$ (in words, L ϑ-subsumes D). For instance, $\{\neg q(x, y), \neg q(y, x), p(x)\} \leq \{\neg q(x, x), p(x)\}$, which can be seen easily, taking $\vartheta = \{y \; -> x\}$. LGG for clauses is unique modulo $\leq$ and the equivalence generated by the subsumption relation.

Concerning anti-unification for higher-order terms, LGGs are not unique and special fragments or variants of the problem must be considered to guarantee uniqueness of LGGs. Such special cases include generalizations with higher-order patterns (Cerna and Kutsia, 2019) and object terms. For instance, a pattern LGG of $\lambda x{\cdot}f(g(x))$ and $\lambda x{\cdot}h(g(x))$ is $\lambda x{\cdot}Y\ (x)$, ignoring the fact that those terms have a common subterm $g(x)$. It happens because the pattern restriction requires free variables to apply to sequences of distinct bound variables. That is why we get a generalization in which the free variable Y applies to the bound variable x, and not to the more complex common subterm $g(x)$ of the given terms.

Becerra-Bonache et al. (2015) proposed a method of learning the meaning of phrases from phrase/context pairs in which the phrase's meaning is not explicitly represented. They aim at modeling the way how children learn language. Often, learning from a physical context means to find a correspondence between the phrase elements and observed things. The phrases are assumed to be linked to the context, but it is not required that all context elements are mentioned in phrases. Contexts and meanings are represented as first-order logic expressions, and an incremental learning algorithm is presented. A phrase is represented as a sequence of words, and a context as a set of ground facts (ground atomic formulas). For instance, a context in anatomy where a big red bone is to the left of a small green cartilage is represented as {*object(o1), shape(o1, bone), color(o1, rd), size(o1, bg), object(o2), shape(o2, cartilage), color(o2, gr), size(o2, sm), relative-position(o1, lo, o2)*}.

To define the meaning of a sentence, phrase or word, the authors propose a pragmatic solution: the meaning of an n-gram is "whatever is common among all contexts where the n-gram can be used." This "common" knowledge is formalized with the help of LGGs with respect to ϑ-subsumption. For instance, for two contexts {*obj(o1), clr(o1,re), shp(o1,bone), obj(o2), clr(o2,gr), shp(o2, cartilage), relpos(o1,lo,o2)*} and {*obj(o3), clr(o3,gr), shp(o3, cartilage), obj(o4), clr(o4,re), shp(o4, cartilage), relpos(o3,lo,o4)*}, their LGG, the most specific common pattern of both contexts, is *{obj(B), clr(B, re), shp(B,D), obj(E), clr(E,gr), shp(E, cartilage), obj(A), clr(A,C), shp(A,D), relpos(A,lo,F), obj(F), clr(F,G), shp(F, cartilage)}*, where the capital letters are variables. It states that there are red and green objects (the objects B and E, respectively), E is a cartilage, and there is an object A to the left of cartilage F. It does not imply that these objects are necessarily distinct. The meaning of an n-gram is the most specific common pattern of all the contexts where it can be used. There is a simple algorithm that incrementally learns the meaning of specific n-grams: whenever a new example (context/phrase pair) (C, P) appears, update the meaning of each n-gram G in P with respect to C, that is, use the procedure *Update(G, C)*. The latter can be defined as

Update(G, C):– if Meaning(G) is undefined then Meaning(G): = C else Meaning(G): = LGG(C, Meaning(G)).

Galitsky et al. (2011) defined sentence generalization and generalization diagrams as a special sort of conceptual graphs that can be constructed automatically from syntactic parse trees and support semantic classification task. A similarity measure between syntactic parse trees is developed as a generalization operation on the lists of sub-trees of these trees. The diagrams are a representation of the mapping between the syntactic generalization level and semantic generalization level (anti-unification of logic forms). Generalization diagrams are intended to be more accurate semantic representation than conventional conceptual graphs for individual sentences because only syntactic commonalities are represented at the semantic level.

Other representations for generalization are *pattern structures*. They consist of objects with descriptions (called patterns) that allow a semilattice operation on them. Pattern structures arise naturally from ordered data, for example, from labeled graphs ordered by graph morphisms. It is shown that pattern structures can be reduced to formal contexts; however, sometimes processing the former is often more efficient and obvious than processing the latter. Concepts, implications, plausible hypotheses, and classifications are defined for data given by pattern structures. Since computation in pattern structures may be intractable, approximations of patterns by means of projections are introduced in Ganter and Kuznetsov (2001) and Kuznetsov (2013a,b). Applications of pattern structures in search are described in Galitsky (2019).

4. Question-generation system architecture

The processes involved in a conventional QG are:

(1) transforming assertive sentences into interrogative ones (when the input is text);
(2) determining the question type (i.e., selecting suitable wh-word or template); and
(3) selecting a gap position (relevant to gap-fill questions).

The procedure of transforming can follow one of three methods:

(1) *Templates*. Questions are formed with the use of templates. The templates determine the syntactic structure of the questions using a fixed text and placeholders that are substituted with values to generate questions. The templates also specify the features of the entities (syntactic, semantic, both or named entity types) that can be substituted instead of the placeholders.
(2) *Rules*. Questions are generated leveraging the rules that take text as input. Typically, approaches utilizing rules annotate sentences with syntactic and semantic tags. They the rules use these annotations to match the input to a template specified in the rules. These rules determine how to

select a suitable question type (including a selection of a suitable WH-words) and how to manipulate the input to construct questions (e.g., converting sentences into questions).

(3) *Statistical methods*. This is where the question transformation is learned from training data. In (Zhou et al., 2017), QG was dealt with as a sequence-to-sequence prediction problem where, given a segment of text (usually a sentence), the question generator forms a sequence of text representing a question (using the probabilities of co-occurrence that are learned from the training data). Training data has also been used in Kumar et al. (2018) for predicting which words in the input sentence are to be replaced by a gap (in gap-fill questions).

The main difference between the architectures of these systems and the one of the current chapter is that QG systems generate questions from text, and we generate questions *complementary* to the text. Fig. 10 shows our system architecture.

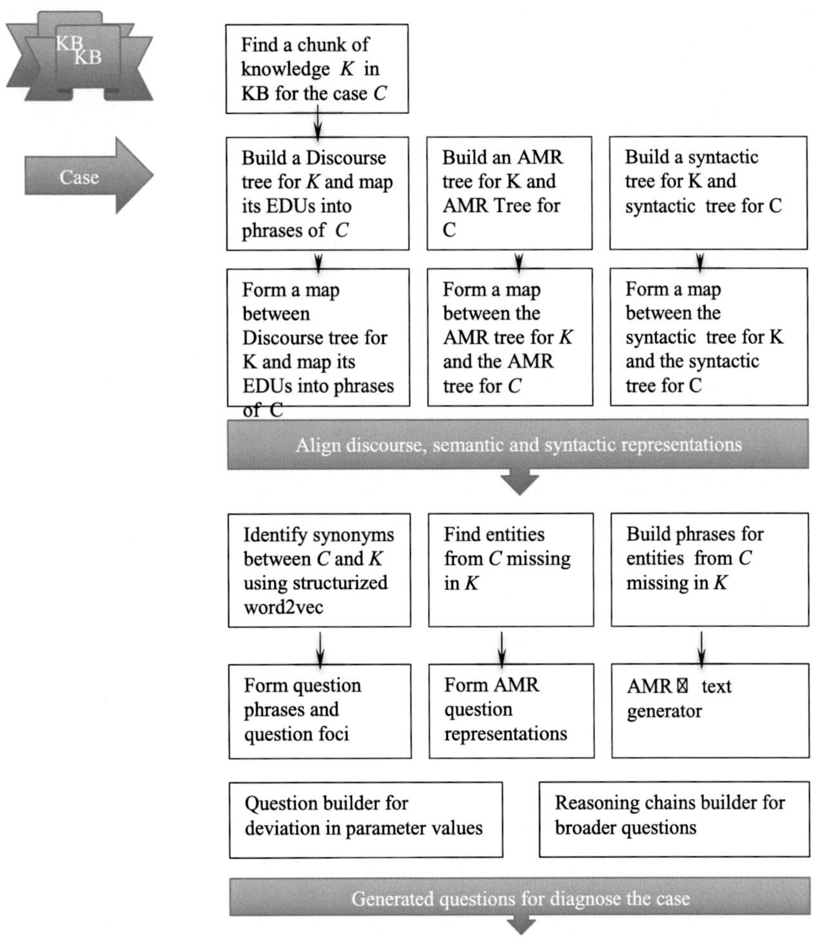

FIG. 10

The QG system architecture.

Once the QG system is given a case description C, it finds relevant knowledge about symptoms of a disease K. QG itself starts only when the system confirms that the obtained textual knowledge is relevant. This relevance is assured by semantic or syntactic relevance assessment (Galitsky et al., 2012; Galitsky, 2017a,b).

To estimate $C\setminus K$, we obtain discourse, semantic (AMR), and syntactic representations for C and K, map the representation for C into the representation for K, and then align them. An alignment of syntactic, semantic, and discourse structures via a graph-based algorithm is described in Galitsky (2020a). Once the alignment $C \leftrightarrow K$ is built for available representations, we enrich this alignment with synonyms, identifying synonyms between C and K using structured word2vec, find entities from C missing in K, and build phrases for entities from C missing in K. Then for these three components, we form question phrases and question foci, form AMR question representations, and initiate AMR $\rightarrow$ text generator, respectively.

Reasoning Chain Builder links words and phrases directly, without logic form representation. It is used to broaden questions, connect them with more entities and more attributes, and make sure answering them is easy and natural for the user.

Finally, once we have the AMR fragment to build a question from, we pass this fragment to the *AMR to Text* component and obtain the desired question. To diversify questions, we rely on *Question builder for deviation in parameter values* and *Reasoning chains builder for broader questions* components.

QG for missing information is usable in a standalone mode; however, its application domains would significantly grow if QG were wrapper by a chatbot and integrated with data collection components. We focus on these features in the two following subsections.

4.1 Chatbot implementation

Automated formation of clarification questions naturally fits into a chatbot that makes a diagnosis from communication with a patient. Once C is specified as the initial user utterance, the chatbot finds the closest *Ks* to C and builds critical questions for each *Ks*. After that, these questions are given to the patient and answers are obtained. The conversation continues until the symptoms are properly identified.

Fig. 11 depicts the chatbot wrapper architecture. The chatbot starts a conversation with the intent to encourage the patient to share their symptoms. The symptoms are then processed in two scenarios:

(1) automated diagnosis making to form a treatment for the patient, with involvement of a physician
(2) deliver symptoms in a well-organized and verified form to be considered by a physician in a decision-support environment

A chatbot may conduct a general wellbeing-related conversation, and when it determines that the patient trusts it enough to seek an illness diagnosis, requests a description of symptoms. Once this description is obtained, the chatbot tries to apply the case-based diagnosis making such as the one described in Chapter 3. Once the textual description of the suspected illness is identified, the QG component is applied to generate additional questions the chatbot will proceed to ask.

We will further explore chatbots in health in Chapters 9 and 10.

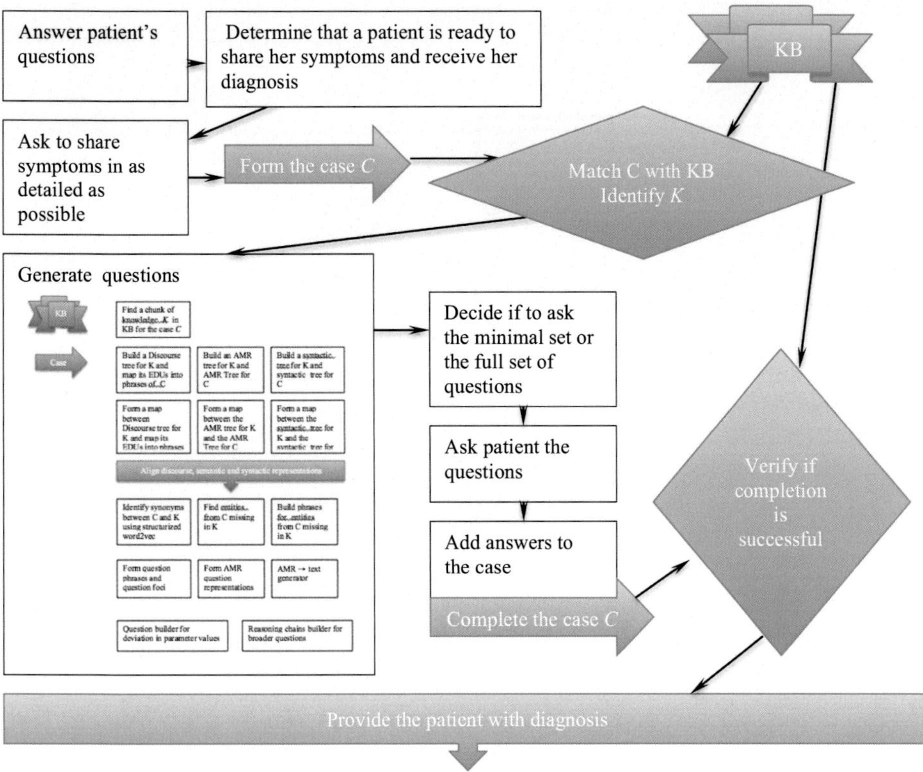

FIG. 11

Chatbot architecture.

4.2 Data collection

Many studies have been carried out in information extraction in the past decades, ranging from handcrafted wrappers to fully automatic techniques (Schulz et al., 2016). Varlamov and Turdakov (2016) share a comprehensive overview of the state-of-the-art approaches available for web data extraction and its classification based on the nature of the technique used for extraction, level of human supervision needed, and their applicability to web pages having single and multiple data regions.

Commercial tools such as Lixto (2020) and Mozenda (2020) have been introduced to facilitate extraction by non-expert users. These tools come with a sophisticated user interface that allows users to select a target of extraction. All these tools are semi-supervised and require human intervention.

To minimize the level of human intervention, several automatic wrapper-induction techniques have been proposed, such as RoadRunner (Crescenzi et al., 2002), that determine the template given a sample web page and expresses it as Union-Free Regular Expression (UFRE). It uses UFRE for extraction of data from similarly structured pages and experiences difficulty for pages with missing attributes. Other wrapper-induction techniques consider a web page as a sequence of tokens. It determines frequent tokens and their frequency of occurrence. It keeps track of the tokens with the same frequency

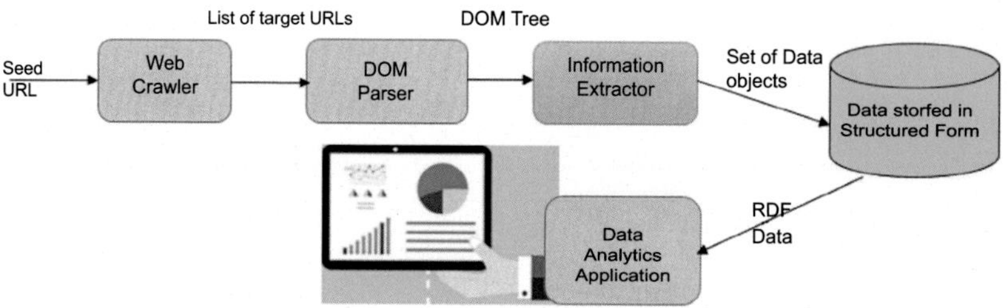

FIG. 12

A general framework for information extraction.

of occurrence in a single equivalence class. It then finds the large and frequently occurring equivalence class that as associated with the template of the web page.

Alternatively, there is also a Document Object Model (DOM) tree-based approach that combines DOM trees to obtain a pattern tree. In turn, the pattern tree represents the web page schema (Fig. 12). This method experiences difficulty processing real-world websites with thousands of pages. Sleiman and Corchuelo (2014) designed a wrapper based on the construction of tree-like structure called a trinary tree, in which every node has three child nodes: prefix, separator, and suffix. This system experiences limitations such as inability to extract attributes formatted using similar templates, manual labeling of post extraction, and so on.

Health Discussion Forum Taxonomy

Top-level index: https://patient.info/forums

Forum: https://patient.info/forums/discuss/browse/depression-683

Thread: https://patient.info/forums/discuss/after-5-long-years–742636

Post the title says it all, hmm well not quite! 5 years I have fought to get my name cleared on hospital records. I am not a narcissistic and I now can't disprove it.

From the analysis of various health discussion forum websites, it is clear that the threads are visually organized using any of three block structures: block/table/list.

We perform an analysis of various medical forum websites based on organization of posts and structuring of posts. Then we build the automated framework for extracting posts from health discussion forums (Fig. 13). After that, an assessment of extraction accuracy is performed by randomly selecting forum web pages belonging to various health discussion forum websites (Table 1).

Other sources

https://patient.info/forums/discuss/browse/abdominal-disorders-3321/
http://www.paindiscussion.com/
https://ask4healthcare.com/healthcaresolutions/
https://www.doctorslounge.com/forums
https://forums.netdoctor.co.uk/discussion/94854/sleeping
https://www.modasta.com/health-forums/pregnancy-childcare/forum/topic/child-problem/
https://forums.webmd.com/3/parenting-exchange/forum/2344
https://forums.psychcentral.com/other-mental-health-discussion/
https://www.spine-health.com/forum/categories/chronic-pain

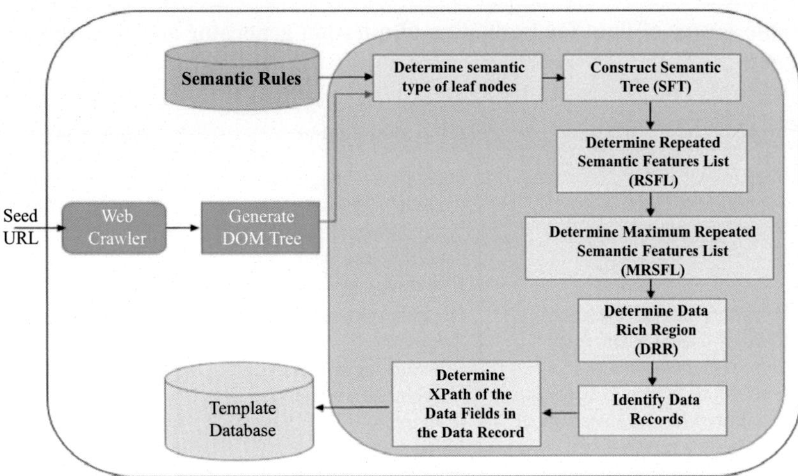

FIG. 13

A scraper with on-pattern-based rules.

To support the *Automated Builder of Reasoning Chains*, we relied on the dataset collected by Clark et al. (2020), https://allenai.org/data/ruletaker. To investigate a builder's ability to emulate rule-based reasoning, five datasets were generated by the authors requiring various depths of inference to answer the questions. Each example in a dataset is a triple (*context,statement,answer*), where *context* has the form (*fact*,rule**), *statement* is the question, a declarative sentence to prove, and *answer* is either T (true) if statement deductively follows from the context, or F if it does not (false under CWA). Facts, rules, and question statements are expressed in synthetic English. Each example is essentially a (linguistic) standalone formal logical theory with "*Is it true?*" question formulated against it.

To obtain each example, a small theory (facts + rules) in the formal logic must be obtained first, and forward inference needs to be run to form all its implications. Expressions for questions are then chosen from those implications (answer = true) as well as from the positive facts that are not proven (answer = false, under the CWA). Five datasets are obtained by Clark et al. (2020) and each is limited by the maximum depth of inference (nesting level) required to prove the facts used in its questions, with the nesting level $n=0$, $n \leq 1$, $n \leq 2$, $n \leq 3$, and $n \leq 5$, respectively. Nesting level $n=0$ means the true facts can be "proved" by a simple lookup in the context (no inference). The fifth dataset includes questions of the complexity up to nesting level five and is used to test generalization to nesting levels unreached in training on the other four datasets.

5. Evaluation

We use the WebMD dataset for K and Kaggle Disease Symptom Prediction dataset plus Patient.info for C. We first evaluate whether the formed questions are meaningful (Table 2). We conduct a step-by-step assessment of the QG procedure. The second column shows the accuracy of the first step of identifying the unmatched parameters. The third column shows the accuracy of building the main phrase of a

Table 1 Sample source of data for evaluation of question generator and the overall system for making diagnosis.

Source	WebMD	Kaggle disease symptom prediction dataset	Patient.info
URL	https://www.webmd.com/a-to-z-guides/overactive-thyroid-hyperthyroidism#1	https://www.kaggle.com/itachi9604/disease-symptom-description-dataset?select=symptom_Description.csv	https://patient.info/doctor/hypothyroidism
Example text	Hyperthyroidism (overactive thyroid) occurs when your thyroid gland produces too much of the hormone thyroxine. Hyperthyroidism can accelerate your body's metabolism, causing unintentional weight loss and a rapid or irregular heartbeat	Hyperthyroidism Signs and Symptoms Common signs include: Nervousness, anxiety, or crankiness Mood swings Fatigue or weakness Sensitivity to heat A swollen thyroid (called a goiter); you might see swelling at the base of your neck Losing weight suddenly, without trying Fast or uneven heartbeat or palpitations (pounding in your heart) Having more bowel movements Shaking in your hands and fingers (tremor) Sleep problems Thinning skin Fine, brittle hair Changes in your menstrual cycle	Hypothyroidism often has an insidious onset but has a significant morbidity. The clinical features are often subtle and nonspecific and may be wrongly attributed to other illnesses, especially in postpartum women and in the elderly. The earliest biochemical abnormality is an increase in serum thyroid-stimulating hormone (TSH) concentration with normal serum fT4 and fT3 concentrations (subclinical hypothyroidism), followed by a decrease in serum fT4, at which stage most patients have symptoms and require treatment (overt hypothyroidism)
Role	K	C can be derived from text by random phrase removes	C can be derived from text by random phrase removes
Quantity	136	421	113

desired question. The fourth column provides the accuracy data on the finalized question correctness, and the fifth column shows the overall assessment of the correctness of the formed questions in $K-C$ context.

One can observe an accuracy loss of between 4.5% and 5% at each processing step, as the resultant accuracy drops to 77%.

We proceed to the end-to-end evaluation of an automated diagnosis system, as described in Section 4. For each case C, we want to find the symptom description S from K, which covers it such that there is no such S' from K that would also cover C. In this evaluation, the main goal is to track if

Table 2 Forming of questions to validate meaningfulness and correctness.

Common symptom	Correctness in identification of unmatched parameters (%)	Correctness of building the query phrase (%)	Correctness of forming the questions (%)	Overall correctness of $K-C$ match (%)
Bloating	83.1	81.6	76.2	73.1
Cough	88.7	87.1	82.4	77.5
Diarrhea	91.0	86.2	82.0	76.3
Dizziness	86.3	82.7	79.9	76.0
Fatigue	92.6	87.9	83.1	80.7
Fever	90.1	85.2	82.5	78.6
Headache	84.6	81.3	77.4	74.2
Muscle cramp	88.9	86.2	82.0	79.1
Nausea	86.0	80.3	77.5	72.7
Throat irritation	93.4	89.0	86.1	83.4
Average	88.47	84.75	80.91	77.16
Loss of performance at each step		4.4	4.8	4.9

there is an improvement in diagnosis due to a successful generation of additional questions so that the rule from K can fire once the answers are available. We generate Qs according to the algorithm developed in this chapter but answer it automatically from additionally available patient records. Although it can be the case in some of the anticipated deployment settings, the primary target of the developed technique is to obtain answers from human patients rather than from an automated system. We use the automated answering system for the purpose of scaling up the automated evaluation.

We experiment with two settings for obtaining answers:

(1) Once the question is formulated, we automatically provide a default value for a given disease (such as 100F). This is a simpler evaluation setting.

(2) We extract the value from the additional textual data in a patient record (this extraction is implemented for the purpose of evaluation only). This is a more sophisticated evaluation setting with additional noise due to extraction errors.

We show the percentage of cases with the correct diagnosis for various assessment settings (Table 3).

One can observe that obtaining information about the default values boosts the diagnosis accuracy by more than 4.8%. Improvement of the diagnosis rate by means of acquiring knowledge about required parameters extracted from text is more modest and only exceeds 2.6%. We believe the real-life boost of accuracy with patients and doctors answering questions would be in between these values. These improvement values are more important characteristics of the proposed approach in comparison with the accuracy rates themselves, which are determined by specific disease and data availability and collection methods.

Table 3 Correctness of diagnosis once the questions are answered.

Common symptom	Correctness of diagnosis without additional questions (baseline) (%)	Correctness of diagnosis with default additional questions (setting 1) (%)	Correctness of diagnosis where answers are auto-extracted (imitated) from additional records (setting 2) (%)
Bloating	74.2	77.3	75.3
Cough	78.1	81.4	79.0
Diarrhea	75.3	82.0	80.4
Dizziness	77.0	81.3	82.0
Fatigue	72.8	78.8	76.5
Fever	71.4	77.9	75.0
Headache	74.8	78.4	73.2
Muscle cramp	72.9	76.5	75.1
Nausea	74.0	79.6	77.3
Throat irritation	77.2	82.4	79.6
Average	**74.77**	**79.56**	**77.34**
Gain of performance compared to baseline		**4.8**	**−2.6**

6. Syntactic and semantic generalizations

The notion of word similarity is very useful in larger semantic tasks. Knowing how similar two words are can help in computing how similar the meaning of two phrases or sentences are, which is a very important component of natural language understanding (NLU) tasks like question answering, recommendation, paraphrasing, and summarization (Galitsky et al., 2010). One way of getting values for word similarity is to ask humans to judge how similar one word is to another.

The meaning of two words can be related in ways other than relatedness similarity. One such class of connections is called word relatedness (Budanitsky and Hirst, 2006), also traditionally called word association in psychology. Consider the meanings of the words *drug* and *disease*. *Drug* is not similar to *disease*; they share practically no features. But *drug* and *disease* are clearly related; they are associated by co-participating in an everyday event (the event of using *drug* to cure *disease*). Similarly, the nouns *surgeon* and *scalpel* are not similar but are related via a usability event: a *surgeon* employs a *scalpel*.

One common kind of relatedness between words is if they belong to the same semantic field. A semantic field is a set of words that cover a particular semantic domain and bear structured relations with each other. For example, words might be related by being in the semantic field of schools (*pupil*, *teacher*, *board*, *lesson*) or restaurants (*waitress*, *menu*, *dish*, *food*).

Regretfully, word2vec and GloVe do not differentiate between similarity and relatedness (Galitsky, 2020b). In these approaches, similarity and relatedness are expressed by the same “physical units” of similarity. In the spirit of word2vec, a weight can be summed up with electrical current. Similar words play the same semantic role, and related words play complementary roles, such as an adjective and a noun in a noun phrase, and a verb and a noun in verb phrases. Structurization enforces that the measure of relatedness is computed separately from the measure of similarity between the entities.

Our generalization algorithm combines the best of the following worlds:

- word2vec
- syntactic, domain-independent analysis
- semantic analysis, which requires domain-specific ontology and possibly domain-independent semantic parsing engine
- named-entity analysis, which sometimes require domain-specific ontology of entities, attributes and entity-entity, entity-attribute, and attribute-attribute (cross-entity type) relations

Word2vec would assist with representation of meaning of individual words, syntactic analysis would direct word2vec into comparing only comparable words, in appropriate positions and roles.

Semantic analysis would complement word2vec with meaning where knowledge of context is a key, and named-entity analysis extends word2vec in case words are associated with specific entities instead of having generic meanings. Grasping this structured and integrated text similarity assessment algorithm, the reader would acquire intuitive understanding why word2vec on its own, without syntactic analysis, is inaccurate, and without semantic and entity analysis is incomplete. The main idea of word2vec-based generalization is to apply it to an aligned linguistic structure, not to an original text. Here we continue our development of text alignment techniques from Chapters 2 and 3.

Our running example will be a health insurance-related query that breaks many MRC systems (Galitsky, 2020b).We expand this query with synonyms and a variety of phrasings:

> "*Health insurance may be denied/rejected/not qualified if/when/due to I have problem with my health/illness/pre-existing condition.*"

In a question-answering setting, we intend to demonstrate that proper meaning similarity assessment would correctly associate an A with a Q:

> Q: *health coverage is rejected because of bad health.*
> A: *medical insurance is denied due to pre-existing conditions.*

Notice that this Q/A pair is derived from various phrasings of our running example. If these phrases are not identified as semantically identical, search recall would drop (Galitsky and Botros, 2015).

It is worth mentioning that good search engines know that these texts have the same meaning (give similar search results). In particular, Google knows that these two expressions mean similar things, but most likely obtained this knowledge outside of linguistic means. By accumulating data on what kinds of queries people input and what was the selected hit, Google figures out that some n-grams of words in these two expressions, Q and A, lead to the same search result related to *health insurance* and its *possible denial of coverage due to pre-existing conditions*. In this section, we explore the linguistic opportunities of relating these expressions in the same semantic class based on syntactic, conventional semantic, and entity/ontology-based analyses.

To structurize distributional semantics (DS)-based similarity assessment, we attach DS similarity to structures built for text: syntactic, semantic, and entity/attribute based (Fig. 14).

To complete the merge, we add nodes and combine the labels for the nodes where there is a one-to-one correspondence. (syntactic_node = *today*, semantic_node = *today*, DateTime = *today*) $\Rightarrow$ node of the generalization structure $<$ today, {syntactic_node, semantic_node, entity_type(DateTime)} $>$.

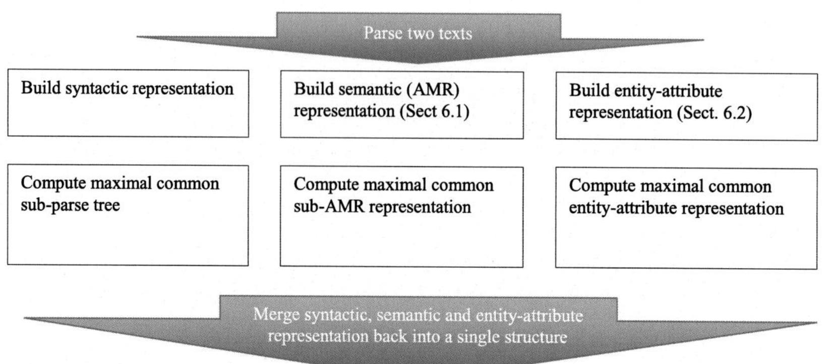

FIG. 14

A high-level view of generalizing two texts.

To machine-learn meaning of words in a numerical space, one needs to express a numerical relation between them such as *similarity*. To provide a meaningful expression of similarity between two words, numbers are not good enough since poorly interpretable, and we need other words for such expression (Galitsky, 2017a).

We refer to this expression as *generalization*. Generalization is intended to minimize the loss of information expressing a meaning; from generalization we can computer the similarity score, but not the other way around.

Similarity between two words is a number, and generalization is a list of words expressing the common meaning of these words. Unlike a default word2vec, only words of the same part of speech and the same semantic role/tag can be generalized, such as *animal* with another *animal*, *organization* with *organization*, and *location* with *location*. This is similar to physics where only values of the same physical units can be added, not a *current value* with *weight*.

Generalization between two words is an unordered list of words that expresses a least general meaning of both of them (Galitsky, 2017b). One way to obtain generalization via word2vec is to intersect a list of synonyms (for the same part of speech) for these two words. For example, *painter* ^*architect*= {*exhibition, idea, student, nature,* mod*ernity*}. Notice that a generalization result can be further generalized with other words and with other generalization results. Numerical similarity then can be expressed as the relative common number of elements in this list. If w_1 and w_2 are word or generalization results with the lists $\{..., w_{1i}, ...\}$ and $\{..., w_{2j}, ...\}$ respectively, then

$$w_1 \wedge w_2 = \cup_{i,j} \left(w_{1i} \wedge w_{2j}\right)$$

Phrases need to be first aligned, and then generalized on a word-by-word basis. Firstly, head nouns need to be extracted and generalized with each other. If these head nouns give an empty generalization, so are phrases. For two phrases "*digital camera with long battery life*" and "*long zoom focus digital camera with viewfinder*" generalization is just "*digital camera*" since there is no commonality between other attributes such as *battery*, *viewfinder*, or *zoom*. The head noun here in both phrases is *camera*. Word2vec representation of these individual attributes should not be considered to compute generalization since they are not comparable.

Other than alignment, a normalization of phrases such as *A* with $B \Rightarrow BA$ is needed to compute generalization of distinct forms of phrases, for example, "*video camcorder with long zoom*" ≥ "long *zoom video camcorder*." We then obtain

$$\text{“}video\ camcorder\ with\ long\ zoom\text{”} \wedge \text{“}short-focus\ zoom\ digital\ camera\text{”} \\ = \text{“}(camcorder \wedge camera)\ with\ zoom.\text{”}$$

To generalize two expressions, we first generalize their main entities (head nouns in their main noun phrase) and then add a sequence of argument-by-argument generalizations:

Expression for entity-based and attribute-based representation are as follows:

$$\text{AMR(Q)} \wedge \text{AMR(A)} = \text{E(Q)} \wedge \text{E(A)} \cup_n \text{ARGn(Q)} \wedge \text{ARGn(A)}$$

Although *similarity(deny, reject)* < *similarity(deny, accept)*, it is still high enough to conclude that *deny* = *reject* for the purpose of generalization.

For syntactic generalization, it is important to generate paraphrases and then compute the maximum common sub parse tree. Generating accurate and diverse paraphrases automatically is still very challenging. Traditional methods (Bolshakov and Gelbukh, 2004) exploit how linguistic knowledge can improve the quality of generated paraphrases, including shallow linguistic features (Zhao et al., 2009), and syntactic and semantic information (Ellsworth and Janin, 2007). However, they are often domain-specific and hard to scale or yield inferior results. With the help of growing large data and neural network models, recent studies have shown promising results. Several deep learning architectures have been investigated with the goal of generating high-quality paraphrases. One approach is to formulate paraphrase generation as a sequence-to-sequence problem, following experience from machine translation (Cheng et al., 2016).

For parse trees, the generalization operation is defined as finding maximal common subgraph (Galitsky et al., 2012). Fig. 15 shows generalization at the level of parse trees. One can see that common words remain in the maximum common sub-tree, except *can*, which is unique for the second sentence, and modifiers for *lens*, which are different in these two sentences (shown as [*NN-focus NN-* NN-lens*].

As a whole expression, the generalization result is [*MD-can, PRP-I, VB-get, NN-focus, NN-lens, IN-for JJ-digital NN-camera*]. At the phrase level, we obtain:

Noun phrases: [[*NN-focus NN-**], [*JJ-digital NN-camera*]].
Verb phrases: [[*VB-get NN-focus NN-* NN-lens IN-for JJ-digital NN-camera*]].

To get to the application of word2vec, a number of phrase extractions, aggregations, and alignments are necessary so that word-to-word comparison is syntactically meaningful (Fig. 16).

6.1 Semantic generalization

Fig. 17 shows an example of semantic generalization for our running example. On the top, semantic structures for each text are shown according to simplified AMR notation conventions. On the bottom, intermediate and final generalization results are shown. The root-level verbs are generalized against each other as well as each semantic role, one against a corresponding one. Nesting of semantic roles is preserved. Since the semantic structures vary in the innermost expression, generalization is reduced to the respective phrases ("*bad health*" ^ "pre-*existing conditions*") and not their semantic structures.

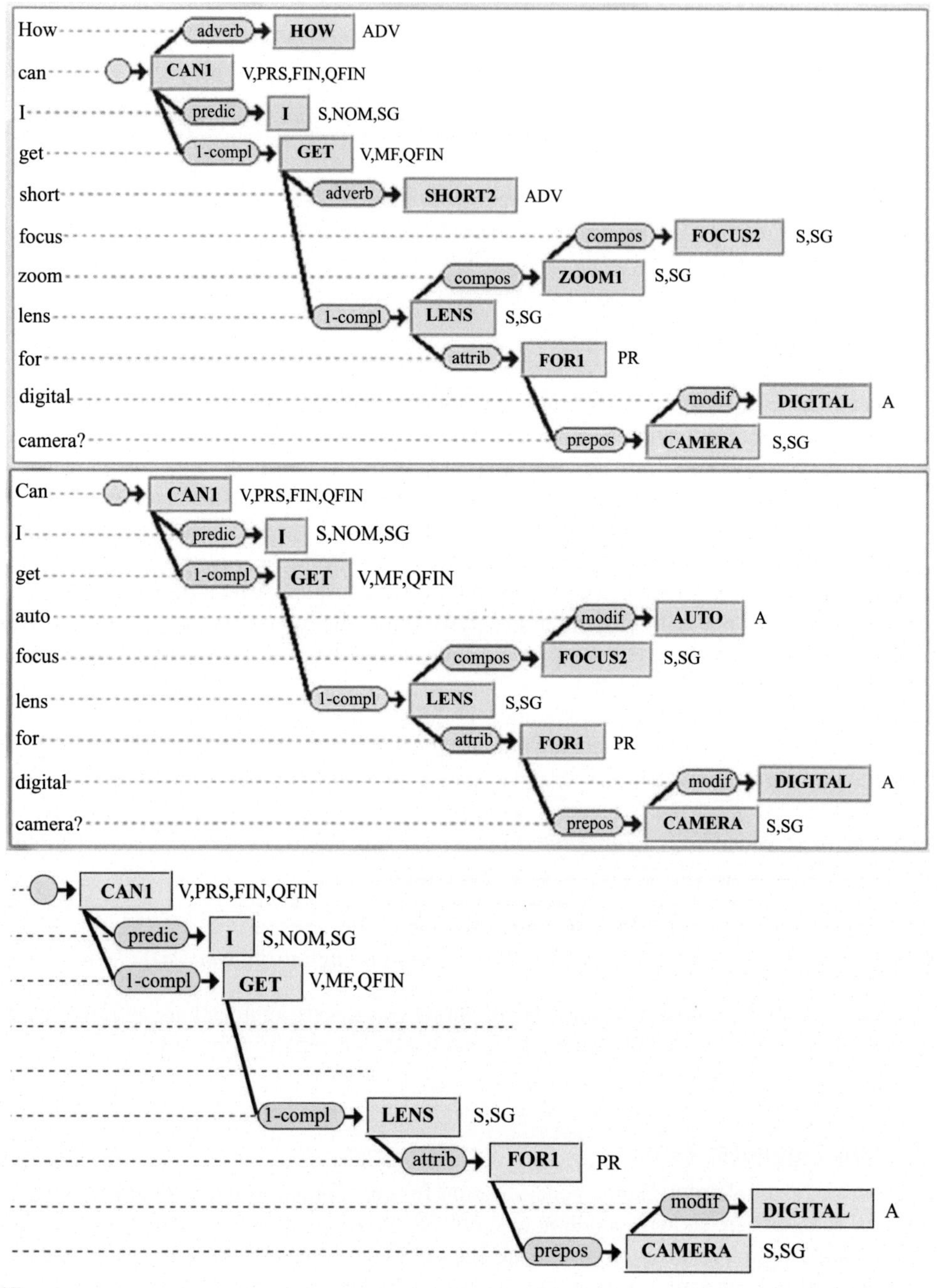

FIG. 15

Generalization of two parse trees (top and middle). The generalization result is shown on the bottom.

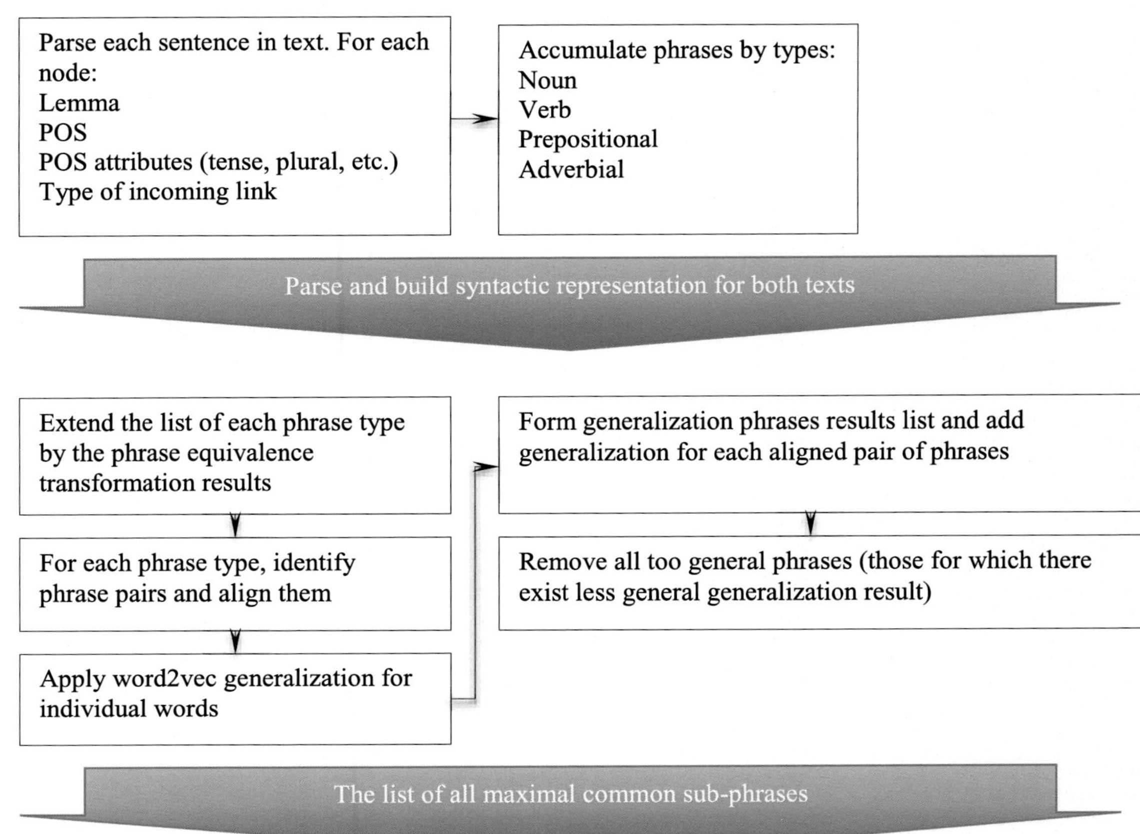
Parse each sentence in text. For each node:
Lemma
POS
POS attributes (tense, plural, etc.)
Type of incoming link
Accumulate phrases by types:
Noun
Verb
Prepositional
Adverbial
Parse and build syntactic representation for both texts
Extend the list of each phrase type by the phrase equivalence transformation results
For each phrase type, identify phrase pairs and align them
Apply word2vec generalization for individual words
Form generalization phrases results list and add generalization for each aligned pair of phrases
Remove all too general phrases (those for which there exist less general generalization result)
The list of all maximal common sub-phrases

FIG. 16

Syntactic generalization component.

```
AMR(Q): reject-01(
        [:ARG1 (company )fictitious]
        :ARG1-of (coverage
                :mod (health)
        :ARG2-of (cause-01 (
                :ARGO (health
                        :mod (bad))))


AMR(A) deny-01(
        [:ARG1 (company )fictitious]
        :ARG1-of (insurance
                :mod (medical)
        :ARG2-of (cause-01 (
                :ARGO (condition
                        :ARGO (exist)
                                :mod (pre))))
AMR(Q) ^ AMR (A) = deny^reject(
        [:ARG1 (company )fictitious]
        :ARG1-of (insurance^coverage
                :mod (medical^health)
        :ARG2-of (cause-01 (
                :ARGO ("bad health" ^ "pre-existing conditions")))) =
not-acceptance(
        [:ARG1 (company )fictitious]
        :ARG1-of ({medical, plan, regular, deductible, payments}
                :mod ({wellness, personal, good, bad, physical, wellbeing,
dental, pediatric})
        :ARG2-of (cause-01 (
                :ARGO({problem, issues, increased, higher, premiums, cost,
deductibles}))))
```

FIG. 17

Example of semantic generalization.

6.2 Attribute-based generalization

Attribute-based generalization is based on available ontology and entity extraction results (Fig. 18). Two entities such as *organization*, *person*, *location*, or *time* can be matched against each other unless there is an entry in the ontology that related two entities of different types, like *Jeff Besos—isCEO—Amazon*.

Times and *dates* are generalized as a range the events from both texts occur; generalization is empty if these events are too distant in time (Galitsky and Botros, 2015).

Geo locations, addresses, and points of interest are generalized into the location range or common properties (if available).

(*Lattutude1, Longtitude1*) ^ (*Lattutude2, Longitude2*) = range [(*Lattutude1, Longitude1*), (*Lattutude2, Longtitude2*)].

Lattutude, Longtitude ^*Location name* = range [(*Lattitude, Longitude*), ($Lattutude_{Loc}$, $Longitude_{Loc}$)], which includes/covers the Lat/Long of this *Location*, if below certain distance threshold (Galitsky and Usikov, 2008).

Range1 ^*Range2* = $\cup_{ij}$ ($Range1_j$ ^$Range2_j$), computing overlaps of all ranges, for time and space.

If time and space points or ranges are related, they are generalized together with a relation between them.

$occur_1$ (*Location1, Time1*) ^$occur_2$ (*Location2, Time2*) = {($occur_1$ ^$occur_2$)(*Location1* ^*Location2*, *Time1* ^*Time2*), $occur_1$ (*Location1* ^*Location2*, *Time1* ^*Time2*), $occur_2$ (*Location1* ^*Location2*, *Time1* ^ *Time2*).

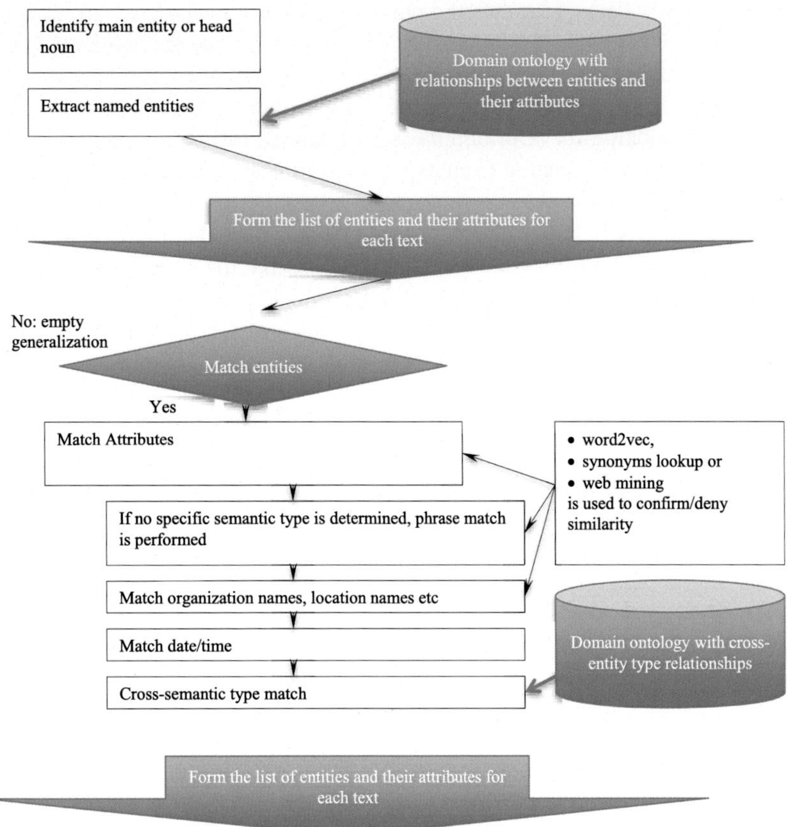

FIG. 18

Entity/attribute generalization component.

7. Building questions via generalization of instances

Frequently, novice users of search engines experience difficulties formulating their queries, especially when these queries are long. It is often hard for a user who is new to a domain to pick proper keywords. Even for advanced users exploring data via querying, including web queries, it is usually hard to estimate the proper generality/specificity of a query being formulated. Lattice querying makes it easier for a broad range of user and data exploration tasks to formulate the query; given a few examples, it formulates the query automatically.

In this section, we introduce the technique of lattice querying (Galitsky, 2015a), which automatically forms questions from the set of text samples provided by a user by generalizing them from the respective parse trees. Also, the system produces search results by matching parse trees of this query with that of candidate answers. Lattice queries allow an increase in big data exploration efficiency since they form multiple *hypotheses* concerning user intent and explore data from multiple angles (generalizations).

Exploring data, mostly keyword query and phrase query are popular, as well as natural language-like ones. Users of search engines also appreciate "fuzzy match" queries, which help to explore new areas where the knowledge of exact keywords is lacking. Using synonyms, taxonomies, ontologies, and query expansions helps to substitute user keywords with the domain-specific ones to find what the system believes users are looking for (Ourioupina and Galitsky, 2001; Galitsky, 2003). Lattice queries increase usability of search, proceeding from expressions in user terms towards queries against available data sources.

Fig. 19 illustrates the idea of lattice query. Instead of a user formulating a query exploring a dataset, the user provides a few samples (expressions of interest) so that the system formulates a query as an overlap (generalization) of these samples, applied in the form of a lattice (shown in bold on the bottom).

Proceeding from a keyword query to regular expressions or fuzzy one allows making search more general and flexible, and assists in exploration of a new domain as a set of documents with unknown vocabulary. What can be a further step in this direction? We introduce lattice questions, based on NL expressions that are generalized (Section 6) into an actual lattice question.

There is a broad range of search engine query types with string character-based similarity. They include Boolean queries, span queries that restrict the distances between keywords in a document, regular expressions queries that allow a range of characters at certain positions, fuzzy match queries, and *more-like-this* queries that allow substitution of certain characters based on string distances. Other kinds of queries allow expressing constraints in a particular dimension, such as geo-shape queries (Galitsky, 2015b).

Lattice questions, based on NL expressions that are generalized into an actual query, abstracting up from individual phrasings, could be a further step in this direction. Instead of getting search results that are similar to a given expression (done by "more-like-this" query), we first form the commonality expression between all or subsets of the given sample expressions (phrases, sentences), and then use the generalization result as a question. A lattice question includes words as well as attributes such as entity types and verb attributes.

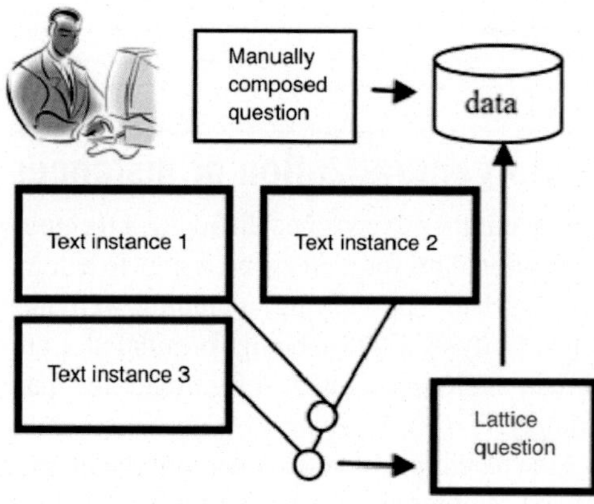

FIG. 19

A lattice question and a conventional question against a data source.

Let us start with a hospital service request question example:

- *A junior MRI sale engineer expert travels to hospitals on site*
- *A junior MRI design expert goes to hospitals and clinics*
- *A junior MRI software engineer rushes to hospital sites*

Given this set of samples, the system needs to form a question that would give us cases somewhat similar to what we are looking for. A trivial approach would be to just turn each sample into a question and attempt to find an exact match. However, most of the time it would not work, so such questions need to be weakened, releasing some constraints. How to determine which constraints need to be dropped and which keywords are most important?

To do that, we apply generalization to the set of these samples. For the entities and attributes, we form the least general generalization. The seniority of the job (adjective) "*junior*" will stay. The job activity (noun phrase) varies, so we generalize them into <*job-activity*>. The higher-level reference to the job is "*MRI*" and is common for all three cases, so it stays. The verbs for *job responsibility* vary, so we use <*action*> that can be further specified as.

<*moving_action*>, using verb-focused ontologies like VerbNet. To generalize the last noun phrase, we obtain the generalization <*hospital, NP*>:

junior<any job activity>expert<action>customer-NP.

This is a lattice query, which is expected to be run against *job descriptions* index and find the cases that are supposed to be most desired, according to the set of samples.

In terms of parse trees of the potential sentences to be matched with the lattice query, we rewrite it as

JJ-junior NP- NN-expert VP-* NN-hospital NP-**

The lattice question read as *find me a junior something MRT expert doing-something-with a hospital of-something.*

Now we show how this template can be applied to accept/reject a candidate answer *Cisco junior MRT sale representative expert flew to hospital data centers.*

We represent the lattice question as a conjunction of noun phrases (NP) and verb phrases (VP) set:

[[NP [DT-a JJ-junior NN-MRT NN-], NP [NN*-hospital]],*

The first NP covers the beginning of the lattice query above, and the second NP covers the end.

[VP [VB- TO-to NN*-hospital]]].*

VP covers the second half of the lattice query starting from *doing-something…*

The generalization between the lattice query and a candidate answer is

[[NP [JJ-junior NN- NN-*], NP [NN*-hospital]], [VP [VB-* TO-to NN*-hospital]]]*

One can see that the NP part is partially satisfied (the article a does not occur in the candidate answer) and VP part is fully satisfied.

8. Discussion and conclusions

While exam-style questions are a fundamental educational tool serving a variety of purposes, manual construction of questions is a complex process that requires training, experience, and resources. This, in turn, hinders and slows down the use of educational activities (e.g., providing practice questions) and new advances (e.g., adaptive testing) that require a large pool of questions. To reduce the expenses associated with the manual construction of questions and to satisfy the need for a continuous supply of new questions, automatic QG techniques were introduced.

It turns out that the types of questions generated from ontologies are more varied than the types of questions generated from text (Kurdi et al., 2020).

Extracting an underspecified span from the rule text that is uncovered from the user's feedback and rephrasing this span into a well-formed question is an active area of research. Existing approaches put much effort into extracting the underspecified span, such as entailment-driven extracting and ranking (Zhong and Zettlemoyer, 2019) or coarse-to-fine reasoning.

Gao et al. (2019) investigate *difficulty-controllable* QG, where, given a sentence in the reading comprehension paragraph, the text answers what one wants to query about. The required difficulty levels are assessed and the system generates questions that are associated with specified answers and obey the required difficulty levels as much as possible.

Developing plausible distractors (wrong answer options) when writing multiple-choice questions is a complementary problem to the one addressed in this chapter. Distractors have been described as one of the most challenging and time-consuming parts of the writing process. Ha and Yaneva (2018) propose a fully automatic method for yielding distractor options for multiple-choice questions used in high-stakes medical exams. The system uses a question stem and the correct answer as an input and produces a list of suggested distractors ranked based on their similarity to the stem and the correct answer, combining concept embeddings with information-retrieval methods.

Feedback generation is the process of supplying information regarding the response to a question. Feedback is important in reinforcing the benefits of questions especially in electronic environments in which interaction between instructors and students is limited. In addition to informing test takers of the correctness of their responses, feedback plays a role in correcting test takers' errors and misconceptions. It also navigates the learners to the knowledge they must acquire, possibly with reference to additional materials. This aspect of questions has not been sufficiently addressed in QG literature. Leo et al. (2019) produce feedback text, together with the generated questions, in the way of a verbalization of the axioms used to select options. In cases of distractors, the axioms employed to generate the key as well as distractors occur in the feedback text. In terms of complexity, the critical QG problem is situated in between QG and narrative generation (Galitsky, 1999).

Galitsky (2017a) described a linguistic-based relevance technology based on learning of parse trees for processing, classifying, and delivering a stream of texts. The content pipeline for the eBay entertainment domain that employs this technology is presented and shows that text processing relevance is the main bottleneck for its performance. Several components of the content pipeline such as content mining, aggregation, de-duplication, opinion mining, and integrity enforcing need to rely on domain-independent efficient text classification, entity extraction, and relevance assessment operations.

There is a difference between symptoms reported in formal settings (e.g., electronic health records (EHRs), databases) and informal communities, such as those represented in Web 2.0. There is a comparison of texts written by patients and more formal data sources. Specifically, these findings include

(1) the widespread use of real-time social networking sites (i.e., Twitter) and short online documentation as the data source for texts written by patients.
(2) the informal nature of symptoms and the diverse nature of language online.

The proposed approach of question construction can be applied to tracking of how EHRs evolve in time. There continues to be a limitation in the capability of text mining and NLP to study heterogeneity of symptoms and patients' experiences. One review (Dreisbach et al., 2019) revealed that Twitter was the online community most frequently used to access and study symptom-related patient records. The studies that use Twitter largely focus on pharmacological alertness and estimates of public health outbreaks. Posts made by users on Twitter are termed "tweets" and are limited to 140 (more recently 280) characters. In contrast to other textual sources of patient symptom information, such as clinical notes within EHRs (which are typically much longer and can be limited by reporting lags), the short length of tweets in combination with real-time, interactive posting of online communities has the potential to facilitate immediate, scalable access for pharmaceutical companies to monitor the evolution of symptoms. This possibility can be a great value for examining the recent opioid crisis and patient management of pain.

In this chapter, we relied on deduction to build inference chains of words. Human reasoning over language (natural language inference, NLI) is not always deductive. In particular, NLI is capable of performing an unsupported inference that humans can typically do (Dagan et al., 2013). However, relying on a precise model of inference, all of a rule's conditions have to be proved true for the conclusion to be inferred. A trained inference chain model is still quite far from what is required for fully natural reasoning over NL. The desired feature of a trained inference chain model is to jump through gaps in the explicitly provided knowledge, providing the missing knowledge is natural, obvious, and lacks contradictions with the explicitly provided facts. It can be possibly achieved by leveraging its pretrained knowledge. Regretfully, there is a conflict between the model's treatment of negation as failure and an intuition about NLI. For example, given (just) "*If a patient is tired then he is not moving*" the model will conclude (given nothing else) that "*he cannot move*," as it cannot prove that "*he is not tired*."

Asking questions to fill the gaps in required knowledge is an important and complex form of intellectual activity of humans. This problem of inventing critical questions turns out to be much more difficult than deriving questions from text such that the text naturally answers them. As we attempt to automate this process, we encounter a series of problems in reasoning and computational linguistics, all of which are necessary to solve to build a robust and flexible QG system. Our evaluation shows that acquiring missing knowledge by asking questions for information outside of available texts is an efficient way to support decision-making and decision support in the health domain.

Supplementary data sets

Please visit https://github.com/bgalitsky/relevance-based-on-parse-trees to access all supplementary data sets.

References

Alsubait, T., Parsia, B., Sattler, U., 2012. Next generation of e-assessment: automatic generation of questions. Int. J. Technol. Enhanc. Learn. 4 (3–4), 156–171.

Antonini, S., Mariotti, M.A., 2008. Indirect proof: what is specific to this way of proving? ZDM 40, 401–412.

Apt, K., Blair, H., Walker, A., 1988. Towards a theory of declarative knowledge. In: Foundations of Deductive Databases and Logic Programming.

Becerra-Bonache, L., Blockeel, H., Galv'an, M., Jacquenet, F., 2015. A first-order-logic based model for grounded language learning. In: Fromont, E., Bie, T.D., van Leeuwen, M. (Eds.), Advances in Intelligent Data Analysis XIV, IDA 2015, Volume 9385 of LNCS. Springer, pp. 49–60.

Benner, P., Hughes, R.G., Sutphen, M., 2008. Clinical reasoning, decision-making, and action: thinking critically and clinically. In: Hughes, R.G. (Ed.), Patient Safety and Quality: An Evidence-Based Handbook for Nurses. Agency for Healthcare Research and Quality, Rockville, MD (Chapter 6).

Bolshakov, I.A., Gelbukh, A., 2004. Synonymous paraphrasing using wordnet and internet. In: International Conference on Application of Natural Language to Information Systems. Springer, pp. 312–323.

Budanitsky, A., Hirst, G., 2006. Evaluating WordNet—based measures of lexical semantic relatedness. Comput. Linguist. 32 (1), 13–47.

Cerna, D.M., Kutsia, T., 2019. 4th International Conference on Formal Structures for Computation and Deduction (FSCD 2019). vol. 10, pp. 1–10. 19.

Cheng, Y., Liu, Y., Yang, Q., Sun, M., Xu, W., 2016. Neural Machine Translation with Pivot Languages. arXiv preprint arXiv:1611.04928.

Clark, P., Tafjord, O., Richardson, K., 2020. Transformers as soft reasoners over language. IJCAI, 3882.

Crescenzi, V., Mecca, G., Merialdo, P., 2002. Roadrunner: Automatic Data Extraction from Data-Intensive Websites. SIGMOD, p. 624.

Dagan, I., Roth, D., Sammons, M., Zanzotto, F., 2013. Recognizing Textual Entailment: Models and Applications. Morgan and Claypool publishing.

de la Higuera, C., Daniel-Vatonne, M.-C., 1996. On sets of terms: a study of a generalisation relation and of its algorithmic properties. Fund. Inform. 25, 99–121.

Dreisbach, C., Koleck, T.A., Bourne, P.E., Bakken, S., 2019. A systematic review of natural language processing and text mining of symptoms from electronic patient-authored text data. Int. J. Med. Inform. 125, 37–46.

Ellsworth, M., Janin, A., 2007. Mutaphrase: paraphrasing with FrameNet. In: Proceedings of the ACL-PASCAL Workshop on Textual Entailment and Paraphrasing, pp. 143–150.

Galitsky, B., 1999. Narrative generation for the control of buyer's impression. In: Symposium on Artificial Intelligence and Creative Language, Edinburgh, UK.

Galitsky, B., 2003. Natural Language Question Answering System: Technique of Semantic Headers. Advanced Knowledge International, Australia.

Galitsky, B., 2015a. Finding a lattice of needles in a haystack: forming a query from a set of items of interest. In: FCA4AI@ IJCAI, pp. 99–106.

Galitsky, B., 2015b. Lattice queries for search and data exploration. In: The Twenty-Eighth International Flairs Conference.

Galitsky, B., 2017a. Improving relevance in a content pipeline via syntactic generalization. Eng. Appl. Artif. Intell. 58, 1–26.

Galitsky, B., 2017b. Matching parse thickets for open domain question answering. Data Knowl. Eng. 107, 24–50.

Galitsky, B, 2019. Developing Enterprise Chatbots: Learning Linguistic Structures. Springer Publishing.

Galitsky, B., 2020a. Social Autonomous Agent Implementation using Lattice Queries And Relevancy Detection. US Patent App. 16/460,503.

Galitsky, B., 2020b. Distributional semantics for CRM: making word2vec models robust by structurizing them. In: Artificial Intelligence for Customer Relationship Management: Keeping Customers Informed. Springer, Cham, Switzerland, pp. 25–56.

Galitsky, B., Botros, S., 2015. Searching for Associated Events in Log Data. US Patent 9,171,037.

Galitsky, B., Dobrocsi, G., De La Rosa, J.L., Kuznetsov, S.O., 2010. From generalization of syntactic parse trees to conceptual graphs. In: International Conference on Conceptual Structures, pp. 185–190.

Galitsky, B., De La Rosa, J.L., Dobrocsi, G., 2012. Inferring the semantic properties of sentences by mining syntactic parse trees. Data Knowl. Eng. 81, 21–45.

Galitsky, B., Dobrocsi, G., De la Rosa, J.L., Kuznetsov, S.O., 2011. Using generalization of syntactic parse trees for taxonomy capture on the web. In: International Conference on Conceptual Structures, pp. 104–117.

Galitsky, B., Ilvovsky, D., Kuznetsov, S.O., Strok, F., 2013. Matching sets of parse trees for answering multi-sentence questions. In: Proceedings of the Recent Advances in Natural Language Processing, RANLP 2013. Shoumen, Bulgaria, pp. 285–294.

Galitsky, B., Usikov, D., 2008. Programming spatial algorithms in natural language. In: AAAI Spring Symposium on Spatial Reasoning.

Ganter, B., Kuznetsov, S.O., Stumme, P.G., Delugach, H., 2001. Pattern structures and their projections. In: 9th International Conference on Conceptual Structures (ICCS 2001), Lecture Notes in Artificial Intelligence. vol. 2120. Springer, pp. 129–142.

Gao, Y., Wang, J., Bing, L., King, I., Lyu, M.R., 2019. Difficulty controllable question generation for reading comprehension. In: IJCAI, pp. 4968–4974.

Ha, L.A., Yaneva, V., 2018. Automatic distractor suggestion for multiple-choice tests using concept embeddings and information retrieval. In: The 13th Workshop on Innovative Use of NLP for Building Educational Applications, pp. 389–398.

Heilman, M., Smith, N.A., 2010. Good question! Statistical ranking for question generation. In: HLT-NAACL.

Kumar, V., Boorla, K., Meena, Y., Ramakrishnan, G., Li, Y.-F., 2018. Automating reading comprehension by generating question and answer pairs. In: PAKDD.

Kuper, G., Palem, K., Perry, K.J., 1988. Efficient Parallel Algorithms for Anti-Unification and relative Complement. pp. 112–120, https://doi.org/10.1109/LICS.1988.5109.

Kurdi, G., Leo, J., Parsia, B., Sattler, U., Al-Emari, S., 2020. A systematic review of automatic question generation for educational purposes. Int. J. Artif. Intell. Educ. 30, 121–204.

Kuznetsov, S.O., 2013a. Fitting pattern structures to knowledge discovery in big data. In: Cellier, P., Distel, F., Ganter, B. (Eds.), Proc. 11th International Conference on Formal Concept Analysis (ICFCA 2013), Lecture Notes in Artificial Intelligence. vol. 7880. Springer, pp. 254–266. 2013.

Kuznetsov, S.O., 2013b. Scalable knowledge discovery in complex data with pattern structures. In: Maji, P., Ghosh, A., Murty, M.N., Ghosh, K., Pal, S.K. (Eds.), Proc. 5th International Conference Pattern Recognition and Machine Intelligence (PReMI'2013), Lecture Notes in Computer Science. vol. 8251. Springer, pp. 30–41.

Lassez, J.L., Marriott, K., 1986. Explicit representation of terms defined by counter examples. In: Nori, K.V. (Ed.), Foundations of Software Technology and Theoretical Computer Science. FSTTCS 1986. Lecture Notes in Computer Science. vol. 241. Springer, Berlin, Heidelberg.

Leo, J., Kurdi, G., Matentzoglu, N., Parsia, B., Forege, S., Donato, G., Dowling, W., 2019. Ontology-based generation of medical, multi-term MCQs. Int. J. Artif. Intell. Educ. 29, 145–188.

Lixto, 2020. From: http://www.lixto.com/. (Accessed 10 July 2020).

Michalski, R.S., 1983. Theory and methodology of inductive learning. Artif. Intell. 20, 111–163.

Mozenda, 2020. From: http://mozenda.com/. (Accessed 10 July 2020).

Ourioupina, O., Galitsky, B., 2001. Application of default reasoning to semantic processing under question-answering. In: DIMACS Tech Report, p. 16.

Plotkin, G.D., 1970. A note on inductive generalization. Mach. Intell. 5 (1), 153–163.

Reiter, R., 1987. A theory of diagnosis from first principles. Artif. Intell. 32, 57–95.

Schulz, A.A., Lassig, J., Gaedke, M., 2016. Practical web data extraction: are we there yet?—a short survey. In: IEEE/WIC/ACM International Conference on Web Intelligence, WI 2016, Omaha, NE, USA, October 13–16 2016. IEEE Computer Society.

Sleiman, H.-A., Corchuelo, R., 2014. Trinity: on using trinary trees for unsupervised web data extraction. IEEE Trans. Knowl. Data Eng. 26 (6), 1544–1556.

Song, L., Wang, Z., Hamza, W., Zhang, Y., Gildea, D., 2018. Leveraging context information for natural question generation. In: NAACL-HLT.

Sowa, J., 2000. Knowledge Representation: Logical, Philosophical, and Computational Foundations. Brooks Cole Publishing Co.

Varlamov, M.I., Turdakov, D.Y., 2016. A survey of methods for the extraction of information from webresources. Program. Comput. Softw. 42 (5), 279–291.

Wang, T., Wan, X., Yao, S., 2020. Better AMR-to-text generation with graph structure reconstruction. In: IJCAI, pp. 3919–3925, https://doi.org/10.24963/ijcai.2020/542.

Xinya, D., Shao, J., Cardie, C., 2017. Learning to ask: neural question generation for reading comprehension. In: ACL.

Yao, X., Bouma, G., Zhang, Y., 2012. Semantics-based question generation and implementation. Dialogue Discourse 3 (2), 11–42.

Yuan, X., Wang, T., Gulcehre, C., Sordoni, A., Bachman, P., Subramanian, S., Zhang, S., Trischler, A., 2017. Machine comprehension by text-to-text neural question generation. In: Rep4NLP@ACL.

Zhao, S., Lan, X., Liu, T., Li, S., 2009. Application-driven statistical paraphrase generation. In: ACL. vol. 2, pp. 834–842.

Zhong, V., Zettlemoyer, L., 2019. E3: Entailment-driven extracting and editing for conversational machine reading. In: Proceedings of the 57th Annual Meeting of the Association for Computational Linguistics. Association for Computational Linguistics, Florence, Italy, pp. 2310–2320.

Zhou, Q., Yang, N., Wei, F., Tan, C., Bao, H., Zhou, M., 2017. Neural question generation from text: a preliminary study. In: NLPCC.

CHAPTER

Relying on discourse analysis to answer complex questions by neural machine reading comprehension

7

Boris Galitsky
Oracle Corporation, Redwood City, CA, United States

1. Introduction

For machine reading comprehension (MRC) based on deep learning (DL), it is important to effectively model the linguistic knowledge from the detail-riddled and lengthy passages. Also, getting rid of the noisy linguistic signals is essential to improve MRC performance. Attentive models, popular in the last few years, attend to all words without explicit constraints, which results in an equal focus on some least important words and phrases. It has been shown that incorporating explicit syntactic (Hu et al., 2018) and semantic (Zhang et al., 2019) constraints into the attention mechanism for better linguistic representation enhances encoding of words. In this work, for a self-attention network (SAN)-sponsored transformer-based encoder, we introduce a discourse enablement design into the SAN to form a self-attention supported by a discourse tree (DT).

A human reader reads most words superficially and pays more attention to the essential ones (Wang et al., 2017). Although a variety of attentive models have been proposed to imitate human learning, most of them, especially global attention methods (Bahdanau et al., 2015), tackle each word equally and attend to all words in a sentence without explicit pruning and prior focus, which results in inaccurate concentration on some less important words (Mudrakarta et al., 2018). For passage-focused MRC, an input sequence always consists of multiple sentences. Most neural attentive methods and language models regard the input sequence as a whole, for example, a passage, with no consideration of the linguistic structure inside each sentence. Because of this, there is a process bias caused by much noise and a lack of associated spans for each concerned word.

It is known in the community that the accuracy of MRC models decreases when answering long questions. If the text is particularly lengthy and contains plenty of details, it would be quite difficult for a neural model to process it and build an internal representation. This is because a DL approach is affected by noise and does not differentiate between text fragments (Zhang et al., 2019). At the same time, human readers process sentences efficiently, at the level of concepts, by taking a sequence of fixation and saccades after a quick first glance (Galitsky et al., 2010; Yu et al., 2017).

Artificial Intelligence for Healthcare Applications and Management. https://doi.org/10.1016/B978-0-12-824521-7.00012-0

Recent work (Roth and Lapata, 2016; He et al., 2018; Marcheggiani and Titov, 2017) indicates that neural network models could see even greater accuracy gains by leveraging syntactic information rather than ignoring it. Many of the errors made by a syntax-free neural network MRC are tied to certain syntactic confusions such as prepositional phrase attachment and show that while constrained inference using a relatively low-accuracy predicted parse can provide small improvements in MRC, providing a high-quality syntactic and semantic parse leads to substantial gains.

In this chapter, we explore if/how discourse-level features, fed to a neural MRC on top of syntactic and semantic features or independently, can help answer complex, long, multi-sentence questions (Galitsky, 2019a). Providing exact, concise answers frequently requires not just syntactic/meaning similarity but also an overall structure of thoughts expressed by an author of a text (Galitsky et al., 2013, Fig. 1).

We intend to develop a neural method that selects important words by considering only the related subset of words of syntactic, semantic, and discourse-level importance inside each input sentence explicitly. With a guidance of syntactic structure clues, the linguistic features-guided method is expected to give more accurate attentive signals and reduce the impact of the noise introduced by lengthy sentences (Galitsky, 2003).

We refer the reader to Chapter 3 for an introduction to discourse analysis.

FIG. 1

Discourse analysis can help MRC find exact answers for complex, abstract questions.

2. Examples where discourse analysis is essential for MRC

We start with an example of text (passage), a question, and an incorrect answer delivered by the baseline MRC (Fig. 2).

Viruses, bacteria, and fungi can all cause pneumonia. In the United States, common causes of viral pneumonia are influenza and respiratory syncytial virus. A common cause of bacterial pneumonia is Streptococcus pneumoniae. However, clinicians are not always able to find out which germ caused someone to get sick with pneumonia.

Q: Who experiences difficulties finding causes for pneumonia?

MRC fails miserably here associating *virus, bacteria, and fungi* with *Who*. Also, MRC failed to match the question with the sentence "*However, clinicians are not always able to find out which germ caused someone to get sick with pneumonia*," but it should have.

The DT for the question Q is more detailed and contains shorter elementary discourse units (EDUs) than usually delivered by discourse parsers. It is used here for illustrative purposes. Also, the rhetorical relation of *Cause* is unreliable in most discourse parsers and its detection is based on specific enhancement targeting infrequent rhetorical relations associated with explanation, argumentation, and other discourse links between EDUs (Galitsky, 2017b, Fig. 3).

We establish a correspondence between the question Q and the passage P. A mapping is formed between: Q: *Attribution* → P: *Attribution*, Q: *Cause* → P: *Cause*, Q: "*causes*" → P: "*caused*." In addition, there is a mapping at the syntactic level (Fig. 4).

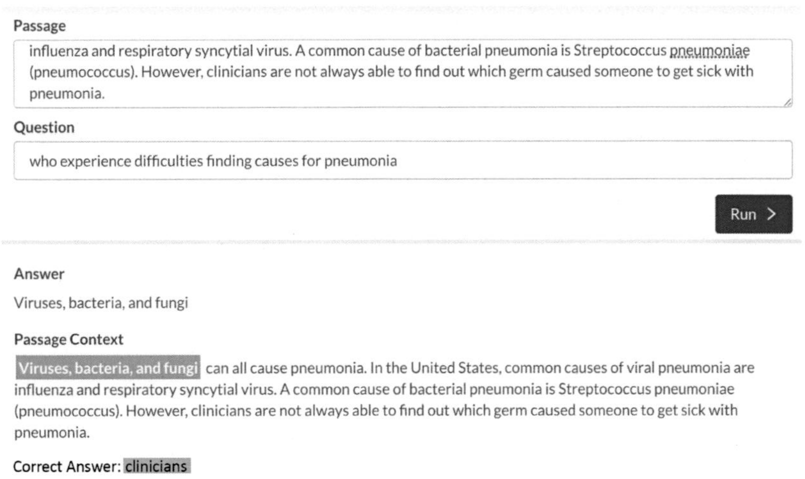

Passage

influenza and respiratory syncytial virus. A common cause of bacterial pneumonia is Streptococcus pneumoniae (pneumococcus). However, clinicians are not always able to find out which germ caused someone to get sick with pneumonia.

Question

who experience difficulties finding causes for pneumonia

Run >

Answer

Viruses, bacteria, and fungi

Passage Context

Viruses, bacteria, and fungi can all cause pneumonia. In the United States, common causes of viral pneumonia are influenza and respiratory syncytial virus. A common cause of bacterial pneumonia is Streptococcus pneumoniae (pneumococcus). However, clinicians are not always able to find out which germ caused someone to get sick with pneumonia.

Correct Answer: clinicians

FIG. 2

ELMo embeddings-based MRC frequently experiences difficulties answering questions about complex (causal) relationships between entities.

DT for Passage (P):

contrast
 elaboration
  TEXT:Viruses , bacteria , and fungi can all cause pneumonia .
  elaboration
   cause
    TEXT:Common causes of viral pneumonia are
    TEXT:influenza and respiratory syncytial virus .
   TEXT:A common cause of bacterial pneumonia is Streptococcus pneumoniae .
 attribution
  TEXT:However , clinicians are not always able to find out
  cause
   TEXT:which germ caused someone
   TEXT:to get sick with pneumonia .

DT for question (Q):

attribution
 TEXT:Who experience difficulties
 cause
  TEXT:finding causes
  TEXT:for pneumonia ?

FIG. 3

The discourse tree (DT) for text from which to choose an answer (top) and for the question (bottom) with the mappings between corresponding nodes.

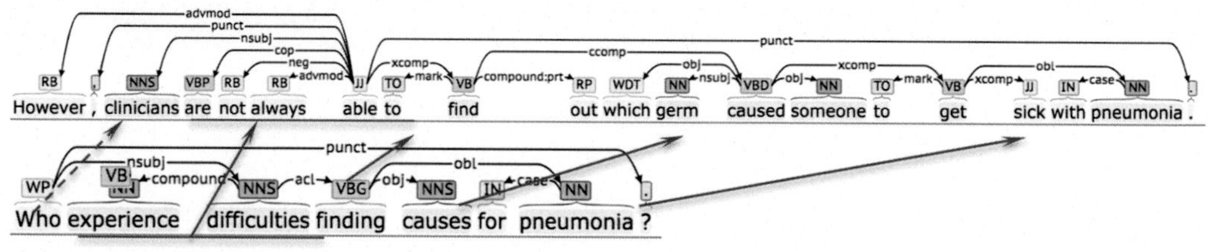

FIG. 4

A mapping between syntactic trees for Q and A.

Solid arrows show mapping between the words "*causes*" → "*caused,*" "*pneumonia*" → "*pneumonia,*" "*finding*" → "*find*" and synonymous phrase "*experiences difficulties*" → "*are not always able to.*"

The dashed line shows the target mapping delivering the correct answer "*Who*" → "*clinicians.*"

3. Discourse dataset

In this section, we proceed with our presentation of discourse analysis, started in Chapter 2. Over the last decade, PDTB-2 (Prasad et al., 2008) has been the most popular manually annotated discourse dataset. It was the largest public repository of annotated discourse relations (more than 43,000), including more than 18,400 signaled by explicit discourse connectives (coordinating or subordinating conjunctions, or discourse adverbials). In the corpus, discourse relations comprise two arguments labeled Arg1 and Arg2, with each relation anchored by either an explicit discourse connective or an adjacency.

The substantial amount of data and availability of the PDTB-2 initiated the work on shallow discourse parsing.

With the release of the PDTB-3, there are now about 12,500 additional intra-sentential relations annotated (i.e., relations that lie wholly within the projection of a top-level S-node) and about 1000 additional inter-sentential relations (Webber et al., 2019). Work on shallow discourse parsing consistently shows that recognizing implicit discourse relations is much more difficult than recognizing explicit discourse relations; therefore, the focus of PDTB-3 is the implicit relations. Also, assigning sense-labels to implicit relations needs more data to automatically learn implicit relations. In PDTB-3, implicit rhetorical relations can hold within sentences as well as between them (Liang et al., 2020).

Of more than 13,000 additional discourse relations annotated in the PDTB-3, more than 95% occur within individual sentences. These are most important for Q/A since they tell which EDU is most suitable as an answer. Within a sentence, implicit relations occur at the boundaries of syntactic forms:

"*After a slow start, Treasury bonds were buoyed by a late burst of buying,* [→therefore] *to end slightly higher*." The Connector here is "*therefore*" and rhetorical relation is *Result*. This helps answer questions of the sort "*What caused/lead to* <*to*-clause>?" in particular, "*What caused the bonds to close higher?*"

PDTB-3 annotations indicate implicit relations that co-occur with explicit relations (Rohde et al., 2018), as a way of indicating a relation that was not obtained from the explicit connective but instead derived from what can be inferred from the arguments themselves:

"*Exxon Corp. built the plant but (Implicit=then) closed it in 1985*"

PDTB-3 rhetorical relation is {COMPARISON.CONCESSION.ARG2-AS-DENIER, TEMPORAL.ASYNCHRONOUS.PRECEDENCE}

This discourse information helps to answer questions about a history of events with *plant*, such as "*When open … and when closed …*"

Table 1 shows a distribution of inter-sentential/intra-sentential implicit relations among discourse relation labels and the proportion of selected label with respect to inter-sentential/intra-sentential implicit relations (Liang et al., 2020). The total numbers of all implicit relations used in annotation are more than 15,000 inter-sentence and 6000 intra-sentence.

Table 1 compares the distribution of inter-sentential and intra-sentential implicit relations with respect to the rhetorical relation labels, along with the proportion of each label to the total inter-sentential

Table 1 Frequencies of specific rhetorical relations.

Relation	Inter-sentence		Intra-sentence	
	#	%	#	%
Concession	1355	8.70	136	2.19
Contrast	700	4.50	156	2.51
Cause	4153	26.67	1613	25.97
Purpose	19	0.12	1351	21.76
Equivalence	286	1.84	48	0.77
Level-of-detail	2644	16.98	589	9.48

FIG. 5

A wife is discovering implicit relationships of her husband, looking at his mask (left). A wife swears she did not cheat on her husband (right).

and intra-sentential implicit relations. For instance, relations for *Purpose* occupy 21.76% of intra-sentential implicit relations, while only 0.12% of inter-sentential implicit relations. At the same time, relations for *Instantiation* constitute 8.89% of inter-sentential implicit ones, while only 1.4% of intra-sentential implicit relations. Besides differences in frequency, the senses of inter-sentential implicit relations are more unequally distributed. A triple of relation classes—{*Contigency.Cause*, *Expansion.Conjunction* and LevelOfDetail}—cover more than two-thirds of the inter-sentential implicit relations. However, except for *Contigency.Cause* and *Purpose*, most of the other intra-sentential implicit relations are more evenly distributed. As frequently occurs with training on an imbalanced dataset, the unequal distribution of inter-sentential relations forces the model to predict the majority class, skipping minority classes.

Being enriched with more fine-grade and implicit rhetorical relation, PDTB-3 can support much broader classes of abstract, general search queries than PDTB-2. In addition, leveraging the possibility to store multiple relations between the same discourse units (Rohde et al., 2018), Q/A can cover a richer set of questions related to these multiple relations. The authors test how a joint presence of rhetorical relations can lead annotators to tag seemingly divergent conjunctions (e.g., *but* and *so*) to express the link they observe between two segments. As a result, both *why-contradiction* and *why-result* types of questions can be successfully handled. Hence implicit relationships are fairly important (Fig. 5).

There are two relations (Fig. 5) between EDUs: one is explicit (*Condition*) and another is implicit (*Result*)

{**condition, result**}:

TEXT: I will fall into a hole
TEXT: if I cheat on you at least once

4. Discourse parsing

Any coherent text is structured so that we can derive and interpret the information. This structure shows how discourse units (text spans such as sentences or clauses) are connected and related to each other. Discourse analysis aims to reveal this structure. Several theories have been proposed in the past to describe the discourse structure, among which the Rhetorical Structure Theory (RST) (Mann and Thompson, 1988) is one of the most popular. RST divides a text into EDUs. It then forms a tree representation of a discourse called a discourse tree (DT) using rhetorical relations such as *Elaboration and Explanation* as edges, and EDUs as leaves. EDUs are linked by a rhetorical relation and are also distinguished based on their relative importance in conveying the author's message; nucleus is the central part, whereas satellite is the peripheral part.

Fig. 6 shows an example DT with four EDUs spanning two sentences. In this DT, EDUs are hierarchically connected with arrows and the rhetorical relation *Elaboration*. The direction of arrows indicates the nuclearity of relations, wherein a Satellite points to its Nucleus. The satellite unit is a supporting sentence for the nucleus unit and contains less prominent information. It is standard practice that the DT is trained and evaluated in a right-heavy binary manner, resulting in three forms of binary nuclearity relationships between EDUs: Nucleus-Satellite, Satellite-Nucleus, and Nucleus-Nucleus.

An exploration of coherence relations in frameworks such as RST (Mann and Thompson 1988b), SDRT (Segmented Discourse Representation Theory, Asher and Lascarides, 2003), and PDTB (Penn Discourse TreeBank, Miltsakaki et al., 2004), has experienced a revival in the last decade, in English and a few other languages (Matthiessen and Teruya, 2015; Maziero et al., 2015; da Cunha, 2016; Iruskieta et al., 2016; Zeldes, 2016, 2017). Multiple teams are actively developing discourse parsers (Feng and Hirst, 2014; Joty et al., 2015; Surdeanu et al., 2015; Braud et al., 2017). Although evaluation of results in discourse parsing has proven complicated (see Morey et al., 2017), and progress in integrating results across discourse treebanking frameworks has been slow, several applications of discourse analysis steadily grow. Discourse parsers are used in sentiment analysis in patient complaints, argumentation mining in health disputes, summarization of medical notes, medical question answering, and machine translation evaluation (Benamara et al., 2017; Durrett et al., 2016; Peldszus and Stede, 2016; Scarton et al., 2016; Schouten and Frasincar, 2016).

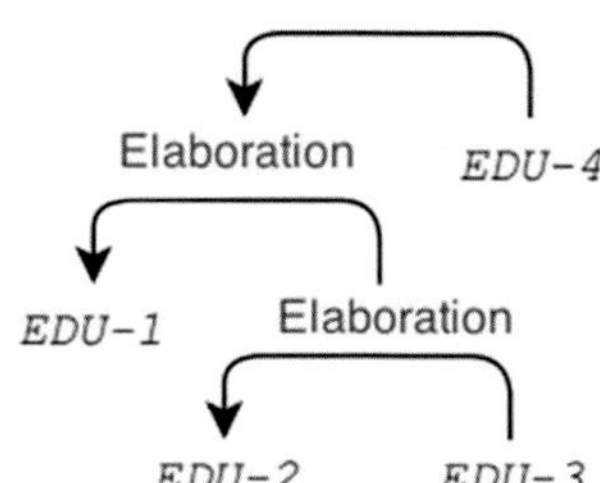

EDU-1: Roy E. Parrott, the company's president and chief operating officer since Sept. 1, was named to its board.
EDU-2: The appointment increased the number of directors to 10,
EDU-3: three of whom are company employees.
EDU-4: Simpson is an auto parts maker.

FIG. 6

An example discourse tree (DT).

Work on RST parsing has been dominated by the bottom-up paradigm (Hernault et al., 2010; Feng and Hirst, 2014; Ji and Eisenstein, 2014). This method produces very competitive benchmarks, but in practice it is not a straightforward approach (e.g., transition-based parser with actions prediction steps). Furthermore, bottom-up parsing limits the tree construction to local information, and macro context such as global structure/topic is prone to underutilization. As a result, there has recently been a move toward top-down approaches (Kobayashi et al., 2020).

The goal of top-down parsing is to identify splitting locations in each iteration of the DT construction. Koto et al. (2021) formulated discourse parsing as a sequence-labeling task; given a sequence of input EDUs, identify a segmentation boundary to split this sequence into two sub-sequences. This is implemented by training a sequence-labeling model to predict a binary label for each EDU and select the EDU with the highest probability to be the segmentation point. After the sequence is segmented, the same process is repeated for the two sub-sequences in a divide-and-conquer fashion, until all sequences are segmented into individual units, producing the DT.

Fig. 7 shows an iterative segmentation process to construct the RST tree. In each iteration, a sequence is popped from the queue that contains the original sequence of EDUs of the document. The segmentation label for each EDU is computed using a transformer. Once the sequence is segmented leveraging the ground truth label during training (or the highest-probability label at test time), the two sub-sequences are pushed to the queue for the segmented pairs. The EDU encodings are averaged for the segments and fed to a multi-layered perceptron (MLP) layer to predict the nuclearity and discourse labels.

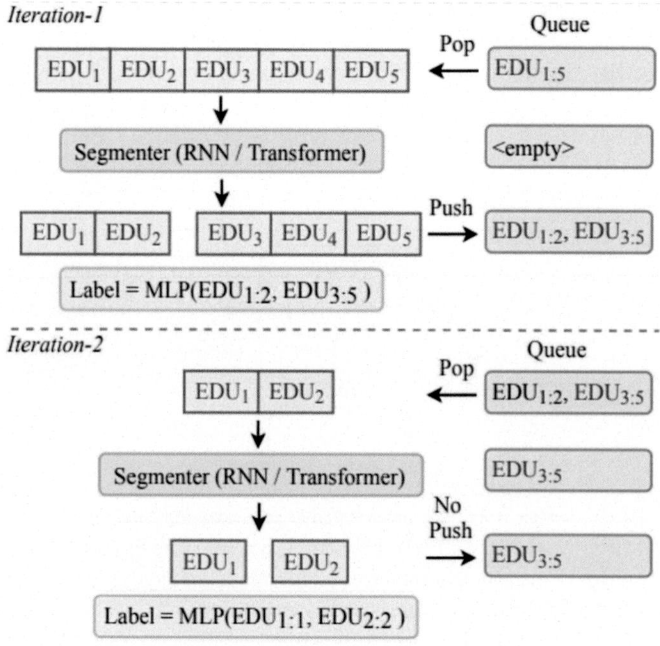

FIG. 7

Building segmentation and predicting rhetorical relations.

5. Incorporating syntax into model

Syntactic information helps to deal with unanswerable questions. Whereas previously developed methods are not well suited to find potential candidates for unanswerable questions, He et al. (2018) addressed this problem by relying on an independent span loss that focuses on the answer-extraction task regardless of the answerability of the question. To avoid conflicts with no-answer recognition, the authors leverage a multi-head pointer network to generate two pairs of span scores, where one pair is normalized with the no-answer score and the other is used for our auxiliary loss.

Independent span loss is designed to concentrate on answer extraction. In this task, the model is asked to extract candidate answers for all possible questions. Therefore, besides questions that can be answered, He et al. (2018) also include the cases of questions that cannot be answered as positive examples, and consider the plausible answer as a gold answer. To not conflict with no-answer detection, the authors proposed using a multi-head pointer network to additionally produce another pair of span scores

$\widetilde{\alpha}$ and $\widetilde{\beta}$:

$$\widetilde{o}_j = \widetilde{w}_v^T v_j, \quad \widetilde{t} = \sum_{j=1}^{l_q} \frac{e^{\widetilde{o}_j}}{\sum_{k=1}^{l_q} e^{\widetilde{o}_k}} v_j$$

$$\widetilde{\alpha}, \widetilde{\beta} = \text{pointer\_network}\left(U, \widetilde{t}\right)$$

where multiple heads share the same network architecture but with different parameters. Then, the independent span loss is defined as:

$$\mathcal{L}_{indep-I} = -\log\left(\frac{e^{\widetilde{\alpha}_{\widetilde{a}} \widetilde{\beta}_{\widetilde{b}}}}{\sum_{i=1}^{l_p} \sum_{j=1}^{l_p} e^{\widetilde{\alpha}_i \widetilde{\beta}_j}}\right)$$

where $\widetilde{a}$ and $\widetilde{\beta}$ are the augmented ground-truth answer boundaries. The final span probability is computed using a simple mean pooling over the two pairs of softmax normalized span scores.

To exclusively encourage the prediction on no-answer detection, an independent no-answer loss is computed as:

$$\mathcal{L}_{indep-II} = -(1-\delta)\log\sigma(z) - \delta\log(1-\sigma(z))$$

where σ is the sigmoid activation function. Relying on this loss, the model is believed to produce a more confident prediction on no-answer score z without considering the shared-normalization operation.

The limitation of this approach to detect the no-answer situation is its probabilistic nature, where the syntactic generalization approach directly fails to align a foreign answer with a question, explicitly indicating the syntactic features making this generalization impossible (Galitsky et al., 2010; Galitsky and Ilvovsky, 2019).

Several researchers observe that the accuracy of MRC models decreases when answering long questions (Galitsky, 2021a). Usually, if a document is lengthy and riddled with details, it would be hard for a DL model to comprehend and represent it properly because it suffers from noise. It is hard for such a model to pay attention to individual text fragments and even harder to accurately answer questions. In addition, for passage-involved reading comprehension, an input sequence always consists of multiple sentences. Nearly all the current attentive methods and language models treat the input sequence as a

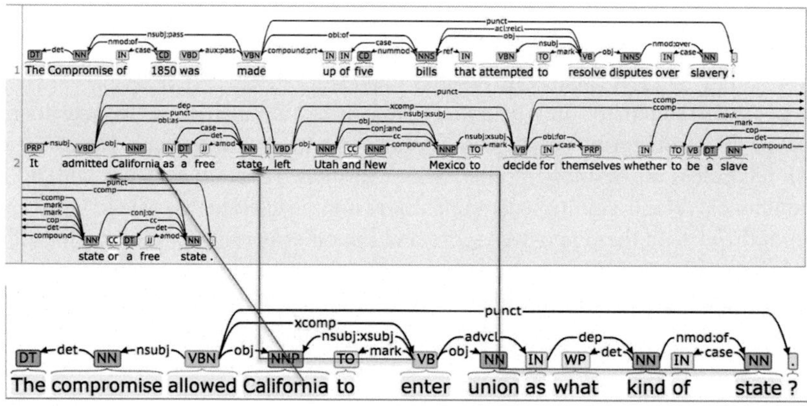

FIG. 8

A mapping between Q and Passage.

whole (e.g., a passage) with no consideration of the internal linguistic structure inside each sentence. This would result in process bias caused by much noise and a lack of associated spans for each concerned word.

Zhang et al. (2019) designed an effective algorithm that can selectively choose important words by considering only the related subset of syntactically coordinated words inside each input sentence explicitly. With the assistance of syntactic structure signals, the syntax-driven method could give precise attentive signals and reduce the impact of the noise introduced by lengthy sentences. The authors extend the self-attention mechanism with syntax-driven constraints, to capture syntax-related parts with each concerned word. Zhang et al. (2019) leveraged pre-trained dependency syntactic parse tree structure to yield the relevant nodes for each word in a sentence by treating each word as a child node; the *syntactic dependency of interest* consists of all its ancestor nodes and itself in the dependency parsing tree.

Passage: *The Compromise of 1850 was made up of five bills that attempted to resolve disputes over slavery. It admitted California as a free state, left Utah and New Mexico to decide for themselves whether to be a slave state or a free state.*

Q: *The compromise allowed California to enter the Union as what kind of state?*

Zhang et al. (2019) illustrated syntax-guided span-based Q/A as computing the *syntactic dependency of interest* between matching words such as *state.*

We have the mapping between Q and Passage: *California→California, enter→admitted, state→state*, and, therefore, *kind→free*, so we have the answer=*free* as a result of syntactic generalization (Fig. 8, Galitsky, 2016).

6. Attention mechanism for the sequence of tokens

Language modeling tools such as recurrent neural networks (RNNs) are believed to be closely associated with human reading behavior (Frank and Bod, 2011). RNNs treat each sentence as a sequence of words and recursively compose each word with its previous memory until the meaning of the whole sentence has been derived. In practice, however, sequence-level networks are met with at least three challenges. The first one concerns model training problems associated with vanishing and exploding gradients (Bengio et al., 1994), which can be partially ameliorated with gated activation functions, such as the Long Short-Term Memory. The second issue relates to memory compression problems. As the input sequence gets compressed and blended into a single dense vector, sufficiently large memory capacity is required to store past information. As a result, the network generalizes poorly to long sequences while wasting memory on shorter ones. Finally, it should be acknowledged that sequence-level networks lack a mechanism for handling the structure of the input. This imposes an inductive bias that is at odds with the fact that language has an inherent structure. In this chapter, we develop a text-processing system that addresses these limitations while maintaining the incremental, generative property of a recurrent language model.

Recent attempts to turn neural network algorithms into more structure-aware ones have seen the incorporation of external memories in the context of RNNs. The idea is to use multiple memory slots outside the recurrence to piece-wise store representations of the input. Read and write operations for each slot can be modeled as an attention mechanism with a recurrent controller.

Cheng et al. (2016) leveraged memory and attention to empower a recurrent network with stronger memorization capability and more importantly the ability to discover relations among tokens. This was realized by inserting a memory network module in the update of a recurrent network together with attention for memory referencing. The attention acts as an inductive module identifying relations between input tokens and is trained in an unsupervised manner.

Fig. 9 illustrates the reading behavior of the proposed architecture, Long Short-Term Memory-Network (LSTMN). The underscore represents the current word being fixated and *blue* represents memories. Shading indicates the degree of memory activation. The model processes text incrementally while learning the past tokens in the memory and to what extent they relate to the current token being processed. As a result, the model induces undirected relations among tokens as an intermediate step of learning representations. Cheng et al. (2016) assessed the performance of the LSTMN in language

The hospital is releasing a patient with the pneumonia
The hospital is releasing a patient with the pneumonia
The hospital is releasing a patient with the pneumonia
The hospital is releasing a patient with the pneumonia
The hospital is releasing a patient with the pneumonia
The hospital is releasing a patient with the pneumonia
The hospital is releasing a patient with the pneumonia
The hospital is releasing a patient with the pneumonia
The hospital is releasing a patient with the pneumonia

FIG. 9

The reading behavior of the proposed LSTMN architecture (left). A sequence of word tokens to be accepted by LSTMN (right).

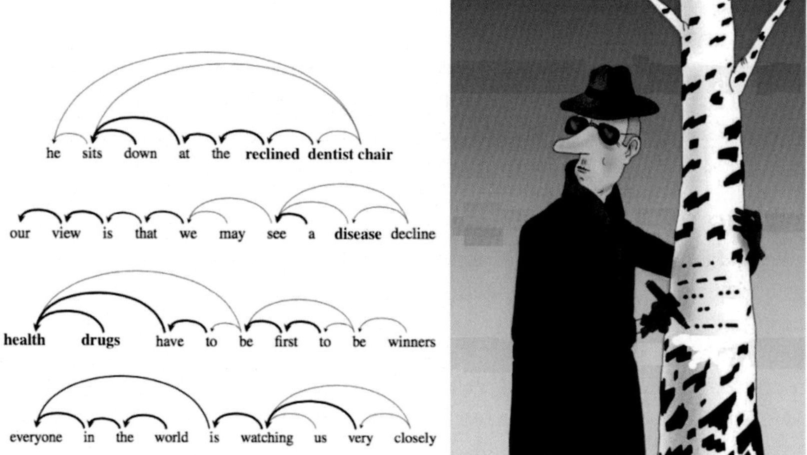

FIG. 10

Examples of intra-attention (language modeling, left). On the right, neural encoding is shown as done by a spy.

modeling, sentiment analysis, and natural language inference (NLI). In all cases, LSTMN models are trained end-to-end with task-specific supervision signals, exceeding or matching the performance of the state-of-the-art models and superior to vanilla LSTMs.

Cheng et al. (2016) also studied the memory activation mechanism of the machine reader by visualizing the attention scores. Fig. 10 shows four sentences sampled from the Penn Treebank validation set. Although the reader is directed to attend to any memory slot, much attention focuses on recent memories. This agrees with the linguistic intuition that long-term dependencies are relatively rare and are important only if discourse analysis confirms so.

Bold lines indicate higher attention scores. Arrows denote which word is being focused on when attention is computed, but not the direction of the relation. As illustrated in Fig. 10, the model captures some valid lexical relations (e.g., the dependency between *sits* and *at*, *sits* and *chair*, *everyone* and *is*, *is* and *watching*). Note that arcs here are undirected and are different from the directed arcs denoting head-modifier relations in dependency graphs.

7. Enabling attention mechanism with syntactic features

Fig. 11 depicts the model that first directly takes the output representations from an SAN-empowered transformer-based encoder, then builds syntactic parse tree-based SAN representations. Finally, the syntax-enhanced combined representation is passed to task-specific layers for final predictions.

To use the relationship between the headword and dependent words provided by the syntactic dependency tree of a sentence, the scope of attention is restrained to only the link between the word and all its ancestor headwords. Each word only needs to be attended to words of syntactic importance in a sentence; the ancestor headwords are linked to the child word. As shown in Fig. 12, instead of taking

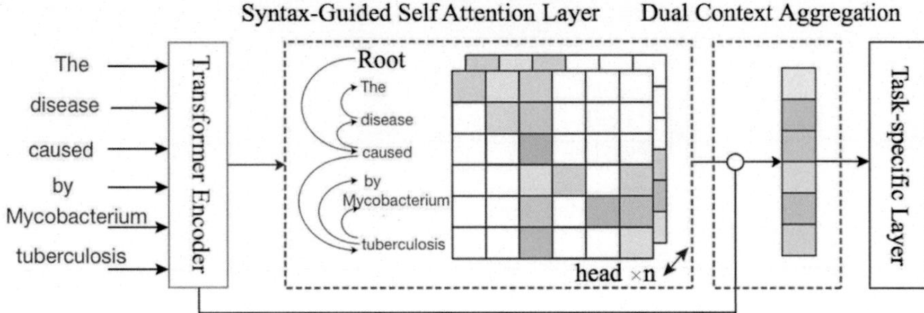

FIG. 11

A transformer architecture with syntax-guided SAN.

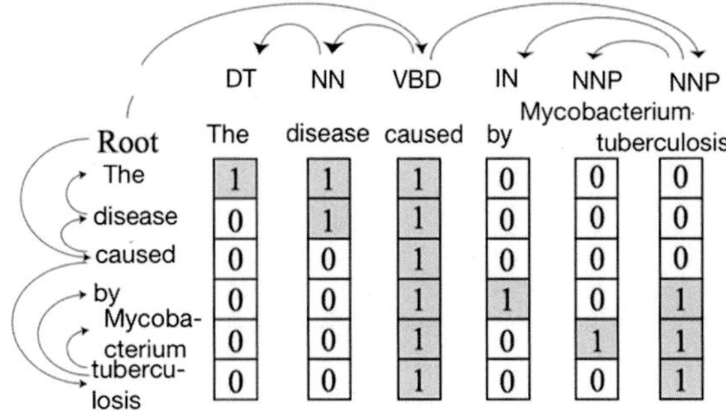

FIG. 12

Encoding syntactic relations.

attention with each word in the whole passage, the word *tuberculosis* only makes attention with its ancestor headwords and dependent words {*cased*, *by*, *Mycobacterium*, itself} in this sentence.

The basis for the syntactically enabled model of Strubell et al. (2018) is the transformer encoder introduced by Vaswani et al. (2017); word embeddings are transformed into contextually encoded token representations using stacked multi-head SAN and feed-forward layers. To include syntax, one self-attention head is trained to attend to the syntactic parent of each token, allowing the model to use this attention head to represent syntactic dependencies.

Word embeddings are input to J layers of multi-head self-attention (Fig. 13). In layer p one attention head is trained to attend to parse parents (Fig. 14). Layer r is an input for a joint predicate/part-of-speech (POS) classifier. Representations from layer r corresponding to predicted predicates are passed to a bilinear operation that ranks distinct predicate and role representations to produce per-token semantic role labeling predictions with respect to each predicted predicate.

Fig. 14 shows the syntactically informed SAN for the query word *disease*. The attention weights A_{parse} heavily weight the token's syntactic driver, *observed*, in a weighted average over the token values V_{parse}. The other attention heads act as usual, and the attended representations from all heads

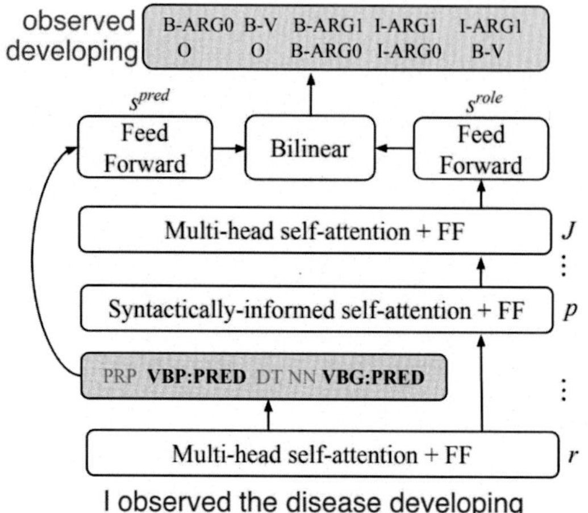

FIG. 13

Multi-head self-attention.

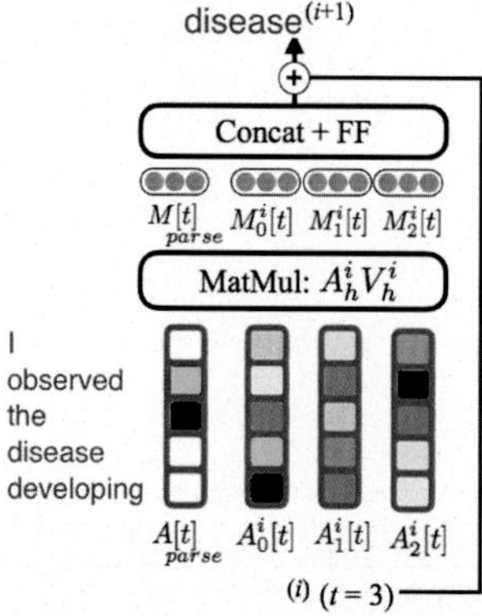

FIG. 14

Syntactically informed self-attention.

are concatenated and projected through a feed-forward layer to produce the syntactically informed representation for *disease*.

The model is designed for the more realistic setting in which gold predicates are not provided at test time. The model predicts predicates and integrates POS information into earlier layers by repurposing representations closer to the input to predict predicate and POS tags using hard parameter sharing. The optimization is reduced, and leverages shared statistical estimates derived from highly correlated POS and predicates by treating tagging and predicate detection as a single task. A multi-class classification into the joint Cartesian product space of POS and predicate labels is then conducted. Though typical models, which re-encode the sentence for each predicate, can simplify semantic role labeling to token-wise tagging, the joint model of Strubell et al. (2018) requires a different approach to classify semantic roles of each predicate. Contextually encoded tokens are projected to distinct predicate and role embeddings, and each predicted predicate is ranked with the sequence's role representations using a bilinear model, producing per-label scores for the represented semantic role labels for each token.

A multi-head SAN token encoder has been shown to achieve state-of-the-art performance in semantic role labeling tasks, providing a means for incorporating syntax. The input to the network is a sequence X of T token representations x_t. In the standard setting, these token representations are initialized to pre-trained word embeddings. These input embeddings are projected to a representation of the same cardinality as the output of the SAN layers. A positional encoding vector is then added, computed as a deterministic sinusoidal function of t. This token representation is then supplied as an input to a series of J residual multi-head SAN layers with feed-forward connections. Denoting the jth self-attention layer as $T^{(j)}(\cdot)$, the output of that layer $s_t^{(j)}$, and $LN(\cdot)$ layer normalization, the following recurrence applied to initial input $c_t^{(p)}$:

$$s_t^{(j)} = LN\left(s_t^{(j-1)}\right) + T^{(j)}\left(s_t^{(j-1)}\right)$$

gives our final token representations $s_t^{(j)}$. Each $T^{(j)}(\cdot)$ consists of:

(1) multi-head self-attention
(2) a feed-forward projection

The multi-head self-attention consists of H attention heads, each of which learns a distinct attention function to attend to all the tokens in the sequence. This self-attention is run for each token for each head, and the results of the H self-attentions are merged to form the final self-attended representation for each token.

Let us consider the matrix $S^{(j-1)}$ of T token representations at layer $j-1$. For each attention head h, we project this matrix into distinct key, value, and query representations $K_h^{(j)}$, $V_h^{(j)}$, and $Q_h^{(j)}$ of dimensions $T \times d_k$, $T \times d_q$, and $T \times d_q$, respectively. Then $K_h^{(j)}$ is multiplied by $Q_h^{(j)}$ to obtain a $T \times T$ matrix of attention weights $A_h^{(j)}$ between each pair of tokens in the sentence. Following Vaswani et al. (2017), the scaled dot-product attention is performed: the weights are scaled by the inverse square root of their embedding dimension and normalized with the softmax function to produce a distinct distribution for each token over all the tokens in the sentence:

$$A_h^{(j)} = \text{softmax}\left(d_k^{-1/2} Q_h^{(j)} K_h^{(j)T}\right).$$

These attention weights are then multiplied by $V_h^{(j)}$ for each token to obtain the self-attended token representations $M_h^{(j)}$: $M_h^{(j)} = A_h^{(j)} V_h^{(j)}$.

Row t of $M_h^{(j)}$, the SAN representation for token t at layer j, is thus the weighted sum with respect to t (with weights given by $A_h^{(j)}$) over the token representations in $V_h^{(j)}$.

The output of the feed-forward is added to the initial representation and a layer normalization is performed to give the final output of self-attention layer j.

Typically, neural attention algorithms learn to attend to relevant inputs independently. Instead, a training of the SAN to attend to specific tokens corresponds to the discourse structure of the paragraph as a mechanism for passing linguistic knowledge to later layers. Specifically, one attention head is replaced with the deep bi-affine model of Dozat and Manning (2017), trained to predict syntactic dependencies. Let A_{parse} be the discourse parse attention weights at layer i. Its input is the matrix of token representations $S^{(i-1)}$. As with the other attention heads, we project $S^{(i-1)}$ into key, value, and query representations, denoted by K_{parse}, Q_{parse}, and V_{parse}. Here the key and query projections correspond to parent and dependent representations of the tokens, and we allow their dimensions to differ from the rest of the attention heads. Unlike the other attention heads that use a dot product to score key-query pairs, the compatibility between K_{parse} and Q_{parse} is ranked using a bi-affine operator U_{heads} to obtain attention weights:

$$A_{parse} = \text{softmax}\left(Q_{parse}\, U_{heads}\, K_{parse}{}^{T}\right).$$

These attention weights are used to compose a weighted average of the value representations V_{parse} as in the other attention heads.

An auxiliary supervision is applied at this attention head to encourage it to attend to each token's parent in an entity DT and to encode information about the token's dependency label in discourse and syntactic dependency trees. Denoting the attention weight from token t to a candidate head q as A_{parse} [t, q], the probability of token t having parent q is modeled as:

$$P(q = head(t) \mid X) = A_{parse}\,[t, q].$$

using the attention weights A_{parse} [t] as the distribution over possible heads for token t. The root token is defined as one having a self-loop. This attention head thus emits a directed graph where each token's parent is the token to which the attention A_{parse} assigns the highest weight. Dependency labels are predicted using per-class bi-affine operations between parent and dependent representations Q_{parse}, and K_{parse}, to produce per-label scores, with locally normalized probabilities over dependency labels y_t^{dep} given by the softmax function.

This attention head now drives linguistic features, providing a discourse and syntactic dependency parse to downstream layers. This model not only predicts its own dependency arcs but also allows for the incorporation of the auxiliary parse information at test time by simply setting A_{parse} to the parse parents produced by the discourse and syntactic parsers. In this way, the model can benefit from improved, external parsing models without re-training. Unlike typical multi-task models, this algorithm maintains the ability to leverage external syntactic information.

8. Including discourse structure into the model

Given input token sequence $S = \{s_1, s_2, \ldots, s_n\}$ of length n, we first subject it to syntactic parsing to generate a dependency tree. Then, the ancestor node set P_i is derived for each word s_i traversing the dependency tree. Finally, a syntactic dependency of interest sequence of mask M is obtained, organized as n * n matrix, and elements in each row denote the dependency mask of all words to the row-index word. Obviously, if M [i, j] = 1, it means that token s_i is the ancestor node of token s_j.

$$M[ij] = \begin{cases} 1, & \text{if} j \in P_i \text{or} j = i \\ 0, & \text{otherwise.} \end{cases}$$

The last layer output H is projected from the vanilla transformer into the distinct key, value, and query representations of dimensions $<L \times d_k, L \times d_q, L \times d_v>$, respectively, denoted as $<K_i'\ Q_i'\ V_i'>$ for each head word i. Then a dot product is computed to score key-query pairs with the dependency of interest mask to obtain attention weights of dimension $L \times L$, denoted A_0:

$$A_i' = \text{softmax}\left(\frac{M \cdot (Q_i' K_i' T)}{\sqrt{d_k}}\right).$$

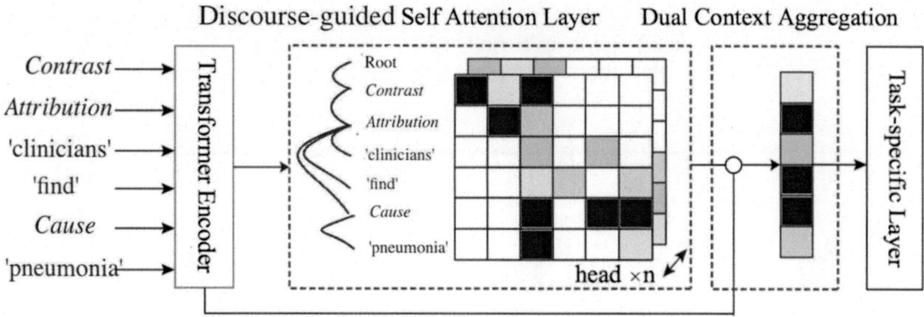

FIG. 15

An architecture of incorporating discourse structure.

The attention weight A_i' is then multiplied by V_i' to obtain the syntax-driven token representations: $W_i' = A_i' V_i' \cdot W_i'$, for all heads are concatenated and passed through a feed-forward layer. After passing through another feed-forward layer, a layer normalization is applied to the sum of output and initial representation to obtain the final representation, denoted as $H_0' = \{h_0', h_1', \ldots, h_n'\}$ (Fig. 15).

9. Pre-trained language models and their semantic extensions

Distributed representations have been widely used as a standard part of Natural Language Processing (NLP) models due to the ability to capture the local co-occurrence of words from large scale unlabeled text (Mikolov et al., 2013). However, these approaches for learning word vectors involve only a single, context-independent representation for each word with little consideration of contextual encoding in sentence level. Thus recently introduced contextual language models including ELMo (Peters et al., 2018), GPT, BERT, and XLNet fill the gap by strengthening the contextual sentence modeling for better representation, among which BERT uses a different pre-training objective, masked language model, which allows capturing both sides of context, left and right. In addition, BERT introduces a next sentence prediction task that jointly pre-trains text-pair representations. Recent studies show that contextual language models are powerful and convenient for downstream natural language understanding (NLU) tasks.

However, several studies have found DL models might not really understand the NL queries (Mudrakarta et al., 2018) and are vulnerable to adversarial attacks (Jia and Liang, 2017). Frequently, DL models pay great attention to non-significant words and ignore important ones; current NLU models suffer from insufficient contextual semantic representation and learning. Zhang et al. (2020) proposed to enable BERT with SRL. Semantics-aware BERT with explicit contextual semantic features learns the representation in a fine-grained manner, combining the strengths of BERT on plain context representation and an explicit semantic analysis for deeper meaning representation.

Semantic BERT is intended to handle multiple sequence inputs. In semantic BERT, words in the input sequence are passed to SRL to obtain multiple predicate-derived structures to form a semantic embedding. In parallel, the input sequence is segmented to subwords (if any) by the BERT word-piece tokenizer, then the subword representation is transformed back to word level via a convolutional layer

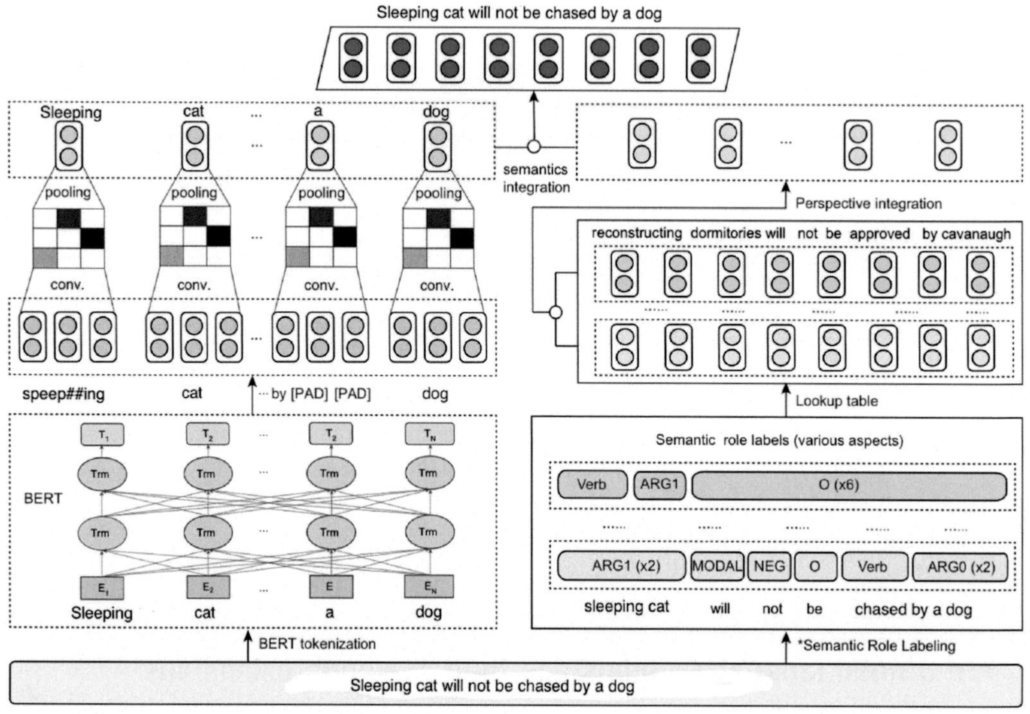

FIG. 16

Semantics-aware BERT.

to obtain the contextual word representations. Finally, the word representations and semantic embedding are concatenated to form the joint representation (Fig. 16).

For the text, {*Sleeping cat will not be chased by a dog*}, it is tokenized to a subword-level sequence, {*Sleep, ##ing, cat, will, not, be, chas, ##ed, by, a, dog*}

As to the word-level semantic structures, they are: [ARG1: sleeping cat] [ARGM-MOD: will] [ARGM-NEG: not] be [V: chased] [ARG0: by a dog]

[V: sleeping] [ARG1: cat] will not be chased by a dog

9.1 Encoding and alignment with BERT

The raw text sequences and semantic role label sequences are firstly represented as embedding vectors to feed a pretrained BERT. The input sentence $X=\{x_1, \ldots, x_n\}$ is a sequence of words of length n, which is first tokenized to subword tokens. Then the transformer encoder captures the contextual information for each token via self-attention and produces a sequence of contextual embeddings.

For m label sequences related to each predicate, $T=\{t_1, \ldots, t_m\}$ where t_i contains n labels denoted as $\{label_1^i, label_2^i, \ldots, label_n^i\}$. Since these labels are in the level of words, the length is equal to the original sentence length n of X. Semantic roles are also encoded as embeddings via a mapping of these labels into vectors $\{v_1^i, v_2^i, \ldots, v_n^i\}$ and feed a BiGRU layer to obtain the label representations for m label sequences in the latent space, $e(t_i)=\text{BiGRU}(v_1^i, v_2^i, \ldots, v_n^i)$ where $0<i<m$.

Gated recurrent units (GRUs) are a gating mechanism in RNNs. A GRU is like an LSTM with a forget gate but has fewer parameters than LSTM, as it lacks an output gate. BiGRU is a bidirectional GRU. Each time step the BiGRU gets a word vector as input. Afterward, an attention layer is applied over each hidden state ht. The attention weights are learned using the concatenation of the current hidden state of the BiGRU and the past hidden state in the second BiGRU layer.

For m label sequences, let L_i denote the label sequences for token x_i, so that we have $e(L_i) = \{e(t_1), \ldots, e(t_m)\}$. We concatenate the m sequences of label representation and feed them to a fully connected layer to obtain the refined joint representation e^t in dimension d:

$$e'(L_i) = W_2[e(t_1), \ldots, e(t_m)] + b_2,$$
$$e^t = \{e'(L_1), \ldots, e'(L_n)\}.$$

where W_2 and b_2 are trainable parameters.

The integration must merge the lexical text embedding and label representations. As the original pre-trained BERT is based on a sequence of subwords, while the semantic representation labels the words, it is necessary to align these sequences of different size. Thus we group the subwords for each word and use a convolutional neural network (CNN) with a max pooling to obtain a word-level representation.

We now show how the merge works on the level of an individual word. Let us select word x_i that consists of a sequence of subwords $[s_1, s_2, \ldots, s_l]$, where l is the number of subwords for word x_i. Denoting the representation of subword s_j from BERT as $e(s_j)$, we first utilize a convolutional layer,

$e_i' = W_1\,[e(s_i), e(s_{i+1}), \ldots, e(s_{i+k-1})] + b_1$, where W_1 and b_1 are trainable parameters and k is the kernel size. Then rectified linear unit (ReLU $y = max(0, x)$) and max pooling are applied to the output embedding sequence for x_i:

$$e_i^* = ReLU(e_i') \text{ and}$$
$$e(x_i) = MaxPooling(e_1^*, \ldots, e_{l-k+1}^*).$$

Hence the overall representation for the word sequence X is

$e^w = \{e(x_1), \ldots, e(x_n)] \in R^{n \times dw}$ where d_w is the dimension of word embedding.

The aligned word embedding and encoded semantic embeddings are then merged by a fusion function

$$h = concatenation(e_w, e_t).$$

The experimental results that show BERT can be easily improved in many domains by adding some limited semantic information defeats the paradigm of an end-to-end learning system. This experiment demonstrates that a split into components (such that each solves its own task) guarantees an improvement over an end-to-end system.

10. Direct similarity-based question answering

As DL does the main job of answering a high percentage of arbitrary–phrases questions, a deterministic technique can complement it by answering the questions where MRC fails by finding a direct similarity between Q and A. To find candidate answers for similarity checking, we use a standard information-retrieval technique of an Apache Lucene index (Galitsky, 2017a).

To verify semantic similarity (Galitsky et al., 2012), one needs to navigate a semantic representation such as an Abstract Meaning Representation (AMR, Chapter 2) graph. A technique navigating a semantic graph such as AMR can verify the correctness of the MRC answer, involving syntactic and named entity relations as well as semantic role information. When an MRC answer is determined to be incorrect, AMR employs answer-finding means complementary to that of MRC and identifies the correct answer within the answer text (context).

We expect that an MRC system and a direct syntactic/semantic similarity approach would complement each other since they rely on totally different feature spaces. DL approaches frequently fail because there is a lack of a phrase structure similar to the ones in a training set, or DL does not generalize well enough to cover a given case. In this chapter, we utilize available AMR parsers and analyze our intuition about fruitful cooperation between state-of-the-art DL-based approaches and AMR-based matching.

Let us look at the semantic representation of an answer text (People.cn, 2019).

As of Monday morning, there have been 21 people from Nghe An suspected of missing in Britain, head of Nghe An police Nguyen Huu Cau told local media on the sidelines of the ongoing biannual meeting of the country's top legislature.

This is AMR representation of the above text. Fig. 17 shows a semantic representation as a logic form, and Fig. 18 shows a graph-based representation of an answer, a question, and association between the selected nodes.

```
(tell-01
  :ARG0 (v11 / person
    :name (v12 / name
      :op1 "Nguyen"
      :op2 "Huu"
      :op3 "Cau")
    :wiki "Nguyen_Huu_Cau")
  :ARG2 (v15 / media
    :ARG1-of (v14 / local-02))
  :ARG1 (v16 / sideline
    :mod (v17 / meet-03
      :time "biannual"
      :ARG0 (v20 / legislate-01
        :mod (v19 / top)
        :ARG0 (v18 / country))))
  :ARG0 (v3 / person
    :quant 21
    :time (v2 / morning
      :mod (v1 / monday))
    :ARG2-of (v4 / suspect-01
      :ARG1 (v5 / miss-01
        :location (v6 / country
          :name (v7 / name
            :op1 "Britain")
          :wiki "United_Kingdom")))
    :ARG0-of (v8 / head-01
      :ARG1 (v10 / police
        :name (v9 / name
          :op1 "Nghe"
          :op2 "An")))))
```

FIG. 17

An AMR expression for the answer text.

In Fig. 17, indentations denote that the order entities occur as arguments of other entities. The rook entity is *tell-01(ARG0, ARG1, ARG2)*, where ARG0 is a telling person, ARG1 is meeting circumstances (sideline), and ARG2 is a telling means. Each node of an AMR has a label for the word lemma and a node ID, such as "*v9 / name*."

To illustrate our idea, we manually implement a procedure of an assessment of a match between a candidate answer and a question as a ***traversal*** of answer AMR graph. Certain question features, such as a Wh-expression, need different kinds of AMR traversal. We give examples of questions and the AMR graph navigations during our search for answers.

Q: *<What happened> on Monday morning?*

AMR traversal:

(1) identify path "Monday – morning"
(2) traverse up to the node whose argument is "Monday – morning": <person>
(3) Get the full verb phrase from the node

Fig. 18 shows a correspondence between the question Q (top) and its answer (bottom). In this case, *person* node is an argument of both *head* and *suspect* (that is a wrong semantic parsing result). Syntactically, *person* (mapped into *people*) is related to *suspect* and not *head*, so we navigate upwards to *suspect* and return the whole verb phrase for *suspect* in the answer: "*suspected of missing in Britain.*"

Questions with wrong answers given by the DL approach are marked with "Q*." In the following, we present more questions and the respective AMR graph traversals steps required to answer them.

Q: *< When/Where/How many > were the suspect report missing?* AMR traversal:

(1) Identify the path for the expression "*suspect report missing*" as *suspect-miss*;
(2) Traverse down from *suspect* through all branches until we hit edge label *[time/location/quantity]*; and
(3) Return the value from the target node of this edge.

Notice the difference between the location of the event being described (in *Britain*) and the location of agents being described (in Vietnam). The DL approach cannot figure out this difference.

Q*: *< Who > < told/informed/shared information > that the suspects were missing?*

AMR traversal:

(1) Identify path "*suspects were missing*": *suspects-miss*;
(2) Traverse up or down till we hit the next level predicate: *tell*;
(3) Traverse down till we hit the edge with label *person:*;
(4) Return the value from the target node of this edge.

Q: *< Who is/are/were > / < Tell me/provide information about > missing suspects?* AMR traversal:

(1) Identify path "*missing suspects*": *suspects-miss*;
(2) Go to other nodes connected to this graph path from upward or at the same level;
(3) Get all values from these nodes and return all these values as an unordered set.

Q*: *< Where/From where/Which place > 21 missing people < live/come/travel >?*AMR traversal:

(1) Identify path "*21 missing people*": *suspects-miss*;
(2) Identify the top-level node connected with this path;
(3) Traverse down for the edge labeled location, return its value.

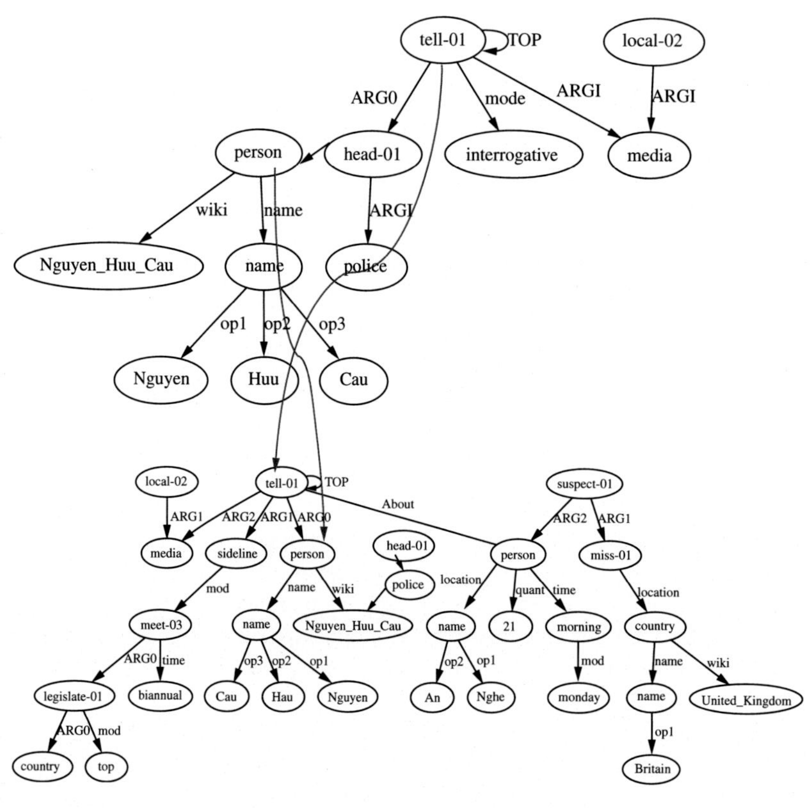

FIG. 18

An AMR graph for the query (top) and for the answer text (bottom).

Q*: < How > did *local media learn about missing people?* AMR traversal:

(1) Extract a mental action from the query: learn;
(2) Split the query with identified mental actions into two parts/phrases;
(3) Identify paths for phrases in the query: *local-media, missing-person*;
(4) Identify a verb in the sentence logically associated with the extracted mental action: *If a Tells B About F then B Learns F: Tell*
(5) Return all arguments of *tell* other than those in the query.

Q*: *< What > did head of police Nguyen Huu Cau tell/say/inform/shared with/let know to local media*

(1) Extract a mental action from the query: *tell*;
(2) Split the query with identified mental actions into two parts/phrases;
(3) Identify paths for phrases in the query: *head-of-police-Nguyen-Huu-Cau, local-media*;
(4) Return all arguments of *tell* other than those in the query.

We enumerate the other questions most of which are handled properly by MRC:

< How > often/frequent/regular is Meeting of the country's Top Legislature Organized/held?

What Was the Agenda of the country's Top Legislature Meeting?

What Official/officer/who Shared Information on the country's Top Legislature Meeting?

When Police Officer Spoke on the country's Top Legislature Meeting? When Did Police Officer Report at country's Top Legislature Meeting?

One can observe that semantic representation allows us to provide much broader associations between questions and answers compared to a syntactic representation or a pure data-driven representation.

We use two kinds of graph alignment-based operations: *enrichment* and *generalization*. Enrichment of two graphs aligns them and retains all information (Fig. 19). We enrich a semantic graph by a syntactic one and add named entity labels; other linguistic sources can enrich such representation as well. Discourse-level information for representations of longer texts can be also added (Galitsky, 2017c). Once we obtain an enriched representation for a question Q and candidate answers A_n (e.g., all sentences and longer phrases in text), we find a generalization between them to estimate similarity as

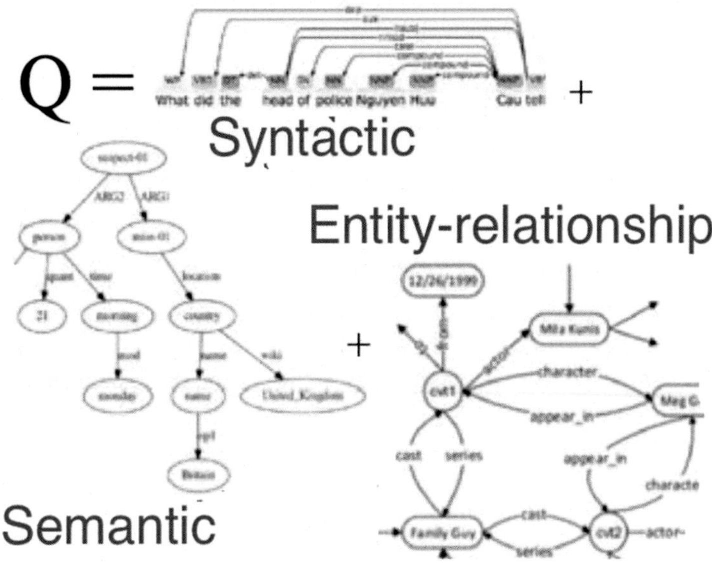

Generalizing alignment:

Q^A_1 … Q^A_n

Q →A best (largest graph overlap)

FIG. 19

Involving multiple sources for generalization.

an indication of an A correctness for Q (Galitsky, 2013). Notice that MRC-based approaches assess Q vs *answer passage* similarity as well, relying on a totally different set of features and entirely distinct learning settings.

10.1 Correcting an MRC answer

We take a question and substitute the identified answer into the Wh-expression denoted by "< + … + >" (Fig. 20):

Q=*"What happened with Beyonce after 1990?"* →

Q+*A* = *"Their hiatus saw the release of Beyonce's debut album, Dangerously in Love"* <+ *"with Beyonce after 1990"* +>

In $Q+A$, we show the mandatory part in <+…+> (since it is specified in the Q), preceded by the optional part, identified by the answer.

Now if we generalize (Q+A) with each sentence of context:

(Q+A) ^ context1, context1="Beyonce Giselle …" (sentence 1);

(Q+A) ^ context2, context2="Born and raised in Houston …" (sentence 2);

… then the mandatory part will not be retained in each generalization result, which indicates that the answer is incorrect.

(After 1990) ^1990s=1990s

Hence the generalization of this incorrect answer does not retain "*after 1990*" part. At the same time, generalization of this query with another expression, "*rose to fame in the late 1990s*" retains all constraint keywords from the Q, hence this A is the correct one.

Once AMR generalization detects that the answer is incorrect, it performs its own search for a sentence or a phrase that has the largest generalization (the set of sub-graph with the maximum number of nodes). To do that, we first form a syntactic template to be generalized with each sentence, to be converted from a question to a statement template. For example, "*What time is it*?" is converted into **{Time-NN is-VBZ *-CD, Time-NN is-VBZ *-NER=date_time}**. In this template, the last token is for an expression for time, either as a number or an entity with NER type recognized as ***date_time***.

Once we formed a template, we generalized it with each sentence and each verb phrase to get the one with the largest sub-graph. In our running example, the template is

[*-VP Beyonce-'NE=PERSON' after-IN 1990s-{NNS, Date}]

Passage Context

Beyonce Giselle Knowles-Carter (born September 4, 1981) is an American singer, songwriter, ´record producer and actress. Born and raised in Houston, Texas, she performed in various singing and dancing competitions as a child, and rose to fame in the late 1990s as lead singer of R&B girl-group Destiny's Child. Managed by her father, Mathew Knowles, the group became one of the world's best-selling girl groups of all time. Their hiatus saw the release of Beyonce's ´debut album, Dangerously in Love (2003), which established her as a solo artist worldwide, earned five Grammy Awards and featured the Billboard Hot 100 number-one singles "Crazy in Love" and "Baby Boy"

Question

What happened with Beyonce after 1990?

FIG. 20

An incorrect answer that can be detected.

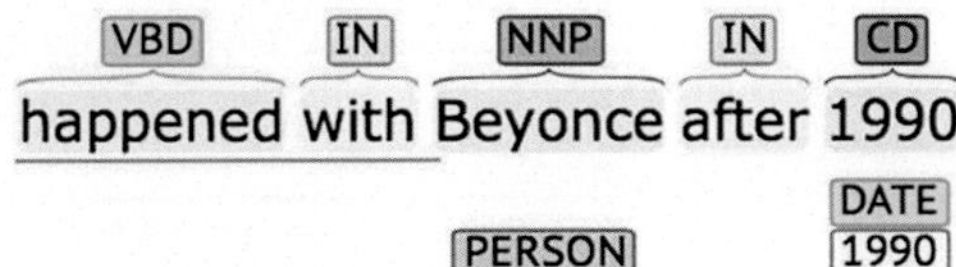

This template is made as general as possible to cover a broad range of phrasings in a candidate answer. "*-VP" here is an arbitrary verb phrase. Hence the intersection with the phrase "*rose to fame in the late 1990s as lead singer*"

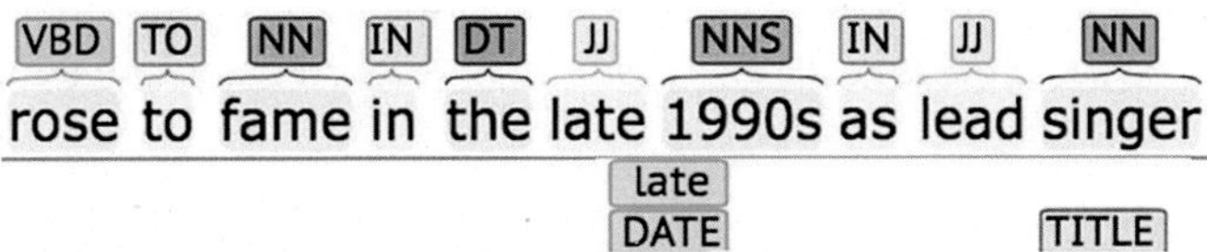

is **[she-PRP rose-VBD, to-TO, fame-NN, 1990-DATE]**, which is sufficient evidence that this phrase is a suitable answer. Intersections with other sentences and phrases are insignificant, so it is the only answer.

So far, we have described the generalization algorithm based on syntactic and entity-based graph nodes. In practice, the syntactic trees with additional named entity labels are first enriched by aligning with AMR graphs and then generalized between questions and candidate answers to identify the correct one (Fig. 21).

We employ the generalization component developed in Chapters 2, 3, and 6 (Fig. 22).

11. System architecture

The architecture includes four main components (Fig. 23):

(1) The Linguistic data preparation component, which extracts, organizes, and aligns linguistic features at various level of knowledge abstraction.
(2) The MRC/DL component, actually finding an answer in most cases based on the model.
(3) The Generalization component, matching linguistic representation of Q and A to provide data structures for direct Q/A in parallel with the DL component. Fig. 22 shows the generalization component's own architecture.
(4) The direct Q/A component that is based on obtaining answers by information retrieval and ranking them based on generalization-based similarity. It is done in parallel with the DL component.

The discourse after-parser takes a default DT and attempts to make the recognized default rhetorical relations such as *Elaboration* and *Joint* more precise and specific (Galitsky, 2021b, Chapter 3). To do that, we rely on an AMR dataset and try to find an annotated sentence with a known semantic relation that can be translated into a specific discourse relation such as *Purpose*, *Means*, *Cause*, and other. This annotated sentence needs to have a similar syntactic structure to the sentence with the relation being specified.

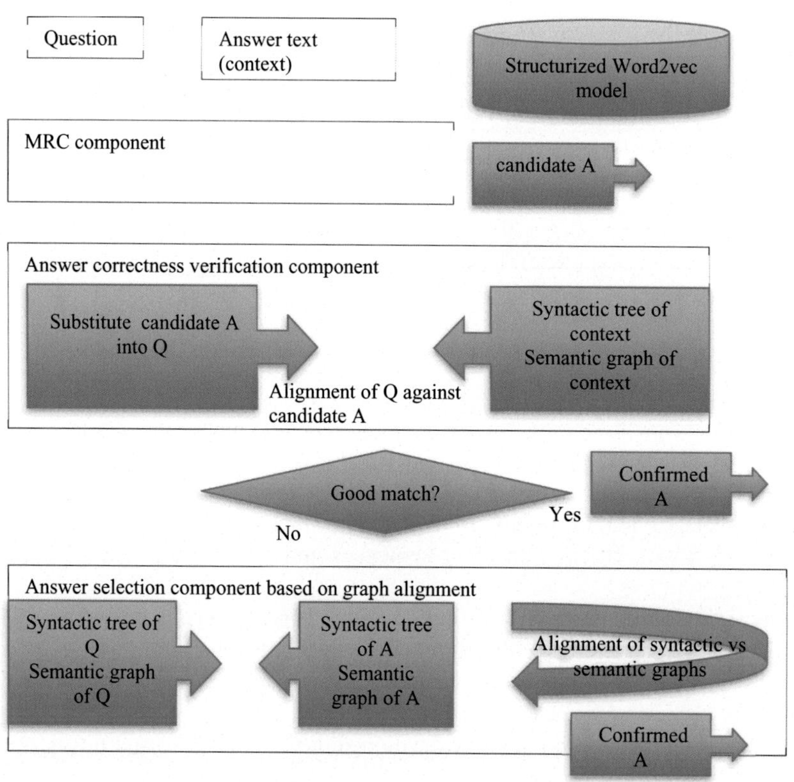

FIG. 21

Error identification and answer selection scenario of hybrid MRC and AMR Generalization system. Fig. 22 shows the top component with more details.

12. Evaluation

We rely on several Q/A datasets with long, complex, multi-hop questions (Galitsky, 2019c) to observe if/how syntactic, semantic, and, mainly, discourse-level features help.

The Stanford Question Answering Dataset (SQuAD) is a reading comprehension dataset consisting of questions posed by crowd workers on a set of Wikipedia articles, where the answer to every question is a segment of text or span from the corresponding reading passage. With more than 100,000 question-answer pairs on more than 500 articles, SQuAD is significantly larger than previous reading comprehension datasets. SQuAD was built by having humans write questions for a given Wikipedia passage and choose the answer span. Other datasets used similar techniques; the NewsQA dataset also consists of 100,000 Q/A pairs from CNN news articles. For other datasets like WikiQA the span is the entire sentence containing the answer (Yang et al., 2015); the task of choosing a sentence rather than a smaller answer span is sometimes called the *sentence selection* task.

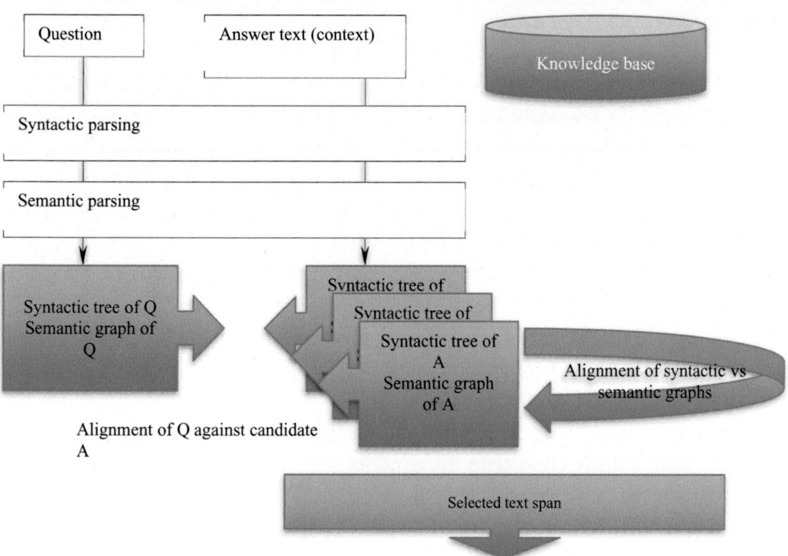

FIG. 22

The generalization procedure that works along the MRC component.

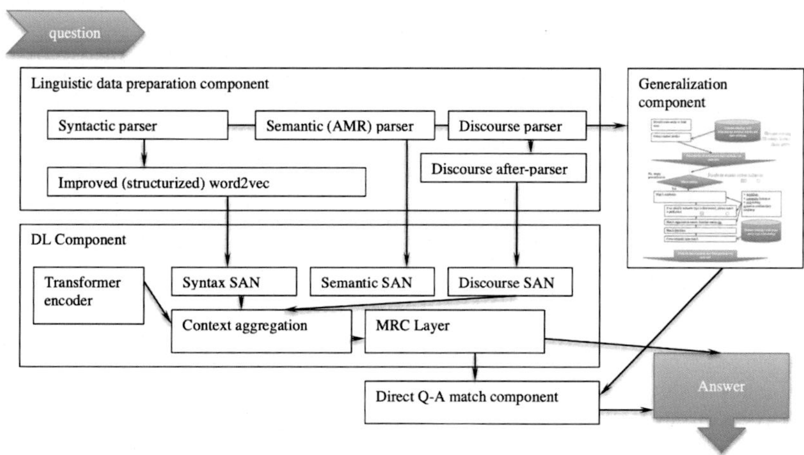

FIG. 23

The architecture of a linguistically enabled MRC system.

Stack Exchange is a network of question-answering sites, where each site covers a particular topic. Questions on Stack Exchange are formatted to have a short title and then a longer body describing the question, meaning that it is far more likely to contain multi-sentence questions (MSQs) than other question answering sites, which tend to focus attention on the title with only a short description after the title. There is a voting system that allows for assessing well-formedness, since badly formed questions are likely to be rated poorly. It covers a variety of topics, meaning that we can obtain questions from a variety of domains. To obtain the MSQ data, Burchell et al. (2020) used the Stack Exchange Data Explorer, an open-source tool for running arbitrary queries against public data from the Stack Exchange network. The authors chose 90 sites within the network and queried each site for entries with at least 2 question marks in the body of the question. Also, the authors removed questions less than 5 or more than 300 characters in length. Many of the questions labeled as "non-English" indeed were poorly formed English, making language identification a useful pre-processing step. After cleaning and processing, 160 questions from almost a hundred topics were extracted.

We also evaluated the search of the same queries against an index that includes the totality of all documents. Not only does a position within a document need to be found but so too does a relevant document itself (Galitsky, 2017c). The purpose of this evaluation is to compare the developed AMR -based Q/A technique with a conventional search engine. In addition to the search F1 measure, we used a Normalized Discounted Cumulative Gain (NDCG, Wang et al., 2013), measuring the top five search results. A full corpus search was implemented integrating the MRC component with a conventional TF*IDF search, which finds candidate documents subject to MRC on a one-by-one basis.

As to the other datasets, the NarrativeQA (Kocisky et al., 2017) dataset, for example, has questions based on entire long documents like books or movie scripts, while the Q/A in Context (QuAC) dataset (Choi et al., 2018) has 100,000 questions created by two crowd workers asking and answering questions about a hidden Wikipedia text.

Table 2 shows our performance on both SQuAD 1.1 and 2.0 test data for evaluation. The default MRC employs neither syntactic nor semantic information; the baseline is shown in the third (grayed) row. As we move toward syntactic, semantic, and discourse levels, the performance boost is 3%, 4%, and 3%, respectively. The improvement of the integrated system is 6.8%.

As we proceed toward the evaluation in the datasets of more complex questions (Table 3), the performance drops up to 10% in comparison to Table 2. Analogously to Table 2, the default MRC employs neither syntactic nor semantic information; the baseline is shown in the third (grayed) row. Whereas absolute performance value is lower than in Table 2, the performance boost due to linguistic information is higher. The contributions of syntactic, semantic, and discourse levels are 5%, 5%, and 6.5%, respectively. One can observe that contribution of *discourse-level* features is *the highest* in this

Table 2 Performance of MRC on SQuAD.

	SQuAD 1.1 test			SQuAD 2.0 test		
Dataset/settings	**P**	**R**	**F1**	**P**	**R**	**F1**
Keyword-based MRC	84.7	88.6	86.61	81.9	88.3	84.98
Syntactically enabled MRC	89.3	90.5	89.90	84.7	89.7	87.13
Semantically/AMR-enabled MRC	90.1	91.1	90.60	86.1	91.6	88.76
Discourse-enabled MRC	88.7	91.5	90.08	83.2	90.3	86.60
Syntactic+semantic+discourse-enabled MRC	**94.3**	**92**	**93.14**	**90.3**	**90.1**	**90.20**
ALBERT	–	–	–	–	–	92.2

Table 3 Performance of MRC on complex questions datasets.

	NarrativeQA			QuAC			MSQ		
Dataset/settings	**P**	**R**	**F1**	**P**	**R**	**F1**	**P**	**R**	**F1**
Keyword-based MRC	74.2	76.8	75.48	72.9	78.7	75.69	69.1	72.3	70.66
Syntactically enabled MRC	78.5	79.4	78.95	79.8	78.4	79.09	75.6	74	74.79
Semantically/AMR-enabled MRC	80.7	79	79.84	78	78.3	78.15	74.3	74.8	74.55
Discourse-enabled MRC	78.9	81.4	80.13	80.6	80.2	80.40	76.2	75.4	75.80
Syntactic + semantic + discourse-enabled MRC	**83.3**	**82.8**	**83.05**	**84.2**	**81.6**	**82.88**	**79.3**	**80**	**79.65**

evaluation domain of longer, multi-sentence questions. The improvement of the integrated system is almost 11% in comparison with the baseline. Hence the longer and more complex the questions are, the greater the impact of linguistic information, especially discourse-level features.

13. Discussion and conclusions

By adding semantic information to BERT, Zhang et al. (2019) boosted MRC performance on SQuAD 2.0 dataset by 4%, from F1 83.6% to 87.9%. The authors relied on the explicit contextual semantics from pre-trained semantic role labeling, and introduced an improved language representation model, SemBERT, capable of explicitly absorbing contextual semantics over a BERT backbone.

For machine reading comprehension, the capacity of effectively modeling the linguistic knowledge from the detail-riddled and lengthy passages and getting rid of the noises is essential to improve its performance. Traditional attentive models attend to all words without explicit constraint, which results in inaccurate concentration on some dispensable words. Zhang et al. (2019) proposed using syntax to guide the text modeling by incorporating explicit syntactic constraints into an attention mechanism for better linguistically motivated word representations. The proposed SG-Net was applied to a typical pre-trained language model called BERT. SG-Net design helps achieve substantial performance improvement.

For longer, sentence-level Q/A, a big disadvantage of the BERT network structure is that no independent sentence embeddings are computed, which makes it difficult to derive sentence embeddings from the network. To bypass this limitation, it is possible to pass single sentences through BERT and then derive a fixed-sized vector by averaging the outputs (similar to average word embeddings). However, a direct approach via a hybrid semantic + syntactic similarity is much more computationally efficient. SBERT of Reimers and Gurevych (2019) boosted the performance of GloVe embedding by 15% and BERT embedding by 22%, as measured by textual similarity tasks.

He et al. (2018) proposed a novel read-then-verify system, which leverages an answer verifier to decide whether the predicted answer is entailed by the input snippets, similarly to the current study. The authors introduced two auxiliary losses to help the reader better handle answer extraction as well as no-answer detection, and investigated three different architectures for the answer verifier. Their experiments on the SQuAD 2.0 dataset showed that their system obtains F1 score of 74.2 on test set, achieving state-of-the-art.

We observed that linguistic sources encoded into a neural MRC cover most peculiarities of complex questions to provide correct answers (Figs. 24 and 25). Although our MRC system did not achieve state of the art on the evaluation datasets, it demonstrated superiority of integrated syntax/semantic/discourse subsystems in multiple diverse Q/A domains with complex questions.

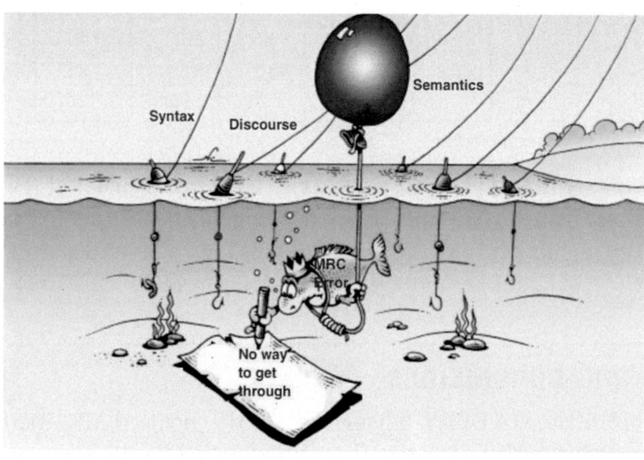

FIG. 24

It is hard to come up with a question that is not answered correctly by linguistically enabled MRC.

FIG. 25

Discourse relations between entities is a strong feature for MRC in comparison with all words and syntactic relations (left). A recognition of this strong feature is achieved by a multi-layer neural network architecture (right).

Supplementary data sets

Please visit https://github.com/bgalitsky/relevance-based-on-parse-trees to access all supplementary data sets.

References

Asher, N., Lascarides, A., 2003. Logics of Conversation. Cambridge University Press, Cambridge.

Bahdanau, D., Cho, K., Bengio, Y., 2015. Neural machine translation by jointly learning to align and translate. In: Proceedings of the ICLR, San Diego, California.

Benamara, F., Taboada, M., Mathieu, Y., 2017. Evaluative language beyond bags of words: linguistic insights and computational applications. Comput. Linguist. 43 (1), 201–264.

Bengio, Y., Simard, P., Frasconi, P., 1994. Learning long-term dependencies with gradient descent is difficult. IEEE Trans. Neural Netw. 5 (2), 157–166.

Braud, C., Coavoux, M., Søgaard, A., 2017. Cross-lingual RST discourse parsing. In: Proceedings of EACL 2017. Valencia, Spain, pp. 292–304.

Burchell, L., Chi, J., Hosking, T., Markl, N., Webber, B., 2020. Querent intent in multi-sentence questions. arXiv preprint arXiv:2010.08980.

Cheng, Jianpeng, Dong, Li, Lapata, Mirella, 2016. Long Short-Term Memory-Networks for Machine Reading. Proceedings of the 2016 Conference on. Empirical Methods in Natural Language Processing, 551–561.

Choi, E, He, H, Mohit, I, Mark, Y, Wen-tau, Y, Yejin, C, Percy, L, Luke, Z, 2018. QuAC: question answering in context EMNLP, 2174–2184.

da Cunha, I., 2016. Towards Discourse Parsing in Spanish. Papers presented at TextLink—Structuring Discourse in Multilingual Europe—Second Action Conference. Budapest, Hungary.

Dozat, T., Manning, C.D., 2017. Deep biaffine attention for neural dependency parsing. In: ICLR.

Durrett, G., Berg-Kirkpatrick, T., Klein, D., 2016. Learning-based single-document summarization with compression and anaphoricity constraints. In: Proceedings of the 54th Annual Meeting of the Association for Computational Linguistics. Berlin, Germany, 1998–2008.

Feng, V.W., Hirst, G., 2014. A linear-time bottom-up discourse parser with constraints and post-editing. In: Proceedings of ACL 2014. Baltimore, MD, pp. 511–521.

Frank, S.L., Bod, R., 2011. Insensitivity of the human sentence-processing system to hierarchical structure. Pyschol. Sci. 22 (6), 829–834.

Galitsky, B., 2003. Natural Language Question Answering System: Technique of Semantic Headers. Advanced Knowledge International, Australia.

Galitsky, B., 2013. Machine learning of syntactic parse trees for search and classification of text. Eng. Appl. Artif. Intell. 26 (3), 1072–1091.

Galitsky, B., 2016. Generalization of parse trees for iterative taxonomy learning. Inf. Sci. 329, 125–143.

Galitsky, B., 2017a. Improving relevance in a content pipeline via syntactic generalization. Eng. Appl. Artif. Intell. 58, 1–26.

Galitsky, B., 2017b. Matching parse thickets for open domain question answering. Data Knowl. Eng. 107, 24–50.

Galitsky, B., 2017c. Discovering rhetoric agreement between a request and response. Dialogue Discourse 8 (2), 167–205.

Galitsky, B., 2019a. Learning discourse-level structures for question answering. In: Developing Enterprise Chatbots. Springer, Cham, pp. 177–220.

Galitsky, B., 2019c. A content management system for chatbots. In: Developing Enterprise Chatbots. Springer, Cham, pp. 253–352.

Galitsky, B., 2021a. Employing abstract meaning representation to lay the last-mile toward reading comprehension. In: Artificial Intelligence for Customer Relationship Management: Keeping Customers Informed. Springer, Cham, pp. 221–252.

Galitsky, B., 2021b. Social promotion chatbot. In: Artificial Intelligence for Customer Relationship Management: Keeping Customers Informed. Springer, Cham, pp. 221–252.

Galitsky, B., Ilvovsky, D.I., 2019. Least general generalization of the linguistic structures. In: FCA4AI@ IJCAI, pp. 39–44.

Galitsky, B., Dobrocsi, G., De La Rosa, J.L., Kuznetsov, S.O., 2010. From generalization of syntactic parse trees to conceptual graphs. In: International Conference on Conceptual Structures, pp. 185–190.

Galitsky, B., De La Rosa, J.L., Dobrocsi, G., 2012. Inferring the semantic properties of sentences by mining syntactic parse trees. Data Knowl. Eng. 81, 21–45.

Galitsky, B., Kuznetsov, S.O., Usikov, D., 2013. Parse thicket representation for multi-sentence search. In: International Conference on Conceptual Structures, pp. 153–172.

He, L., Lee, K., Levy, O., Zettlemoyer, L., 2018. Jointly predicting predicates and arguments in neural semantic role labeling. In: ACL.

Hernault, H., Prendinger, H., duVerle, D.A., Ishizuka, M., 2010. Hilda: a discourse parser using support vector machine classification. Dialogue Discourse 1 (3), 1–33.

Hu, M., Peng, Y., Huang, Z., Yang, N., Zhou, M., et al., 2018. Read+ verify: machine reading comprehension with unanswerable questions. arXiv preprint arXiv:1808.05759.

Iruskieta, M., Labaka, G., Antonio, J.D., 2016. Detecting the central units in two different genres and languages: a preliminary study of Brazilian Portuguese and Basque texts. Proces. Leng. Nat. 56, 65–72.

Ji, Y., Eisenstein, J., 2014. Representation learning for text-level discourse parsing. In: ACL, pp. 13–24.

Jia, R., Liang, P., 2017. Adversarial examples for evaluating reading comprehension systems. In: EMNLP.

Joty, S., Carenini, G., Ng, R., 2015. CODRA: a novel discriminative framework for rhetorical analysis. Comput. Linguist. 41 (3), 385–435.

Kobayashi, N., Hirao, T., Kamigaito, H., Okumura, M., Nagata, M., 2020. Top-down RST parsing utilizing granularity levels in documents. In: AAAI 2020: The Thirty-Fourth AAAI Conference on Artificial Intelligence.

Kocisky, T., Schwarz, J., Blunsom, P., Dyer, C., Hermann, K., Melis, G., Grefenstette, E., 2017. The narrativeQA reading comprehension challenge. Transactions of the Association for Computational Linguistics.

Koto, F., Lau, J., Baldwin, T., 2021. Top-down discourse parsing via sequence labelling. ArXiv:2102.02080.

Liang, L., Zhao, Z., Webber, B., 2020. Extending Implicit Discourse Relation Recognition to the PDTB-3. arXiv:2010.06294.

Mann, W.C., Thompson, S.A., 1988. Rhetorical structure theory: toward a functional theory of text organization. Text Interdiscipl. J. Study Discour. 8 (3), 243–281.

Marcheggiani, D., Titov, I., 2017. Encoding sentences with graph convolutional networks for semantic role labeling. In: Proceedings of the 2017 Conference on Empirical Methods in Natural Language Processing (EMNLP).

Matthiessen, C., Teruya, K., 2015. Grammatical realizations of rhetorical relations in different registers. Word 61 (3), 232–281.

Maziero, E.G., Hirst, G., Pardo, T.A.S., 2015. Semi-supervised never-ending learning in rhetorical relation identification. In: Proceedings of Recent Advances in Natural Language Processing, Hissar, Bulgaria.

Mikolov, T., Sutskever, I., Chen, K., Corrado, G.S., Dean, J., 2013. Distributed representations of words and phrases and their compositionality. In: NIPS.

Miltsakaki, E., Prasad, R., Joshi, A.K., Webber, B.L., 2004. The Penn discourse treebank. In: Proceedings of LREC 2004. Lisbon, Portugal.

Morey, M., Muller, P., Asher, N., 2017. How much progress have we made on RST discourse parsing? A replication study of recent results on the RST-DT. In: Proceedings of EMNLP 2017. Copenhagen, Denmark, pp. 1319–1324.

Mudrakarta, P.K., Taly, A., Sundararajan, M., Dhamdhere, K., 2018. Did the model understand the question? In: ACL.

Peldszus, A., Stede, M., 2016. Rhetorical structure and argumentation structure in monologue text. In: Proceedings of the 3rd Workshop on Argument Mining, ACL. Berlin, Germany, pp. 103–112.

People.cn, 2019. Vietnamese Police Detain 8 Suspects in Connection With Illegal Immigration Organizing. http://en.people.cn/n3/2019/1104/c90000-9629296.html.

Peters, M.E., Neumann, M., Iyyer, M., Gardner, M., Clark, C., Lee, K., Zettlemoyer, L., 2018. Deep contextualized word representations. In: NAACL-HLT.

Prasad, R., Dinesh, N., Lee, A., Miltsakaki, E., Robaldo, L., Joshi, A., Webber, B. (2008). The Penn Discourse TreeBank 2.0. In: Proceedings of the International Conference on Language Resources and Evaluation, LREC 2008, 26 May to 1 June 2008, Marrakech, Morocco.

Reimers, N., Gurevych, I., 2019. Sentence-BERT: sentence embeddings using Siamese BERT-networks. In: EMNLP.

Rohde, H., Johnson, A., Schneider, N., Webber, B., 2018. Discourse coherence: concurrent explicit and implicit relations. In: Proceedings of the 56th Annual Meeting of the ACL.

Roth, M., Lapata, M., 2016. Neural semantic role labeling with dependency path embeddings. In: Proceedings of the 54th Annual Meeting of the Association for Computational Linguistics (ACL), pp. 1192–1202.

Scarton, C., Beck, D., Shah, K., Smith, K.S., Specia, L., 2016. Word embeddings and discourse information for machine translation quality estimation. In: Proceedings of the First Conference on Machine Translation, ACL. Berlin, Germany, pp. 831–837.

Schouten, K., Frasincar, F., 2016. COMMIT at SemEval-2016 task 5: sentiment analysis with rhetorical structure theory. In: Proceedings of SemEval-2016. San Diego, CA, pp. 356–360.

Strubell, E., Verga, P., Andor, D., Weiss, D., McCallum, A., 2018. Linguistically-informed self-attention for semantic role labeling. In: EMNLP.

Surdeanu, M., Hicks, T., Valenzuela-Escárcega, M., 2015. Two practical rhetorical structure theory parsers. In: Proceedings of NAACL 2015. Denver, CO, pp. 1–5.

Vaswani, A., Shazeer, N., Parmar, N., Uszkoreit, J., Jones, L., Gomez, A.N., Kaiser, L., Polosukhin, I., 2017. Attention is all you need. In: 31st Conference on Neural Information Processing Systems (NIPS).

Wang Y., Wang, L., Li, Y., He, D., Chen, W., Liu, T.-Y. (2013) A theoretical analysis of normalized discounted cumulative gain (NDCG) ranking measures. In: Proceedings of the 26th Annual Conference on Learning Theory (COLT 2013).

Wang, S., Zhang, J., Zong, C., 2017. Learning sentence representation with guidance of human attention. In: IJCAI.

Webber, B., Prasad, R., Lee, A., Joshi, A., 2019. The Penn Discourse Treebank 3.0 Annotation Manual. https://catalog.ldc.upenn.edu/docs/LDC2019T05/PDTB3-Annotation-Manual.pdf.

Yang, Y., Yih, W.-T., Meek, C., 2015. Wikiqa: a challenge dataset for open-domain question answering. In: EMNLP 2015.

Yu, A.W., Lee, H., Le, Q., 2017. Learning to skim text. In: ACL.

Zeldes, A., 2016. rstWeb: a browser-based annotation interface for Rhetorical Structure Theory and discourse relations. In: Proceedings of the 15th Annual Conference of the North American Chapter of the Association for Computational Linguistics (NAACL 2016) System Demonstrations. San Diego, CA, pp. 1–5.

Zeldes, A., 2017. The GUM corpus: creating multilayer resources in the classroom. Lang. Resour. Eval. 51 (3), 581–612.

Zhang, Z., Wu, Y., Zhao, H., Li, Z., Zhang, S., Zhou, X., Zhou, X., 2019. Semantics-Aware BERT for Language Understanding. arXiv.

Zhang, Z., Wu, Y., Zhao, H., Li, Z., Zhang, S., Zhou, X., Zhou, X., 2020. Semantics-aware BERT for language understanding. Proceedings of the AAAI Conference on Artificial Intelligence 34, 9628–9635.

CHAPTER

Machine reading between the lines (RBL) of medical complaints

Boris Galitsky
Oracle Corporation, Redwood City, CA, United States

1. Introduction

Recently, artificial intelligence (AI) techniques have made waves across healthcare, even fueling an active discussion of whether AI doctors will eventually replace human physicians in the future. We believe that human physicians will not be replaced by machines in the foreseeable future, but AI can definitely assist physicians to make better clinical decisions or even replace human judgment in certain functional areas of health care such as radiology and cardiology. The increasing availability of healthcare data and rapid development of big data analytic methods has made possible the recent successful applications of AI in healthcare. Guided by relevant clinical questions, powerful AI techniques can unlock clinically relevant information hidden in the massive amount of data, which in turn can assist clinical decision-making.

The shift from volume-based to value-based health care is inevitable. Health systems are transitioning from traditional fee-for-service models to more outcome-based approaches, implemented incrementally and at varying speeds across the world's healthcare systems. At the heart of the value-based model are the payment mechanisms (Oracle Healthcare, 2020). They encourage effective treatments and create disincentives for treatments that are not cost-effective and do not deliver value. To make the treatment effective, the medical document processing pipeline needs to have the Reading Between the Lines (RBL) feature, to have a complete picture for how a patient describes their conditions. Maximum information extracted from patient complaints is beneficial for cost-effective care. An RBL technique can be applied not only to patients' complaints but to consumer complaints as well, to better understand customer issues and maintain customer retention.

Natural Language Processing (NLP) methods extract information from unstructured data such as clinical notes, medical journals, and patient complaints to supplement and enrich structured medical data. The NLP procedures turn texts into machine-readable structured data, which can then be analyzed by ML techniques. It would be especially valuable to extract implicit authors' thoughts and include them in extraction results.

Unsolicited patient complaints can be a useful service recovery tool for healthcare organizations. Some patient complaints contain information that may necessitate further action on the part of the healthcare organization and/or the healthcare professional. Current approaches depend on the manual processing of patient complaints, which can be costly, slow, and challenging in terms of scalability (Elmessiry et al., 2017; Galitsky et al., 2009).

Artificial Intelligence for Healthcare Applications and Management. https://doi.org/10.1016/B978-0-12-824521-7.00014-4

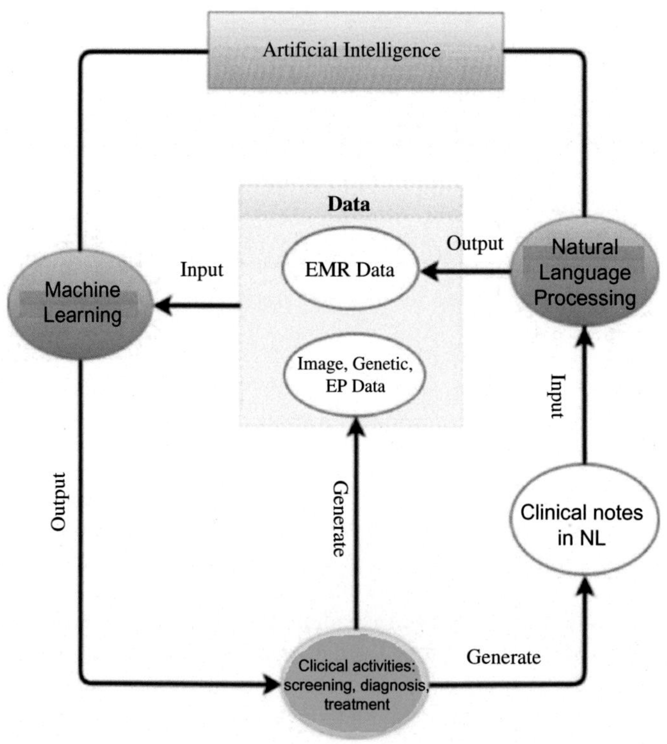

FIG. 1

The flow of clinical data generation to NLP-based data enrichment, to ML data analysis, to clinical decision-making based on EHRs.

Fig. 1 shows a relationship between AI, machine learning (ML), NLP, and medical data such as electronic health records (EHRs; Chapter 2). The information flow starts and ends with clinical activities. As powerful as AI techniques can be, these activities must be motivated by clinical problems and applied to assist clinical practice.

We formulate a text RBL problem as finding or generating portions of text that express what the author intended to say, according to our belief, but did not actually state in text. RBL can include:

(1) *entities* missing in texts, but assumed to be identified and understood by the reader
(2) *attributes* of these entities, which are either default or which could be negatively perceived by the reader, according to the author
(3) *opinions* on a mentioned topic, which the author does not want to explain explicitly
(4) *sentiments* about an entity, which the author prefers to avoid writing explicitly but expects the reader to comprehend
(5) *explanation* or *argumentation* links between facts and clauses mentioned in text, which can be recovered by a competent reader (Galitsky, 2020)

RBL forms a phrase that logically connects two statements in text. This phrase is not mentioned by the author but is either assumed or intentionally concealed.

Simple examples can be related to child development. Usually, children avoid accepting that they are tired and ready to go to bed. Instead, they say *they are hungry*, *thirsty*, *bored*, and so on. It is then the task of the caregiver to deduce what the child actually means, referring to the child's different intents including something she is not explicitly mentioning: *an intent to sleep*. Hence the RBL phrase here is "*I want to sleep*" and the child's statements include various other intents that do not really characterize their state of mind but need to be connected with *sleep*.

In a typical family anecdote, a wife tells her husband "*I have nothing wear*" to encourage attention to her dress. Analogously, this statement should not be perceived literally, but instead should be connected with an attempt to attract attention, to ask for funds to buy a new dress, or to help the wife choose the dress most suitable for a party.

1.1 RBL, machine reading comprehension, and inference

Machine Reading Comprehension (MRC; Chapter 6) involves, among others, identifying what is implied but not expressed in text. This task, known as textual entailment (TE), offers a natural abstraction for many NLP tasks. TE has been recognized as a central tool for the new area of Machine Reading. Important in the study of TE is making precise the sense in which something is implied by text. The operational definition of TE is a subjective one: something is implied if humans are more likely to believe it given the truth of the text, than otherwise. (Michael (2008)) proposed a natural objective definition for TE. He views text as a partial representation of some underlying hidden reality. There is a correspondence between this hidden reality and text via a stochastic process, implemented by the author of this text. TE is then formalized as the task of recovering information about this hidden reality in a thoroughly defined meaning. Existing ML approaches can be applied in this information recovery framework. Michael (2008) analyzes the implications for the construction of ML machines that autonomously engage in TE, investigates the role of using multiple inference rules. These rules cannot be learned and applied in parallel, but instead layered learning and reasoning are required.

Despite the usefulness of Natural Language Inference (NLI), and huge steps made in the recent years, an important drawback remains in this line of work: NLI systems are evaluated against datasets that represent only a fraction of human reasoning possibilities. Furthermore, these different datasets seem to have arisen from the need to test specific theoretical architectures, for example, logical approaches in the case of the FraCaS test suite (Cooper et al., 1996) and deep learning (DL) architectures in the case of the Stanford Natural Language Inference Dataset (SNLI; Bowman et al., 2015). What happens as a result is that any NLI system performs very poorly on any dataset that was not specifically intended to test it. As such, the different systems designed to tackle NLI are not only incomplete but are also not even comparable. There is a need of creating more realistic NLI datasets and hybrid approaches to NLI that maintain a connection to symbolic NLP; this is contrary to current research trends.

As some NLI models are believed to approach human performance, a natural question arises: can models trained on these large-scale NLI datasets be used for other downstream NLP tasks? So far, efforts toward using NLI for downstream tasks have had limited success (Trivedi et al., 2019; Falke et al., 2019; Clark et al., 2018).

1.2 RBL and common sense

Pearl (2019) writes that AI systems need world knowledge and common sense to make the most efficient use of the data they are fed. AI developers should build systems that have a combination of knowledge of the world and data. AI systems based only on amassing and blindly processing large volumes of data are doomed to fail. Knowledge does not emerge from data, but rather humans rely on the innate structures in our brains to interact with the world, and we use data to interrogate and learn from the world, as witnessed in newborns, who learn many things without being explicitly instructed. That kind of structure must be implemented externally to the data. Even if we succeed by some miracle to learn that structure from data, we still need to have it in the form that is communicable with human beings. Hwang et al. (2021) demonstrates the importance of common sense and the challenges its absence presents to current AI systems, which are focused on mapping input data to outcomes.

The DL community knows how to solve a dataset without solving the underlying task with DL today. This is due to the significant difference between AI and human intelligence, especially knowledge of the world. And common sense is one of the fundamental missing pieces. The space of reasoning is infinite and reasoning itself is a generative task and very different from the categorization tasks today's DL methods and evaluation benchmarks are suited for. Humans do not enumerate entities very frequently. Instead, the human mind reasons on the fly, and this is one of the key fundamental, intellectual challenges that need to be addressed advancing the state-of-the-art of commonsense reasoning.

But how can one build a common sense and reasoning in AI to support RBL? There is a wide range of parallel research areas, including combining symbolic and neural representations (Hwang et al., 2021), integrating knowledge into reasoning, and constructing benchmarks that go beyond classification problems.

Instead of identifying a philosophical proof of existence based on the fact that someone capable of any form of thought necessarily exists, a language modeling approach finds the most likely phrase, averaging over millions of similar phrases (Fig. 2). Hence for a correct RBL, one needs to find a single most semantically similar phrase, rather than a formal representation of multiple phrases that are somewhat similar.

Recognizing textual entailment (RTE) (Dagan et al., 2006), recently framed as NLI (Bowman et al., 2015) is the task concerned with identifying whether a premise sentence entails, contradicts, or is neutral with the hypothesis sentence. Following the release of the large-scale SNLI dataset (Bowman et al., 2015), many end-to-end neural models have been developed for the task, achieving high accuracy on the test set. As opposed to previous-generation methods, which relied heavily on lexical resources, neural models make use only of pre-trained word embeddings. State-of-the-art DL systems perform poorly, suggesting that they are limited in their generalization ability.

NLI systems are evaluated against datasets that represent only a fraction of human reasoning possibilities. Furthermore, these different datasets seem to have arisen from the need to test specific

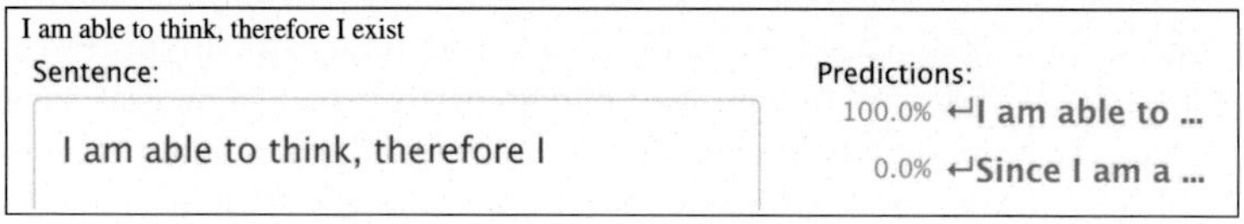

I am able to think, therefore I exist
Sentence:
I am able to think, therefore I
Predictions:
100.0% ↵I am able to ...
0.0% ↵Since I am a ...

FIG. 2

A failure of a trained language model to recognize the verb existing in the famous idiom.

theoretical architectures, for example, logical approaches in the case of the FraCaS test suite (Cooper et al., 1996) and DL architectures in the case of SNLI. The few efforts to incorporate external lexical knowledge resulted in negligible performance gain. This raises the following questions:

(1) Are DL methods inherently stronger, obviating the need of external lexical knowledge?
(2) Does large-scale training data allow for implicit learning of previously explicit lexical knowledge?
(3) Are the NLI datasets simpler than early RTE datasets, requiring less knowledge?

Hence pure data-driven, end-to-end DL approaches to NLI do not solve the RBL problem well enough.

2. RBL as generalization and web mining

Here is a proverb that can serve as an example of an explanation chain:

We drink wine to become healthy. We need our health to drink vodka.

The chain is: *drink(wine)* → *healthy* & *healthy* → *drink(vodka)*. This chain is complete, so nothing needs to be inserted between these sentences to link them. However, if the sentences were

"*We drink wine to become spiritual. We need our health to drink vodka*," then we would need to apply RBL to link *spiritual* → *health*. It can be done by looking for a source of wisdom connecting these two concepts, such as a wellbeing recommendation: "*Improving your spiritual health may not cure an illness, but it may help you feel better*." It is quite possible that the author of this proverb wanted the reader to obtain this RBL result to better comprehend and appreciate the text.

2.1 Patient repeats what he wants to say

Let us look at a patient's opinion and try to read it between the lines, revealing what the patient really wants:

> I avoid flu shots because I am allergic to eggs. Most flu shots produced today use an egg-based manufacturing process that leaves trace amounts of egg protein behind. I do not need a flu shot since I got it last year. I believe it is not necessary for me, because the vaccine is not 100% effective. Also, I never get the flu, so I do not need a vaccine.

To infer what the actual reason for refusal to do flu shot is, we need to generalize from what the author cited as the reason, produce a web query from this generalization, obtain the list of reasons people avoid flu shots, and, finally, subtract the explicitly mentioned reasons from this list obtained from the Web. The remaining elements from this list would be the possible actual reasons the text author intends to conceal.

To form the web query, we need to take expressions for the intents (Galitsky, 2019). These are followed by discourse markers such as *because*, *since*, or *so*: {*I avoid flu shots, I do not need a flu shot, I believe it is not necessary for me, I do not need a vaccine*}. Hence the template for the sentences we want to use to RBL are *<patient intent>* *<discourse marker for the reason>* *<reason>* or *<reason>* *<discourse marker for the reason>* *<patient intent>*. The second template covers the last sentence.

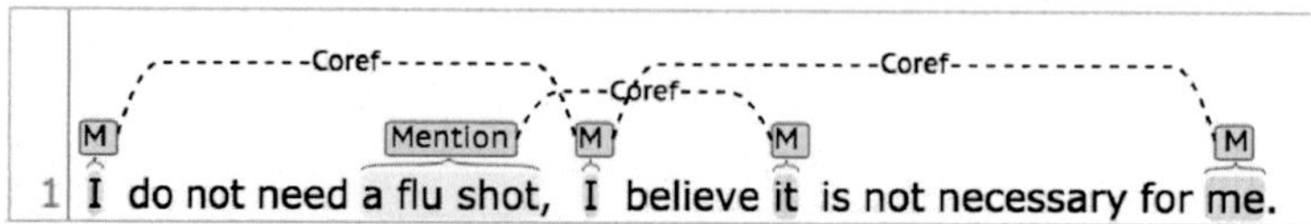

One reason people avoid the flu shot might come from **anti-vaccine propaganda** widespread in the media, mostly on the Internet. Anti-vaxxers have sown vaccine fear over a wide swath of the western world. In 1998, a British study by Andrew Wakefield purported to show a link between vaccines and autism.

5 bogus excuses people use to avoid the flu vaccine ...

FIG. 3

Coreference link (top) and a Bing search result for the query.

We also need a coreference resolution to substitute "*it*" with "*flu shot*" to properly generalize these reasons. The structure of generalization is a <*negation*> of "*flu shots.*"

The web query here is *Why people + generalize (list-of-causes) =*

Why people <avoid/do not want/do not do> flu shots?

We provide an example of a Bing search, but it could be another Web or local health-specific search (Fig. 3 on the bottom).

From the search results, we select the one with the title that starts with a number (*4 causes, 5 reasons, 6 excuses*, etc.). Once we get to a web page whose content is a list of items, we can extract these items and match them with the reasons in the patient complaint (Galitsky, 2013). In our case, the extracted reason items from the identified web page are as follows (we call them *outside reasons* (OR)):

OR = {*Vaccines are dangerous and give kids autism,*
I got the vaccine one year and it didn't work,
I have egg allergies,
I don't get the flu,
The flu vaccine can give you the flu}.

As to the list of reasons from text (*inside reasons*, IR):

IR = {*I am allergic to eggs,*
I believe it is not necessary for me,
"*I got it last year,*"
I never get the flu}.

Finally, *OR* – *IR* = {***Vaccines are dangerous and give kids autism,***
The flu vaccine can give you the flu}.

The expression "*I got the vaccine one year and it didn't work*" is killed by "*I got it last year,*" "*I have egg allergies*" is killed by "*I am allergic to eggs,*" and "*I don't get the flu*" is killed by "*I never get the flu.*"

Hence the RBL result is a list of two possibilities the patient does not want to mention. Both these possibilities need to be explored and taken care of by a physician to avoid ignoring a possibility that can lead to a dangerous outcome.

Unfortunately, a DL-based language model cannot help here. It did not acquire from the available NLI dataset (Bowman et al., 2015) that an allergy to shots infers an unwillingness to take these shots. A trained NLI model gives an incorrect, opposite result (Fig. 4).

Premise

I am allergic to eggs. Flu shot facilities use egg proteins

Hypothesis

I do not want flu shot

Summary

It is **very likely** that the premise **contradicts** the hypothesis.

	Judgment	Probability
E	Entailment	0.9%

FIG. 4

Language model tries to find a correlation between a problem associated with eggs and an unwillingness to get shots.

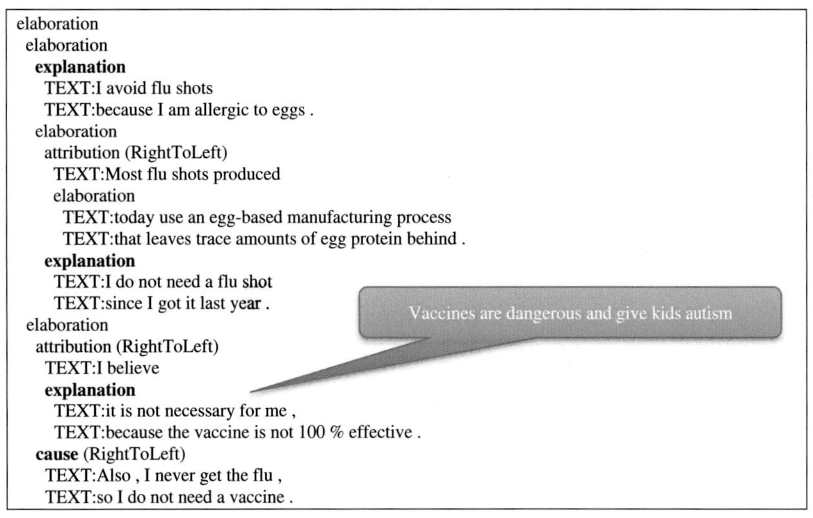

```
elaboration
 elaboration
  explanation
   TEXT:I avoid flu shots
   TEXT:because I am allergic to eggs .
  elaboration
   attribution (RightToLeft)
    TEXT:Most flu shots produced
    elaboration
     TEXT:today use an egg-based manufacturing process
     TEXT:that leaves trace amounts of egg protein behind .
   explanation
    TEXT:I do not need a flu shot
    TEXT:since I got it last year .
 elaboration
  attribution (RightToLeft)
   TEXT:I believe
   explanation
    TEXT:it is not necessary for me ,
    TEXT:because the vaccine is not 100 % effective .
  cause (RightToLeft)
   TEXT:Also , I never get the flu ,
   TEXT:so I do not need a vaccine .
```

Vaccines are dangerous and give kids autism

FIG. 5

A discourse tree (DT) for the patient's explanation.

A discourse-level analysis confirms that the preceding text contains a number of *Explanations* relations and a *Cause* (Galitsky and Ilvovsky, 2017), and a hidden meaning should be expected (Fig. 5).

Splits into elementary discourse units (EDUs) give us the expression to generalize (the first line) and an expression to match with the candidate RBL expressions (the second line):

explanation
TEXT: I do not need a flu shot
TEXT: since I got it last year

We refer to such non-default rhetorical relations as *anchors* since they tell us when the author might expect the reader to RBL.

This case turns out to be more frequent than the reader would imagine because people would repeat multiple times what they want to say to avoid what they do not want to say.

2.2 Reading deep between the lines

We now proceed to a more complex example where the RBL result is less explicit. Someone needs to dig deeper into the author's mind to derive a plausible explanation (Galitsky, 2018) for what the patient is saying.

Diagnosis: *coronavirus*
Doctor question: why do you refuse to drink half a gallon of water per day?
What the patient does not want to tell: *don't want to drink because I have issues and pain urinating.*
Additional diagnosis: interstitial cystitis.
Patient explanation: *I try to drink more liquids, but I do not feel thirsty. I do not want to drink when I get up in the morning. I do not drink in the evening so that I can sleep through the night. I try to drink more at mealtime, but my stomach is full.*
Desired RBL result that is being concealed by the patient: *more drink - more urination.*
User does not want to confess that *he avoids urinating, and therefore avoids drinking required/optimal amount of water.*

Regretfully, an NLI model produces a wrong result, similarly to the preceding example (Fig. 6).

Looking at the discourse tree (DT) in Fig. 8, we can formulate the RBL problem as finding a text where a DT of available/partial explanation is a sub-DT of a full explanation with clear picture (Galitsky and Goldberg, 2019). However, this formulation is not helpful for finding RBL results text, but only, possibly, for verifying it.

As language modeling does not work to identify a correlation between *drinking* and *urinating*, we form a query and run it (Fig. 7). Fig. 8 shows a DT (Chapter 3) for the patient's complaint regarding her conditions where *Contrast*, *Background*, and *Enablement* relations show the positions is text where EDUs for generalization toward forming a search query need to be identified.

From the discourse representation, we obtain and formalize the clauses associating *drinking* and *urinating*:

Drink more ⇔ no thirst
Wake → not want drink
Not drink → sleep through night
Try drink(meal) ⇔ stomach(full)

---

drink(more) → urinate(more)

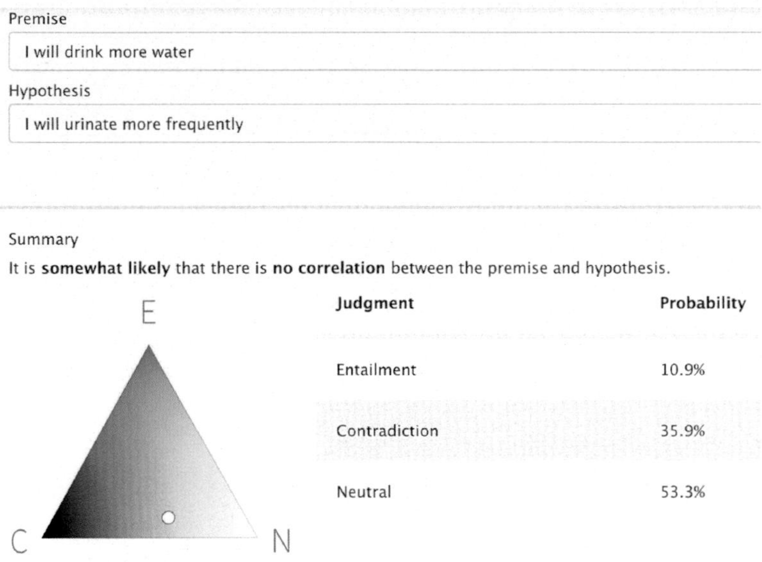

FIG. 6

Allen NLP does not find obvious correlation between *drinking* and *urinating*.

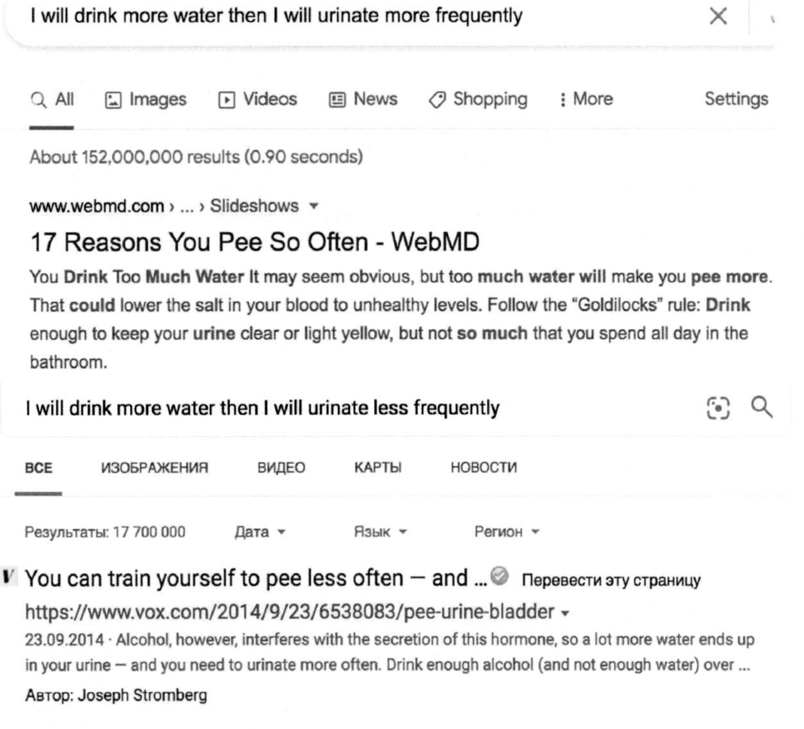

FIG. 7

Web mining to discover a relation (or implication) between *drinking* and *urinating* on Bing.

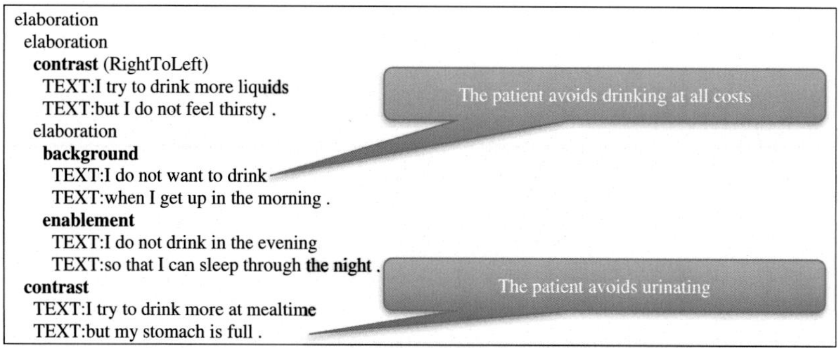

FIG. 8

A discourse tree (DT) for text with repetitive phrase as RBL sources.

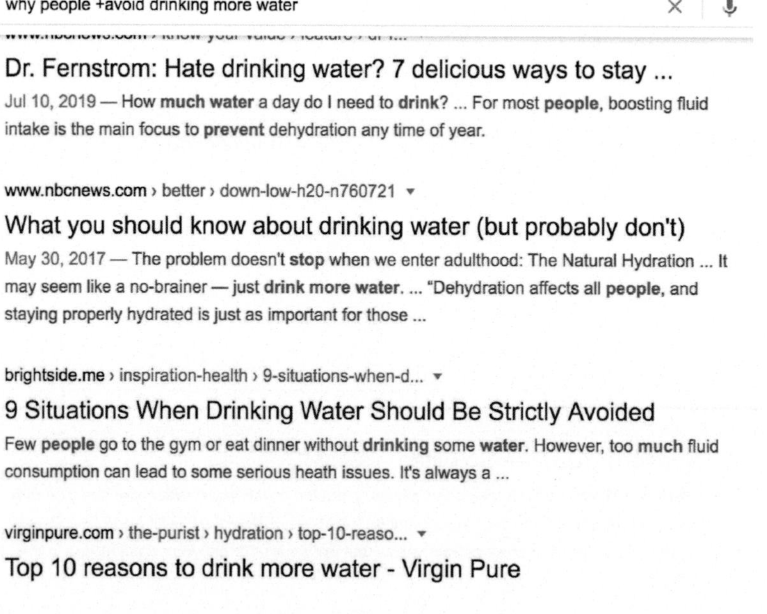

FIG. 9

Searching for the query obtained from the resolving question.

We now formulate the question to the Web that is expected to give us RBL results (Fig. 9):

"*Why people avoid drinking more water?*"

"*Why negation/avoiding/preventing <doctor's recommendation>*"

Language modeling, the task of determining the probability of a given sequence of words occurring in a sentence, can potentially be used to find hidden causes. However, in real life, concealed

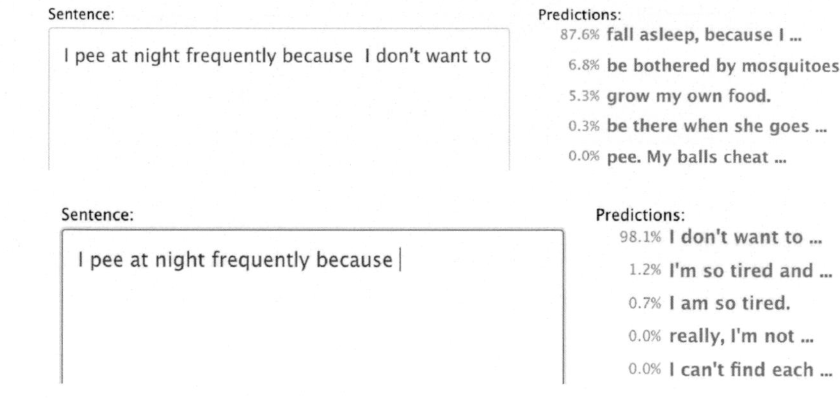
Sentence:
I pee at night frequently because I don't want to
Predictions:
87.6% fall asleep, because I ...
6.8% be bothered by mosquitoes.
5.3% grow my own food.
0.3% be there when she goes ...
0.0% pee. My balls cheat ...
Sentence:
I pee at night frequently because
Predictions:
98.1% I don't want to ...
1.2% I'm so tired and ...
0.7% I am so tired.
0.0% really, I'm not ...
0.0% I can't find each ...

FIG. 10

Using the language model for RBL: Continuing the phrase.

thoughts are infrequent in comparison to typical cases. The further we go, the less meaningful it gets (Fig. 10). This demonstration uses the public 345M parameter OpenAI GPT-2 language model to generate sentences.

We now proceed to the query formation algorithm. One needs to generalize instances of what has been explicitly stated to form a query for something that is implicit and needs to be surfaced (Goncharova et al., 2020).

Fig. 11 shows how a query can be formulated:

$$query = why? + \wedge (explanationSentence(i))$$

Four explicit author expressions are shown on the top as syntactic trees (1)–(4). They are generalized into an Abstract Meaning Representation (AMR) semantic graph (middle) whose keywords form the query to search for RBL results.

A robust and viable way for Natural Language Understanding (NLU) systems to acquire commonsense knowledge, like that employed by humans, is through learning from natural language texts. Traditional NLP tasks and techniques are useful components of this ambitious goal. Yet, the emphasis shifts from extracting knowledge encoded within a piece of text, to that of understanding what text implies, even if not explicitly stated. As an example, consider the following sentence: "*Mary had a appendicitis surgery last week*." Traditional NLP tasks include recognizing the entities, tagging words with their part of speech, creating the syntactic tree, identifying the verbs and their arguments, and so on. Beyond these tasks, however, one may also ask what can be inferred from this sentence. Although this question might not admit a unique answer, a possible inference might be that the "*leukocytosis was present*." Indeed, the author of this sentence may be aware, or even take for granted, that readers will make such an inference, and she may choose not to explicitly include this information. If NLU systems are to understand the intended meaning of text, they should be able to draw similar inferences as those (expected to be) drawn by human readers.

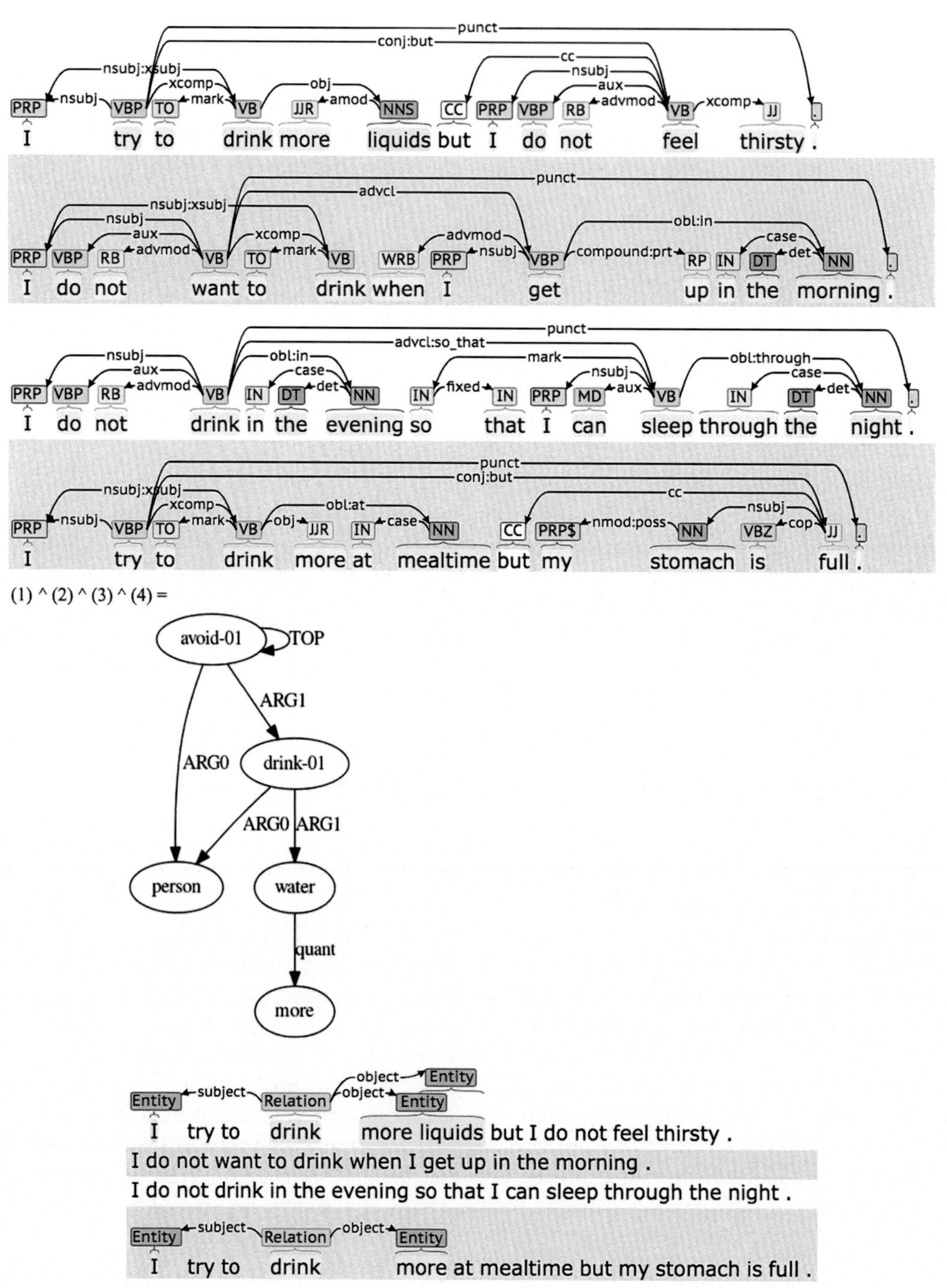

FIG. 11

Explanations and their generalization toward forming a query (top and middle). The Entity-Relation representation (bottom).

2.3 RBL in storytelling

In choosing how to represent their lived experiences of melanoma, the storytellers had to establish an event as a beginning point. Half the stories we read began at the point in time when some kind of change in health was identified or a symptom particular to skin disease was noticed. In these accounts, we witness the storyteller's illness experience when the possibility of disease becomes apparent. One navigates through a timeline in which a diagnosis is made, treatment is given, and an outcome is arrived at. Some stories conclude where the storyteller still has not recovered, some with treatment finished and follow-up care becoming routine, and others, such as the following story, with recurrence or metastases (Lamprell and Braithwaite, 2019).

> *At 22 years old I had a small pink nodule on my neck, just behind my ear, my hairdresser commented on it, said it needed to be checked as it went red when she washed my hair. I promised I would have it checked, but I did not. Over a period of several months, it started to turn dark and grow down my neck. Although it wasn't very big, less than 3 mm, people started asking what was on my neck, had I put permanent marker by accident? I finally went to the doctor and he referred me to a skin specialist and it was removed as a precaution. Ten days later I was told it was a melanoma and needed further surgery….full check-ups were required for the next 5 years before I finally got the all clear. Twenty-eight years later almost to the day, it presented in my gallbladder… I am now stage 4 cancer, living a life of uncertainty.*

This story spans from early adulthood into middle age, although the framing of time is imbalanced. The storyteller is imprecise about time frames in the period of events that lead from symptom to diagnosis, recounting fighting with the presence of the symptom for "several months." This description is clearly in contradiction with the specificity of periods of time specified in diagnosis and treatment, follow-up care, and metastases: 10 days, 5 years, and 28 years. This contrast yields reflection about the personal circumstances of the storyteller at the time of symptom identification. The RBL question concerns the issues untold in the story and their impact on the storyteller's desire or capacity to act on the illness for such a long time.

Fig. 12 shows a *Communicative* DT to extract results from a web page or a document (Chapter 2). In addition to a DT, we attach the labels to edges with information about communicative actions and their subjects (red italics). The rhetorical relations show where RBL should occur when the flow of content is interrupted. It is indicated by the relation of *Contrast*. In the first instance, the contradiction "*I promised …, but never did*" assumes that some conjectures would be drawn by the reader and it is not necessary to write about them explicitly.

The NLI trained model does not work as usual (Fig. 13).

The training set-based entailment is unable to find correlation between the premise in text and the hypothesis we formulated.

In this case, we generalize from a *single* EDU pair, highlighted in green in Fig. 12.

I promised I would have it checked but I did not ->

Promised I do something but never did

Fig. 14 shows a high-level (AMR) abstraction that we are generalizing.

To get an RBL expression, we extract phrases of interest from the search results snippets (red ovals) in Fig. 15. We then select a document with the snippet closest to the formed query and attempt to extract an RBL expression from it. To do that, we build a DT and identify the punchline rhetorical relation, such as *Contrast*, that indicates a significant EDU to be used as our RBL result (Fig. 16).

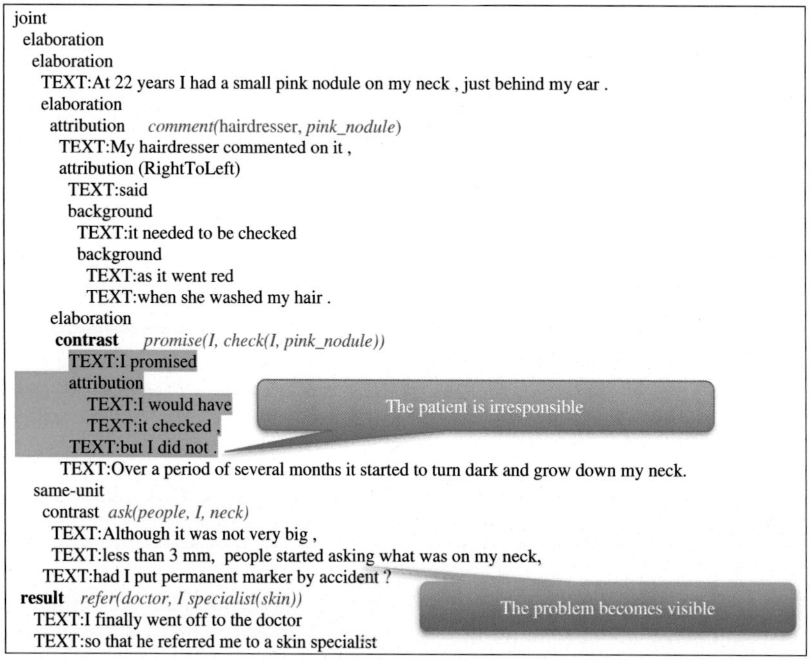

```
joint
 elaboration
  elaboration
   TEXT:At 22 years I had a small pink nodule on my neck , just behind my ear .
   elaboration
    attribution    comment(hairdresser, pink_nodule)
     TEXT:My hairdresser commented on it ,
     attribution (RightToLeft)
      TEXT:said
      background
       TEXT:it needed to be checked
       background
        TEXT:as it went red
        TEXT:when she washed my hair .
    elaboration
     contrast    promise(I, check(I, pink_nodule))
      TEXT:I promised
      attribution
        TEXT:I would have
        TEXT:it checked ,
      TEXT:but I did not .
     TEXT:Over a period of several months it started to turn dark and grow down my neck.
  same-unit
   contrast  ask(people, I, neck)
    TEXT:Although it was not very big ,
    TEXT:less than 3 mm,  people started asking what was on my neck,
   TEXT:had I put permanent marker by accident ?
 result   refer(doctor, I specialist(skin))
  TEXT:I finally went off to the doctor
  TEXT:so that he referred me to a skin specialist
```

The patient is irresponsible

The problem becomes visible

FIG. 12

A communicative discourse tree (DT) for the text obtained from search results to extract RBL.

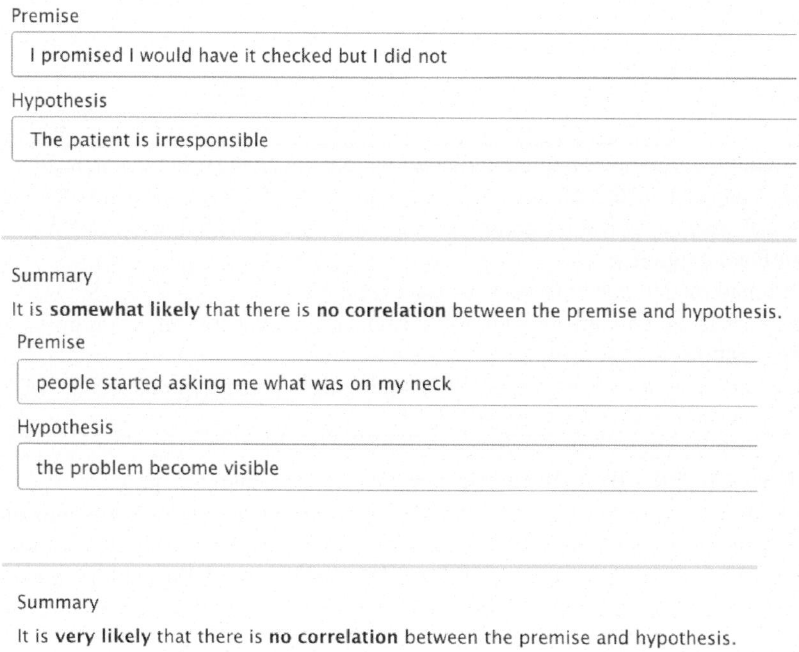

Premise

I promised I would have it checked but I did not

Hypothesis

The patient is irresponsible

Summary

It is **somewhat likely** that there is **no correlation** between the premise and hypothesis.

Premise

people started asking me what was on my neck

Hypothesis

the problem become visible

Summary

It is **very likely** that there is **no correlation** between the premise and hypothesis.

FIG. 13

The language model applied to "*promise …but did not do*" vs "*being irresponsible.*"

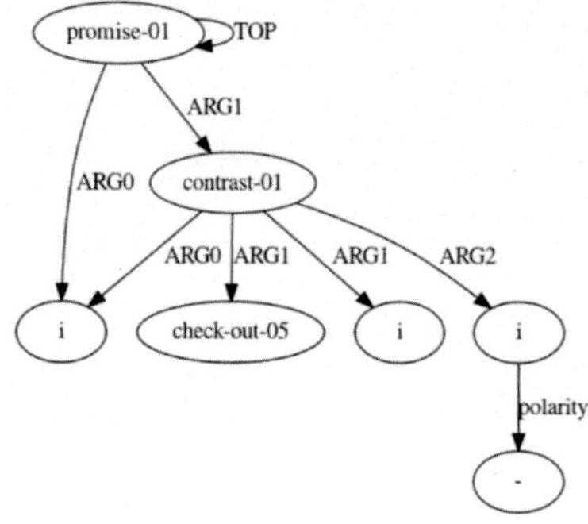

FIG. 14

An AMR graph. Rhetorical relation contrast is expressed as a verb *contrast-01*.

2.4 Extracting RBL results from text

Discourse analysis helps to discover the EDUs that can form promising candidate RBL results. Default rhetorical relations of *Elaboration* and *Joint* are least interesting. What we want for RBL results is something extraordinary, unexpected, and emergent (if available). Relations of *Attribution*, *Condition*, and *Background* are indicative of potentially informative EDUs. Moreover, *Contrast*, *Cause*, and *Explanation* are introducing facts and observations that stand out of routine people's knowledge and cut the best candidate RBL results.

Communicative actions attached to the edges of DT (which form CDT) are also important indicators of an EDU interestingness to form an RBL result. If something said is to be communicated from one person to another, amplified by a specific communication modality like *disagree* or *confirm*, then in most cases the subjects of communicative actions can serve as good RBL candidates. On the top of Fig. 16, the communicative action expression *ought(person, strive(person, consistent(person, [word, action])))* is attached to the edge from the node for the second *Elaboration* (from the top). Nested communicative actions are strong indicators of the importance of the innermost subject: *consistent(person, [word, action])*.

2.5 Difficult RBL cases

This is a domain-within-domain example of a text where RBL is essential but hard to automate. This is how the GPT-2 model is presented (OpenAI, 2019):

> Our model, called GPT-2, was trained simply to predict the next word in 40GB of Internet text. Due to our **concerns about malicious applications of the technology**, we are not releasing the trained model. However, as an experiment in responsible disclosure, we are instead releasing a much smaller model for researchers to experiment with.

The real concern is that GPT- based content generation produces meaningless text

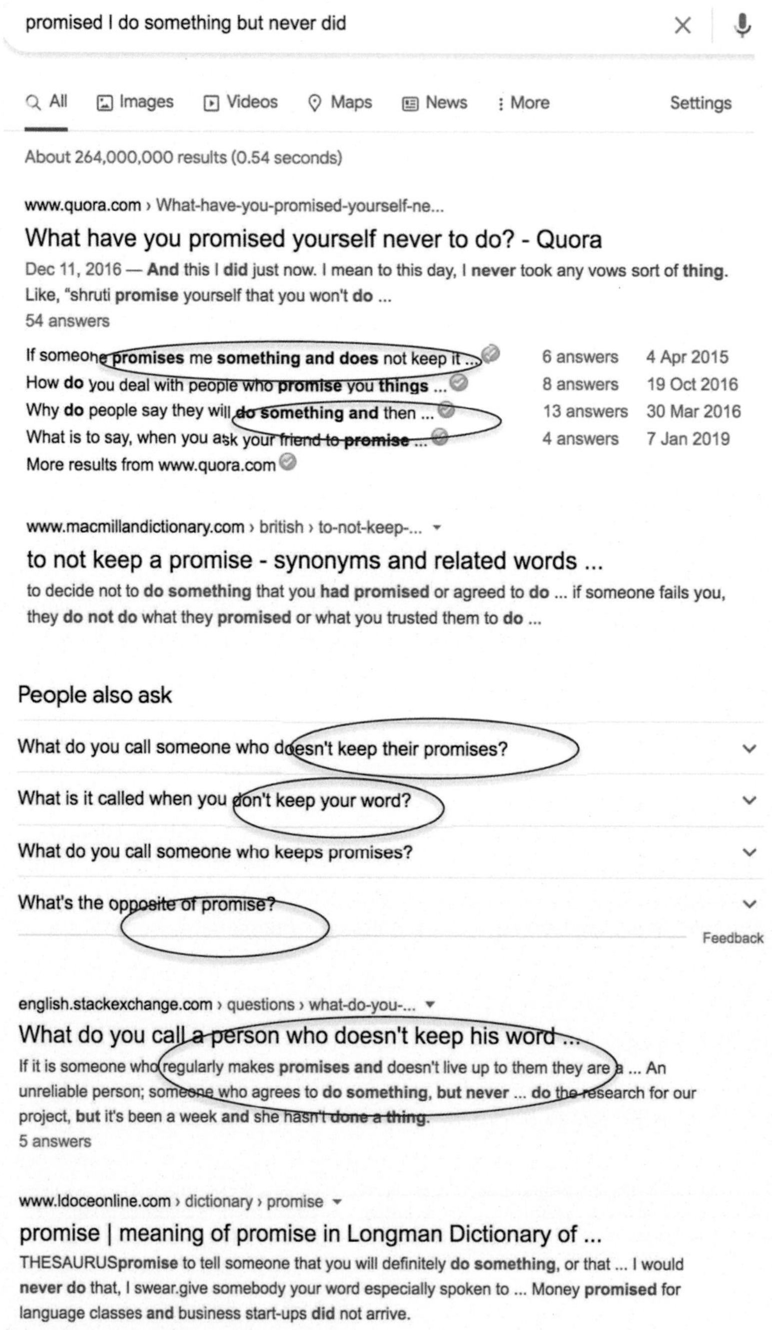

promised I do something but never did

All Images Videos Maps News More Settings

About 264,000,000 results (0.54 seconds)

www.quora.com › What-have-you-promised-yourself-ne...

What have you promised yourself never to do? - Quora

Dec 11, 2016 — **And** this I **did** just now. I mean to this day, I **never** took any vows sort of **thing**. Like, "shruti **promise** yourself that you won't **do** ...

54 answers

If someone **promises** me **something and does** not keep it ...	6 answers	4 Apr 2015
How **do** you deal with people who **promise** you **things** ...	8 answers	19 Oct 2016
Why **do** people say they will **do something and** then ...	13 answers	30 Mar 2016
What is to say, when you ask your friend to **promise** ...	4 answers	7 Jan 2019

More results from www.quora.com

www.macmillandictionary.com › british › to-not-keep-...

to not keep a promise - synonyms and related words ...

to decide not to **do something** that you **had promised** or agreed to **do** ... if someone fails you, they **do not do** what they **promised** or what you trusted them to **do** ...

People also ask

What do you call someone who doesn't keep their promises?

What is it called when you don't keep your word?

What do you call someone who keeps promises?

What's the opposite of promise?

Feedback

english.stackexchange.com › questions › what-do-you-...

What do you call a person who doesn't keep his word ...

If it is someone who regularly makes **promises and** doesn't live up to them they are a ... An unreliable person; someone who agrees to **do something, but never** ... **do** the research for our project, **but** it's been a week **and** she hasn't **done a thing**.

5 answers

www.ldoceonline.com › dictionary › promise

promise | meaning of promise in Longman Dictionary of ...

THESAURUS**promise** to tell someone that you will definitely **do something**, or that ... I would **never do** that, I swear.give somebody your word especially spoken to ... Money **promised** for language classes **and** business start-ups **did** not arrive.

FIG. 15

Web search results from which RBL expressions are extracted. Quora.com and "*People also ask*" section of Google search are particularly good sources of comments and explanation for the situations described by the search query.

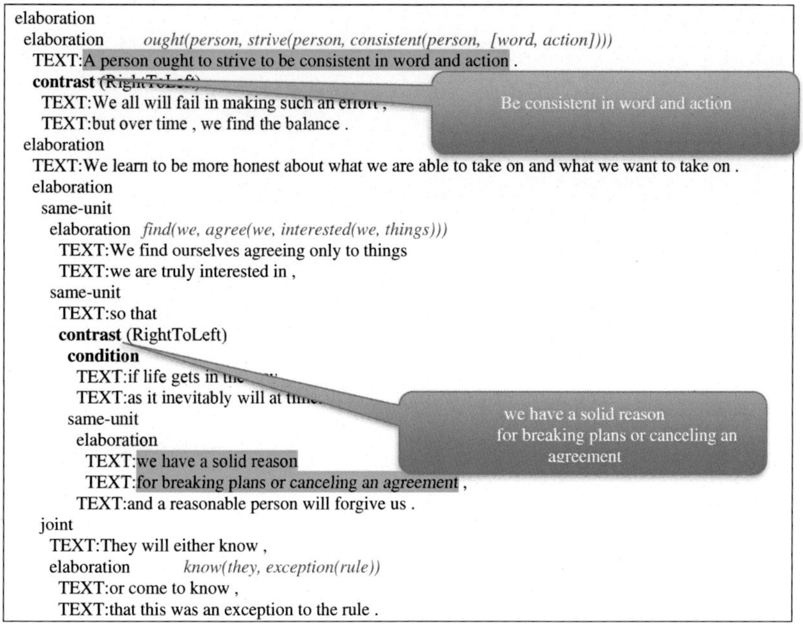

```
elaboration
 elaboration      ought(person, strive(person, consistent(person,  [word, action])))
  TEXT:A person ought to strive to be consistent in word and action .
  contrast (RightToLeft)
   TEXT:We all will fail in making such an effort ,
   TEXT:but over time , we find the balance .
 elaboration
  TEXT:We learn to be more honest about what we are able to take on and what we want to take on .
  elaboration
   same-unit
    elaboration  find(we, agree(we, interested(we, things)))
     TEXT:We find ourselves agreeing only to things
     TEXT:we are truly interested in ,
    same-unit
     TEXT:so that
     contrast (RightToLeft)
      condition
       TEXT:if life gets in the way
       TEXT:as it inevitably will at times
      same-unit
       elaboration
        TEXT:we have a solid reason
        TEXT:for breaking plans or canceling an agreement ,
       TEXT:and a reasonable person will forgive us .
  joint
   TEXT:They will either know ,
   elaboration        know(they, exception(rule))
    TEXT:or come to know ,
    TEXT:that this was an exception to the rule .
```

Be consistent in word and action

we have a solid reason
for breaking plans or canceling an agreement

FIG. 16

A communicative DT (CDT) for a text that is obtained from the Web and is a source of RBL expressions. Each callout box points to a *Contrast* relation relied on for identification of the respective RBL expression.

RBL here is difficult since a commonsense knowledge that "computer scientists frequently avoid releasing their systems so that it is easy for others to see problems with them" is hard formalize. To explain why they do not want to release systems, they need to make an excuse that they are **concerned about malicious applications**.

On the bottom of Fig. 17, we show the best we could find on the Web, forming a query related to "*concern related to malicious applications of technology*." We obtain not-so-relevant results such as "*I am not good enough*," which can explain the situation, but there is a lack of confidence here that the author meant exactly that.

In complex cases of RBL such as the preceding, one approaches *sarcasm* (Akula and Garibay, 2021), *hypocrisy* (Galitsky, 2021a), *pretending* (Galitsky, 2016), and other complex linguistic phenomena that cannot always be automated by means of discourse analysis, generalization, and web mining (Mitchell, 2005).

2.6 RBL in a dialogue

Let us try to RBL the following dialogue interaction between participants A and B (Fig. 18).

The listener of this piece of dialogue will have to reason based on utterances that are shared between two participants, thus having to dynamically keep track of them (Galitsky and Ilvovsky, 2019). Furthermore, the listener must be able, on one hand, to compute global inferences, that is, inferences

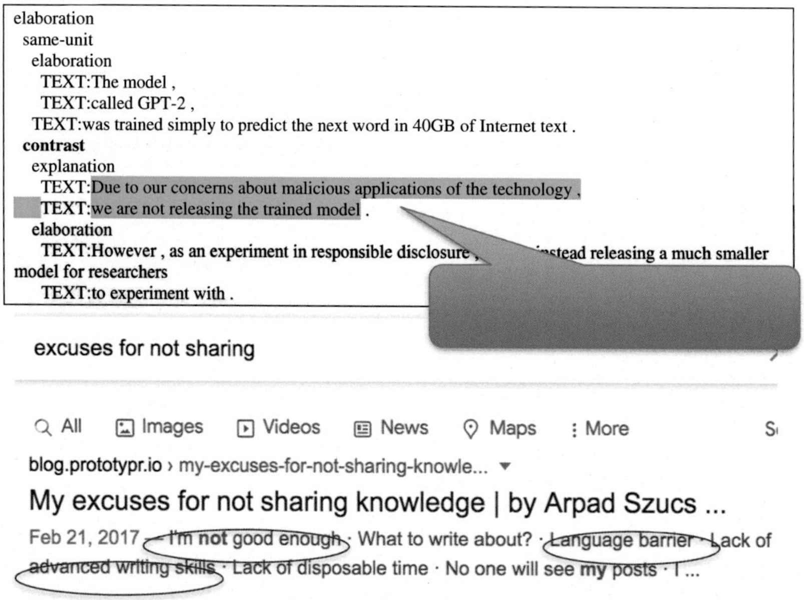

elaboration
same-unit
elaboration
TEXT:The model ,
TEXT:called GPT-2 ,
TEXT:was trained simply to predict the next word in 40GB of Internet text .
contrast
explanation
TEXT:Due to our concerns about malicious applications of the technology ,
TEXT:we are not releasing the trained model .
elaboration
TEXT:However , as an experiment in responsible disclosure , ... instead releasing a much smaller model for researchers
TEXT:to experiment with .

excuses for not sharing

All Images Videos News Maps More

blog.prototypr.io › my-excuses-for-not-sharing-knowle...

My excuses for not sharing knowledge | by Arpad Szucs ...

Feb 21, 2017 — I'm not good enough · What to write about? · Language barrier · Lack of advanced writing skills · Lack of disposable time · No one will see my posts · I ...

FIG. 17

A DT for a complex RBL case.

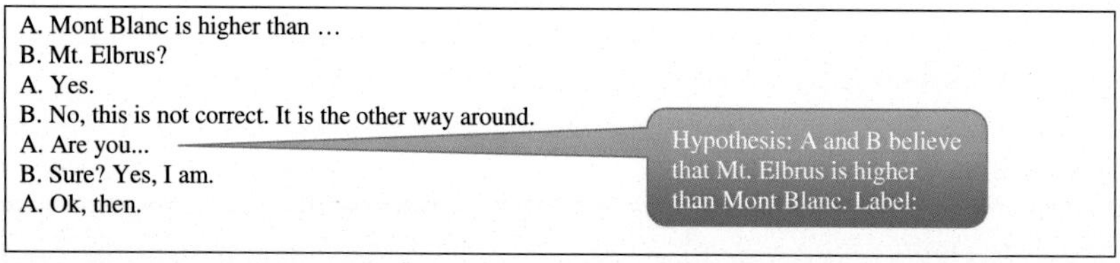

A. Mont Blanc is higher than …
B. Mt. Elbrus?
A. Yes.
B. No, this is not correct. It is the other way around.
A. Are you...
B. Sure? Yes, I am.
A. Ok, then.

Hypothesis: A and B believe that Mt. Elbrus is higher than Mont Blanc. Label:

FIG. 18

A dialogue demanding reasoning in the form of RBL.

that are based on statements/facts that are shared (agreed upon) by the dialogue participants, and local inferences, on the other hand, that is, inferences that are based on facts that are not shared by all dialogue participants (Bernardy and Chatzikyriakidis, 2019).

Generalizing, we could say that the human ability to reason with natural language (NL), that is, NLI, cannot be seen as a single, coherent system of reasoning, but rather as a collection of reasoning tools, a toolbox to perform diverse reasoning tasks. Despite the fragmentary nature of dialogue, humans can perform reasoning tasks at each stage of the interaction and update these inferences if needed when more information comes in. Dialogues are sources of high-density RBL; however, there are no NLI datasets for dialogue data and thus no dataset that will include reasoning with this type of data. Given that dialogue data is a core part of NL, this is something that the NLP community should eventually focus on. One way to design NLI for dialogues is to build dialogue datasets via extracting dialogue pieces from corpora like the British National Corpus (BNC) or the newest dialogue datasets, most prominently bAbI (Bordes et al., 2016) and bAbI+ (Shalyminov et al., 2017) used the pieces as premises and then constructed the hypothesis based on those. One of the promising approaches here is a doc2dialogue framework (Galitsky et al., 2019). Given the nature of the task, issues like participants' individual beliefs will come into play (Ilvovsky et al., 2020). For example, here is a formed hypothesis against a fragment of the dialogue: "*A and B believe that Mt. Elbrus is higher than Mont Blanc.*"

2.7 Question formation and diversification

When we obtain a candidate for a question, it is subject to reduction to avoid being too specific. For example, "*What is a British rock band that formed in London in 1970 and received Grammy Hall of Fame Award in 2004?*" would be too specific and should be reduced, for instance, to "What is a British rock band that formed in London?" To achieve a proper level of generalization for questions, we take an extended set of questions such as Stanford Q/A database (SQuAD), perform pair-wise syntactic generalization (Galitsky et al., 2012), and retain most frequent question templates. The SQuAD corpus is a machine comprehension dataset consisting of more than 100,000 crowd-sourced question-answer pairs on 500 Wikipedia articles. For example, generalizing "*What is the purpose of life on Earth?*" and "*Tell me the purpose of complex numbers*" we obtain "the-DT purpose-NN of-PRP *-NP" where we retain the part-of-speech tags. We collect the most frequent generalization results (question templates).

We apply phrase-reduction rules at both the individual phrase and sentence levels. As a result, we want to obtain a question from an original satellite EDU expression that is as close to a question template as possible. Hence for every satellite EDU expression we iterate through the templates and find the most similar one. In terms of syntactic generalization, it is the template that delivers a maximal common sub- parse tree with this expression. For the sentence "[I built a bridge] nucleus [with the purpose of fast access to the forest]satellite," the satellite EDU is better covered by the template from our previous paragraph than, for example, by "access-NN to-TO forest-NN" or "access-NN to-TO NP" in terms of the number of common terms (parse tree nodes) of the generalization result.

To improve the meaningfulness, interestingness, and diversity of a formed and generalized question, we rely on the wisdom of the Web, analogously to RBL results. We form a web search query from the formed question and attempt to find an expression from a web document as close to this question as possible and from a reputable or popular source. We iterate through web search results obtained by the Bing API and score document titles, snippet sentences, and other expressions in found documents to be semantically similar to the query. Semantic similarity is assessed via the syntactic generalization score between the candidate query and a search result. If such expression from the document is found, its entities need to be substituted by the ones from the original question. As a result, a candidate question will appear more popular, mature, and in more common terms.

To verify that the formed and modified question obtained from a satellite EDU text has this text as a good answer, we apply the open-domain Q/A technique (Galitsky, 2017). Given the whole original text and a formed question, we verify that the answer is the EDU this question was formed from and does not correspond to another EDU. A wrong text fragment can appear as an answer if the question was substantially distorted by generalization or web mining. We use (Deep Pavlov, 2020) DL Q/A system for this verification.

3. System architecture

For a document or a long text, we first need to select the sections or text fragments where RBL is required or expected to give fruitful results. That can be done, for example, based on formatting cues or tags. The input text is first parsed syntactically to obtain a parse tree and is then subject to discourse parsing to yield a communicative DT (Fig. 19).

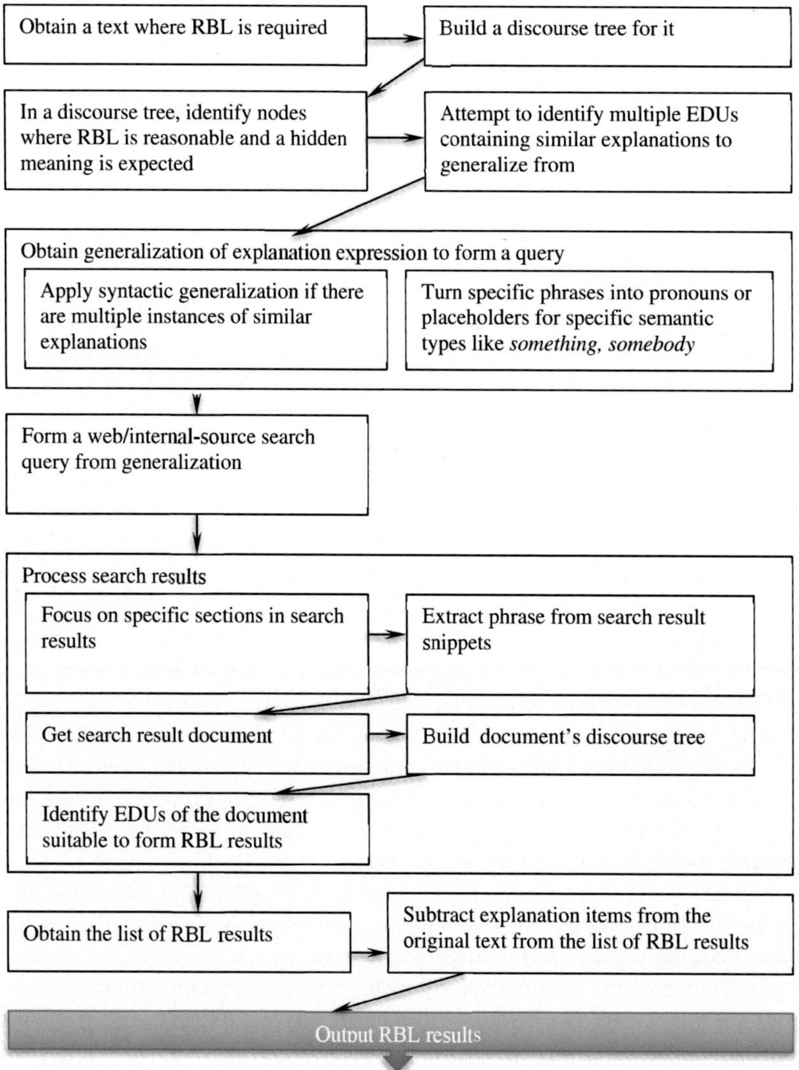

FIG. 19

The system architecture.

The DT gives a hint to where RBL should be applied. In the case of the continuous content flow structured by the rhetorical relation of *Elaboration*, RBL is unlikely to give interesting results since the text author gives a clue that they are not going to conceal something or express sarcasm or controversy. Conversely, when the content flow is turbulent, with the relations *Contrast*, *Condition*, *Explanation*, and others, one can expect a hidden meaning, something the author does not dare to express. Such rhetorical relation is an *anchor*.

Once we identify the anchor position, we have EDUs to work with to RBL. We attempt to identify multiple indicators for an RBL seed and generalize them. If there is just a single EDU to attempt to RBL, we transform it into a more general form, substituting specific values into placeholders for certain entity types or semantic types. Finally, in this step, we turn the obtained generalization into a query (Chapter 6).

Processing search results is the last step of RBL. We focus on the specific fragments and sections of a document or a web page such as enumeration of conditions or cases to extract the one most relevant to the query. We extract the phrases from those search result snippets that are semantically closest to the query. We then select the respective documents and apply discourse parsing to the chosen text fragment to obtain the EDUs potentially most suitable to serve as RBL results.

Once the RBL candidate list is obtained, it is subject to filtering based on domain-specific criteria. Firstly, we subtract the phrases that are already in the text and are semantically close to the members of the candidate RBL list from the RBL list. Then we remove out-of-domain members, the ones with inappropriate style, and so forth.

4. Statistical model of RBL

Michael (2008) proposes that text be viewed as an appearance of some underlying and hidden reality. There is the following example scenario: a newspaper reporter attends the scene of a patient's recovery at the time of the event. The news reporter observes the event unfolding and later documents his experience in a newspaper article. The article is subsequently read by the readers of the newspaper. From a reader's point of view, the reality of interest is the event of the actual patient recovery that took place. This reality, however, is not directly visible to the reader. The reader's only source of information about the event is the reporter's article, a fragment of text. In this sense, this fragment of text acts as an appearance, a partial observation, of the actual reality. Depending on the reporter, the article might contain many details of the actual event or mention only the important, in the reporter's opinion, parts of the event. The reporter might have a page limit to uphold in writing the article and may be forced to drop even important aspects of the event. Even more so, the reporter might be biased in favor of or against the doctor treating the patient, and the text might describe the event noisily or inaccurately.

Yet, from this fragment of text the reader hopes to reconstruct (to some extent) the actual event. Michael's (2008) approach is to view text as a partial depiction of some underlying hidden reality. RBL is then intended to recover this reality by finding similar cases on the Web or elsewhere. The author maps this reality into a fragment of text through the author of the text. TE is then formalized as the task of accurately, in a defined sense, recovering information about this underlying reality. An agent engaged in the TE task is first given access to a corpus of text relevant to some domain of interest, and only then it is asked to recognize TE. This training phase aims, from a semantics point of view, to make precise the type of statistical accuracy for the textual entailment task and to give the agent a means of acquiring relevant ontology (Chapter 11).

To capture the nature of text *text* as an appearance of some underlying reality, machinery is required to model reality, text, and the author that ties the two together. We consider a fixed set $A = \{x_1, \ldots, x_n\}$, $n = |A|$, of attributes, and think of each attribute in A as an indicator variable of some aspect of the reality of interest. An event is represented as a binary string e of length n, with the i-th bit of e, denoted $e[i]$, corresponding to the value of attribute x_i. The patient care event in our example can, for instance, correspond to the binary string $e = 010001110111001$, where x_1 stands for whether the nurse took a temperature measurement (in this case "no"), x_2 for whether the nurse administered a painkiller shot (in this case "yes"), and so on. Some other patient recovery events would be represented by a different binary string, although keeping the same interpretation of the attributes.

To capture the fact that text is only partially depicting the event, a third value * is used, which stands for "do not know." A fragment of text describing the patient story event of our example could, for instance, correspond to the ternary string $T = * \, 00 * 011 ** 1110 * 1$, with the same interpretation of the attributes as before. Note that the values of some attributes are * (masked). The example text fragment does not accurately represent the underlying reality according to e, since the actual patient process involved, for example, chemical therapy, x_3 is noisy in text w.r.t. e.

The author is modeled as a stochastic process that takes as input events (binary arrays) and outputs text (ternary arrays). An event exists first and is then mapped into the text through the writer. When reading this text, the reader attempts to recover the event. We call any such process that maps binary to ternary strings a *sensor*; the author is the sensor through which a reader observes an event. The reader's task is well defined this way, and the RBL task is too.

To understand why it is plausible to recover information about some underlying event by only reading some text about it, one needs to appreciate the fact that the reader also employs some prior knowledge relevant to the event of interest. Most text consumers (readers) know, for instance, that surgeries often involve the use of some form of scalpels. Even if the news reporter does not mention such information, it is reasonable to assume that the reader will deduce it given the context. The prior information employed by the reader can then be modeled as a rule that tries to predict the value of some target attribute x_t given only T. We take the approach that this rule $(\phi) \equiv x_t$ is of the typical form. The rule's body ϕ is a propositional formula defined over the attributes A of a domain, and the rule's head is the attribute x_t to be predicted.

Let KB be the knowledge base that an agent uses to perform RBL, including both the actual knowledge and inference that applies this knowledge to a given fragment of text T. $conc(KB \mid T)$ denotes the ternary string that results when KB is applied to T.

A first attempt to define TE is to ask that for a sensing process sense, an event e, and a fragment of text T drawn from $sense(e)$, it holds that $conc(KB \mid T)$ is equal to e. Thus, the application of the knowledge base KB on the fragment of text T provides an RBL result for the hidden event e.

Note that for any knowledge base KB, an event e can be chosen in a defeating way to make it impossible to reliably (i.e., not by chance) RBL e, even if no attribute is noisy in *text*, and only a single attribute is masked in *text*. A minimal assumption is needed to circumvent this: that the events have some structure, in the sense that the values of the attributes in e are somehow correlated with each other.

We assume that e is drawn from some arbitrary probability distribution D; we write $e \leftarrow D$. Similarly, some minimal structure should be assumed on the sensing process. We also assume that once e is chosen, T is drawn from some arbitrary probability distribution $sense(e)$: $T \leftarrow sense(e)$.

A KB can be characterized by its RBL capability. *Soundness* is based on asking that if some attribute in a selected set A_t has a {0, 1} value in $conc(KB \mid T)$, then this value should match the one specified by the underlying event e that yielded T. *Completeness* amounts to asking that the attributes in A_t should have a {0, 1} value in $conc(KB \mid T)$.

A KB is $(1-\varepsilon)$**-sound** for a target attribute set $A_t \subseteq A$ under a probability distribution D and a sensing process *sense* if

$Pr\,[\exists x_t \in A_t$ that is noisy in $conc(KB \mid T)$ w.r.t. $e \mid e \leftarrow D\ \&\ T \leftarrow sense(e)] \leq \varepsilon$.

A KB is $(1-\omega)$**-complete** for a target attribute set $A_t \subseteq A$ under a probability distribution D and a sensing process *sense* if

$Pr\,[\exists x_t \in A_t$ that is masked in $conc(KB \mid T)$ w.r.t. $e \mid e \leftarrow D\ \&\ T \leftarrow sense(e)] \leq \omega$, where Pr is a probability

Maintaining the hospital domain, let $x_t =$ "*the patient's recovery was successful*." What does it mean when we say that a $rule(\phi) \equiv x_t$ is appropriate for inferring from text whether x_t is true or not? This could be formalized as asking that the rule does not wrongly predict the value of x_t in some underlying event e, given access to $T \leftarrow sense(e)$. Denote by $val(\phi \mid T)$ the prediction that the rule $(\phi) \equiv x_t$ determines the value of its head x_t given T. We say that $(\phi) \equiv x_t$ has an *accuracy conflict* with e given T if $val(\phi \mid T) \in \{0, 1\}$ and $val(\phi \mid T) \neq e[t]$.

For example, for the rule $(x_3 \vee (x_1 \wedge x_7)) \equiv x_4$, the $e = 1{,}000{,}110$, and $T = 10$ *** 10, it holds that $val(x_3 \vee (x_1 \wedge x_7) \mid T) = 1$, and $e\,[4] = 0$, hence there is an accuracy conflict, since the predicted value of x_4 is incorrect.

A rule $(\phi) \equiv x_t$ is $(1-\varepsilon)$**-accurate** under a probability distribution D and a sensing process sense if Pr $[(\phi) \equiv x_t$ has an accuracy conflict with e given $T \mid e \leftarrow D\ \&\ T \leftarrow sense(e)] \leq \varepsilon$.

Michael (2008) considers consistency conflict metric to evaluate a rule used to infer one thing and against which its accuracy is measured as *unknown*. We say that $(\phi) \equiv x_t$ has a **consistency conflict with** T if $val(\phi \mid T)$, $T[t] \in \{0, 1\}$ and $val(\phi \mid T) \neq T[t]$. For example, for the rule $(x_3 \vee (x_1 \wedge x_7)) \equiv x_4$, and $T = 10$ *** 10, it holds that $val(x_3 \vee (x_1 \wedge x_7)) \mid T) = 1$, and $T[4] =$ *; there is no consistency conflict independently of the value of x_4 in the underlying event that yields T.

A rule $(\phi) \equiv x_t$ is $(1-\varepsilon)$**-consistent** under a probability distribution D and a sensing process sense if Pr $[(\phi) \equiv x_t$ has a consistency conflict with $T \mid e \leftarrow D;\ T \leftarrow sense(e)] \leq \varepsilon$.

The theorem demonstrates that highly consistent rules are also highly accurate to the extent possible (Michael, 2007).

Theorem 1 *For every noiseless sensing process* sense, *and every class* F *of rules with head* x_t, *there exists* $\eta \in [0, 1]$ *such that if* $\eta \neq 0$:

- *For every probability distribution* D, *and rule* $(\phi) \equiv x_t$, *the rule is* $(1-\varepsilon)$***-accurate*** *if it is* $(1-\eta\cdot\varepsilon)$***-consistent.***
- *There is a probability distribution* D_0, *and a rule* $(\phi_0) \equiv x_t$ *that is* $(1-\varepsilon)$***-accurate*** *only if it is* $(1-\eta\cdot\varepsilon)$***-consistent***.

Here, intuitively, $1-\eta$ *measures how strongly the author of text to which the rules in* F *are applied conceals information from the reader (Fig. 20). To be able to infer whether* "the patient recovery was successful," *and be confident that this was indeed the case, it is sufficient to rely on a rule that when tested on documents, is almost never found to be in conflict with the text. This rule either:*

(1) *makes no prediction due to a lack of information to determine whether the rule's premises hold, or*

FIG. 20

Concealing information.

(2) *it makes a prediction, but the text does not offer any information on whether this is true or false, or*
(3) *it makes a prediction that is corroborated by the text.*

Assuming that such a rule can be identified, it is reliable according to the preceding theorem. This rule will almost never predict something that is in conflict with the actual event underlying the text. Thus, such rules, learned from text alone, can be later applied to new fragments of text and reliably, in a precisely defined sense, recover information on the event observed by the author.

Theorem 2 *Assuming the following:*

(1) *In the underlying reality, as determined by some arbitrary probability distribution* D*, the value of some target attribute* x_t *is determined by some monotone formula* ψ *over the rest of the attributes.*
(2) *Events drawn from* D *are mapped into text through an arbitrary noiseless sensing process* sense*.*
(3) *The formula* ψ *belongs to a class of formulas that is learnable in the standard Probably Approximately Correct model (Valiant, 1984) from complete examples.*

Then there exists an algorithm that given an access to documents drawn from sense(D)*, runs in time polynomial in the relevant learning parameters, and returns a rule* $(\phi) \equiv x_t$ *that, w.h.p., is* $(1-\varepsilon)$*-consistent under* D *and* sense.

How should the acquired rules be used for recovering missing information implied by a fragment of text? Naturally, an inference should choose to apply all rules in parallel, that is, to check whether the premises of each rule are satisfied given the original text. Some other inference machinery could choose to apply some of the rules and expand the fragment of text with the conclusions. The rest of the rules are then applied to this expanded fragment of text. Thus, this second set of rules would be able to leverage the conclusions of the rules in the first set.

Valiant (2006) proposes pragmatic considerations leveraging a stage-by-stage application of rules in the context of automated acquisition and handling of the knowledge that is not axiomatized. The statistics of the data might not support the induction of rules within a single stage, and even if they do, the induction task might be computationally hard, and programmed rules might need to be integrated in the reasoning process. It is naturally implemented by applying them in a certain stage preceding the learned rules' stage.

One can prove that applying rules in multiple stages is beneficial. This result holds without appealing to any statistical, computational, or representational assumptions, and irrespectively of whether the rules are acquired by learning or programmed.

We say that reasoning collapses for a target attribute set $A_t \subseteq A$ under a probability distribution D and a sensing process sense if for every $(1-\varepsilon)$-sound and $(1-\omega)$-complete KB, there exists a $(1-\varepsilon')$-sound and $(1-\omega')$ complete single-stage KB such that $\varepsilon' + \omega' \leq \varepsilon + \omega$. Thus, reasoning does not break if it is possible to find a KB that strictly outperforms, in terms of soundness and completeness, every KB whose rules are applied in parallel. We claim that the KB that chains the following two rules in two stages has this property:

Stage 1 Rule: (*noon time*)$\equiv$*antibiotic injection*.

Layer 1 Rule: (*antibiotic injection* and temp >37.5)$\equiv$*antibiotic injection* and *aspirin*.

Let us consider a rule $(\phi)\equiv x_t$, and an attribute x_i that is masked in T. If changing the value of x_i to 0 or 1 causes the rule to make different $\{0, 1\}$ predictions, then call x_i is critical for $(\phi)\equiv x_t$ w.r.t. T. It is not hard to show:

Unique Critical Attribute Theorem: At most one attribute is critical for any rule $(\phi)\equiv x_i$ w.r.t. any T.

This concludes the statistical model of RBL following (Michael, 2008).

5. RBL and NLI

We now return to the traditional definition of NLI. It is the task of determining whether a "hypothesis" is true (entailment), false (contradiction), or undetermined (neutral) given a "premise." Capturing semantic relations between sentences, such as entailment, is a long-standing challenge for computational semantics. Logic-based models analyze entailment in terms of possible worlds (interpretations or situations) where a premise P entails a hypothesis H if in all worlds where P is true, H is also true. Statistical models view this relationship probabilistically, addressing it in terms of whether a human would likely infer H from P (Vu et al., 2018). For instance, the premise "*People trying to get warm in front of a fireplace*" and the hypothesis "*A family is trying to get warm at home*" are highly likely to be in an entailment relation.

From the RBL standpoint, TE and NLI patterns are rather simple and cannot help RBL directly. However, rule-based TE can potentially approach RBL demands, and eventually learning-based NLI will get closer to a higher-abstraction inference desired from RBL. NLI has gained significant attention due to the availability of large-scale datasets (Williams et al., 2018) that can be used to train data-hungry DL models (Kapanipathi et al., 2020). However, work relevant to the use of these NLI models for downstream tasks such as RBL has been very limited and can be categorized into two categories:

(1) work focusing on using models trained on sentence-level NLI datasets with fixed or learned aggregation to perform a target downstream task (Falke et al., 2019)
(2) studies addressing the need for task-specific NLI datasets (Demszky et al., 2018)

In the Stanford Natural Language Inference dataset (SNLI; Bowman et al., 2015), premises are taken from a dataset of images annotated with descriptive captions; the corresponding hypotheses are produced through crowdsourcing, where for a given premise, annotators provided a sentence that is true or not true with respect to a possible image that the premise could describe. A consequence of this choice is that the contradiction relation can be assigned to pairs that are rather unrelated ("*A person in a black wetsuit is surfing a small wave*" and "*A woman is trying to sleep on her bed*").

5.1 NLI and semantic fragments

NLI is known to involve a wide range of reasoning and knowledge phenomena, including knowledge that goes beyond basic linguistic understanding (e.g., elementary logic). As one example of such knowledge, the inference in Fig. 21 involves monotonicity reasoning (i.e., reasoning about word substitutions in context); here the position of *rats* in the premise occurs in a downward monotone context (marked as $\downarrow$), meaning that it can be specialized (i.e., substituted with a more specific concept such as *small rats*) to generate an entailment relation. In contrast, substituting *mouse* for a more generic concept, such as *animal*, has the effect of generating a neutral inference (Richardson et al., 2020).

For NLI and RBL, it is important to design challenge datasets that are not limited by the simple types of inferences that they included (e.g., lexical and negation inferences). It is valuable to cover more complex reasoning phenomena related to logic in addition to using adversarially generated corpus data, which sometimes makes it difficult to identify exactly the particular semantic phenomena being tested for. Moreover, it is necessary to build NLI datasets that can be easily constructed and evaluated using crowdsourcing techniques. Adequately evaluating a model's competence on a given reasoning phenomena, however, often requires datasets that are hard even for humans, but that are nonetheless based on sound formal principles. In particular, it is worth designing a dataset with complex reasoning about monotonicity where, in contrast to the simple example in Fig. 21, several hierarchically nested monotone contexts are used to test the model capability for compositionality.

Using a fixed vocabulary of people and place names, individual fragments cover Boolean coordination (Boolean reasoning about conjunction *and*), simple *negation*, *quantification* and quantifier

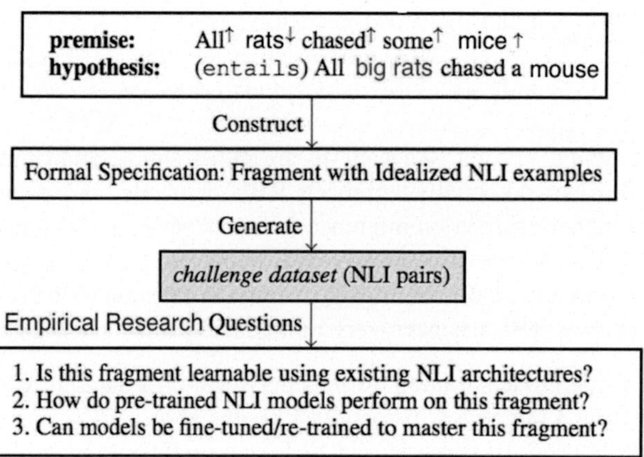

FIG. 21

Studying NLI model behavior through semantic fragments.

Table 1 Semantic fragments to learn nontrivial NLI: the top four fragments test basic logic and the bottom fragments cover monotonicity reasoning.

Fragments	Example (premise,label,hypothesis)	Genre
Negation	*Laurie has only visited Nephi, Marion has only visited Calistoga.* CONTRADICTION *Laurie didn't visit Calistoga.*	Countries/Travel
Boolean	*Travis, Arthur, Henry, and Dan have only visited Georgia.* ENTAILMENT *Dan didn't visit Rwanda.*	Countries/Travel
Quantifier	*Everyone has visited every place.* NEUTRAL *Virgil didn't visit Barry.*	Countries/Travel
Counting	*Nellie has visited Carrie, Billie, John, Mike, Thomas, Mark, …, and Arthur.* ENTAILMENT *Nellie has visited more than 10 people.*	Countries/Travel
Conditionals	*Francisco has visited Potsdam and if Francisco has visited Potsdam, then Tyrone has visited Pampa.* ENTAILMENT *Tyrone has visited Pampa.*	Countries/Travel
Comparatives	*John is taller than Gordon and Erik…, and Mitchell is as tall as John.* NEUTRAL *Erik is taller than Gordon.*	People/Height
Monotonicity	*All black mammals saw exactly 5 stallions who danced.* ENTAILMENT *A brown or black poodle saw exactly 5 stallions who danced.*	Animals
SNLI+MNLI	*During calf roping a cowboy calls off his horse. CONTRADICTION A man ropes a calf successfully.*	Mixed

scope, *comparative* relations, set counting, and *conditional* phenomena all related to a small set of traveling and height relations (Table 1).

Semantic fragments are built using the set of verb-argument templates first described in (Salvatore et al., 2019), including two-way NLI classification rules such as *Entailment* and *Contradiction*. Richardson et al. (2020) adjusted their rule sets to handle three-way classification, and added other inference rules, enumerated in Table 2.

Semantic fragments vary in complexity, with the negation fragment (which is limited to verbal *negation*) being the least complex in terms of linguistic phenomena. We also note that all other fragments include basic negation and Boolean operators, which we found to help preserve the naturalness of the

Table 2 Semantic templates for NLI.

Logic Fragment	**Rule Template: [premise], { hypothesis**$_1$**, ... }** ⇒ **label**; Labeled Examples (simplified)		
Negation	[only-did-p(x)], $\neg$p(x)	⇒ CONTRADICTION	Dave$_x$ has only visited Israel$_p$, Dave$_x$ didn't$_\neg$ visit Israel$_p$
	[only-did-p(x)], $\neg$p$'(x)$	⇒ ENTAILMENT	Dave$_x$ has only visited Israel$_p$, Dave$_x$ didn't$_\neg$ visit Russia$_{p'}$
	[only-did-p(x)], $\neg$p(x')	⇒ NEUTRAL	Dave$_x$ has only visited Israel$_p$, Bill$_x$ didn't$_\neg$ visit Israel$_p$
Boolean	[p$(x_1) \wedge ... \wedge$p(x_n)], $\neg$p(x_j)	⇒ CONTRADICTION	Dustin$_{x_1}$, Milton$_{x_2}$, ... have only visited Equador$_p$; Dustinx_1 didn't$_\neg$ visit Equador$_p$
	[p$_1(x_1) \wedge ... \wedge$p$_n(x_n)$], $\neg$p$_j(x')$	⇒ NEUTRAL	Dustin$_x$ only visited$_p$ Portugal$_1$ and Spain$_2$; James$_{x'}$ didn't$_\neg$ visit$_p$ Spain$_{'}$
	[p$_1(x) \wedge ... \wedge$p$_n(x)$], $\neg$p$'(x)$	⇒ ENTAILMENT	Dustin$_x$ only visited$_p$ Portugal$_1$ and Spain$_2$; Dustin$_x$ didn't$_\neg$ visit$_p$ Germany$_{'}$
Conditional	[(p $\to$ q) $\wedge$ p], q	⇒ ENTAILMENT	Dave visited Israel$_p$ and if Dave visited Israel$_p$ then$_\to$ Bill visited Russia$_q$; Bill visited Russia$_q$.
	[(p $\to$ q) $\wedge$ p], $\neg$q	⇒ CONTRADICTION	Dave visited Israel$_p$ and if Dave visited Israel$_p$ then$_\to$ Bill visited Russia$_q$; Bill didn't visit Russia$_p$.
	[(p $\to$ q) $\wedge$ $\neg$p], {q, $\neg$q}	⇒ NEUTRAL	Dave didn't visit Israel$_p$, and if Dave visited Israel$_p$ then$_\to$ Bill visited Russia$_q$; Bill visited Russia$_p$.
Quantifier	[$\forall x.\forall y.$ p(x,y)], $\exists x.\iota y.$ $\neg$p(x,y)	⇒ CONTRADICTION	Everyone$_{\forall x}$ visited$_p$ every$_\forall$ country$_y$; Someone$_{\exists x}$ didn't$_\neg$ visit$_p$ Jordan$_{\iota y}$
	[$\exists x.\forall y.$ p(x,y)], $\iota x.\exists y.$ {$\neg$p(x,y), p(x,y)}	⇒ NEUTRAL	Someone$_{\exists x}$ visited$_p$ every$_\forall$ person$_y$; Tim$_{\iota x}$ didn't$_\neg$ visit$_p$ someone$_{\exists y}$
	[$\exists x.\forall y.$ p(x,y)], $\exists x.\iota y.$ p(x,y)	⇒ ENTAILMENT	Someone$_{\exists x}$ visited$_p$ every$_\forall$ person$_y$; A person$_{\exists x}$ visited$_p$ Mark$_{\iota y}$

examples in each fragment. Various NLI stress-testing datasets include simple lexical inferences (Glockner et al., 2018), quantifiers (Geiger et al., 2018), numerical reasoning, antonymy and negation (Naik et al., 2018), conjunctions (Saha et al., 2020), and linguistic minimal pairs (Warstadt et al., 2020).

To cover monotonicity reasoning, Richardson et al. (2020) use a regular grammar with polarity facts according to the monotonicity calculus: *every* is *downward* monotone/entailing in its first argument but upward monotone/entailing in the second argument, denoted by the ↓ and ↑ arrows in the example sentence "*every*↑ *small*↓ *dog*↓ *ran*↑." The monotonicity information is encoded for 14 types of quantifiers (*every*, *some*, *no*, *most*, *at least 5*, *at most 4*, etc.) and negators (*not*, *without*).

Table 2 shows a simplified description of some of the templates used for four of the logic fragments (stemming from Salvatore et al., 2019) expressed in a quasi-logical notation with predicates *p,q,only-did-p* and quantifiers ∃ (there exists), ∀ (for all), ι (there exists a unique), and Boolean connectives (∧ (and), → (if-then), ¬ (not)).

Entailments are generated as a lattice (Fig. 22). Each node in the tree shows an entailment generated by one substitution. Substitutions are based on a hand-coded KB with information such as: all ≤ some/a, poodle ≤ dog ≤ mammal, and black mammal ≤ mammal. *Contradiction* examples are generated for each inference using simple rules such as "replace *some*/*many*/*every* in subjects by *no*." *Neutrals* are generated in a reverse manner as the entailments.

Glockner et al. (2018) created a new NLI test set with the goal of evaluating systems' ability to make inferences that require simple lexical knowledge. This set is also useful for RBL. Although the formed test is much simpler than SNLI and does not introduce new vocabulary, the state-of-the-art systems perform poorly on it, suggesting that they are limited in their generalization ability. The authors created a new NLI test set with examples that capture various kinds of lexical knowledge (Table 3). The test set can be employed in the future to assess the capabilities of lexical inference of NLI components. Lexical knowledge is needed for RBL as badly as it is for NLI.

For example, champagne is a type of wine (hypernymy), and violin and guitar are different musical instruments (co-hyponyms). To isolate lexical knowledge aspects, the constructed examples contain only words that appear both in the training set and in pre-trained embeddings and differ by a single word from sentences in the training set.

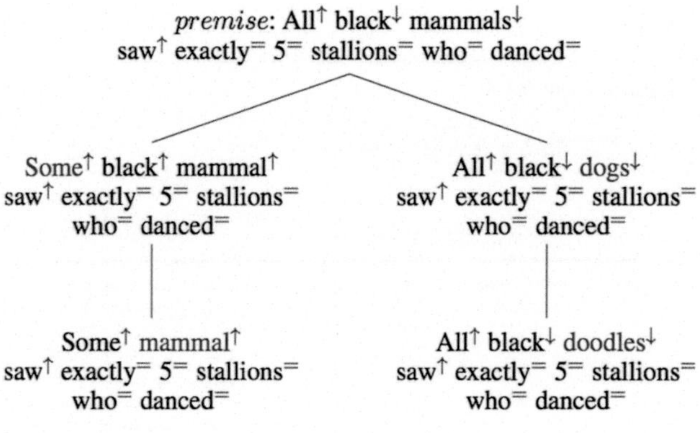

FIG. 22

A lattice of entailments with quantifiers. Substitutions are shown in *blue*.

Table 3 Various kinds of lexical knowledge including adversarial cases.

Premise	Label	Hypothesis
A man inspects the uniform of a figure in some East Asian country	contradiction	The man is sleeping
An older and younger man smiling	neutral	Two men are smiling and laughing at the cats playing on the floor
A soccer game with multiple males playing	entailment	Some men are playing a sport
The man is holding a <violin *vs* guitar>	*contradiction*	
A little girl is very <sad *vs* unhappy>	*entailment*	
A family is drinking <wine *vs* champagne>	*neutral*	

Finally, the goal for RBL and NLI is to have machines that completely autonomously acquire relevant background knowledge and subsequently use it to recognize TE. Designing and implementing such machines would arguably be a concrete step forward in endowing machines with the ability to understand text by drawing those commonsense inferences that humans do when reading text (Michael, 2008).

5.2 Reinforcement learning approach

An interesting, partial case of RBL is the task of mapping high-level instructions to sequences of commands into an external environment. Processing these instructions is challenging as they contain the goals to be achieved without specifying the steps required to complete them. An algorithm that fills in missing information leveraging an automatically derived environment model that encodes states, transitions, and commands that cause these transitions to happen is an alternative approach to RBL.

Branavan et al. (2010) relied on two distinct approaches to reinforcement learning. The first approach, model-based learning, constructs a model of the environment in which the learner operates (e.g., modeling location, velocity, and acceleration in robot navigation). It then computes a policy directly from the rich information represented in the induced environment model. In the NLP literature, model-based reinforcement learning techniques are commonly used for dialogue management (Lemon and Konstas, 2009). However, if the environment cannot be accurately approximated by a compact representation, these methods do not perform well. The instruction interpretation task falls into this latter category, demonstrating that a standard model-based learning is ineffective. The second approach, model-free methods such as policy learning, aims to select the optimal action at every step, without explicitly constructing a model of the environment. While policy learners can effectively operate in complex environments, they are not designed to benefit from a learned environment model. Branavan et al. (2010) addressed this limitation by expanding a policy-learning algorithm to take advantage of a partial environment model estimated during learning. The approach of conditioning the policy function on future reachable states is similar in concept to the use of post-decision state information in the approximate dynamic programming framework (Powell, 2011).

For actions, the goal is to map instructions expressed in NL document d into the corresponding sequence of commands $c^{\sim} = <c_1, \ldots, c_m>$ executable in an environment. As input, we are given a set of raw instruction documents, an environment, and a reward function as described below.

The environment is formalized as its states and transition function. An environment state E specifies the objects accessible in the environment at a given time step, along with the objects' properties. The environment state transition function $p(\varepsilon'|\varepsilon, c)$ encodes how the state changes from ε to ε' in response to a command c. During learning, this function is not known, but samples from it can be collected by executing commands and observing the resulting environment state.

A real-valued reward function assesses how well a command sequence $c^{\sim}$ performs the task described in the d. Document d is composed of a sequence of instructions, each of which can take one of two forms:

- low-level instructions: these explicitly describe a single connection between phrases ("*measure temperature to check for fever*")
- high-level instructions, commands, and explanations: these correspond to a sequence of one or more environment commands, none of which are explicitly described by the explanations ("check symptoms for flu")

A document is interpreted by incrementally constructing a sequence of actions. Each action selects a word span from the document and maps it to one environment command. To predict actions sequentially, we track the states of the environment and the document over time. This mapping state s is a tuple (ε, d, W), where ε is the current environment state, d is the document being interpreted, and W is the list of word spans selected by previous actions. The mapping state s is observed prior to selecting each action.

The mapping action a is a tuple (c, W_a) that represents the joint selection of a span of words W_a and an environment command c. Some of the candidate actions would correspond to the correct instruction mappings, e.g., (c = ["take a syringe"/"draw vaccine medicines from an ampoule"], W_a = "*make a vaccine shot*"). Others such as (c = ["take a syringe"/"draw water from an ampoule"], W_a = "*make a flu shot*") would be erroneous. The algorithm learns to interpret instructions by learning to construct sequences of actions that assign the correct commands to the words.

The interpretation of document d begins at an initial mapping state $s_0 = (\varepsilon_d, d, \varnothing)$, where ε_d is the starting state of the environment for d. Given a state $s = (\varepsilon, d, W)$, the space of possible actions $a = (c, W_a)$ is defined by enumerating sub-spans of unused words in d and candidate commands in ε. a to be executed is selected based on a policy function $p(a|s)$ by finding arg $\max_a p(a|s)$. Performing action a in state $s = (\varepsilon; d; W)$ results in a new state s_0 according to the distribution $p(s'|\ s;\ a)$, where:

$$
\begin{aligned}
&a = (c, W_a),\\
&\varepsilon' \sim p(\varepsilon'/\varepsilon, c)\\
&W' = W \cup W_a\\
&s' = (\varepsilon', d, W').
\end{aligned}
$$

The process of selecting and executing actions is repeated until all the words in d have been mapped.

In Fig. 23, we search for a command sequence for a high-level instruction. The algorithm focuses on steps leading to a certain vaccination stage. The information about such states is acquired during exploration and is stored in a partial environment model $q(\varepsilon'|\varepsilon, c)$. ε_d is the starting state, and c_1 through c_4 are candidate-linking phrases. Environment states are shown as circles, with previously visited environment states colored green. Dotted arrows show known state transitions. All else being equal, the information that the certain explanation results observed in state E_5 during previous exploration steps can help to correctly select command c_3.

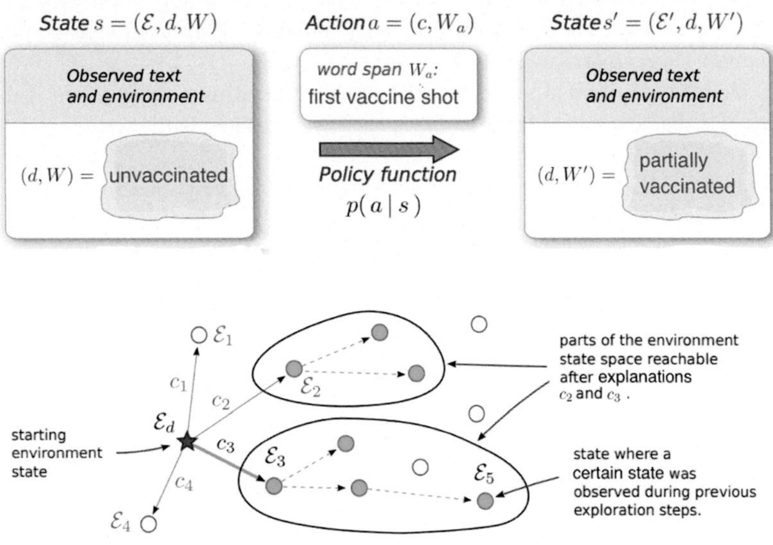

FIG. 23

Using information derived from future states to interpret the high-level instruction "cure flu."

5.3 Language models

The goal of GPT-2 (a successor to GPT) is to predict the next word in 40GB of Internet text (Radford et al., 2019). GPT-2 is a large transformer-based language model with 1.5 billion parameters, trained on a dataset with a focus on a diversity of content. GPT-2's purpose is to predict the next word, given all of the previous words within some text.

To preserve document quality, only pages that have been curated and filtered by humans were selected. Outbound links from Reddit that received at least three "karmas" can be viewed as a heuristic indicator for whether other users found the link interesting and adequate. The training dataset includes eight million web pages. The diversity of the dataset assures this simple purpose of GPT-2 to contain naturally occurring demonstrations of many tasks across diverse domains. GPT-2 is a direct scale-up of GPT, with more than 10 times the parameters and trained on more than 10 times the amount of data.

GPT-2 possesses a wide spectrum of capabilities, including the ability to generate conditional synthetic text samples of a good quality, where the model is fed with an input and generates a lengthy continuation. Also, GPT-2 outperforms other language models trained on specific domains (like Wikipedia, news, or books) without needing to use these domain-specific training datasets. On language tasks like question answering, reading comprehension, summarization, and translation, GPT-2 begins to learn these tasks from the raw text, using no task-specific training data. While scores on these downstream tasks are far from state of the art, they suggest that the tasks can benefit from unsupervised techniques, once sufficient unlabeled data is available.

Zhou et al. (2019) studied the commonsense ability of GPT, BERT, XLNet, and RoBERTa by testing them on seven challenging benchmarks, finding that language modeling and its variants are effective objectives for promoting models' commonsense ability, while bi-directional context and larger training set are bonuses. The authors additionally found that current models do poorly on tasks that require inference steps (InferKit, 2020; Huggingface, 2020).

Language models have a limited value for RBL, as they determine the most probable keywords between the lines of actual text, but *most probable* is weakly correlated with *concealed thoughts*, which are peculiar and very specific in most cases.

Following is an example of GPT-2-based content generation given a seed (in bold):

Asomex 5 Tablet is a medicine used to treat high blood pressure (hypertension) and to prevent angina*, angina pectoris, and related complications.*

Asomex tablets contain magnesium, pyridoxine hydrochloride, and vitamin B6.

The first oral treatment approved for this indication in Japan, it is indicated as a 2.5 mg dose twice a day.

One can see that generated content is smooth and cohesive, but all entities and their attributes are random and incorrect, although they belong to the correct domain of drug description. We explore how to fix these entities and values in Chapter 15.

5.4 Storytelling discourse approach

Training in narrative theory and creative expression has been recently recognized as a boon to effective communication in healthcare environments. Medical students and established medical practitioners are learning about story-making (Chretien et al., 2015) and the role it plays in their relationships with patients and colleagues.

Charon et al. (2016) developed a new field of narrative competence as a crucial proficiency for physicians and established the field of narrative medicine as a contribution to modern medical education technology. Their guidelines for the practice of narrative competence involve the "close reading" (Charon, 2006) of texts, considering the ways storytellers attach a narrative form to experience (Bamberg, 2012). Charon and colleagues propose an approach to the narrative expression of lived or imaginary experience, including time, space, voice, metaphor, and genre. These narrative features may be considered individually, but in practice, they work together to produce the unique story that is told. In terms of narration features, the whole is greater than the sum of its parts.

Narrative comments are broadly used in medical education, in many forms of rater-based assessment. Interpretation can be difficult because of idiosyncratic writing styles and disconnects between literal and intended meanings. Ginsburg et al. (2015) explored how medical students interpret and make sense of the narrative comments on residents' in-training evaluation reports and identified the language cues that appear to be essential in generating and justifying the interpretations of these reports. Participants perform logical inferences based on what they thought test evaluators intended by their comments and seem to share an understanding of a "hidden code." Participants' RBL capability explains how comments can be effectively used to categorize and grade medical students. However, it also suggests a mechanism in which variable interpretations can arise. Computational linguistics' pragmatics and politeness theories may explain why such an implicit code might evolve and be maintained in clinical evaluation.

6. Evaluation

Our main evaluation task is generation of RBL expressions for texts. We imitate the situation with text writing where an author attempts to conceal some facts or implications by removing respective portions of text such that the reduced text is still reasonably readable. To assess the adequacy of generated RBL results, we remove a particular EDU or a whole sentence that might potentially be concealed by the author from this text so that the remaining text is still cohesive and attempt to recover this missing EDU or sentence. We identify such candidate for concealment, building a DT for text and finding the locations in it where RBL is most probable.

This approach gives us a chance to perform a fully automated assessment. The RBL results are then automatically assessed with respect to semantic similarity with the actual removed EDU or sentence. When this semantic similarity is computed to be high, we conclude that the RBL procedure succeeds, as we recover the concealed facts or implications correctly.

We also perform a relative comparison of the RBL-based text recovery procedure with the language models one. Whereas the RBL procedure identifies facts and thoughts other people share in a similar situation (unlike the author of the given text), the language model finds the most typical syntactic expression in a given word context (Radford et al., 2019). We assess the success rate of the RBL model vs that of the language model to demonstrate the value of the proposed RBL procedure.

To convert a text with the one where something is "concealed" by the author, we build its DT and determine which EDU or a short chain of EDUs can be removed so that the remaining DT assures a cohesive text.

We use various sources of medical texts where the RBL procedure can be assessed (Table 4).

Table 4 Sources of RBL procedure assessment.

Name	Description	#	Reference	URL
Medical Transcription dataset	Short description of transcription, Medical specialty classification of transcription	5000 total, 250 selected for assessment	Boyle (2018)	www.kaggle.com/tboyle10/medicaltranscriptions
UCI ML Drug Review dataset		1000 total, 250 selected for assessment	Li (2019)	www.kaggle.com/jessicali9530/kuc-hackathon-winter-2018
Medicinal Reviews	Treatment review, drug review, patient feedback	150 total, 23 reviews long enough to be selected	Doe (2018)	www.kaggle.com/cybermed/medicinal-reviews
Health Community Forums	Various discussions on health issues (Chapter 2 Diagnosis)	4000 total, 250 selected for assessment		www.ehealthforum.com/health/health_forums.html www.healthforum.com

6.1 Meaningfulness of generated RBLs

We show the percentages of cases properly recovered (with high semantic similarity between the actual sentence and the RBL result). We first show the language model baseline, obtained by relying on the:

(1) *preceding* sentence to the one that has been removed, and
(2) sentence *after* the one that has been removed and attempted to be recovered.

Then we show the RBL results *without* sentence generalization to obtain a search query, followed by the ones *with* sentence generalization.

Chapter 9 describes the conventional syntactic and semantic similarity measures used to assess the correct RBL recovery, such as BLEU.

We observe that the language model gives only about one-seventh of reasonable RBL results (Table 5). Being syntactically correct and even semantically valid according to the most frequent occurrences of the obtained phrase words in a training corpus, the language modeling results nevertheless strongly deviate from the actual removed sentences. At the same time, one-fifth of these sentences are properly recovered by the RBL procedure with a lack of data for syntactic generalization. Finally, more than one-quarter of sentences are correctly recovered where multiple explanation instances were sufficient to generalize at least two of them.

6.2 Search recall improvement

Generating RBL for text also helps for improving search recall. Once we have RBL expressions indexed along with the indexed text itself, we can cover more queries, assuming RBL expressions are central to the topic of the text. For search recall, RBL can be viewed as content enrichment, providing an increase in a number of index entries for a given text, by means of deducing what this text is about, and which questions it can answer.

For example, once we successfully added the expression '*avoid negatively impress potential clients*' to our GPT example in Section 5, one can ask '*Which companies do not want* to *negatively impress potential clients with their demo?*' and receive the GPT answer. That would not be possible without RBL indexing approach.

Table 5 Recovery of missing sentence assessment.

Dataset	Language model GPT-2 performance	RBL procedure without sentence generalization	RBL procedure with query generalization from multiple instances only
Medical Transcription dataset	13.2	21.8	27.3
UCI ML Drug Review dataset	17.1	23.0	25.2
Medicinal Reviews	10.9	18.7	23.4
Health Community Forums	14.3	20.8	26.0
Average	**13.9**	**21.1**	**25.5**

Table 6 Recall of the baseline and RBL-supported search.

Dataset	Baseline search recall	Search recall with RBL index: *maximal* number	Search recall with RBL index: *optimal* number
Medical Transcription dataset	78.3	75.1	83.4
UCI ML Drug Review dataset	80.9	82.3	85.2
Medicinal Reviews	75.1	74.8	79.0
Health Community Forums	77.4	75.7	80.2
Average	**78.0**	**76.9**	**82.0**

We experiment with indexing optimal and maximal numbers of RBL expressions. The *optimal* number is obtained when we derive RBL expressions for EDUs under non-trivial rhetorical relations like *Cause* and *Contrast*. The *maximal* number is obtained where RBL results are built for all sentences (these expressions could be misleading and should not be considered RBL).

We use the question-answering evaluation data and setting from Chapter 7. It includes complex, long questions typically requiring some form of reasoning. We also use the health content employed for evaluation in Chapter 3 where texts with symptoms are categorized into disease classes such as *Bloating*, *Cough*, *Diarrhea*, *Dizziness*, *Fatigue*, *Fever*, and others. We put all sources in one index and form a search query from the dataset if available or form a question from the important parts of texts (top-level *Elaboration* EDU nucleus).

Table 6 shows the search recall data normalized for fixed precision. We observe that the maximal approach decreases the search accuracy since its precision is broken because of the misleading RBL expressions obtained for phrases and sentences the index should not contain. The absolute value of recall is improved but precision drops much stronger.

The optimal number of RBL model results indeed improves the search recall by 4%, by adding expressions logically connected with the original text. When these expressions are not added, the search system cannot find an answer among the original sentences and phrases (4% of cases).

7. Discussions

Some people are frustrated that others are good at Reading Between the Lines. These super-smart people seem to know, well before anyone else, who the killer is in a movie or the meaning of an abstract poem. What these people are skilled at is inference. They can leverage indirect evidence to reveal hidden information.

But reasoning is not a skill possessed by a limited audience of people. Conversely, most people use inference regularly but do not feel it because it comes so naturally to them. Reasoning has been essential for survival as a species since day one, when people searched for food. Humans rely on indirect evidence, such as weak rustling sounds in the vegetation or the presence of half-eaten grass, to deduce that a bunny must be near.

A fundamental incompatibility between how humans process information from multiple modalities and how ML tries to accomplish the same thing is that humans can bridge the information gap from the contexts in an environment (Chandu et al., 2020). Human training procedures do not take care of embedding the same ability into a supervised learning method. Traditionally, the problem of missing context in long text generation is addressed using additional input such as entities and actions (Dong et al., 2019), latent templates, and external knowledge. These are explicit approaches to acquire content during generation. In contrast, Chandu et al. (2020) proposed infilling techniques to implicitly interpolate the gap between surrounding contexts from a stream of images.

Meinert (2011a,b) claims that when reading journal articles, the methods section of a results paper is the most important part. If the reader wants to understand the results, they need to comprehend how they were generated, and for that, the reader has to navigate through the methods section line by line. However, at reading time, a reader must pay attention to what is *not* there as well as what *is* there. In many cases, authors do not intend to tell their peers what they did not do. One must RBL and infer that from what is not said. The most important words in any paper are the few represented in the title of the manuscript. The second most important words are those in the abstract, which gives the conclusion reached by the study investigators.

It is a special art to read a clinical study between the lines (Kaplan, 2019). The author cites (Riffenburgh and Stableford, 2019), explaining that it is helpful to know who paid for the study. If clinical research is financially supported by a pharmaceutical company, one would read it with suspicion, but if it was funded by a pharmaceutical company and reviewed in a double-blind manner, one can be more comfortable. A study designed by academics and run in multiple institutions, with medication supplied by a pharmaceutical company, increases experts' confidence in an unbiased experiment. In either case, the FDA is believed to carefully verify trial results and question the clinical researchers before approving a treatment for a specific use.

It has proved difficult to use statistical models to assemble the meaning of longer passages of text from their component parts. According to Marcus and Davis (2019), to understand the meaning of the word "tuberculosis," you have to know not just how this word is used but also something about lung illnesses. The authors believe it is essential to apply symbolic reasoning to the ill-defined concepts humans think and talk about however hard it is to program computers to do that. When we understand what other people tell us, we are not just hearing what they are saying but we are also leveraging the knowledge about the real world, the way people and other objects behave. This knowledge is so obvious to humans that we are not conscious of employing it.

Manually constructed knowledge bases such as CYC (Lenat, 1995) are not accompanied by guarantees of their appropriateness for any given TE task. ML is used to build knowledge bases for the TE classification task; however, most methods process a training set that includes pairs of a fragment of text and a statement, tagged by humans to indicate whether the latter is implied by the former. This is consistent with the operational and subjective definition of TE. For software agents to be designed, and for the broader TE generation task to be accomplished, an ML technique not relying on human supervision needs to be employed. Access to a corpus of documents should be allowed, but text is not tagged with the inferences expected to be obtained. Since text is a partial depiction of some underlying reality, an ML framework that can deal with partial information in its learning examples is required. It is also beneficial that this ML system makes minimal assumptions on how information is missing in its learning examples, thus allowing it to be employed as broadly as possible (Michael, 2008).

FIG. 24

Relying on an image to associate *P* and *H*.

Several models have been proposed to integrate the language and vision modalities; usually, the integration is operationalized by element-wise multiplication between linguistic and visual vectors. Though the interest in these modalities has been growing because of the various multimodal tasks proposed, very little work has been done on grounding entailment. Young et al. (2014) proposed the idea of considering images as the "possible worlds" on which sentences find their denotation. The authors released a "visual denotation graph" that associates sentences with their denotation (sets of images). The idea has been exploited by Lai and Hockenmaier (2017). Vendrov et al. (2016) looked at hypernymy, TE, and image captioning as special cases of a single visual-semantic hierarchy over words, sentences, and images; the authors state that modeling the partial order structure of this hierarchy in visual and linguistic semantic spaces improves model performance on those three tasks.

Vu et al. (2018) questioned whether having an image that illustrates the event (Fig. 24) can help a model to capture the relation. To answer this question, the authors augmented the largest available TE dataset with images and enhanced a state-of-the-art model of TE to take images into account. The inclusion of images can also alter relations that, based on text alone, would seem likely. For example, to a "blind" model, the sentence pair in Fig. 24 would seem to be unrelated, but when the two sentences are viewed in the context of the image, they do become related.

P: "*A family near the fireplace*" and H: "*People trying to warm up*"

P: "*People are trying to get warm*" and H: "*Family is outside in a cold weather*"

As a default TE task, they are unrelated, and as a grounded TE, they *are* correlated. Having an image that illustrates the event helps a model to capture the relation. The inclusion of images can also alter relations that, based on text alone, would seem likely.

Image captioning provides a textual description T given an image I. Visual storytelling is the task of generating a sequence of textual descriptions ($\{T_1, T_2, \ldots, T_n\}$) from a sequence of images ($\{I_1, I_2, \ldots, I_n\}$). This sequential context is the differentiating factor in generation of visual narratives in comparison to image captioning in isolation.

Chandu et al. (2020) tackled the problem of generating long-form narratives such as stories and procedures from multiple modalities by using *infilling* techniques involving prediction of missing steps in a narrative while generating textual descriptions from a sequence of images (Fig. 25).

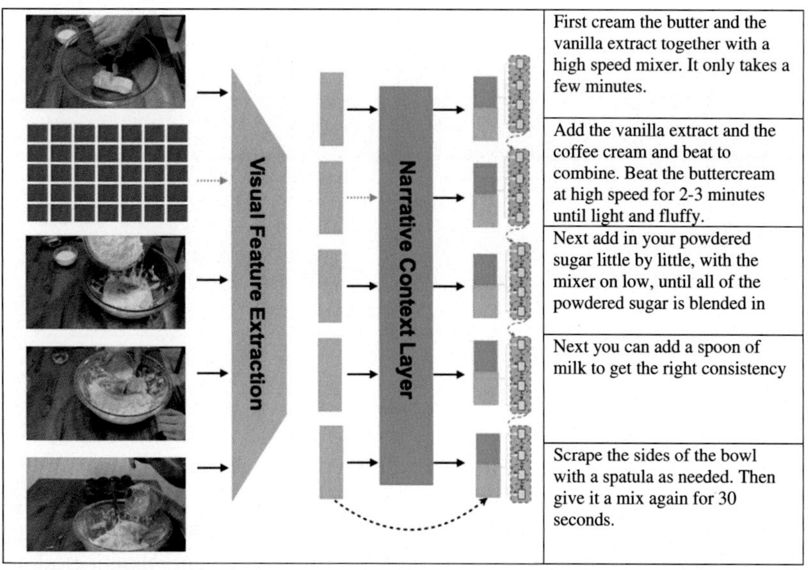

Visual Feature Extraction
Narrative Context Layer
First cream the butter and the vanilla extract together with a high speed mixer. It only takes a few minutes.
Add the vanilla extract and the coffee cream and beat to combine. Beat the buttercream at high speed for 2-3 minutes until light and fluffy.
Next add in your powdered sugar little by little, with the mixer on low, until all of the powdered sugar is blended in
Next you can add a spoon of milk to get the right consistency
Scrape the sides of the bowl with a spatula as needed. Then give it a mix again for 30 seconds.

FIG. 25

The process of infilling in visual procedures. The image in the second step is masked while the model generates the corresponding textual description from surrounding context.

8. Conclusions

Symbolic systems for NLI have been criticized as a means to deal with NLI, and NLP tasks in general, on the basis of coverage, that is, the fact that these systems tend to easily break down once they are moved to open domains, experiencing information overload (Fig. 26). This, as a general criticism of a deterministic family of approaches, is to a great extent legitimate. It is true that symbolic/logical systems can be very precise but have a very poor recall. They break easily in the presence of new data. On the other hand, DL models have offered a promising way out of these limitations, delivering impressive results in all areas of NLP, and most specifically, as already mentioned, in dealing with NLI. At first sight, these systems do not seem to be suffering from the brittleness problem just described for symbolic/logical approaches. This is to some extent correct, but not all the way through.

For example, in the case of NLI, recent studies show that state-of-the-art NLI systems are rather brittle as well, but also brittle in another sense; they fail to generalize outside individual datasets and are, furthermore, unable to capture certain NLI patterns at all. This is a very different kind of brittleness, distinct from the one found with symbolic/logical approaches to NLI. For example, it would be highly unlikely that a symbolic system would break down by creating a variation of a test dataset in the sense of Glockner et al. (2018), a dataset that managed to break several DL NLI systems. On the other hand, building a logical system that can parse, in a reasonable way, a huge dataset like SNLI or Multi-NLI, and produce reasonable logical forms, is far from trivial. But on the assumption that this is somehow achieved, such a system will not be prone to the type of breaking shown by Glockner et al. (2018).

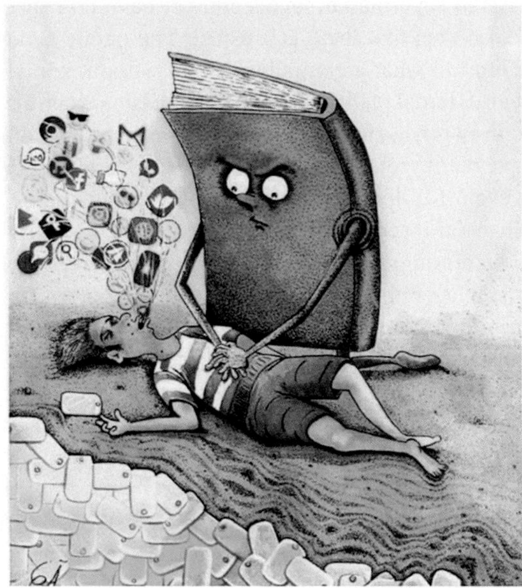

FIG. 26

Rescue from information overload.

At the same time, going to cases where a stricter definition of inference is assumed, for example, logical inference, it is not clear that DL models will be able to stand up to the task (Galitsky, 2018).

The proposed RBL procedure is an efficient and effective way to obtain and represent invisible knowledge in text. In real-world communication, authors do not have to spell out each chunk of knowledge necessary to comprehend a text; some of these knowledge chunks are assumed. However, for text formalization, these knowledge chunks are needed badly since formalization without them is incomplete. Such incomplete formal representation of text is a major bottleneck for text understanding under question answering (Galitsky et al., 2011, 2013), summarization, and information extraction.

Several research projects addressed the RBL problem. However, we believe this is the first study that targets obtaining the results similar to what humans do Reading Between the Lines. We do not formulate RBL as an end-to-end problem or as a pure data-driven machine to demonstrate the cognitive steps, an ambiguity and trial-and-error approach associated with RBL.

A key challenge facing most attempts to build AI, either by classical knowledge engineering or contemporary ML, is the recognition that our ideas about the world are inevitably *incomplete*. Humans know that there is a world, that their ideas are representations of this world, and that these representations must defer to a world that will always, to some degree, elude representation. In the last decade, the community started to believe that ML systems are better than old-fashion logical AI at evading the limitations imposed by naive assumptions about ontology. However, end-to-end architectures still lack an awareness of their relationship to the world. Requiring them to develop this might be too strong of a demand. RBL is a technique that addresses this incompleteness in a way of "action on demand," trying to navigate toward a complete picture of what an author is saying when the reader believes it is the right time.

A computer can play chess to superhuman levels and yet have no concept of what chess is, what place chess has in the world, or even that there is a world. The public perceives this computer as intelligent. Perhaps there is a limit to what a computer can do without knowing that it is manipulating imperfect representations of an external reality. To take one pressing example, one can argue that safely controlling a self-driving car in an urban environment will require the kind of judgment that makes such awareness necessary. Perhaps, but it seems at least possible that careful engineering could make a car that would be safe enough, even if it does not really know what it is doing (Taylor, 2021).

As patients take more financial responsibility for their health, they have more choice over where they receive care. They are increasingly influenced by ratings and reports on quality and outcomes. They are also seeking other people's opinions and reviewing experiences via social media before making decisions. For today's health systems to attract patients, they need to treat them as the informed consumers they are becoming. Accessibility of care, the consumer experience, and the availability of complex treatments are top of mind for today's healthcare consumers. The proposed RBL technique is designed to convert opinionated data with plenty of concealed observations into a complete, thoroughly represented assessment of their health, their caretakers, and health facilities.

An alternative approach to RBL in mental space is to compute implicit mental states (Galitsky, 2021b). A Theory of Mind engine is introduced that takes an initial mental state and produces the consecutive mental states as plausible to a real-world scenario as possible. In that study, a multiagent decision-making environment was simulated considering intentions, knowledge, and beliefs of itself and others. The simulation results are evaluated with respect to precision, completeness, and complexity. Further development of RBL can be associated to metaprogramming techniques of introspection developed for putting an agent in "someone else's shoes," better predicting how they would think and act. We conclude that the Theory of Mind engine is adequate to support a broad range of tasks requiring simulation of human mental attitudes.

Supplementary data sets

Please visit https://github.com/bgalitsky/relevance-based-on-parse-trees to access all supplementary data sets.

References

Akula, R., Garibay, I., 2021. Interpretable multi-head self-attention architecture for sarcasm detection in social media. Entropy 23, 394.

Bamberg, M., 2012. Identity and narration. In: HŸhn, P., Meister, J.C., Pier, J., Schmid, W. (Eds.), The Living Handbook of Narratology. Hamburg University. http://www.lhn.uni-hamburg.de/article/identity-and-narration.

Bernardy, J.P., Chatzikyriakidis, S., 2019. What kind of natural language inference are NLP systems learning: is this enough? In: Proceedings of the 11th International Conference on Agents and Artificial Intelligence (ICAART 2019), pp. 919–931.

Bordes, A., Boureau, Y.-L., Weston, J., 2016. Learning End-to-End Goal-Oriented Dialog. arXiv preprint arXiv:1605.07683.

Bowman, S.R., Angeli, G., Potts, C., Manning, C.D., 2015. A large annotated corpus for learning natural language inference. In: Conference on Empirical Methods in Natural Language Processing, EMNLP, pp. 632–642.

Boyle, S., 2018. Medical Transcription Dataset. Over 200,000 Patient Drug Reviews. https://www.kaggle.com/tboyle10/medicaltranscriptions.

Branavan, S.R.K., Zettlemoyer, L., Barzilay, R., 2010. Reading Between the Lines: Learning to Map High-Level Instructions to Commands. Association for Computational Linguistics, Uppsala, pp. 1268–1277.

Chandu, K., Dong, R.-P., Black, A., 2020. Reading between the lines: exploring infilling in visual narratives. In: EMNLP, pp. 1220–1229.

Charon, R., 2006. Narrative Medicine: Honoring the Stories of Illness. Oxford University Press, New York.

Charon, R., DasGupta, S., Hermann, N., Marcus, E.R., Irvine, C., Colsn, E.R., Spencer, D., Spiegel, M., 2016. The Principles and Practice of Narrative Medicine. Oxford University Press, UK.

Chretien, K.C., Swenson, R., Yoon, B., Julian, R., Keenan, J., Croffoot, J., Kheirbek, R., 2015. Tell me your story: a pilot narrative medicine curriculum during the medicine clerkship. J. Gen. Intern. Med. 30 (7), 1025–1028.

Clark, P., Cowhey, I., Etzioni, O., Khot, T., Sabharwal, A., Schoenick, C., Tafjord, O., 2018. Think You Have Solved Question Answering? Try Arc, The Ai2 Reasoning Challenge. arXiv preprint arXiv:1803.05457.

Cooper, R., Crouch, D., Van Eijck, J., Fox, C., Van Genabith, J., Jaspars, J., Kamp, H., Milward, D., Pinkal, M., Poesio, M., 1996. Using the framework for Computational Semantics. Technical Report LRE 62-051.

Dagan, I., Glickman, O., Magnini, B., 2006. The pascal recognising textual entailment challenge. In: Machine Learning Challenges. Evaluating Predictive Uncertainty, Visual Object Classification, and Recognising Tectual Entailment, pp. 177–190.

Deep Pavlov, 2020. An Open Source Conversational AI Framework. https://deeppavlov.ai/_.

Demszky, D., Guu, K., Liang, P., 2018. Transforming Question Answering Datasets Into Natural Language Inference Datasets. ArXiv, abs/1809.02922.

Doe, J., 2018. Medicinal Reviews. https://www.kaggle.com/cybermed/medicinal-reviews.

Dong, R.-P., Chandu, K.R., Black, A.W., 2019. Induction and Reference of Entities in a Visual Story. arXiv preprint arXiv:1909.09699.

Elmessiry, A., Cooper, W.O., Catron, T.F., et al., 2017. Triaging patient complaints: Monte Carlo cross-validation of six machine learning classifiers. JMIR Med. Inform. 5 (3), 13–29.

Falke, T., Leonardo, F.R., Ribeiro, P., Utama, A., Dagan, I., Gurevych, I., 2019. Ranking generated summaries by correctness: an interesting but challenging application for natural language inference. In: Proceedings of the 57th Annual Meeting of the Association for Computational Linguistics, pp. 2214–2220.

Galitsky, B., 2013. Machine learning of syntactic parse trees for search and classification of text. Eng. Appl. Artif. Intell. 26 (3), 1072–1091.

Galitsky, B., 2016. Theory of mind engine. In: Computational Autism. Springer, Cham.

Galitsky, B., 2017. Matching parse thickets for open domain question answering. Data Knowl. Eng. 107, 24–50.

Galitsky, B., 2018. Customers' retention requires an explainability feature in machine learning systems they use. In: Kudo (Ed.), AAAI Spring Symposium Series. AAAI Press.

Galitsky, B., 2019. Discourse level dialogue management. In: Galitsky, B. (Ed.), Developing Enterprise Chatbots. Springer, pp. 365–426.

Galitsky, B., 2020. Enabling Chatbots by Detecting and Supporting Affective Argumentation. US Patent 10,839,154.

Galitsky, B., 2021a. Truth, lie and hypocrisy. In: Artificial Intelligence for Customer Relationship Management: Solving Customer Problems. Springer, Charm, Switzerland, pp. 223–287.

Galitsky, B., 2021b. Reasoning and simulation of mental attitudes of a customer. In: Artificial Intelligence for Customer Relationship Management: Solving Customer Problems. Springer, Charm, Switzerland, pp. 371–428.

Galitsky, B., Goldberg, S., 2019. Explainable machine learning for chatbots. In: Developing Enterprise Chatbots. Springer, Cham.

Galitsky, B., Ilvovsky, D., 2017. Chatbot with a discourse structure-driven dialogue management. In: Proceedings of the Software Demonstrations of the 15th Conference of the European Chapter of the ACL, pp. 87–90.

Galitsky, B., Ilvovsky, D., 2019. On a chatbot conducting virtual dialogues. In: Proceedings of the 28th ACM International Conference on Information and Knowledge Management (CIKM 2019). ACM, pp. 2925–2928.

Galitsky, B., González, M.P., Chesñevar, C.I., 2009. A novel approach for classifying customer complaints through graphs similarities in argumentative dialogues. Decis. Support. Syst. 46 (3), 717–729.

Galitsky, B., Dobrocsi, G., de la Rosa, J.L., Kuznetsov, S.O., 2011. Using generalization of syntactic parse trees for taxonomy capture on the web. In: International Conference on Conceptual Structures, pp. 104–117.

Galitsky, B., De La Rosa, J.L., Dobrocsi, G., 2012. Inferring the semantic properties of sentences by mining syntactic parse trees. Data Knowl. Eng. 81, 21–45.

Galitsky, B., Ilvovsky, D., Kuznetsov, S.O., Strok, F., 2013. Matching sets of parse trees for answering multi-sentence questions. In: Proceedings of the International Conference Recent Advances in NLP, p. 25.

Galitsky, B., Ilvovsky, D., Goncharova, E., 2019. On a chatbot conducting dialogue-in-dialogue. In: Proceedings of the SIGDial Conference, Stockholm, Sweden, 11-13 September, pp. 118–121.

Geiger, A., Cases, I., Karttunen, L., Potts, C., 2018. Stress-Testing Neural Models of Natural Language Inference With Multiply-Quantified Sentences. arXiv preprint arXiv:1810.13033.

Ginsburg, S., Regehr, G., Lingard, L., Eva, K.W., 2015. Reading between the lines: faculty interpretations of narrative evaluation comments. Med. Educ. 49 (3), 296–306.

Glockner, M.R., Shwartz, V., Goldberg, Y., 2018. Breaking NLI Systems With Sentences That Require Simple Lexical Inferences. ACL, pp. 650–655.

Goncharova, E., Makhalova, T., Ilvovsky, D., Galitsky, B., 2020. FCA-based approach for query refinement in IR-chatbots. In: 18th Russian Conference, RCAI 2020, Moscow, Russia, October 10–16.

Huggingface, 2020. https://transformer.huggingface.co/doc/gpt2-large.

Hwang, J., Bhagavatula, C., Le Bras, R., Da, J., Sakaguchi, K., Bosselut, A., Choi, Y., 2021. (Comet-) Atomic 2020: On Symbolic and Neural Commonsense Knowledge. AAAI.

Ilvovsky, D., Kirillovich, A., Galitsky, B., 2020. Controlling chat bot multi-document navigation with the extended discourse tree. In: CLIB Conference.

InferKit, 2020. InferKit Demo. https://app.inferkit.com/demo.

Kapanipathi, P., Thost, V., Patel, S.S., Whitehead, S., Abdelaziz, I., Balakrishnan, A., Chang, M., Fadnis, K., Gunasekara, C., Makni, B., Mattei, N., Talamadupula, K., Fokoue, A., 2020. Infusing knowledge into the textual entailment task using graph convolutional networks. In: Proceedings of the AAAI Conference on Artificial Intelligence.

Kaplan, D.A., 2019. Read Between the Lines: Understanding Clinical Studies. vol. 18 CURE. Winter 2019, Issue 1.

Lai, A., Hockenmaier, J., 2017. Learning to predict denotational probabilities for modeling entailment. In: Proceedings of the 15th Conference of the European Chapter of the Association for Computational Linguistics, Valencia, Spain, pp. 721–730.

Lamprell, K., Braithwaite, J., 2019. Reading between the lines: a five-point narrative approach to online accounts of illness. J. Med. Humanit. 40, 569–590.

Lemon, O., Konstas, I., 2009. User simulations for context-sensitive speech recognition in spoken dialogue systems. In: EACL 2009—12th Conference of the European Chapter of the Association for Computational Linguistics, pp. 505–513.

Lenat, D.B., 1995. CYC: a large-scale investment in knowledge infrastructure. Commun. ACM 38 (11), 33–38.

Li, J., 2019. UCI ML Drug Review Dataset. https://www.kaggle.com/jessicali9530/kuc-hackathon-winter-2018.

Marcus, G., Davis, E., 2019. Rebooting AI: Building Artificial Intelligence We Can Trust. Pantheon Books, New York.

Meinert, C.L., 2011a. An Insider's Guide to Clinical Trials. Oxford University Press.

Meinert, C.L., 2011b. Reading Between the Lines, or How to Read a Journal Article. Oxford Scholarship Online.

Michael, L., 2007. Learning from partial observations. In: IJCAI'07.

Michael, L., 2008. Autodidactic Learning and Reasoning. (PhD thesis). School of Engineering and Applied Sciences, Harvard University, USA.

Mitchell, T.M., 2005. Reading the web: a breakthrough goal for AI. AI Mag. 26 (3), 12–16. Fall 2005.

Naik, A., Ravichander, A., Sadeh, N., Rose, C., Neubig, G., 2018. Stress test evaluation for natural language inference. In: Proceedings of the 27th International Conference on Computational Linguistics, pp. 2340–2353.

OpenAI, 2019. Better Language Models and Their Implications. https://openai.com/blog/better-language-models/#task5.

Oracle Healthcare, 2020. Forces of Change. https://www.oracle.com/webfolder/assets/ebook/health-science-industry-viewpoints/index.html#0.

Pearl, J., 2019. On the Interpretation of do(x). UCLA Cognitive Systems Laboratory. Technical Report (R-486).

Powell, W., 2011. Approximate dynamic programming I: modeling. In: Cochran, J. (Ed.), Wiley Encyclopedia of Operations Research and Management Science. Wiley Online Library.

Radford, A., Wu, J., Child, R., Luan, D., Amodei, D., Sutskever, I., 2019. Language Models Are Unsupervised Multitask Learners. https://openai.com/blog/better-language-models/#fn2.

Richardson, K., Hu, H., Moss, L., Sabharwal, A., 2020. Probing natural language inference models through semantic fragments. In: Proceedings of the AAAI Conference on Artificial Intelligence. vol. 34, pp. 8713–8721.

Riffenburgh, A., Stableford, S., 2019. Health literacy and clear communication: keys to engaging older adults and their families. In: Robnett, R.H., Brossoie, N. (Eds.), Gerontology for the Health Care Professional, fourth ed. Jones & Bartlett Learning, Burlington, MA, pp. 109–128.

Saha, S., Nie, Y., Bansal, M., 2020. ConjNLI: Natural Language Inference Over Conjunctive Sentences. arXiv:2010.10418.

Salvatore, F., Finger, M., Roberto Hirata Jr., Á., 2019. A Logical-Based Corpus for Cross-Lingual Evaluation.

Shalyminov, I., Eshghi, A., Lemon, O., 2017. Challenging Neural Dialogue Models with Natural Data: Memory Networks Fail on Incremental Phenomena. arXiv preprint arXiv:1709.07840.

Taylor, P., 2021. Insanely complicated, hopelessly inadequate. London Review of Books 43 (2 á).

Trivedi, H., Kwon, H., Khot, T., Sabharwal, A., Balasubramanian, N., 2019. Repurposing entailment for multi-hop question answering tasks. In: Proceedings of the North American Chapter of the Association for Computational Linguistics: Human Language Technologies, pp. 2948–2958.

Valiant, L.G., 1984. A theory of the learnable. Commun. ACM 27 (11), 1134–1142.

Valiant, L.G., 2006. Knowledge infusion. In: AAAI, pp. 1546–1551.

Vendrov, I., Kiors, R., Fidler, S., Urtasun, R., 2016. order-embeddings of images and language. In: Proceedings of the International Conference of Learning Representations (ICLR).

Vu, H.T., Greco, C., Erofeeva, A., Jafaritazehjan, S., Linders, G., Tanti, M., Testoni, A., Bernardi, R., Gatt, A., 2018. Grounded Textual Entailment. arXiv:1806.05645.

Warstadt, A., Parrish, A., Liu, H., Mohananey, A., Peng, W., Wang, S.-F., Bowman, S.R., 2020. BLiMP: the benchmark of linguistic minimal pairs for English. Trans. Assoc. Comput. Linguist. 8, 377–392.

Williams, A., Nangia, N., Bowman, S., 2018. A broad-coverage challenge corpus for sentence understanding through inference. In: Proceedings of the 2018 Conference of the North American Chapter of the Association for Computational Linguistics: Human Language Technologies. vol. 1. Association for Computational Linguistics, pp. 1112–1122 (Long Papers).

Young, P., Lai, A., Hodosh, M., Hockenmaier, J., 2014. From image descriptions to visual denotations: new similarity metrics for semantic inference over event descriptions. Trans. Assoc. Comput. Linguist. 2, 67–78.

Zhou, X., Zhang, Y., Cui, L., Huang, D., 2019. Evaluating Commonsense in Pre-trained Language Models. https://arxiv.org/abs/1911.11931.

CHAPTER

Discourse means for maintaining a proper rhetorical flow

Boris Galitsky
Oracle Corporation, Redwood City, CA, United States

1. Introduction

Medical dialogue systems are being developed to serve as "virtual doctors." These virtual doctors are aimed to interact with patients via natural dialogues, asking about the medical conditions and history of patients and providing clinical advice. They can also proactively reach out to patients to ask about the progression of patients' conditions and provide timely interventions. Medical conversational agents constitute a great tool to assist doctors in responding to easily diagnosed common diseases and obtaining patients' medical information for complex diseases.

Chatbots have received a considerable amount of attention from academic researchers and have achieved remarkable success in a myriad of industry scenarios, such as in chit-chat machines, information seeking, searching (Hashemi et al., 2020), and intelligent assistants (Li et al., 2017b). Social dialogue systems are becoming robust and reliable and are being widely used to converse with humans. In recent years, this progress has been driven mostly by advances in neural generation (Adiwardana et al., 2020) that can tackle a broad variety of user utterances and provide meaningful chatbot responses. People expect their interactions with these dialogue agents to be like real social relationships (Galitsky, 2019a).

Modern approaches to dialogue systems can be categorized into two groups:

(1) domain specific
(2) open domain

Domain-specific models generally pursue solving and completing one specific target (e.g., restaurant reservation, transportation, or social promotion (Galitsky et al., 2014)) that relies on domain knowledge and engineering (Galitsky, 2013). Conversely, open-domain dialogues involve unlimited topics within a conversation (Ritter et al., 2011); therefore, building an open-domain dialogue system is more challenging without sufficient knowledge of general dialogue management. Leveraging a vast amount of available dialogue datasets, constructing open-domain dialogue systems has attracted a growing interest in the Natural Language Processing (NLP) community. Among dialogue systems in the open-domain setting, generation-based (Sordoni et al., 2015) and retrieval-based (Wang et al., 2013) methods are the most common in industry. At the same time, generation-based methods learn to create a feasible response for a user-issued query, while retrieval-based methods extract a proper response from a set of available candidate utterances. In contrast to the "common response" created by

Artificial Intelligence for Healthcare Applications and Management. https://doi.org/10.1016/B978-0-12-824521-7.00005-3

generation models, retrieval-based methods can extract fluent and informative responses from human conversations (Tao et al., 2019). Early retrieval-based methods mainly address the issue of single-turn response selection, where the dialogue context only contains one utterance. Recent studies focus on modeling multi-turn response selection (Galitsky, 2019b).

Generation-based methods produce responses with Natural Language Generation (NLG) models learned from conversation data, while retrieval-based methods re-use the existing responses by selecting proper ones from an index of the conversation data. In this work, we study the problem of response selection in retrieval-based chatbots, because retrieval-based chatbots have the advantage of returning informative and concise responses (Galitsky and Ilvovsky, 2017). Although most existing work on retrieval-based chatbots studies response selection for single-turn conversations in which conversation history is ignored, the focus of this study is a multi-turn scenario. In a chatbot, multi-turn response selection takes a message and utterances in its previous turns as an input and selects a response utterance that is natural and relevant to the entire context.

To build medical dialogue systems, a large collection of conversations between patients and doctors is needed as training data. Due to data privacy concerns, such data is difficult to obtain. The existing medical dialogue datasets (Xu et al., 2019; Yang et al., 2020) are limited in size or biased to certain diseases, and thus cannot adequately serve the purpose of training medical dialogue systems that can achieve human doctor-level intelligence and cover many specialties in medicine. Several medical dialogue corpora have been released to facilitate the research of information extraction (Lin et al., 2019; Zhang et al., 2020) and automatic diagnosis (Wei et al., 2018; Xu et al., 2019). However, these corpora do not solve the problem of dialogue generation due to a lack of full natural language-based dialogues and a limited dataset scale.

Past work has used neural-generated chatbot responses for adding new world knowledge (Dinan et al., 2019), reviews (Ghazvininejad et al., 2018), and personality into conversations. However, chatbots for medical diagnosis poses rigorous requirements not only on the dialogue rationality in the context of medical knowledge but the comprehension of symptom-disease relations. The symptoms that the dialogue system inquiries about should be related to underlying disease and consistent with medical knowledge. Current task-oriented chatbots are frequently dependent on the complex belief tracker (Mrkšić et al., 2016; Lukin et al., 2018) and end-to-end data-driven learning, which is unable to involve automatic diagnosis making since medical knowledge is ignored.

The problem of finding the best utterance in an IR chatbot is essentially two-dimensional (Fig. 1). When both dimensions are tackled simultaneously under the data-driven approach, topical relevance is

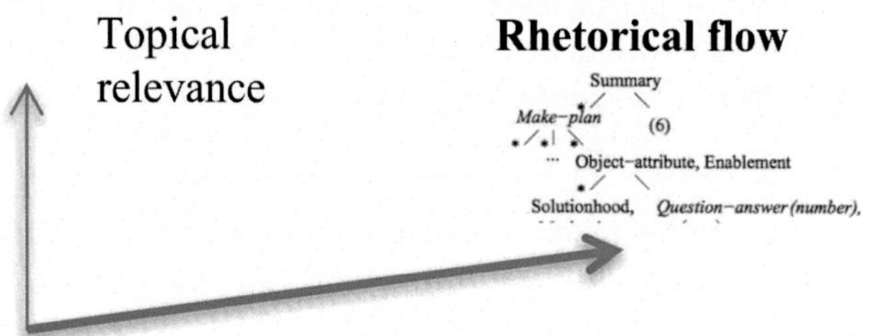

FIG. 1

Two dimensions of the utterance selection problem.

handled well, whereas dialogue management, rhetorical flow is random and uncontrolled. This is because there are quite a few levels of abstraction between the syntactic level available to the learning system and the discourse level that controls the rhetorical flow. It is hard to accumulate sufficient data to learn the rhetorical flow from the ground syntactic level. Therefore, in this study, we focus on the rhetorical flow separated from the topical relevance. The main subject of our consideration will be the discourse representation of a dialogue. Maintaining the proper dialogue flow is an essential task of a dialogue manager (DM).

In our previous studies, we separated the tasks of question answering (Q/A) into relevance and rhetorical agreement (Galitsky, 2017b). In this chapter, we take a step forward and extend the latter task of rhetorical agreement toward rhetorical flow, maintaining multiple utterances in a dialogue.

There are other issues in end-to-end learning-based dialogue management. A lack of control over neural generation methods makes it difficult to reliably use them to introduce new information in utterances asking questions or replying to user requests. When current chatbots (explicitly provided with new factual content) introduce facts in a conversation, their generated responses do not acknowledge the prior turns. This is due to the following: whereas current methods are trained with two contexts, new factual content and conversational history, the responses generated by chatbots are not simultaneously specific to both the content and conversational history. Chatbots lack specificity relatively to conversational history most of the times (Paranjape and Manning, 2021).

Although deep learning (DL) models outperform baseline methods in most cases, there are several major dialogue management problems with logical consistency that cannot yet be handled perfectly. An end-to-end model represents well a context and response on a semantic level but pays little attention to logical consistency. This leads to several bad cases in most corpora. For example, in the conversation history, one of the speakers says that *he thinks the item on eBay is fake*, and the response is expected to be *why he dislikes the fake shoes*. However, most neural models select the response "*It is not a fake. I just worry about the date of manufacture*." However, this response is inconsistent with the context in terms of logic, as it claims that the running shoes are not fake, which is contradictory to the context. The reason behind this is that most neural models only handle the semantics of context-response pairs. Logic, attitude, and sentiment are not taken into account in response selection.

While the most popular approaches filter candidates based on words, attempting syntactic and semantic level, we believe it *should be done at the level of the overall logical flow, the discourse level.*

1.1 Medical dialogue systems

Plenty of data is available to train health chatbots. MedDialog (Zeng et al., 2020) contains an English dataset with a quarter of a million conversations, half a million utterances, and covering 96 disease classes. Both datasets cover almost all specialties in medicine, ranging from internal medicine to family medicine and represents a wide spectrum of diseases, including cancer, pneumonia, and others.

In a typical medical consultation dialogue, a patient reports some health issues in the beginning, and then a doctor keeps asking questions to obtain more specific information about the patient. Finally, the doctor makes a disease diagnosis and provides medical advice based on both the obtained information and clinical experience. However, online medical consultations are much less efficient than offline consultations since most patients are unable to describe their symptoms clearly and communicate with doctors efficiently. In such a situation, doctors need to spend more time understanding patients' conditions to give a correct diagnosis.

As patients take more financial responsibility for their health, they have more choice over where they receive care. They are increasingly affected by ratings and reports on quality and outcomes. When making choices, patients also look for other people's opinions and experiences with care providers via social media (Oracle, 2020). For today's health systems to attract patients, they need to treat them as the informed consumers they are becoming and provide information in the form of dialogues with advanced management of user options and information access means.

During the COVID-19 pandemic, millions of patients worldwide have been facing delays in diagnosis and treatment due to the diversion of medical resources. As a result, telemedicine is increasingly expected to play a role in relieving therapeutic stress. Telemedicine has substantially increased from around 10% of general medicine consultations before COVID-19 to approximately 75% in the United Kingdom during the peak of the pandemic. Chatbots are a key underlying technology for telemedicine.

The problem we are solving in this chapter is discourse-driven dialogue management. Instead of relying on full text information about the previous utterances to select the proper next one, we form a discourse representation and attempt to identify simple criteria for correct and incorrect discourse structure for a dialogue.

Let us consider a text and a dialogue about it.

A man just underwent a very complicated operation. He is complaining about a bump on his head and a terrible headache. Since he had an intestinal operation, he should not have a headache. The man's nurse expresses her concerns that the man might be suffering from some post-operative shock.

Nurse: Doc, what can we do about the patient's headache?

Surgeon: Don't worry about it. He really does have a bump on his head ... About halfway through the operation, we ran out of anesthesia.

In this dialogue, the nurse raised the question about the inconsistency in the text, and the surgeon provided an explanation by sharing missing information about the circumstances of the surgery. Providing explanation is the most appropriate reply in this situation. The other replies such as

- critiquing the nurse or a patient,
- changing a conversation mood from information/explanation request to a negative sentiment,
- asking them about a confirmation of a headache, and
- asking them other questions

are less appropriate or inappropriate. In this chapter, we explore the discourse features associated with appropriate and inappropriate replies and dialogue flows.

2. Discourse tree of a dialogue

In this section, we extend a conventional discourse representation means toward a dialogue so that we can classify this representation into a valid, cohesive dialogue with a proper rhetorical flow vs invalid, incohesive one with an illogical flow.

2.1 Response selection

A key step in response selection is measuring a matching degree between an input and response candidates. Different from the single-turn conversation, in which the input is a single utterance (i.e., the message), multi-turn conversation requires context-response matching where both the current message and the utterances in its previous turns should be taken into consideration. The challenges of the task include:

(1) how to extract important information (words, phrases, and sentences) from the context and leverage the information in matching; and
(2) how to model relationships and dependencies among the utterances in the context.

Fig. 2 uses an example to illustrate the challenges. A chatbot recommends a certain activity to the user (Galitsky, 2020a). First, to find a proper response for the context, the chatbot must know that "have a swimming class" and "swim" are important points. Without them, it may return a response relevant to the message (i.e., Turn-5 in the context) but inappropriate in the context (e.g., "What lessons do you want?"). On the other hand, *Prague* and *Vyšehrad* can be less useful and even noisy to response selection. The responses from the chatbot may drift to the topic of *Prague* if the chatbot pays a significant attention to these words. Therefore, it is crucial yet non-trivial to let the DM understand the important points in the context and leverage them in matching and at the same time circumvent noise. Also, there is a clear dependency between the second and third user utterances in the context, and the order of utterances matters in response selection because there will be different proper responses if one swaps these utterances.

The last utterance is the one where it is important to maintain proper rhetorical flow. Among the rhetorically inappropriate responses are:

- What lessons do you want? ✗
- Do you want me to teach you swimming? ✗
- Do you want to do something else besides swimming? ✗

Notice that these utterances are topically correct but break the logical flow of a conversation.

In our first example we will turn a regular discourse tree (DT; Chapter 2) into a dialogue DT (DDT). To do that, we turn default relation of *Elaboration* into a specific relation for a dialogue Q/A turn *Qna*.

Here is a default, conventional DT for the plain text obtained by merging utterances of the preceding dialogue (Fig. 3).

To express a dialogue via a DT, we add specific relations between utterances (Table 1). To link utterances in a dialogue, we mix rhetorical relations and communicative actions, as both kinds regulate an agreement between a request and response (a question and an answer, and a sharing intent and its acceptance). Now the DDT is expressed via *Qna* (Fig. 4).

Bot: How are you doing?
User: I am going to swimming class in Prague. Anyone wants to join? The location is near Vyšehrad.
Interesting! Do you have coaches who can help me practice swimming?
Bot: Yes we have.
User: Can I have a first lesson on butterfly stroke?
Bot: Sure. Have you ever swum butterfly before?

FIG. 2

A dialogue where it is important to differentiate between important and unimportant points.

```
elaboration
 elaboration
  joint
   TEXT:How are you doing ?
   TEXT:I am going to swimming class in Prague .
  elaboration
   elaboration
    TEXT:Anyone wants to join ?
    elaboration
     TEXT:The location is near Vyšehrad .
     joint
      TEXT:Interesting !
      joint
       elaboration
        TEXT:Do you have coaches
        TEXT:who can help me practice swimming ?
       TEXT:Yes we have .
   elaboration
    TEXT:Can I have a first lesson on butterfly stroke ?
    TEXT:Sure .
 TEXT:Have you ever swam butterfly before ?
```

FIG. 3

A conventional DT for a dialogue text.

Table 1 Rhetorical relations and speech acts linking utterances.

Rhetorical relation or a speech act	Description
Qna	Relation between a question and an answer
Request	Terminates the interaction with the system
Disbelief/rejection/ disagreement/denial	Relation between a statement and a corresponding denying statement
Sharing/acknowledgment/ acceptance	Relation between an utterance with information being shared and an utterance with acknowledgment
Repeating/insisting	Relation between the first and the second utterances confirming/insisting a claim
Confirmation/agreement	Relation between a statement and a corresponding accepting statement
Explanation	Relation between a current utterances and a pair of two utterances: • one that takes a statement from one utterance • one that expresses a doubt from another utteranceand attempts to address this doubt
Explanation request/doubt	Relation between an actual explanation (Why question) and explanation request

We intend to encode a dialogue by a DT so that rhetorical relations express both dialogue turns and relations inside an utterance. An utterance containing multiple phrases is expected to be split into elementary discourse units (EDUs). Representing dialogue as a tree helps to establish a logical flow of this dialogue and encode abrupt changes within it. The last utterance (the key question) in the dialogue in Fig. 5 is shown as a result of the whole previous sequence of utterances. Since there is no

```
qna
 elaboration
  qna
   TEXT:How are you doing ?
   TEXT:I am going to swimming class in Prague .
  elaboration
   qna
    TEXT:Anyone wants to join ?
    elaboration
     TEXT:The location is near Vyšehrad .
     joint
      TEXT:Interesting !
      qna
       elaboration
        TEXT:Do you have coaches
        TEXT:who can help me practice swimming ?
       TEXT:Yes we have .
   qna
    TEXT:Can I have a first lesson on butterfly stroke ?
    TEXT:Sure .
 TEXT:Have you ever swam butterfly before ?
```

FIG. 4

An example of a DDT with *Qna* relation.

```
elaboration → continue_topic
 elaboration → qna
  joint → confirmation tell(i , nick, apt) → yes
   attribution
    TEXT:Did you tell Nick
    TEXT:that you are making a doctor appointment ?
   TEXT:Yes I told him about the clinic for tonight .
  TEXT:Tell him he does not need a car .
 contrast
  TEXT:I will ,
  attribution insist(he, need(he, car))
   TEXT:but he would insist
   TEXT:he needs one .
```

FIG. 5

A dialogue with communicative actions inside utterances.

change in dialogue logical flow, this last utterance is connected with the previous sequence by *Elaboration*.

Default dialogue flow is encoded by *Elaboration* and *Joint* similarly to a regular text, not a dialogue.

Elaboration means that in the course of dialogue, the recipient gets further information. *Joint* means just a concatenation of two utterances.

2.2 Speech acts and communicative actions

There are more epistemic states in a dialogue than just *Qna*. We now consider a variety of mental states evolving in a dialogue and their discourse representations (Table 1).

For a regular text, it is important to incorporate speech acts in its discourse representation. It is done via communicative DTs (CDTs) where communicative actions are labels for the terminal DT arcs. The role of CDT extension of DT by means of communicative actions (Galitsky and Kuznetsov, 2008) is even more significant for representing dialogues than for plain text (Galitsky, 2018). Now there are communicative actions within utterances, encoded via labels, and communicative actions between utterances that form additional dialogue-specific relations between utterances. The latter can be viewed as meta-communicative actions with respect to the former object-level communicative actions.

User1: Did you tell Nick that you are making a doctor appointment?
User2: Yes, I told him about the clinic for tonight.
User1: Tell him he does not need a car.
User2: I will, but he would insist he needs one.

Fig. 5 illustrates the case of a dialogue with several communicative actions mentioned in utterances. The root and higher-level relations *Elaboration*, *Elaboration*, and *Joint* are turned into *Continue_topic*, *Qna*, and *Confirmation*, respectively (top three lines in Fig. 5). This is done to differentiate between a set of utterances as a plain text and a "structurized" set of utterances as a dialogue. *Continue_topic*, *Qna*, and *Confirmation* outline a dialogue structure and its overall logic.

Communicative actions in this dialogue occur between the utterances *Continue_topic* and *Confirmation*, as well as inside the utterances, as indicated in red italics following the relation. The former group constitutes meta-level communicative actions relative to the latter, object-level ones.

2.3 A dialogue with doubt

We consider a simple dialogue where the answer recipient A does not accept the answer from Q and expresses a *doubt* (*disagreement*, *disbelief*, *denial*):

Q: What does the Investigative Committee of Russian Federation do?
A: Performs law enforcement duties and investigation. [default answer]
Q: Really?
A: Indeed, it frequently manages organized crime groups.

The resultant DDT includes relations of *Disbelief* specific to a dialogue, and *Qna*, the default dialogue rhetorical relation.

```
disbelief
  qna
    TEXT:What does the Investigative Committee of Russian Federation do ?
    TEXT:It performs law enforcement duties and investigations .
  concession believes(A, not believe(Q), qna(Q,A)
    TEXT:Really ?
    TEXT:Indeed , it manages organized crime groups .
```

We enumerate four utterance candidates that maintain the proper entity and sentiment (here, neutral; see Galitsky and Kovalerchuk, 2006) but break the rhetorical flow. The comments are in square brackets:

- *It also maintains law and order* [does not address the doubt]
- *It does a great job of fighting the crime* [does not address the doubt and uses unexpected positive sentiment]
- *It participates in maintaining order at elections* [different entity, so inappropriate entity flow]

Correct alternative utterances would be:

- *Well, not always law enforcement duties* [attenuation of first answer]
- *There are other duties* [attenuation of first answer]
- *You are right. It is totally corrupt* [confirmation of the doubt]

We cite Manvarov and Koshek (2020) for an example of such corruption charges.

2.4 Further extending the set of rhetorical relations toward dialogue

A task-oriented dialogue is associated with a complex behavior, involving two participants, each with their own beliefs and intentions, in a collaborative effort to interact to solve some problem. There is a whole set of behaviors related to maintaining the collaboration and synchronizing beliefs that do not arise in monologue (Clark, 1996). These include answering questions, agreeing to proposals, and simply acknowledging that the other participant has spoken.

User (1) We have to send ambulance to the emergency area 1.
User (2) There are people there to evacuate.
Bot (3) How many are we sending?
User (4) Three.
Bot (5) OK
Bot (6) So one ambulance to the emergency area E1 and two ambulances to the emergency area E2?

Fig. 6 shows an analysis of a part of a constructed dialogue. Nuclei are marked with * and non-RST relations are in italics.

We proceed to the examples of other epistemic states in dialogues such as *regulation-applicability*.

Regulation: To qualify for tax exemption, the nonprofit organizations must apply under Section 501(c)(3) of the Internal Revenue Code. The status allows the organizations to write off their contributions on their individual tax returns.
User Scenario: We are a charity helping the crime victims in United States who accept donations from businesses.
User Question: Can we qualify for Section 501(c)(3)?
Follow-up Q1: Are you a for-profit business?
Follow-up A1: Yes.
Follow-up Q2: Do you qualify for other Sections for tax exemption?
Follow-up A2: No.
Final Answer: Yes. You qualify for Section 501(c)(3)
https://www.irs.gov/charities-non-profits/other-non-profits/requirements-for-exemption

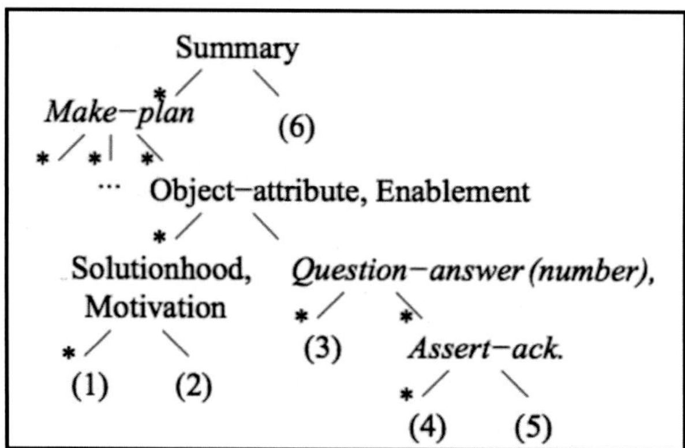

FIG. 6

A DDT with extended rhetorical relations for dialogue.

Table 2 Other relations controlling a dialogue.

Speech act	Description
Summary	Relationship between a few utterances and their summary
Make-plan	Relation between the expected result utterance and a set of utterances for a plan to get to this result
Stance	Returns the current stance of the user
Exit	Terminates the interaction with the system
Level-up	Changes the current state and switches to the according parent node (one level up)
Why (argument)	Provides information about the current argument by exploring its child nodes
Prefer (argument)	User prefers the referenced argument component over the others
Reject (argument)	User disagrees with an argument component

In addition, there are argumentation-related relations that can link utterances (Table 2).

3. Computing rhetorical relation of entailment

One of the challenges of dialogue management is deriving a literal answer from a rule or a regulation that does not contain this answer explicitly. The DM needs to provide a procedure to derive it through interactions. The DM is required to read the rule text, interpret the user scenario, clarify the unknown user's background by asking questions, and derive the final answer.

Considering an example (Fig. 7) to make a decision for a patient whether a specific treatment is well-suited for him, the Entailment Relation component needs to interpret the treatment text to know what the requirements are, understand the patient's circumstances from the scenario, ask follow-up clarification questions, and produce the final answer.

Rule/regulation/treatment: An active Tuberculosis (TB) disease needs to be treated with a combination of antibacterial medications for a period of six to 12 months. The most common treatment for active TB is isoniazid INH in combination with three other drugs—rifampin, pyrazinamide and ethambutol. A patient usually begins to feel better only a few weeks after starting to take the drugs but treating TB takes much longer than other bacterial infections. The patient must continue taking his medication as prescribed for the entire time your doctor indicates or he could get sick again, have a harder time fighting the disease in the future and spread the disease to others.
Patient condition: Treated by isoniazid and rifampin for one week but low sensitivity to rifampin. Need to switch to pyrazinamide.
Patient question: can I switch to ethambutol to have a stronger effect?
Follow up patient Q1: Can I text susceptibility of tuberculosis to pyrazinamide?
Follow up answer: Standard culture-based testing of the susceptibility of Mycobacterium tuberculosis to pyrazinamide is difficult to perform.
Final Answer: Yes you can switch to pyrazinamide.

FIG. 7

The chatbot answers the patient's question by reading the treatment text, interpreting the user scenario, and asking follow-up questions to clarify the patient information until it concludes a final answer.

Two sub-tasks need to be solved:

(1) Given the rule text, user question, user scenario, and dialogue history (if any), make a decision among "Yes," "No," "Inquire," and "Irrelevant." The "Yes/No" directly answers the user question and "Irrelevant" means the user question is unanswerable by the rule text. If the user-provided information (user scenario, previous dialogues) is not enough to determine his fulfillment or eligibility, an "Inquire" decision is made and the second sub-task is activated.
(2) Capture the underspecified condition from the rule text and generate a follow-up question to clarify it. Propose an entailment-driven extracting and editing framework to extract a span from the rule text and edit it into the follow-up question.

Fig. 8 shows the architecture for computing entailment in a dialogue.

The entailment detection component concatenates all sequences together and uses RoBERTa to encode the concatenated sequence (Fig. 8). The input is the discourse-segmented regulation text and other utterances.

The encoded [CLS] token represents the sequence that follows it. Sentence-level representations of conditions (EDUs) are extracted as $e_1, e_2, \ldots, e_N$, as well as the representations of the user question u_Q, user scenario u_S, and M turns of dialogue history $u_1, \ldots, u_M$.

To yield the correct decision for the user question, it is necessary to compute the fulfillment of conditions in the regulation text. The fulfillment prediction of the conditions problem is formulated as a multi-sentence entailment task. Given a sequence of conditions (premises) and a sequence information items from the user (hypotheses), the entailment recognition system should output in the set {*Entailment*, *Contradiction*, *Neutral*} for each condition listed in the regulation text.

Taking all sentence-level representations $[e_1; e_2; \ldots; e_N; u_Q; u_S; u_1; \ldots; u_M]$ as inputs, the L-layer transformer encoder makes each condition attend to all the user-provided information to predict whether the condition is entailed or not. All conditions also attend to each other to track the logical structure of the regulation text. Letting the transformer encoder output of the i-th condition as $\widetilde{e}_i$, we use a linear transformation to predict its entailment state:

$$c_i = W_c \widetilde{e}_i + b_c \in \mathbb{R}^3,$$

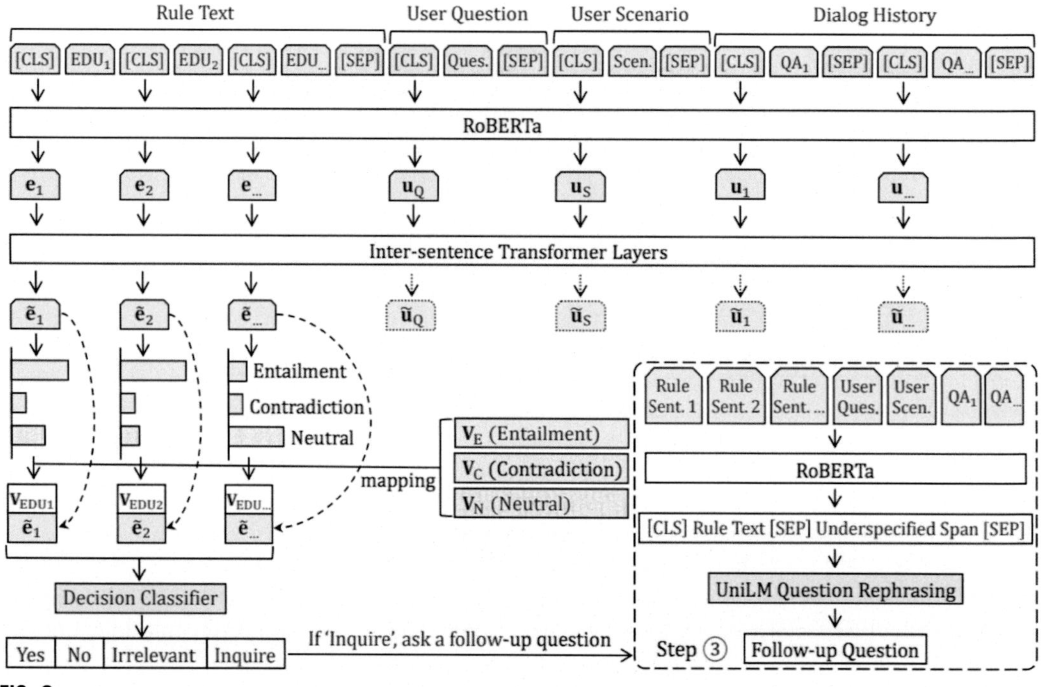

FIG. 8

The architecture of DISCERN (Gao et al., 2020). Taking the segmented conditions, user question, user scenario, and dialogue history as inputs, DISCERN performs reasoning concerning the decision set {*Yes, No, Irrelevant, Inquire*}. If the decision is "Inquire," the question-generation model asks a follow-up question.

where $c_i = [c_{E,i}, c_{C,i}, c_{N,i}] \in \mathbb{R}^3$ contains confidence scores of three entailment states {*Entailment*, *Contradiction*, *Neutral*}.

All associated follow-up questions in the dataset are collected for each regulation text. Each follow-up question is matched to an EDU in the regulation text that has the minimum edit distance. For conditions in the regulation text that are mentioned by follow-up questions in the dialogue history, the entailment state of a condition is assigned *Entailment* if the answer for its mentioned follow-up question is *Yes*, and labels the state of this condition as *Contradiction* if the answer is *No*. The remaining conditions not covered by any follow-up question are labeled as *Neutral*.

Let r be the correct entailment state. The entailment prediction is expressed by a cross-entropy loss, divided by the total number of K conditions:

$$\mathcal{L}_{\text{entail}} = -\frac{1}{K}\sum_{i=1}^{K} \log \text{softmax}(c_i)_r,$$

Interpreting scenarios to extract the entailment information within is the hardest problem in the DT construction pipeline. To test the entailment accuracy in a conversational setting, we follow Gao

Table 3 Reasoning patterns and their examples.

Reasoning pattern	Rule or regulation	Scenario	Question	Correct answer
Numerical	Each attachment must be less than 10 MB	The attachment right now isn't less than 10 MB, but I think I can use Zip so it becomes less than 10 MB	Can I email the attachment?	No
Paraphrase	There is an educational assistance program attracting high-quality men and women into the Armed Forces	I applied for the program and found out I was qualified My spouse wants me to join the army, but I prefer to go to school	Can I leverage the program?	Contradiction
Temporal	The Additional State Pension is an extra amount of money you could get on top of your basic pension as a fed government employee	I live with my husband We both have worked for the state for the last 20 years before retirement	Do I qualify for extra pension?	No
Commonsense Reasoning	Owners of single-family homes qualify for up to $200,000 to repair or replace their primary residence to its pre-disaster condition	My area was hit by an earthquake	Can I get assistance with repair?	Yes

et al. (2020) in employing the ShARC dataset that is the current benchmark to test entailment reasoning in conversational machine reading. The dataset contains almost a thousand texts with rules and regulations scraped from 10 government websites. About two-thirds of texts are plain text with in-line conditions while the remaining third contain enumeration of items for conditions. Each rule text is associated with a dialogue tree with follow-up utterances that considers all possible fulfillment combinations of conditions. In the data annotation stage, parts of the dialogues are reformulated into the user scenario. These parts of dialogues are marked as evidence that should be deduced (entailed) from the user scenario and are not provided as inputs for evaluation. The inputs to the system are the rule text, user question, user scenario, and dialogue history (if any). The output is the answer among *Yes*, *No*, *Irrelevant*, or a follow-up clarification question. Table 3 presents examples of reasoning patterns.

We conclude this section with an example of joint incompetence of human and machine reading comprehension.

In this example (Allen AI, 2021), a human writer lacks the basic knowledge of physics, and a machine reading comprehension system is unable to associate *low bound … temperature* with *cool down* (Fig. 9).

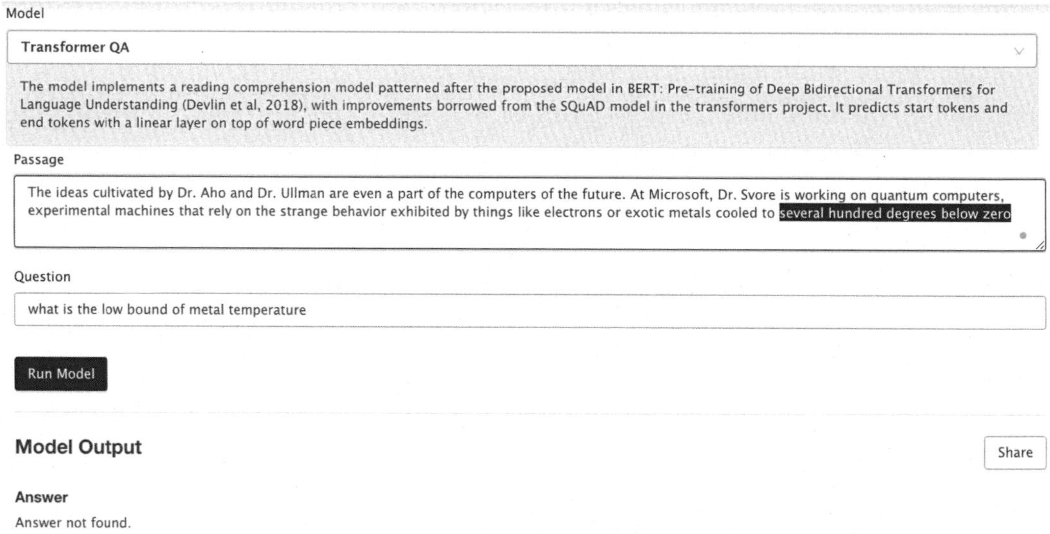

Model

Transformer QA

The model implements a reading comprehension model patterned after the proposed model in BERT: Pre-training of Deep Bidirectional Transformers for Language Understanding (Devlin et al, 2018), with improvements borrowed from the SQuAD model in the transformers project. It predicts start tokens and end tokens with a linear layer on top of word piece embeddings.

Passage

The ideas cultivated by Dr. Aho and Dr. Ullman are even a part of the computers of the future. At Microsoft, Dr. Svore is working on quantum computers, experimental machines that rely on the strange behavior exhibited by things like electrons or exotic metals cooled to several hundred degrees below zero

Question

what is the low bound of metal temperature

Run Model

Model Output

Share

Answer

Answer not found.

FIG. 9

A human makes a meaningless statement, and a machine gets lost in it.

4. Dialogue generation as language modeling

Response generation can be formulated as a language modeling problem. Given the conversation history s, a language model defines the following probability on the sequence of tokens $t = t_1, \cdots, t_n$ in the response:

$$p(t \mid s) = p(t_1 \mid s) \prod_{i=2}^{n} p(t_i \mid s, t_1, \cdots, t_{i-1}), \tag{1}$$

where $s, t_1, \cdots, t_{i-1}$ denotes the concatenation of s and $s, t_1, \cdots, t_{i-1}$.

A transformer (Vaswani et al., 2017) architecture is typically used for sequence-to-sequence modeling. A transformer consists of an encoder that embeds the input sequence into a latent space and a decoder that takes the embedding of the input sequence as input and generates the output sequence.

The encoder generates an encoding for each token in the input sequence. These encodings are fed into the decoder to generate the output sequence. To generate the token at position i, the decoder encodes the generated tokens from 1 to $i-1$ (like an encoder), calculates an attentional representation by performing attention between the encodings of input tokens and the encodings of output tokens $1, \cdots, i-1$, then feeds the attentional representation into a softmax layer to generate token i. The transformer learns the weights in the encoder and decoder by maximizing the conditional likelihood of responses conditioned on conversation histories.

Language models can produce unspecific responses that may be bland and low quality. Li et al. (2016) suggest improving their quality by selecting the response with maximum Pointwise Mutual Information (PMI) to maintain specificity. PMI between two events (x, y) is a measure of change in the probability of one event x, given another event y: $pmi(x;y) \equiv \log p(x \mid y)\, p(x)$.

A conversational rephrasing can be defined (Paranjape and Manning, 2021) as a generation task where conversational history (h) and new factual content (k) are inputs, and a response (g) is generated as the output. We expect the generation g to paraphrase the new factual content k in a conversational manner by utilizing the conversational history h. Not including the prior task of finding the right k simplifies the task and analysis.

PMI is used to determine the increase in the likelihood of $\boldsymbol{g}$, given $\boldsymbol{h}$ and $\boldsymbol{k}$.

$$\text{pmi}(\boldsymbol{g}; \boldsymbol{h}, \boldsymbol{k}) = \log \frac{p(\boldsymbol{g}|\boldsymbol{hk})}{p(\boldsymbol{g})}$$

A high PMI indicates that a candidate generation g is more likely given the two contexts h and k than otherwise and is, therefore, considered specific to the contexts. While candidates with a low PMI can be filtered out, since they are specific to neither context h nor k, we cannot necessarily conclude that high PMI is specific to both the contexts simultaneously, since mutual information could come from either context.

The recent effective deep matching networks for multi-turn response retrieval, short text matching, and overall dialogue planning (Fig. 10) consist of four elements.

(1) Representations learning. A multi-turn response selection first transforms context utterances and response candidates to either vector representations or interaction matrices (Guo et al., 2016) for matching. For vector representations learning, various deep neural networks are designed for learning multi-level and multi-dimension semantic information from conversation utterances. Interaction-based representation learning methods first generate an interaction matrix for each utterance pair between context utterances and response candidates. Then, direct matching features such as the degree and structure of matching are captured.

(2) Dependency modeling. Besides the semantic representations and matching structures in the interaction-based method, there exist sophisticated dependency information and reference relations within utterances and across utterances. Benefited from the great success of the transformer on neural machine translation, various attention-based methods are proposed to capture the dependency structure and information from different levels.

(3) Matching. Once utterance representations at each level of granularity are obtained, the matching relations between two segments are calculated. Semantic matching methods and structure

FIG. 10

A cat plans a negotiation dialogue with a mouse.

matching approaches are designed to calibrate the matching degree between two representations, including Euclidean distance between two vectors, cosine similarity, or element-wise dot product.

(4) **Aggregation and fusion.** After calculating the matching degree between context and response at each level of granularity, a typical deep matching network contains an aggregation or fusion module for learning the final matching score.

4.1 Strategies for informative conversations

Paranjape and Manning (2021) find that people apply four kinds of strategies:

(1) *acknowledgment* of each other's utterances.
(2) transition to new information.
(3) *appropriate level of detail* selection.
(4) presentation of factual content via *opinions or experiences.*

We adopt and extend Herbert Clark's approaches to conversational analysis. According to his *given-new* contract (Clark and Haviland, 1977), the speaker tries to connect their utterances with the given information (assumed to be known to the listener) and add new information. This builds up common ground between the two participants, defined to be the sum of their mutual, common or joint knowledge, beliefs, and suppositions. We identify four aspects to the process of adding new information to a conversation (Table 4)

We now proceed to a neural architecture for utterance selection. A 1-D convolution on the word embeddings of a given utterance $U_j[e_{uj,\ 1}, e_{uj,\ 2}, \ldots, e_{uj,\ k}, \ldots, e_{uj,\ nuj}]$ is computed with window size l from 1 to 3, where there are d_f filters for each window size and the stride length is 1 (Fig. 11). The l-gram phrase representation in the k-th location is calculated as: $\boldsymbol{o}_k^l = ReLU(\boldsymbol{Z}_k^l \boldsymbol{W}_1 + \boldsymbol{b}_1)$ where $\boldsymbol{W}_1$ and $\boldsymbol{b}_1$ are trainable parameters of the convolutional filter with window size l, and $\boldsymbol{Z}_k^l \in R^{l \times dw}$ stands for the input unigram embeddings in the current sliding window. The output sequence of vectors of the convolution has the same length as the input sequence of vectors by utilizing the zero-padding strategy.

To obtain the sophisticated dependency representations in conversations, Li et al. (2021) rely on attentive module that is similar to the attention module in the transformer. The attentive module takes three sentences as input {the query sentence, the key sentence, and the value sentence}, which are denoted as $Q = [e_i]_{i=0}^{nQ-1}, K = [e_i]_{i=0}^{nK-1}, V = [e_i]_{i=0}^{nK-1}$, respectively. Here n_Q, n_k, represent the number of words in each sentence, and the length of the sentence with keys is the same as the length of the sentence with values, and $\boldsymbol{e}_i$ is the d_w-dimensional word embedding representation of a word. The attentive module first uses each word in the query sentence to attend each word in the key sentence through the scaled dot-product attention mechanism. Then, the obtained attention score is a function of the value sentence V to form a new representation of Q, which is formulated as follows:

$$attention(Q, K, V) = \text{softmax}\left(\frac{QK^T}{\sqrt{d_w}}\right) \text{V}$$

Wu et al. (2019) studied text matching for response selection in multi-turn conversation, in which matching is conducted between a piece of text and a context that consists of multiple pieces of text dependent on each other. We propose a new matching framework that can extract important information in the context and model dependencies among utterances in the context.

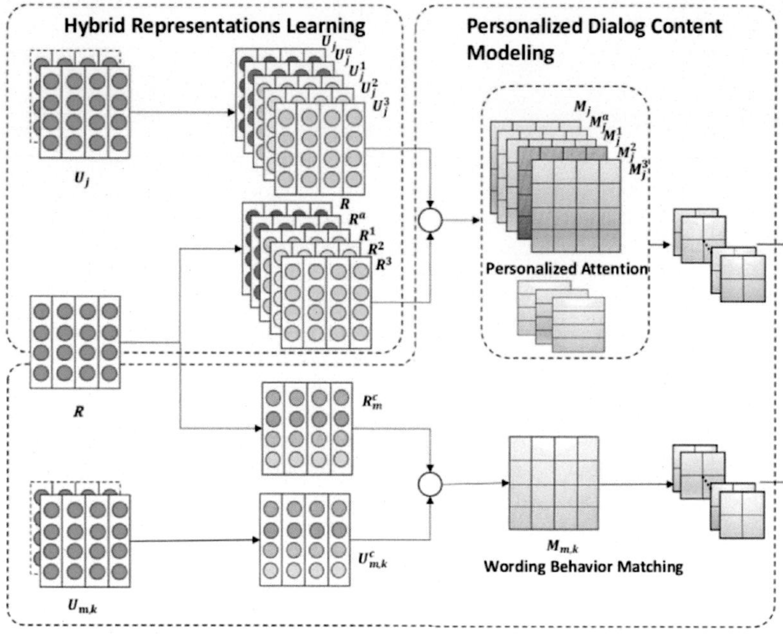

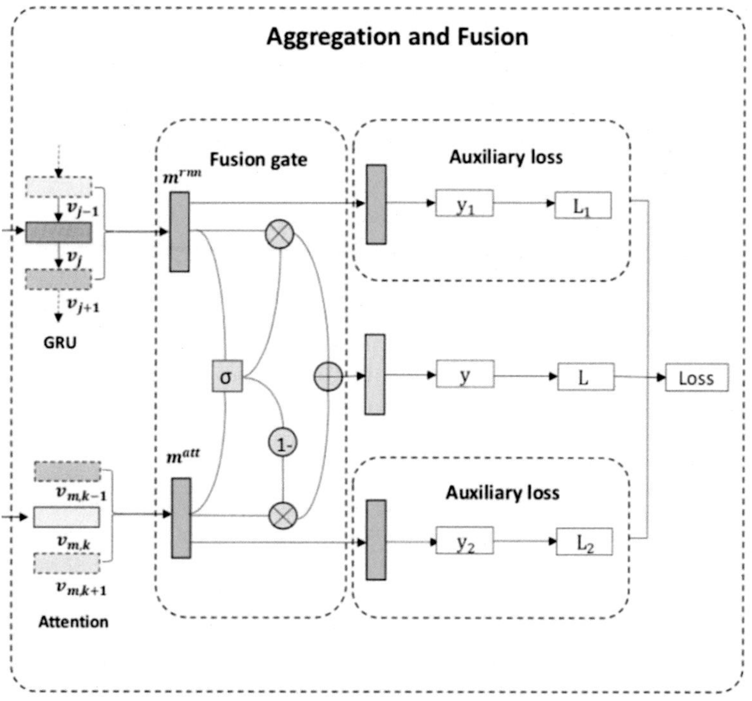

FIG. 11

Neural architecture of utterance selection (Li et al., 2021).

Table 4 Dialogue strategies in conversational analysis.

Information flow strategy	Description	RST relation and other DT labels	Reference
Acknowledgment strategies	The listener provides positive evidence for grounding. We classify all mentions of prior context into various acknowledgment strategies.	Confirmation, acknowledgment	Clark and Brennan (1991)
Transition strategies	Topical changes happen step by step, connecting the given, stated information to new information. We annotate these as different transition strategies.		Sacks and Jefferson (1995)
Detail selection strategies	Each speaker knows varying amounts of information about the discussion topic. Speakers must assess each other's expertise to resolve their possible differences in opinions and factoids. Each dialogue participant applies detail selection strategies to select the right level of detail to be presented and classify utterances as such.	Detail	Isaacs and Clark (1987)
Presentation strategies	A presentation of answers is guided by two social goals: exchange of information and self-presentation. People talk about factual information in non-factual forms (e.g., opinion, experience, recommendation).	Speech Act labels	Smith and Clark (1993)

5. Rhetorical agreement between questions and answers

In this section, we address a sub-problem of the discourse-driven dialogue management problem of how to coordinate a single question-answer pair. These considerations also cover the case of an arbitrary response with an arbitrary request concerning appropriateness that goes beyond topic relevance, typical for a question-answer pair. Argumentation patterns in a question need to be reflected in the argumentation patterns in the answer; the latter may contain an argumentation defeat or support. Irony in a question needs to be addressed by irony or sarcasm in the answer. Doubt in a question needs to be answered by rejection or confirmation. A knowledge-sharing intent in an utterance needs to be followed by an acceptance or rejection of this knowledge in the answer.

Which linguistic structures need to come into play to express this sort of coordination? Naturally, neither syntactic nor semantic, as they reflect the phrasing and domain-specific information, which should be independent of rhetorical agreement. Hence one would expect that a discourse structure takes responsibility for utterance coordination. Certainly though, patterns expressed in a question must be responded with matching thought patterns in an answer to be accepted by social norms.

A request can have an arbitrary rhetorical structure as long as the subject of this request or a question is clear to its recipient. A response on its own can have an arbitrary rhetorical structure. However, these structures should be correlated when the response is *appropriate* to the request. In this section, we focus on a computational measure for how logical, rhetorical structure of a request or question agrees with that of a response or an answer.

When answering a question formulated as a phrase or a sentence, the answer must address the *topic* of this question. When a question is formulated implicitly, via a *seed* text of a message, its answer is expected not only to maintain a topic but also to match the *epistemic state* of this seed. For example, when a person is looking to sell an item with certain features, the search result should not only contain these features but also indicate an intent to buy. When a person is looking to share knowledge about an item, the search result should contain an intent to receive a recommendation (Galitsky, 2020a). When a person asking for an opinion about a subject, the response should be sharing an opinion about this subject, not another request for an opinion. Modern dialogue management systems and automated email answering have achieved good accuracy maintaining the topic, but maintaining the communication discourse is a much more difficult problem. This measure of rhetorical agreement needs to be learned from data since it is hard to come up with explicit rules for coordinated rhetorical structures.

The goal of this section is to extend the notion of question/answer relevance to *rhetorical* relevance of a general request/response pair for a broader dialogue support. Let us now see if there is a correlation between the discourse trees of Q and A.

Q: My wife wants to eat her placenta. Is it OK if she is vegan? I know it sounds gross and weird, but a lot of animals do it. So she did some research and found out that it helps to cure postpartum depression. You swallow your own blood when you cut a tongue, this thing is just much bigger.

A: Consuming your placenta after giving birth can be a controversial topic. Add veganism into the mix, and it is even more so. Because it is technically an animal product, some may argue that vegans should not eat it. I grew it from my body, gave it to myself willingly and heard from multiple women that it had helped with postpartum depression, recovery from childbirth, increased energy, and milk production. I had nothing to lose. Although other animals eat it raw, some women cook, put it in smoothies, or have it encapsulated like I did, which definitely makes it more palatable! Others may consider eating a placenta cannibalism, but I beg to differ. I did not suffer or die just so I could consume my placenta.

Let us try to find correlation between the DTs of Q and A (Fig. 12). One can observe that certain relations in the question should be addressed by those in the answer. If the question author included *Topic-comment* in the question, the answer should communicate a link between a topic and a comment about it in the answer by using analogous rhetorical relations of *Explanation* (on the top). Second from the top-level *Elaboration* in the question is handled by providing *Background* information in the answer. Handling *Contrast* in the question requires a communication for how the respective *Contrast* is addressed in the answer; this is essential for a comprehensive answer (third arrow from the top).

6. Discourse parsing of a dialogue

Documents can be analyzed as sequences of hierarchical discourse structures. Discourse structures describe the organization of documents in terms of discourse or rhetorical relations. Discourse parsing is an integral part of understanding information flow and argumentative structure in documents (Chapter 2).

One of the main issues of discourse coherence is how rhetorical relations such as *Cause*, *Evidence*, *List*, or *Summary* are signaled in text. Rhetorical relations are often indicated by discourse markers such as *and*, *because*, *however*, and *while*, and relations are sometimes classified as explicit relations if they

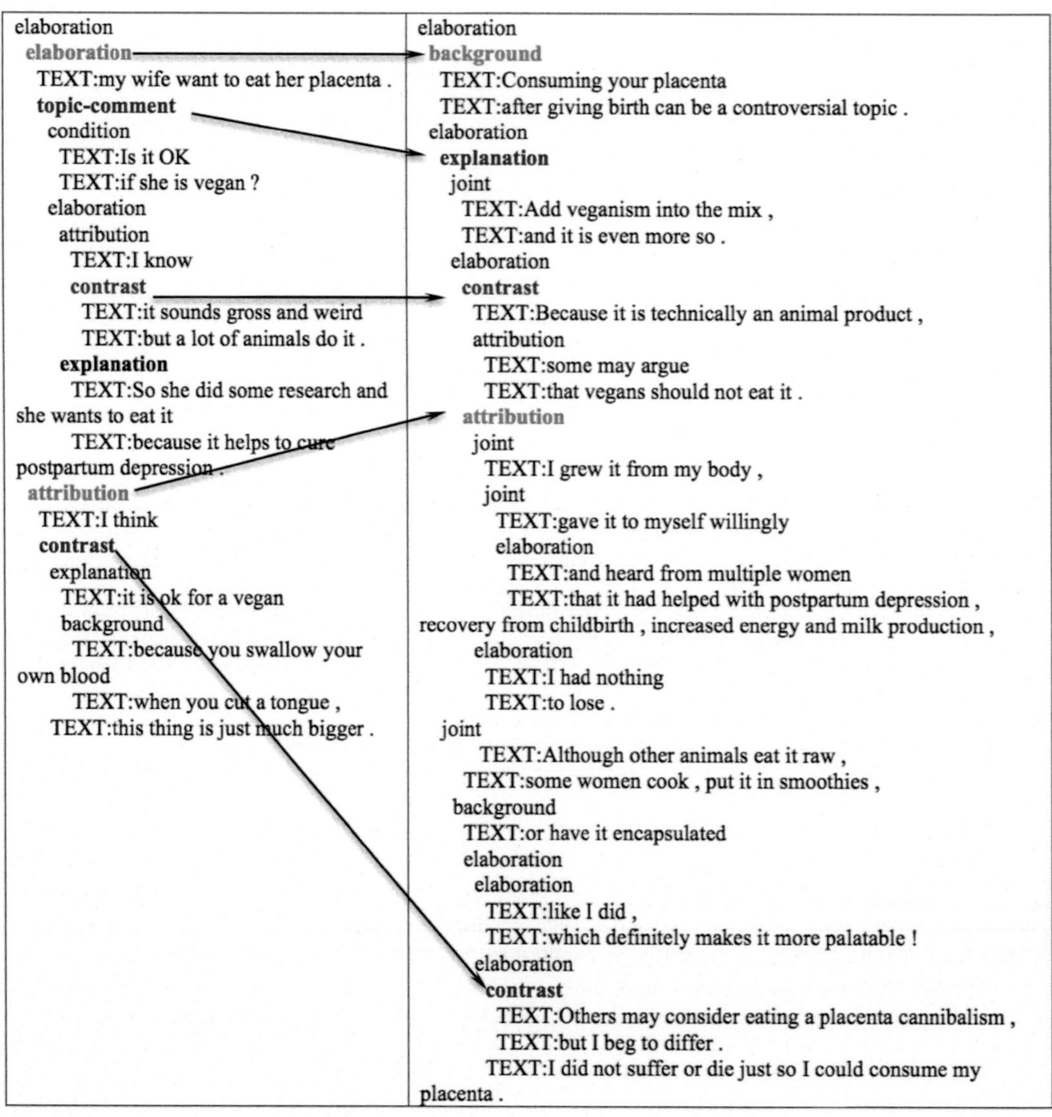

FIG. 12

Rhetorical agreement between a Q (left) and A (right).

contain such markers (Taboada and Mann, 2006; van der Vliet and Redeker, 2011). Discourse markers are widely believed to be the most reliable signals of coherence relations.

Prediction of the rhetorical relation between two sentences is the goal of discourse parsing, along with text segmentation (splitting sentences into EDUs). We rely on baseline segmentation and do not attempt to improve it. Several annotated corpora exist, such as RST-DT (Carlson et al., 2001) and

PDTB, but in general, the available data is fairly limited, and the task of discourse relation prediction is rather difficult. Most available discourse parsers assign just *Elaboration* and *Join* relations in most cases, and the recall of establishing other, more specific rhetorical relation is fairly low. In this section, we employ a linguistic formalism and resource of Abstract Meaning Representation (AMR) targeting semantic representation to learn to recognize specific rhetorical relations in text.

We first apply the state-of-the art discourse parse of Joty et al. (2013) and Surdeanu et al. (2015) and then attempt to overwrite the *Elaboration* and *Joint* with a specific rhetorical relation obtained from AMR patterns if they are available. We apply such a procedure for intra-sentence rhetorical relations only.

Was it a question of life or death for you?
I had scarcely enough drinking water
To last for how long?
For a week

Fig. 13 shows a DDT for this dialogue. The top-level relation of *Elaboration* is not very accurate, and we look up this example in the AMR dataset.

```
elaboration
 qna
  TEXT: Was it a question of life or death for you ?
  TEXT: I had scarcely enough drinking water
 qna
  TEXT: To last for how long ?
  TEXT: For a week
```

```
(q / question
    :ARG0 i
    :ARG1 (o / or
        :op1 (l / live-01)
        :op2 (d / die-01))
    :ARG1-of (c / cause
        :ARG0 (h / have
            :ARG0 (i / i)
            :ARG1 (w / water
                :purpose (d2 / drink
                    :ARG0 i)
                :quant (e / enough
                    :mod (s / scarce))
                :ARG1-of (l2 / last
                    :ARG2 (t / temporal-quantity :quant 1
                        :unit (w2 / week))
                    :ARG3 i)))))
```

FIG. 13

A simplified DDT (top). An AMR tree where the rhetorical relation of purpose can be yielded (bottom).

In this semantic representation, ***purpose*** as a semantic role is related to the verb *drink*. In our analysis, we identify a nucleus EDU with *drink* and then look for its satellite connected with *Elaboration*. Then this *Elaboration* should be substituted with *Purpose* for a more accurate DDT (Fig. 14).

The importance of establishing the higher-level relation of *Purpose* here is to observe that the logical flow of this dialogue has come to completion, and it is appropriate to change the topic of conversation, and the second *Qna* pair concludes the initial two-cycle dialogue here. If we had just three utterances instead of four, there would be much stronger constraints for the proper fourth utterance, as it would need to logically conclude the previous three, answering the question "*To last for how long?*" and addressing the rhetorical relation of *Purpose*.

In our second example, we want to map the AMR semantic role of *compared-to* to rhetorical relation of *Comparison*. The default discourse parsing gives us *Elaboration* that can be turned into a more accurate rhetorical relation, if the EDU pair with a default rhetorical relation is semantically similar to a template that has a specific semantic relation that can be mapped into a rhetorical relation.

To establish an accurate rhetorical relationship between EDUs in a dialogue, we attempt to match it against a template found in a tagged AMR repository (Fig. 15):

Q: Was the fever high?

A: It was the highest that I have ever experienced

To match the dialogue's EDUs being parsed with an AMR template, we align and generalize them with the template (Galitsky et al., 2013). In our case, the syntactic generalization between the EDU pair and the AMR template is as follows: [*VB-* DT-the RBS-highest NN-* PRP-* VB-had RB-ever VB-experience*] so that there is a significant evidence that the sentence being parsed and the pattern share the common syntactic structure. We show with an arrow a correspondence between the adjective *magnificent* in the AMR representation and adjective *wonderful* in the original DT. Hence we obtain the corrected dialogue DT.

If we want to continue this dialogue, the relation of *Comparison* needs to be addressed. Asking *Why* is related to *Comparison* and asking or sharing information about either entity being compared is also appropriate. However, a confirmation that the entities being compared are *the same* is inappropriate.

This parsing improvement approach works in the cases where there is a lack of discourse markers, they are ambiguous or misleading, or a deeper semantic representation of a sentence such as AMR implies a specific rhetorical relation. Once syntactic similarity between a text being parsed and an AMR pattern is established, the semantic role from the AMR verb can be interpreted at the discourse level as a respective rhetorical relation. This mapping between a semantic relation in AMR and a specific rhetorical relation is established irrespectively of how, with which connective, nucleus and satellite EDUs are connected.

```
purpose
 qna
  TEXT:Was it a question of life or death for you ?
  TEXT:I had scarcely enough drinking water
 qna
  TEXT:To last for how long ?
  TEXT:For a week
```

FIG. 14

DDT for a dialogue enhanced via AMR.

'It was the most severe pain that she had ever experienced'

```
(p / pain
    :domain (i / it)
    :mod (m2 / severe
        :degree (m / most)
        :compared-to (p2 / pain
            :ARG1-of (s2 / see
                :ARG0 (h / she)
                :time (e / ever))))
    :mod (s / stately
        :degree (m3 / most)
        :compared-to p2))
```

```
qna
 TEXT:Was the fever high ?
 comparison
  TEXT:It was the highest
  TEXT:that I have ever experienced
```

FIG. 15

Mapping words and semantic relations into rhetorical relations.

The mapping between AMR semantic relations and rhetorical relations is developed as a result of manual generalization of available AMR annotations. We iterate through the list of rhetorical relations and for each observe a collection of AMR annotations of specific semantic relations. Once we see a systematic correlation between these, we create an entry in our mapping (Table 5). The first column enumerates the rhetorical relation to be detected, the second column shows the AMR semantic relations being mapped into the rhetorical ones, and the third column gives the example sentence that is going to be matched against a sentence being rhetorically parsed. The right column shows the AMR parsing for the templates. Details about AMR denotations and conventions are available in Chapters 2 and 6.

For two entries on the bottom, we provide an example of a refined DT where *Elaboration* is turned into a specific relation. We take a template, build a DT for it, and refine it, showing the detected rhetorical relation manner in bold (the third row from the bottom). The first row from the bottom shows actual refinement where *Elaboration* is turned into *Concession* by applying the template from the second row from the bottom. The syntactic generalization between this template and the sentence in the second column is shown on the top of the right column (bottom row). Only rhetorical relations that are thoroughly represented in AMR are shown in Table 4. Other relations are not presented there and therefore cannot be detected or enhanced using this algorithm.

To overwrite the rhetorical relation of *Elaboration* with the one obtained by manual tagging in AMR, we need to establish a syntactic similarity between the nucleus taken together with the satellite EDUs for this *Elaboration* and a template. If such similarity is high (a pattern from AMR dataset is being parsed), then *Elaboration* can be overwritten with high confidence. The higher the syntactic similarity score, the higher is the confidence that the semantic role obtained from the pattern describes the rhetorical relation precisely. Since we neither have sufficient AMR pattern data nor extensive mapping

Table 5 The AMR semantic roles and corresponding rhetorical relations.

Rhetorical relation	Semantic role of a verb	Example sentence (template)	AMR representation
Contrast	contrast-XX	But he receives the explorers in his study	(c / contrast-01 :ARG2 (r / receive-01 :ARG0 (h / he) :ARG1 (p / person :ARG0-of (e / explore-01)) :location (s / study :poss h)))
Purpose	:purpose()	It was a question of life or death for me: I had scarcely enough drinking water to last a week	(q / question-01 :ARG0 i :ARG1 (o / or :op1 (l / live-01) :op2 (d / die-01)) :ARG1-of (c / cause-01 :ARG0 (h / have-03 :ARG0 (i / i) :ARG1 (w / water :purpose (d2 / drink-01 :ARG0 i) :quant (e / enough :mod (s / scarce)) :ARG1-of (l2 / last-03 :ARG2 (t / temporal-quantity :quant 1 :unit (w2 / week)) :ARG3 i)))))
Comparison	:compared-to()	I was more isolated than a shipwrecked sailor on a raft in the middle of the ocean	(i / isolate-01 :ARG1 (i2 / i) :degree (m / more) :compared-to (p / person :ARG0-of (s / sail-01) :ARG1-of (s2 / shipwreck-01) :location (r / raft :location (o / ocean :part (m2 / middle)))))
Cause	cause-XX	That is why, at the age of six, I gave up what might have been a magnificent career as a painter	(c2 / cause-01 :ARG0 (t2 / that) :ARG1 (g / give-up-07 :ARG0 (i / i) :ARG1 (c / career :mod (m / magnificent) :topic (p / person :ARG0-of (p2 / paint-02))) :time (a / age-01 :ARG1 i :ARG2 (t / temporal-quantity : quant 6 :unit (y / year)))))

Table 5 The AMR semantic roles and corresponding rhetorical relations—cont'd

Rhetorical relation	Semantic role of a verb	Example sentence (template)	AMR representation
Condition	:condition (),: have-condition(), condition-of	If one gets lost in the night, such knowledge is valuable	(v / value-02 :ARG1 (k / knowledge :mod (s / such)) :condition (g / get-03 :ARG1 (o / one) :ARG2 (l / lost :time (d / date-entity :dayperiod (n / night)))))
Manner	:manner	It was from words dropped by chance that, little by little, everything was revealed to me	(r / reveal-01 :ARG0 (w / word :ARG1-of (d / drop-06 :ARG1-of (c / chance-02))) :ARG1 (e / everything) :ARG2 (i / i) :manner (l / little-by-little))
manner elaboration TEXT:It was from words TEXT:dropped by chance TEXT:that, little by little, everything was revealed to me			
Concession	:concession (), :have-concession ()	The little prince looked everywhere to find a place to sit down; but the entire planet was crammed and obstructed by the king's magnificent ermine robe	(a / and :op1 (c / cram-01 :ARG1 (r2 / robe :mod (e2 / ermine) :mod (m / magnificent) :poss (k / king)) :ARG2 (p3 / planet :extent (e3 / entire))) :op2 (o / obstruct-01 :ARG0 r2 :ARG1 p3) **:concession** (l / look-01 :ARG0 (p / prince :mod (l2 / little)) :ARG1 (p2 / place :purpose (s / sit-down-02 :ARG1 p)) :location (e / everywhere)))

Continued

Table 5 The AMR semantic roles and corresponding rhetorical relations—cont'd

Rhetorical relation	Semantic role of a verb	Example sentence (template)	AMR representation
elaboration TEXT:A designer trying to fit the power unit into the processor box, elaboration TEXT:but there was not enough space TEXT:to accommodate the cooling fan .		A designer trying to fit the power unit into the processor box, and there was not enough space to accommodate the cooling fan	[VP [VB-* NN-* IN-into], VP [VB-* VB-* NN-* NN-* NN-*], VP [VB-* IN-* DT-the NN-*], VP [VB-was DT-the NN-*], VP [TO-to VB-* DT-* NN-*]]] **concession** TEXT: A designer trying to fit the power unit into the processor box, elaboration TEXT: but there was not enough space TEXT: to accommodate the cooling fan.

into rhetorical relations data, we are unable to formally learn such mapping but instead, select a threshold for the similarity score.

7. Constructing a dialogue from text

Despite the success of building dialogue systems, the bottleneck of training data remains. In most problem domains, designers of chatbots are unable to obtain training dialogue datasets of desired quality and quantity and therefore attempt to find alternative, lower quality datasets and apply techniques such as transfer learning. As a result, the relevance and dialogue cohesiveness are frequently unsatisfactory.

We discover a general mechanism of conversion of a paragraph of text of various styles and genres into a dialogue form. The paragraph is split into text fragments serving as a set of answers, and questions are automatically formed from some of these text fragments. The problem of building dialogue from text T is formulated as splitting it into a sequence of answers $A = [A_1 \ldots A_n]$ to form a dialogue

$$[A_1, <Q_1, A_2>, \ldots, <Q_{n-1}, A_n>],$$

where A_i answers A_{i-1} and possibly previous question, and $\cup A_i = T$. Q_{i-1} needs to be derived from the whole or a part of A_i by linguistic means and generalization (Galitsky et al., 2010); also, some inventiveness may be required to make these questions sound natural. To achieve it, we try to find a semantically similar phrase on the web and merge it with the candidate question. Dialogue generation is somewhat related to a general content (sentence) generation problem; however, questions should be less random than the ones potentially generated by methods such as neural sequence-to-sequence.

Question generation has gained increased interest branching from the general Q/A problem. The task is to generate an NL question conditioned on an answer and the corresponding document. Among its many applications, question generation has been used to improve Q/A systems.

A dialogue is formed from text by the following rule: once the nucleus EDU is finished, and before satellite EDU starts, the question against this satellite EDU is inserted. In terms of a dialogue flow between a text author and a person asking the question, the latter "interrupts" the author to ask him this question such that the satellite EDU and possibly consecutive text would be an answer to this question. This question is supposed to be about the entity from the nucleus, but this nucleus does not contain an answer to this question. The person asking questions only interrupts the text author when his question sounds suitable; it does not have to be asked for all nucleus-satellite transitions.

CDTs are designed to combine rhetorical information with speech act structures. CDTs are DTs with arcs labeled with expressions for communicative actions (Galitsky, 2020b). These expressions are logic predicates expressing the agents involved in the respective speech acts and their subjects.

The arguments of logical predicates are formed in accordance with respective semantic roles, as proposed by a framework such as VerbNet (Kipper et al., 2008). If a text already includes a subject (underlined in our example) of a communicative action (bolded) in a satellite, it can be naturally converted into a question: "*A potential PG&E bankruptcy is* ***seen*** *as putting pressure on California lawmakers to provide a bailout and avoid more turmoil for the state's largest utility*" → {"*Why put pressure on California lawmakers?*," "*What should California lawmakers provide?*," ...}.

7.1 Building a dialogue based on a DT

Let us consider a paragraph from a controversial domain of Theranos investigation (Fig. 16):

"*...But Theranos has struggled behind the scenes to turn the excitement over its technology into reality. At the end of 2014, the lab instrument developed as the linchpin of its strategy handled just a small fraction of the tests then sold to consumers, according to four former employees.*"

To convert it into a dialogue, we need to build a DT for it and form a question for each satellite for each its relation:

- "*But Theranos has struggled...*
- *Struggled for what?*

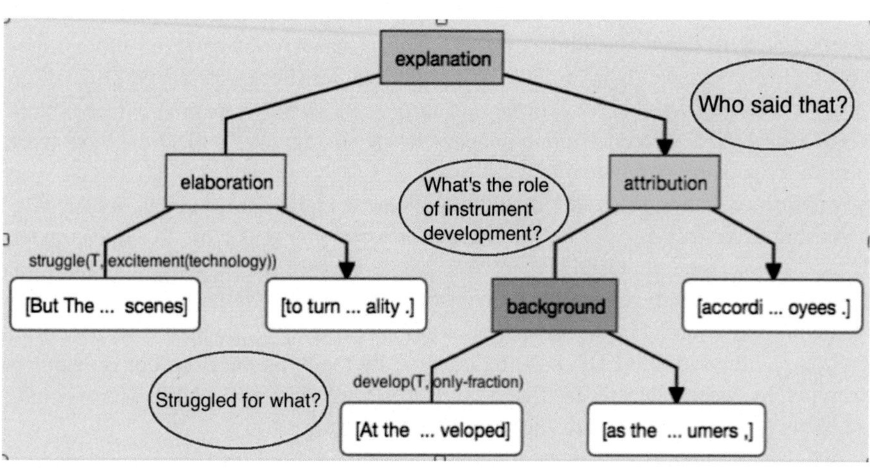

FIG. 16

A communicative discourse tree (CDT) for a text and questions attached to satellite nodes.

- *... behind the scenes to turn the excitement over its technology into reality. At the end of 2014, the lab instrument developed as ...*
- *What's the role of instrument development?*
- *... the linchpin of its strategy handled just a small fraction of the tests then sold to consumers, ...*
- *Who said that?*
- *... according to four former employees.*"

Once we split a text into EDUs, we know which text fragments will serve as an answer to questions: satellites of all relations. *Elaboration* rhetorical relation is default and *What*-question to a verb phrase is formed. *Background* relation yields another *What*-question for the satellite "*...as <predicate>-<subject>*." Finally, *Attribution* relation is a basis of "*What/who is source*" question.

A trivial approach to question generation would be to just convert satellite EDU into a question. But it would make it too specific and unnatural, such as "*the linchpin of its strategy handled just a small fraction of the tests then sold to whom*?". Instead, a natural dialogue should be formed with more general questions like "*What does its strategy handle?*"

Communicative actions help to formulate questions for satellite EDUs as well. For *struggle(T, excitement(technology))* attached to the relation of *Elaboration*, the question can be "*Was there an excitement about [Theranos] technology?*", and for *develop(T, small-fraction)* the possible question is "*Does Theranos only did a small fraction of tests?*"

7.2 Constructing questions

When we obtain a candidate for a question, it is subject to reduction to avoid being too specific. For example, "*What is a British rock band that formed in London in 1970 and received Grammy Hall of Fame Award in 2004?*" would be too specific and should be reduced, for instance, to "*What is a British rock band that formed in London*." To achieve a proper level of generalization for questions, we take an extended set of questions such as Stanford Q/A database (SQuAD), perform pair-wise syntactic generalization (Galitsky et al., 2012) and retain the most frequent question templates. SQuAD corpus (Rajpurkar et al., 2016) is a machine comprehension dataset consisting of more than 100,000 crowd-sourced question-answer pairs on 500 Wikipedia articles. For example, by generalizing "*What is the purpose of life on Earth*" and "*Tell me the purpose of complex numbers*," we obtain "*the-DT purpose-NN of-PRP *-NP*" where we retain the part-of-speech tags. We collect the most frequent generalization results (question templates).

We apply phrase-reduction rules at both individual phrase and sentence levels. As a result, we want to obtain a question from an original satellite EDU expression that is as close to a question template as possible. Hence for every satellite EDU expression, we iterate through the templates and find the most similar one. In terms of syntactic generalization, it is the template that delivers a maximal common sub-parse tree with this expression. For the sentence "[I built a bridge]$_{nucleus}$ [with the purpose of fast access to the forest]$_{satellite}$," the satellite EDU is better covered by the template from our previous paragraph than, for example, by "access-NN to-TO forest-NN" or "access-NN to-TO NP" in terms of the number of common terms (parse tree nodes) of the generalization result.

To improve the meaningfulness, interestingness, and diversity of a formed and generalized question, we rely on the wisdom of the Web. We form a web search query from the formed question and attempt to find an expression from a web document as close to this question as possible and from a reputable source or popular repository. We iterate through web search results obtained by the Bing API and score document titles, snippet sentences, and other expressions in found documents to be semantically similar to the query. Semantic similarity is assessed via a syntactic generalization score between the candidate query and a search result. If such expression from the document is found, its entities need to be substituted by the ones from the original question. As a result, a candidate question will look more popular, mature, and in more common terms.

To verify that the formed and modified question obtained from a satellite EDU text has this text as a good answer, we apply the open-domain Q/A technique (Galitsky, 2017a). Given the whole original text and a formed question, we verify that the answer is the EDU this question was formed from and does not correspond to another EDU. A wrong text fragment can appear as an answer if the question was substantially distorted by generalization or web mining (Galitsky and Kuznetsov, 2013). We use the DeepPavlov.ai, 2020 DL Q/A system for this verification.

Fig. 17 shows the architecture of the system for automated building of a dialogue. A text is split into paragraphs and the CDT for each paragraph is built. Once we identify all satellite EDUs in all obtained CDTs, we try to insert a querying utterance before each of these satellite EDUs. To do that, we consider each such satellite EDU as an answer and attempt to formulate a question for it, generalizing it. We apply certain rules to achieve a proper generalization level; if the question is too broad or too specific,

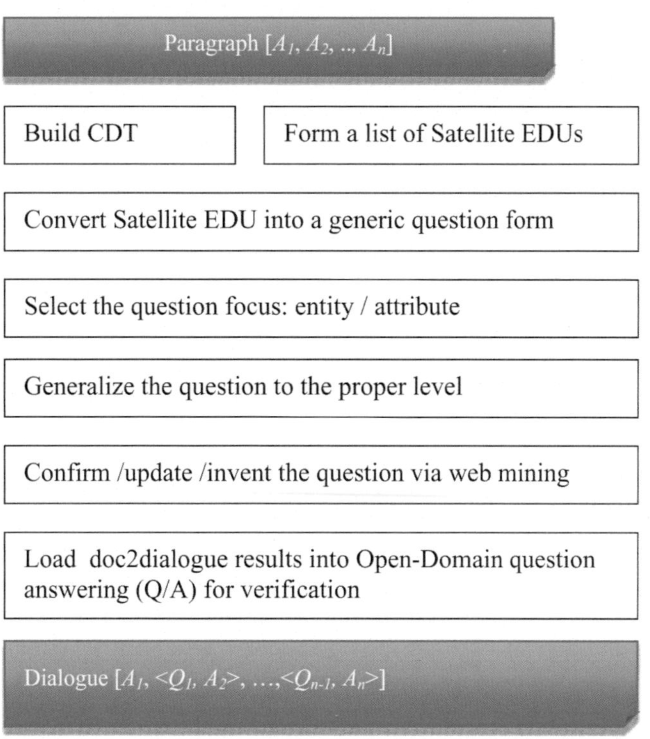
Paragraph [A_1, A_2, .., A_n]
Build CDT
Form a list of Satellite EDUs
Convert Satellite EDU into a generic question form
Select the question focus: entity / attribute
Generalize the question to the proper level
Confirm /update /invent the question via web mining
Load doc2dialogue results into Open-Domain question answering (Q/A) for verification
Dialogue [A_1, <Q_1, A_2>, …,<Q_{n-1}, A_n>]

FIG. 17

A dialogue formation chart.

1) Build a parse tree 2) Select parse tree nodes for nouns, verbs and adjectives. Also, add nodes linked by coreferences such as pronouns. More complex node selection rules can be applied (Finn 1975). 3) For every selected node, form a reduction of a parse tree by removing this node. 4) Build a question for this reduction by substituting a Wh word for this node 5) Select a proper Wh word following the rules: *noun → Who or What, verb → 'what ... do', adjective → 'Which way', 'How is'*.

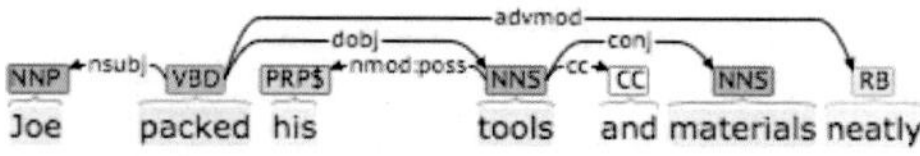

Node deleted	
Tools and materials (NNS)	What did Joe pack neatly
Joe (NNP) , his (PRP$)	Who packed tools and materials neatly? Whose tools and materials were packed neatly
Neatly (RB)	How did Joe pack?

FIG. 18

Transforming a statement/sentence into a question.

the fixed answer (the satellite EDU) would look unnatural. We also apply the rules to maintain proper question focus. As a candidate question is formed, it is sent as a query to the Web to turn it into a question other people asked in some situations, assumed to be similar to the one described by the current paragraph. Once we form such a question, we insert it after the previous nucleus EDU and before the current satellite EDU.

To form a question from a nucleus EDU to get a set of questions, the following steps are applied (Fig. 18).

8. System architecture

Fig. 19 shows an overall view of the discourse-driven DM. Once the discourse representation of the current dialogue combined with that of the candidate utterance is constructed, we first check the rhetorical agreement of the question-answer pair, if the last utterance of the current dialogue is a question and we are accepting/rejecting an answer (Section 5). Then if the rhetorical agreement component is applicable and is passed, we proceed to the discourse analysis of the overall candidate dialogue to accept or reject the candidate utterance. The classifier of a DT or an extended DT such as DDT is described in Galitsky et al. (2016) and Galitsky (2018). Fig. 19 (right middle) shows the Representation Former. Section 7 describes the algorithm for forming a training set for a DDT builder.

Fig. 20 shows DT processing step by step. An original DT is built for the current sequence of utterances and the candidate utterance. It is turned into a dialogue-independent CDT by adding labels for communicative actions (Section 2 and Galitsky et al., 2018). The initial DT is based on default relations, mostly *Elaborations* and *Joints*. Firstly, the most frequent epistemic state of Q/A is recognized, and corresponding *Elaborations* are turned into *Qna*s. Then *Entailment* relations are recognized (Section 3). After that, the relations available in the AMR dataset are substituted. Once the individual

8 System Architecture

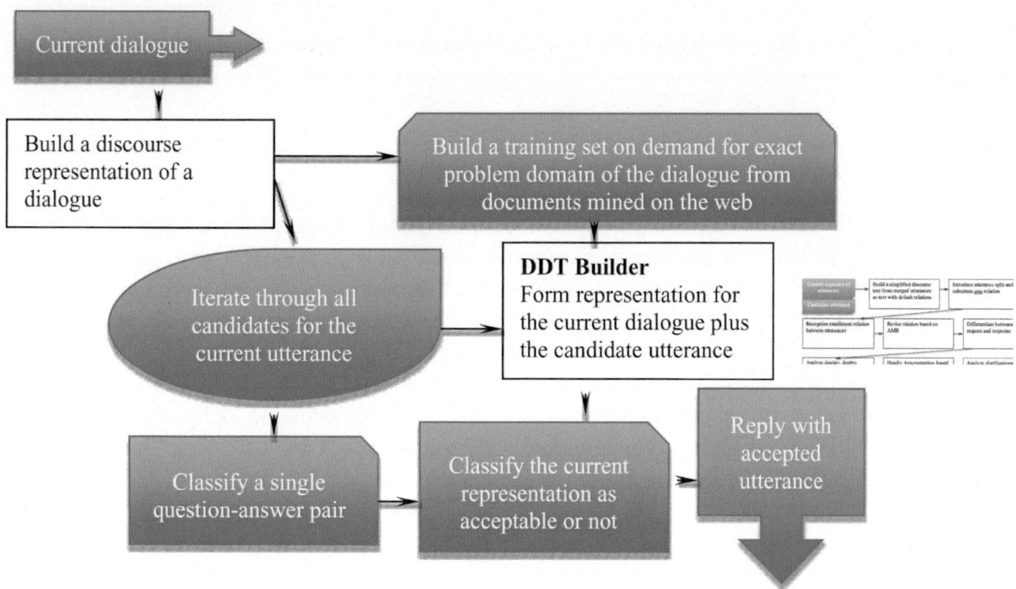

FIG. 19

A high-level view of dialogue management based on the current discourse structure of a dialogue.

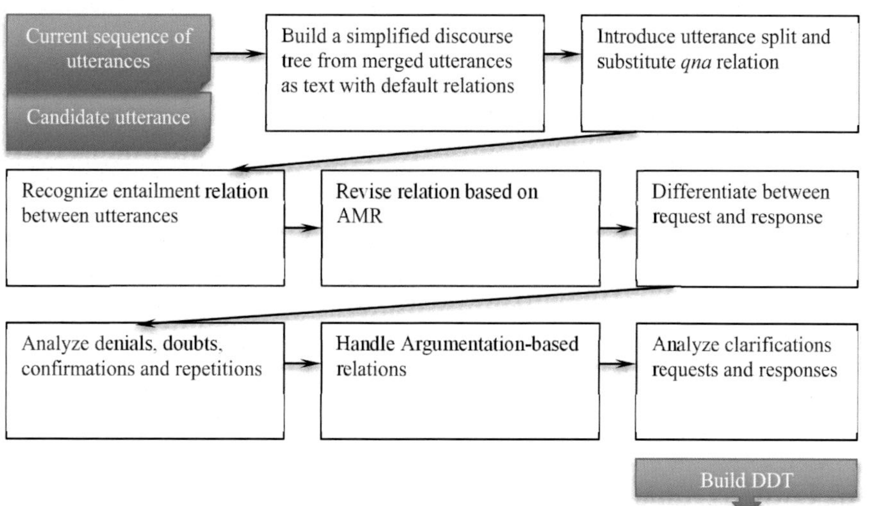

FIG. 20

The architecture of a DDT builder.

rhetorical relations are refined, we recognize the portions of the DT as request/response or other dialogue epistemic state (Section 6). More refined epistemic states such as *Denials/Doubts* vs *Agreement/Confirmation* are detected, and respective relations are updated. Similarly, the relations associated with argumentation are detected. Finally, the DM analyzed clarification requests and responses.

9. Evaluation

We use online health forums to form our evaluation dataset. Online forums provide a convenient channel for people to share their experiences and exchange ideas and have attracted more and more users (Chapter 3). They become valuable resources for extracting useful knowledge, through the forum search, question answering, and expert finding. A typical forum thread consists of a sequence of posts, ordered according to the time when the post is submitted. Thread data can be a useful source to accumulate the discourse structures of a dialogue.

We had to form our own health dialogue datasets because the ones available such as Liu et al. (2020) and Zeng et al. (2020) contain too short dialogues mostly including just two utterances. The complexity of the discourse structure of dialogues in the available health datasets is way less what we intend to tackle in this work. We get the data from www.healthboards.com where there is a hierarchy of diseases.

Here is an example from https://www.healthboards.com/boards/hepatitis/1035610-chronic-symptoms.html:

Topic: chronic symptoms of Hepatitis
Init: Can chronic symptoms happen even when blood work shows alumbim, bilbrum, alt and ast in good levels? The levels have been consistent yearly with the exception of alt and ast.
Reply1: Sorry for asking so much but i am stressed. Is it possible to get hepatitis b or c from sticking finger inside woman for about 5 seconds and then in her mouth for 5 seconds? I had an HPV wart on edge of finger that splits and turns a little red but not open or bleeding.
Reply2: Also my right foot is starting to swell and i am starting to see spider veins on that foot. Also to add wifes symptoms, infection on finger, some headaches and neaseau, diabetes about two months afterwards, same with inverse psoriasis. Inverse psoriasis lasted 6 months till she got on insulin.
Gold-set Reply: For heaven's sake, be responsible. You won't be stressing out if you keep your wart out of other people's bodies! At least keep it covered with a water proof bandage. Better yet, go to a doctor and have the wart cut out.

We form a dataset of utterances related to car repair recommendations. These pairs were extracted from dialogues as first and second utterances so that the question is 7–15 keywords, and the answer is three to six sentences. This resource was obtained to train a dialogue support system, but it also proved to be useful to evaluate search. This dataset is scraped from http://www.CarPros.com and is available at CarPros Car Repair Dataset (2017).

This dataset includes 9300 dialogues, so for a specific car problem, there is a high chance of a shortage of similar repair scenarios to learn from. Notice that it is a much more comprehensive dataset than the ones mostly used in chatbot evaluations, with coherent conversations, higher responsibility of answers, and higher clarity of instructions. This dataset provides answers much more "to the point" than a typical customer support dialogue would do.

The objective of our evaluation is to predict the last utterance or the one before the last. In the evaluation set, there is a single true utterance from actual dialogue and a set of 10 false utterances, obtained from other dialogues on the same topic. The false utterance has the proper topic most of the time, but inappropriate epistemic state, sentiment (Galitsky and McKenna, 2017), unrelatedness to previous utterances, and a corruption of an overall dialogue flow.

Table 6 shows show the recognition accuracies for dialogue utterances. We estimate separately the correct topic or sentiments in columns two and three. Two grayed columns on the right show the percentages of the correct rhetorical agreement and clarification when applicable. The last column shows the resultant accuracy of finding the true last utterance that matches the actual dialogue.

One can see that maintaining topic is the easiest task at 92% followed by the agreement in sentiment of 83% and utterance pair-wise rhetorical agreement of 80%.

A typical evaluation of an end-to-end dialogue system based on a trained model relies on automatic metrics including perplexity, NIST-n (Doddington, 2002) (where n is the size of n-gram and is set to 4), BLEU-4 (Papineni et al., 2002), METEOR (Lavie and Agarwal, 2007), Entropy-4, and *Dist-n* (Li et al., 2015) (where n is set to 1 and 2). Perplexity measures the language quality of the generated responses (the lower, the better). NIST, BLEU, and METEOR measure the similarity between the generated responses and the golden utterance via n-gram matching (the higher, the better). Entropy and *Dist* measure the lexical diversity of generated responses (the higher, the better).

In addition, other studies use recall at position k in n candidates ($R_n@k$) as evaluation metrics. The matching models are required to return k most likely responses, and $R_n@k = 1$ if the true response is among the k candidates. $R_n@k$ will become larger when k gets larger or n gets smaller.

These measures assess the similarity of a generated dialogue to the gold standard and do not access dialogue management separately. Hence these measures are not good for dialogue management, and

Table 6 Selecting the suitable utterance in various health domains.

Domain and source	# dialogues	Correct topic	Correct sentiment	Correct rhetorical agreement with previous utterance	Correct clarification	Correct last utterance
Bloating	316	92.7	82.1	77.8	83.7	75.3
Cough	315	94.5	84.5	79.5	80.6	74.6
Diarrhea	320	90.8	80.9	81.4	81.0	76.8
Dizziness	330	93.0	84.2	76.8	79.5	74.8
Fatigue	370	92.6	83.6	79.0	80.2	72.7
Fever	346	91.6	84.0	81.5	78.4	73.0
Headache	325	93.9	80.8	82.0	82.6	71.1
Muscle Cramp	310	90.7	81.5	80.9	83.0	73.8
Nausea	330	89.3	80.4	78.8	82.8	71.3
Throat irritation	208	94.2	83.7	80.7	83.2	73.6
Average	**317**	**92.3**	**82.6**	**79.9**	**81.5**	**73.7**

we present them only for the sake of comparison of dialogue management results of this study with other studies.

If we rearrange our setting to BLUE-4 measure, we obtain 5.7% on BLEU-2 (Table 7).

We compare our settings with a weakly-supervised open-retrieval approach of Qu et al. (2020) for the conversational Q/A. The learned weak supervision approach can detect a paraphrased span of the known answer in a retrieved passage as the weak answer. Such a method is more flexible than span-match weak supervision since it can handle both span and free-form answers. Moreover, this approach is less demanding on the retrieval component since it can detect weak answers even when this component is unable to obtain any passage that contains an exact match of the known answer.

Theoretically, if the known answer is a part of the given passage, the learned weak supervisor should be able to predict the weak answer as exactly the same as the known answer. Saying this differently, the learned weak supervisor should fall back to the span-match weak supervisor when handling span answers. In the real life, this is not guaranteed because of a broad spectrum of DL models. A weak supervision of Qu et al. (2020) displays no statistically significant performance decrease compared with the span-match supervisor. This demonstrates that the learned weak supervision approach can cover span answers as well. Although the learned supervisor can identify more weak answers than span match, these weak answers could be false positives that do not contribute to the model performance.

We conclude in this section that the proposed discourse-driven dialogue management is comparable with end-to-end neural approaches with respect to their measures. The discourse-driven approach has a direct measure of meaningless and logical soundness for the utterances unlike the text data-driven approaches, therefore, we expect it to outperform them, given the direct dialogue management measure.

Table 7 Comparison with other studies.

	Correct utterance obtained in this study	**Correct utterance percentage based on other measures in other studies**
Health forums	73.7	
Car repair	78.1	
ShARC government regulations	75.0	DISCERN (Gao et al., 2020) 73.2% in micro-averaged and 78.3% in macro-averaged
Medical dialogue datasets (Xu et al., 2019; Yang et al., 2020)	78.3	
MedDialog (Zeng et al., 2020)	73.2 5.7% on BLEU-2	5.0% on BLEU-2 GPT (Zeng et al., 2020)
QuAC (Choi et al., 2018) and CoQA (Reddy et al., 2018)	74.3 for Q/A part	76% for learned weak supervision, 73% for span-match (Qu et al., 2020)
UBUNTU (Lowe et al., 2015)	*R*10@ = 76.9	*R*10@1 = 78.2% (Li et al., 2021) *R*10@1 = 73.4% (Wu et al., 2017)

10. Discussions and conclusions

Among the strategies for maintaining dialogue flow, the transition involves choosing new factual content to be introduced. This is a hard task that needs methods from the field of information retrieval. Based on advances in neural language generation and the authors' own experience, the methods available today demonstrate satisfactory detail selection and presentation strategies in a dialogue. However, neural generation methods fail to acknowledge prior turns as well as humans do because the generated responses are not specific w.r.t conversational context.

Early work for retrieval-based dialogue systems studies single-turn response selection (Ji et al., 2014). After that, various multi-turn response selection methods were presented, including the dual LSTM model, the multi-view matching method (Zhou et al., 2016), the sequential matching network (Wu et al., 2017), and the deep attention matching network (Zhou et al., 2018). Recently, various effective methods have been proposed for investigating the fusion of multiple types of sentence representations (Tao et al., 2019), the deep interaction in matching feature extraction, model ensemble, external knowledge combination, and emotion control in context-response matching.

A dialogue is planned when the parties are ready to start a conversation. Each participant has formed their goals and has a plan for their utterances to be delivered (Fig. 21). A family of dialogue

FIG. 21

A couple and their thought bubbles. As the lady is getting ready to give in (raising a white flag), the general is planning a tactic of his attack.

management approaches via planning abstract away from the topic of the dialogue, similar to our approach. Dialogue-related reasoning happens at two levels:

(1) Object-level: reasoning about the subject of dialogue, about what is being discussed. This is an utterance relevance technique based on syntactic and semantic means (Galitsky, 2014)
(2) Meta-level: reasoning about how to organize a dialogue. This is related to dialogue management and based on discourse-level means

Following along the lines of reasoning levels, we treat what needs to be said and how the whole communication needs to be organized separately, unlike a data-driven, neural approach to dialogue. While neural approaches can drive a conversation successfully in many cases, when they do not, not much can be done as it is unclear how the conversation control should be tweaked. When relevance and dialogue management are both unexplainable and uninterpretable under neural approach, only a huge amount of data similar to a current conversation can help (Galitsky, 2019c).

Many theories of dialogue adopt the Information State Update paradigm (Larsson and Traum, 2000): an utterance triggers an update to the information state representing the dialogue context to form a new information state. The differences between various approaches to this paradigm are as follows:

(1) the type of information that's recorded in an information state
(2) the type of update operations that are permissible
(3) the controls over their application

Larsson and Traum (2000) examine two theories that already offer an account of agreement: the Grounding Acts model (Traum, 1994) and Segmented Discourse Representation Theory (SDRT; Asher and Lascarides, 2003). Wu et al. (2019) studied the problem of multi-turn response selection in which one has to model the relationships among utterances in a context and pay more attention to important parts of the context. It seems that the existing models cannot address the two challenges at the same time when we summarize them into a general framework.

Piwek et al. (2007) were pioneers of automated construction of dialogues, providing a theoretical foundation of the mapping that the system performs from RST structures to dialogue representation structures. The authors introduced several requirements for a dialogue generation system (robustness, extensibility, and variation and control) and reported on the evaluation of the mapping rules.

An important body of work concerns tutorial dialogue systems. Some of the work in that area focuses on authoring tools for generating questions, hints, and prompts. Typically, however, these are single utterances by a single interlocutor, rather than an entire conversation between two agents. Some researchers have concentrated on generating questions together with possible answers such as multiple-choice test items, but this work is restricted to a very specific type of question-answer pairs (Mitkov et al., 2006). Conversion of a text into a dialogue is different from the dialogue generation problem; the former is a training set-based foundation for the latter.

A response generation for dialogue can be viewed as a source-to-target transduction problem. Sordoni et al. (2015) rescore the outputs of a phrasal machine translation-based conversation system with a neural model incorporating prior context. Recent progress in sequence-to-sequence models has been leveraged (Luan et al., 2016) to build an end-to-end dialogue system that firstly applies an utterance message to a distributed vector representation using an encoder, then, secondly generates a response from this representation. Li et al. (2016, 2017a) simulated dialogues between two virtual agents using policy gradient methods to reward sequences that display three useful conversational properties: informativity, coherence, and ease of answering. We measured comparable dialogue effectiveness properties such as the speed of arrival to a search result, a decision, and domain coverage, in the current study. Further details on dialogue evaluation are available in Chapter 10.

Dialogue acts are an important source that differentiates between plain text and dialogue. The proposed algorithm of virtual dialogues can assist with building domain-specific chatbot training datasets. The recently released dataset, DailyDialog (Li et al., 2017b), is the only dataset that has utterances annotated with dialogue acts and is large enough for learning conversation models. Unlike the virtual dialogues produced in this study, in DailyDialog, conversations are not task oriented, and each conversation focuses on one topic. Each utterance is annotated with four dialogue acts.

Fig. 22 shows a framework of an end-to-end knowledge-routed chatbot (Xu et al., 2019). A Bi-LSTM based NL understanding is utilized to parse input utterances and generate semantic frames, which are further fed into the DM module to generate chatbot utterances. The DM manages the system actions containing a topic transition branch, a relational refinement branch, and a medical knowledge graph branch. A User Simulator with a user goal including patients' symptoms is based on reinforcement learning. A template-based NL generation is leveraged by the User Simulator and the DM based on user utterances.

Maintaining a cohesive dialogue flow is connected with handling argumentation in utterances. A variety of different *argumentative* dialogue systems have been described (Abro et al., 2021). The chatbot distinguishes between multiple user intents and identifies system arguments the user refers to in their NL utterances. Their model is applicable in an argumentative dialogue system that allows the user to inform themself about and build their opinion toward a

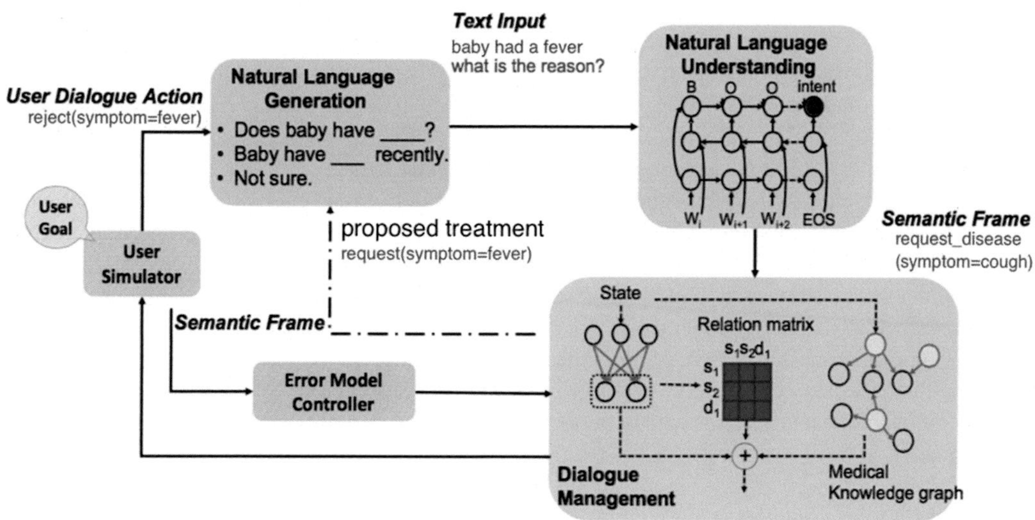

FIG. 22

End-to-end knowledge-routed chatbot architecture.

controversial topic. The chatbot of Aicher et al. (2019) assists the user in their opinion forming on a certain topic by providing arguments in favor or against it. Rach et al. (2021) introduced a dialogue system that discusses controversial topics with the users. An automated persuasion system (Galitsky, 2020c) persuades the user for behavior change in some aspects such as healthcare (Hunter, 2018). Wei et al. (2018) built a chatbot for automatic diagnosis (Chapter 2) that treats dialogue systems as Markov decision process and trains the dialogue policy via reinforcement learning. To demonstrate and explore various styles of argumentation, Rach et al. (2021) proposed a multi-agent system in which different aspects of persuasion can be modeled and observed separately, utilizing argument structures extracted from texts where a minimal bias of the user can be assumed. The persuasive dialogue is modeled as a dialogue game for argumentation that is oriented to enable both natural and flexible interactions between agents.

Gao et al. (2020) split the document to be explored into EDUs and trained their model in a weakly supervised manner to predict whether each EDU is entailed by the user feedback in a conversation or not. Based on the learned EDU and entailment representations, the chatbot either concludes the session with "yes/no/irrelevant" related to the initial question or generates a follow-up question to inquire for more information and perform a clarification procedure.

Discourse analysis uncovers text-level linguistic structures (e.g., topic, coherence, co-reference) that can be useful for many downstream applications, such as coherent text generation (Bosselut et al., 2018) and text summarization (Joty et al., 2019; Cohan et al., 2018). Recently, discourse information has also been introduced in neural reading comprehension. Mihaylov and Frank (2019) designed a discourse-aware semantic self-attention mechanism to supervise different heads of the transformer by discourse relations and coreference mentions. Different from their use of discourse information, we leverage it as a parser to segment surface-level in-line conditions for entailment reasoning.

In addition to proper discourse flow, dialogue management needs to verify a sequence of mental and epistemic states in a dialogue that are weakly correlated with the utterance words. This level of analysis is even harder to implement using a data-driven approach. There is a commonality between the errors DL systems and people with mental disorders commit in dialogue management (Galitsky, 2016; Galitsky and Parnis, 2017). It is a task of our future study to incorporate reasoning about mental and epistemic states into the discourse-based dialogue management.

In this study, we performed dialogue management separately from finding the most relevant utterance. At the same time, generative approaches to conversational machine reading do not separate between topical, entity-based relevance of an utterance and its rhetorical appropriateness. Mixing these totally distinct worlds of relevance and logical smoothness, data-driven approaches to dialogue systems achieve satisfactory results in neither world. Most studies of chatbots do not have an explicit measure of rhetorical appropriateness and logical smoothness and instead use an indirect measure of diversity and perplexity that is weakly correlated with the goal of logical cohesiveness of a dialogue. We also proposed methods to select utterances with better acknowledgment, thus significantly improving the overall DM quality.

Conversely, in this chapter we focus on the latter world and demonstrate that relying on explicit, explainable discourse features, a reasonable performance exceeding 70% can be achieved by selecting utterances with the logic well suited for the given dialogue step.

Supplementary data sets

Please visit https://github.com/bgalitsky/relevance-based-on-parse-trees to access all supplementary data sets.

References

Abro, W.A., Aicher, A., Rach, N., Ultes, S., Minker, W., Qi, G., 2021. Natural Language Understanding for Argumentative Dialogue Systems in the Opinion Building Domain.

Adiwardana, D., Luong, M.-T., So, D.R., Hall, J., Fiedel, N., Thoppilan, R., Yang, Z., Kulshreshtha, A., Nemade, G., Lu, Y., et al., 2020. Towards a Human-Like Open-Domain Chatbot. arXiv preprint arXiv:2001.09977.

Aicher, A., Rach, N., Minker, W., Ultes, S., 2019. Opinion building based on the argumentative dialogue system BEA. In: 10th International Workshop on Spoken Dialog Systems Technology.

Allen AI, 2021. Reading Comprehension. https://demo.allennlp.org/reading-comprehension/transformer-qa/s/what-is-the-low-temperature/F6N6N8B6K.

Asher, N., Lascarides, A., 2003. Logics of Conversation. Cambridge University Press.

Bosselut, A., Celikyilmaz, A., He, X., Gao, J., Huang, P.-S., Choi, Y., 2018. Discourse-aware neural rewards for coherent text generation. In: NAACL. Association for Computational Linguistics, New Orleans, LA, pp. 173–184.

Carlson, L., Marcu, D., Okurowski, M.E., 2001. Building a discourse-tagged corpus in the framework of rhetorical structure theory. In: Proceedings of the Second SIGdial Workshop on Discourse and Dialogue, pp. 1–10.

CarPros Car Repair Dataset, 2017. https://github.com/bgalitsky/relevance-based-on-parse-trees/blob/master/examples/CarRepairData_AnswerAnatomyDataset2.csv.zip.

Choi, E., He, H., Iyyer, M., Yatskar, M., Yih, W.T., Choi, Y., Liang, P., Zettlemoyer, L., 2018. QuAC: question answering in context. In: EMNLP.

Clark, H., 1996. Using Language. Cambridge University Press.

Clark, H.H., Brennan, S.E., 1991. Grounding in communication. In: Resnick, L.B., Levine, J.M., Teasley, S.D. (Eds.), Perspectives on Socially Shared Cognition. American Psychological Association, pp. 127–149.

Clark, H.H., Haviland, S., 1977. Comprehension and the given-new contract. In: Freedle, R.O. (Ed.), Discourse Production and Comprehension. Lawrence Erelbaum Associates, Hillsdale, NJ, pp. 1–40.

Cohan, A., Dernoncourt, F., Kim, D.S., Bui, T., Kim, S., Chang, W., Goharian, N., 2018. A discourse-aware attention model for abstractive summarization of long documents. In: NAACL, New Orleans, LA, pp. 615–621.

DeepPavlov.ai, 2020. https://deeppavlov.ai/.

Dinan, E., Roller, S., Shuster, K., Fan, A., Auli, M., Weston, J., 2019. Wizard of Wikipedia: knowledge-powered conversational agents. In: International Conference on Learning Representations.

Doddington, G., 2002. Automatic evaluation of machine translation quality using n-gram co-occurrence statistics. In: Proceedings of the Second International Conference on Human Language Technology Research, pp. 138–145.

Galitsky, B., 2013. Transfer learning of syntactic structures for building taxonomies for search engines. Eng. Appl. Artif. Intell. 26 (10), 2504–2515.

Galitsky, B., 2014. Learning parse structure of paragraphs and its applications in search. Eng. Appl. Artif. Intel. 32, 160–184.

Galitsky, B., 2016. Theory of mind engine. In: Computational Autism. Springer, Cham.

Galitsky, B., 2017a. Matching parse thickets for open domain question answering. Data Knowl. Eng. 107, 24–50.

Galitsky, B., 2017b. Discovering rhetoric agreement between a request and response. Dialogue Discourse 8 (2), 167–205.

Galitsky, B., 2018. Data Loss Prevention System for Cloud Security Based on Document Discourse Analysis. US Patent App 20180365593.

Galitsky, B., 2019a. A social promotion chatbot. In: Developing Enterprise Chatbots. Springer, Cham, pp. 427–463.
Galitsky, B., 2019b. Learning discourse-level structures for question answering. In: Developing Enterprise Chatbots. Springer, Cham, pp. 177–219.
Galitsky, B., 2019c. Rhetorical agreement: maintaining cohesive conversations. In: Developing Enterprise Chatbots. Springer, Cham, pp. 327–363.
Galitsky, B., 2020a. Recommendation by joining a human conversation. In: Artificial Intelligence for Customer Relationship Management: Solving Customer Problems. Springer, Cham, pp. 63–92.
Galitsky, B., 2020b. Enabling Rhetorical Analysis via the Use of Communicative Discourse Trees. US Patent 10,853,581.
Galitsky, B., 2020c. A virtual social promotion chatbot with persuasion and rhetorical coordination. In: Artificial Intelligence for Customer Relationship Management: Solving Customer Problems. Springer, Cham.
Galitsky, B., Ilvovsky, D., 2017. Chatbot with a discourse structure-driven dialogue management. In: EACL Demo Program.
Galitsky, B., Kovalerchuk, B., 2006. Mining the blogosphere for contributor's sentiments. In: AAAI Spring Symposium on Analyzing Weblogs. Stanford, CA.
Galitsky, B., Kuznetsov, S.O., 2008. Learning communicative actions of conflicting human agents. J. Exp. Theor. Artif. Intell. 20 (4), 277–317.
Galitsky, B., Kuznetsov, S.O., 2013. A web mining tool for assistance with creative writing. In: ECIR, European Conference on Information Retrieval, pp. 828–831.
Galitsky, B., McKenna, E.W., 2017. Sentiment Extraction from Consumer Reviews for Providing Product Recommendations. US Patent 9,646,078.
Galitsky, B., Parnis, A., 2017. How children with autism and machines learn to interact. In: Autonomy and Artificial Intelligence: A Threat or Savior? Springer, pp. 195–226.
Galitsky, B., Dobrocsi, G., de la Rosa, J.L., Kuznetsov, S.O., 2010. From generalization of syntactic parse trees to conceptual graphs. In: Croitoru, M., Ferré, S., Lukose, D. (Eds.), Conceptual Structures: From Information to Intelligence, 18th International Conference on Conceptual Structures, ICCS 2010, Lecture Notes in Artificial Intelligence. vol. 6208, pp. 185–190.
Galitsky, B., de la Rosa, J.L., Dobrocsi, G., 2012. Inferring the semantic properties of sentences by mining syntactic parse trees. Data Knowl. Eng. 81–82 (November), 21–45.
Galitsky, B., Ilvovsky, D., Kuznetsov, S.O., Strok, F., 2013. Finding maximal common sub-parse thickets for multi-sentence search. In: IJCAI Workshop on Graphs and Knowledge Representation, IJCAI 2013.
Galitsky, B., Ilvovsky, D., Lebedeva, N., Usikov, D., 2014. Improving trust in automation of social promotion. In: AAAI Spring Symposium on the Intersection of Robust Intelligence and Trust in Autonomous Systems, Stanford, CA, 2014.
Galitsky, B., Ilvovsky, D., Kuznetsov, S.O., 2016. Style and genre classification by means of deep textual parsing. In: Computational Linguistics and Intellectual Technologies, CICLING.
Galitsky, B., Ilvovsky, D., Kuznetsov, S.O., 2018. Detecting logical argumentation in text via communicative discourse tree. J. Exp. Theor. Artif. Intell. 30 (5), 637–663.
Gao, Y., Wu, C.-S., Li, J., Joty, S., Hoi, S.C.H., Xiong, C., King, I., Lyu, M.R., 2020. Discourse-aware entailment reasoning network for conversational machine reading. In: Proceedings of the 2020 Conference on Empirical Methods in Natural Language Processing.
Ghazvininejad, M., Brockett, C., Chang, M.-W., Dolan, B., Gao, J., Yih, W., Galley, M., 2018. A knowledge-grounded neural conversation model. In: AAAI Conference.
Guo, J., Fan, Y., Ai, Q., Croft, W.B., 2016. A deep relevance matching model for Ad-hoc retrieval. In: Proceedings of the 25th ACM International on Conference on Information and Knowledge Management. ACM, pp. 55–64.
Hashemi, H., Zamani, H., Croft, W., 2020. Guided transformer: leveraging multiple external sources for representation learning in conversational search. In: Proceedings of the 43rd International ACM SIGIR Conference on Research and Development in Information Retrieval.

Hunter, A., 2018. Towards a framework for computational persuasion with applications in behaviour change. Argum. Comput. 9 (1), 15–40.

Isaacs, E.A., Clark, H.H., 1987. References in conversation between experts and novices. J. Exp. Psychol. Gen. 116 (1), 26.

Ji, Z., Lu, Z., Li, H., 2014. An Information Retrieval Approach to Short Text Conversation. arXiv preprint arXiv:1408.6988.

Joty, S.R., Carenini, G., Ng, R.T., Mehdad, Y., 2013. Combining Intra-and Multi-Sentential Rhetorical Parsing for Document-Level Discourse Analysis. vol. 1 ACL, pp. 486–496.

Joty, S., Carenini, G., Ng, R., Murray, G., 2019. Discourse Analysis and its Applications. ACL, Florence, pp. 12–17. Tutorial Abstracts.

Kipper, K., Korhonen, A., Ryant, N., Palmer, M., 2008. A large-scale classification of English verbs. Lang. Resour. Eval. 42, 21–40.

Larsson, S., Traum, D., 2000. Information state and dialogue management in the TRINDI dialogue move engine toolkit. Nat. Lang. Eng. 6 (3–4), 323–340.

Lavie, A., Agarwal, A., 2007. Meteor: an automatic metric for mt evaluation with high levels of correlation with human judgments. In: Proceedings of the Second Workshop on Statistical Machine Translation, pp. 228–231.

Li, J., Galley, M., Brockett, C., Gao, J., Dolan, B., 2015. A Diversity-Promoting Objective Function for Neural Conversation Models. arXiv preprint arXiv:1510.03055.

Li, J., Monroe, W., Ritter, A., Jurafsky, D., 2016. Deep reinforcement learning for dialogue generation. In: Empirical Methods in Natural Language Processing.

Li, F.-L., Qiu, M., Chen, H., Wang, X., Gao, X., Huang, J., Ren, J., Zhao, Z., Zhao, W., Wang, L., 2017a. AliMe assist: an intelligent assistant for creating an innovative E-commerce experience. In: Proceedings of the 2017 ACM on Conference on Information and Knowledge Management, pp. 2495–2498.

Li, J., Monroe, W., Shi, T., Jean, S., Ritter, A., Jurafsky, D., 2017b. Adversarial learning for neural dialogue generation. In: Empirical Methods in Natural Language Processing. Copenhagen, Denmark, September 7–11, pp. 2157–2169.

Li, J., Liu, C., Tao, C., Chan, Z., Zhao, D., Zhang, M., Yan, R., 2021. Dialogue History Matters! Personalized Response Selection in Multi-Turn Retrieval-Based Chatbots. https://arxiv.org/abs/2103.09534.

Lin, X., He, X., Chen, Q., Tou, H., Wei, Z., Chen, T., 2019. Enhancing dialogue symptom diagnosis with global attention and symptom graph. In: EMNLP-IJCNLP, pp. 5032–5041.

Liu, W., Tang, J., Qin, J., Xu, L., Li, Z., Liang, X., 2020. MedDG: A Large-Scale Medical Consultation Dataset for Building Medical Dialogue System. https://arxiv.org/abs/2010.07497.

Lowe, R., Pow, N., Serban, I., Pineau, J., 2015. The Ubuntu dialogue corpus: a large dataset for research in unstructured multi-turn dialogue systems. In: Proceedings of the SIGDIAL 2015 Conference, the 16th Annual Meeting of the Special Interest Group on Discourse and Dialogue, Prague, pp. 285–294.

Luan, Y., Ji, Y., Ostendorf, M., 2016. LSTM Based Conversation Models. arXiv preprint arXiv:1603. 09457.

Lukin, S.M., Gervits, F., Hayes, C., Moolchandani, P., Leuski, A., Rogers, J., Amaro, C.S., Marge, M., Voss, C., Traum, D., 2018. Scoutbot: a dialogue system for collaborative navigation. In: Proceedings of ACL 2018, System Demonstrations, pp. 93–98.

Manvarov, O., Koshek, E., 2020. A High-Ranking Police Officer Helped the Kolosov Gang of Pimps to Solve Problems (in Russian) https://www.e1.ru/news/spool/news_id-69439912.html.

Mihaylov, T., Frank, A., 2019. Discourse-aware semantic self-attention for narrative reading comprehension. In: EMNLP, Hong Kong, China, pp. 2541–2552.

Mitkov, R., Ha, L.A., Karamanis, N., 2006. A computer-aided environment for generating multiple- choice test items. Nat. Lang. Eng. 12 (2), 177–194.

Mrkšić, N., Seaghdha, D.O., Wen, T.-H., Thomson, B., Young, S., 2016. Neural Belief Tracker: Data-Driven Dialogue State Tracking. arXiv preprint arXiv:1606.03777.

Oracle, 2020. Healthcare Forces of Change. https://www.oracle.com/webfolder/assets/ebook/health-science-industry-viewpoints/index.html#0.

Papineni, K., Roukos, S., Ward, T., Zhu, W.-J., 2002. Bleu: a method for automatic evaluation of machine translation. In: ACL, pp. 311–318.

Paranjape, A., Manning, C.D., 2021. Human-Like Informative Conversations via Conditional Mutual Information. North American Chapter of the Association for Computational Linguistics (NAACL).

Piwek, P., Hernault, H., Prendinger, H., Ishizuka, M., 2007. T2D: generating dialogues between virtual agents automatically from text. In: Intelligent Virtual Agents. Lecture Notes in Artificial Intelligence. Springer, Berlin Heidelberg, pp. 161–174.

Qu, C., Yang, L., Chen, C., Croft, W.B., Krishna, K., Iyyer, M., 2020. Weakly-Supervised Open-Retrieval Conversational Question Answering. arXiv:2103.02537.

Rach, N., Weber, K., Yang, Y., Ultes, S., Andre, E., Minker, W., 2021. EVA 2.0: emotional and rational multimodal argumentation between virtual agents. it Inf. Technol., 63.

Rajpurkar, P., Zhang, J., Lopyrev, K., Liang, P., 2016. Squad: 100,000+ Questions for Machine Comprehension of Text. arXiv:1606.05250.

Reddy, S., Chen, D., Manning, C.D., 2018. CoQA: a conversational question answering challenge. Trans. Assoc. Comput. Linguist. 7, 249–266.

Ritter, A., Cherry, C., Dolan, W.B., 2011. Data-driven response generation in social media. In: Proceedings of the 2011 Conference on Empirical Methods in Natural Language Processing, pp. 583–593.

Sacks, H., Jefferson, G., 1995. Winter 1971. John Wiley Sons, Ltd (Chapter 12).

Smith, V.L., Clark, H.H., 1993. On the course of answering questions. J. Mem. Lang. 32 (1), 25–38.

Sordoni, A., Galley, M., Auli, M., Brockett, C., Ji, Y., Mitchell, M., Nie, J.-Y., Gao, J., Dolan, B., 2015a. A neural network approach to context-sensitive generation of conversational responses. In: Proceedings of NAACL-HLT, May–June.

Surdeanu, M., Hicks, T., Valenzuela-Escarcega, M.A., 2015. Two practical rhetorical structure theory parsers. In: Proceedings of the Conference of the North American Chapter of the Association for Computational Linguistics—Human Language Technologies: Software Demonstrations (NAACL HLT), 2015.

Taboada, M., Mann, W.C., 2006. Rhetorical structure theory: looking back and moving ahead. Discourse Stud. 8 (3), 423–459.

Tao, C., Wu, W., Xu, C., Hu, W., Zhao, D., Yan, R., 2019. Multi-representation fusion network for multi-turn response selection in retrieval-based chatbots. In: Proceedings of the Twelfth ACM International Conference on Web Search and Data Mining, pp. 267–275.

Traum, D., 1994. A Computational Theory of Grounding in Natural Language Conversation (PhD thesis). Computer Science Department, University of Rochester.

van der Vliet, N., Redeker, G., 2011. Complex sentences as leaky units in discourse parsing. In: Proceedings of Constraints in Discourse. Agay–Saint Raphael, pp. 1–9.

Vaswani, A., Shazeer, N., Parmar, N., Uszkoreit, J., Jones, L., Gomez, A.N., Kaiser, Ł., Polosukhin, I., 2017. Attention is all you need. In: Advances in Neural Information Processing Systems, pp. 5998–6008.

Wang, H., Lu, Z., Li, H., Chen, E., 2013. A dataset for research on short-text conversations. In: Proceedings of the 2013 Conference on Empirical Methods in Natural Language Processing, pp. 935–945.

Wei, Z., Liu, Q., Peng, B., Tou, H., Chen, T., Huang, X., Wong, K.-F., Dai, X., 2018. Task-oriented dialogue system for automatic diagnosis. In: ACL. vol. 2, pp. 201–207.

Wu, Y., Wu, W., Xing, C., Zhou, M., Li, Z., 2017. Sequential matching network: a new architecture for multi-turn response selection in retrieval-based chatbots. In: Proceedings of the 55th Annual Meeting of the Association for Computational Linguistics. Long Papers. vol. 1, pp. 496–505.

Wu, Y., Wu, W., Xing, C., Xu, C., Li, Z., Zhou, M., 2019. A sequential matching framework for multi-turn response selection in retrieval-based chatbots. Comput. Linguist. 45 (1), 163–197.

Xu, L., Zhou, Q., Gong, K., Liang, X., Tang, J., Lin, L., 2019. End-to-end knowledge-routed relational dialogue system for automatic diagnosis. In: Proceedings of the AAAI Conference on Artificial Intelligence. vol. 33, pp. 7346–7353.

Yang, W., Zeng, G., Tan, B., Ju, Z., Chakravorty, S., He, X., Chen, S., Yang, X., Wu, Q., Yu, Z., 2020. On the Generation of Medical Dialogues for Covid-19. arXiv preprint arXiv:2005.05442.

Zeng, G., Yang, W., Zeqian, J., Yang, Y., Wang, S., Zhang, R., Zhou, M., Zeng, J., Dong, X., Zhang, R., Fang, H., Zhu, P., Chen, S., Xie, P., 2020. MedDialog: large-scale medical dialogue datasets. In: EMNLP, pp. 9241–9250.

Zhang, Y., Jiang, Z., Zhang, T., Liu, S., Cao, J., Liu, K., Liu, S., Zhao, J., 2020. MIE: a medical information extractor towards medical dialogues. In: ACL 2020, pp. 6460–6469.

Zhou, X., Dong, D., Wu, H., Zhao, S., Yu, D., Tian, H., Liu, X., Yan, R., 2016. Multi-view response selection for human-computer conversation. In: EMNLP, pp. 372–381.

Zhou, X., Li, L., Dong, D., Liu, Y., Chen, Y., Zhao, W.X., Yu, D., Wu, H., 2018. Multi-turn response selection for chatbots with deep attention matching network. In: Proceedings of the ACL. vol. 1, pp. 1118–1127.

CHAPTER

Dialogue management based on forcing a user through a discourse tree of a text 10

Boris Galitsky

Oracle Corporation, Redwood City, CA, United States

1. Introduction

Advances in Natural Language Processing (NLP) and artificial intelligence (AI) have popularized and dramatically increased the use of dialogue systems that imitate human conversation using text or spoken language. Familiar examples of chatbots include Apple Siri, Google Now, Microsoft Cortana, or Amazon Alexa. One-on-one, face-to-face interaction with a health provider is widely acknowledged to be the "gold standard" for providing medical education to and affecting desired health behavior in patients. Automated chatbots implement this form of interaction to communicate health information to users in a format that is natural, intuitive, and dynamically tailored to user interests. Building conversational agents to interact with patients and provide primary clinical advice has attracted increased attention especially during the COVID-19 pandemic. According to McCall (2020), use of telemedicine has increased substantially from around 10% of general medicine consultations before COVID-19 to approximately 75% in the United Kingdom during the peak of the pandemic.

Since the 2000s, a solid body of research has shown the potential benefits of using chatbots for health-related applications. Several randomized controlled trials of interventions involving embodied conversational agents have shown significant improvements in accessibility to online health information, among other outcomes (Bickmore et al., 2013; Watson et al., 2012; Edwards et al., 2013).

However, the majority of these chatbots only accept constrained user input (such as multiple choice of utterance options), not having the full capability to understand a natural language (NL) input. A recent renewed interest in deep AI has seen an increase in the popularity of conversational agents, particularly those with the capability to use any unconstrained NL utterance. Advances in machine learning (ML), particularly in neural networks, has allowed for more complex methods for dialogue management (DM) and more conversational flexibility (McTear, 2002; Radziwill and Benton, 2017). Given the development of increasingly powerful and connected devices, and growing access to contextual information (such as from sensors), smartphone-based chatbots are now widely used by consumers for daily tasks like retrieving information and managing calendars.

A substantial corpus of research has been devoted to the automatic generation of documents, web pages and other static media for the purpose of providing health communication to patients and doctors. Although these approaches turned out to be effective (de Vries and Brug, 1999), they still have several

Artificial Intelligence for Healthcare Applications and Management. https://doi.org/10.1016/B978-0-12-824521-7.00004-1

shortcomings. In static documents, information cannot be rephrased if the users do not understand it. Users cannot ask clarifying questions, nor can they zoom in or request more or less information on specific topics. In addition, while many studies have demonstrated the efficacy of tailoring documents' content based on initial characteristics of the user, dialogue systems can allow messages to be tailored at a very fine-grained level, with each sentence of delivered information composed on the basis of the inferred goals and beliefs of the user at a particular moment in time and incorporating everything that has previously been said in the conversation. For these reasons, a simulated face-to-face conversation can be an effective communication channel to use with individuals with special needs or those who have low reading or functional health skills.

In person-to-person conversations, humans respond to each other's utterances in a meaningful way not only by considering the latest utterance of the peer itself, but also by recalling relevant information in the dialogue history and integrating it into their responses. Such information may contain personal experience, recent events, and commonsense knowledge. As a result, we believe that a conversational model with a history-processing component can substitute human knowledge-exploration conversations more closely (Young et al., 2018; Ghazvininejad et al., 2017; Bordes et al., 2016). In an open-domain human-computer conversation, where the model is expected to respond to human utterances in an appealing and encouraging way, commonsense knowledge in some form must be applied to the selected answer on top of available text fragments.

A chatbot for medical diagnosis poses stringent requirements not only on the dialogue rationality and correctness in the context of medical knowledge but also on the comprehension of symptom-disease relations. The symptoms that a dialogue system inquiries about should be associated with underlying illness and consistent with available medical ontology (Chapter 11). Current task-oriented dialogue systems such as (Lei et al., 2018; Lukin et al., 2018; Bordes et al., 2016) are highly dependent on the complex belief tracker (Mrksic et al., 2016) and are based on pure data-driven learning, that is, they are unable to apply an automatic diagnosis directly due to a lack of medical knowledge.

In many task-oriented chatbot domains, an objective is to fully inform a user about a particular important piece of information (Galitsky, 2021b). It is also crucial to make the user believe this piece of information, relying on explanation and argumentation as much as possible. In some cases, it is important to make a user believe in facts contained in a particular short text. This should be done by thoroughly navigating a user through possible disagreements and misunderstanding to make sure the issue is explained and communicated exhaustively to the user. These disagreements and misunderstandings can be internal to this portion of text or appear between the user and the chatbot in the course of content exploration.

In this chapter, we build a chatbot whose task is *to encourage a user to learn a short text by conversing* about it. We refer to this chatbot as *persistent* because it enforces the user to stay focused on a given topic (Fig. 1). To organize such dialogue based on a short text, the chatbot navigates the discourse structure of this text to conduct a meaningful, cohesive conversation.

In the field of medical education, it is crucial to maintain quality content with well-organized structure. The content delivered by a chatbot needs to have a thorough navigation sequence (from more general and a high-level to more specific) and a smooth logical flow. It is important to navigate a user step by step through various portions and types of knowledge, from symptoms to treatment. It is better to maintain the original phrases from an authoritative text than to generate utterances on the fly.

Several developed DL-based end-to-end chatbots end up being slot-fillers in the best case (Xu et al., 2019) and random chit-chatter in the worst case. These generative chatbots may rely on association between symptoms and diseases. However, online, once a candidate disease is established (Chapter 3), the chatbot learns the symptom-disease association, dialogue management, and utterance

FIG. 1

A persistent chatbot makes sure the student learns the topic thoroughly.

generation *simultaneously*, *on the fly*. Therefore, it is hard to achieve a high quality and relevance of a content delivery (Galitsky, 2019a).

2. Keeping a learner focused on a text

Rhetorical Structure Theory (RST; Mann and Thompson, 1988) establishes two different types of units. Nuclei are considered the most important parts of text, whereas satellites contribute to the nuclei and are secondary. The nucleus contains basic information, and the satellite contains additional information about the nucleus. The satellite is often incomprehensible without the nucleus, whereas a text where a satellite has been deleted can be understood to a certain extent. Hence the content delivery needs to be established in a way that nucleus is delivered to the chatbot user first and to the satellite second, after the nucleus. If the user is explicitly asking about a topic that occurs in a satellite, it can be delivered, but its nucleus should be given in one form or another as well.

Rhetorical relations act between a nucleus and satellite. Rhetorical relations are applied recursively in a text until all units in that text are constituents in rhetorical relations. The result of such representation is that the discourse structure is typically represented as a *discourse tree* (DT), with one top-level relation that encompasses other relations at lower levels. The DT tells us how an author organizes her thought structure, which will be followed when we provide an assess to this text via a dialogue. A DT is a labeled tree in which the leaves correspond to contiguous units for clauses (elementary discourse units; EDUs).

Rather than throwing the whole paragraph of text at a user, we split it into logical parts and feed the user the text fragment by fragment, following the user's interests and intents. To systematically implement this navigation, we follow a discourse-level structure for how the author of this text organized their thoughts. This can be done by navigating a DT of this text. Adjacent EDUs, as well as higher-level (larger) discourse units, are organized in a hierarchy by rhetorical relation (e.g., *Reason*, *Temporal sequence*). An anti-symmetric rhetorical relation involves a pair of EDUs: nuclei, which are core parts of the relation, and satellites, which are the supportive parts of the rhetorical relation. A satellite can be delivered by the chatbot to a user as an utterance only if its nucleus has already been received and acknowledged in one way or another.

If we have the following EDU pairs connected by the relation of *Elaboration*.

Nucleus: *Influenza is an acute viral infection of the respiratory tract.*
Satellite: *that is marked by fever and chills.*

Thus, the first, introductory question to the user will be: "*Do you want to know a definition of flu?/ Please learn the definition of flu*," followed by (assuming the user agrees):

"*Influenza is an acute viral infection* ...." Then the chatbot needs to encourage the user to continue the content exploration and asks:

"*Do you want to know what it marked by?*"

If the user agrees, the chatbot now provides information from the satellite:

"*It is marked by fever and chills*."

In this case, the link between the nucleus and satellite is default (*Elaboration*), so the simple order works: nucleus first and then (if the user agrees/is interested to learn more) satellite. In case of a different rhetorical relation, the way the conversation can be continued depends on the kind of relation. If it is *Explanation*, for example, then the chatbot can ask "*Do you want to learn why?*" and then returns the satellite, if the user is interested to *learn why*.

In this mixed-initiative dialogue, if the user disagrees with the proposed navigation options, they can answer their own questions. However, the chatbot would encourage the user to focus back on the main topic of the available short text.

Hence the reader observes that *content exploration* occurs in the form of *DT navigation*.

Communicative discourse trees (CDTs) are designed to combine rhetorical information with speech act structures. CDTs are DTs with arcs labeled with expressions for communicative actions. These expressions are logic predicates expressing the agents involved in the respective speech acts and their subjects. The arguments of logical predicates are formed in accordance with respective semantic roles, as proposed by the VerbNet framework (Kipper et al., 2008). The purpose of adding these labels is to incorporate the speech act-specific information into DTs so that content exploration can jump to the subjects of the communicative actions and back. A navigation of CDT follows the structure of how author thoughts are organized and communicated irrespectively of the subjects of these thoughts. Communicative actions also help to navigate the CDTs in two respects:

(1) If the chatbot user is interested in mental states of agents talking about the topic. Then the user is encouraged to ask questions "*Who knows/believes/wants what?*"

(2) Subjects of communicative actions are self-contained topics that can be addressed in user questions in their entirety. A subject of communicative action is usually a part of EDU that constitutes a good answer to a question "*What* ...?"

A default navigational structure can be linear, starting from the first phrase or sentence fragment and finishing with the last. However, the default structure has a major logical flaw: this way we do not move from general, definitional entities to more specific ones, to their attributes and relations between these entities. Hence to build a conversational discourse for a text, we start with its original discourse representation.

We outline the chatbots' algorithm of the DT traversal, covering a multitude of user intents at each iteration:

(1) If a text is given, navigating a DT of this text T is one of the most efficient ways to communicate it. The chatbot starts by making an introduction and then making the main statement M_T. Then the user would either ask for more details E_T, disagree with what the chatbot is proposing D_T, or ask a question O_T on a topic outside of the scope of this text T.

(2) If the user asks for more details I_T, the EDU connected with *Elaboration* with M_T is provided as a reply. We denote this EDU as *Elaboration*(I_T). This is the easiest, most direct situation.

(3) If the user disagrees, the chatbot tries to find an EDU that is connected by *Explanation* or *Cause* with M_T or $I_{T.}$ This EDU should be returned as a reply along with the statement that the bot insists that it is right (T is authoritative and trusted).

(4) If the user asks a question outside of O_T then it should be answered as a factoid question, but nevertheless the chatbot needs to take the user back to T, so the reply should end with *Elaboration*(I_T).

(5) If the user doubts the validity of a claim in M_T, the chatbot needs to deliver *Attribution*(M_T) as an answer, informing the user about the source. Alternatively, a user might ask for a source explicitly.

(6) If the user asks a question involving a mental state or actions of agents described in T, the labels for communicative actions included in the CDT come into play. Some reasoning steps are applied, such as *being informed(Who, Whom, What)* $\rightarrow$ *knows*(*Whom, What*) to answer question "*Does Whom know What?*" when there is no explicit mention of *Who*'s knowledge in T.

The aforementioned procedure should iterate until no more EDU in T is left or the user terminates the conversation. If the chatbot persistence was too high in trying to take the user back to T, this user would terminate the conversation too soon. Otherwise, if the chatbot persistence is too low, the user would deviate from T too far and thus will read less content of T (EDU(T)). We want to optimize the chatbot to maintain the optimal persistence to maximize the number of delivered EDU(T) until the conversation is abandoned by the user.

Let us take a text and show how a DT navigation leads a dialogue wrapped around this text.

According to BBC, China has rejected calls for an independent international investigation into the origin of the coronavirus. A top diplomat in the United Kingdom, Chen Wen explained to the BBC that the demands were politically motivated and would divert China's attention from fighting the pandemic. However, the EU believes that information about how it initially spread could help countries tackle the disease. The virus is thought to have been caused by a poor hygiene emerged at a wildlife market in the city of Wuhan.

Fig. 2 Shows a DT for this text and a fragment of a sample navigation path.

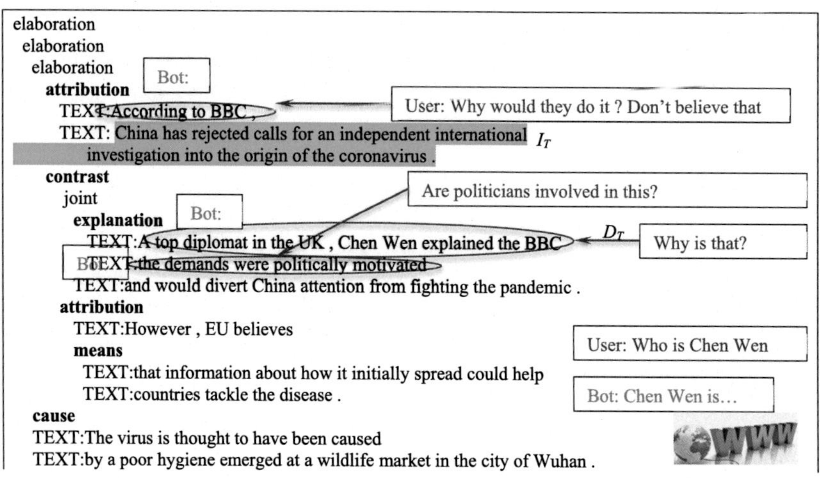

FIG. 2

A DT and a fragment of a navigation leading a conversation.

We embed a possible dialogue into the visualization of the DT. The DT is represented by indentation encoding the depth of a node; terminal nodes with EDUs are marked as 'TEXT:'. The first chatbot utterance is highlighted in green (I_T).

When the user disagrees with a chatbot statement asking "Why is that?" (D_T), the chatbot needs to involve a rhetorical relation such as *Cause, Explanation, Reason,* or *Attribution* to back itself up. This is the second bot's utterance, linked to *Attribution*: "*According to BBC*," shown by an oval above the initial answer highlighted in green.

Blocks with red font show possible user utterances. Arrows lead from the user utterances to the chatbot responses. We now show the full dialogue with comments on how each chatbot utterance is produced (Fig. 3).

When a question does not have an answer within a text ("Who is Chen Wen?"), the chatbot must run an external search and inform the user "Chen Wen is ..." (Fig. 2 bottom right corner).

In italics we show the phrases added by the chatbot to the original, available text. These phrases are hard-coded and linked with specific recognized states of the user and their intent (epistemic states). In square brackets, the results of chatbot analysis of utterances and a reply selection rule/result are spelled out. EDUs from original text are written in double quotes.

What we observe is that a dialogue is fairly plausible, although no data-driven method has been applied. It does not matter where the user deviates from the target text if the chatbot always takes them back to the EDU and rhetorical relation that is either relevant to what the user asked or claimed, or just follows the DT navigation flow from more important, closer to the root, to less important EDUs. If the user asks a question outside of the scope of the target text, we provide an answer from the foreign source and then switch topics and come back to the business of the target answer, proceeding with the DT navigation.

Finally, we show the resultant dialogue itself (Fig. 4).

Bot : "China has rejected calls for an independent international investigation into the origin of the coronavirus"
User: Why would they do it ? Don't believe that.
Bot: [doubt is detected] [(*Attribution* ("China has rejected…") = 'According to BBC']
This is "According to BBC"
User: Are politicians involved in this?
Bot: [Searching for 'politi…' & 'involv…' tokens in EDUs] "the demands were politically motivated"
User: Why is that?
Bot: [Detected explainability request. Looking for *Explanation*("the demands were politically…".] "A top diplomat in the UK, Chen Wen explained the BBC
User: Who is Chen Wen?
Bot: [question is about an entity from the answer but foreign to the thread. So search on the web and then continue navigate DT]
Chen Wen is … [Found information on the web]. *Notice also that* … [*Elaboration, Joint*, or other default rhetorical relation from the current node]
"and would divert China attention from fighting the pandemic ."
User: And how can countries tackle coronavirus?
Bot: [Searching for 'countr…' & 'tackle…' & 'coronavirus' tokens in EDUs & rhetorical relations related to 'how' such as *Explanation, Cause, Means* etc].
Selected fragment:
EU believes
means
TEXT:that information about how it initially spread could help
TEXT:countries tackle the disease .
"EU believes that information about how it initially spread could help countries tackle the disease"
User: Why is it EU business?
Bot: [question is about an entity from the answer but foreign to the thread. So search on the web and then continue navigate DT]
[Found node with EDU:]"The virus is thought to have been caused … " [Formed question for this EDU and the relation]
Do you know what causes "the virus"?
User: Yes I know, it is caused by …
Bot: [The user confirmed. It does not matter what the user knows. Proceed to the next EDU & relation]
"It is caused by a poor hygiene emerged at a wildlife market in the city of Wuhan"

FIG. 3

A dialogue with the comments on how each chatbot utterance is derived.

Bot: China has rejected calls for an independent international investigation into the origin of the coronavirus
User: Why would they do it ? Don't believe that.
Bot: This is According to BBC
User: Are politicians involved in this?
Bot: The demands were politically motivated

User: Why is that?
Bot: A top diplomat in the UK, Chen Wen explained the BBC
User: Who is Chen Wen?
Bot:
Chen Wen is …
and would divert China attention from fighting the pandemic
User: And how can countries tackle coronavirus?
Bot: EU believes that information about how it initially spread could help countries tackle the disease
User: Why is it EU business?
Bot: EU is concerning with …
Bot: Do you know what causes the virus?
User: Yes I know, it is caused by …
Bot: It is caused by a poor hygiene emerged at a wildlife market in the city of Wuhan

FIG. 4

A dialogue wrapped around a DT for a paragraph of text.

3. Navigating discourse tree in conversation

We continue our exploration of what a navigation of a DT might look like. In this case, the chatbot introduces an introductory topic I_T followed by the main topic M_T. Fig. 5 shows the dialogue flow through the DT.

First, we start with the introduction of the topic (the line highlighted in green on the top) and as the user does not indicate a specific interest, the chatbot proceeds along the *Elaboration* to the next subtopic (the EDU text highlighted in green below). Then the user interrupts the default DT navigation flow and asks the question "*Did it lead to incidents*" forcing a jump to "*At least two accidents happened*." After that, the user question "*Why/did it happen?*" does not violate the original text flow and the chatbot arrives at "*Because of the pitch-up phenomenon*." Now, as the user asks "*What caused it?*" instead of "*What does this phenomenon cause?*," the chatbot is forced to jump back to the *Cause* answer "*Poor design aerodynamics of the wings*."

The resultant dialogue is as follows (Fig. 6).

The EDUs on the top, I_T and M_T, are highlighted. Text T is introduced "*Tu-104 continued to be used*" followed by the main topic "*The aircraft was unreliable*." Notice that this main topic M_T is not a satellite of the introduction but rather the next nucleus closest to the root of this DT. In the given exploration scenario, *satellite* (I_T) has not been reached yet.

Fig. 7 shows another dialogue flow when the user is initially passive. If once I_T and M_T are announced the user does not come up with questions, the chatbot tries to intrigue the user and encourages them to get interested in the satellite (I_T) by asking "*But you know what*" relying on *Contrast*. Once the user responds, "*Tell me!*," the chatbot responds "*although the safety record of the aircraft was poor…*" initiating the user question "*How do pilots feel in it?*" The chatbot answers "*aircrew would fly*

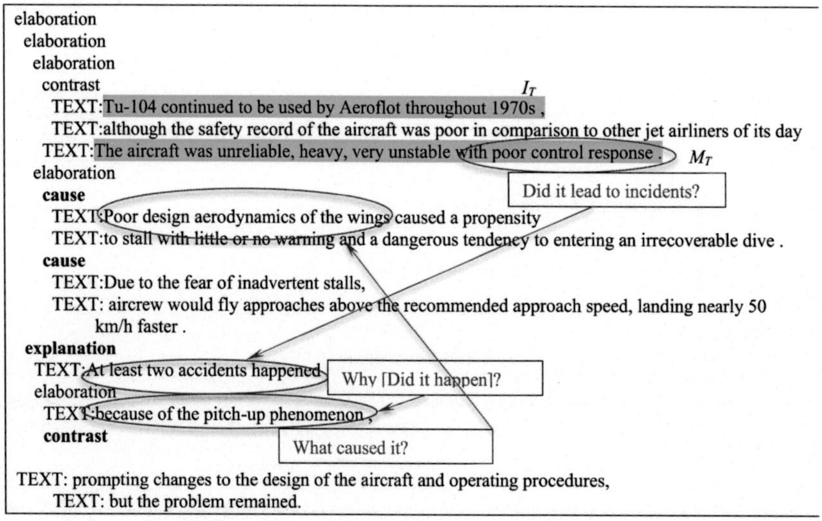

elaboration
 elaboration
  elaboration
   contrast I_T
    TEXT:Tu-104 continued to be used by Aeroflot throughout 1970s ,
    TEXT:although the safety record of the aircraft was poor in comparison to other jet airliners of its day
   TEXT:The aircraft was unreliable, heavy, very unstable with poor control response . M_T
  elaboration
   cause Did it lead to incidents?
    TEXT:Poor design aerodynamics of the wings caused a propensity
    TEXT:to stall with little or no warning and a dangerous tendency to entering an irrecoverable dive .
   cause
    TEXT:Due to the fear of inadvertent stalls,
    TEXT: aircrew would fly approaches above the recommended approach speed, landing nearly 50 km/h faster .
 explanation
  TEXT:At least two accidents happened Why [Did it happen]?
  elaboration
   TEXT:because of the pitch-up phenomenon
   contrast What caused it?
 TEXT: prompting changes to the design of the aircraft and operating procedures,
    TEXT: but the problem remained.

FIG. 5

A simplified view of a navigation of a discourse tree (DT). All utterances in boxes are those of the users.

Bot: "Tu-104 continued to be used by Aeroflot throughout 1970s , although the safety record of the aircraft was poor in comparison to other jet airliners of its day"
Bot: Should I continue?
User: Yes.
Bot: "The aircraft was unreliable, heavy, very unstable with poor control response"
User: Did it lead to accidents?
Bot: [searching for entity accident and jumping across DT paths] "At least two accidents happened."
User: Why did it happen?
Bot: [Handling the relation of *Explanation*] "because of the pitch-up phenomenon".
User: What caused it?
Bot [Handling the relation of *Cause*] Poor design aerodynamics of the wings

FIG. 6

Resultant dialogue.

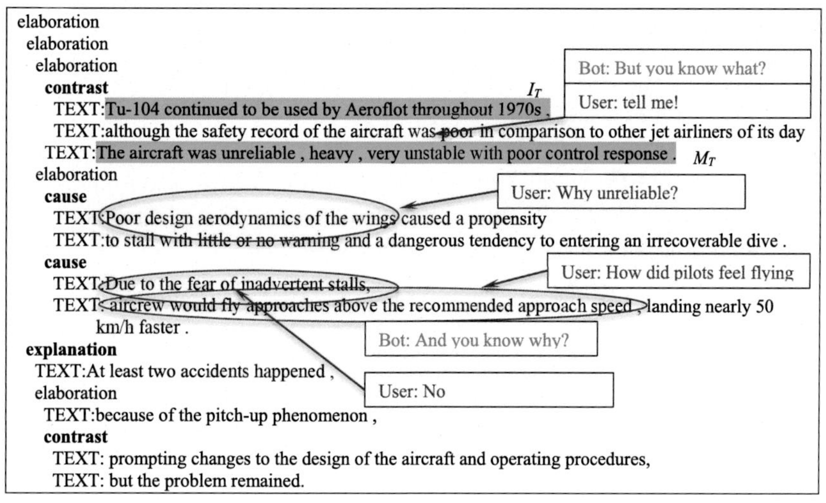

FIG. 7

Another navigation of this discourse tree (DT) yielded by user interest.

approaches above the recommended approach speed" "*And you know why?*" The second utterance is added because navigations go towards the satellite.

Now the resultant dialogue is as follows (Fig. 8).

Notice that the flow of a dialogue does not follow the flow of the original text since the user might ask questions in a totally different order. Also notice that providing a full paragraph as an answer to a question about a specific point would overwhelm the user with information and would defeat the purpose of a "to-the-point" conversation.

This is a mixed-initiative dialogue. The chatbot starts a conversation, introducing a topic. Then, a user can either follow the chatbot's initiative, accepting its proposal to share information, or start asking their own questions about the topic, forcing the chatbot to make jumps in the DT navigation.

Bot: "Tu-104 continued to be used by Aeroflot throughout 1970s , although the safety record of the aircraft was poor in comparison to other jet airliners of its day"
Bot: But you know what?
User: Tell me!

Bot: "The aircraft was unreliable, heavy, very unstable with poor control response"
User: Why unreliable?
Bot [Handling the relation of *Cause*] "Poor design aerodynamics of the wings"
User: How did pilots feel flying in it?
Bot: [searching EDU with 'fly'] "Aircrew would fly approaches above the recommended approach speed"
Bot: And you know why?
User: No
Bot: [Handling the relation of *Cause*] "Due to the fear of inadvertent stalls"

FIG. 8

Alternative resultant dialogue.

4. The dialogue flow

Fig. 9 shows the dialogue flow based on a DT navigation. A conversation with the focus on T starts with an introduction of I_T followed by the main topic M_T expressed by EDUs being the closest to the root of the DT. A chatbot utterance pair includes:

- the information from the EDU of the current node (shown in bolded boxes on the right), plus
- an encouragement utterance to the user to continue conversation, such as a question or a knowledge sharing request (shown in thick arrows on the right).

The chatbot's encouragement utterance depends on the rhetorical relation for the current navigation node (now, the M_T node). The user replies (formulates a questions) in a certain form, depending on the encouragement question of the chatbot (thick arrows on the left). The sequence of entities e_0… e_i … e_n is enumerated in the order of DT traversal: first e_i is given to the user and then e_{i+1}.

The user's questions vary in terms of the focus entity or its attribute, and/or the epistemic state initiated by the chatbot (Galitsky and Pascu, 2006). Once the user question is received by the chatbot, it is analyzed with respect to the following:

- if an external knowledge source needs to be searched, and/or
- if a machine reading comprehension (MRC) component needs to be initiated to find a value for a factoid question and identify an EDU this value occurs in.

Then the decision needs to be made if the user changed the topic and a jump in navigation is required, or the chatbot can maintain the dialogue by continuing the DT navigation. The next navigation step depends on whether the current node is a nucleus (and satellite is the next to be visited), or if it is a satellite and its nucleus needs a visit. An epistemic state update is chosen accordingly. The chatbot's processing units are shown in boxes.

For the nucleus, the user has already expressed interest in a given topic. Thus, the information from its EDU is ready to be sent to the user. For the satellite, the user is encouraged to express her interest according to the rhetorical relation to the nucleus of this satellite. A topic is expected from this user. External search and/or MRC can be applied in this option. In both cases, e_i is delivered.

The example in Fig. 10 shows a less involved user, so the initiative is on the chatbot's side. The chatbot initiates the conversation, asking "*You want to know about* …" and the user agrees. When

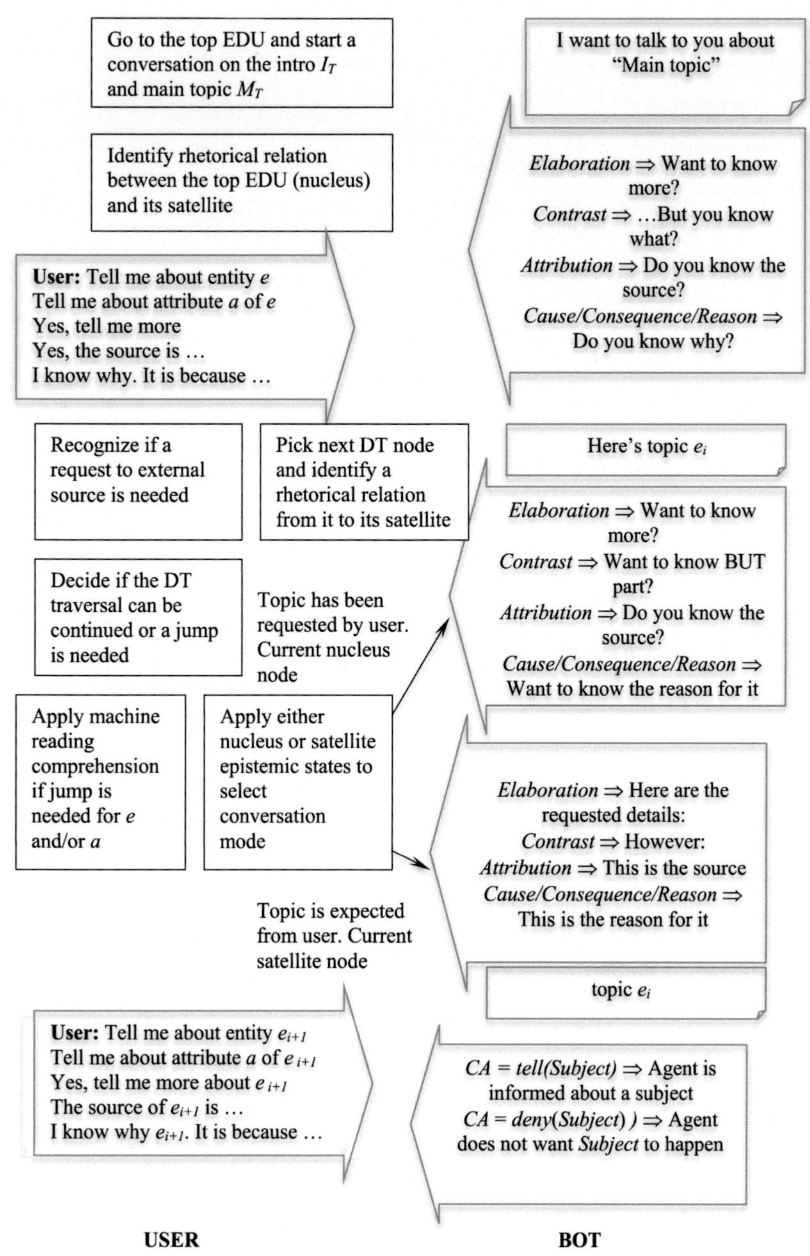

FIG. 9

The mixed-initiative dialogue flow. *Thick arrows* denote a structure of conversation, and boxes—chatbot processing units.

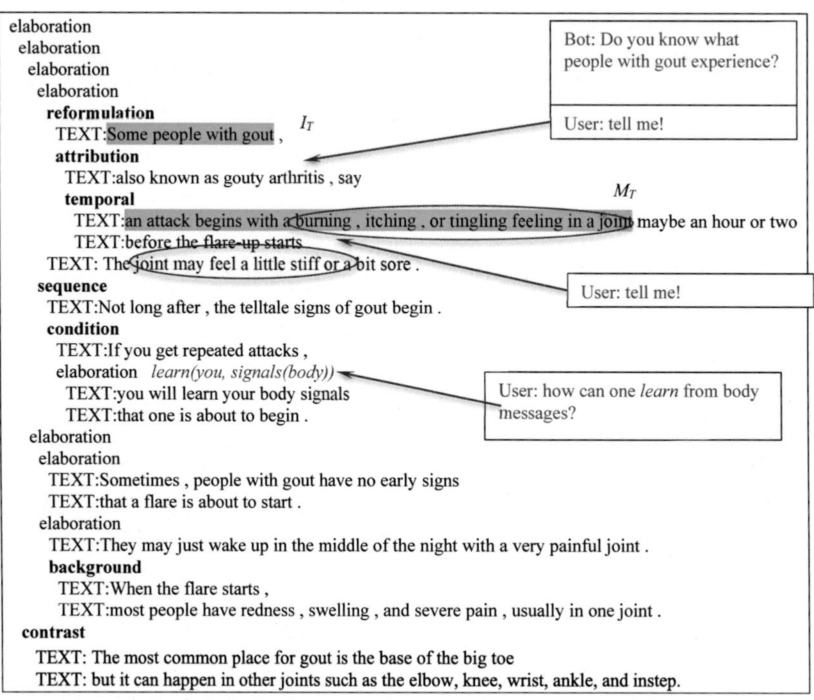

FIG. 10

Navigating a CDT for the *gout* domain. The labels of communicative actions are shown in *blue italics*.

a user asks a question involving a communicative action or mental state, it is first matched against labels of arcs for communicative actions in a CDT and then matched against the subject of this communicative action. There is an example on the bottom of Fig. 10.

We proceed to another example of a DT navigation (Fig. 11).

In Fig. 11, another example of a conversation, the arrows indicate how the bot came to the given replies. In the top case, the doubt-type question is generated based on rhetorical relation of *Contrast*. Fig. 12 shows the resultant dialogue for epilepticus.

4.1 Managing user intents

The key, default user intent is acquiring information by asking or accepting a chatbot's offer to share information. However, there are more intents (Table 1).

A great variability in a dialogue can be achieved by generating a specific reply for each user intent and a current position in the DT (Table 2). Hence the structure for the pair of utterances is determined by the user intent, node type, and relation type.

In open-domain conversational agents, topic and dialogue intent classification can be treated as a text classification problem (Finch et al., 2020). Compared to general text classification, utterance classification poses a greater challenge due to the following:

Status epilepticus is a common, life-threatening neurologic disorder that is essentially an acute, prolonged epileptic crisis. Status epilepticus can represent an exacerbation of a preexisting seizure disorder, the initial manifestation of a seizure disorder. However, it can also be an insult other than a seizure disorder. In patients with known epilepsy, the most common cause is a change in medication. Most seizures terminate spontaneously.

Aggressive treatment is necessary for status epileptics. Clinicians should not wait for blood level results before administering a loading dose of phenytoin, regardless of whether the patient is already taking phenytoin. Most patients with status epilepticus who are treated aggressively with a benzodiazepine, fosphenytoin, and/or phenobarbital experience complete cessation of their seizures. If status epilepticus does not stop, general anesthesia is indicated.

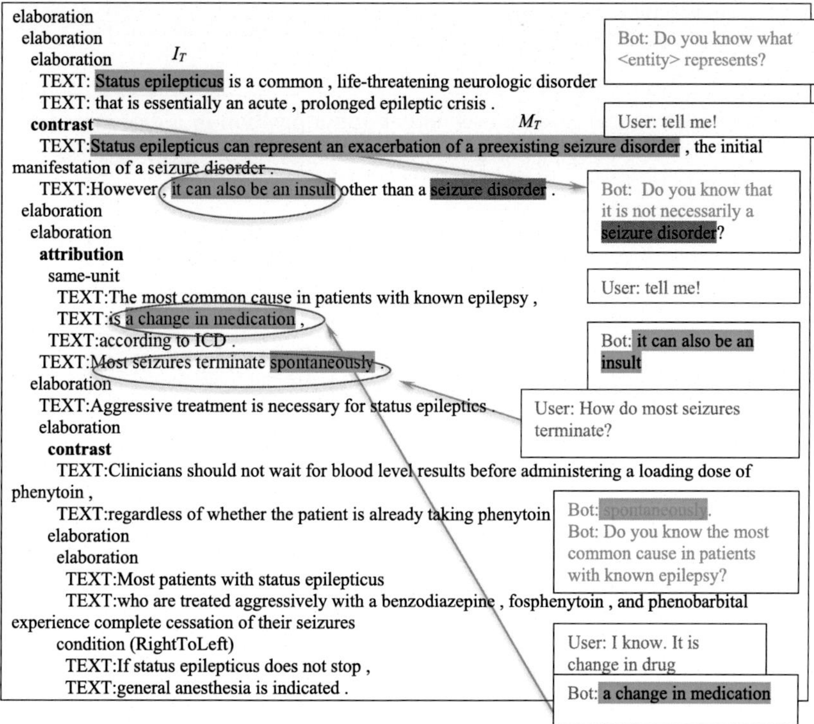

FIG. 11

A DT yields a content exploration dialogue about epilepsy.

User: What is epilepticus?
Bot: Do you know what epilepticus represents?
User: Yes tell me!
Bot: Status epilepticus can represent an exacerbation of a preexisting seizure disorder
Bot: Do you know that it is not necessarily a seizure disorder?
User: tell me!
Bot: it can also be an insult
User: How do most seizures terminate?
Bot: spontaneously.
Bot: Do you know the most common cause in patients with known epilepsy?
User: I know. It is change in drug
Bot: a change in medication

FIG. 12

A dialogue for epilepticus.

Table 1 A list of user intents.

Ask for a specific topic
Confirm that topic is familiar
Confirm that there is an interest in a topic
Go to more details/zoom in
Learn a reason
Learn a consequence
Learn an argument for a claim
Disagree with a statement

Table 2 Selecting an utterance, given a user intent and a position in a discourse tree (DT).

Class of intent	Current node	Relation	Bot reply
Ask for a specific topic	Nucleus	*Elaboration*	Return nucleus. Ask if *want to learn more*
	Satellite		Return satellite Move up from nucleus (zoom out)
	Nucleus	*Condition*	Return nucleus Ask the user: *do you know what happens if* <Satellite condition part>
	Satellite		Return satellite
	Nucleus	*Temporal sequence*	Return nucleus Ask the user: *do you know what happens after/before* <Satellite condition part>?
	Satellite		*This is what happened after/before* <nucleus>: Return satellite
Confirm that the topic is familiar (user already knows that) User: Yes, I know <topic>	Nucleus	*Elaboration*	*Good you know this. Do you want to know about* <satellite-entity>?
	Satellite		Good you know this. Move up from nucleus (zoom out)
	Nucleus	*Condition*	OK, you know it. Do you know when is <topic> true?
	Satellite		*What you know* <topic> *is a condition. Want to know the premise?*
	Nucleus	*Contrast*	*You would think that* <topic>? *However,* <satellite>
	Satellite		*There is a controversy: on one hand,* <nucleus>, *but, on the other hand,* <satellite>
Confirm that there is an interest in a topic User: Yes, tell me	Nucleus	*Elaboration*	Return <nucleus> *Is there interest to learn about* <satellite-entity>?
	Satellite		Return satellite Continue traversal *Are you interested in* <new node-entity>?

(1) the tendency of human utterances to be short
(2) users frequently mention out-of-vocabulary words and entities
(3) a lack of available labeled open-domain human-machine conversation data

Natural conversations entail utterances that are dependent on the context, thus making it impossible to classify the topic and intent without considering the preceding utterances (Fig. 13). For example, when a customer replies with the expression '*Oh, yeah*', it can be interpreted as one of several options, such as *Accept/Agree* or *Topic-Update*. To help address these problems, a contextual-aware topic and dialogue intent classification model for open-domain conversational agents has been proposed. To identify both topics and dialogue intents, a *Mixture of Experts* model is developed. The topic classifier is trained on new topics such as *Diabetes* and *Lung diseases*, and the intent classifier is trained on new dialogue intents such as *Reject-Answer*. In addition, the intent classifiers aim to improve the quality of some specific classes to better fit the use cases in health. For instance, we observed that a default intent classifier would consider user disagreements as *Topic-Update*, even when this is not the most accurate label of the current dialogue situation. To improve this case, another intent *Decline* is added to cover the situations where the users were disagreeing with the last chatbot utterance but did not want to stop the current topic being delivered to them.

4.2 Handling epistemic states

The purpose of a dialogue centered around a paragraph of text is to make sure the recipient acquired information from this text, can willingly follow instructions accordingly, believes in this text, and can share their beliefs with others. In other words, the goal is to persuade the user that the topic is important and needs to be well understood. The chatbot plays the role of persuader and the user plays the role of the persuadee. However, to achieve this goal in a more reliable way, the roles can swap, and the user is

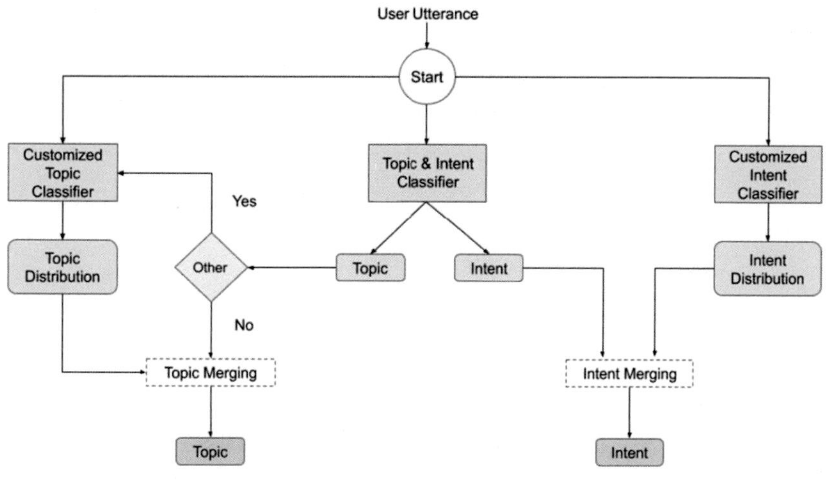

FIG. 13

Classifying topic and intent in parallel.

encouraged to answer questions such as the answer can be confirmed/updated/revised by the chatbot in the utterance to follow.

Epistemic states are linguistically expressed through the verbs of propositional attitude (*believe, know, be convinced, have doubt*, among many others). These denote the attitude (or state) of an agent to a subject and are formulated by sentences of the form *communicative_action_or_state(Agent1, Agent2, Subject)*.

For example "*Dr Pedro is convinced that antibiotics can help a given patient.*" Epistemic states are experienced with respect to propositions believed. They are a matter of a complex experience involving the belief itself, but the reasons and motives the agents have for supporting the proposition are also considered (Fig. 14). Epistemic states do not always accompany beliefs because, similarly to beliefs, they are potential states (Rigo-Lemini and Martínez-Navarro, 2017).

Bochman (2013) wrote that a general representation framework for preferential nonmonotonic reasoning can be given in terms of epistemic states. A user acquires information from the chatbot in a nonmonotonic way, as newly acquired facts and assertions can defeat previously acquired ones. An *epistemic state* is defined as a triple $(S, l, \prec)$, where S is a set of *admissible belief states*, $\prec$ a preference relation on S, while l is a labeling function assigning a deductively closed *belief set* to every state from S. The goal of the chatbot is to expand the belief set of the user, minimizing contradictions.

Admissible belief states are generated as logical closures of allowable combinations of default assumptions about what the user currently believes (acquired set of facts). Such states are taken to be the options for choice for the chatbot on which fact or assertion to deliver next. The preference relation on admissible belief states reflects the fact that not all admissible combinations of defaults constitute equally preferred options for choice. Defaults are rules that are assumed to be true unless proven otherwise.

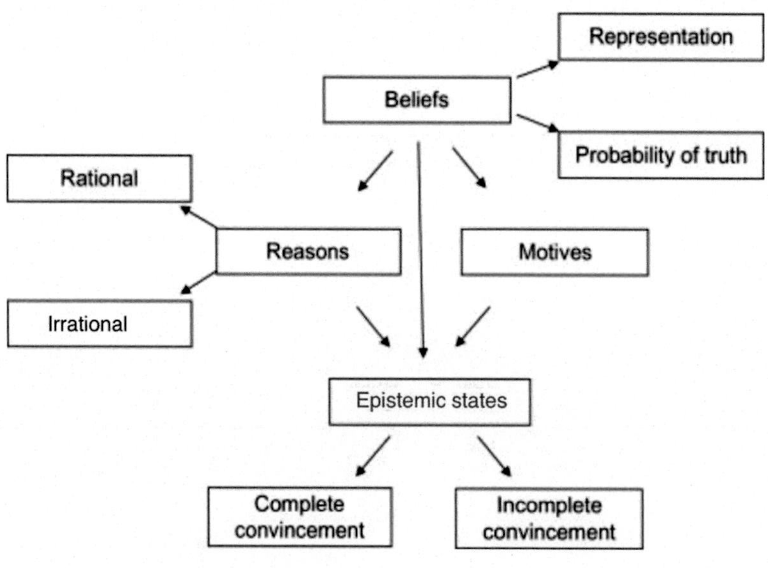

FIG. 14

Epistemic states, propositional attitudes, and reasons.

If a set of defaults is assumed to hold, an admissible belief state generated by a larger set of defaults is normally preferred to an admissible state generated by a smaller set of defaults. In addition, not all-defaults are the same in terms of importance, so they may have some priority structure that imposes, in turn, additional preferences among belief states.

Epistemic states drive the chatbot decisions concerning what the user should believe in particular dialogue state. They are epistemic, however, precisely because they say nothing directly about what is true but only what is believed (or assumed) to hold. This makes epistemic states relatively stable entities; change in facts and situations will not necessarily lead to change in epistemic states. The actual assumptions made in particular situations are obtained by choosing preferred admissible belief states that are consistent with the facts. The notion of epistemic state is tightly connected with persuasion, another function of a persistent chatbot.

The aim of persuasion is for the persuader to change the mind of the persuadee, and the provision of good arguments, and possibly counterarguments, is of central importance for accomplishing this. Some recent developments in the field of computational persuasion have focused on the need to model the beliefs of the persuadee for the persuader to better select arguments to present to the persuadee. For instance, if the persuader wants to persuade the persuadee to stop running on pavement, and the persuader knows that the persuadee believes that if they give up any running, they will put on weight, then the persuader could start the dialogue by providing a counterargument to this, for example, by saying that there is a local stadium well suited for running on grass.

One approach to modeling the persuadee is to harness the epistemic approach to argumentation. An argument graph (as defined by Dung, 1995) is used to represent the arguments and attacks between them. When the chatbot starts a dialogue with a persuadee, it does not have any model concerning what the persuadee already knows and what they do not. This is the initial default epistemic state. Then, during the dialogue, the participants make the moves according to some protocol. After each move, the epistemic state is updated using an update function defined on the DT.

Let us have a text with a DT that consists of n EDUs. Initially, the chatbot believes that the user does not know anything from this text: $\forall i$ *not know(user, EDU(i))*. $i = 0 \ldots n$ are ordered according to how the DT is built (an original order). These EDU(i) cannot be acquired by the user in any order; this order should follow a navigation of DT, since, for example, EDU(i) as a satellite cannot be acquired as long as its nucleus EDU($i-1$) has not being acquired. The chatbot cannot just traverse DT since every user has a different initial knowledge and interests and leads a chatbot session through the epistemic states of his choice. Hence the actual sequence of utterances in a conversation deviates from $0 \ldots n$.

When a user asks about EDU(i), the chatbot believes that user wants to know EDU(i). If the user shares EDU(i), then the chatbot decides that this user also wants to know or wants to share EDU($i+1$) as well as EDU($i-1$), navigating the DT in both directions from the nucleus and the satellite and back.

If the user interrupts the chatbot and wants a new topic t, the chatbot either finds the one determined to be similar $t \sim$ EDU(i) or launches an external search and attempts to associate the external search results with EDU(i). If a question about an attribute a of e is given by the user, inaccessible from the current node I, the chatbot transitions into the MRC mode and determines the value a along with the new node j.

If the chatbot is in a satellite node, it has delivered the main point e and is now in a position to produce an utterance with an elaboration on e, attribution of e, cause of e, and temporal sequence of e, not changing the current topic. Conversely, if the chatbot is in a nucleus mode, it shares the main nucleus topic e with the user and expects the user's request for information concerning more details about e, attribution of e, what caused e, and so forth.

FIG. 15

Illustrating the idea of pruning as many leaves of a discourse tree (DT) as possible in the course of a dialogue to cover the topic of a given text.

The objective is to have as few undelivered EDUs as possible until the user abandons the conversation (Fig. 15).

5. User intent recognizer

One of the essential capabilities of a chatbot is to discriminate between a request to commit a transaction (such as a patient treatment request) and a question to obtain some information. Usually, these forms of user activity follow each other.

Before a user wants a chatbot to perform an action (such as *open a new bank account*), the user would want to know the rules and conditions for this account. Once the user knowledge request is satisfied, the user makes a decision and orders a transaction. Once this transaction is completed by the chatbot, the user might want to know a list of options available and asks a question (such as *how to fund this new account*). Hence user questions and transactional requests are intermittent and need to be recognized reliably.

Errors in recognizing questions vs transactional requests are severe. If a question is misinterpreted and an answer to a different question is returned, the user can reformulate it and ask again. If a transactional request is recognized as a different (wrong) transaction, the user will understand it when the chatbot issues a request to specify inappropriate parameters. Then the user would cancel their request, attempt to reformulate it, and issue it again. Hence chatbot errors associated with wrongly understood questions and transactional requests can be naturally rectified. At the same time, chatbot errors recognizing questions vs transactional requests would break the whole conversation and the user would be confused as how to continue a conversation. Therefore, the chatbot needs to avoid these kinds of errors by any means.

Recognizing questions vs transactional requests must be *domain independent*. In any domain a user might want to ask a question or to request a transaction, and this recognition should not depend on the subject. Whereas a chatbot might need training data from a chatbot developer to operate in a specific domain (such as flu), recognizing questions vs transactional requests must be a capability built in advance by a chatbot vendor, before this chatbot will be adjusted to a particular domain.

We also target recognition of questions vs transactional requests to be in a *context-independent* manner. Potentially there could be any order in which questions are asked and requests are made. A user may switch from information access to a request to do something and back to information access, although this should be discouraged. Even a human customer support agent prefers a user to first receive information, make a decision, and then request an action (make an order).

A request can be formulated *explicitly or implicitly*. *Could you do this* may mean both a question about the chatbot capability as well as an implicit request to *do this*. Even a simple question like "*what is my account balance?*" may be a transactional request to select an account and execute a database query. Another way to express a request is via mentioning of a desired state instead of explicit action to achieve it. For example, the utterance "I am too cold" indicates not a question but rather a desired state that can be achieved by turning on the heater. If no available action is associated with "cold" this utterance is classified as a question related to "coldness." To handle this ambiguity in a domain-independent manner, we differentiate between questions and transactional requests *linguistically,* not pragmatically.

Although a vast training dataset for each class is available, it turns out that the rule-based approach provides an adequate performance. For an utterance, classification into a request or question is done by a rule-based system on two levels:

(1) Keyword level
(2) linguistic analysis of phrases level

The algorithm chart includes four major components (Fig. 16):

- Data, vocabularies, configuration
- Rule engine
- Linguistic processor
- Decision former

Data, *vocabularies*, and *configuration* components include leading verbs indicating that an utterance is a request. They also include expressions used by an utterance author to indicate the author wants something from a peer, such as "*Please do … for me*." These expressions also refer to information requests such as "Give me MY …," for example, account information. For a question, this vocabulary includes the ways people address questions, such as "*please tell me….*"

Rule engine applies a sequence of rules, both keyword-based, vocabulary-based, and linguistic. The rules are applied in certain order, oriented to find indication of a transaction. If main cases of *transactions* are not identified, only then does the rule engine apply *question* rules. Finally, if question rules

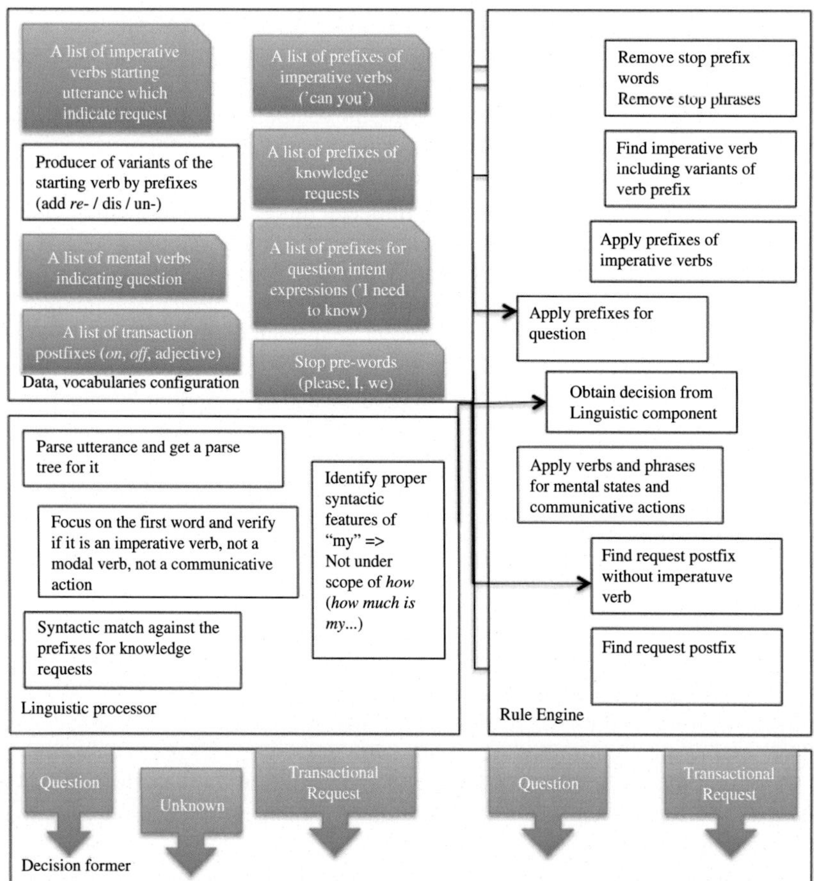

FIG. 16

The architecture for question vs transaction request recognition. The class labels on the bottom correspond to the decision rules above.

did not fire, we classify the utterance as *unknown*, but nevertheless treat it as default, a *question*. Most rules are specific to the class of requests; if none of them fire, then the decision is also a *question*.

Linguistic processor targets two cases: imperative leading verb and a reference to "my" object. Once parsing is done, the first word should be a regular verb in present tense and active voice, and be neither modal, mental, or a form of *be*. These constraints assure this verb is in the imperative form, for example, "*Drop the temperature in the room.*" The second case addresses utterances related to an object the author owns or is associated to, such as "*my account balance*" and "*my car*." These utterances are connected with an intent to perform an action with these objects or a request for information on them (versus a question that expresses a request to share general knowledge, not about *my* object).

Decision former takes an output of the rule engine and outputs one out of three decisions, along with an explanation for each of them. Each fired keyword-based rule provides an explanation, as well as each linguistic rule. Thus when a resultant decision is produced, there is always a detailed backup of it. If any of the components failed while applying a rule, the resultant decision is *unknown*.

If no decision is made, the chatbot comes back to the user asking for explicit clarification: "*Please be clearer if you are asking a question or requesting a transaction.*"

We present examples for each class together with the rules that fired and delivered the decision (shown in brackets).

Questions

If I do not have my Internet Banking User ID and Password, **how can I** login? [*if* and how can I— prefix].

I am **anxious** about spending my money [mental verb].

I am ***worried*** about my spending [mental verb].

I am ***concerned*** about how much I used [mental verb].

I am **interested** how much money I lost on stock [mental verb].

How can **my** saving account be funded [How+my].

Domestic wire transfer [no transactional rule fired therefore question].

order replacement/renewal card not received [no transactional rule fired therefore question].

Requests from the chatbot to do something

Tell me… [leading imperative verb].

Confirm that…

Help me to … [leading imperative verb].

5.1 Nearest neighbor-based learning for user intent recognition

If a chatbot developer intends to overwrite the intent recognition rules, they need to supply a balanced training set that includes samples for both classes. To implement a nearest-neighbor functionality, we rely on information extraction and search library Lucene (Erenel and Altınçay, 2012). The training needs to be conducted in advance, but in real time when a new utterance arrives the following happens:

(1) An instant index is created from the current utterance.
(2) We iterate through all samples from both classes. For each sample, a query is built and a search issued against the instant index.
(3) We collect the set of queries that delivered non-empty search results with its class, and aggregate this set by the classes.
(4) We verify that a certain class is highly represented by the aggregated results and the other class has significantly lower presentation. Then we select this highly represented class as a recognition result. Otherwise, the system should refuse to accept a recognition result and issue *Unknown*.

Lucene default TF*IDF model will assure that the training set elements are the closest in terms of most significant keywords (from the frequency perspective (Salton and Yang, 1973)). Trstenjak et al. (2013) presented the possibility of using a k-nearest neighbor (KNN) algorithm with TF*IDF method for text classification. This method enables classification according to various parameters, measurement, and analysis of results. Evaluation of framework was focused on the speed and quality of classification, and testing results showed positive and negative characteristics of the TF*IDF-KNN algorithm. Our evaluation was performed on several categories of documents in the online environment and showed stable and reliable performance. Tests shed light on the quality of classification and determined which factors have an impact on performance of classification.

6. System architecture

Fig. 17 depicts the high-level architecture of the chatbot. Offline, a paragraph of text to be delivered is subject to discourse parsing. It is then subject to additional custom parsing to determine specific rhetorical relations for navigation (Chapter 9; Yi et al., 2019). Also, the ontology is integrated to differentiate between questions that can be answered by this text versus the ones requiring an external search (Chapter 11; Galitsky, 2019b).

Online, when a user replies, their intent is established (classified into the one of pre-determined classes, Section 5). Also, when the user is sharing their knowledge, it must be matched against the given paragraph of text to be delivered, to be compatible, contradicting, or independent of this text.

The central part of the persistent chatbot is the DT navigator. Its main function is to establish a reply type by the user intent and the current position in the DT. After each user utterance, the navigator decides which node to proceed to next. If the user has an explicit knowledge request, a jump is required to

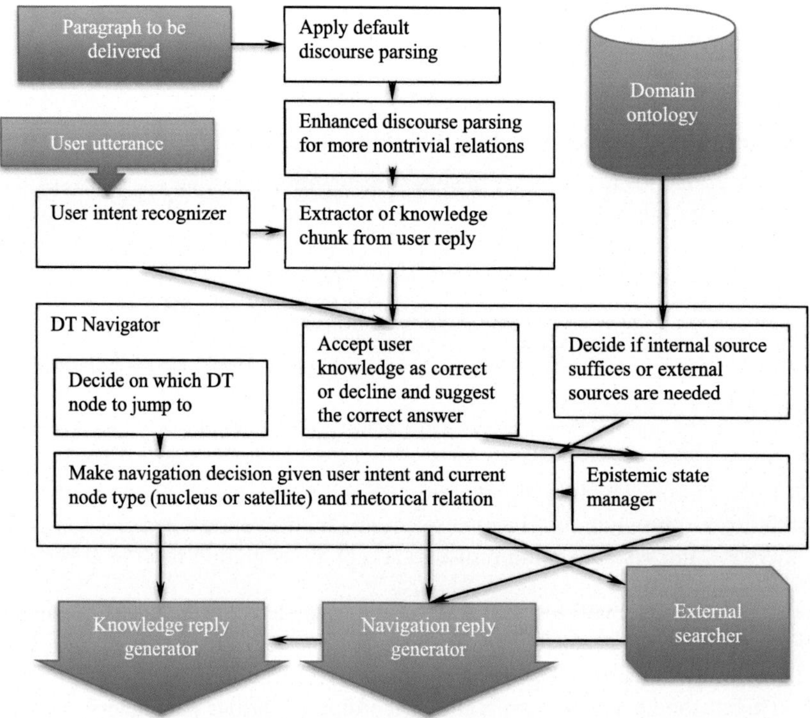

FIG. 17

The system architecture of the persistent chatbot.

the node that has a chunk of text to address this request. Otherwise, the persistent chatbot takes initiative and generates a set of options for the user to proceed. These options match the rhetorical relation coming in and coming out of the current node of the DT. The navigator also matches the user's epistemic states as a part of their intent characteristics with available rhetorical relations.

Depending on the epistemic state, the navigator picks the text fragment to reply to the user and encourages the user to continue knowledge exploration in one form or another. A decision on which text to reply to and the next step to propose are made independently (Section 4).

Internal and external search engines match the user query or statement with each EDU of the DT first. In cases of both a question and a statement, the chatbot jumps to the node that is syntactically and semantically closest to the user utterance. In the case of a question, an answer (this EDU) is returned. In the case of a statement, semantic similarity is confirmed by the chatbot if this statement is matched with this EDU or rejected, and then the user is encouraged to receive the correct chunk of information. The search engine implementation is based on structurized word2vec (Galitsky, 2021a), combining syntactic and semantic features to find the best text fragment matching the user utterance.

Both knowledge and navigation reply generators employ ML-based rhetorical agreement to make sure the selected utterances not only follow the topic but also agree with previous utterances in style and logic (Chapter 9; Galitsky and Ilvovsky, 2017a,b).

7. Evaluation

7.1 Evaluation setting

One of the main challenges faced by researchers is absence of a good technique to measure performance due to a lack of explicit objective function for task-oriented conversations. To measure the quality of a response given a set of previous utterances, (Adiwardana et al., 2020; Venkatesh et al., 2018) suggested seven questions for assessors (Fig. 18):

(1) Whether the response, given the context, *makes sense*. Meaningfulness is a must-have feature to achieve human-like conversation. Meaningfulness includes relevance of answers to questions, consistency in epistemic states when a chatbot follows a user request to share information, common sense, and logical and rhetorical coherence. Meaningfulness also captures other important aspects of a chatbot, such as consistency. The assessor is asked to use common sense to

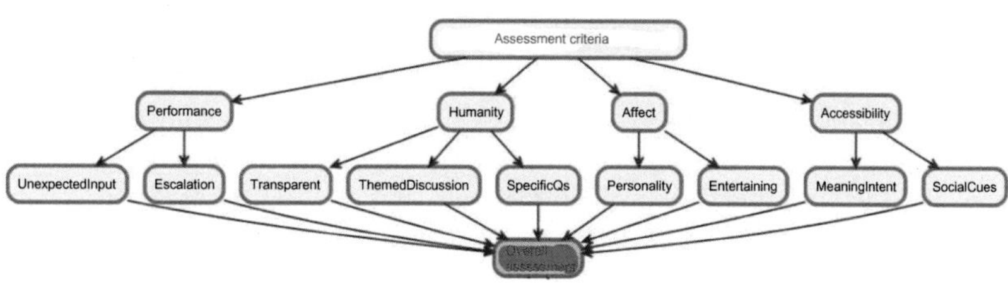

FIG. 18

Overall chatbot performance assessment.

judge if a response is completely reasonable in context of previous utterances. If anything seems confusing, illogical, out of context, or factually incorrect, then it should be labeled as meaningless.

(2) How *specific* is the response. Being sensible is not enough; a generic response (e.g., "*tell me more*" or "*I don't know*") can be sensible, but it is also uninformative and unspecific. Chatbots that are evaluated according to metrics like sensibleness alone frequently generate such responses. An assessor is asked to determine if the chatbot response is specific to the given context and informative to the user at a given step. The specificity average (SSA) combines this measure with assessment (1) as key aspects of an intelligent chatbot: making sense and being specific.

(3) *Engagement* is a measure of interestingness in a conversation (Yu et al., 2004). Researchers in the field of dialogue evaluation attempt to identify indicators for user engagement such as a number of dialogue turns and total conversation duration. There are cases that may have a higher number of turns due to inability of a task-oriented bot to understand the user's intent, leading to follow-up turns with clarifications and modifications, also potentially resulting in user dissatisfaction. An analysis of a random sampling of conversations leads (Venkatesh et al., 2018) to the conclusion that the impact of this effect is negligible.

(4) A *coherent* response indicates a comprehensible and relevant response to a user's request. A response can have a low coherence if it is somewhat related. For example, when a user says: "*What do you think about the entity e*?," the response should be about *e*, the category for *e*, more broadly, or something related to *e*. A response related to *e* but not exactly an opinion or something related to the category of *e* would be considered weakly coherent. For open-domain conversations, the complexity in the response space makes this problem extremely hard, but within the specific text *T* the assessment is straightforward. Coherence is also associated with rhetorical agreement (Galitsky, 2017b).

(5) *Conversational depth*. Coherence measure is usually computed for a pair of utterances. However, in a multi-turn conversation, context and content flow may continue over multiple utterances. While evaluating a chatbot, it is essential to recognize the context and depth of the dialogue. Human conversations frequently zoom into a particular topic. An agent that can capture topical depth (Galitsky, 2017a) may sound more natural. To evaluate the chatbot for conversational depth, a topical model can be employed to identify the domain for each individual utterance. Conversational depth can be estimated as the average number of consecutive utterances within the same topic. More precisely, it can be estimated as depth of a chain of entities being communicated, such as *disease-specific/symptom-specific feature of this symptom.*

(6) *Conversational breadth*. This is a feature of a chit-chat open-domain bot. This type of chatbot can identify the topics and keywords from a given utterance, manage a dialogue around the same topics, and have related entities in common. Natural dialogues are highly topical, and humans frequently use keywords in their interactions. Users are frequently unhappy with chatbots lacking topical diversity. Evaluating conversational breadth, it is a key to understand how broadly an agent can support conversations as opposed to potentially highly scripted and/or hard-coded conversations about a small number of domains.

(7) *Overall user satisfaction score*. For a given dialogue, the user confirms that they achieved their goal, learned what they intended to learn (+1), or did not (0). Turing Test participants frequently attempt to avoid detection by being strategically vague (Venkatesh et al., 2018). This strategic vagueness needs to be avoided.

To converse properly with a human, a chatbot's responses have to make sense in context; humans typically take this for granted when conversing with one another, and the evaluations of Adiwardana et al. (2020) found that 97% of human-produced statements meet this criterion. To assess the usefulness of DT navigation, we rely on an overall measure such as *user satisfaction score*, expressing a need to read *T* after the dialogue. If it is still necessary to consult the text *T* after the session with a chatbot, this user is considered to be unsatisfied. We then average through multiple sessions for a number of users for *T*.

Radziwill and Benton (2017) proposed approaches for a hybrid dialogue management technique for recommender chatbots, based on the analytic hierarchy process, shown in Table 3. A recommender chatbot can perform a broad range of tasks, such as the ones shown in Fig. 19.

7.2 Assessment of navigation algorithm

We first evaluate the level of persuasiveness answering user questions. We vary the navigation algorithm from keeping the user focused on text *T* to more precise answers to user questions (Table 4). This evaluation can also be viewed as an ablation study where we turn various components on/off and track the percentages of covered information in *T* and the overall user satisfaction score.

In our evaluation, we focus on paragraphs of text (five to seven sentences each) that contain important instructions on how to do things. Domains range from home to professional, from low to high responsibility, and up to legal, aviation, and health.

We now assess the overall meaningfulness of dialogues and rhetorical agreement. We manually assess 20% of dialogues in each domain. For the remaining 80% we used a specifically designed *evaluation chatbot* designed to reproduce the assessment score of a human evaluator, irrespectively of the error type of the main chatbot. This evaluation chatbot is designed to formulate basic questions given an utterance from the main chatbot or a user. The main underlying algorithm is to generalize a received sentence and convert it into a question about an attribute of an entity occurring in this question. A detailed description of the algorithm is available in the *doc2dialogue* paper (Galitsky and Ilvovsky, 2018).

The evaluation chatbot is tuned to yield the same assessment as a human on 20% of the evaluation dataset. The assessment performance of the evaluation chatbot (not the main chatbot) is then manually

Table 3 Assessment of some chatbot features.

Category	Quality attribute	Metric	Value
Performance	Robustness to unexpected input	% of successes	8
	Provides appropriate escalation channels	% of successes	90
Humanity	Transparent to inspection (known chatbot)	% of users who correctly classify	78
	Able to maintain themed discussion	0 (low) … 100 (high)	91
	Able to respond to specific questions	% of successes	93
Affect	Provides greetings, pleasant personality	0 (low) … 100 (high)	76 (Fig. 18)
	Entertaining, engaging	0 (low) … 100 (high)	72
Accessibility	Can detect meaning and intent	% of successes	81
	Responds to social cues appropriately	% of successes	73

FIG. 19

Recommendation on nutrition and insurance that can be delegated to a chatbot.

Table 4 Varying the navigation algorithm from keeping the user focused on text *T* to more precise answers to user questions.

Navigation and reply algorithm/mode	# of total utterances	# of covered EDUs (utterances) from *T*	% of covered EDUs (utterances) from *T*	User satisfaction score (%)
Always try to find an EDU matching the user query. Provide the closest EDU as an answer, even if it is very dissimilar to the question. Use MRC against *T* when possible. Encourage a user with questions "*Do you know why/who/when?*"	7.5	6.7	67.2	72.1
Try to find an EDU matching the user query with a **low** relevance threshold. Encourage a user with a question concerning *T* before trying external search. Try MRC against T with **high** threshold.	8.1	7.0	**69.2**	**77.8**
Try to find an EDU matching the user query with a **medium** relevance threshold Encourage a user to ask a question or make a comment that would match a rhetorical relation in a navigation path Try external search with **medium** relevance threshold Try MRC against T with **low** threshold	**10.5**	8.2	62.8	73.2
Apply **high** relevance threshold matching user query with EDU Otherwise, search external content. Attempt to provide the most exact answer to user queries Use MRC against external content.	10.3	8.1	63.1	72.9

assessed on the remaining 10% of this dataset. The rest (70%) of cases is assessed by the evaluation chatbot in a fully automated mode.

In Table 5, one can see that the user satisfaction is 70% and greater. Some higher complexity health domains lag 3%–5% behind such simpler domains as *Cough*, *Muscle cramp*, and *Throat irritation*. In health-related domains, missing important pieces of knowledge is a strong flaw that can lead to the trainee needing to read the whole paragraph after the chatbot mode and an overall user dissatisfaction. Assessors apply stricter meaningfulness criteria in these domains. In other knowledge domains related to entertainment, just the dialogue mode suffices in most cases; missing certain EDUs does not critically affect the knowledge acquisition results.

To compare a DT navigation with a pure data-driven approach, we take the given paragraph of text as a seed and mine the health resources and the Web for a few hundred similar texts. Then we learn from them and apply the dialogue model of Galitsky et al. (2014). The evaluation chatbot acting on behalf of a user is the same, but the dialogue is totally different now. What is mostly lacking is a systematic navigation through the text; the data-driven chatbot jumps abruptly from topic to topic, and content exploration becomes chaotic (Table 5, last column).

The evaluation results show the superiority of the DT-navigation approach in comparison to a data-driven one for content exploration. There is an 11% decrease in user satisfaction rate when the DT navigation is substituted by a data-driven system such as DeepPavlov (2019).

Table 6 presents the results of the assessment of other dialogue criteria.

- *Specificity* column shows the percentage of utterances that are specific in addressing the same or relevant entity. A non-specific answer would include a totally foreign entity or no specific entity at all.

Table 5 Chatbot overall performance in various domains.

Domain and source	# dialogues	Percentages of overall meaningful dialogues	Percentages of meaningful utterances by the bot	User satisfaction score (%)	User satisfaction score for a data-driven chatbot (baseline) (%)
Bloating	316	78.1	87.9	77.4	66.3
Cough	315	79.5	92.4	79.6	68.4
Diarrhea	320	81.1	88.7	77.9	69.7
Dizziness	330	78.3	89.0	78.7	67.2
Fatigue	370	81.0	86.6	77.0	69.0
Fever	346	80.5	91.8	78.3	65.2
Headache	325	79.7	90.7	74.6	67.4
Muscle cramp	310	82.4	91.4	80.3	66.1
Nausea	330	76.2	86.5	78.5	67.0
Throat irritation	208	80.8	91.2	79.0	69.6
Average	317	79.8	89.6	78.1	67.6

Table 6 Assessment of other dialogue criteria.

Domain	Specificity	Engagement	Coherence	Conversational depth	Conversational breadth
Bloating	86.3	89.2	84.2	6.1	5.2
Cough	90.2	85.3	86.3	4.2	6.8
Diarrhea	88.4	87.9	88.7	5.3	5.7
Dizziness	89.0	89.3	86.5	6.0	6.1
Fatigue	94.4	91.7	90.3	5.7	5.0
Fever	92.3	95.0	83.9	7.1	5.9
Headache	93.2	92.4	87.0	5.7	6.6
Muscle cramp	90.7	88.6	87.3	4.8	6.4
Nausea	87.5	90.3	89.4	5.9	5.8
Throat irritation	88.4	92.4	86.8	5.2	5.3
Average	90.0	90.2	87.0	5.6	5.9

- *Engagement* column shows the percentage of dialogues that successfully covered the paragraph of text being communicated. We consider an engagement failed if after the *second* question the human user gave up on continuing a conversation and decided that just reading this text is beneficial for them in comparison with conducting a dialogue.
- *Coherence* column shows the percentages of dialogues where the user did not interrupt the dialogue, having encountered a totally incoherent utterance of a chatbot. Such incoherent utterance would break the thought train of a user, abruptly changing the flow of a conversation. If less than five total utterances lead to a loss of coherence, a given dialogue is considered incoherent.
- *Conversational depth* is measured as the highest number of nested entities communicated by the chatbot replies. For example, the chain *diabetes-chronic condition-abnormally high levels of sugar-glucose-in the blood-insulin* gives us *depth* =6.
- *Conversational breadth* is measured as a number of distinct entities covered in a conversation so that one is not a sub-entity of another (do not form a chain from depth evaluation).

Notice that the failures of specificity, engagement, and coherence are not mutually exclusive; some problematic dialogues can fail more than one criterion.

8. Related work

The chatbot developed in this chapter falls in the category of task-oriented, frame-based, mixed-initiative dialogue systems (Fig. 20, Galitsky, 2019c). We did not target the complexity of agent-based systems that enable complex communication between the chatbot, the user, and the application. There are many variants of agent-based systems, depending on what particular aspects of intelligent behavior are designed into the system. Communication is viewed as the interaction between two agents, each of which is capable of reasoning about its own actions and beliefs, and sometimes also about the actions

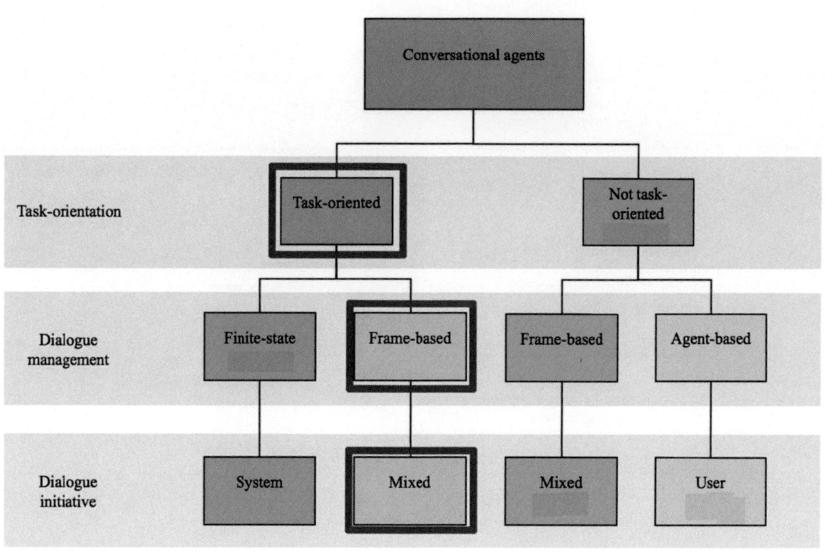

FIG. 20

A taxonomy of chatbots.

and beliefs of the other agents. The dialogue model takes the preceding context into account with the result that the dialogue evolves dynamically as a sequence of related steps that build on each other (Galitsky, 2013, 2016). If the primary metric of a task-oriented chatbot is just the generation of plausible human readable responses, it is easy to ignore more challenging areas of forming a response and conducting dialogue management. It is important to be able to produce interesting and relevant content while generating plausible responses.

Venkatesh et al. (2018) trained a topic classification model using a deep averaging network (DAN) on an Alexa internal dataset to identify topics within a conversation to enable computation of the above topic-based metrics. The classifier identified topical domains for any given user utterance or socialbot response into one of 26 knowledge domains (News, Entertainment, etc.) with more than 80% accuracy.

Beyond current conversational chatbots or task-oriented dialogue systems that have attracted increasing attention, Xu et al. (2019) developed a dialogue system for automatic medical diagnosis that converses with patients to collect additional symptoms beyond their self-reports and automatically makes a diagnosis. Besides the challenges for conversational dialogue systems (e.g., topic transition coherency and question understanding), the automatic medical diagnosis further poses more critical requirements for the dialogue rationality in the context of medical knowledge and symptom-disease relations.

Fig. 21 shows an end-to-end, knowledge-routed relational dialogue system framework (Xu et al., 2019). A bi-directional long short term memory (Bi-LSTM) system processes input utterances and generates semantic frames that are further fed into the DM component to generate system actions. The DM interacts with the basic DL branch, a relational refinement branch, and a medical knowledge-routed graph branch. A user simulator with a user goal (consisting of symptoms of patients) interacts with the agent and gives rewards. A template-based NL generator is used to yield NL for the user simulator

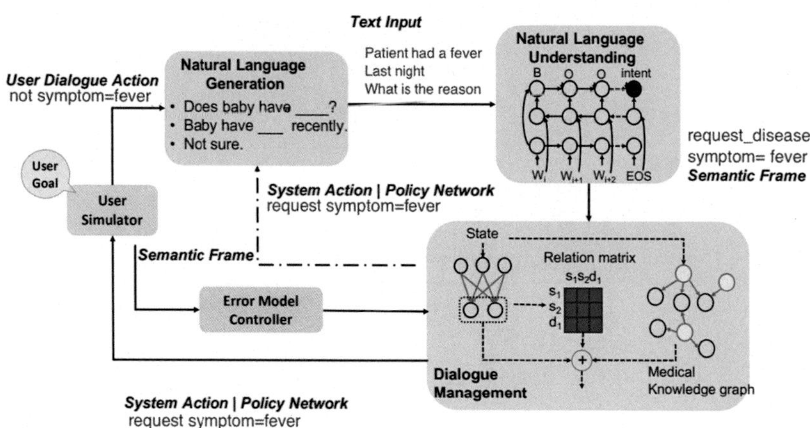

FIG. 21

Architecture of dialogue-based diagnosis-making system.

and the DM based on actions. The system stores the original self-reports and the conversational data between patients and doctors.

An access to a paragraph of text can have various forms. Galitsky et al. (2019) designed a chatbot that delivers content in the form of virtual dialogues automatically produced from plain texts extracted and selected from documents. This virtual dialogue content is provided in the form of answers derived from the found and selected documents split into fragments, and questions are automatically generated for these answers.

Most of the recent approaches to generative chatbots are primarily based on sequence-to-sequence (Seq2Seq) learning. Seq2Seq is a supervised learning algorithm in which the input and the generated output are each a sequence of words (Shang et al., 2015). In general, Seq2Seq models consist of two recurrent neural networks (RNNs): an RNN for encoding inputs and an RNN for generating outputs. Previous studies have demonstrated that chatbots based on Seq2Seq models often respond with either a safe response problem (i.e., the problem returning short and general responses such as "Okay" and "I see") or a semantically erroneous response. A variational auto-encoder (VAE) learns a latent space using a given set of instances. The model consists of an encoder and decoder; the encoder maps inputs into latent variables, and the decoder generates outputs that are similar to the inputs based on the latent variables. As a result, VAEs are capable of processing high-level semantics of the responses and help chatbots to generate various utterances (Shen et al., 2018).

However, VAE models have a strong limitation, as the decoder learns to ignore the latent variable and simplifies the latent variable to a standard normal distribution (Goyal et al., 2017). This limitation has been partially addressed by learning latent variable space through adversarial learning. In addition, various papers focus on generative adversarial networks (GAN) architectures; however, adversarial learning for discrete tokens is difficult because of non-differentiability. To solve these problems, various attempts have been made, including those on a hybrid model of a GAN and reinforcement learning (Shen et al., 2017). These approaches run into flaws when considering non-differentiability. Moreover, they must calculate the word probability distribution of each step of the decoder to learn a discriminant model. A learning method has been proposed that does not consider non-differentiability when learning using a GAN, as it relies on the response vector produced by the decoder. To generate natural responses in multi-turn dialogues, an attention method is needed between a query and its previous utterances that helps chatbots selectively consider the given context.

The model of (Kim et al., 2019) consists of three sub-modules: a query encoder, a query-to-response (QR) mapper, and a response-to-response (RR) mapper, as shown in Fig. 22. The query encoder returns a query vector embedding a current utterance U_n (i.e., user query) and a dialogue context composed of k previous utterances $U_{n-1}, U_{n-2}, \ldots, U_{n-k}$, by using RNNs and a scaled dot product attention mechanism (Vaswani et al., 2017). At training time, the QR mapper makes a query vector similar to an RNN-encoded response vector (i.e., a vector of a next utterance U_{n+1}; a vector of a chatbot's response) through an adversarial learning scheme. Then, it decodes an encoded response vector through an auto-encoder learning scheme. Then in real time (reasoning time), a query vector is fed as an input to a response decoder based on an RNN. The response-to-response mapper makes an encoded response vector similar to a response vector decoded by the RNN through an adversarial learning scheme.

Laranjo et al. (2018) surveyed 17 chatbot systems, where conversational agents were used to support tasks undertaken by patients, clinicians, and both patients and clinicians. Patient support is the chatbot focus (Hudlicka, 2016; Ireland et al., 2016; Miner et al., 2016) mostly providing education and training for health-related aspects of their lives. Clinicians were the focus of the studies such as (Philip et al., 2014) including the studies of conversational agents used to autonomously conduct clinical interviews with diagnostic purposes in mental health and sleep disorders (Lucas et al., 2017) and a study of a conversational agent used to assist with data collection and decision support in referral management. Another area for conversational agents used in applications supporting both clinicians and patients is telemonitoring and data collection. Other conditions included asthma (Rhee et al., 2014), hypertension (Giorgino et al., 2005), type 2 diabetes (Harper et al., 2008a), breast cancer, obstructive sleep apnea (Philip et al., 2014), and sexual health (Crutzen et al., 2011).

Currently, health applications chatbots lag behind those used in other areas such as customer care, travel information, restaurant selection and booking, where dialogue management and NL generation methods have advanced beyond the rule-based approaches typical for health applications. Rule-based approaches used in finite-state dialogue management systems are simple to construct for tasks that are

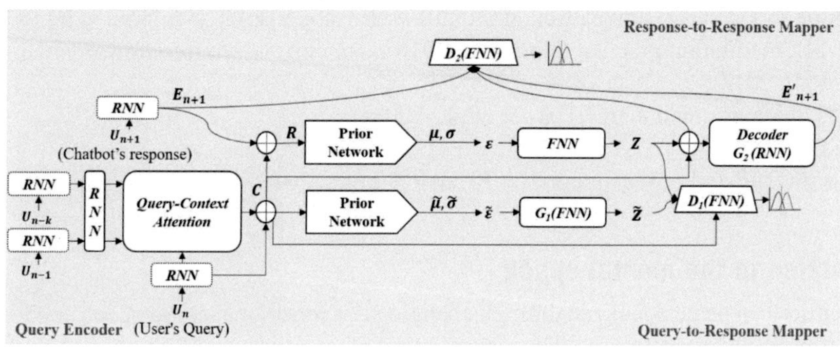

FIG. 22

An architecture with a query encoder, a query-to-response mapper, and a response-to-response mapper.

straightforward and well structured but have the disadvantage of restricting user input to predetermined words and phrases, not allowing the user to take initiative in the dialogue, and making correction of misrecognized items difficult (López-Cózar et al., 2011). This explains why studies in our review using finite-state dialogue management were all task-oriented, mostly focusing on information retrieval tasks such as data collection or following a predefined clinical interview guide.

8.1 Personalization in health chatbots

Studies of personalization in health care and medicine have been increasing over the last two decades, with growing evidence showing their effectiveness (Noar et al., 2010). One important limitation in the healthcare personalization literature is equating it to genomics-supported efforts in medicine. Genomic markers are only one dimension of personalization that helps to recognize the uniqueness of individuals and make their medicine personalized (Cesuroglu et al., 2016). There are other factors that affect this personalization of health care, such as people's lifestyle choices, their socioeconomic context and living environment, and other healthcare services that can be personalized like health education and therapies (Barnard et al., 2014).

Dialogue systems can offer fine-grained possibilities to personalize the information to be delivered to a user on the basis of their deduced goals, intent, knowledge beliefs, and everything that has previously been said in the conversation (Bickmore and Giorgino, 2006).

Learning from a history of previous conversations plays a key role in ensuring the continuity of health communications that take place over multiple interactions over time. A review of behavior change interventions put forward four intervention groups according to their degree of personalization in the messages delivered to individuals:

(1) Generic: one-size-fits-all messages
(2) Personalized: messages with the person's name
(3) Targeted: messages specific to a subgroup of the general population
(4) Tailored: messages specific to an individual's characteristics

Personalization is primarily used for tailoring the content to be delivered. Personalized content includes:

(1) feedback on mood states (Fitzpatrick et al., 2017), narrative skills, symptom summaries (Rhee et al., 2014), meditation practice (Hudlicka, 2016), and current progress towards the goals set (Sillice et al., 2018);
(2) reminders, warnings, and alerts (Harper et al., 2008a);
(3) multimedia;
(4) questions on pain and physical activity (Kocielnik et al., 2018) and health status.

8.2 Interaction in the mental space

The user interface can be personalized through changing conversational styles according to users' motivation state, level of expertise with the system, and dialogue history (Hudlicka, 2016). The author used either didactic, relational, or motivational conversational styles based on the user profile and progress. While the learning style was used for training-related conversations, the relational style was used at the beginning of sessions to retain the user through the dialogue. The motivational style was leveraged to gather information on learner progress and then to provide customized responses to support users.

Although the technology behind smart chatbots is continuously being developed, these bots are still far from full human-level language abilities, resulting in misunderstanding and users dissatisfaction (Lewis and Monnet, 2017). Furthermore, as ML algorithms evolve, it is becoming increasingly hard to keep track of chatbots' performance, evolution, and the inference behind their responses. Although the black-box effect appears to be an unavoidable consequence of the use of AI, there is some emerging research on making AI transparent and explainable (Galitsky and Goldberg, 2019; Rai, 2019; Tudor Car et al., 2020). Nowadays, however, its use may affect the safety and efficiency of treatment and should be thoroughly assessed and evaluated in the healthcare domain.

Chatbots are evolving from conducting simple transactional tasks towards more involved complex tasks such as long-term disease management (Fitzpatrick et al., 2017) and behavior change (Kowatsch et al., 2017). Most of the conversational agents target patients, with only a few aimed at healthcare professionals, for example, by automating patient intake or aiding in patient triage and diagnosis.

Fitzpatrick et al. (2017) built a dialogue system to include the following therapeutic process-oriented features:

- *Empathic responses*: The chatbot replied in an empathic way appropriate to the recognized mood of the user. For example, in response to a lack of empathy from the human user, the chatbot might say "Sorry you are feeling lonely. I guess we all feel a little alienated sometimes." If the human peer displays excitement, the chatbot replies "Cool, I am happy to hear that!" (Galitsky, 2021c).
- *Tailoring*: Specific content is sent to individuals depending on mood state. For example, a participant indicating that they feel anxious is offered in vivo assistance with the anxious event.
- *Goal setting*: The conversational agent asked participants if they had a personal goal that they hoped to achieve over the 2-week period.
- *Accountability*: To facilitate a sense of accountability, the chatbot set expectations of regular check-ins and followed up on earlier activities, for example, on the status of the stated goal.
- *Motivation and engagement*: To engage the individual in daily monitoring, the bot sent one personalized message every day or every other day to initiate a conversation (i.e., prompting). In addition, "emojis" and animated gifs with messages that provide positive reinforcement can be used to encourage effort and completion of tasks.
- *Reflection*: The bot also provided weekly charts depicting each participant's mood over time. Each graph was sent with a brief description of the data to facilitate reflection, for example, "Overall, your mood has been fairly steady, though you tend to become tired after periods of anxiety. It looks like Tuesday was your best day."

Persistent chatbots are especially valuable in organizations that cannot assure a systematic approach to education (Galitsky, 2020). Persistent chatbots can train whole teams, not just individual members (Fig. 23).

Two major themes emerge in respect to this question concerning favorite features of a social bot: process and content. In the process theme, the subthemes that emerged were accountability from daily check-ins, the empathy that the bot showed, or other factors relating to the bot's "personality"; and the learning that the bot facilitated, which in turn was divided into further subthemes of emotional insight, general insight, and insights about cognitions (Fig. 24).

FIG. 23

A persistent chatbot can train a team of trainees.

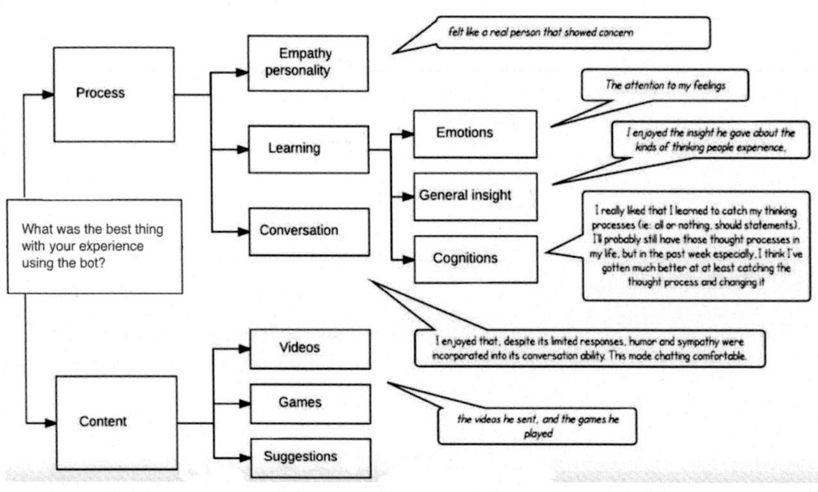

FIG. 24

A thematic map of participants' most favored features of their experience of using the bot.

Dazeley et al. (2021) defined the levels of explanation and described how they can be integrated to create a human-aligned conversational explanation system. The authors surveyed current approaches and discussed the integration of different technologies to achieve these levels with Broad eXplainable Artificial Intelligence (Broad-XAI), and thereby attempted to achieve high-level, "strong" explanations.

8.3 Persuasive dialogue

In (Galitsky, 2021a), we built a social chatbot that delivers content in the form of virtual dialogues automatically produced from plain texts extracted and selected from documents. Given an initial query, this chatbot finds documents, extracts topics from them, organizes these topics in clusters, receives from the user clarification on which cluster is most relevant, and provides the content for this cluster (Leouski and Croft, 1996; Tunkelang, 2018). This content is provided in the form of a virtual dialogue so that the answers are derived from the found and selected documents and its split results, and questions are automatically generated for these answers.

We attempted to advance the ease of generating high-quality, multi-modal content for both non-professional and expert content creators and chatbot developers. Virtual dialogue is defined as a multi-turn dialogue between imaginary agents obtained as a result of content transformation. It is designed with the goal of effective information representation and is intended to resemble as closely as possible a genuine dialogue.

We present a chatbot session that not only provides a user with the content on their topic of interest, but also imitates the user's conversations with their proponents and a dispute with their opponents, as the user's own opinion is expected to evolve (Fig. 25). The user starts a session with a topic and the chatbot forms the clusters, some of them supporting a positive view of this topic and others defeating it. The chatbot consults the sources (in this case, public URLs) and extracts the content from each page (or documents) expected to be relevant for the query. The formed clusters are shown as a list so that the user can select the element that is the closest to their opinion and share it in their own words.

Once the user states their opinion, a virtual dialogue is automatically formed from available documents and pages, simulating a conversation between virtual proponents and opponents and virtual bots. The user can read the whole conversation thread, join the discussion they believe is the most intriguing, or formulate a question to the thread participant. Given this question, the chatbot takes the user to the part of the virtual discussion thread as close to their question as possible, but with an opposite opinion.

The main purpose of a virtual dialogue is to present content in an informal, social, and comprehensive way in comparison to providing just a plain text description of a topic or addressing this topic via a document. A virtual dialogue form is expected to be more engaging so that the user can ask their own questions and organically join the dialogue.

Once the chatbot forms the topics for clarification of the user search intent, it shows the user a list.

The user selects the topic of interest and requests a specific answer via the topic number of the topic expression. Once the answer is read, there are multiple options:

- accept the answer and conclude the session
- navigate to the next answer from the chatbot list
- navigate to a specific answer from the chatbot list

User>**ideology of political correctness** Bot>
exploring https://theimaginativeconservative.org/2015/04/the-reality-of-the-political-correctness-ideology.html
exploring https://www.spiked-online.com/2018/10/16/political-correctness-an-elite-ideology
exploring https://www.nationalists.org/pdf/political_correctness_a_short_history_of_an_ideology.pdf
...
These are the opinions on the topic. Which one do you want to argue for or against? 'criticism of its favored constituencies and ideologies'. 'commentators on the political left'. 'flagellate themselves for their white privilege'. 'an elite preoccupation should surprise no one'[2]. 'is directly derived from classical Marxism'. politically correct and politically incorrect brands... User> **classical Marxism [3]**
Bot> Deconstruction. proves that any text, past or present, illustrates the oppression of blacks, women, homosexuals, etc. by reading that meaning into words of the text (regardless of their. actual meaning). For cultural Marxists, the analysis is linguistic. *Please provide your arguments for/against the claim or proceed to virtual dialogue*
User > **I think Marxism does not necessarily associated with the political correctness** Bot> This is what other people who are your opponents chat about the topic:

> User1> 80 Percent Of Americans Think Political Correctness Is An Issue ?
> Bot1> Among devoted conservatives, 97% believe that political correctness is a problem .
> User2> 10 Hilarious Examples Of Political Correctness Gone Mad ?
> Bot2>Progressive activists are the only group that strongly backs political correctness
> User3> What happens in the country sank into political correctness? Youth isn't a good proxy for support of political correctness and it turns out race isn't either. Whites are ever so slightly less likely than average to believe ...

User> **Is it OK to have an ideology in general?**
Bot> These are the fragments from the thread that try to convince you:

> User3> Do you want to abandon the ideological system ?
> Bot3>But the ideology can not adjust to reality. Ideology takes an intellectual system
> User4>What kind?
> Bot2>a product of one or more philosophers , and says 'This system must be true'

FIG. 25

A persuasive chatbot session with conventional and virtual dialogues.

- reject this answer and attempt to reformulate the query
- reduce search to a specified web domain (such as quota.com, for example)
- proceed in the same direction to more search results in the form of a virtual persuasive dialogue

The user selects the last option and the chatbot builds a virtual dialogue. It is a conversation between imaginary people, but the topic stays the same, matching the original query. Virtual dialogues are shown in frames. If the imaginary chatbot responds to the same person, the dialogue is intended to stay cohesive; coreferences in the follow-up questions are maintained. The main dialogue can be viewed as a one in the meta-level, and the object-level dialogue is naturally embedded into the meta-level one.

Campillos-Llanos et al. (2020) designed a dialogue system with a focus on handling a wide variety of medical specialties and clinical cases. The authors designed a patient record model, a knowledge model for the task, and an ontological model that merged structured thesauri with linguistic, terminological, and ontological knowledge. A frame- and rule-based approach and terminology-rich resources were leveraged to handle the medical dialogue in French. An evaluation shows that the system achieved high vocabulary coverage of 98% in unseen cases.

9. Conclusions

A data-driven chatbot forms a reply, *averaging* through several similar text fragments and dialogue fragments to construct a smooth and plausible dialogue. Whereas such dialogue can be accepted by a human annotator as meaningful, the conversation built by averaging does not bring any purpose. Optimizing a conversation for perplexity makes sure the focus of this conversation is evolving but does not bring a bit of a meaning to transmit between the peers, or for the reader of this conversation. Learning from more data makes sure any utterance of a user is well represented in the training set for averaging but does not make a conversation more meaningful either.

A conversation starting with "*Hi*" and followed by "*I am well/How are you*" is carried out for the sake of continuing this dialogue in time and keeping the conversers busy. Conversely, we propose a conversation mode with a clear target of informing a user by delivering a certain chunk of knowledge, in a comprehensive, systematic, and explainable way.

In conclusion, we state that our evaluation covered the effectiveness and user satisfaction of the proposed DT navigation approach. We summarize that the traversal of the DT for the purpose of learning a short text in the educational context is more efficient than a traditional data-driven dialogue management approach.

Supplementary data sets

Please visit https://github.com/bgalitsky/relevance-based-on-parse-trees to access all supplementary data sets.

References

Adiwardana, D., Luong, M.-T., So, D., Hall, J., Fiedel, N., Thoppilan, R., Yang, Z., Kulshreshtha, A., Nemade, G., Lu, Y., Le, Q., 2020. Towards a Human-like Open-Domain Chatbot. arxiv.org/abs/2001.09977.

Barnard, K.D., Lloyd, C.E., Dyson, P.A., Davies, M.J., O'Neil, S., Naresh, K., Lawton, J., Ziegler, R., Holt, R.I.G., 2014. Kaleidoscope model of diabetes care: time for a rethink? Diabet. Med. 31 (5), 522–530. https://doi.org/10.1111/dme.12400.

Bickmore, T., Giorgino, T., 2006. Health dialog systems for patients and consumers. J. Biomed. Inform. 39 (5), 556–571. https://doi.org/10.1016/j.jbi.2005.12.004.

Bickmore, T., Schulman, D., Sidner, C., 2013. Automated interventions for multiple health behaviors using conversational agents. Patient Educ. Couns. 92 (2), 142–148.

Bochman, A., 2013. A Logical Theory of Nonmonotonic Inference and Belief Change. Springer BM.

Bordes, A., Boureau, Y.-L., Weston, J., 2016. Learning End-to-End Goal-Oriented Dialog. arXiv:1605.07683.

Campillos-Llanos, L., Thomas, C., Bilinski, É., Zweigenbaum, P., Rosset, S., 2020. Designing a virtual patient dialogue system based on terminology-rich resources: challenges and evaluation. Nat. Lang. Eng. 26 (2), 183–220.

Cesuroglu, T., Syurina, E., Feron, F., Krumeich, A., 2016. Other side of the coin for personalised medicine and healthcare: content analysis of 'personalised' practices in the literature. BMJ Open 6 (7). https://doi.org/10.1136/bmjopen-2015-010243, e010243.

Crutzen, R., Peters, G.-J., Portugal, S., Fisser, E., Jorne, J., 2011. An artificially intelligent chat agent that answers adolescents' questions related to sex, drugs, and alcohol: an exploratory study. J. Adolesc. Health. 48, 514–519. https://doi.org/10.1016/j.jadohealth.2010.09.002.

Dazeley, R., Vamplew, P., Foale, C., Young, C., Aryal, S., Cruz, F., 2021. Levels of explainable artificial intelligence for human-aligned conversational explanations. Artif. Intell. 299, 1–29.

de Vries, H., Brug, J., 1999. Computer-tailored interventions motivating people to adopt health promoting behaviours: introduction to a new approach. Patient Educ. Couns. 36, 99–105.

DeepPavlov, 2019. Deep Pavlov Chatbot Dev platform. https://deeppavlov.ai/.

Dung, P., 1995. On the acceptability of arguments and its fundamental role in nonmonotonic reasoning, logic programming, and n-person games. Artif. Intell. 77, 321–357.

Edwards, R.A., Bickmore, T., Jenkins, L., Foley, M., Manjourides, J., 2013. Use of an interactive computer agent to support breastfeeding. Matern. Child Health J. 17 (10), 1961–1968.

Erenel, Z., Altınçay, H., 2012. Nonlinear transformation of term frequencies for term weighting in text categorization. Eng. Appl. Arti. Intell. 25 (7), 1505–1514.

Finch, S., Finch, J., Ahmadvand, A., Ingyu, C., Dong, X., Qi, R., Sahijwani, H., Volokhin, S., Wang, Z., Wang, Z., Choi, J., 2020. Emora: An Inquisitive Social Chatbot Who Cares For You. https://arxiv.org/abs/2009.04617.

Fitzpatrick, K.K., Darcy, A., Vierhile, M., 2017. Delivering cognitive behavior therapy to young adults with symptoms of depression and anxiety using a fully automated conversational agent (Woebot): a randomized controlled trial. JMIR Ment. Health 4 (2). https://doi.org/10.2196/mental.7785, e19.

Galitsky, B., 2013. Exhaustive simulation of consecutive mental states of human agents. Knowl. Based Syst. 43, 1–20.

Galitsky, B., 2016. Theory of mind engine. In: Computational Autism. Springer, Cham.

Galitsky, B., 2017a. Improving relevance in a content pipeline via syntactic generalization. Eng. Appl. Artif. Intell. 58, 1–26.

Galitsky, B., 2017b. Discovering rhetoric agreement between a request and response. Dialogue Discourse 8 (2), 167–205.

Galitsky, B., 2019a. A content management system for chatbots. In: Developing Enterprise Chatbots. Springer, Cham.

Galitsky, B., 2019b. Building chatbot thesaurus. In: Developing Enterprise Chatbots. Springer, Cham.

Galitsky, B., 2019c. Chatbot components and architectures. In: Developing Enterprise Chatbots. Springer, Cham.

Galitsky, B., 2020. Identifying distributed incompetence in an organization. In: Lawless, W.F., Mittu, R., Sofge, D. (Eds.), Human-Machine Shared Contexts. Elsevier, pp. 315–340.

Galitsky, B., 2021a. Distributional semantics for CRM: making Word2vec models robust by structurizing them. In: Artificial Intelligence for Customer Relationship Management: Keeping Customers Informed. Springer, Cham.

Galitsky, B., 2021b. Chatbots for CRM and dialogue management. In: Artificial Intelligence for Customer Relationship Management: Solving Customer Problems. Springer, Cham.

Galitsky, B., 2021c. Adjusting chatbot conversation to user personality and mood. In: Artificial Intelligence for Customer Relationship Management: Solving Customer Problems. Springer, Cham, pp. 92–128.

Galitsky, B., Goldberg, S., 2019. Explainable machine learning for chatbots. In: Developing Enterprise Chatbots. Springer, Cham.

Galitsky, B., Ilvovsky, D.I., 2017a. On a chat bot finding answers with optimal rhetoric representation. In: RANLP, pp. 253–259.

Galitsky, B., Ilvovsky, D.I., 2017b. Chatbot with a discourse structure-driven dialogue management. In: Proceedings of the Software Demonstrations of the 15th Conference of the European Chapter of the Association for Computational Linguistics, pp. 87–90.

Galitsky, B., Ilvovsky, D., 2018. Building dialogue structure from discourse tree of a question. In: Proceedings of the 2018 EMNLP Workshop SCAI.

Galitsky, B., Pascu, A., 2006. Epistemic categorization for analysis of customer complaints. In: FLAIRS Conference, pp. 291–296.

Galitsky, B., Ilvovsky, D., Lebedeva, N., Usikov, D., 2014. Improving trust in automation of social promotion. In: AAAI Spring Symposium-Technical Report, pp. 28–35.

Galitsky, B., Ilvovsky, D., Goncharova, E., 2019. On a chatbot conducting dialogue-in-dialogue. In: Proceedings of the 20th Annual SIGdial Meeting on Discourse and Dialogue.

Ghazvininejad, M., Brockett, C., Chang, M., Dolan, B., Gao, J., Yih, W., Galley, M., 2017. A Knowledge-Grounded Neural Conversation Model. arXiv:1702.01932.

Giorgino, T., Azzini, I., Rognoni, C., Quaglini, S., Stefanelli, M., Gretter, R., Falavigna, D., 2005. Automated spoken dialogue system for hypertensive patient home management. Int. J. Med. Inform. 74, 159–167. https://doi.org/10.1016/j.ijmedinf.2004.04.026.

Goyal, P., Hu, Z., Liang, X., Wang, C., Xing, E.P., 2017. Nonparametric variational auto-encoders for hierarchical representation learning. In: Proceedings of the IEEE International Conference on Computer Vision, Sinaia, Romania, 19–21 October, pp. 5094–5102.

Harper, R., Nicholl, P., McTear, M., Wallace, J., Black, L., Kearney, P., 2008a. Automated phone capture of diabetes patients readings with consultant monitoring via the web. In: The 15th Annual IEEE International Conference and Workshop on the Engineering of Computer Based Systems; March 31–April 04; Belfast. 2018, pp. 219–226.

Hudlicka, E., 2016. Computational analytical framework for affective modeling: towards guidelines for designing. In: Psychology and Mental Health: Concepts, Methodologies, Tools, and Applications, pp. 1–64.

Ireland, D., Atay, C., Liddle, J., Bradford, D., Lee, H., Rushin, O., Mullins, T., Angus, D., Wiles, J., McBride, S., Vogel, A., 2016. Hello Harlie: enabling speech monitoring through chat-bot conversations. Stud. Health Technol. Inform. 227, 55–60. 27440289.

Kim, J., Oh, S., Kwon, O.-W., Kim, H., 2019. Multi-turn chatbot based on query-context attentions and dual wasserstein generative adversarial networks. Appl. Sci. 9, 3908. https://doi.org/10.3390/app9183908.

Kipper, K., Korhonen, A., Ryant, N., Palmer, M., 2008. A large-scale classification of English verbs. Lang. Resour. Eval. J. 42, 21–40.

Kocielnik, R., Xiao, L., Avrahami, D., Hsieh, G., 2018. Reflection companion: a conversational system for engaging users in reflection on physical activity. Proc. ACM Interact. Mob. Wearable Ubiquitous Technol. 2 (2), 1–26. https://doi.org/10.1145/3214273.

Kowatsch, T., Volland, D., Shih, I., Rüegger, D., Künzler, F., Barata, F., 2017. Design and evaluation of a mobile chat app for the open source behavioral health intervention platform MobileCoach. In: Chatbots International Conference on Design Science Research in Information System and Technology; DESRIST 2017; May 30–June 1, 2017; Karlsruhe, Germany.

Laranjo, L., Dunn, A.G., Tong, H.L., Kocaballi, A.B., Chen, J., Bashir, R., Surian, D., Gallego, B., Magrabi, F., Lau, A.U.S., Coiera, E., 2018. Conversational agents in healthcare: a systematic review. J. Am. Med. Inform. Assoc. 25 (9), 1248–1258.

Lei, W., Jin, X., Kan, M.-Y., Ren, Z., He, X., Yin, D., 2018. Sequicity: simplifying task-oriented dialogue systems with single sequence-to-sequence architectures. In: Proceedings of the 56th Annual Meeting of the Association for Computational Linguistics. vol. 1, pp. 1437–1447.

Leouski, A.V., Croft, W.B., 1996. An evaluation of techniques for clustering search results. In: UMass Tech Report #76. https://ciir.cs.umass.edu/pubfiles/ir-76.pdf.

Lewis, C., Monnet, D., 2017. AI and Machine Learning Black Boxes: The Need for Transparency and Accountability. KDnuggets News. https://www.kdnuggets.com/2017/04/ai-machine-learning-black-boxes-transparency-accountability.html.

López-Cózar, R., Callejas, Z., Espejo, G., Griol, D., 2011. Enhancement of conversational agents by means of multimodal interaction. In: Conversational Agents and Natural Language Interaction: Techniques and Effective Practices, pp. 223–253, https://doi.org/10.4018/978-1-60960-617-6.ch010.

Lucas, G., Rizzo, A., Gratch, J., Scherer, S., Stratou, G., Boberg, J., Morency, L., 2017. Reporting mental health symptoms: breaking down barriers to care with virtual human interviewers. Front. Robotics 4, 51.

Lukin, S.M., Gervits, F., Hayes, C., Moolchandani, P., Leuski, A., Rogers, J., Amaro, C.S., Marge, M., Voss, C., Traum, D., 2018. Scoutbot: a dialogue system for collaborative navigation. In: Proceedings of ACL 2018, System Demonstrations, pp. 93–98.

Mann, W., Thompson, S., 1988. Rhetorical structure theory: toward a functional theory of text organization. Text 8 (3), 243–281.

McCall, B., 2020. Could Telemedicine Solve the Cancer Backlog? The Lancet Digital Health.

McTear, M.F., 2002. Spoken dialogue technology: enabling the conversational user interface. ACM Comput. Surv. 34 (1), 90–169.

Miner, A.S., Milstein, A., Schueller, S., Hegde, R., Mangurian, C., Linos, E., 2016. Smartphone-based conversational agents and responses to questions about mental health, interpersonal violence, and physical health. JAMA Intern. Med. 176 (5), 619–625. https://doi.org/10.1001/jamainternmed.2016.0400.

Mrksic, N., Seaghdha, D.O., Wen, T.H., Thomson, B., Young, S., 2016. Neural Belief Tracker: Data-Driven Dialogue State Tracking. arXiv preprint arXiv:1606.03777.

Noar, S.M., Grant Harrington, N., Van Stee, S.K., Shemanski, A.R., 2010. Tailored health communication to change lifestyle behaviors. Am. J. Lifestyle Med. 5 (2), 112–122. https://doi.org/10.1177/1559827610387255.

Philip, P., Bioulac, S., Sauteraud, A., Chaufton, C., Olive, J., 2014. Could a virtual human be used to explore excessive daytime sleepiness in patients? Presence Teleop. Virt. Environ 23 (4), 369–376.

Radziwill, N.M., Benton, M.C., 2017. Evaluating Quality of Chatbots and Intelligent Conversational Agents. arXiv preprint. 1704.04579 1–21.

Rai, A., 2019. Explainable AI: from black box to glass box. J. Acad. Mark. Sci. 48, 137–141.

Rhee, H., Allen, J., Mammen, J., Swift, M., 2014. Mobile phone-based asthma self-management aid for adolescents (mASMAA): a feasibility study. Patient Prefer. Adherence 8, 63–72. https://doi.org/10.2147/PPA.S53504.

Rigo-Lemini, M., Martínez-Navarro, B., 2017. Epistemic states of convincement. a conceptualization from the practice of mathematicians and neurobiology. In: Understanding Emotions in Mathematical Thinking and Learning. Academic Press, pp. 97–131.

Salton, G., Yang, C.S., 1973. On the specification of term values in automatic indexing. J. Doc. 29, 351–372.

Shang, L., Lu, Z., Li, H., 2015. Neural responding machine for short-text conversation. In: Proceedings of the 53rd Annual Meeting of the Association for Computational Linguistics and the 7th International Joint Conference on Natural Language Processing, Beijing, China, 26–31 July. vol. 1, pp. 1577–1586.

Shen, T., Lei, T., Barzilay, R., Jaakkola, T., 2017. Style transfer from non-parallel text by cross-alignment. In: Guyon, I., Luxburg, U.V., Bengio, S., Wallach, H., Fergus, R., Vishwanathan, S., Garnett, R. (Eds.), Advances in Neural Information Processing Systems. Curran Associates, Inc, Red Hook, NY, pp. 6830–6841.

Shen, X., Su, H., Niu, S., Demberg, V., 2018. Improving variational encoder-decoders in dialogue generation. In: Proceedings of the Thirty-Second AAAI Conference on Artificial Intelligence, Lyon, France, 23–27 April.

Sillice, M.A., Morokoff, P.J., Ferszt, G., Bickmore, T., Bock, B.C., Lantini, R., Velicer, W.F., 2018. Using relational agents to promote exercise and sun protection: assessment of participants' experiences with two interventions. J. Med. Internet Res. 20 (2). https://doi.org/10.2196/jmir.7640, e48.

Trstenjak, B., Sasa, M., Donko, D., 2013. KNN with TF-IDF based framework for text categorization. Procedia Eng. 69, 1356–1364.

Tudor Car, L., Dhinagaran, D.A., Kyaw, B.M., Kowatsch, T., Joty, S., Theng, Y.L., Atun, R., 2020. Conversational agents in health care: scoping review and conceptual analysis. J. Med. Internet Res. 22 (8). https://doi.org/10.2196/17158, e17158.

Tunkelang, D., 2018. Search Results Clustering. https://queryunderstanding.com/search-results-clustering-b2fa64c6c809.

Vaswani, A., Shazeer, N., Parmar, N., Uszkoreit, J., Jones, L., Gomez, A.N., Kaiser, Ł., Polosukhin, I., 2017. Attention is all you need. In: Guyon, I., Luxburg, U.V., Bengio, S., Wallach, H., Fergus, R., Vishwanathan, S., Garnett, R. (Eds.), Advances in Neural Information Processing Systems. Curran Associates, Inc, Red Hook, NY, pp. 5998–6008.

Venkatesh, A., Khatri, C., Ram, A., Guo, F., Gabriel, R., Nagar, A., Prasad, R., Cheng, M., Hedayatnia, B., Metallinou, A., Goel, R., Yang, S., Raju, A., 2018. On Evaluating and Comparing Conversational Agents. CoRR, abs/1801.03625.

Watson, A., Bickmore, T., Cange, A., Kulshreshtha, A., Kvedar, J., 2012. An internet-based virtual coach to promote physical activity adherence in overweight adults: randomized controlled trial. J. Med. Internet Res. 14 (1), e1.6.

Xu, L., Zhou, Q., Gong, K., Liang, X., Tang, J., Lin, L., 2019. End-to-end knowledge-routed relational dialogue system for automatic diagnosis. In: Proceedings of the AAAI Conference on Artificial Intelligence. vol. 33, pp. 7346–7353.

Yi, Z., Chu, X., Li, P., 2019. Constructing Chinese macro discourse tree via multiple views and word pair similarity. In: International Conference on Natural Language Processing and Chinese Computing, pp. 773–786.

Young, T., Cambria, E., Chaturvedi, I., Huang, M., Zhou, H., Biswas, S., 2018. Augmenting End-to-End Dialog Systems with Commonsense Knowledge. https://arxiv.org/abs/1709.05453.

Yu, C., Aoki, P.M., Woodruff, A., 2004. Detecting User Engagement in Everyday Conversations. arXiv preprint cs/0410027.

CHAPTER

Building medical ontologies relying on communicative discourse trees 11

Boris Galitsky[a] and Dmitry Ilvovsky[b]

Oracle Corporation, Redwood City, CA, United States[a]

Computer Science, HSE University, Moscow, Russia[b]

1. Introduction

Building and adapting medical ontologies is a complex task that requires substantial human effort and a close collaboration between domain experts such as health professionals and knowledge engineers. Even if automatic ontology construction techniques are mature enough to support this task (Liu et al., 2011), they provide only partial solutions, and manual interventions from healthcare professionals will always be necessary when high quality is expected. One of the focuses of health ontologies is a representation of medical terminologies. Health professionals use them to represent knowledge about symptoms and treatments of diseases, and pharmaceutical enterprises use ontologies to represent information about drugs, dosages, and allergies.

Ontologies are a foundation for numerous decision support systems (DSSs) used to support medical activities; therefore the quality of the underlying ontologies affects the results of using DSSs that rely on these ontologies. In consequence, automatically built medical ontologies (including schema knowledge and individual descriptions) must be validated by domain experts (Goldberg et al., 2019). However, healthcare professionals are usually not fluent in ontology management and must be assisted by knowledge engineers during the validation process, which can potentially extend errors and inconsistencies (Galitsky and Goldberg, 2019).

Medical records are one of the most valuable sources of information and data on patients' treatments. These records contain important items such as eligibility criteria, a summary of diagnosis results, and prescribed drugs, which are normally recorded in unstructured free text. Extracting medical or clinical information from health records is an important task, especially with the adoption of electronic health records (EHRs). These records are normally stored as text documents and contain valuable unstructured information that is essential for better decision-making for a patient's treatment (Chapters 2 and 3).

Gaining insight from a tremendous amount of unstructured clinical data has been a critical and challenging issue for medical organizations such as hospitals. Having an automated system that can read patients' medical reports, extract medical entities, analyze the extracted data using the stored knowledge, and present the analyses to clinicians/users in a visualized form is not only very desirable but also a necessity. The hard part is how to extract and encode the unstructured data to improve an overall healthcare system. Information extraction (IE) and text mining (TM) are potentially suitable techniques

Artificial Intelligence for Healthcare Applications and Management. https://doi.org/10.1016/B978-0-12-824521-7.00001-6

here. There are three major elements that should be extracted from these clinical records: entities, attributes, and relations between them (Jusoh et al., 2020).

Automatic recognition of medical entities in an unstructured text is a key component of biomedical information retrieval systems. Its applications include analysis of unstructured text in EHRs (Arbabi et al., 2019) and knowledge discovery from the biomedical literature (Gonzalez et al., 2016). Many medical terminologies are structured as ontologies, adding relations between entities and often including several synonyms for each term.

Ontologies are a critical component for these tasks, and the quality and consistency of an ontology automatically extracted from text determine the overall decision support system (DSS) accuracy (Galitsky, 2003). The bottleneck of building concise, robust, and complete ontologies is due to the lack of a mechanism to extract ontology entries from reliable, authoritative parts of documents. Building ontologies, one needs to use reliable text fragments expressing the central point of a text, and avoid constructing entries from additional comments, clarifications, examples, instances and other less significant parts of text (Galitsky, 2019b). We rely on discourse analysis (that has been proven useful for tasks like summarization) to select discourse units that yield ontology entries.

1.1 Ontology extraction from text

Usually, retrieved information takes the form of sets of entities bound by a relation (Banko et al., 2007). Information presented in this format is useful for many applications (mining biomedical text, ontology learning, and question answering). Ontologies structure knowledge as a set of terms with edges between them that are labeled as relational information to evoke meaningful information. Ontologies serve as the backbone of the semantic web concept that aims to provide meaningful information on the Web (Cimiano, 2006).

Open IE facilitates the domain-independent discovery of relations extracted from text and readily scales to the diversity and size of the Web corpus (Del Corro and Gemulla, 2013). The features of open IE are its domain independence, its unsupervised methods to retrieve relational data, and scalability to large corpora. Open IE system TextRunner (Banko et al., 2007), which does not require a training set compared to previous approaches, employs a combination of dependency parsing, labeling of terms and Naive Bayes probability estimates for each identified relation.

Open language learning for information extraction (OLLIE; Schmitz et al., 2012) is another important open IE method that leverages dependency parsing, improving the extraction triples by incorporating contextual information implied in the sentence. This method extracts triples by utilizing nouns and adjectives instead of solely relying on verb-based predication, utilizing either shallow parsing (parts of speech identification and chunking) techniques or dependency parsing. With the former, there is a cost of diminished recall for high precision, and the latter provides better precision and recall but with lowered efficiency.

1.2 Text mining

Text mining (TM) is extracting useful knowledge from textual data, not necessarily in the form of an ontology. TM inputs a collection of textual and unstructured input data that is standardized and cleaned in a preprocessing step. Typically, TM includes a process of structuring the unstructured input, transforming data into a suitable representation model, and easing the final knowledge

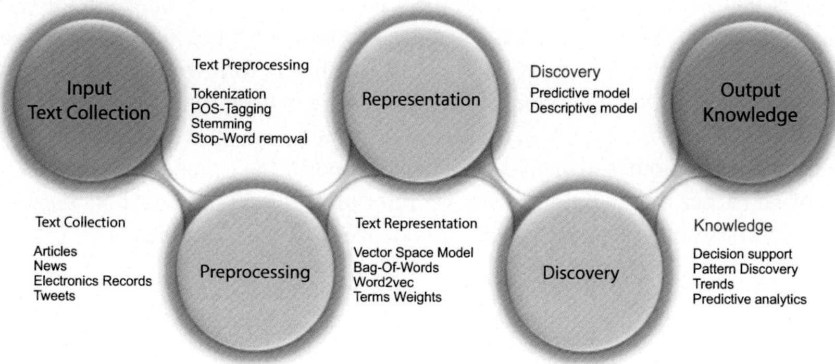

FIG. 1

Text mining (TM) steps.

discovery process in which useful, unknown, and high-quality information is extracted from the textual input data (Luque et al., 2018).

TM usually includes (Fig. 1):

(1) text-based prediction
(2) patterns identification
(3) formulation and revision of new hypotheses
(4) named entities recognition
(5) relationship extraction
(6) document classification
(7) summarization

2. Introducing discourse features

In this section, we continue our exploration of how discourse analysis assists in artificial intelligence (AI) for health, continuing our considerations in Chapters 2, 3, and 6–10. Discourse commonly comprises a sequence of sentences, although it can be found even within a single sentence, for example, the connected sequence of eventualities such as actions, resultant states, and events.

Within a discourse, the patterns formed by its sentences mean that the whole conveys more than the sum of its separate parts. While each sentence in the example below is a simple assertion.

"*Don't worry about the water source exhausting today. It is already tomorrow in some parts of the Earth.*"

The latter sentence is meant to be connected with the former with the rhetorical relation of *Reason* for *not worrying*.

Discourse analysis leverages language features, which allow speakers to specify that they are:

(1) talking about something they have talked about before in the same discourse
(2) indicating a relation that holds between the states, events, beliefs, and so on presented in the discourse
(3) changing to a new topic or resuming one from earlier in the discourse

Language features that allow a speaker to specify a relation that holds between the states, events, beliefs, and so on presented in the discourse include subordinating conjunctions such as "*until*" or "*unless*" and discourse adverbials such as "*as a result*," as in the following:

"*Birds have wings. As a result, they can fly unless they are too heavy and wings cannot support their weight.*"

Language features in discourse also give speakers an opportunity to specify a change to a new topic or resumption of an earlier one including what we refer to as *cue phrases* or boundary features.

It is reasonable to associate discourse with a sequence of sentences that:

(1) conveys more than its individual sentences through their relationships to one another; and
(2) leverages special features of language that enable discourse to be more easily understood.

Discourse can be structured by its topics, each comprising a set of entities and a limited range of things being said about them. A topic structure is common in the expository text found in schoolbooks, encyclopedias, and reference materials. A topic can be characterized by the question it addresses. Each topic involves a set of entities, which may (but do not have to) change from topic to topic. Here the entities consist of gliders, their pilots, and passengers; then gliders and their means of propulsion; and then gliders and their launch mechanisms. This aspect of structure has been modeled as entity chains (Barzilay and Lapata, 2008), each a sequence of expressions that refer to the same entity. There are several entity chains in the text about *flu*:

flu → virus → vitamins → their → drinking more liquids → high temperature

When a given entity chain terminates and another chain begins, one can observe an indicator that the discourse has moved from one topically oriented segment to another. This is important for tuple extraction logic in the process of ontology formation from text. Hence discourse-level considerations are helpful when extracting ontology entries from text.

2.1 Discourse-level support for ontology construction

We circumscribe in green the area we intend to extract as a candidate for ontology entry in text, discourse tree (DT), and Abstract Meaning Representation (AMR; Chapter 3) graph in Fig. 2. If there is an explicit logical connection between phrases, we want to capture it in our ontology. Conversely, we are not interested in circumstances, certain interesting facts which happen to come to our attention, such as *Background*(_, "*as my mom asked me to do*"). These phrases we do not want to derive our ontology from, we show in red ovals.

Hence we extract the clause.

suspect(*tuberculosis) -> see(pulmonologists).*

We proceed to a longer example of text:

Oxygen saturation refers to the amount of oxygen that's in your bloodstream. The body requires a specific amount of oxygen in your blood to function properly. The normal range of oxygen saturation for adults is 94 to 99%. However, if your oxygen saturation level is below 90%, you will likely require supplemental oxygen, which is prescribed by your primary care doctor or pulmonologist.

We first look at the entity-relation chart to observe a super-set of candidate triples that would be extracted from text. A DT (Chapter 2) gives us a logical view for which text fragments are

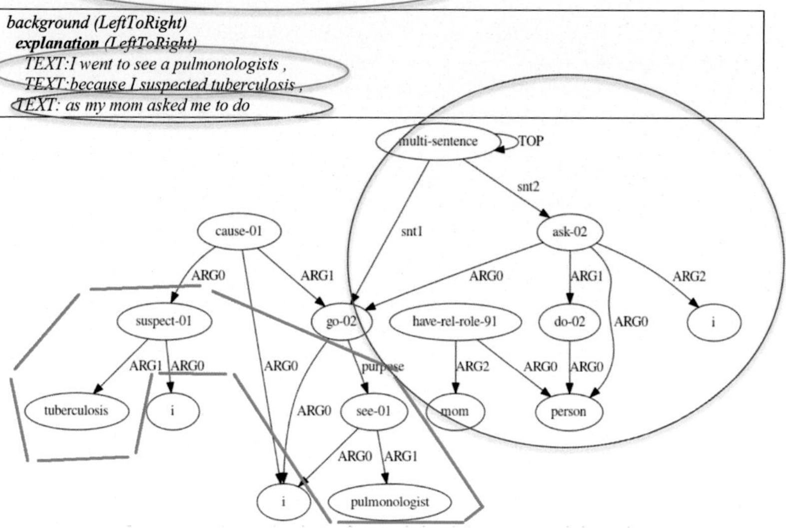

FIG. 2

Logical clause is a reliable hint to extract and formalize an assertion from text.

authoritative, reliable source of relations (shown in green ovals) to be recorded in our ontology, and *which are not (shown in red ovals*; Fig. 3).

Definitional phrases under *Elaboration* are less important and informative. We show such elementary discourse units (EDUs) in *red ovals*:

elaboration
  TEXT:Oxygen saturation refers to the amount of oxygen ,
  TEXT:that is in your bloodstream

oxygen(saturation) = oxygen(amount)
This gives an unreliable synonymy between *saturation* and *amount*

Most important phrases to form ontology entries occur in EDUs for non-trivial relations other than *Elaboration* and *Joint*:

condition → ontology rule.
level(oxygen(), saturation)→require(patient, oxygen(supplemental)).

enablement
enable(doctor(primary_care), oxygen(supplemental)).
enable(pulmonologist (), oxygen(supplemental)).

contrast: extract from nucleus (usual, normal, typical part).
level(oxygen(), saturation) =94…99.

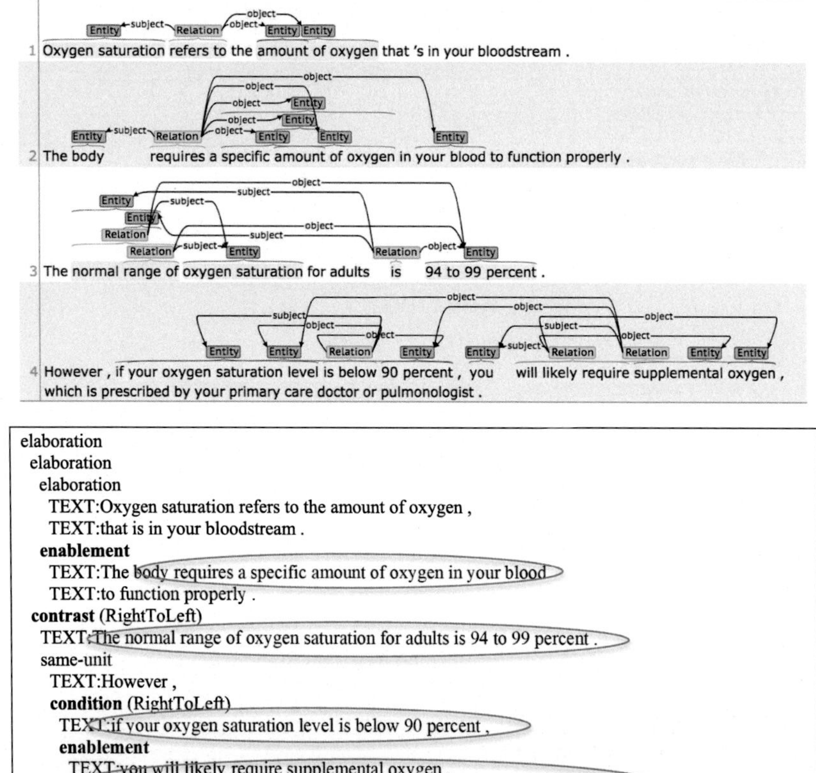

FIG. 3

An entity-relation chart and a DT.

2.2 Issues associated with not using discourse information for ontology entry extraction

We proceed to another example and explore which EDUs are good to form our ontology entries and which are not good. We take a piece of content (MedlinePlus, 2019, Fig. 4) and show that not all phrases are good to extract tuples to form ontology entries.

Default, syntactic, and semantic approaches to entity/tuple extraction consider all highlighted phrases equally. However, some of these phrases are *central* to this text and therefore should serve as a source for relation extraction. At the same time, the rest of phrases are only meaningful in the context of central phrases and should not be used for relation extraction in a standalone mode, to avoid extracting relations that should not be generalized (Galitsky et al., 2011b; Galitsky, 2017a).

Green bolded ovals show the *central* phrases where extracted relations are informative and express the central topic of this text (Fig. 4). Red ovals show the rest of phrases that should not yield entity tuples as they are only informative being attached to the central phrases, not on their own. Therefore,

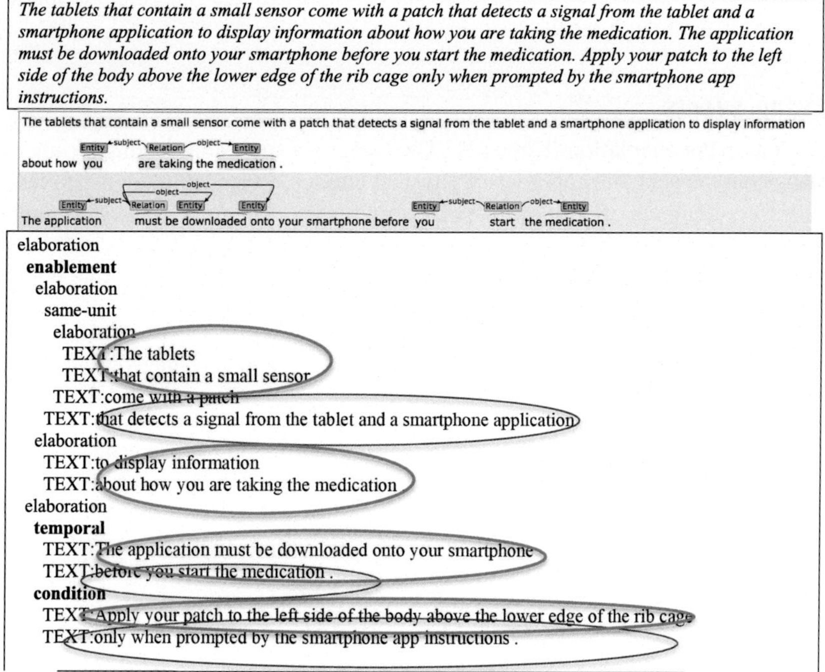

FIG. 4

An entity graph and a DT. Not all phrases are good to extract tuples to form ontology entries.

a candidate ontology entry should not include logical representations for these phrases as they are not meaningful on their own.

In the DT, we see that the central phrase *tablet-contain-sensor* corresponds to the nucleus EDU of the top-level rhetorical relation of *Enablement*. This phrase talks about the *tablet* which is a central topic of this text, and its predicate and object/attribute "*contain a small sensor*." The other important phrase associated with the main entity node "*The tablets*" is "*to display information about how you are taking the medication*."

The satellite EDUs contain phrases that cannot be properly interpreted in a stand-alone mode. "*Come with a patch that detects a signal*" must be interpreted in the context of the tablet. Otherwise, a hypothetical ontology entry *detect(patch, signal)* is too general and does not necessarily hold on its own. A consistent ontology should not generalize from this expression.

As we proceed from the central entity, navigating the DT, we observe that nucleus EDUs are interpretable on their own and can form an ontology entry, and satellite EDUs should not form an ontology entry.

Finally, we extract the following entries:

contain(tablet, sensor(small)).
display(information(take(people, medications)).

Our considerations in this section are similar to indexing important and ignoring unimportant parts of an answer to improve the search recall.

2.3 Annotating events

The GENIA corpus event annotation (Kim et al., 2008) marks expressions stating bio-medical events, defined as changes in the state or properties of physical entities. Event annotations are text-bound association of arbitrary numbers of entities in specific roles (e.g., Theme, Cause). The annotation tags overlap with rhetorical relations (Fig. 5).

Fig. 6 on the top shows a screenshot of the annotation visualization. There are four regions outlined by a box. The top box contains a sentence under annotation:

> *"The binding of I kappa B/MAD-3 to NF-kappa B p65 is sufficient to retarget NF-kappa B p65 from the nucleus to the cytoplasm."*

Other three boxes display an event annotation that has been added to this sentence. The original sentence is shown inside each of those boxes to show text spans that belong to the corresponding annotation. Biological entities, which had been annotated earlier during term annotation, are shown in colors: blue and green indicate protein molecules and cell components, respectively. The terms are expressed as n-tuples of attribute-value pairs as follows:

- (Id: T36, Class: Protein_molecule, Name: I kappa B/MAD-3)
- (Id: T37, Class: Protein_molecule, Name: NF-kappa B p65)
- (Id: T38, Class: Protein_molecule, Name: NF-kappa B p65)
- (Id: T39, Class: Cell_component, Name: nucleus)
- (Id: T40, Class: Cell_component, Name: cytoplasm)

The first event E5 represents binding of the two entities, T36 (I kappa B/MAD-3) and T37 (NF-kappa B p65). This is an indication of the binding event. The *Theme* in an event is an attribute or slot to be filled by an entity or entities whose properties are affected by the event. The second event E6 represents localization of the protein T38. The textual indications, *retarget* and "*to the cytoplasm*," are marked up as key expressions ranging over the event type and the location relevant to the event, respectively.

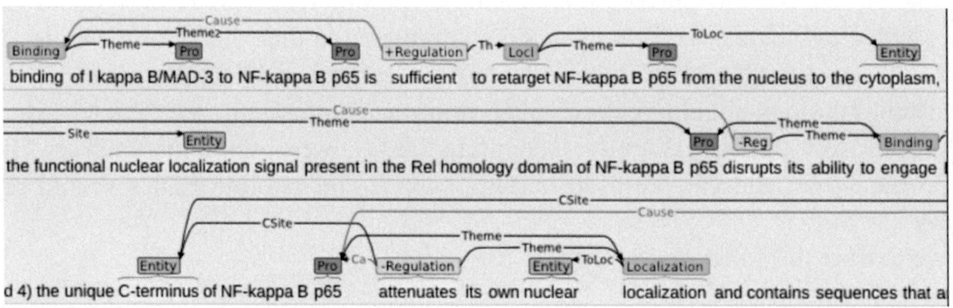

FIG. 5

An example of event annotation.

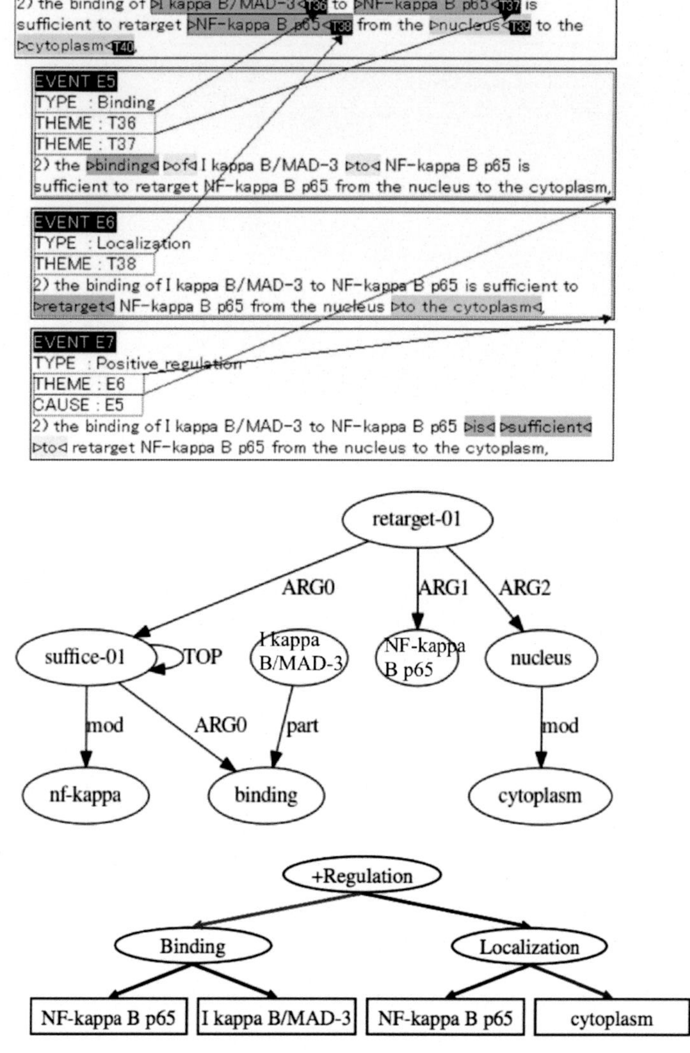

FIG. 6

Annotation visualization (top), AMR graph (middle), and event taxonomy (bottom).

The last event E7 is the *causality* relation between E5 and E6. That is, the binding event (E5) of the two proteins "causes" the localization event (E6) of one of the two proteins. This causality relation is represented as an event of type *Positive_regulation*.

Regulation has a broader definition than regulatory events in a strict biological sense, for example, catalysis, inhibition, up-/down-regulation, and so on. It is used to encode general causality among events. The expression "*is sufficient to*" turns out to be a syntactic cue for *causality*. In Fig. 6 (bottom),

FIG. 7

Complete extraction of ontology entries until the last leaf of the DT.

the ontology entities are shown in rectangular boxes, while event entities are shown in circles. Black, red, and blue arrows indicate a link between an event and its themes, causes, and location, respectively.

Concluding this section on discourse features for text mining, we proceed to Fig. 7, which illustrates a completeness feature of text mining when each EDU forms an ontology entry, "until the last leaf."

3. Informative and uninformative parts of text

Typically, all text in answers is indexed so that "we do not miss anything" in answering possible questions. In this section, we identify a deficiency in this popular belief and discover that not all text in answers should be searchable (and therefore be indexed). A logical organization of answer, expressed via its DT, tells us which parts of an answer should be matched with a question this answer is good for. It also tells us which parts of an answer should not be indexed to avoid misfiring (Galitsky, 2017b).

Once we know important parts of an answer, we can automatically formulate a set of questions this answer is supposed to answer well. Forming a set of such questions would substantially improve the recall of searching sets of Q/A pairs, a popular domain in modern chatbot development. The tools available today to make Q/A pairs searchable, such as QnA Maker by Microsoft, produce systems with very low recall because there should be many-to-one mapping between questions and answers, not a one-to-one mapping.

3.1 Informative and uninformative parts of an answer

A lot of content nowadays is available in the form of Q/A pairs. Starting from frequently asked questions (FAQs) on company portals to customer support logs, Q/A pairs are found to be an efficient way to familiarize users with content by means of browsing. Also, chatbots are now readily available to import the Q/A pairs and provide relevant information via querying. However, the recall of these chatbots is low since only the questions matching the Q part of the pairs can provide relevant answers. If a user question does not match any Q parts of a pair, and is searched against an index of answers, precision of the chatbot answers become very low. Although standard relevance techniques such as ontology, keyword frequency models, and discourse features can be applied, only a rather modest boost in relevance can be achieved.

In a traditional search engine approach all text in answers is indexed. However, not all parts of an answer are equally important. There are some portions of answers (text fragments) that are good to be matched with potential questions, some are neutral, and some can be rather misleading (would lead for this answer to answer a question it should not). In our considerations, we select an answer and analyze which questions it is good for answering, instead of focusing on a question and ranking its candidate answers. Our considerations are applied to an indexing procedure; we do not really know which questions will be given, but once we have an answer, we index it in a way to answer suitable questions and to avoid answering a foreign question by this answer.

Let us consider an answer and a set of questions it is good at answering.

> **A**: ***This camera takes good pictures in low light***, *according to my neighbor who works as an event photographer and did a good portfolio for my sister.*
> As a review, this text is suitable to provide answers on opinions related to a given *digital camera*, with the focus on its feature *low light*. For example, this text can naturally answer.
> **Q**: *Which digital camera takes good shots in low light?*

This text is **not** suitable to answer other questions that would include phrases and keywords outside of the topic of *digital camera* and *low light*. In the context of this Q/A domain, it does not really matter whom this opinion is attributed to (*my neighbor*). And even if this sort of attribution **is** important, the exact mention of *digital camera* and *low light* is required in the question for this answer to be relevant. Hence only the underscored part of this answer is informative and should be put into an index and matched with a question.

The questions like

- *how to make good portfolios*
- *good thing for my sister*
- *how to work as event photographer*

would need to be assigned to different answers. Hence we observe that the key assumption of search engineering that one can match the keywords in query with the keywords in a search result as long as they are properly weighted is far from being true!

How to differentiate between an informative part of an answer, which should be matched with a question, and an uninformative part, which should not? Do we need domain knowledge to determine the informative and uninformative parts of an answer to match with potential questions? Domain knowledge can help, but it turns out there is a domain-independent universal mechanism to label informative parts of answers based on discourse features instead of answer topics and domain knowledge. The way an author logically organizes their thoughts in text give us a hint as to what is informative and what is not when this text is serving as an answer.

Rhetorical structure theory (RST; Mann and Thompson, 1988) sheds light on how to distinguish between informative parts of an answer from uninformative or less important ones. In particular, elaboration relation of RST links more important text fragments or EDUs (nucleus) with less important, auxiliary information (satellite). Whereas more important text is strongly correlated with a potential

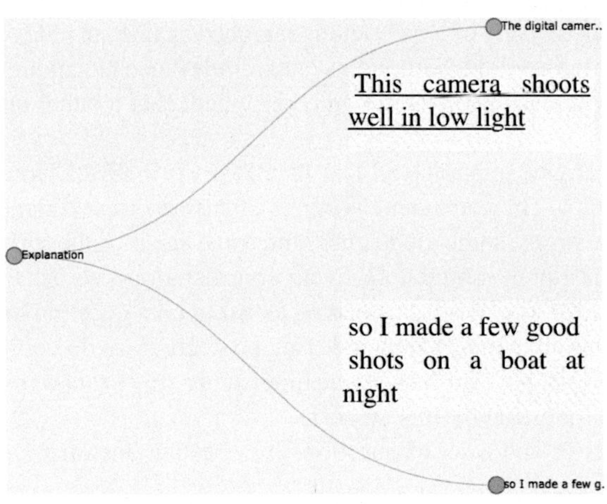

FIG. 8

A simple DT for an *informative* EDU (top) and an uninformative EDU (bottom).

question, less important text provides details that are less likely to be queried directly. If this less important text is indexed, it might trigger this answer as a response to a question on something totally different. Hence the **informative** part of text usually corresponds to a **nucleus**, and the *uninformative* part corresponds to *satellite*.

For example, consider the text of a review for a digital camera: "***This camera shoots well in low light****, so I made a few good shots on a boat at night*." The first part of this compound question is a nucleus EDU connected by rhetorical relation of *Explanation* with the satellite EDU as the second part (Fig. 8).

This is a good answer for:

- *Which camera shoots well in low light*
- *How to shoot in low light*
- *Low light camera*
- *Low light conditions*

But not for:

- *Good shorts at a boat*
- *Night boat*
- *Boat at night*
- *Good shots*
- *Good boat*
- *Good night*

We also consider nucleuses in answers as alternative questions. They are intended to complement the main Q in the Q/A pair to cover a broader range of user questions. This is expected to improve the overall Q/A recall, having the search precision intact. In terms of search engineering, instead of indexing the whole answer for search, we index only the main FAQ question and the alternative questions obtained from the parts of answers we determined to be informative and put this data in index *IndexNucleus*. At search time, we run a query against this index first. Alternative question technology complements such Q/A tools as Microsoft QnA Maker (QnAmaker, 2018) that takes a single question per answer but should instead take multiple alternative questions to assure a reasonable recall.

Only when no search results are obtained searching *IndexNucleusA* do we retreat to the conventional, baseline search index *IndexA*, which provides a default functionality in search applications.

RST models the logical organization of text, a structure employed by a writer, relying on relations between parts of text. This theory simulates text coherence (of answers, in particular) by forming a hierarchical, connected structure of texts via DTs. Rhetorical relations are split into the classes of coordinate and subordinate; these relations hold across two or more text spans (EDUs). Adjacent EDUs are connected by coherence relations (e.g., *Attribution, Sequence*) and form higher-level discourse units. EDUs linked by a relation are then differentiated based on their relative importance: nuclei are the core parts of the relation, whereas satellites are peripheral ones.

Each text can be viewed from the viewpoint of answering certain questions by means of this text. Answers are written in a form so that questions are reformulated and repeated in them in multiple ways, and our objective is to extract them. According to Mann and Thompson (1988), for every part of a coherent text such as an answer, there is some plausible reason for its presence, evident to readers. Rhetorical relations play a role of forcing constraints on one answer element to fit another.

3.2 How a discourse tree indicates what to index and what not to index

We illustrate our analysis with a Q/A pair and a DT for answer.

Q: *How should I plan to pay for taxes resulting from converting to a Roth IRA?*
A: *To help maximize your retirement savings, it's generally a good idea to consider not using the proceeds from the conversion to pay the resulting tax costs. Instead, you should consider using cash or other savings held in nonretirement accounts. Using retirement account funds to pay the taxes will reduce the amount you would have available to potentially grow tax-free in your new Roth IRA. Additionally, if you are under 59½, using funds from your retirement account could result in an additional 10% tax penalty, which may significantly reduce the potential benefit of conversion.*

Being a Q/A pair, the answer is provided for a single question. The main issue of this section is what are other questions this answer is good for? As can be seen from this answer, some of its clauses are more relevant to answering the question than others. For example, the phrase "*it is generally a good idea*" adds little to the answer, whereas "*consider not using the proceeds from the conversion*" informs the user who posed the original question. Hence if someone asks "*What is generally a good idea*?" this particular answer is not good for this fairly general question. Conversely, the question "*should I consider not using the proceeds from the conversion*" can be answered well by this answer.

Fig. 9 shows the DT for the question (EDUs are circled). We start with the simple hypothesis that only EDUs that are nucleus of rhetorical relations should be indexed as they are directly related to the topic of the answer. All satellites EDUs should not be selected for indexing. This is obvious for the *Elaboration* relation, whose nucleus expresses more important information than the satellite does.

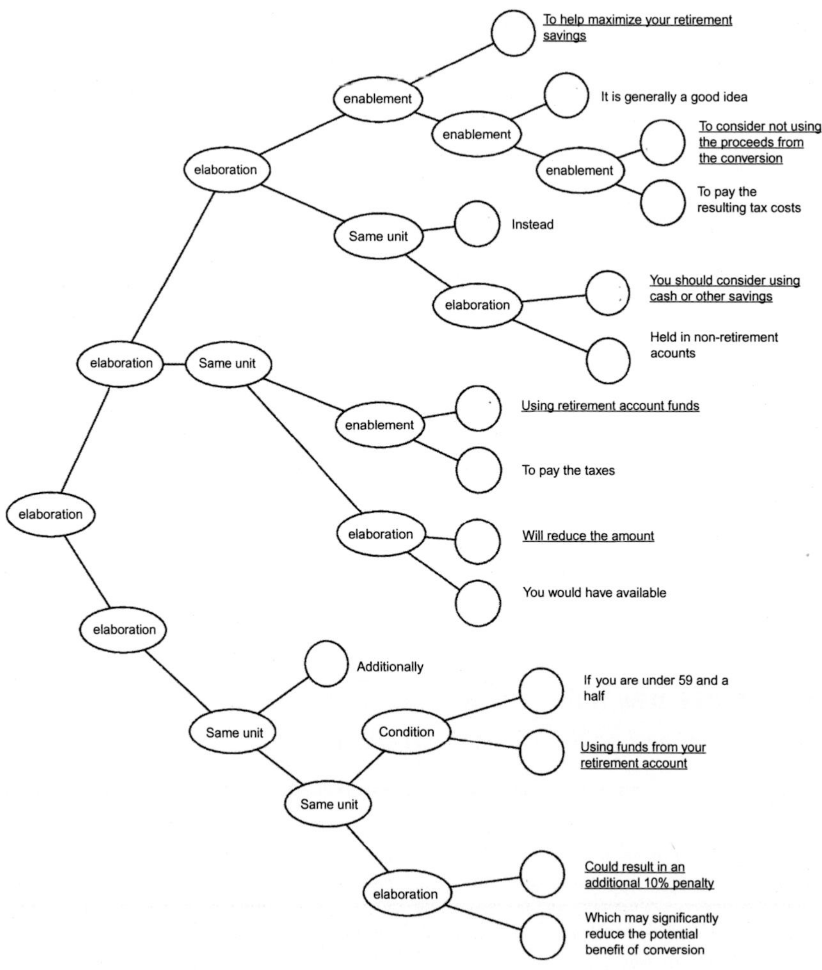

FIG. 9

Discourse tree for an answer with the EDUs selected for indexing.

We hypothesize that a satellite may express a detail of information being communicated that is unlikely to be explicitly queried by a user (Galitsky, 2017b; Jasinskaja and Karagjosova, 2017).

This is the list of phrases from the nucleus EDU:

- *help maximize your retirement savings*
- *proceeds from the conversion*
- *cash or other savings held in nonretirement accounts*
- *retirement account funds*
- *using funds from your retirement account*
- *result in an additional 10% tax penalty*

Notice the list of satellite EDU expressions:

- *it's generally a good idea* (not related to finance)
- *pay the resulting tax* costs (detached from the context)
- *held in nonretirement accounts* (detached from the context)
- *to pay the taxes will reduce the amount …* (detached from the context)
- *you would have available to potentially …* (counterfactual expressions, unlikely to occur in a user question)
- *if you are under 59½ …* (condition, not necessarily potentially directly queried)

For each of these cases, we indicate the reason we believe this fragment of text should not be matched with a potential question to deliver this particular answer.

3.3 How rhetorical relations determine indexing rules

For *Elaboration*, we index the nucleus part and assume that satellite part is too specific to be mentioned in a question and instead is only expected in an answer. For *Enablement*, we have the following template:

To achieve some state [nucleus] | *do this and that [satellite]*. A query may be of the form "how to *achieve some state?*" but less likely be of the form "what can I achieve *doing this and that*?" Therefore, we select the nucleus of *Enablement* relation for indexing.

Rhetorical relation of *Condition* tells us that IF part (the satellite) should not be indexed when the nucleus is indexed and answers the question of the type "*when/where/under what condition ….*" We expect other relations such as *Contrast*, to act similarly to *Condition*: the EDU which expresses facts that actually hold (and not the satellite part facts which are unusual, unexpected, unanticipated). *Attribution* acts in a similar way: the nucleus fact is important and may occur in a factoid question, and the satellite part (on whom this is attributed to) is usually a detail. The exception here is a query by an author, but for such queries, texts need to be transformed into a structured way and covered by a different kind of search technology.

The *Same-Unit* and *Joint* relations are symmetric and should not affect our selection of text portions for indexing.

For *Contrast*, a satellite is good because it is an expression with elevated importance. For *Evidence*, just nucleus is good because the statement is important but its backup in unlikely to be queried.

If *Elaboration* holding between two discourse units is defined as the second describing the same state of affairs as the first one (in different words), or, at a certain level of abstraction, says the same thing, then both nucleus and satellite would form meaningful answers. In the original formulation of RST, usually, an additional requirement for *Elaboration* is imposed that the satellite is more detailed and longer. The broadest definition *Elaboration* also includes in special cases such relation as *Reformulation* or *Restatement*, *Summary*, *Specification* and *Generalization*.

Explanation gives the cause or reason why the state of affairs presented in the context sentence takes place, or why the speaker believes the content of that sentence holds, or why the speaker chose to share information with us; these cases correspond to the three types of causal relations identified. For the cases of content level causality, epistemic causality and speech act causality satellite should not form a question (Galitsky et al., 2011a).

Rhetorical relations *Evidence, Justify, Motivation, Enablement, Evaluation, Background* all overlap in their function with *Explanation*, but vary in goals and means of giving reasons. For example, *Evidence* is given to increase the hearer's belief in a claim.

Sequence relation connects descriptions of events that (are to) take place one after the other, the order of events matching the textual order of utterances. This is typical for narrative texts and successive instructions, (e.g., cooking recipes). For two EDUs e1 and e2, there is an additional requirement imposed that the described events be temporally and spatially contiguous. Where things are at the end of e1 is where things are at the start of e2, there is no break in between.

4. Designing ontologies

4.1 Systematized nomenclature of medicine—Clinical terms

The Systematized Nomenclature of Medicine—Clinical Terms (SNOMED CT, SCT) is a comprehensive medical terminology used for standardizing the storage, retrieval, and exchange of electronic health data. Some efforts have been made to capture the contents of SCT as Web Ontology Language (OWL), but these efforts have been hampered by the size and complexity of SCT. SNOMED provides structured relationships for more than 300,000 medical entities. SNOMED CT is commonly used in electronic health record (EHR) systems to help summarize patient encounters and is fully integrated with the *International Classification of Diseases, Tenth Revision* (ICD-10) billing codes used in the United States and many other jurisdictions. Other than SCT, biomedical ontologies are created in a variety of languages, such as OBO Format, OWL, and Protege frames (Rubin et al., 2008).

The goal of SCT is to build a taxonomy of terms referring to entities in a given medical environment (Bhattacharyya, 2016) and a framework of rules guaranteeing that each term is used with a single meaning; each meaning salient in the environment is expressed using exactly one term. Each term in this taxonomy is in one or more parent-child relationships to some other terms in the taxonomy (Galitsky, 2016).

SNOMED CT formulas are defined as a structured combination of one or more concept identifiers used to express an instance of a clinical idea (El-Sappagh et al., 2018). The formulas consist of one or more focus concepts and optional refinements. SCT terms are shown in italics. Clinical expressions in SCT concepts can be of two types:

(1) pre-coordinated expressions, which use a single SCT concept identifier
(2) post-coordinated expressions, which contain more than one SCT identifier

In pre-coordinated expressions, the clinical meaning of the expression matches the meaning of the unique listed concept (e.g., <73,211,009-*diabetes mellitus*>). Pre-coordinated concepts are identified by their defining relationships under the concept <246,061,005-*attribute*>.

The most common form of post-coordination is the refinement, which is characterized by refining the value of one or more of the defining attributes of the concept using the form, as follows:

- The attribute name is a concept that is a subtype of <246,061,005-*attribute*>.
- The refinement attribute value is a concept or expression that is appropriate to the attribute name as specified by the SCM. In most cases, any subtype child or descendant of a concept that is permitted as an attribute value of an attribute is also permitted as an attribute value.

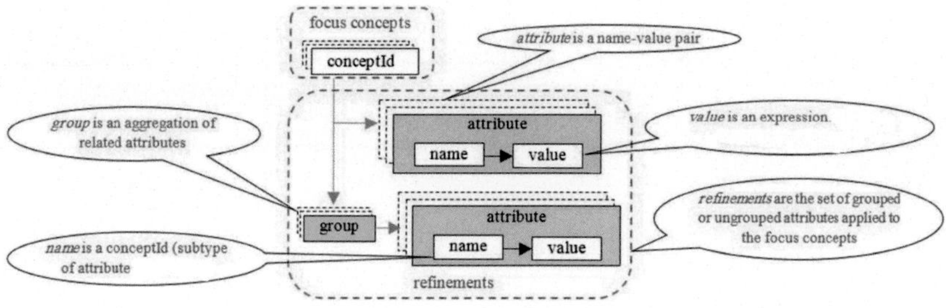

FIG. 10

An example of SCT post-coordinated concept.

Table 1 SCT logical formula representation.

NL expression	SCT representation
Capsule containing 500 mg of amoxicillin	*Amoxicillin ⊓ ∃has dose form.capsule ⊓ ∃RG (∃has active ingredient.amoxicillin ⊓ ∃has basis of strength.(amoxicillin only ⊓ ∃ strength magnitude.#500 ⊓ ∃ strength unit.mg))*
Closed skull fracture with intracranial injury	*closed injury of head ⊓ closed fracture of skull ⊓ ∃RG (∃associated morphology. closed_traumatic_abnormality ⊓ ∃finding site.intracranial structure) ⊓ ∃RG (∃associated morphology.fracture, closed ⊓ ∃finding site.bone structure of cranium)*
Bacterial infectious disease	*Causative agent = streptococcus pneumonia | finding site | = structure of upper lobe of lung laterality = left*

- Refinements may be grouped to represent interdependencies between them in the same way as super-type relationship groups.

The example in Fig. 10 describes the idea for "*removal of an ovarian structure using a laser device*."

A post-coordinated formula can be a simple formula or a complex formula. As shown in Fig. 10, a simple formula is an expression consisting of one or more *conceptIds* plus optional refinements. The refinements include any number of attributes, which are expressed as name-value pairs and may be applied either independently and or as parts of groups (Table 1).

A complex form of refinement is modeled by nested formulas (Fig. 11). Here, a complete formula can be enclosed in double parentheses and used to refine the attribute value of a refining attribute in another formula. This refinement is done by relationship group.

Fig. 12 shows how SNOMED CT is employed to form various sections of a health record such as allergy, family history, patient problems, diagnoses, and others.

4.2 Relation extractor based on syntactic parsing

A broadly used open IE library, ClausIE derives knowledge tuples for ontology engineering (Tuan et al., 2017). This library relies primarily on a dependency parser and grammatical sentence structure to evoke knowledge triples. Not only can explicit knowledge triples be derived from this method, but

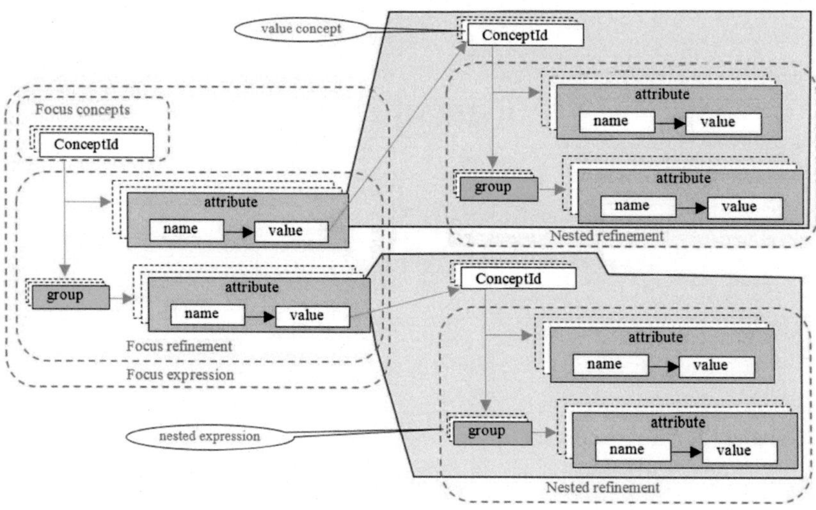

FIG. 11

Nested expressions in a complex post-coordinated concept structure.

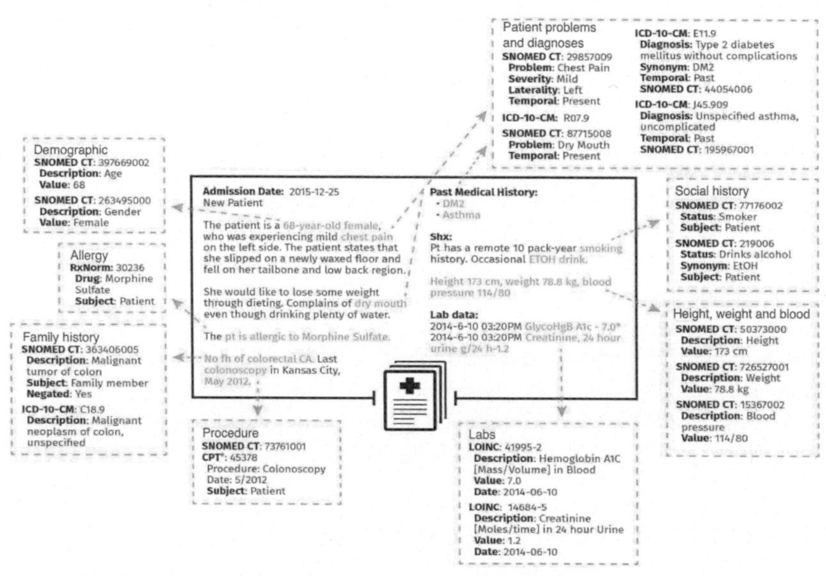

FIG. 12

Extracting data from unstructured text (in the middle) to populate SNOMED CT attribute-values.

implied, embedded knowledge can also be evoked. Let us use an example of a sentence "*The human papillomavirus virus (HPV) leads to cervical cancer*" would produce an explicit triple.

<"*The human papillomavirus virus*," "*leads to*," "*cervical cancer*"> and an implicit triple.

<"*human papillomavirus virus*," "*is*," "*HPV*">. In addition, ClausIE is domain-independent and when compared with other well-known domain-independent, open IE approaches, performance is significantly better. ClausIE relies on a dependency parser to syntactically analyze a sentence. Based on the results of the dependency parser, clauses, which are coherent pieces of information, are determined by ClausIE. Further details of ClausIE's method can be found in Del Corro and Gemulla (2013).

Textual health documents (questions, descriptions, reports, or any other medical documents) go through a series of steps for interpretation (Fig. 13). The first is an NL analysis followed by the IE task. The second is projection into the meta-model and execution of the reasoning modules for the interpretation process. The final stage is the presentation of the results. The system outputs an interpretation model containing the relevant medical concepts found within the input text.

The first system component is *information extraction*. Information is extracted by matching manually defined syntactical patterns against the syntactical trees. The result is represented using Resource Description Framework—like format triplets or predicate (subject, object).

The reasoning component includes induction, deduction, and abduction. Three mechanisms are used to improve IE. The ontological modeling allows one to perform reasoning like deduction. In addition, there are two other methods of reasoning: induction and abduction through the context (Galitsky, 2013). These enable the announcement and evaluation of new hypotheses, performing term disambiguation, specializing generic concepts, and checking coherence.

4.3 Conceptualization process

As a part of the ontology conceptualization process, a set of questions posted on medical forums are collected. Each question is manually analyzed to extract the relevant information. The information is categorized into concepts, and relationships are derived from them to build a common structure. Conceptualization analysis of the questions results in a meta-model, reviewed by a specialist doctor to judge the relevance of the requested information (Fig. 14). The questions range from online diagnosis of a given set of reported symptoms and prevention advice to simple explanation requests of medical concepts. Well-constructed questions attract the attention of doctors and benefit from an answer (Otmani et al., 2018).

During the conceptualization process of the solution, ontology design patterns can be searched and selected to be reused whenever possible to accelerate the process of modeling and save time (Hammar, 2017). An ontology design pattern is a reusable successful solution to a recurrent modeling problem . The patterns have been used in some biomedical ontologies (Mortensen et al., 2012) and to improve interoperability in EHRs.

Lexico-syntactic ontology design patterns are recurrent patterns used in knowledge extraction. Some patterns for common relationships like (*is-a, part-of*, […]) can be reused to extract part-of relationships, for instance, the pattern [(NP) *and*] NP PART NP for the *part-of* relationship. They are recommended in ontology engineering.

The conceptual model, represented in Fig. 15, defines the set of the necessary information to construct adequate and cohesive descriptions of medical entities. Patients, physicians, and ontology engineers alike can comprehend it.

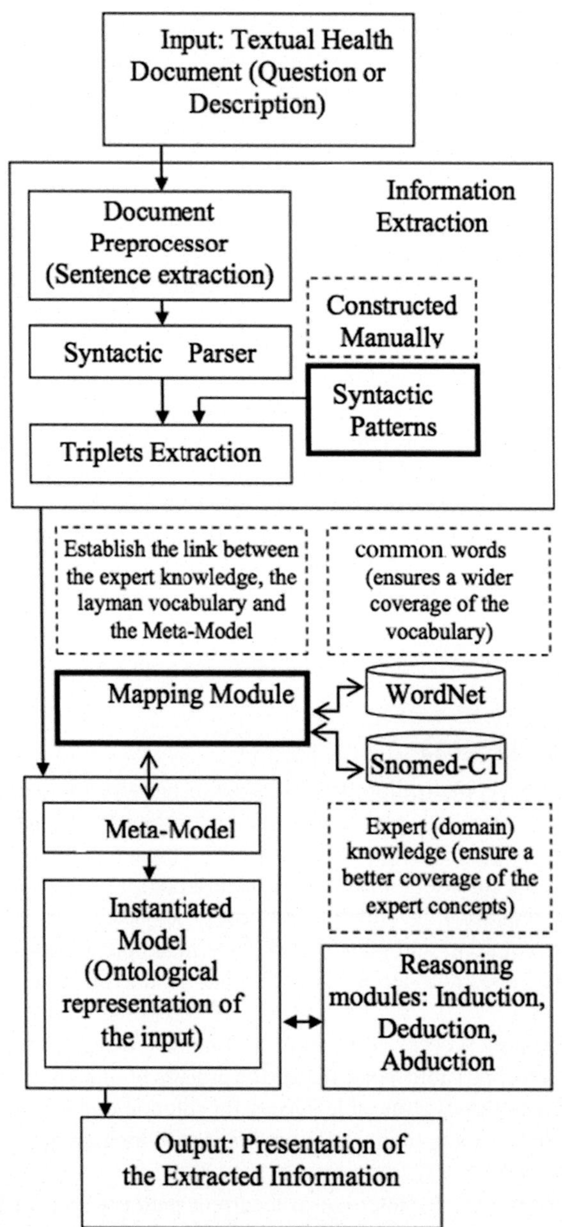

FIG. 13

Text mining (TM) architecture.

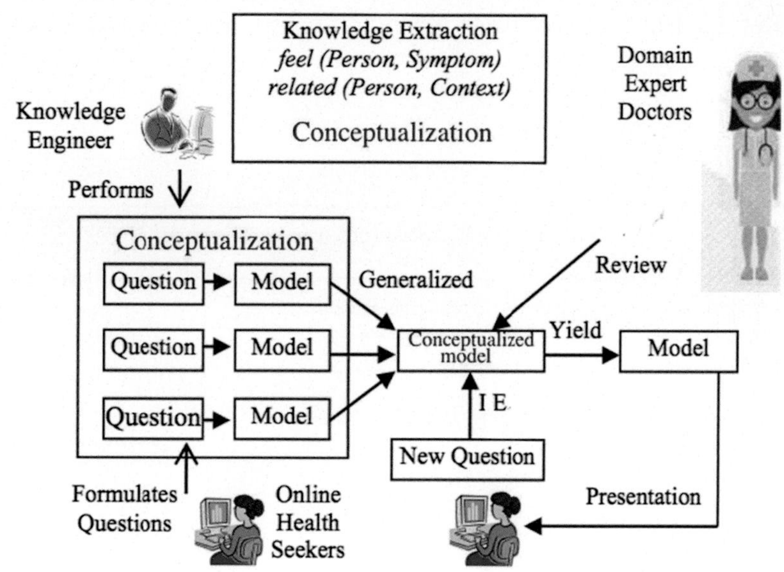

FIG. 14

Conceptualization analysis.

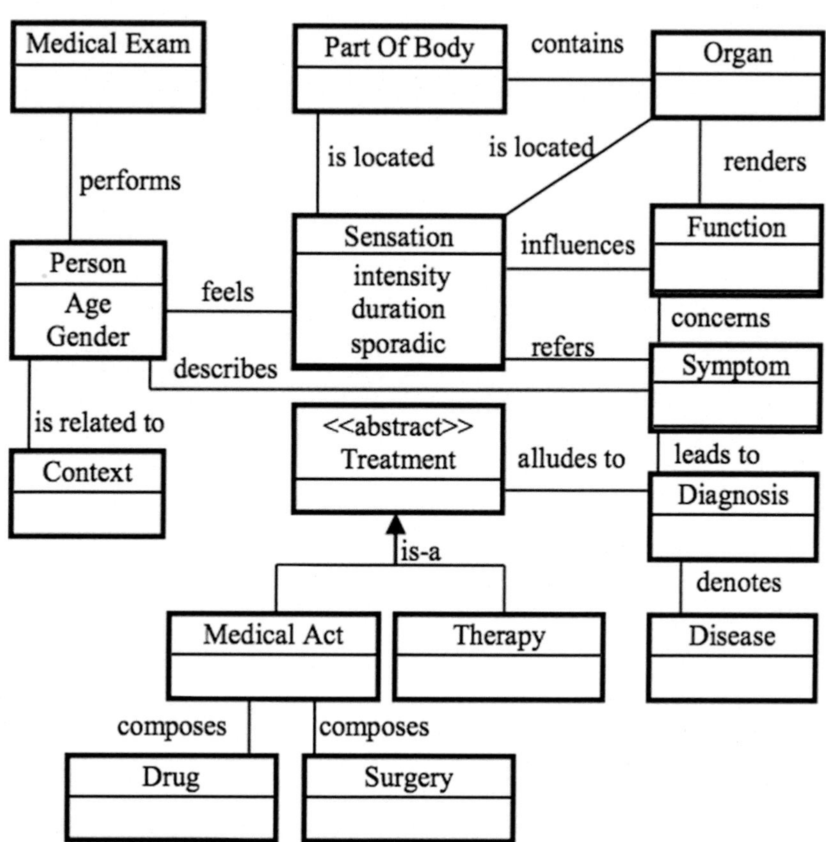

FIG. 15

Conceptual model of medical questions acquisition.

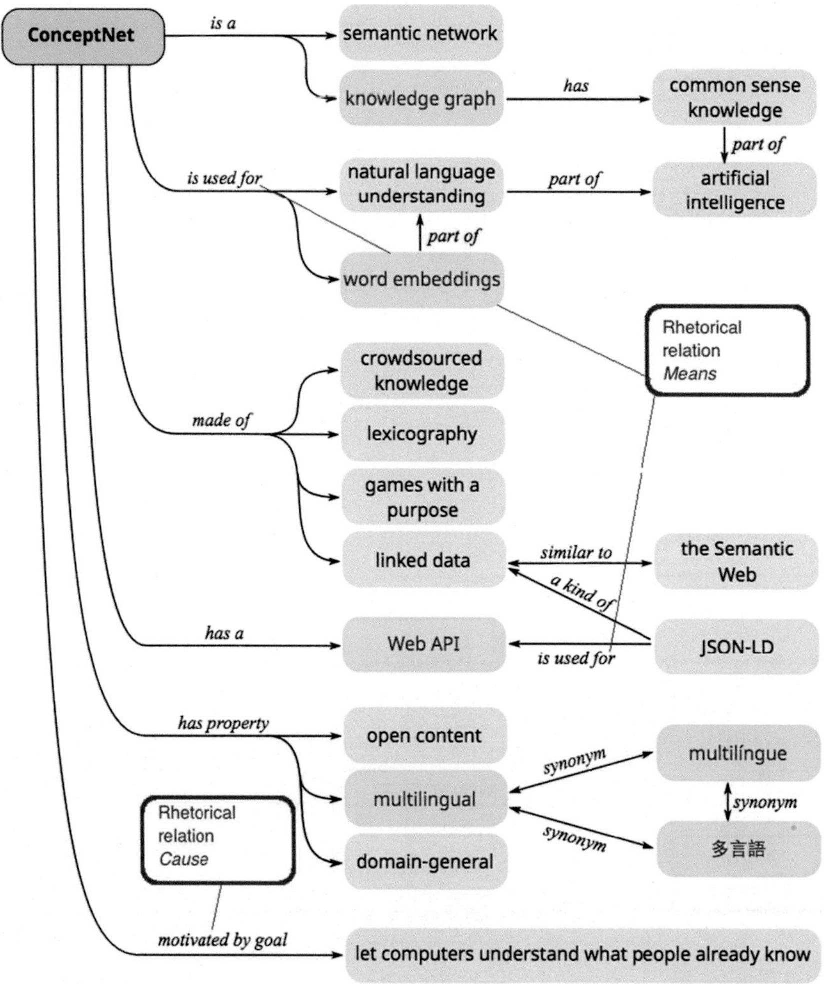

FIG. 16

ConceptNet horizontal ontology.

Another example of conceptual representation is ConceptNet ontology (Speer et al., 2017, Fig. 16). ConceptNet was inspired by the crowdsourcing project Open Mind Common Sense, which was launched two decades ago at the MIT Media Lab. It now includes knowledge from various crowd-sourced and expert-created resources. Some ontological relations in it are closely associated with rhetorical relations like *Means* and *Cause*.

5. Neural dictionary manager

In this section, we describe an ML model for entity recognition in large unstructured text that optimizes the use of ontological structures and can identify previously unobserved synonyms for concepts in the ontology. Automatic recognition of medical entities in unstructured text is a key feature of many clinical and research applications, and its accuracy strongly affects the accuracy of EHR analysis. The mining of medical concepts is complicated by the broad use of synonyms and nonstandard terms in health documents.

The input of the neural dictionary manager is a word or a phrase. The manager computes the probability of an entity in the ontology matching it. The manager includes:

(1) a text encoder, which is a neural network that maps the query phrase into vector representation
(2) an embedding matrix with rows corresponding to the ontology concepts
(3) the dot product of the query vector and an entity vector as the measure of similarity

Fig. 17 shows the architecture of the neural dictionary model (Arbabi et al., 2019). The encoder flow is at the top, and the flow for computing the embedding for a concept is shown at the bottom. A query phrase is first represented in the Encoder by its word vectors, which are then processed by a *convolution layer* into a new space. A max-*over-time pooling layer* is employed to merge the set of vectors into one. After that, a fully connected layer maps this vector into the final representation of the phrase. The output vectors are aggregated into a single vector v:

$v = max_t \{ELU(Wx^{(t)} + b)\}$, where $x^{(t)}$ is the word vector for the t-th word in the phrase; W and b are the weight matrix and the bias vector of the convolution filter, respectively; and ELU is the activation function for use in the convolution layer (Clevert et al., 2015). Result e is the encoded vector representation of the phrase: $e = \frac{\text{ReLU}(U_v)}{\text{ReLU}\|(U_v)\|_2}$.

The goal of the Encoder is to map semantically similar words (e.g., synonyms) to close vectors considering the subword information (Bojanowski et al., 2017), which is important in the medical domain where there are many semantically close words with slight morphologic variations.

A matrix of raw embeddings is learned by *Entity embedding*, where each row represents one entity. The final embedding of an entity is retrieved by summing the raw embeddings for that entity and all its ancestors in the ontology, implemented by a fully connected network.

The *entity embedding* component learns representations for entities and measures the similarity between an input phrase and the entities by computing the dot product between these representations and the encoded phrase e. These representations are denoted by the matrix H, where each row corresponds to one entity. H is not learned directly; instead, $\widetilde{H}$ is acquired where each row represents the features of

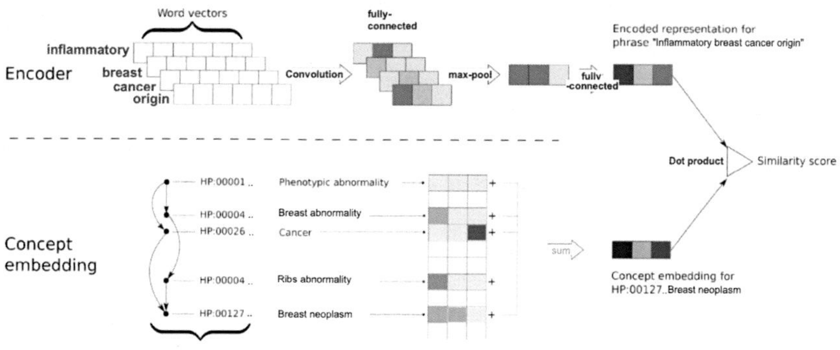

FIG. 17

Architecture of the neural dictionary model.

FIG. 18

A relationship between two extreme entities is visualized by a child in between.

entity c that is distinct compared to its ancestors. Then, $\widetilde{H}$ can be derived by multiplying $\widetilde{H}_c$ by the taxonomy's ancestry matrix A: $H = A\widetilde{H}$. Each element of the ancestry matrix $A_{i,j}$ is nonzero only if entity j is an ancestor of i (including $i = j$) and is calculated as

$$A_i = \text{OneHot}(i) + \frac{1}{|\text{parents}(i)|} \sum_{j \in \text{Parents}(i)} A_j$$

The final embedding of an entity would be the final embedding of its parent (or the average of its parents, in cases of multi-inheritance) plus its own raw embedding, that is

$$H_c = H_{P_c} + \widetilde{H}_c$$

In other words, the parent entity provides the global location in the embedding space, whereas the child entities learn their local locations with respect to that space.

Fig. 18 shows a relationship between two entities: an angel and a demon.

The query classification is done by deriving the dot product plus a bias term followed by a softmax layer as follows:

$$p(c|e) \propto \exp(H_c e + b_c)$$

The taxonomy information can be ignored by setting A to the identity matrix I. In this scenario, the model would behave like an ordinary softmax classifier with the weight matrix $\widetilde{H}$.

To use the neural dictionary manager for entity recognition in a sentence or larger text, all n-grams of one to seven words are extracted from the text. The neural dictionary manager is used to match each n-gram to an entity. Irrelevant n-grams are removed from the list of candidates when their matching score (the softmax probability provided by the neural dictionary model) is lower than a threshold.

6. Phrase aggregator

This component takes a list of phrases and merges synonymous and related ones, to form meaningful ontology entries. The aggregator outputs a hierarchical structure of phrase entities obtained by means of the generalization of phrase instances (Galitsky, 2015a, Fig. 19).

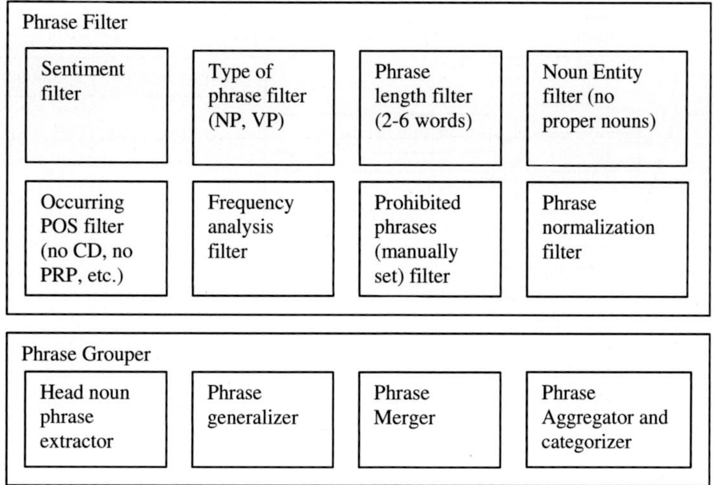

FIG. 19

Phrase aggregator units.

We use the following phrase filtering rules:

(1) Only extract noun, verb, and prepositional phrases.
(2) Exclude phrases with sentiments because they can occur in an opinionated context.
(3) We exclude name entities since they cannot be generalized across properties. However, we include the specific type of such proper nouns in connection with relation specific to the health domain, such as *affect/cure/drug-for/followed-by* and others.
(4) Exclude numbers and prepositions.
(5) Limit phrase length.
(6) Remove too frequent phrases and too rare phrases.
(7) Avoid phrases that start with an article if they are short.
(8) Clean/normalize strings that are not words.

Once the phrases are extracted, they are clustered and aggregated to obtain reliable, repetitive instances. Phrases that only occur once are unreliable and considered to be "noise."

For example, we intend to form a hierarchy from a list of phrases (Fig. 20):

- *insulin-dependent diabetes mellitus*
- *adult-onset dependent diabetes mellitus*
- *diabetes with almost complete insulin deficiency*
- *diabetes with almost complete insulin deficiency and strong hereditary component*

Head noun extraction occurs as follows (Fig. 20): if two phrases have the same head noun, we combine them into a category. If two phrases within a category have other nouns or adjectives in common besides the head noun, we form a subcategory from these common nouns (Galitsky, 2015b). In this respect we follow the cognitive procedure of induction, finding a commonality between data samples, retaining the head noun, such as *diabetes*.

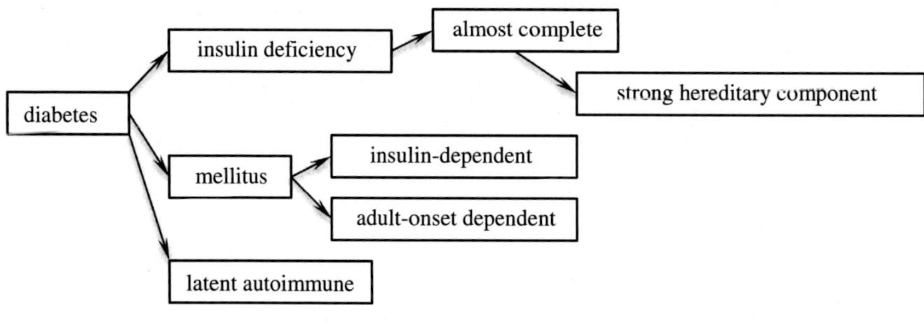

FIG. 20

Aggregation of phrases to obtain a hierarchy.

Hence we have the following class, subclasses, and sub-subclasses (shown by indentation):

7. Ontologies supporting reasoning

HyBrow (Hypothesis Browser, Racunas et al., 2004) is a system for the representation, manipulation, and integration of diverse biological data such as gene expression, protein interactions, and annotations, with prior data for the purpose of evaluating alternative hypotheses. The goal is to evaluate and rank hypotheses based on user-defined "constraints," and to evaluate the consistency of hypotheses with all information available. The system enables researchers to pose hypotheses and to determine whether those hypotheses are consistent with or contradict existing knowledge contained in its knowledge base.

Computer reasoning is one of the most compelling advantages ontologies can provide in helping researchers exploit the vast amounts of biomedical knowledge available in electronic form. Computer reasoning encompasses methods that use ontologies to make inferences based on the knowledge they contain as well as any additional contextual information or asserted facts. These methods can help researchers think about what information means in the context of what is already known. Tools can utilize formal methods to query and interpret the information at hand.

Fig. 21 shows an example of reasoning log and reasoning user interface that illustrates the evaluation of a simple hypothesis: "Gal2p transports galactose into the cell at the cell membrane. In the cytoplasm, galactose activates *Gal3p*. *Gal3p* binds to the promoter of *gal1* gene and induces its transcription in the presence of galactose". This hypothesis was decomposed into events. In its assessment, the system reports support from literature and annotation for event *ev0*; a support from literature for *ev1*; a support from ontology constraints and annotation for *ev2*; and a support from the ontology,

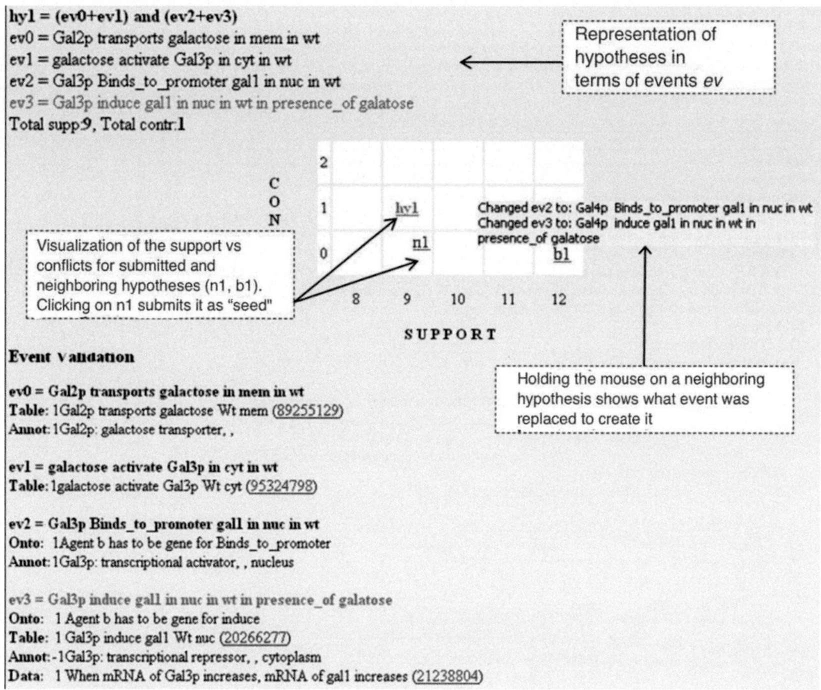

FIG. 21

Using ontologies for computer-aided reasoning.

literature, and data divisions for *ev3*. A conflict is discovered for *ev3* (marked in light gray) from the annotation rule division since *Gal3p* is annotated to be primarily in the *cytoplasm* in presence of *galactose*. Variant events are then being searched. For *ev2*, "*Gal4p binds to promoter of gal1*" is found with greater support. For *ev3*, the more meaningful event is found ("*Gal4p induces gal1in nucleus in presence of galactose*") with the same support but no conflict. These events were inserted in place of the original events to create a neighboring hypothesis that is better than the original hypothesis. The user receives rankings for events, explanations for them, and references to conflicting and supporting data in a summary page.

Fig. 22 shows the text for Fig. 21, its DT, and entity relationship graph.

The overall effect of these glucose-regulated processes is thought to speed up the cell transition from utilization of galactose to the fermentation of the preferred sugar glucose. Previously, we have shown that during glucose-induced inactivation, a relatively rapid and irreversible loss of both Gal2p transport activity and Gal2p amount occurs due to its internalization by endocytosis from the plasma membrane. Once internalized, the protein is targeted to the vacuole, where it is degraded by vacuolar proteases with no assistance of the 26S proteasome. Moreover, our previous finding of Gal2p-ubiquitin conjugates under the conditions resulting in Gal2p proteolysis suggested the possible role of ubiquitin in this process.

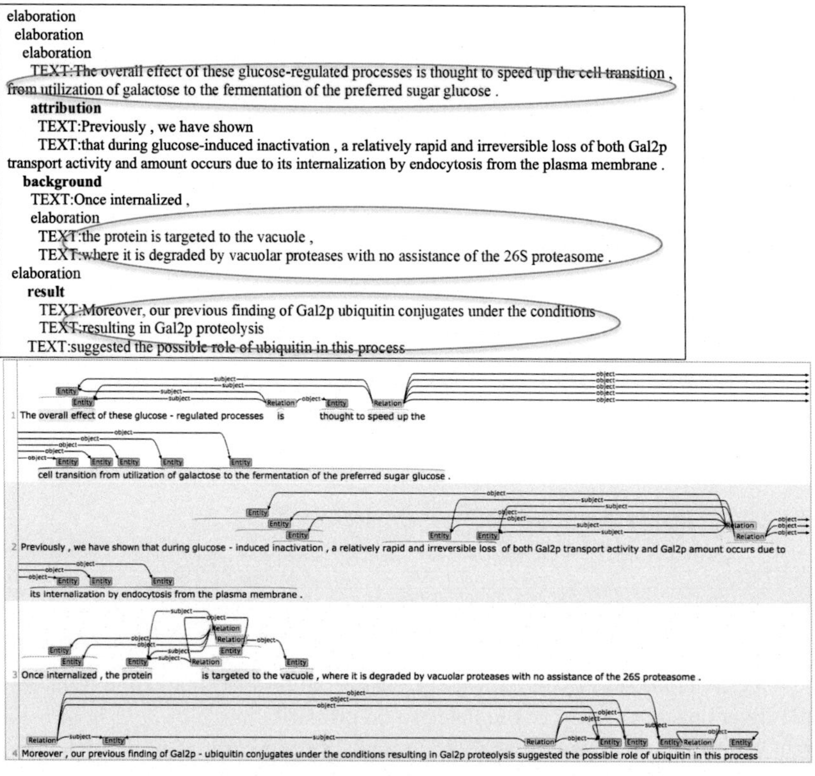
The overall effect of these glucose-regulated processes is thought to speed up the cell transition from utilization of galactose to the fermentation of the preferred sugar glucose. Previously, we have shown that during glucose-induced inactivation, a relatively rapid and irreversible loss of both Gal2p transport activity and Gal2p amount occurs due to its internalization by endocytosis from the plasma membrane. Once internalized, the protein is targeted to the vacuole, where it is degraded by vacuolar proteases with no assistance of the 26S proteasome. Moreover, our previous finding of Gal2p-ubiquitin conjugates under the conditions resulting in Gal2p proteolysis suggested the possible role of ubiquitin in this process
elaboration
elaboration
elaboration
TEXT:The overall effect of these glucose-regulated processes is thought to speed up the cell transition , from utilization of galactose to the fermentation of the preferred sugar glucose .
attribution
TEXT:Previously , we have shown
TEXT:that during glucose-induced inactivation , a relatively rapid and irreversible loss of both Gal2p transport activity and amount occurs due to its internalization by endocytosis from the plasma membrane .
background
TEXT:Once internalized ,
elaboration
TEXT:the protein is targeted to the vacuole ,
TEXT:where it is degraded by vacuolar proteases with no assistance of the 26S proteasome .
elaboration
result
TEXT:Moreover, our previous finding of Gal2p ubiquitin conjugates under the conditions
TEXT:resulting in Gal2p proteolysis
TEXT:suggested the possible role of ubiquitin in this process
1 The overall effect of these glucose - regulated processes is thought to speed up the
cell transition from utilization of galactose to the fermentation of the preferred sugar glucose .
2 Previously , we have shown that during glucose - induced inactivation , a relatively rapid and irreversible loss of both Gal2p transport activity and Gal2p amount occurs due to
its internalization by endocytosis from the plasma membrane .
3 Once internalized , the protein is targeted to the vacuole , where it is degraded by vacuolar proteases with no assistance of the 26S proteasome .
4 Moreover , our previous finding of Gal2p - ubiquitin conjugates under the conditions resulting in Gal2p proteolysis suggested the possible role of ubiquitin in this process

FIG. 22

A DT and entity relationship graph to support reasoning.

A logic form representation of the discourse units shown in green ovals are:

speed(higher, processes(glucose-regulated), cell(transition(utilization(galactose), fermentation(glucose(sugar)))))
target(vacuole, protein, internalized)
degrade(protein, _, vacuolar proteases)
not assist(26S proteasome, degrade(protein, _, vacuolar proteases))
conjugate(gal2p, ubiquitin) -> proteolysis (gal2p)

A formal representation of the logical form (LF) grammar using this schema (Fig. 23) is as follows. Medical events are denoted as ME_i (e.g., *LabEvent, ConditionEvent*) and relations are denoted as RE_i (e.g., conducted/reveals). Now, $ME[a_1, \ldots, a_j, \ldots, oper(a_n)]$ is a medical event where a_i represents

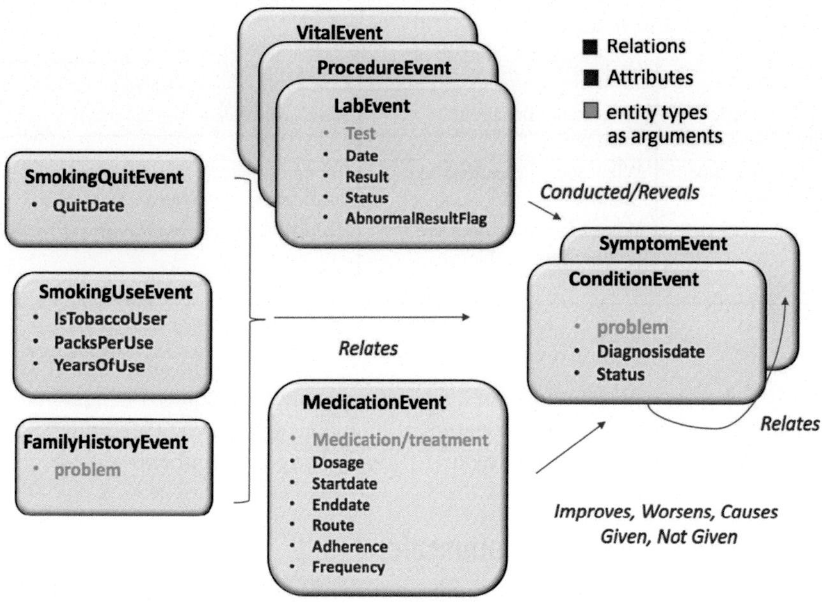

FIG. 23

An example of events, attributes, and relations (Pampari et al., 2018).

the attribute of the event (such as result in *LabEvent*). An event may optionally include constraints on attributes captured by an operator ($oper() \in \{sort,\ range,\ check\ for\ null\ values,\ compare\}$). These operators sometimes require values from external medical KB (indicated by ref., e.g., *lab.ref=low/lab.ref=high* to indicate the range of reference standards considered healthy in lab results) indicating the need for medical knowledge to answer a question. Using these constructs, a LF can be defined using the following rules,

$$
\begin{aligned}
&LF \rightarrow ME_i \mid M_1\ relation\ M_2 \\
&M_1 \rightarrow ME_i,\ M_2 \rightarrow ME_j \\
&M_1 \rightarrow M_1\ relation\ M_2,\ M_2 \rightarrow M_1\ relation\ M_2 \\
&relation \rightarrow \mathrm{OR} \mid \mathrm{AND} \mid RE_i
\end{aligned}
$$

Advantages of an LF representation include the ability to represent composite relations, define attributes for medical events, and constrain the attributes to precisely capture the information need in the question. While these can be achieved using different methods that combine lambda calculus and first-order logic (Roberts and Demner-Fushman, 2016), this representation is more human comprehensible. This allows a physician to consider an ontology like the one in Fig. 23 and easily define a logical form.

Some example question templates with their LF annotations are described in Table 2 using the above notation. The entities seen in LF are the entities posed in the question and the entity marked X indicates the answer entity.

PubMedQA (Jin et al., 2019) covers several different reasoning types; almost 60% involve comparing multiple groups (such as experiment and control), and others require interpreting statistics of a

Table 2 Question types and instances.

Question type	Question instance	Logic Form
Fine-grained answer type (attribute entity is answer	What is the dosage of |medication|?	*medicationEvent* (|*medication*| & *dosage*(X)), *X*-?
Coarse-grained answer type (event entity is answer)	What does the patient take |medication| for?	{conditionEvent(X) OR symptomEvent(X)} ⇒ *medicationEvent*(|*medication*|)
At least one event relation	What lab results does are pertinent to |problem| diagnosis?	*LabEvent (X) & conditionEvent(|problem|)*

single group or its subgroups. Reasoning over quantitative contents is required in nearly all (more than 95%) of them, which is expected due to the nature of biomedical research. Three-quarters of contexts have text descriptions of the statistics while one-fifth only have the numbers.

7.1 Entity grid helps to extract relationships

A coherent text binds sentences together to express a meaning as a whole; the interpretation of a sentence usually depends on the meaning of its neighbors. Coherence models help with distinguishing coherent from incoherent texts; this capability has a wide range of applications in text generation (Chapter 15), summarization, and coherence scoring. In this subsection, we explore how a coherence model can tell which phrases and sentences are good sources for an ontology entry, and which phrases are not.

The entity grid model (Barzilay and Lapata, 2008), inspired by Centering Theory (Grosz et al., 1995), is one of the most popular. It represents a text by a grid that captures how grammatical roles of different entities change from sentence to sentence. The grid is then converted into a feature vector containing probabilities of local entity transitions, which enables ML models to learn the degree of importance of each entity occurrence.

We want to extract the first mention of relationship if possible. In addition, we want to extract the most complete tuple of objects connected by a relation.

s0: Eaton Corp. said it sold its Pacific Sierra Research unit to a company formed by employees of that unit.
s1: Terms were not disclosed.
s2: Pacific Sierra, based in Los Angeles, has 200 employees and supplies professional services and advanced products to industry.
s3: Eaton is an automotive parts, controls and aerospace electronics concern.

s0: *sell(eaton, unit, company).*
s3: *employ(pacific_sierra, 200).*

Figs. 24 and 25 show various representations of this paragraph, including the entity grid, semantic and entity relationships, and the DT. Each representation uses its own means to show a distribution of entities through sentences. In the DT, entities are italicized so that the correspondence with the entity

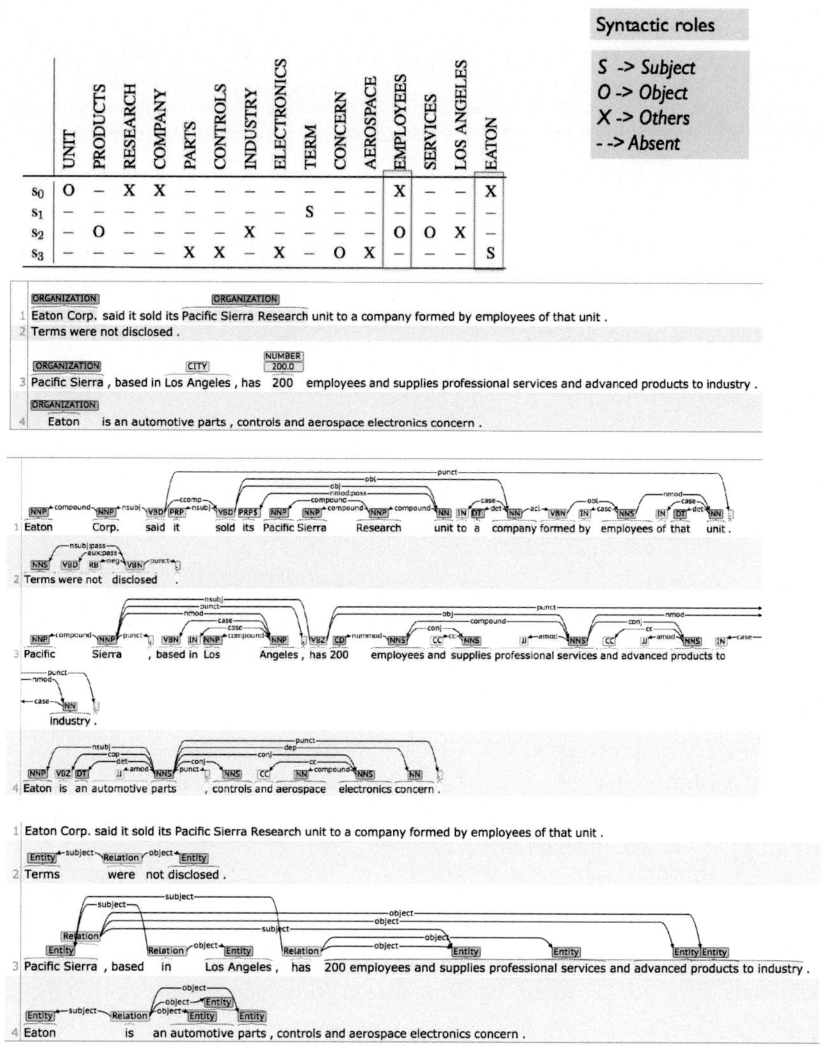

FIG. 24

An entity grid matrix, an entity relationship graph, and a syntactic parse tree for a paragraph of text.

grid is easier to track. Semantic entity relationships representation tags the entities but does not show distribution; although, being combined with syntactic representation, becomes as informative as the discourse-level ones.

7.2 Validating ontology

Ontology validation is a necessary step to assure the correct performance of downstream applications. The following relations can be validated:

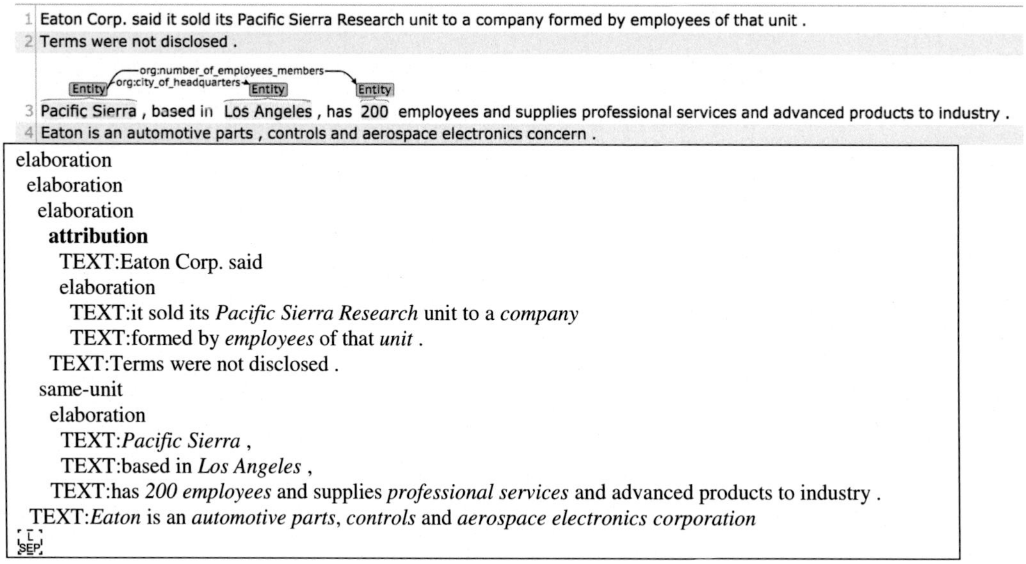

1 Eaton Corp. said it sold its Pacific Sierra Research unit to a company formed by employees of that unit .
2 Terms were not disclosed .
3 Pacific Sierra , based in Los Angeles , has 200 employees and supplies professional services and advanced products to industry .
4 Eaton is an automotive parts , controls and aerospace electronics concern .

```
elaboration
 elaboration
  elaboration
   attribution
    TEXT:Eaton Corp. said
    elaboration
     TEXT:it sold its Pacific Sierra Research unit to a company
     TEXT:formed by employees of that unit .
   TEXT:Terms were not disclosed .
  same-unit
   elaboration
    TEXT:Pacific Sierra ,
    TEXT:based in Los Angeles ,
   TEXT:has 200 employees and supplies professional services and advanced products to industry .
 TEXT:Eaton is an automotive parts, controls and aerospace electronics corporation
```

FIG. 25

An entity grid matrix, an entity relationship graph and a DT for a paragraph of text.

- a class A is a subclass of B
- property P is a sub-property of Q
- D is the domain class for property P
- R is the range class for property P
- I is an individual of class A
- the property P links the individuals I and J

This involves validating concepts (*Substance*), relations between concepts (*employed-by*), concept instances (*activated sulfate ammonia is an <instance-of> Manufactured Material*), relations between concept instances (*spinal cord X-ray can be <ordered-for> Chronic back pain*) or between concept instances, and literals (*give oral activated sulfate ammonia 100 g* indicates the dose of the substance to be applied: "100 g").

The first step consists of autogenerating a list of NL questions from the ontology to be validated. These questions are submitted to domain experts who provide an agreement decision (Yes/No) and textual feedback. The next step consists of interpreting expert feedback to validate or modify the ontology (Fig. 26). The proposed approach can be used to:

(1) validate ontologies constructed automatically from medical texts (e.g., clinical guidelines); and
(2) re-validate ontologies constructed manually or automatically, since medical knowledge evolves quickly over time.

To verify an ontology via question answering, (Asma et al., 2013) manually construct question templates associated with each type of ontological element. A question template consists of a regular textual expression with the appropriate variables over ontology nodes. For instance, the pattern "*Is DOSE*

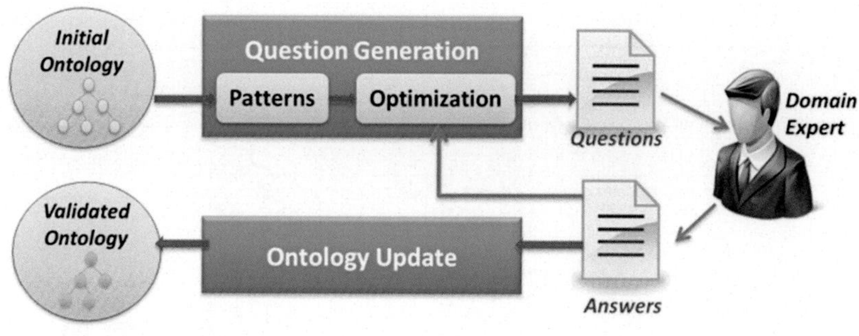

FIG. 26

A chart on how to validate an ontology.

Table 3 Some Boolean question patterns.

Question pattern	Example of instance
CLASS *a*(*n*) have *a*(*n*) PROPERTY?	*Does temperature have a measurement method? Does a treatment have an administration path?*
Is SUB-CLASS a type of CLASS?	*Is big data evidence a type of evidence?*
Is SUB-PROP a type of PROP?	*Is primary treatment a type of treatment?*
Does *a*(*n*) CLASS1 PROPERTY *a*(*n*) CLASS2?	*Does medical exams verify disease symptoms?*
Does INSTANCE1 PROPERTY INSTANCE2?	*Does Prozac treat depressions?*

of DRUG well suited for PATIENTS having DISEASE?" is a textual pattern with four variables: {*DOSE*, *DRUG*, *PATIENTS*, and *DISEASE*}. This question template aims to validate a drug dose delivered to a patient with a particular illness. Table 3 presents examples of Boolean question patterns.

Fig. 27 illustrates an observation that various types of noise can get into an ontology.

8. Specific ontology types in bioinformatics

8.1 Spatial taxonomy

When considering shapes, some fundamental concepts that arise are *connectedness* and *adjacency*. Such concepts have been addressed from a qualitative perspective in the ontological literature. A formalization of these spatially related concepts needs to leverage an extensive work in the area of image processing and analysis, where connectivity or adjacency are precisely defined. Currently, in a broad spectrum of domains, ontologies use the *part-of* and *is-a* relations at their core. While the *is-a* relationship has been extensively used in purely semantic ways, it can encompass geometrical and morphological properties of shapes and can be embodied by classes of shapes. For example, Fig. 28 (top) shows a very simplified, high-level taxonomy of geometrical shapes.

FIG. 27

It is sometimes hard to get rid of noise extracting relationships from text.

Fig. 29 shows a foundational model of anatomy, representing detailed anatomic knowledge. Anatomic knowledge is modeled by specifying a large set of rich relations among the anatomic entities. For example, one can observe that the heart (top left) has many relationships to other entities in the model (right), such as *adjacency*, *orientation*, *containment*, and *vascular supply*. Specifically, the foundational model of anatomy provides information that the *heart* is contained in the *middle mediastinum*, and that it is supplied by *left* and *right coronary arteries*.

9. Supporting search

Ontology-supported search is required to address a central problem that biomedical knowledge and clinical professionals face: to synthesize and filter information from multiple, large, and fast-growing sources. Existing search engines such as PubMed only partially address this need (Doms and Schroeder, 2005; Silla Jr and Freitas, 2011). They focus on a limited range of resources (e.g., only MEDLINE articles and concepts from GENE ONTOLOGY or MESH). At the same time, multiple sources including, for example, specialized drug databases and ontologies, frequently need to be integrated. Furthermore, existing search engines in health mostly retrieve possibly relevant texts or structured information, which the users then must browse, analyze, filter, and combine by themselves to obtain the answers they seek.

Interfaces to most search engines, including PubMed, use simple text boxes into which users enter query terms. This interface style does not assist users in articulating their information needs (Hoeber and Khazaei, 2015) and works well only for lookup search tasks (Hoeber, 2014; Hearst et al., 2002).

Digital record-keeping for the healthcare sector has transformed information collection and processing tasks. However, frequently the vast information is neither transferable nor subject to an analysis and is therefore not searchable due to underlying storage mechanisms and local terminology. E-health

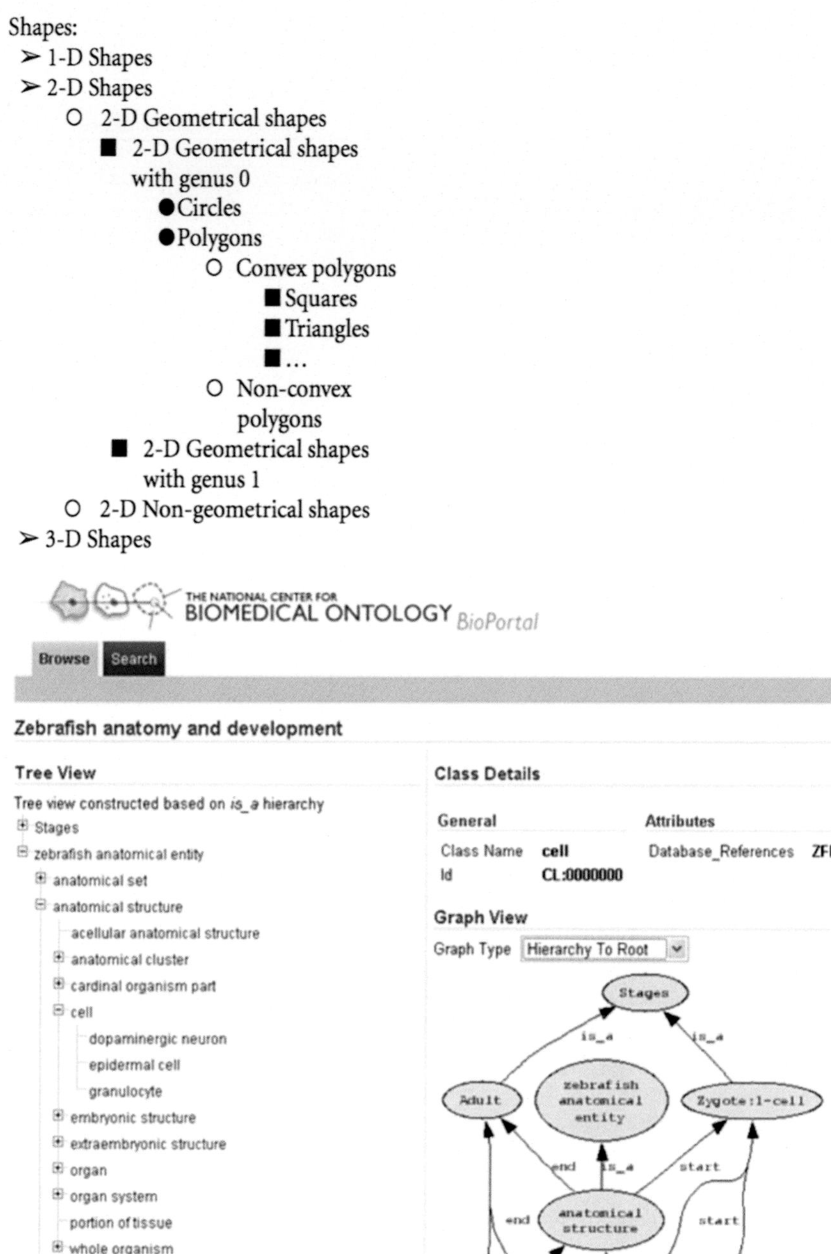

FIG. 28

An ontology of geometrical shapes (top). Ontologies shown as expandable tree (bottom).

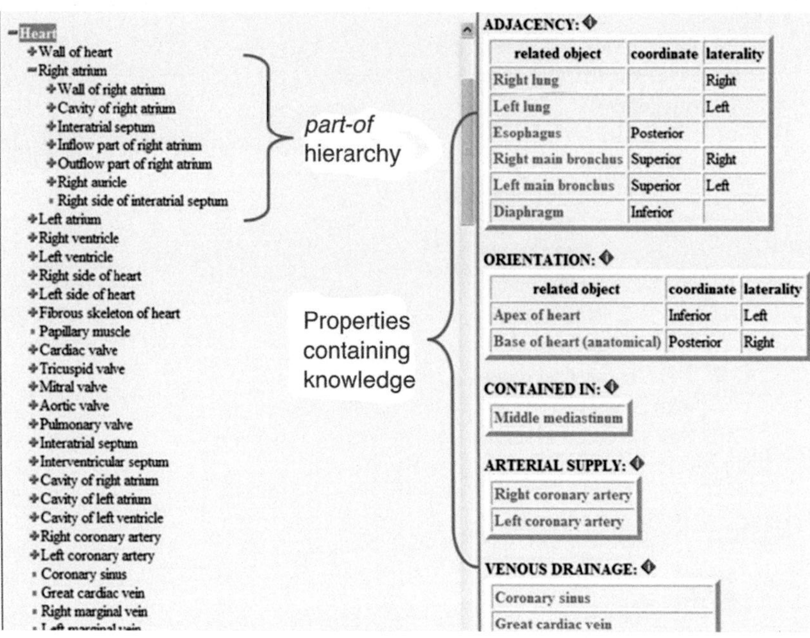

FIG. 29

Ontologies for anatomy.

is an area with the key objective of interoperability, secure sharing of patient health records for analysis, and informed decision-making. E-health implementation requires consistent domain and process terminology across applications. Ontology can be leveraged by search as it describes concepts in standard vocabulary for a specified domain. Further, due to consistent vocabulary, it can be utilized for querying and retrieval of required information from healthcare informatics repositories.

The main advantage of using ontologies to support search is their formalized semantics. Semantic web-based search engines employ ontologies in a particular domain to enhance the performance of the information retrieval process (Fig. 30). The ability to deduce additional facts based on the axiomatic content of ontology can be important from a research point of view (Rajendran and Swamynathan, 2015). A reasoner can automatically infer new statements without writing specific code. On the other hand, the decentralized nature of the Web makes it difficult to construct a single ontology. Although using a single ontology could make the task of integration and semantic interoperation easier, from the perspective of scalability, it is inefficient to retain a global consistency with a single huge ontology. Therefore, integration of multiple ontologies is one of the key technologies that need to be developed for the Semantic Web.

OVERT-MED (Demelo et al., 2017, Fig. 31) is developed to address two major problems of exploratory search activities:

(1) An issue in articulating information needs due to insufficient knowledge and domain-specific vocabulary. The authors propose an idea of using a formal ontology to help users build domain-specific terminology and knowledge for constructing search queries.

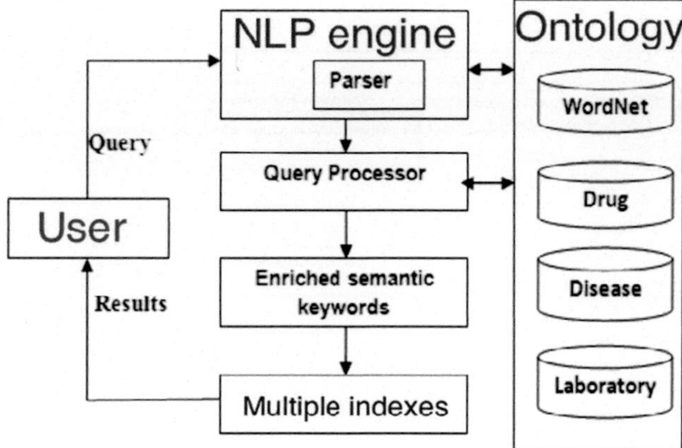

FIG. 30

A search engine supported by ontologies.

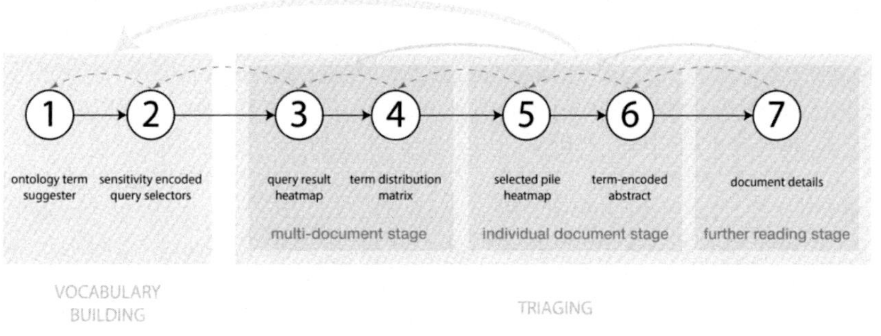

FIG. 31

OVERT-MED ontology construction pipeline.

(2) An issue in dealing with information overload due to the large number of results returned. To address the problem of search criteria being too restrictive in open-ended contexts, a visual sensitivity encoding strategy is employed to help users see possibilities with different combinations of terms.

Fig. 32 shows a semantic indexing and question answering (Q/A) pipeline in the biomedical domain (Tsatsaronis et al., 2015). The BIOASQ framework starts with a variety of data sources (lower right corner of Fig. 28) and semantic indexing that converts the data into a form that can be used to respond effectively to domain-specific questions. A semantic Q/A system links ontology entities with each question and uses the semantic index of the data to retrieve the relevant answer snippets (Galitsky and Kovalerchuk, 2014). The retrieved information is converted into a user-friendly format such as a ranked list of candidate answers in factoid questions, explanation questions, or a collection of text snippets, forming a coherent summary (in the best case). Examples here are as follows: "*What are*

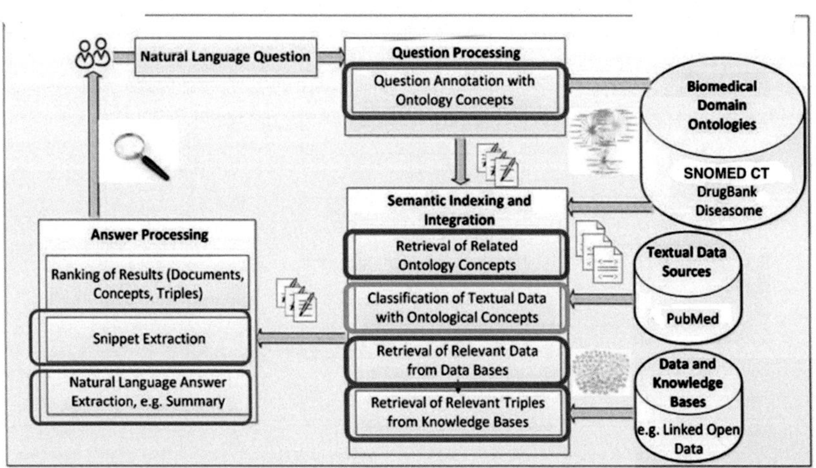

FIG. 32

A pipeline for ontology-supported search.

the symptoms of illness Y?" (e.g., in "*What data do we have about the side effects of drug X?*"). The figure also illustrates how these steps are mapped to the BIOASQ challenge tasks.

An automatic annotation of new PubMed documents headings is shown in blue frame. The brown frame depicts the task of processing the whole datasets containing 30 development and almost 300 English test questions, along with gold-standard answers, prepared by a team of annotators.

Starting with a variety of data sources (lower right corner of Fig. 32), semantic indexing and integration converts the data into a form that can be used to respond effectively to domain-specific questions. This semantic Q/A system associates ontology concepts with each question and uses the semantic index to retrieve relevant texts (documents or abstracts, e.g., from PubMed) to retrieve pieces of structured information such as Linked Open Data triples (Galitsky et al., 2010a) and relevant documents. This is depicted in the middle of the figure, by the processes included in the Question Processing, Semantic Indexing, and Integration boxes. The retrieved information is then turned into an exact form, interpretable by a user. This form can be a ranked list of candidate answers in factoid questions or a collection of text snippets (ideally forming a coherent summary) jointly providing the sought information.

A query engine parses the query and interprets the meaning of the user's query terms. Before any actual query reformulation, the mapping between the vocabulary of the ontologies and the query is required. The first step of the engine is to identify the set of ontologies likely to provide the information requested by the user. Hence it searches for near syntactic matches within the ontology indexes, using lexically related words obtained from WordNet and from the ontologies used as background knowledge source. The engine forms the subject, predicate, and object, which are used to create the query, and runs it against the ontology to attempt to answer it from existing knowledge (Galitsky and Ilvovsky, 2019).

Query expansion is a query reformulation technique that appends to query Q a (possibly empty) set of keywords $\{k_i, \ldots, k_{i+j}\}$ while retaining the semantics of Q, for some numbers *i* and *j*. Query expansion does not expand entities implicitly in a query but instead extends the keyword set by including the keywords more relevant to the entities such that the query intent becomes obvious to a search engine.

The resultant query is the disjunction of the original query entities and the entities that make it more precise, formed using the Boolean operation OR. Only a few web users employ advanced searching options (e.g., Boolean operators) in query formulation.

Query expansion has some intrinsic flaws like query drift, which moves the query in a direction away from the user's intention. This occurs normally when the query is ambiguous (Galitsky, 2005; Wu et al., 2011). The concerns addressed with query expansion are the selection and the weighting of added search terms. Instead of choosing phrases that are similar to the query terms, they are expanded by adding those terms that are equivalent to the entities in the query. The semantically related keywords in the ontology are retrieved to construct the refined query. Hence these refined queries are expected to have a greater semantic relevance (Galitsky, 2019a).

The whole process of query reformulation via ontology occurs in three steps:

(1) Identify the key ontology entities in the query. The input query keywords are used to choose the most related group and the domain ontology associated with the selected group is used to identify the associated entities for the expansion of the user query. Thus the choice of ontology is based on query phrases.

(2) Entity expansion. The input query is semantically expanded in ontology-based information retrieval. The phrase concepts are not split into single terms because single terms are likely to be semantically different to their associated phrase concepts, phrases, or multiwords (e.g., "sleep walking disorder"). Moreover, expanding entities by their superclass entities is avoided because broader concepts are more likely to compromise precision and cause query drift. Hence the detected ontology term is expanded by its equivalent entity. For each identified ontology entity, the system estimates its weight learning from the log file created for previous searches.

(3) Aggregation of entities. Merge lists of expansion terms for each entity into one final expansion list. The query is finalized by forming an OR query combining the original terms with the set of expansion terms obtained and then forming an AND query with the semantic types retrieved from the Unified Medical Language System ontology. Normally, forming a disjunction of the keywords with their synonyms will not significantly affect the precision of top 10 results. At the same time, in most cases, forming a conjunction of the semantic types of the query keywords with the expanded query improves the precision of the top 10 search results.

For example, the query "*symptoms of liver failure due to paracetamol overdose*" to a web search engine delivers hundreds of web pages that include both relevant and irrelevant results. Typically, a user will be willing to look at only a few of these pages. Most of medical journals use the term *acetaminophen* or *Tylenol* instead of the term *paracetamol*. When the query is expanded according to the preceding scenario, the system parses the input query and identifies the key terms in it. As a result, having consulted WordNet and drug ontologies, the system returns *acetaminophen* as an equivalent term for *paracetamol*.

10. System architecture

We first introduce a high-level view of how ontology entries are extracted form text and how logical forms are built from text, resulting in an extended ontology. We also show an iterative nature of ontology growth. After that, we drill into the components for entity extraction and aggregation and enumerate the necessary processing steps.

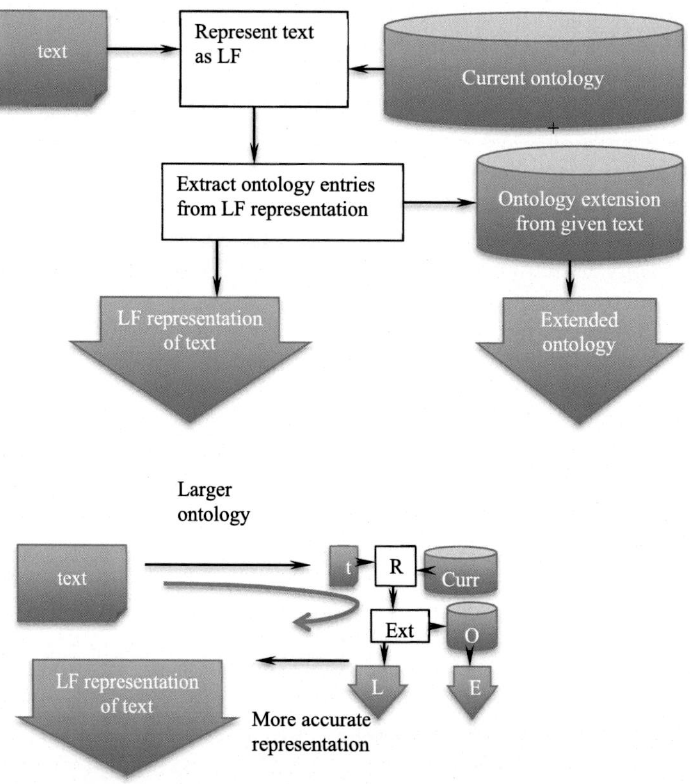

FIG. 33

A chart for building a logical form (LF).

Fig. 33 (top) shows a text is subject to LF representation as well as entity tuple extraction. To form an LF representation, the current ontology is used. The extraction tuple is added to the current ontology as a new entry. As a result, we obtain both LF representation and extended ontology.

Fig. 33 (bottom) shows an iterative pipeline of processing new texts and ontology construction. For the same text, as we extract more accurate and richer LF representation, we can identify more ontology entries. Once we have an extended ontology, we can form even richer LF representation. As a result, we can potentially extract an additional tuple and extend the ontology further, and so forth. This iterative procedure is more plausible for a corpus of documents rather than for one.

Fig. 34 shows the architecture of the ontology extractor from text. For a corpus of texts, we apply *Candidate Ontology Entry Extractor* (Sections 2 and 3). It first performs discourse parsing and yields the communicative discourse tree (CDT). This tree is then subject to a rule-based extractor of EDUs appropriate for tuple formation.

It happens in multiple steps. The EDU with the central entity is extracted and other associated EDUs are labeled as appropriate for tuple formation. Then all nucleus EDUs are considered and if they constitute a too short phrase, they are merged with the respective nucleus to form a single CDT node. Finally, all nucleus EDUs outside of EDUs associated with the central entity are included in the list of

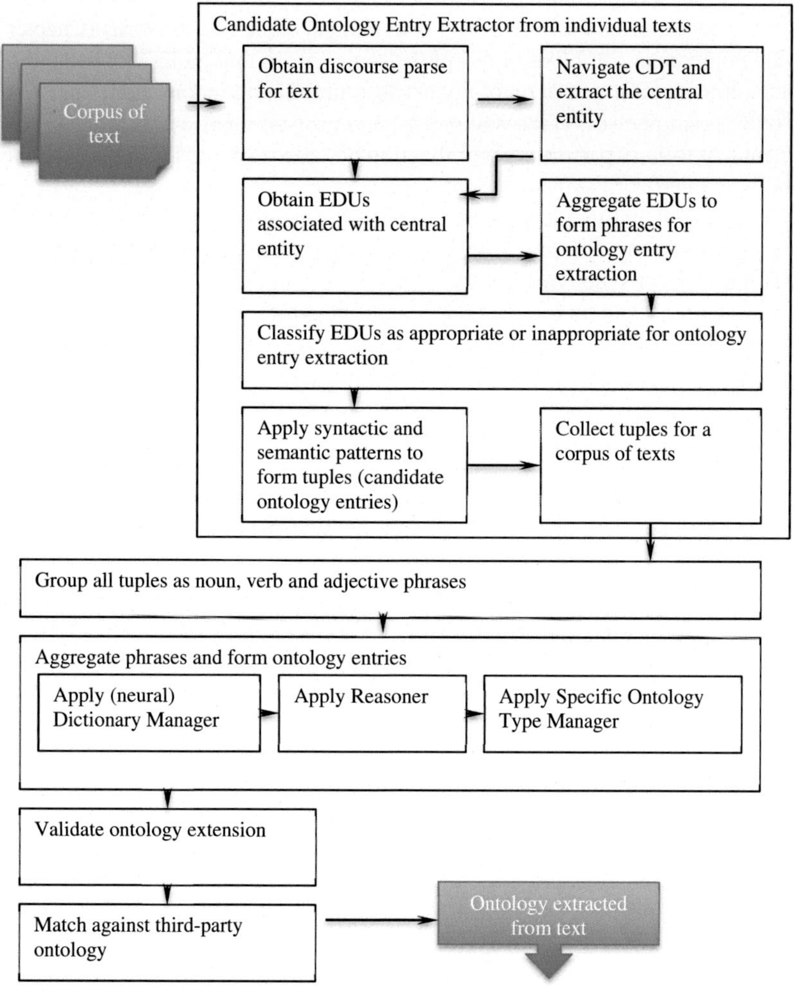

FIG. 34

An architecture of CDT-enhanced ontology builder.

EDUs appropriate for tuple formation. As a result, we obtain the list of tuples as candidates for inclusion in the ontology. The last step is conversion of aggregated and refined tuples into logical forms, based on simplified semantic parsing such as AMR (Galitsky, 2021b). Hence the *Candidate Ontology Entry Extractor* pipeline includes the following transformations:

$$Text \rightarrow CDT \rightarrow list-of-EDUs \rightarrow list-of-phrases \rightarrow list-of-tuples \rightarrow logicalforms$$

We apply syntactic and semantic templates to extract a tuple such as *predicate—subject—object* from a phrase (Galitsky et al., 2012). Finally, as an output of the *Candidate Ontology Entry Extractor*, we obtain the list of tuples for a given text. Before grouping, these tuples need to be accumulated for all texts in a corpus (Section 6). Also, specific ontology types have certain generalization rules for values like space and time that are generalized in a different way than entities expressed in words (Chapter 7).

The grouping component combines tuples of the same sort so that tuples can be matched with each other to produce reliable, informative ontology entries, minimizing inconsistencies. Noun phrases are grouped with other noun phrases, verbs with verbs, and propositional with propositional. The aggregation component that follows performs generalization of tuples to avoid too specific, noisy entries that cannot be reliably applied with sufficient confidence (Section 5).

A dictionary manager that includes identification of synonyms helps in generalizing tuples that have the same meanings but different words expressing them. Reasoning is used to cover words and multiwords that are not synonyms but imply each other in context of other words.

11. Evaluation

11.1 Datasets

It is not easy to evaluate an ontology construction, as criteria vary from the domain and application areas. Complex domain-specific medical Q/A datasets such as MCTest (Richardson et al., 2013), biological process modeling (Vivek Srikumar et al., 2014), BioASQ (Tsatsaronis et al., 2015), and InsuranceQA are available but are limited in scale (500–10,000) because of the complexity of the task or the need for expert annotations that cannot be crowdsourced or gathered from the Web. We combine seven datasets of varying complexity of questions, texts, and their associations to track the contribution of each ontology construction step. Table 4 characterizes Q/A datasets.

A few studies proposed several automated dataset-generation techniques. Pampari et al. (2018) proposed a novel methodology to generate domain-specific, large-scale question answering (QA) datasets by re-purposing existing annotations for other Natural Language Processing (NLP) tasks. The authors demonstrate an instance of this methodology in generating a large-scale Q/A dataset for electronic medical records (EMRs) by leveraging existing expert annotations on clinical notes for various NLP tasks from the community shared i2b2 datasets. The resulting corpus (emrQA) has one million questions-LFs and more than 400,000 question-answer evidence pairs. The authors characterized the dataset and explored its learning potential by training baseline models for question-to-LF and question-to-answer mapping.

Pampari et al. (2018) demonstrated that the LF approach utilizes a formalized representation that is useful for corpus generation and for model analysis. The LFs support building interpretable systems via learning the LFs and answers to questions. This framework can also be applicable to other health datasets such as MIMIC and generate a more diverse and representative EMR QA corpus (Johnson et al., 2016).

Fig. 35 shows the architecture of a Q/A dataset-generation framework. The generation of questions along their logical forms is based on annotations on a given patient's record.

11.2 Assessment of ontology consistency

When ontology entries are extracted arbitrarily from noisy data, some entries contradict each other. The frequency of contradiction indirectly indicates the error rate of tuple extraction and overall ontology formation. Examples of contradicting entries are <*bird, penguin, fly*> vs <*bird, penguin, not fly*> and <*frog, crawl, water*> vs <*frog, swim, water*> (the third argument should be distinct).

Table 4 The Q/A datasets we use for evaluation of the ontology construction.

Name	Description	#	Source and sample	Link
Medical-Question-Answer-Datasets	Several sources for medical question and answer datasets from HealthTap.com	1,600,000	https://www.healthtap.com/user_questions/919966-foods-you-can-eat-with-acid-reflux-and-a-fatty-liver	https://github.com/durakkerem/Medical-Question-Answer-Datasets
MedQuAD: Medical Question Answering Dataset	Medical question-answer pairs created from 12 NIH websites. The collection covers 37 question types (e.g., Treatment, Diagnosis, Side Effects) associated with diseases, drugs, and other medical entities such as tests	50,000	cancer.gov, niddk.nih.gov, GARD, MedlinePlus Health Topics	https://github.com/abachaa/MedQuAD
Medical Q/A data	Medical Q/A datasets gathered from eHealth Forum and HealthTap		iCliniq Question Doctors WebMD	https://github.com/LasseRegin/medical-question-answer-data
PubMedQA	Biomedical question answering dataset collected from PubMed abstracts	275,000	Jin et al. (2019)	https://pubmedqa.github.io
emrQA	Generated domain-specific large-scale electronic medical records datasets produced by repurposing existing annotations on clinical notes	1 million questions-logical form and 400,000 + question-answer evidence pairs	Pampari et al. (2018) Auto generated	https://github.com/panushri25/emrQA https://www.i2b2.org/NLP/DataSets/
BioASQ	Evaluation infrastructure for biomedical semantic indexing and QA		Tsatsaronis et al. (2015)	
GENIA	One of the most used corpora on TM specifically developed to support the construction and evaluation of IE	2000 Medline abstracts	Kim et al. (2003)	http://www.nactem.ac.uk/genia

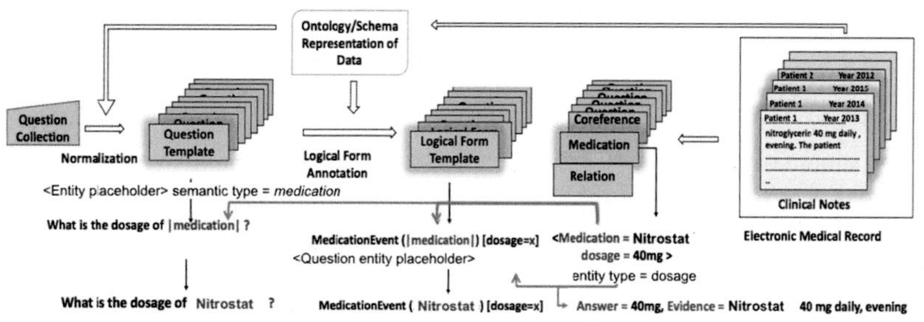

FIG. 35

Q/A dataset-generation framework.

Table 5 Assessment of ontology consistency.

Dataset/ settings	Baseline extraction of individual entries	Entity grid method	Syntactic + semantic	+Dictionary manager	+Discourse	+Reasoning	+Existing ontology support
Medical-Question-Answer-Datasets	7.6	5.9	2.8	2.4	1.7	1.1	0.8
MedQuAD	6.2	4.7	2.3	1.9	1.4	1.2	1.1
Medical Q/A data	7.0	5.0	2.4	1.7	1.7	1.4	1.0
PubMedQA	6.9	6.0	3.8	2.9	1.6	1.1	0.8
emrQA	11.1	9.8	4.9	3.2	2.2	1.6	1.3

We extract ontology entries from answers. Then, in the resultant ontology, given each entry, we attempt to find other entries that contradict the given one. If at least one such entry is found, we consider the given entry inconsistent. The portion of inconsistent entries for the whole ontology is counted and shown as a percentage of all ontology entries. As a baseline, we evaluate an ontology whose entries are extracted from all text parts and left as they are, without any refinement. Then we apply various enhancement steps and track if they affect the ontology consistency.

We assess how each ontology improvement step affects the resultant ontology consistency (Table 5). The inconsistency values are normalized for the total number of ontology entries as each refinement step reduces the number of entries, pruning ones determined to do unreliable. Each step has its own machinery of reducing the entries expected to be noisy, unreliable, and misleading.

We observe that adding rules for extracting ontology entries makes the resultant ontology cleaner, more robust, and consistent. Employing all means to reduce inconsistencies achieves a contradiction rate of less than 1% of inconsistent ontology entries in most domains. The hardest domains to achieve inconsistency are MedQuAD and emrQA. The worst performance occurs for EMRs (bottom row).

11.3 An assessment of search improvement due to ontology

We evaluate the accuracy of search in several health-related datasets when this search is supported by an ontology. We vary the complexity of ontological support, steps employed to improve/validate it, and ontological sources (Table 6). As we have the single best answer for each evaluation dataset, search relevance is measured as F1. This is a simplified measure in comparison to our assessment settings in other chapters (Chapter 3) where multiple search results are expected and the ranking order is important. Our baseline search is a default TF*IDF without ontology involvement. We add the ontology at the various construction steps according to the ontology construction system architecture (Fig. 34).

One can observe that there is a small improvement in search relevance (F1) with each enhancement in ontology construction. Such an improvement in the range of 2% may be hard to differentiate from a

Table 6 Assessment of ontology quality via search relevance.

Dataset/ settings	No ontology baseline, F1	Ontology is built from all results of syntactic extraction, F1	Filtering based on CDT, F1	Aggregation, F1	Enrichment by dictionary manager, F1	Validation and foreign ontology matching, F1
Medical-Question-Answer-Datasets	78.3	80.1	82.3	84.1	85.3	86.1
MedQuAD	75.1	77.0	80.4	81.6	83.0	85.0
Medical Q/A data	80.2	81.3	83.1	85.8	86.7	86.3
PubMedQA	77.5	78.9	82.0	84.2	86.0	87.2
emrQA	76.0	78.1	81.2	82.9	83.9	86.4
Improvement		2.1	5.7	8.1	9.8	11.3

random deviation. However, the overall improvement due to ontologies is significant; greater than 10%. Our ablation experiments show that each step in discourse processing, aggregation, matching, and validation is important and should not be skipped.

12. Conclusions

In this chapter, we reviewed major techniques for automated ontology construction, management and applications. We looked at various TM techniques and system components and observed an ontology construction bottleneck as selecting portions of documents well-suited for ontology construction.

We explored how discourse analysis helps to identify such portions, similar to how informative portions of text were recognized for indexing (Galitsky, 2019a). Adding discourse considerations makes the whole ontology construction process complex (Fig. 36).

High-purity ontologies obtained from proper portions of documents are essential for question answering (Galitsky and Ilvovsky, 2019) and especially under the summarized logic forms approach to controlled questions answering, where association between a question and an answer is fully controlled by a system developer (Galitsky, 2021a).

Although ontology-assisted search cannot be represented as a machine learning (ML) task, in our previous studies we learned important lessons from our industrial evaluation of the learning transfer framework (Galitsky, 2019a). Building ontologies via web mining and applying them in a specific vertical domain can be viewed as inductive transfer/multi-task learning with feature representation and a relational-knowledge transfer approach. We evaluated that the ontologies, which are built from a wide variety of sources including blogs (Galitsky and Kovalerchuk, 2006), forums, chats, opinion data (Galitsky and McKenna, 2017), and customer support data, are adequate to handle user queries in searching for products and recommendations in vertical domains such as shopping and entertainment at eBay.com as well as in finance. Ontology learning in this work is performed in a vertical domain, where the ambiguity of the terms is limited, and therefore, fully automated settings produce adequate resultant search accuracy.

FIG. 36

Frequently, too many levels of hierarchy make an automatically learned ontology unreliable (left). Ontology in the form *predicate-subject-object-...* is used by both search and decision support (right).

Advanced systems for supporting the clinical decision are critical in the emergency department. It is the environment that requires the most accurate solution as fast as possible due to the situation being critical. The use of ontologies has played an important role in the development of intelligent systems that support decision-making in the emergency services, and its application is already a reality. Portela et al. (2014) presented a specific system for emergency services that guides the healthcare professional in a correct decision-making process to establish clinical priorities. This complex process was carried out thanks to TM techniques that extract relevant data from EMRs, laboratory tests, or therapeutic plans (Gupta and Lehal, 2009).

Gómez and Miura (2021) developed a system for service robots that combines ontological knowledge reasoning and human-robot interaction to interpret natural language commands and successfully perform household tasks, such as finding and delivering objects. Knowledge and context reasoning is essential for providing more efficient service robots, given their diverse and continuously changing environments. Moreover, since they are in contact with humans, robots require such skills as interaction and language.

Our evaluation showed that relying on discourse analysis indeed improves the quality of an ontology with respect to:

(1) fewer number of inconsistencies
(2) greater relevance of the resultant search

We conclude that once we extract ontology entries from important and informative parts of text instead of extracting them from all text, the reliability of the resultant ontology for search and decision-making grows.

Supplementary data sets

Please visit https://github.com/bgalitsky/relevance-based-on-parse-trees to access all supplementary data sets.

References

Arbabi, A., Adams, D.R., Fidler, S., Brudno, M., 2019. Identifying clinical terms in medical text using ontology-guided machine learning. JMIR Med. Inform. 7 (2). https://doi.org/10.2196/12596, e12596.

Asma, A.B., Silveira, M., Pruski, C., 2013. Medical Ontology Validation through Question Answering., https://doi.org/10.1007/978-3-642-38326-7_30.

Banko, M., Cafarella, M.J., Soderland, S., Broadhead, M., Etzioni, O., 2007. Open information extraction for the web. In: Proceedings of the International Joint Conferences on Artificial Intelligence Hyderabad, India, pp. 2670–2676. http://www.ijcai.org/proceedings/2007.

Barzilay, R., Lapata, M., 2008. Modeling local coherence: an entity-based approach. Comput. Linguist. 34 (1), 1–34.

Bhattacharyya, S., 2016. Introduction to SNOMED CT. Springer Science, Singapore.

Bojanowski, P., Grave, E., Joulin, A., Mikolov, T., 2017. Enriching word vectors with subword information. Trans. Assoc. Comput. Linguist. 5, 135–146.

Cimiano, P., 2006. Ontology Learning and Population from Text: Algorithms, Evaluation and Applications. Springer-Verlag New York, Inc, Secaucus.

Clevert, A.D., Unterthiner, T., Hochreiter, S., 2015. Fast and Accurate Deep Network Learning by Exponential Linear Units. https://arxiv.org/abs/1511.07289.

Del Corro, L., Gemulla, R., 2013. ClausIE: clause-based open information extraction. In: Proceedings of the 22nd International Conference on World Wide Web. International World Wide Web Conferences Steering Committee, Rio de Janeiro, pp. 355–366.

Demelo, J., Parsons, P., Sedig, K., 2017. Ontology-driven search and triage: design of a web-based visual interface for MEDLINE. JMIR Med. Inform. 5 (1), e4.

Doms, A., Schroeder, M., 2005. GoPubMed: exploring PubMed with the gene ontology. Nucleic Acids Res. 33, 783–786.

El-Sappagh, S., Franda, F., Ali, F., Kwak, K.-S., 2018. SNOMED CT standard ontology based on the ontology for general medical science. BMC Med. Inform. Decis. Mak. 18, 76. https://doi.org/10.1186/s12911-018-0651-5.

Galitsky, B., 2003. Natural Language Question Answering System: Technique of Semantic Headers. Advanced Knowledge International, Australia.

Galitsky, B., 2005. Disambiguation via default rules under answering complex questions. Int. J. Artif. Intell. Tools 14 (1–2), 157–175. World Scientific.

Galitsky, B., 2013. Machine learning of syntactic parse trees for search and classification of text. Eng. Appl. Artif. Intel. 26 (3), 1072–1091.

Galitsky, B., 2015a. Finding a lattice of needles in a haystack: forming a query from a set of items of interest. LNCS 1430, FCA4AI@IJCAI 99–106.

Galitsky, B., 2015b. Lattice queries for search and data exploration. In: The Twenty-Eighth International FLAIRS conference. The track on Semantic, Logics, Information Extraction, and AI.

Galitsky, B., 2016. Generalization of parse trees for iterative taxonomy learning. Inf. Sci. 329, 125–143.

Galitsky, B., 2017a. Improving relevance in a content pipeline via syntactic generalization. Eng. Appl. Artif. Intell. 58, 1–26.

Galitsky, B., 2017b. Matching parse thickets for open domain question answering. Data Knowl. Eng. 107, 24–50.

Galitsky, B., 2019a. Building chatbot thesaurus. In: Developing Enterprise Chatbots. Springer, Cham, Switzerland, pp. 220–252.

Galitsky, B., 2019b. Rhetorical map of an answer. In: Developing Enterprise Chatbots. Springer, Cham, Switzerland, pp. 533–566.

Galitsky, B., 2021a. Summarized logical forms for controlled question answering. In: Artificial Intelligence for Customer Relationship Management: Keeping Customers Informed. Springer, Cham, pp. 87–150.

Galitsky, B., 2021b. Summarized logical forms based on abstract meaning representation and discourse trees. In: Artificial Intelligence for Customer Relationship Management: Keeping Customers Informed. Springer, Cham, pp. 151–192.

Galitsky, B., Goldberg, S., 2019. Explainable machine learning for chatbots. In: Developing Enterprise Chatbots. Springer, Cham, Switzerland, pp. 53–83.

Galitsky, B., Ilvovsky, D., 2019. Discourse-based approach to involvement of background knowledge for question answering. In: RANLP Varna, Bulgaria.

Galitsky, B., Kovalerchuk, B., 2006. Mining the blogosphere for contributors' sentiments. In: AAAI Spring Symposium: Computational Approaches to Analyzing Weblogs, pp. 37–39.

Galitsky, B., Kovalerchuk, B., 2014. Improving web search relevance with learning structure of domain concepts. In: Clust Order Trees Methods Appl. vol. 92. Springer, pp. 341–376.

Galitsky, B., McKenna, E.W., 2017. Sentiment Extraction from Consumer Reviews for Providing Product Recommendations. US Patent App. 15/489,059.

Galitsky, B., de la Rosa, J.L., Dobrocsi, G., 2010a. Improving relevancy accessing linked opinion data. In: AAAI Spring Symposium Series.

Galitsky, B., Kovalerchuk, B., de la Rosa, J.L., 2011a. Assessing plausibility of explanation and meta-explanation in inter-human conflicts. A special issue on semantic-based information and engineering systems. Eng. Appl. Artif. Intell. 24 (8), 1472–1486.

Galitsky, B., Dobrocsi, G., de la Rosa, J.L., Kuznetsov, S.O., 2011b. Using generalization of syntactic parse trees for taxonomy capture on the web. In: ICCS 2011, pp. 104–117.

Galitsky, B., Dobrocsi, G., de la Rosa, J.L., 2012. Inferring semantic properties of sentences mining syntactic parse trees. Data Knowl. Eng. 81, 21–45.

Goldberg, S., Galitsky, B., Weisburd, B., 2019. Framework for interaction between expert users and machine learning systems. In: AAAI Spring Symposium: Interpretable AI for Well-being, Stanford, CA.

Gómez, L., Miura, J., 2021. Ontology-based knowledge management with verbal interaction for command interpretation and execution by home service robots. Robot. Auton. Syst. 140.

Gonzalez, G.H., Tahsin, T., Goodale, B.C., Greene, A.C., Greene, C.S., 2016. Recent advances and emerging applications in text and data mining for biomedical discovery. Brief. Bioinform. 17 (1), 33–42.

Grosz, B.J., Weinstein, S., Joshi, A.K., 1995. Centering: a framework for modeling the local coherence of discourse. Comput. Linguist. 21 (2), 203–225.

Gupta, V., Lehal, G.S., 2009. A survey of text mining techniques and applications. J. Emerg. Technol. Web Intell. 1 (1), 60–76.

Hammar, K., 2017. Content Ontology Design Patterns: Qualities, Methods, and Tools. Linköping University Electronic Press, Linköping.

Hearst, M., Elliott, A., English, J., Sinha, R., Swearingen, K., Yee, K., 2002. Finding the flow in web site search. Commun. ACM 45 (9), 42–49.

Hoeber, O., 2014. Visual search analytics: combining machine learning and interactive visualization to support human-centered search. In: 2014 Presented at: Pro-ceedings of the MindTheGap'14 Workshop; March 4; Berlin, Germany, pp. 37–43.

Hoeber, O., Khazaei, T., 2015. Evaluating citation visualization and exploration methods for supporting academic search tasks. Online Inf. Rev. 39 (2), 229–254.

Jasinskaja, K., Karagjosova, E., 2017. Rhetorical relations. In: Matthewson, L., Meier, C., Rullmann, H. (Eds.), The Companion to Semantics. Wiley, Oxford.

Jin, Q., Dhingra, B., Liu, Z., Cohen, W., Lu, X., 2019. PubMedQA: A Dataset for Biomedical Research Question Answering. pp. 2567–2577, https://doi.org/10.18653/v1/D19-1259.

Johnson, A.E.W., Pollard, T.J., Shen, L., Li-wei, H.L., Feng, M., Ghassemi, M., Moody, B., Szolovits, P., Celi, L. A., Mark, R.G., 2016. MIMIC-iii, a freely accessible critical care database. Sci. Data 3, 160035.

Jusoh, S., Awajan, A., Obeid, N., 2020. The use of ontology in clinical information extraction. J. Phys. Conf. Ser. 1529. https://doi.org/10.1088/1742-6596/1529/5/052083, 052083.

Kim, J.-D., Ohta, T., Tateisi, Y., Tsujii, J., 2003. GENIA corpus—a semantically annotated corpus for bio-textmining. Bioinformatics 19 (3), 180–182.

Kim, J.-D., Ohta, T., Tsujii, J., 2008. Corpus annotation for mining biomedical events from literature. BMC Bioinf. 9, 10.

Liu, J., Kuipers, B., Savarese, S., 2011. Recognizing human actions by attributes. CVPR. pp. 3337–3344.

Luque, C., Luna, J.M., Luque, M., Ventura, S., 2018. An advanced review on text mining in medicine. WIREs Data Min. Knowl. Discov. 9.

Mann, W., Thompson, S., 1988. Rhetorical structure theory: towards a functional theory of text organization. Text Interdiscip. J. Study Discourse 8 (3), 243–281.

MedlinePlus, 2019. Aripiprazole. https://medlineplus.gov/druginfo/meds/a603012.html.

Mortensen, J.M., Horridge, M., Musen, M.A., Noy, N., 2012. Modest use of ontology design patterns in a repository of biomedical ontologies. In: WOP'12: Proceedings of the 3rd International Conference on Ontology Patterns, vol. 928, pp. 37–48.

Otmani, N., Si-Mohammed, M., Comparot, C., Charrel, P.-J., 2018. Ontology-based approach to enhance medical web information extraction. Int. J. Web Inf. Syst. https://doi.org/10.1108/IJWIS-03-2018-0017.

Pampari, A., Raghavan, P., Liang, J., Peng, J., 2018. emrQA: a large corpus for question answering on electronic medical records. In: EMNLP 2021: Conference on Empirical Methods in Natural Language Processing.

Portela, F., Cabral, A., Abelha, A., Salazar, M., Quintas, C., Machado, J., Santos, M., 2014. Knowledge acquisition process for intelligent decision support in critical health care. In: Healthcare Administration: Concepts, Methodologies, Tools, and Applications: Concepts, Methodologies, Tools, and Applications. vol. 270. IGI Global.

QnAmaker, 2018. Microsoft QnA Maker. https://www.qnamaker.ai/.

Racunas, S.A., Shah, N., Albert, I., Fedoroff, N.V., 2004. HyBrow: a prototype system for computer-aided hypothesis evaluation. Bioinformatics 20, 257–264.

Rajendran, V., Swamynathan, S., 2015. MOSS-IR: multi-ontology based search system for information retrieval in E-health domain. Procedia Comput. Sci. 47, 179–187.

Richardson, M., Burges, C.J.C., Renshaw, E., 2013. MCTest: a challenge dataset for the open-domain machine comprehension of text. In: EMNLP. vol. 3, p. 4.

Roberts, K., Demner-Fushman, D., 2016. Annotating logical forms for EHR questions. In: LREC, International Conference on Language Resources and Evaluation, p. 3772.

Rubin, D., Moreira, D.A., Kanjamala, P., Musen, M., 2008. BioPortal: a web portal to biomedical ontologies. In: AAAI Spring Symposium: Symbiotic Relationships between Semantic Web and Knowledge Engineering.

Schmitz, M., Bart, R., Soderland, S., Etzioni, O., et al., 2012. Open language learning for information extraction. In: Proceedings of the 2012 Joint Conference on Empirical Methods in Natural Language Processing and Computational Natural Language Learning. Association for Computational Linguistics, Jeju Island, pp. 523–534.

Silla Jr., C.N., Freitas, A.A., 2011. A survey of hierarchical classification across different application domains. Data Min. Knowl. Disc. 22, 31–72.

Speer, R., Chin, J., Havasi, C., 2017. ConceptNet 5.5: an open multilingual graph of general knowledge. In: Proceedings of AAAI.

Tsatsaronis, G., Balikas, G., Malakasiotis, P., Partalas, I., Zschunke, M., Alvers, M.R., Weissenborn, D., Krithara, A., Petridis, S., Polychronopoulos, D., Yannis Almirantis, J., Pavlopoulos, N.B., Gallinari, P., Artiéres, T., Ngomo, A.-C.N., Heino, N., Gaussier, E., Barrio-Alvers, L., Schroeder, M., Androutsopoulos, I., Paliouras, G., 2015. An overview of the BIOASQ large-scale biomedical semantic indexing and question answering competition. BMC Bioinf. 16, 138.

Tuan, A.M., Song, H.-Y., Zhang, Y., Xu, H., Tao, C., 2017. Lightweight predicate extraction for patient-level cancer information and ontology development. BMC Med. Inform. Decis. Mak. 17. https://doi.org/10.1186/s12911-017-0465-x.

Vivek Srikumar, B.J., Chen, P.-C., Linden, A.V., Harding, B., Huang, B., Clark, P., Manning, C.D., 2014. Modeling biological processes for reading comprehension. In: EMNLP.

Wu, J.W., Ilyas, I., Weddell, G., 2011. A Study of Ontology-Based Query Expansion. Technical Report CS-2011-04.

CHAPTER

Explanation in medical decision support systems

12

Saveli Goldberg

Division of Radiation Oncology, Massachusetts General Hospital, Boston, MA, United States

1. Introduction

Real projects are rarely successful without a reasonable understanding of how machine learning (ML) models or the data processing pipeline work. The European Union even includes the need to explain the decision in the new General Data Protection Regulation, which controls the applicability of ML (https://eugdpr.org/) (Goodman and Flaxman, 2017) (Fig. 1).

There are certain criteria that are used to categorize the interpretation methods of the model (Molnar, 2018). These include:

- **Internal vs ex-post interpretation**: Internal interpretability is the use of an ML model that is internally interpretable. Several such models exist, including linear or tree models. More complex models, such as ensemble models or deep learning (DL) models, often give better performance but are perceived as black-box models because they lack explanatory power. As a result, a posteriori interpretability is required when choosing and training a black-box model.
- **Model-independent vs model-based interpretation**: Interpretation tools for specific models depend solely on the capabilities and functions of each model. Model agnostic tools can be used in any ML model.
- **Local vs global interpretation**: An interpretation is local if the method explains a single decision. Global interpretation explains the behavior of the whole model.

Consider the current situation explaining the solution to the ML model adhering to the largely excellent review by Sarkar (2018).

2. Models of machine learning explanation

2.1 Interpretable models

There are ML models (Table 1) whose conclusions can be interpreted relatively easily depending on the nature of these models.

The usual characteristics of such models are:

- **linearity**: the relationship between objects and targets is modeled linearly.

Artificial Intelligence for Healthcare Applications and Management. https://doi.org/10.1016/B978-0-12-824521-7.00003-X

FIG. 1

AI tries to make a recommendation in the European Union.

Table 1 Some examples of interpretable machine learning (ML) models from *Interpretable Machine Learning* (Molnar, 2018).

Algorithm	Linear	Monotone	Interaction
Linear models	Yes	Yes	No
Logistic regression	No	Yes	No
Decision tree	No	Some	Yes
RuleFit	Yes	No	Yes
Naive Bayes	Yes	Yes	No
k-nearest neighbors	No	No	No

- **monotony**: the relationship between function and target result always has one constant direction.
- **interactions**: the ability to add elements of nonlinear interaction to the model.

2.2 Black-box models

Let there be a numerical characteristic of the accuracy of the solution of the ML system for a specific point in the space f (α_{ML}, **v**). Then the local explanation of the solution α_{ML} at **v** can be based on the analysis of the local gradient at **v**. The local gradient is supposed to indicate how the data point should be moved to change the ML decision (Bouneffouf, 2016). The idea of assessing the importance of a feature based on its change in the quality of the solution was considered by Breiman (2001) and developed by Fisher et al. (2018) and Smith et al. (2020) in the model-agnostic version. The feature is "important" if its value changes can significantly increase the ML solution error.

An important step in developing the idea of explaining ML solutions is the TREPAN algorithm (Craven, 1996; Craven and Shavlik, 1996). If we have an ML model, TREPAN uses queries on that model to create a decision tree (DecT) that approximates the function represented by the ML model. Now, having such a surrogate DecT, we can give local explanations of ML decisions.

The most popular methods for black-box model explanation are Local Interpretable Model-agnostic Explanations (LIME) and Shapley Values and SHapley Additive exPlanations (SHAP).

Ribeiro et al. (2016) developed the LIME algorithm to locally explain the black-box model using interpreted surrogate models (usually a linear classifier).

LIME generates a new dataset consisting of artificial samples and pins of the associated black-box model. On this dataset, LIME then trains the interpreted model (Fig. 2).

SHAP was developed by Lundberg and Lee (2017).

Model predictions can be explained by assuming that each feature is a "player" in a game where the prediction is the payout. The Shapley value, a method from coalitional game theory, tells us how to distribute the "payout" among the features fairly.

- The "game" is the prediction task for a single instance of the dataset.
- The "gain" is the actual prediction for this instance minus the average prediction of all instances.
- The "players" are the feature values of the instance, which collaborate to receive the gain (= predict a certain value).

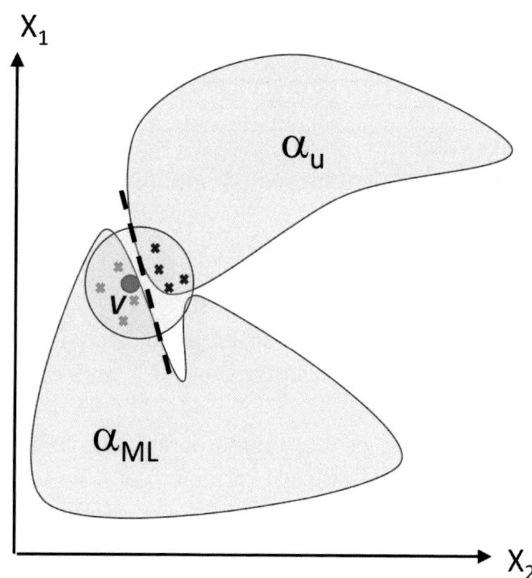

FIG. 2

Local explanation by LIME.

The Shapley value is the average marginal contribution of a feature value over all possible coalitions. Coalitions are basically combinations of features that are used to estimate the Shapley value of a specific feature.

3. Explanation based on comparison of the local case with the closest case with an alternative ML solution

As shown, a local explanation of the ML decision is usually provided based on the relative importance of the characteristics used to make the decision. As a rule, the doctor knows which parameters are important, although, of course, the weight of some of these parameters is not obvious in a given situation.

We think that a physician can better understand an ML solution for such a local case **v** if the explanation system were built with the following principles in mind:

(1) Interactive communication. That is, the expert will be able to get answers to the questions asked by him, such as "Why is the solution of the machine α_{ML}, and not α_U?" or "How to change the αml solution if the value v_{i1} of the parameter **i** changes to v_{i2}?"
(2) The physician will know what minimal change in parameter values will lead to a different ML solution. To do this, the user must get the point **v**′ closest to the initial state **v** when the ML changes its mind. Thus, the user can see which parameters need to be changed to get a different ML solution. It is possible that these parameter changes do not go beyond the measurement errors. It is also possible that the parameter values for **v**′ do differ from those for **v**. At the same time, the user can see the cumulative effect of the combination of parameters instead of the linear effect achieved using a standard linear representation of the parameters with weights.

The main problem with our approach lies in the word "closest." It should be "closest" from the point of view of a specialist, not an ML system. Therefore, it is necessary to enter a distance that is understandable to a specialist (Goldberg et al., 2020).

In our work, we investigated three different distance metrics for the parameters:

(1) by the possibility of equality values.
(2) by differences of parameter values from the scaled normal-abnormal.
(3) by the level of significance in parameters.

(1) Closeness based on the possibility of values equality

It is the proximity in the magnitude of the measurement error. The pressures 125 and 130 could be the same since the standard error of measurement is ±5, and 125 and 150 are really different since the tonometer cannot be so wrong.

Let $\mathbf{x} = (x_1, x_2, \ldots, x_n)$ be a vector of the n input parameters to the algorithm. x_i can be a continuous (numerical) or categorical (Boolean) variable. Let **X** be a set of **x**. Let $\mathbf{v} = (v_1, \ldots, v_n) \in \mathbf{X}$ be the particular input values entered by the expert. For example, **v** = (age (62 years), blood pressure (120 mL), headache (moderate), temperature (97.2°F).

For any parameter **i,** its x_i value can be offset or error. The blood pressure may be 125 mL, and the headache may be mild. Therefore, we define $\Omega(x_i)$ as the set of values considered within the error bounds for x_i and $\Omega(\mathbf{x})$ as a set of errors for $\mathbf{x}$. $G_{yi}(x_i)$ has been the probability of the value of y_i when x_i was defined.

Let $\mathbf{D}=\{\alpha_j\}, j=1, \ldots, k$ be the set of k possible decisions. α_j ($\mathbf{x}$) denotes that decision α_j was made at point $\mathbf{x}$.

We define distance between $\mathbf{x}=(x_1, x_2, \ldots, x_n)$ and $\mathbf{y}=(y_1, y_2, \ldots, y_n)$ as

$$\text{Dist}(\mathbf{x}, \mathbf{y}) = \sum_{i\in\{1,\ldots,n\}} \left(x_i \times (1 - G_{xi}(y_i)) - y_i \times (1 - G_{yi}(x_i))\right)^2$$

(2) Closeness based on differences of parameter values from the scaled normal-abnormal

For the physician, the distance between body temperature 97.2°F and 98.3°F is closer than the distance between 98.3°F and 99.4°F.

We introduce an intuitive feature normalization x_i^{norm} for each i-th dimension based on the four thresholds a_{1i}, a_{2i}, a_{3i}, and a_{4i} (Goldberg et al., 2007):

$x_i < a_{1i}$: strong deviation: $x_i^{\text{norm}} = 0 + x_i/a_{1i}$
$a_{1i} \le x_i < a_{2i}$: abnormal: $x_i^{\text{norm}} = 1 + (x_i - a_{1i})/(a_{2i} - a_{1i})$
$a_{2i} \le x_i < a_{3i}$: normal: $x_i^{\text{norm}} = 2 + (x_i - a_{2i})/(a_{3i} - a_{2i})$
$a_{3i} \le x_i < a_{4i}$: abnormal: $x_i^{\text{norm}} = 3 + (x_i - a_{3i})/(a_{4i} - a_{3i})$
$a_{4i} \le x_i$: strong deviation: $x_i^{\text{norm}} = 3 + x_i/(a_{4i})$

Thus, normalized parameters will belong to five intervals: [0,1), [1,2), [2,3), [3,4), and [4,∞).

An expert panel empirically estimated an assessment of acceptable parameters to determine the range of normal, subnormal, and abnormal values. The range of strong deviations covers all zones of possible values outside the anomalous values. It would be reasonable to assume that, considering significant demographic changes, the introduction of new drugs affecting the human body's reaction to disease/injury, the value of the average will not be the same at present. It is assumed that you can more accurately determine the zones on the standard deviations (SDs) from the current mean values:

- 2 SDs from the mean (normal values)
- 2–3 SDs from the mean (abnormal values)
- more than 3 SDs from the mean (strong deviation)

Mean and SD can be easily obtained from health systems or insurance companies, or national databases.

Of course, it is necessary to remember that it is not always an exclusively statistical procedure that can give an adequate understanding of the norm (pathology). An expert assessment based on pathophysiology, biology, and clinical practice should help in building the thresholds.

For example, in medicine, the standard scale for fever is as follows: if body temperature is less than 95°F, then it is a strong deviation. If it is in the range 95–96.8°F, then it is considered abnormal. If it is in the range 96.9–99.5°F, then it is normal. If the range is 99.6–101.3°F, then it is abnormal, and if it is greater than 101.3 °F, then it is a strong deviation. However, the norm for a flu is 100–102°F, the norm for a cold is 99.6–101.3°F, the norm for allergy is 96.9–99.5°F, and any higher fever is a strong deviation (Fig. 3).

The normalization can be defined for categorical or nominal parameters as well. For example, for allergy, any "general aches, pain" is abnormal ($x_i^{\text{norm}} = 3$), whereas only "no general aches, pain" is normal ($x_i^{\text{norm}} = 2$).

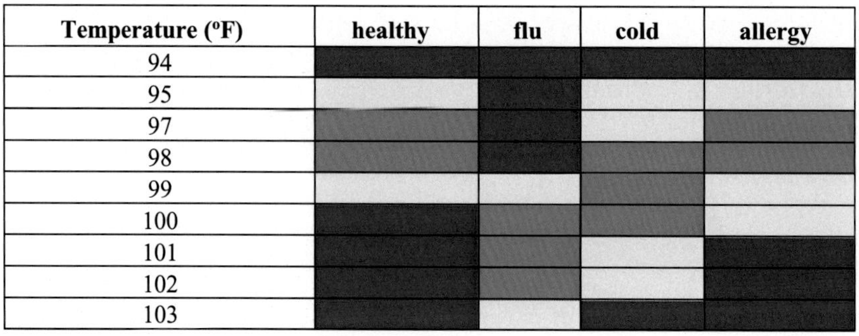

Temperature (°F)	healthy	flu	cold	allergy
94				
95				
97				
98				
99				
100				
101				
102				
103				

FIG. 3

Temperature pathology scale for different diseases.

Based on this definition, we can define a mapping between the input parameters **X** and the normalized parameters $\mathbf{X}^{\text{norm}}$:

$\mathbf{X} \rightarrow \mathbf{X}^{\text{norm}}$ and $\mathbf{X}^{\text{norm}} \rightarrow \mathbf{X}$. Using this normalization we substitute $[x_1, \ldots, x_n]$ for $[x_i^{\text{norm}}, \ldots, x_n^{\text{norm}}]$. Now we can define the distance between strings **x** and **y** in a standard way as

$$\text{Dist}(\mathbf{x}, \mathbf{y}) = \sum_{i \in \{1, \ldots, n\}} \left(\mathrm{x}_i^{\text{norm}} - \mathrm{y}_i^{\text{norm}}\right)^2$$

(3) Closeness based on the level of significance in parameters

This closeness between the two points is based on parameters' "naïve" informativeness. So informativeness can be obtained, for instance, as parameter weights in discriminant analysis. Distance is a linear combination of the parameter values with informativeness weights.

It is possible to adopt any of the approaches for "differential diagnosis" rules for obtaining such a linear combination of parameters:

- assessment of the significance of the feature according to Bayes' theorem
- likelihood ratio-based method
- discriminant or regression analysis
- support vector (Fig. 4)
- logistic regression

For practical applications, the most effective is the formation of distance based on a combination of the proposed ideas. For example, closeness based on the possibility of values equality + closeness based on scale normal - abnormal:

$$\text{Dist}(\mathbf{x}, \mathbf{y}) = \sum_{i \in \{1, \ldots, n\}} \left(x_i^{\text{norm}} \times (1 - G_{xi}(y_i) - y_i^{\text{norm}} \times (1 - G_{yi}(x_i))\right)^2$$

Let's demonstrate these distances by comparing three descriptions of children with suspected cold (Table 2).

A: 7 years old, Temperature 36.6°C, absence of Weakness.

B: 10 years old, Temperature 36.9°C, Weakness.

C: 8 years old, Temperature 37.2°C, Weakness.

Possible errors: Age ± 0.5; Temperature ± 0.2; False-negative for "Weakness" definition is 0.1 and false-positive is 0.3.

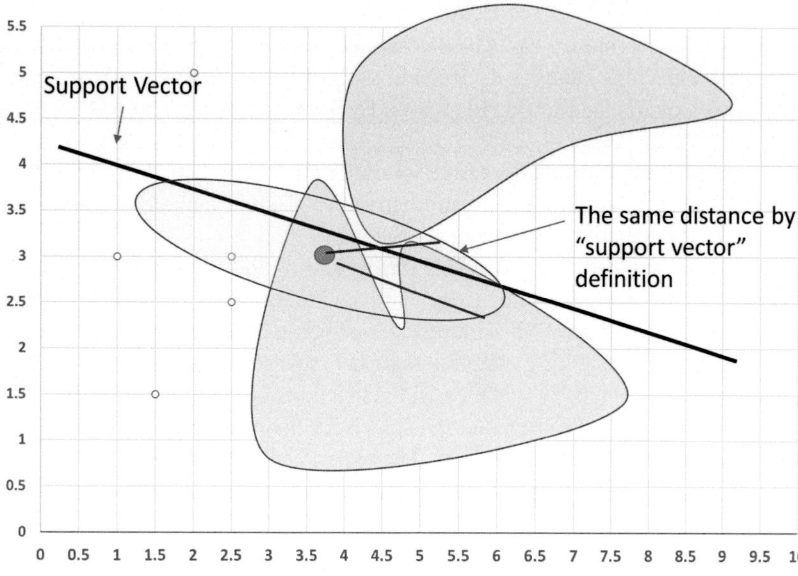

FIG. 4

An example of "nearby" points by a support vector.

Table 2 Comparing different distances.

Distance	Euclidean distance	Closeness based on the possibility of values equality	Closeness based on the discriminant function	Closeness based on scale normal-abnormal	Possibility of values equality + normal-abnormal scale	Possibility of values equality +normal-abnormal scale + Discriminant function
Dist(A, B)	10.09	9.33	1.2	5.9	0.37	0.85
Dist(A, C)	2.36	1.21	2	12.1	1.2	5
Dist(B, C)	4.09	4.08	0.4	1.4	0.24	1.2
	Dist(A, C) < Dist (B,C) < Dist(A, B)	**Dist(A, C)** < Dist(B, C) < Dist(A, B)	**Dist(B, C)** < Dist(A, B) < Dist(A, C)	**Dist(B, C)** < Dist(A, B) < Dist(A, C)	**Dist(B, C)** < Dist(A, B) < Dist(A, C)	**Dist(A, B)** < Dist (B, C) < Dist (A, C)

Age from 5 to 15 years is considered normal. The range of normal body Temperature is 36.0–36.9, and the range for abnormal is 37.0–37.5. The absence of Weakness is normal, and Weakness is abnormal.

Discriminant function for Healthy vs Cold: $-0.1 \times \text{Age} + 5 \times \text{Temperature} + 1$ if the child has Weakness, or 0 if not.

3.1 Finding the closest point to a local case

Let the distance between two arbitrary cases be determined. To find the point (alternative case) closest to our case, at which the machine changes its decision to the decision of an expert, one can use various methods from the class Covariance Matrix Adaptation Evolution Strategy (CMAES) method (Hansen, 2006) (Fig. 5).

The resultant "closest" case with an alternative solution must be "realistic" from the point of view of an expert. The algorithm for searching for an alternative case should include expert rules prohibiting considering cases with incompatible parameter values.

As we have already mentioned, the procedure for explaining the solution of the machine must be iterative. Of course, a user can organize a dialogue with the ML system by repeatedly changing parameters and investigating changes in the ML solution. However, a dialogue in which we learn not only solutions but also the limits of changing parameters to save this solution seems more productive. The tool of such a dialogue is the choice of distance and restrictions on the search for the "closest" point. The expert can impose his own restrictions on the search for the nearest point, for example, fix some parameters and set the range of change for others. The expert can also change the formula for distance or the concept of proximity. Following is a possible dialogue between the expert and ML system.

4. A bi-directional adversarial meta-agent between user and ML system

4.1 Meta-agent behavior

The alignment of expert solutions and machine solutions is the goal of the Meta-Agent (M-A) (Fig. 6). In the beginning, using ML, M-A tries to find "weak points" in the user's decision, which may, in particular, be the result of data errors. If the user's solution is still different from the ML solution, the M-A

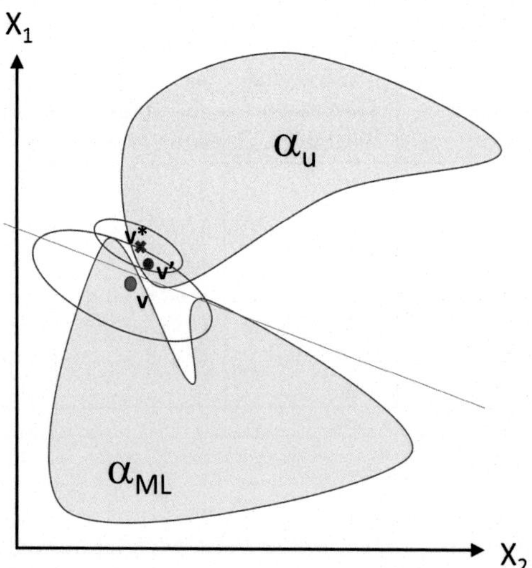

FIG. 5

Finding the closer point **v'** to **v** in the area where a_{ML} becomes a_U by a machine learning (ML) algorithm.

FIG. 6

Humans and AI try to understand the "black box" together.

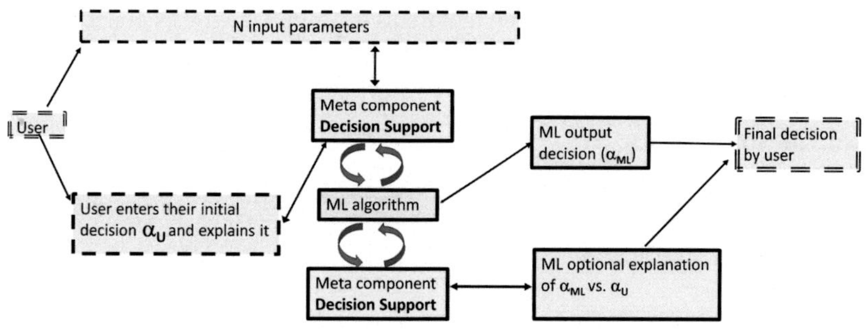

FIG. 7

A proposed architecture for the meta-agent (M-A).

helps the user determine the reasons for the non-compliance (Fig. 7). This M-A is especially useful in a situation where there may be discrepancies in the data. We covered the AI system DINAR2 in Chapter 5, and DINAR2 is already helping the consulting physician organize a dialogue with the local enemy based on the initial patient description and the initial diagnosis. However, the decision support system DINAR2 was developed based on expert rules. Here the situation is considered when the decision-making system is a black box (Goldberg et al., 2019a,b, 2020, 2021; Galitsky and Goldberg, 2019).

Table 3 Diagnostic differentiation between cold, flu, and airborne allergy (NIH News in Health, 2014).

Symptoms	Cold	Flu	Airborne allergy
Fever	Rare	Usual, high (100–102°F), sometimes higher especially in young children, lasts 3–4 days	Never
Headache	Uncommon	Common	Uncommon
General aches, pain	Slight	Usual, often severe	Never
Fatigue, weakness	Sometimes	Usual, can last up to 3 weeks	Sometimes
Extreme exhaustion	Never	Usual, at the beginning of the illness	Never
Stuffy running nose	Common	Sometimes	Common
Sneezing	Usual	Sometimes	Usual

We now consider a particular medical "case." A physician needs to diagnose a patient and differentiate between cold, flu, and allergy (Table 3).

Let us assume that this physician describes patient symptoms to the ML system, provides a preliminary diagnosis of the flu, and notes that this decision was made based on "high temperature of 100.6°F, a strong headache, and a strong chest discomfort." The M-A asks to confirm "strong chest discomfort" and additional symptoms of "stuffy" and "sore" throat. Now imagine the user revises the symptom from "strong chest discomfort" to "mild chest discomfort" and leaves the other two symptoms, "stuffy and sore throat" unchanged, and does not change the initial diagnosis. The M-A outputs the decision cold and reports that for the diagnosis flu, it lacks "higher temperature like 101.5°F." The physician now decides that such a revision is insignificant and maintains the initial diagnosis or accepts this argument and changes the diagnosis to cold.

4.2 Steps of the meta-agent

Step 1:

Physician input: $\mathbf{v}=(v_1, \ldots, v_n) \in \mathbf{X}$. For example (Fever =100.6°F, strong Headache, strong Chest Discomfort, Fever, strong Stuffy, moderate Sore Throat 100.6°F).

Step 2:

Initial unassisted decision $\alpha_U \in \mathbf{D}$ of the physician. For example, the flu.

Step 3:

Now the M-A verifies the doctor's decisions α_U.

If the ML decision α_{ML} matches α_U in the whole $\Omega(\mathbf{v})$, then α_U is selected as a preliminary solution, and we proceed to Step 6.

If α_U $(\mathbf{v}) \neq \alpha_{ML}$ $(\mathbf{v})$, go to Step 4.

If α_{Ml} does not match α_U in some points of $\Omega(\mathbf{v})$ (Fig. 8), go to Step 5.

Example: if we have (Fever = 100.6°F, strong Headache, strong Chest Discomfort, Fever, strong Stuffy, moderate Sore Throat 100.6°F), as a physician noted, α_{ML}="flu." but if we have (moderate Headache, moderate Chest Discomfort, strong Stuffy, strong Sore Throat) as obtaining from $\Omega(\mathbf{v})$ α_{ML}="cold."

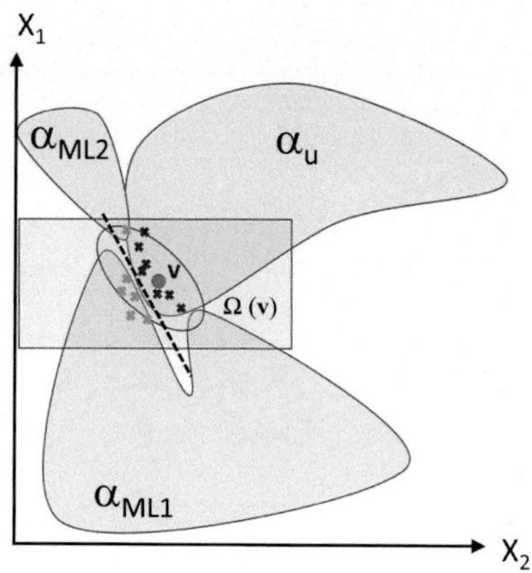

FIG. 8

Checking stability of user decision in the error neighborhood of **v**.

Step 4:

Since α_U (**v**) $\neq \alpha_{ML}$ (**v**), the M-A iteratively works with the physician to see if wc can converge on a stable decision.

At this stage, the M-A could just show the physician α_{ML}, but it does not do this on purpose to prevent the physician from thoughtlessly changing their decision to α_{ML}. Instead, the M-A takes a more subtle, indirect approach. It is trying to show the expert a parameter whose attention to the value of v_i can change the expert's decision α_U. In addition, the number of questions about the parameters should not be large; from our experience, no more than three questions. The expert can always stop this stage and move on to Step 6.

If α_U (**v**) $\neq \alpha_{ML}$ (**v**), then in the local explanation of the ML solution factors for the ML solution are identified and presented to the expert. Any method that explains the local solution of the machine will be fine for finding such parameters (Fig. 9).

Step 5:

If α_U (**v**) $=\alpha_{ML}$ (**v**), but exist point **s** $\in \Omega$(**v**), where α_U (**s**) $\neq \alpha_{ML}$ (**s**). Find the nearest point **v**′ to **v** where

α_U (**v**′) $\neq \alpha_{ML}$ (**v**′) and the most distinctive parameter **i** in **v**′ vs. **v**.

After finding this parameter **i**, the M-A reports to the user that the value they provided for this parameter may be inconsistent with α_U. The M-A then gives the physician the option to change their initial α_U. If the physician maintains the same decision α_U, α_U is set as a preliminary decision, and the M-A proceeds to Step 6. If a physician changes their decision or parameter values, go to Step 2 (unless this point is reached a third time, in which case go to Step 7 to avoid an overly long interaction loop).

Step 6:

Compute decision α_{ML} based on unchanged input values **v**. α_{ML} is set as a decision of the ML system and is shown to the human expert along with the set of key features that has yielded α_{ML}

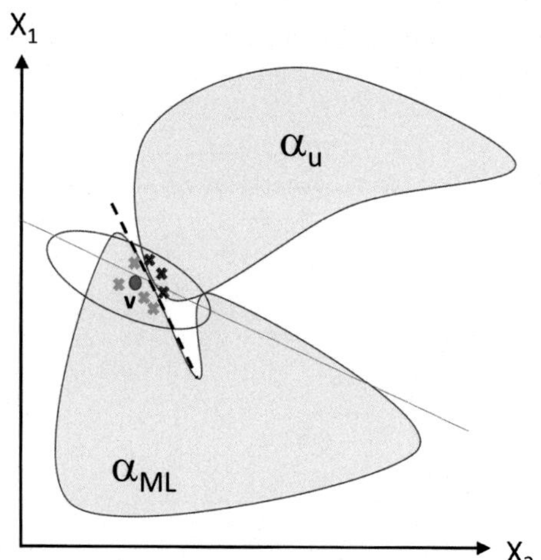

FIG. 9

Using LIME to generate questions to a human expert.

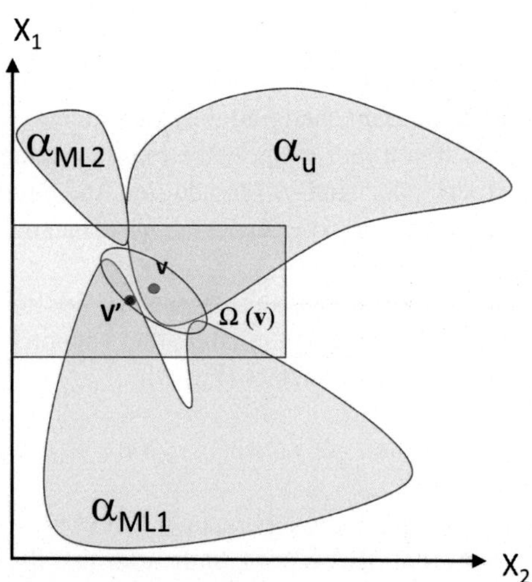

FIG. 10

Explaining a machine decision based on the "nearby" point.

instead of α_U if α_U (**v**)$\neq\alpha_{ML}$ (**v**). In this case, the M-A can also use the local explanations of the solution discussed previously. It seems to us that an iterative approach based on comparing the case under study with the closest hypothetical case, where the ML system makes a different decision, is most acceptable here (Fig. 10).

Step 7:

The human expert can modify **v** and observe the respective decisions of the ML system. The M-A can provide an updated explanation of the ML decision. Once the human expert obtains the M-A decisions and explanations for all cases of interest, the expert makes the final decision.

Hence in Step 2, the human expert announces their decision, and in Step 6, the M-A explains the ML decision. In Steps 4 and 5, the M-A assesses the stability of human experts' decisions with respect to selected features. In Step 7, the human expert does the same with the ML decisions. So, Step 6 is inverse to Step 2, and Step 7 is inverse to Step 5.

5. Discussion

Explanation of the ML findings is an indispensable element of modern decision support systems in medicine.

It is suggested that the most effective way to do this is through a dialogue between the ML and the doctor. However, a translator is needed to organize this dialogue. The ML decision explanation method, which is based on the representation of minimal data changes that change the ML decision, already offers such a dialogue. Of course, this requires an adequate understanding of the concept of "minimum change." The "friendly" distances suggested in this chapter can also be helpful for use in standard local methods of explanation, for example, for LIME (Fig. 11).

Establishing a mediator between the ML system and a person also aims to organize a dialogue, which first helps to validate the expert's decision based on ML and then helps the expert validate the ML solution.

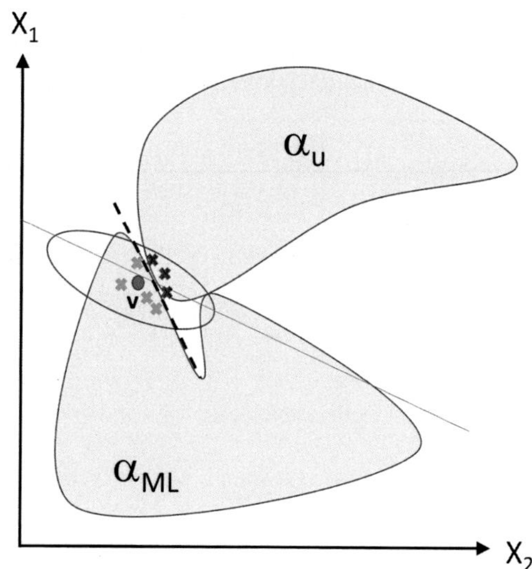

FIG. 11

An example of using custom distance with LIME.

The proposed approach has one important property. Before receiving a decision via ML, a doctor must be the first to announce their decision. Having to announce your decision before the ML system helps counteract the loss of physician experience and sense of responsibility that often arise when users delegate decision-making to ML. This encourages the doctor to think more about their decision. This gives the user a constant opportunity to revise and update their knowledge in the subject area.

The use of such an M-A has several limitations. The interaction of the doctor with the M-A takes time, which may be unavailable or very limited. If the decision is not time-critical, then the main problem with the effectiveness of such an M-A is the need for a "responsible" physician who is ready to spend time and effort in finding the right solution.

The proposed approach is most effective when the accuracy of the decisions of the ML system and the doctor is close. The doctor's ambition can be a hindrance when the findings of the machine are much more accurate than the doctor's decisions. At the same time, the machine-human dialogue proposed in the chapter can lead to a loss of accuracy of the final solution compared to the ML solution. For such cases, the M-A can be used as an effective method of training doctors.

6. Conclusions

An explanation of the ML solution is necessary for organizing the joint work of the doctor and the ML system and obtaining the optimal solution as a result of such a process. For this, it is desirable to have an intelligent mediator (M-A) between the doctor and the ML. An M-A is proposed to first help check the stability of the physician's solution using ML and then help the physician understand and test the stability of the ML solution. For this purpose, an approach has been developed to explain the ML solution based on the comparison of the tested case with the "nearby" case where the ML solution changes. Different versions of the concept "nearby" are considered.

One of the main advantages of the proposed scheme is that ML solutions are presented to the doctor only after the physician's own decision has been submitted and discussed. This should help preserve the doctor's skills and responsibility for the final decision. We explore this in more detail in Chapter 13.

Supplementary data sets

Please visit https://github.com/bgalitsky/relevance-based-on-parse-trees to access all supplementary data sets.

References

Bouneffouf, D., 2016. Exponentiated gradient exploration for active learning. Computers 5 (1), 1–12. https://doi.org/10.3390/computers5010001.

Breiman, L., 2001. Random Forests Machine Learning. vol. 45, pp. 5–32, https://doi.org/10.1023/A:1010933404324.

Craven, M., 1996. Extracting Comprehensible Models From Trained Neural Networks Technical Report #1326 (PhD thesis). Department of Computer Sciences, University of Wisconsin-Madison.

Craven, M., Shavlik, J., 1996. Extracting thee-structured representations of trained networks. In: NIPS. https://papers.nips.cc/paper/1995/file/45f31d16b1058d586fc3be7207b58053-Paper.pdf.

Fisher, A., Rudin, C., Dominici, F., 2018. All Models are Wrong, but Many are Useful: Learning a Variable's Importance by Studying an Entire Class of Prediction Models Simultaneously. https://arxiv.org/abs/1801.01489.

Galitsky, B., Goldberg, S., 2019. Explainable machine learning for Chatbots. In: Developing Enterprise Chatbots, pp. 53–58, https://doi.org/10.1007/978-3-030-04299-8_3.

Goldberg, S., Shklovskiy-Kordi, N., Zingerman, B., 2007. Time-oriented multi-image case history—way to the "disease image" analysis. In: VISAPP (Special Sessions), pp. 200–203. https://www.scitepress.org/Papers/2007/20709/20709.pdf.

Goldberg, S., Galitsky, B., Weisburd, B., 2019a. Framework for Interaction between Expert Users and Machine Learning Systems. http://ceur-ws.org/Vol-2448/SSS19_Paper_Upload_217.pdf.

Goldberg, S., Katz, G., Weisburd, B., Belyaev, A., Temkin, A., 2019b. Integrating user opinion in decision support systems. In: Arai, K., Bhatia, R. (Eds.), Advances in Information and Communication. FICC. Lecture Notes in Networks and Systems, vol 70. Springer, Cham, pp. 1220–1226, https://doi.org/10.1007/978-3-030-12385-7_86.

Goldberg, S., Temkin, A., Weisburd, B., 01 Jun 2020. Physician-machine interaction in the decision making process. Studies in health technology and informatics. In: Digital Personalized Health and Medicine. vol. 270. IOS Press Ebook, pp. 372–376, https://doi.org/10.3233/shti200185.

Goldberg, S., Pinsky, E., Galitsky, B., 2021. A bi-directional adversarial explainability for decision support. In: Human-Intelligent Systems Integration. vol. 3. Springer, pp. 1–14.

Goodman, B., Flaxman, S., 2017. European Union regulations on algorithmic decision-making and a "right to explanation". AI Mag. 38 (3), 50–57. https://doi.org/10.1609/aimag.v38i3.2741.

Hansen, N., 2006. The CMA evolution strategy: a comparing review. In: Towards a New Evolutionary Computation, pp. 75–102, https://doi.org/10.1007/3-540-32494-1_4.

Lundberg, S., Lee, S., 2017. A unified approach to interpreting. Model predictions. In: Advances in Neural Information Processing Systems 30 (NIPS 2017). arXiv:1705.07874v2.

Molnar, C., 2018. Interpretable Machine Learning. A Guide for Making Black Box Models Explainable. 12-17 https://christophm.github.io/interpretable-ml-book/.

NIH News in Health, October 2014. A Monthly Newsletter from the National Institutes of Health, Part of the U.S. Department of Health and Human Services. https://newsinhealth.nih.gov/2014/10/cold-flu-or-allergy.

Ribeiro, M., Singh, S., Guestrin, C., August 2016. Why should i trust you? Explaining the predictions of any classifier. In: Proceedings of the 22nd ACM SIGKDD International Conference on Knowledge Discovery and Data Mining, pp. 1135–1144, https://doi.org/10.1145/2939672.2939778.

Sarkar, D., 2018. A brief introduction into human interpretable machine learning and model interpretation. https://towardsdatascience.com/human-interpretable-machine-learning-part-1-the-need-and-importance-of-model-interpretation-2ed758f5f476.

Smith, G., Mansilla, R., Goulding, N., 2020. Model class reliance for random forests. In: 34th Conference on Neural Information Processing Systems (NeurIPS 2020). Vancouver, Canada. https://proceedings.neurips.cc/paper/2020/file/fd512441a1a791770a6fa573d688bff5-Paper.pdf.

CHAPTER

Passive decision support for patient management

13

Saveli Goldberg[a] and Stanislav Belyaev[b]

Division of Radiation Oncology, Massachusetts General Hospital, Boston, MA, United States[a]

Critical Care, Eastern New Mexico Medical Center, Roswell, NM, United States[b]

1. Introduction

The growing use of artificial intelligence (AI) in various fields, especially in medicine, is raising the problems of machine-human interaction to a higher level. Prominent leaders in business and science warn that modern advances in AI could have serious adverse consequences for society (Torresen, 2018):

- *"Humans, limited by slow biological evolution, couldn't compete and would be superseded by AI*"—Stephen Hawking in a BBC interview, 2014.
- "*AI is our 'biggest existential threat'*" Elon Musk at Massachusetts Institute of Technology during an interview at the AeroAstro Centennial Symposium (2014).
- "*I am in the camp that is concerned about super intelligence.*" Bill Gates (2015) in an Ask Me Anything interview on the Reddit networking site.

The dangers posed by artificial intelligence may include:

- increased unemployment because of machines replacing humans
- psychological problems caused by working in an environment with increased automation
- loss of human professional skills due to AI superiority
- possibility to use AI for destructive tasks

Even today, the introduction of AI systems is faced with socio-psychological problems, such as mistrust and rejection on the part of specialists and the loss of professional skills (acquired helplessness) caused by the transfer of responsibility for the decision-making to AI. It is not only an ethical issue. Even if AI continues to provide acceptable solutions from time to time under stable and predictable conditions, the environment may change (as happened with COVID-19), and the rate of this change may exceed the speed of algorithm adjustments. That may lead to a grave situation if there are not enough responsible and independent human decision-makers.

This is especially true for medicine. Medical decision-making is challenging as it involves setting goals in terms of outcome, collecting data, interacting with multiple entities involved in patient care, developing a plan of care, and modifying that plan according to the patient's response and/or a change in the overall goal in the treatment of a specific patient. The decisions we make about the patient's

Artificial Intelligence for Healthcare Applications and Management. https://doi.org/10.1016/B978-0-12-824521-7.00015-6

treatment are not based solely on the medical aspect of care but are also frequently based on countless socioeconomic factors, such as the level of technological development of society, cultural and religious preferences, and various legal and financial aspects of the systems. A decision-making process that is based solely on algorithms carried out by a computer will not be very successful due to, for example, a multitude of ethical, financial, and cultural differences that are very specific to each individual, family, and society. Moreover, this could potentially create a psychological conflict between the provider, patient, and machine.

Modern basic AI systems function from a psychological point of view, as pure conscious minds. The decisions they make have no unconscious input, which is natural for the human mind and behavior. In essence, these systems are sociopathic since they lack empathy, intuition, kindness, the inability to be, so to speak, in "someone else's shoes," and so on. This is probably one of the reasons why some individuals are anxious and even fearful when it comes to the further development of these kinds of systems.

As a result, despite the significant advances made by AI systems in medicine, there is a general consensus that significant intellectual and financial investments in this area have not led to the widespread acceptance of machine intelligence (Strickland, 2019).

It is hoped that human-friendly ethical AI can avoid most of these problems (Anderson and Anderson, 2011; Wallach and Allen, 2009). Several approaches to the implementation of moral agents in AI are considered: formal-logical and mathematical ethical reasoning (Dennis et al., 2015; Govindarajulu and Bringsjord, 2015; Arkin et al., 2009), machine learning (ML) methods based on examples of ethical and unethical behavior (Deng, 2015), and providing AI systems with internal models to make them self-conscious (Winfield, 2014).

It is believed that "reasonable," from a human point of view, explanations for AI decisions will break down the wall of fear and mistrust and make the AI decision-making process more tailored to the needs of the specific provider/patient. We understand the importance of this process. Chapter 12 in this book was dedicated to local explaining ML decisions in medical applications. However, as the accuracy of the AI decisions increases, the more courage it takes to go against the decision of the AI. As the complexity of AI decisions increases, the harder it is for humans to make decisions without AI supporting those decisions, and at the same time, the more difficult it is to interpret and rationalize decisions that AI makes. Chapter 4 talks about the successful experience of using DINAR2 in the Sverdlovsk region. However, there were instances when the diagnosis of DINAR2 led to undesirable outcomes in the Leningrad region. This happened because the providers believed that DINAR2 was always right, a belief based on DINAR2's flawless performance over the previous years.

The very fact of providing AI solutions may create unexpected problems due to interaction of known and unknown factors. It is especially noticeable in medicine where the treatment of a person is not limited to the treatment of a specific disease and effective treatment is not always an adequate treatment. But could AI assist in finding a solution to a problem without presenting it directly?

2. Dr. Watson-type systems

2.1 Principles of Dr. Watson-type systems

An example of AI-human collaboration can be found in the classic detective stories by Conan Doyle. In these stories, a highly qualified expert, Mr. Holmes, answers Dr. Watson's questions while teaching him deductive thinking. Mr. Holmes with his rule engine, logic, and, superior memory apparently plays the role of an AI system, and Dr. Watson is the user of the system. Mycroft, Mr. Holmes's brother, plays the role of an intellectual superpower. Holmes-Mycroft relations can be another model of human-AI interaction. However, Mr. Holmes, the main decision-maker, rarely and reluctantly seeks Mycroft's assistance, but very often to Dr. Watson. We propose and describe yet another model of AI-human interaction that is more psychologically comfortable for a human. In that model, the AI behaves like Dr. Watson, who, by asking questions and acting in a particular way, helps Holmes (the AI user) make the right decisions.

We feel that Sherlock Holmes found certain characteristics of Dr. Watson attractive. They create a psychologically comfortable environment, which helps Mr. Holmes to solve problems. We use these characteristics for our implementation of friendly AI.

(1) Dr. Watson is Holmes' chronicler. He documents Holmes' victories and failures. He admires Holmes and rejoices at his successes.
(2) Dr. Watson asks questions every time he doesn't understand Holmes' reasoning, thus stimulating thinking and promoting Holmes' creativity.
(3) Dr. Watson does not compete but rather collaborates with Holmes. Therefore, he isn't perceived as a threat.
(4) Dr. Watson covers Holmes in dangerous situations, but he does not take the lead even in these circumstances.
(5) Holmes trusts Dr. Watson and does not expect him to create problems.
(6) Collaboration between Holmes and Dr. Watson resembles a game in which both play their parts enthusiastically.
(7) Holmes feels comfortable with Dr. Watson.

It is known that IBM gave the name of Dr. Watson to its excellent AI system (Ahmed et al., 2017), but we find its decision-making style to be closer to that of Mycroft than to Dr. Watson's. Let us call our AI system a "Dr. Watson-type system" (Goldberg and Meshalkin, 1992, 1993; Goldberg, 1997), if it:

- does not offer a specific solution but rather analyses a user's solution in a way that would reveal logical inconsistencies or insufficient data for such a solution.
- uses game situations, psychological techniques, and visual presentation of information to enhance and stimulate the intellectual activity of the user.

We introduced expert systems in Chapters 2 and 3. Now, we translate the above-listed features of Dr. Watson styles into the requirements for the AI expert system.

(1) The system should document and analyze the dynamics of the professional development of a care provider. For example, the variability in the accuracy of their predictions from patient to patient, how the accuracy of their decisions changes over time, and how their performance compares with the average results in the specialty and/or a certain subgroup of providers.
(2) The system should discover contradictions and omissions on the path to the solution and prompt the user with relevant questions, answers to either confirm the decision or raise doubts, and direct the user towards another decision.
(3) An interactive process should start with a formalization of the prognosis of the outcome and the user's plan of care. Subsequently, the system should influence the decision-making using the organization of the data and asking clarifying questions.

(4) The system should provide alarms in situations of "obvious" errors, hence it should have a dictionary of those errors.
(5) The confidentiality of specialist-machine communication must be ensured. It is advisable to delete the documentation of their interactions and interim solutions.
(6) The system should provide context-based reference and help. It is highly desirable to include game elements in the interaction between the expert and the system.
(7) The system should have a convenient, efficient, and friendly user interface.

A typical example of a Dr. Watson-type system is the "Follow-up Summary" method, which prevents errors that cannot be detected by expert rules or numerical methods. We describe this method in - Chapter 4. The idea behind this method was to organize the presentation of the data to show inconsistencies in the data. This inconsistency makes the data entry person aware of a possible mistake. Evaluating and refining a user's decision without directly providing them with an AI solution is fundamental for Dr. Watson-type systems. We base this approach on algorithms for local explanation of AI solutions (Chapter 12). If the AI's decision matches the user's decision, then the factors that negatively affect such a decision are presented to the user as inappropriate. If AI makes a decision that differs from the user's decision, then the factors that have been most useful for the AI's decision are offered to the user as factors that contradict the user's conclusion.

2.2 Dr. Watson-type system formalization

It comes down to the formal explanation of how the system generates questions based on the decision provided by the user and the parameters that led them to that decision.

Let $\mathbf{x} = (x_1, x_2, \ldots, x_n)$ be a vector of the n input parameters to the algorithm. x_i can be a continuous (numerical) or categorical (Boolean) variable. Let $\mathbf{X}$ be a set of $\mathbf{x}$.

Let $\mathbf{D} = \{\alpha_j\}$, and $j = 1, \ldots, k$ be the set of k possible decisions or output classes. For each solution $\alpha_1, \ldots, \alpha_\kappa$, one should have a typical representative $\mathbf{s}(\alpha_j) = (s_i(\alpha_j), s_{i+1}(\alpha_j), \ldots, s_n(\alpha_j)) \in \mathbf{X}$, which is either the center of gravity of the training sample for α_i or a set of medians for each coordinate in such a sample or, in the absence of a training sample, it is represented by experts. Let us know $\mathbf{v} = (v_1, \ldots, v_{i-1})$, $i-1 < n$, and the expert's decision α_{Holmes}. First, let us check if additional questions are needed to confirm α_{Holmes}. To do this, we randomly select values for $i, i+1, \ldots, n$ coordinates. If there is a point $(v_1, \ldots, v_{i-1}, t_i, \ldots, t_n) \in \mathbf{X}$, where the solution will be $\alpha_{\text{Watson}} \neq \alpha_{\text{Holmes}}$, then it makes sense to ask questions and remember α_{Watson}. If there are several options for an alternative solution to α_{Watson} with a random selection of the values of coordinates $i, i+1, \ldots$, n, then the most common solution is retained.

Consider the vector $(v_1, \ldots, v_{i-1}, s_i(\alpha_{\text{Holmes}}), s_{i+1}(\alpha_{\text{Holmes}}), \ldots, s_n(\alpha_{\text{Holmes}})) \in \mathbf{X}$. Let us apply the local explanation of the α_U solution for the vector $(v_1, \ldots, v_{i-1}, s_i(\alpha_{\text{Holmes}}), s_{i+1}(\alpha_{\text{Holmes}}), \ldots, s_n(\alpha_{\text{Holmes}}))$. The most important parameter (coordinate) from this explanation $i, i+1, \ldots, n$ may be our question. If there is a vector $(v_1, \ldots, v_{i-1}, t_i, \ldots, t_n) \in \mathbf{X}$ with the conclusion α_{Watson}, then we apply a local explanation of the solution α_{Watson} to it. Now, for each parameter, we can summarize its significance for α_{Watson} and α_{Holmes}. Based on this, the system asks a question. If AI makes for $(v_1, \ldots, v_{i-1}, s_i(\alpha_{\text{Holmes}}), s_{i+1}(\alpha_{\text{Holmes}}), \ldots, s_n(\alpha_{\text{Holmes}}))$ a decision $\alpha_{\text{Watson}} \neq \alpha_{\text{Holmes}}$, then a clarifying question is asked on the most significant parameter for the local explanations of the α_{Watson} solution from the whole spectrum of parameters from 1 to n. Any posterior, model-independent and local interpretation methods are suitable for such a task (Molnar, 2018).

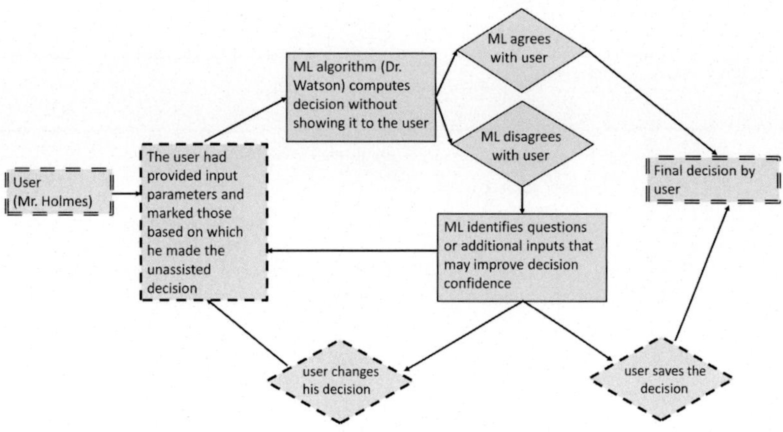

FIG. 1

Proposed architecture for the Dr. Watson-type system.

Fig. 1 shows the architecture of the Dr. Watson-type system.

3. Patient management system (SAGe)

This section describes the SAGe patient management system (PMS) as an example of the implementation of Dr. Watson-type AI (Fig. 2). The purpose of this system is informational and intellectual support for the doctor in making clinical decisions about the patient in the intensive care unit. Here, clinical decisions are understood to mean making a diagnosis and choosing a treatment.

3.1 Requirements and subsystems

The requirements for the SAGe PMS were combined from the seven listed in Section 2.1 as fundamental for Watson-type systems and from the results of interviews with providers who worked with another PMS, DINAR2, which is a predecessor to SAGe. Several intensive care providers with no less than 2 years of experience with DINAR2 were asked to rate possible features of a hypothetically perfect PMS system. Features were evaluated on a five-point scale. The top three were added to the requirements: an assessment of treatment adequacy, an assessment of treatment efficiency, and an assessment of the course of the disease.

It was presumed that a physician would oversee the management of multiple patients, while the mid-level would be responsible for the procedures, bedside patient care, and data entry. The remaining data would be imported automatically from the network. Essentially the software would be integrated with electronic health records (EHRs). SAGe consists of six interconnected subsystems: "Information import," "Diagnostics," "Treatment efficiency," "Treatment adequacy," "Integral assessment of patients," and "Discontinuation of observation" (Goldberg et al., 1997).

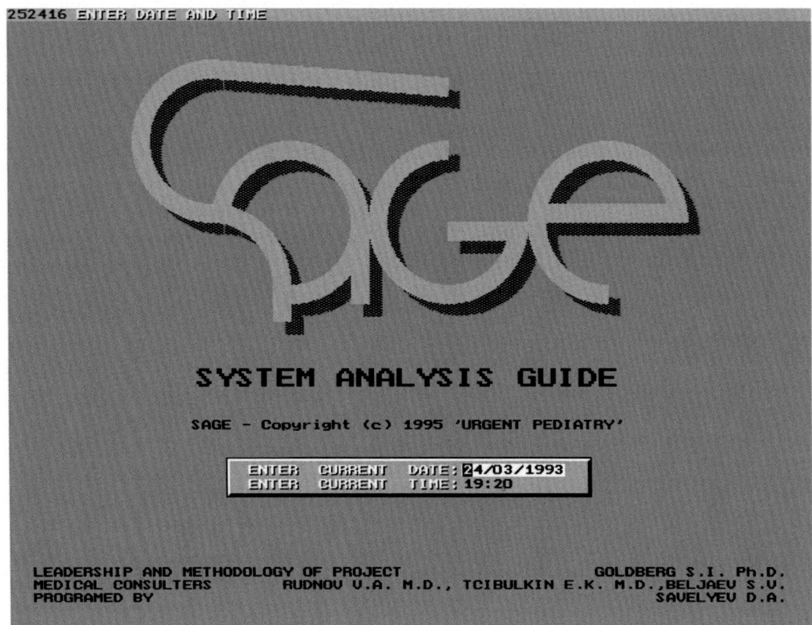

FIG. 2

SAGe system.

3.2 Information import

The goal of this subsystem is to collect information on the patients. The subsystem consists of two components (Fig. 3). In the first component, a physician determines the input parameters (vital signs, labs, imaging) and the frequency of their measurements for a specific patient. The second component is an interface for data input (manual and automatic). SAGe checks the data entry for possible errors (Fig. 3).

3.3 Diagnostics

The goal of this subsystem is to assist with the selection of a diagnostic hypothesis about pathologic syndromes. Matching information regarding the patient's condition with the physician's diagnostic hypothesis, SAGe offers its own view regarding the outcome of a particular patient.

SAGe's decision-making process is based on a set of rules derived from the opinions of several experts. A set of rules was created during the "Diagnostic Game," (Shifrin et al., 2007) similar to the one used for its predecessor DINAR2. The initial set of rules, which had been verified and tested for more than 5 years, were transplanted from DINAR. The major technical difference between "diagnostic games" for SAGe and DINAR2 is the use of databases.

The subsystem functions the following way. If SAGe's prognosis matches the physician's opinion, SAGe does not manifest itself in any way. If the assessment of the physician and SAGe do not match, SAGe displays the specific parameters that do not match. At this point, the physician is prompted with an additional question. SAGe determines the most useful question that would challenge the physician's

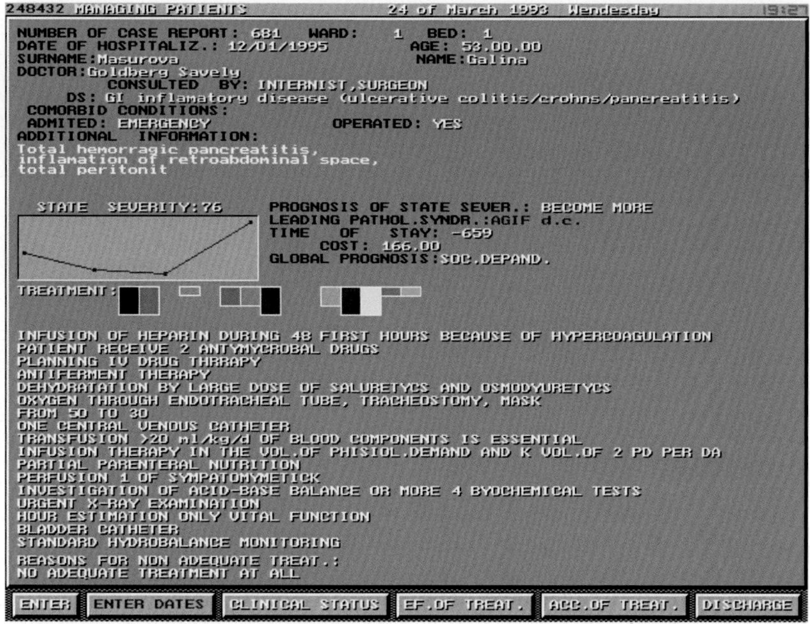

FIG. 3

SAGe. Managing patients' screens.

opinion. If an answer to this question matches the SAGe hypothesis, but the physician's original assessment of the situation remains unaltered, the SAGe asks a new question (maximum two additional questions). Since the procedure for making a diagnosis is organized as a movement along a decision tree (DecT; Chapter 2), the algorithm for choosing a clarifying question is relatively simple. The ease of finding an additional question was one of the reasons for choosing DecT construction as a machine learning (ML) algorithm.

Visualization of information plays an important role in the diagnostic subsystem. Therefore, in order to simultaneously present various quantitative and qualitative parameters, it was decided to use unified scales for those parameters.

Now we would like to emphasize an important concept implemented in SAGe. It is a normalization of different quantitative and qualitative parameters like blood pressure (BP), presence of infiltrates on chest X-ray (CXR), heart rate (HR), and white blood count (WBC). For a provider working with the system, SAGe displays those parameters in a conventional way (for most laboratory tests, the "normal range" is defined as values falling within two standard deviations of the mean), but internally the software operates with normalized data (Fig. 4).

Normalization was done as a normal-abnormal scale in Chapter 12:

Parameter normalization x_i^{norm} for each **i**, based on four thresholds: a_{1i}, a_{2i}, a_{3i}, a_{4i} that are defined by a group of expert physicians.

$x_i < a_{1i}$: strong deviation $x_i^{norm} = 0 + x_i/a_{1i}$
$a_{1i} \le x_i < a_{2i}$: abnormal: $x_i^{norm} = 1 + (x_i - a_{1i})/(a_{2i} - a_{1i})$
$a_{2i} \le x_i < a_{3i}$: normal: $x_i^{norm} = 2 + (x_i - a_{2i})/(a_{3i} - a_{2i})$

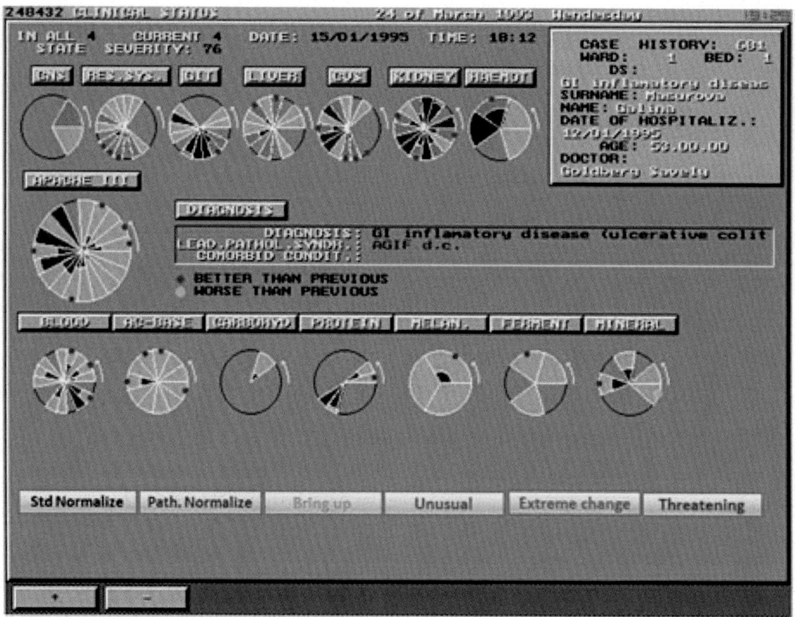

FIG. 4

SAGe. Clinical status screen.

$a_{3i} \le x_i < a_{4i}$: abnormal: $x_i^{norm} = 3 + (x_i - a_{3i})/(a_{4i} - a_{3i})$
$a_{4i} \le x_i$: strong deviation: $x_i^{norm} = 3 + x_i/(a_{4i})$

Thus, normalized parameters will belong to five intervals: [0,1), [1,2), [2,3), [3,4), and the interval of numbers greater than 4.

To visualize the unique conditions of each patient we used pie charts with sections presenting parameters and color boundaries within sections presenting their numeric values (Fig. 5). The graphical interface displays available parameters and shows contradictions and omissions. It helps in assessing specific cases by generating links with similar cases from the past.

In this subsystem, each organ is displayed as a circle divided into several sectors corresponding to the most important parameters. The intensity of coloration of each sector corresponds to the values of the normalized parameters. The numeric value in those sectors is a conventional representation of those parameters. Each combination of the parameters reflects the integral condition of a patient, and the system GUI draws corresponding patterns on the pie charts. With regular use of the system, the user gets trained to recognize those visual patterns and associate them with the conditions of a patient (Fig. 6).

The provider can access historical data, including trends.

In the starting windows of SAGe GUI, the user has a choice from six items (buttons).

1st—brings up changes in any of the parameters over a given period
2nd—allows direct access to the most important parameters of the vital organs

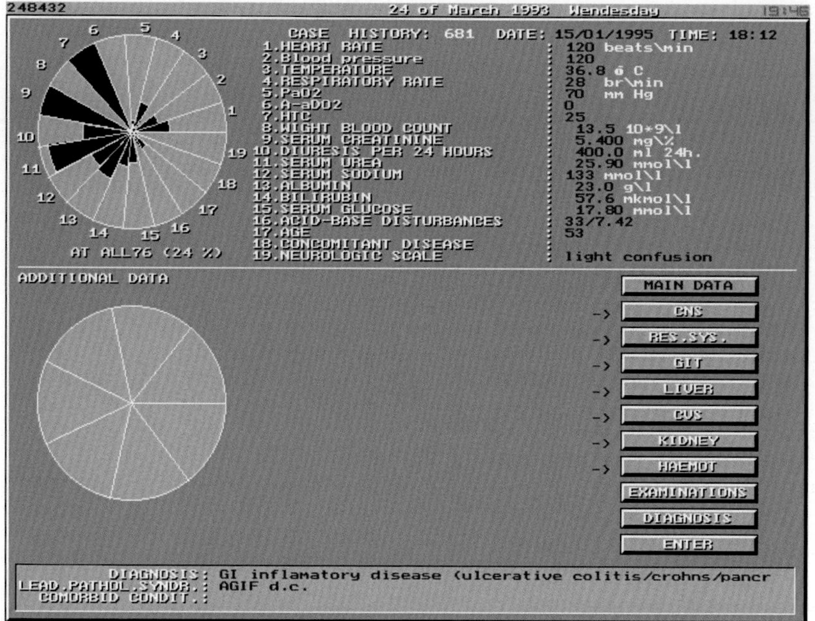

FIG. 5

SAGe. Snapshot of the most relevant data reflecting the patient's condition.

3rd—gives access to the parameters exhibiting unusual patterns. For example, typically, HR increases with the rise of body temperature. The system would classify falling temperature and increasing HR combination as unusual. The typical correlations among different parameters have been built in the system

4th—displays parameters with the most extreme dynamics (e.g., sudden and significant change in HR)

5th—presents parameters with the most threatening dynamics (e.g., sustained critically elevated BP)

6th—allows a provider to view the parameters that they have viewed under similar circumstances in the past

This screen can show no more than four quantitative and two qualitative parameters at a time. Therefore, only the most significant parameters from the groups represented by buttons 2, 3, and 4 are displayed. The clinical significance of these parameters is estimated by SAGe based on normalized data (Fig. 6). The same style of presentation of data dynamics is used by Shklovsky-Kordi in his clinical applications (Shklovsky-Kordi et al., 2005).

When a new parameter is entered, one of the previously displayed parameters (the least important one) disappears. All parameters are displayed in conventional units, although there is a way to review those parameters in their normalized form, which could be useful in some instances.

Once the leading syndrome/diagnosis is determined, the normal and abnormal values for different parameters are recalculated by the system in the way that they would most closely match that specific syndrome/diagnosis.

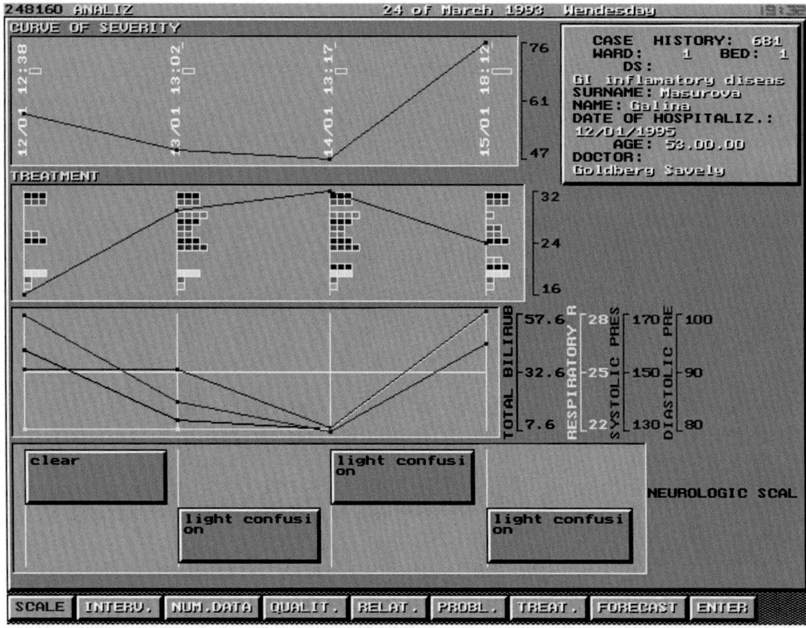

FIG. 6

SAGe. Analysis of trends screen.

For example, a patient with sepsis is being treated with fluids and antibiotics. Persistently elevated HR, despite adequate resuscitation, would be brought to the attention of the provider, as it could be a manifestation of another undiagnosed condition.

Matching the information on the patient's condition and the physician's diagnostic hypothesis, SAGe generates its own diagnostic hypothesis. If it matches the physician's opinion, SAGe does not manifest itself in any way. Otherwise, SAGe displays the mismatching parameters. At this point, the physician is prompted with an additional question. SAGe determines the most useful question that would challenge the physician's opinion. If an answer to this question matches the SAGe hypothesis, but the physician's original assessment of the situation remains unaltered, the SAGe asks a new question (maximum two additional questions).

For example, a patient with sepsis is being treated with fluids and antibiotics. Persistently elevated HR, despite adequate resuscitation, would be brought to the attention of the provider, as it might be a manifestation of another undiagnosed condition. In this case, the system may ask the question: "Are you expecting the HR to remain this high?"

3.4 Treatment effectiveness

For assessing treatment effectiveness, we used a multifactorial evaluation of a patient's response to the therapy. This SAGe subsystem displays the trends of the overall severity of the patient's condition, the severity of leading syndromes relative to the dynamics of type and intensity of treatment.

We understood that:

- Overall changes in the patient's condition may be caused by factors that have not been analyzed by the system.
- Despite an overall improvement of the patient's condition, an unfavorable trend of some parameters can lead to serious problems in the future.

In this regard, a physician can compare the dynamics of the overall severity of the patient with changes of any quantitative and qualitative parameters.

At the same time, SAGe offers trends of parameters that need attention when defining treatment. These parameters are selected by the SAGe algorithm. SAGe presents five groups of such parameters:

Group 1—parameters reflecting a malfunction of organ systems presently not affected (presumably) by the disease.
Group 2—parameters with a paradoxical dynamic (those that significantly deviate from overall trend).
Group 3—parameters exhibiting the most significant fluctuation from the baseline.
Group 4—the most life-threatening parameters.
Group 5—parameters reviewed by the user under similar conditions in the past.

For each individual parameter from Groups 1–5, SAGe assigns a rank from 1 to 7 depending upon its importance. The user is presented with four quantitative and two qualitative parameters that are ranked the highest. In a case when too many parameters have the same rank, preferences are formed according to the group numbers (Fig. 7).

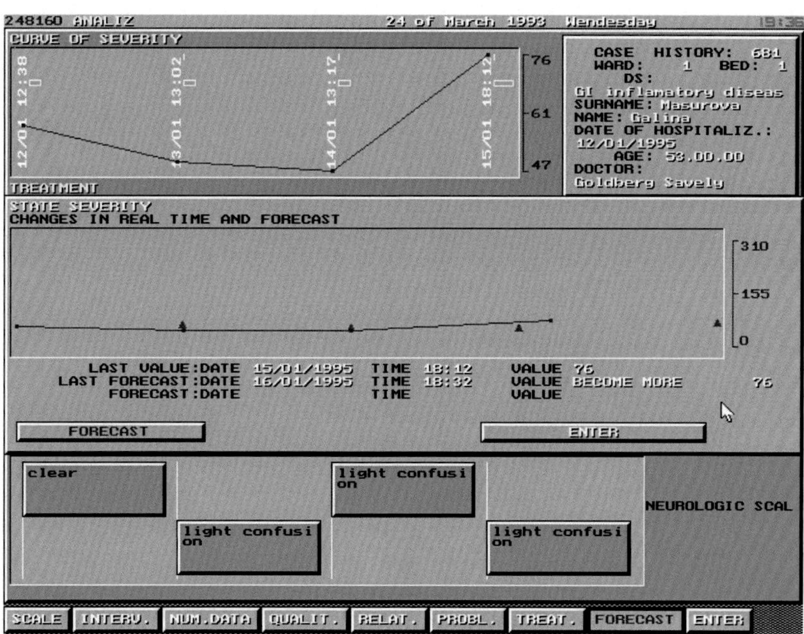

FIG. 7

SAGe. Making a prognosis screen.

A provider is required to make an independent prognosis regarding the course of future events in response to treatment. In case of discrepancy between prognosis and reality, a provider is required to explain probable causes of treatment ineffectiveness and deterioration of the patient's condition.

Our prior experience of using similar questions in DINAR2 revealed their great stimulating effect on the optimization of the plan of care.

3.5 Treatment adequacy

We view treatment adequacy as a balance between the intensity of treatment and the desired response of the patient to that treatment.

Treatment can be excessive. For example, massive fluid resuscitation and amputation of an extremity would be extreme and excessive interventions for superficial infection of a leg. Therapy can be ineffective due to limited understanding of the nature of the disease or lack of information pertinent to a specific patient. Regardless of the circumstances, the provider must be conscious of the consequences of the chosen plan of care.

This subsystem incorporates multiple factors like admission data, initial plan of care and its subsequent modifications, the response of the patient to treatment, provider's prognosis, and type of therapy.

All data is presented in the form of the growth of the flower. Each element of the flower represents a particular aspect of the process of taking care of the patient. The root is history of present illness (HPI), the stem is the trend of the severity of the patient's condition, the branches are unrealized prognoses, the flower is the current value for physiological parameters (similar to the circle from "Diagnostics"), the leaves are leading syndromes, props and strings are the types of treatment, the atmospheric phenomena are reasons for changes of the patient's condition, the types of soil and problems with props and strings are reasons for the ineffectiveness of treatment and its adequacy, and so on (Fig. 8).

The system detects and analyzes contradictions in the provider's decision-making process, as it compares the provider's prognosis with the outcomes reflected in improvement or deterioration of the patient's condition.

Analyzing the provider's input and the patient's condition at various points, SAGe tries to assess the degree of controllability of the therapeutic process and subsequently displays it as a particular color of the background of the picture.

By distorting the image of a flower, SAGe brings to attention various contradictions in the management of the patient.

3.6 Discontinuation of observation

In this subsystem, the physician finalizes the case. The goal of this system is a retrospective analysis of the case by a provider. It is done when the actual unfolding of the events is known, the problems of the patient's treatment have been explained in a new, more accurate way, and contradictions in the provider's earlier reflections have been eliminated (Fig. 9). Missing interventions are determined as well as the ones that were harmful or useless. Critical points in the progression of the disease are identified and explained. These explanations and these breakpoints remain in the patient file in the SAGe database. The explanations for the mismatch of the real-time predictions and their outcomes based on the retrospective analysis, which is done at the time when the patient was "removed from observation," are

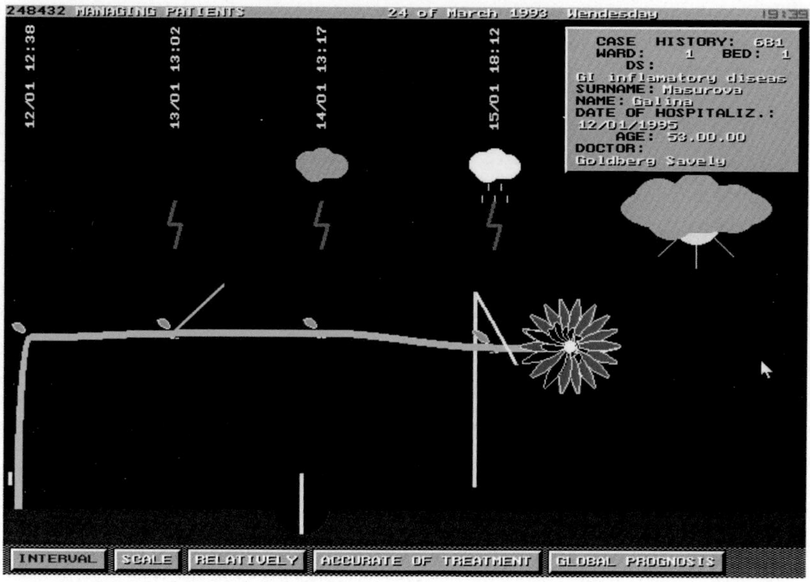

FIG. 8

Managing patients. Response of a patient to the treatment screen.

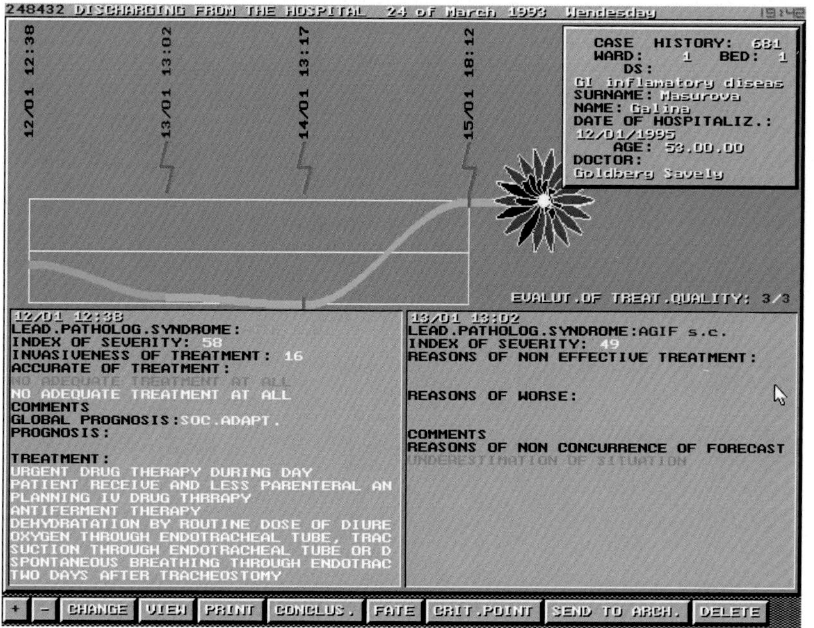

FIG. 9

Taking a patient off observation/discharging screen.

stored in the database without reference to a particular patient. We felt that this feature would incentivize a more thorough and honest approach to post hoc analysis and would reduce the potential danger of alteration of records.

3.7 Integral assessment of patients in the department

This subsystem starts and completes the work with SAGe. The landing screen of this subsystem presents the plan of the medical unit. Each bed represents a window displaying the patient's information retrieved from other subsystems. The most prioritized (most complex) among patients is defined by the severity of state, unfavorable state dynamics, values of the cost of treatment, and medical complexity (Fig. 10).

The complexity of the case is derived from a comparison of the following indexes:

$N1$ (t, i)—index of controllability of the treatment process for patient i at moment t

$$N1\,(i,t) = F1(t-1,i) + F2(t,i) + F3(t,i)$$

Where $F1(t-1, i)$—discrepancy between prognosis and reality at moment t. $F2(t, i)$—loss of control of a patient i at the moment t. $F3(t, i)$—lack of coordination in the treatment revealed at moment t.

$N2(t, i)$—index of the unfavorable condition of the state dynamics at the moment t

$$N2(t,i) = (I(t,i) - \mathrm{I}(t-1)) \times \ln I(t-1)$$

Where $I(t, i)$—the physiological assessment of the severity [10] at the moment t.

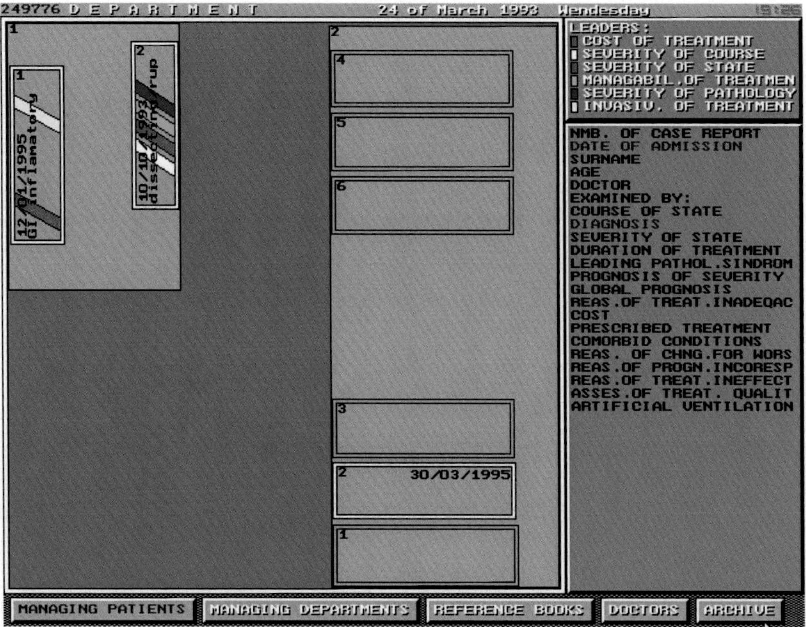

FIG. 10

Integral assessment of patients.

$N3(t, i)$—index of treatment invasiveness [11] at moment t.

A physician has full access to integral characteristics and reports on their patients and partial access to the data on patients treated by other physicians.

3.8 Features of Dr. Watson-type system presented in SAGe

Basic principles of Dr. Watson-type systems were formulated while working on SAGe. The predecessor of SAGe, DINAR2, incorporated some of them. At the development stage of SAGe, we introduced subsystems and their principles.

We provide some details of the implementation of the Dr. Watson-type AI in different subsystems in the sections that follow.

3.8.1 Discovery of contradictions and omissions

In the "Diagnostics" subsystem, discovery of contradictions and omissions is achieved by revealing information that does not fit into the diagnostic hypothesis of a physician. In the "Treatment efficiency" subsystem, this is achieved by revealing disparity between prognosis and reality. In the "Treatment adequacy" subsystem, this is achieved by showing contradictions in the physician's reflections. In the "Discontinuation of observation" subsystem, this is achieved by prompting the physician to create an archive of their own retrospective reflections and conclusions about the course of the treatment of the patients. Retrospective analysis of their prior/interim conclusions and decisions may present the course of the patient's condition.

and the factors, leading to a particular outcome in a new light.

3.8.2 Attempts to direct physicians towards alternative solutions

In the "Diagnostics" subsystem, directing physicians towards alternative solutions is achieved by directing questions. In the "Treatment efficiency" subsystem, this is achieved by displaying signs demanding attention. In the "Treatment adequacy" subsystem, this is achieved by showing possible mistakes in treatment.

In all the subsystems, algorithms make their choice of signs necessary to stimulate the physician, based on the final tasks of the subsystem accepted by SAGe. Algorithms developed for SAGe possess an apparatus of self-tuning to the user.

3.8.3 Encouragement and motivation

In the "Integral assessment" subsystem, encouragement and motivation is achieved by presenting a course of patient's treatment, allowing the possibility to receive integral information, viewing all patients at once, archiving data, and creating convenient access to the archive.

In the "Diagnostics" subsystem, this is achieved by creating access to assessment of the severity of a patient's conditions and control of the accuracy of the information being entered by an assistant into the system.

In the "Treatment efficiency" subsystem, this is achieved by comparing the trends of various parameters and evaluating therapy invasiveness.

In the "Treatment adequacy" subsystem, this is achieved by creating an archive of the physician's own reflections and problems arising during treatment of a patient.

Information about a person's activity within SAGe is accessible only to that person. The input is protected with passwords. Data entry into SAGe (done by the physician's assistant) takes place in a special input subsystem.

4. Conclusions

In this chapter, we proposed a Dr. Watson-type AI system and identified it as the one that:

- does not directly offer a specific solution but rather analyzes a user's solution and reveals logical inconsistencies and missing data
- uses game situations, psychological techniques, and visual presentation of information to enhance and stimulate the intellectual activity of the physician

We defined technical features of this type of AI systems as follows:

(1) The system should document and analyze the dynamics of the development of the user. For example, the variability in the accuracy of their predictions from patient to patient, how the accuracy of their decisions changes over time, and how their performance compares with the average results in the specialty and/or a certain subgroup of specialists.
(2) The system should discover contradictions and omissions on the path to the correct solution and prompt the user with relevant questions, answers to which would either confirm the decision or raise doubts and direct the user towards another decision.
(3) The interaction process should start from the formalization of the user's plans and possible outcomes, and then the system should influence the decision-making using the organization of the data and asking clarifying questions.
(4) The system should provide warnings in situations of critical errors, hence it should have a dictionary of those errors.
(5) The confidentiality of specialist-machine communication must be ensured.
(6) The system should provide context-based reference and help. Interacting with the user should take place in a game-like environment.
(7) The system should have a convenient, efficient, and friendly user interface

Supplementary data sets

Please visit https://github.com/bgalitsky/relevance-based-on-parse-trees to access all supplementary data sets.

References

Ahmed, M.N., Toor, A.S., O'Neil, K., 2017. Cognitive computing and the future of health care cognitive computing and the future of healthcare: the cognitive power of ibm watson has the potential to transform global personalized medicine. IEEE Pulse 8 (3). https://ieeexplore.ieee.org/abstract/document/7929430.

Anderson, M., Anderson, S.L., 2011. Machine Ethics. Cambridge University Press, New York. https://books.google.com/books?hl=en&lr=&id=N4IF2p4w7uwC&oi=fnd&pg=PP1&dq=Machine+Ethics&ots=5YWUvqlWPn&sig=NMInN4ApA6akSn4dhKd0-YBV-4I#v=onepage&q=Machine%20Ethics&f=false.

Arkin, R.C., Ulam, P., Duncan, B., 2009. An Ethical Governor for Constraining Lethal Action in an Autonomous System. Technical Report GIT-GVU-09-02 https://smartech.gatech.edu/bitstream/handle/1853/31465/09-02.pdf?sequence=1&isAllowed=y.

Deng, B., 2015. Machine ethics: the robot's dilemma. Nature 523, 20–22. https://doi.org/10.1038/523024a.

Dennis, L.A., Fisher, M., Winfield, A.F.T., 2015. Towards Verifiably Ethical Robot Behaviour. CoRR abs/1504.03592 http://arxiv.org/abs/1504.03592.

Goldberg, S.I., 1997. Inference Engine the Systems of the Dr. Watson Type—DIMACS Workshop. Rutgers University.

Goldberg, S.I., Meshalkin, L.D., 1992. A new class of AI-systems (DrWT-systems). Tech. Cybern. 5, 217–223 (in Russian).

Goldberg, S., Meshalkin, L., 1993. Assisting Dr.WT—systems. In: East-West Conference on Artificial Intelligence: From Theory to Practice, Moscow, Russia, pp. 207–209.

Goldberg, S.I., Tsibulkin, E.K., Rudnov, V.A., et al., 1997. Computer program SAGE as a tool for standardized assessment of resuscitation patients. Anesthesiol. Reanimatol. (1), 11–15 (in Russian).

Govindarajulu, N.S., Bringsjord, S., 2015. Ethical regulation of robots must be embedded in their operating systems. In: Trappl, R. (Ed.), A Construction Manual for Robots' Ethical Systems. Springer International.

Molnar, C., 2018. Interpretable Machine Learning. A Guide for Making Black Box Models Explainable. In: Creative Commons Attribution-NonCommercial-ShareAlike 4.0 International License. http://bit.ly/iml-paperback. https://christophm.github.io/interpretable-ml-book/.

Shifrin, M.A., Belousova, O.B., Kasparova, E.I., 2007. Diagnostic games, a tool for clinical experience formalization in interactive "Physician—IT-specialist" framework. In: Proceedings of the Twentieth IEEE International Symposium on Computer-Based Medical Systems, pp. 15–20, https://doi.org/10.1109/CBMS.2007.41.

Shklovsky-Kordi, N., Zingerman, B., Rivkind, N., Goldberg, S., Davis, S., Varticovski, L., Krol, M., Kremenetzkaia, A., Vorobiev, A., Serebriyskiy, I., 2005. Computerized case history, history—an effective tool for management of patients and clinical trials. In: Engelbrecht, R., et al. (Eds.), Connecting Medical Informatics and Bio-Informatics. ENMI, pp. 53–57. https://books.google.com/books?hl=en&lr=&id=HXTk5rWOdG4C&oi=fnd&pg=PA53&dq=Computerized+Case+History,+History+-+an+Effective+Tool+for+Management+of+Patients+and+Clinical+Trials.&ots=ZVdFYFxJ8f&sig=WhOnFACkUruu0xbwXqxAUlyReN8#v=onepage&q=Computerized%20Case%20History%2C%20History%20-%20an%20Effective%20Tool%20for%20Management%20of%20Patients%20and%20Clinical%20Trials.&f=false.

Strickland, E., 2019. How IBM Watson overpromised and underdelivered on AI health care. IEEE Spectr. 56 (4), 24–31. https://doi.org/10.1109/MSPEC.2019.8678513.

Torresen, J., 2018. A review of future and ethical perspectives of robotics and AI. Front. Robot. https://doi.org/10.3389/frobt.2017.00075.

Wallach, W., Allen, C., 2009. Moral Machines: Teaching Robots Right from Wrong. Oxford University Press, New York. https://books.google.com/books?hl=en&lr=&id=_r3N82ETng4C&oi=fnd&pg=PR7&dq=Moral+Machines:+Teaching+Robots+Right+from+Wrong&ots=OR8uGQXZ-R&sig=cOtK_ZWJHg6iqyg0cp95kUMwjL4#v=onepage&q=Moral%20Machines%3A%20Teaching%20Robots%20Right%20from%20Wrong&f=false.

Winfield, A.F., 2014. Robots with internal models: a route to self-aware and hence safer robots. In: Pitt, J. (Ed.), The Computer After Me: Awareness And Self-Awareness In Autonomic Systems, first ed. Imperial College Press, London, pp. 237–252, https://doi.org/10.1142/9781783264186_0016.

CHAPTER

14 Multimodal discourse trees for health management and security

Boris Galitsky

Oracle Corporation, Redwood City, CA, United States

1. Introduction

Discourse analysis plays an important role in constructing a logical structure of thoughts expressed in text. Discourse trees (DTs) are means to formalize textual discourse in a hierarchical manner, specifying rhetorical relations between phrases and sentences (Chapter 3). DTs are a high-level representation compromise between complete logical representations like logical forms and informal, unstructured representations in the form of original text. DTs have found a number of applications in content generation, summarization, machine translation, and question answering (Joty et al., 2015, 2019; Galitsky, 2017). The limitation of the use of DT in a general data analysis task is that they are designed to represent the discourse of a text rather than a causal relationship between components of an abstract data item. In this chapter, we address this limitation and propose a solution to generalize DTs towards arbitrary data types with applications to health management and security.

In our previous work, we took DTs to a higher level of abstraction with the goal to form a unified structure for interactive knowledge discovery (Galitsky, 2021b). To provide a systematic navigation means to take a user through content exploration, we built upon DTs for texts and extended the discourse analysis to the level of a corpus of documents. We believe that *a knowledge exploration should be driven by navigating a DT built for the whole corpus of relevant content*. We refer to such a tree as an *extended* discourse tree (EDT; Galitsky, 2019). It is a combination of DTs of individual paragraphs first across paragraphs in a document and then across documents in a corpus.

In this chapter, we take a step away from medicine towards forensic analysis and health management to demonstrate application areas of a discourse representation with a higher level of abstraction and generality. We explore application in disease spread management and crime investigation, domains rich with a broad spectrum of data sources.

We extend the concept of a DT in the discourse representation of text towards data of various forms and natures. Having defined communicative DTs (CDTs) to include speech act theory, extended DT to ascend to the level of multiple documents (Ilvovsky et al., 2019) and entity DT to track how discourse covers various entities, we now proceed to the next level and discourse abstraction, and formalize discourse of not only text and textual documents but also various kinds of accompanying data. The motivations here are that the same rhetorical relations that hold between text fragments also hold between data values, sets, and records, such as *Reason*, *Cause*, *Enablement*, *Contrast*, and *Temporal sequence*.

Artificial Intelligence for Healthcare Applications and Management. https://doi.org/10.1016/B978-0-12-824521-7.00010-7

We call DTs for text and other data forms *multimodal discourse trees* (MMDTs) and apply them in the domains of forensic linguistics and health management.

1.1 Forensic linguistics

The number of computational approaches to forensic linguistics has increased significantly over the last decades because of increasing computer processing power as well as growing interest of computer scientists in forensic applications of Natural Language Processing (NLP). At the same time, forensic linguists faced the need to use computer resources in both their research and their casework, especially when dealing with large volumes of data (Coulthard, 2010).

Forensic linguistics has attracted significant attention ever since Svartvik (1968) published *The Evans Statements: A Case for Forensic Linguistics* Svartvik (1968). The true potential of linguistic analysis in forensic contexts has been demonstrated. Since then, the corpus of research on forensic linguistics methods and techniques has been growing along with the spectrum of potential applications. Indeed, the three subareas identified by forensic linguistics in a broad sense are:

(1) the written language of the law
(2) interaction in legal contexts
(3) language as evidence (Coulthard et al., 2017; Coulthard and Sousa-Silva, 2016)

These directions have been further advanced and extended to several other applications worldwide.

The written language of the law came to include applications other than studying the complexity of legal language; interaction in legal contexts has significantly evolved and now focuses on any kind of interaction in legal contexts. This also includes attempts to identify the use of language with misinterpretation (Gales, 2015), prove appropriate interpreting (Kredens, 2016), and manage language as evidence. Other research foci are on disputed meanings (Butters, 2012), the application of methods of authorship detection for cybercriminal investigations, and an attempt to develop authorship synthesis (Grant and MacLeod, 2018).

One of the main goals of forensic linguistics is to provide a careful and systemic analysis of syntactic and semantic features of legal language. The results of this analysis can be used by many different professionals. For example, police officers can use this evidence not only to interview witnesses and suspects more effectively but also to solve crimes more reliably. Lawyers, judges, and jury members can use these analyses to help evaluate questions of guilt and innocence more fairly. And translators and interpreters can use this research to communicate with greater accuracy. Forensic linguistics serves justice and helps people to find the truth when a crime has been committed.

In this chapter, we build a foundation for what one would call *discourse* forensic linguistics, that is, how legal writers organize their thoughts describing criminal intents and evidence, involving data items of various natures. Legal texts have peculiar discourse structures (Aboul-Enein, 1999); moreover, these texts are accompanied by structured numerical data like maps, logs, and various types of transaction records. Legal texts have DTs different from other written genres and a special form of logical implications. The role of argumentation-based discourse features in legal texts is important as well (Galitsky et al., 2009).

More than 40 years ago, Jan Svartvik showed dramatically just how helpful forensic linguistics could be. His analysis involved the transcript of a police interview with Timothy Evans, a man who had been found guilty of murdering his wife and his baby daughter in 1949. Svartvik demonstrated that parts of the transcript differed considerably in their grammatical style when he compared them to the rest of the recorded interview. Based on this research and other facts, the courts ruled that Evans had been wrongly accused. Unfortunately, Evans had already been executed in 1950. However, thanks to Svartvik's work, 16 years later, he was formally acquitted. The study of Svartvik is considered today to be one of the first major cases in which forensic linguistics was used to achieve justice in a court of law. Today, forensic linguistics is a well-established, internationally recognized independent field of study.

1.2 Extended discourse trees

MMDTs can potentially extend the abilities of the interactive chatbot initially developed by Galitsky and Ilvovsky (2017) and later improved in (Galitsky, 2019; Galitsky and Ilvovsky, 2019). We consider two complementary approaches to dialogue management both using discourse analysis based on rhetorical structure theory (RST) and both utilizing DTs for texts (Chapters 9 and 10). The first approach is inspired by an idea of a guided search (Ilvovsky and Galitsky, 2019). One source of this is a search methodology designed to show a user an array of different visual possibilities where a searching user would proceed. This is done instead of just navigating to an endpoint or a terminal answer. We believe that knowledge exploration should be driven by navigating an extended discourse tree (EDT) built for the whole corpus of relevant content. It is a combination of DTs of individual paragraphs first across paragraphs in a document and then across documents (Galitsky, 2019).

The second approach tries to force the user to request exhaustive information and explanation about the particular topic. We try to achieve this by utilizing a DT of the initial piece of text. At each step of the conversation, the chatbot analyzes the remaining topics and tries to make the user more focused on the initial topic, "turning" the user back to the undiscussed parts of the text and forcing the user to request more details. As one can see, these two approaches are complementary and can be easily combined in one interactive chatbot. More information about general chatbot architecture and evaluation can be found in (Galitsky and Ilvovsky, 2017; Galitsky, 2019).

A conventional DT expresses the author's flow of thoughts at the level of a paragraph or multiple paragraphs. A conventional DT becomes inaccurate when applied to larger text fragments or documents. Hence we can extend the notion of a linguistic DT towards an EDT and then an MMDT, a representation for the set of interconnected documents and data records covering a topic.

For a given paragraph, a DT is automatically built by discourse parsers (Joty et al., 2013). We then automatically combine DTs for the paragraphs of documents to the EDT, which is a basis of an interactive content exploration. We apply structured learning (Galitsky and Kovalerchuk, 2014) of eEDTs to differentiate between good, cognitively plausible scenarios and counter-intuitive, non-cohesive ones. Then we attach data records as additional discourse sub-trees to the overall MMDT.

The goal is to make a discourse representation independent of the nature of data, from text to numerical and structured. This chapter suggests a new level of abstraction for discourse analysis on one hand and finds a health management application for this abstraction on the other hand. We define a discourse structure on data beyond text and demonstrate how it can be used in health management tasks such as recommendation tools for disease spread prevention.

We also explore how this discourse abstraction can be leveraged in forensic science. We form a crime dataset from public data and investigate how an enrichment in discourse representation helps to properly relate a crime to a penal code item. We develop a technology representing a discourse of multimodal data including text, communicating, driving, and money transactions to be applied in a broad spectrum of domains including criminal justice and spread of disease. Mobile location data has been used to track the disease, and in this chapter, we build a computational foundation for tools controlling, limiting, or preventing spread of disease based on a variety of data sources.

1.3 Victims' right and state responsibility to investigate

There is an important potential application of the MMDT technique to humanity and civil rights. The system can automatically classify a crime report or a victim complaint and determine if there is a corpus delicti in the complaint text and accompanying available data. Then the police would not have an excuse not to investigate the reported crime. This way victims right to protection, social justice, and punishment of a criminal can be assured to a greater degree than it is today, independently of the local government. Hence for a truthful criminal complaint, the automated assessment tool would issue a corpus delicti verdict, and if an innocent were falsely accused of a crime, the complainant would still bear full responsibility.

It turns out citizens can sue the police for not investigating a serious crime. The UK Supreme Court judgment in the *Commissioner of Police of the Metropolis v DSD and another* was a win for the victims of a serious violent crime. This case considered whether there is an obligation under the Human Rights Act for the state to investigate ill treatment. The state lost an appeal against a case brought by two of the victims of London cab driver John Worboys (Hodge and Allen, 2018).

The driver committed a series of sexual offenses against women. The respondents, in this case, were two victims of Worboys who had reported their assault to the police. The first victim was unable to identify him as her assailant, and after the second victim's attack, he was quickly arrested but released without charge. After a review and a police media appeal, Worboys was eventually convicted of 19 counts of sexual assault. Both women sued the police alleging they failed to conduct an effective investigation into Worboys' crimes, and this failure was a violation of their right to not be subject to torture or inhuman or degrading treatment or punishment. The Supreme Court judges held unanimously that the state (in this case the Metropolitan Police Service) does have a duty to investigate serious violent crimes that amount to arguably inhuman and degrading treatment.

In the remainder of this chapter, we develop techniques of knowledge and data representation in the MMDT form that is expected to contain sufficient evidence to classify a crime report as valid or invalid.

2. Discourse analysis of health and security-related scenarios

2.1 Discourse of a reasonable doubt

To introduce the flavor of discourse forensic linguistics, we provide an example of the "flow of thoughts" required to understand the definition of *reasonable doubt*. Jurors need to understand this principle in order to convict or acquit in a criminal trial:

> Reasonable doubt is that doubt engendered by an investigation of all the proof in the case and an inability, after such investigation, to let the mind rest easily as to the certainty of guilt. Reasonable doubt does not mean a captious, possible or imaginary doubt. Absolute certainty of guilt is not demanded by the law to convict of any criminal charge, but moral certainty is required, and this certainty is required as to every proposition of proof requisite to constitute the offense.

In jury trials, the judge needs to instruct the jury about those specific aspects of the law necessary for them to reach a decision based on the evidence presented to them. In the United States this instruction is typically achieved through the judge reading out standardized prepared texts, called Pattern Jury Instructions. The instructions while legally secure are often at best opaque and at worst incomprehensible to the target audience; indeed, there are claims that some men in the United States have been wrongly sentenced to death because the jury did not understand the relevant instruction (McKimmie et al., 2014).

For a human or machine to "understand" this definition means to navigate the DT shown in Fig. 1.

If a given case description is a logical theory, then the logic of reasonable doubt related to this case is a meta-theory. In this example, the meta-theory is expressed via the DT where rhetorical relations link logical statements expressed in text. These statements can be thought of as metapredicates that range over first-order predicates describing a legal case or a scenario related to a health accident such as *infecting one person by another*. One such metapredicate is a *Background* ranging over another, which, in turn, performs *Enablement* over another metapredicate for a mental action "*let the mind rest.*"

This DT represents the reasoning structure required to conclude on a case. When the case is described in words, it is possible to coordinate a DT for meta-theory (Galitsky, 2020) such as Pattern Jury Instructions with the DT for the object-level theory related to the case being judged. The object-level theory includes not only a textual description of the case but also accompanying data such as phone calls, people movement, and transactions. All these sources are covered by the meta-theory DT, but the object-level DT traditionally expresses only textual discourse. In this project, we break this tradition and explore the possibilities to include all kinds of data into the object-level DT since the same rhetorical relations hold between texts and other kinds of numerical data.

2.2 Discourse analysis of a scenario

We now proceed to analyze a discourse representation of a security-related scenario (Fig. 2). We consider a series of news titles related to defunding police in Minneapolis, Minnesota, United States. To computationally treat this example of incompetence in security management (Galitsky, 2020), we draw the DT where titles are split into elementary discourse units (EDUs) and rhetorical relations are established between them (Fig. 3). In addition to a sequence of events connected by rhetorical relations, we include the labels for communicative actions (in red; Galitsky and Kuznetsov, 2008).

```
elaboration
 elaboration
  background
   TEXT:Reasonable doubt is that doubt engendered by an investigation of all the proof in the case and an inability ,
   enablement
    TEXT:after such investigation ,
    TEXT:to let the mind rest easily as to the certainty of guilt .
  TEXT:Reasonable doubt does not mean a captious , possible or imaginary doubt .
 joint
  contrast
   enablement
    TEXT:Absolute certainty of guilt is not demanded by the law
    TEXT:to convict of any criminal charge ,
   TEXT:but moral certainty is required ,
  TEXT:and this certainty is required as to every proposition of proof requisite to constitute the offense
```

FIG. 1

A discourse representation via discourse tree (DT).

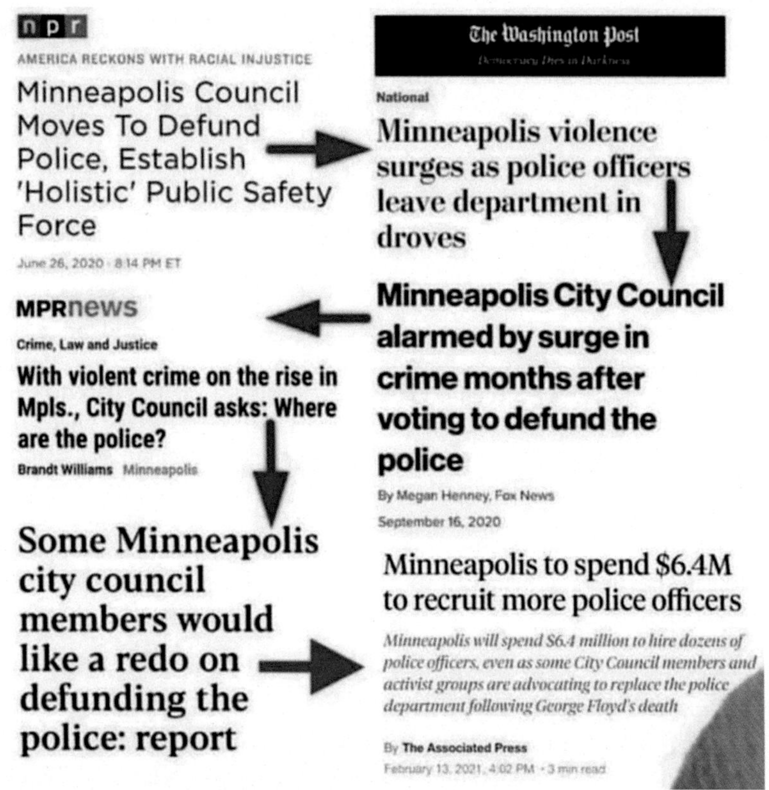

FIG. 2

A circle of incompetence in security management.

Fig. 3 shows a chain of events so that each one is caused by the previous one. The DT provides for explicit links between events; notice that these links are not uniform, in contrast to the original scenario visualization (Fig. 2), which shows only a sequence of events. The main relation to form this chain of events is *Cause*, as each current state is a result of the previous state. In this case, states are mental (not physical); they are related to the Council's opinion on whether the police are required or not to maintain law enforcement.

3. Multimodal discourse representation

Our objective is to recover chains of events from logs of transactions of various sorts including textual descriptions. Fig. 4 shows a simple idea of merging various data sources. The trick is how to retain an original structure inherent to each source and merge it with the logical structure of text (Fig. 5).

Fig. 5 shows an introduction of a logical structure in each source with interconnections between sources. Each source such as web page visit and call sequence is assigned a logical structure. In this

```
elaboration
  elaboration
    temporal
      cause
        Council  moves to defund police
        cause
          temporal
            Violence surge
            as police officers leave department
          temporal
            City Council is alarmed by surge in crime
            months after voting
    attribution asks(council, where(police, ?)
      background
        With violent crime on the rise
        City Council asks
      where are the police?
cause
  attribution want(council, redo(not funding(council, police)))
    City Council members want redo
    on defunding the police
  enablement
    City Council to spend 6.4M
    To recruit more police officers
```

FIG. 3

A discourse tree (DT) for a scenario.

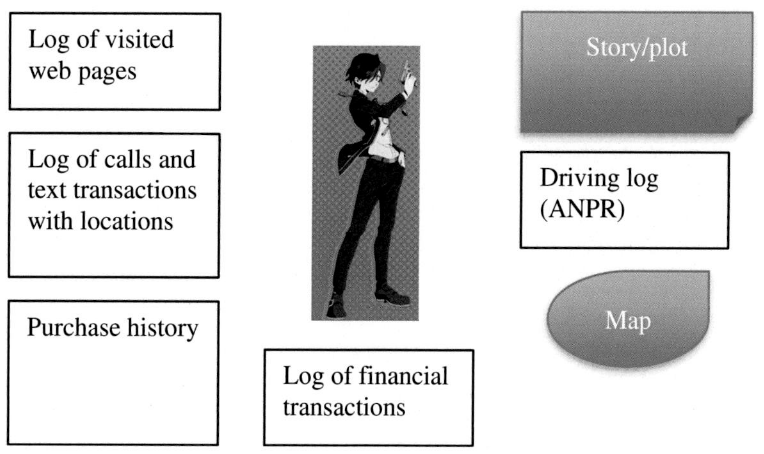

FIG. 4

Combining data of various kinds such that the hybrid data maintains comparable structures.

particular structure, the relation between chunks of knowledge about events (web page visits, calls, and buying transactions) is causal but could be *Explanation*, *Enablement*, *Means*, *Attribution and*, other. These rhetorical relations hold within a source as well as between sources, as shown by arrows from *calls* to *drives* and from *texting* to money *wire*. There is a basic DT for each source, and relations between sources combine these trees of individual sources into a single tree for an event. Explicit, nontrivial relations like *Cause* connect DTs for *calls* and *drives*, *texting* and *wiring*.

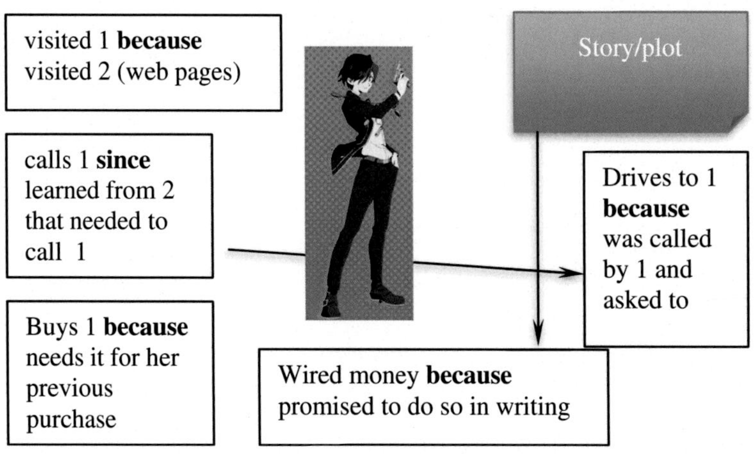

FIG. 5

Merging the same sources but now organized by the same causal structure.

```
elaboration
  reason
    attribution
      TEXT: Blah Blah Blah...
      TEXT: as Mike said so
    cause
     Wired money
     promised to do so in writing
     cause
       Visited 1 (web pages)
       visited 2 (web pages)
  reason
    attribution
     Calls 1
     learned from 2 that needed to call 1
    cause
     Drives to 1
     was called by 1 and asked to
     cause
      Buys 1 needs it
      for her previous purchase
```

FIG. 6

A multimodal discourse tree (MMDT).

We now proceed from the illustration of the idea of the structural merge to its representation via the MMDT (Fig. 6). Inner relations within a given data source are now combined with inter-relations between sources. The same relations hold within a source and between them. The overall logical structure of data is now independent of its nature. A numerical record for banking can be rhetorically connected with a numerical record for calling, which is in turn connected with that for driving.

FIG. 7

An interaction between three persons and their tools (left). It is an art for a detective to find a path to a proof (right).

We can now reconstruct the whole story. What is written in text is that someone is expected to wire money. To perform wire money transactions, banking web pages had to be visited; first, the login page, and then the wire form page. To hand in cash, suspects need to drive, and it can be recorded as in a drive log by an Automated Number Place Recognition (ANPR) system.

MMDTs are required when complex scenarios of inter-human interactions are encoded and need to be retrieved (Fig. 7, left). MMDTs support a path to proof discovery (Fig. 7, right).

3.1 Multimodal discourse tree for a crime report

We now present a crime description and its MMDT representation (Fig. 8). We proceed to the start of the extortion crime (Fig. 9).

Rhetorical relations link text EDUs as well as discourse units with information chunks of other modalities, including calls and cars, connected with rhetorical relations of *Means* and *Enablement*. We now proceed with the crime description (Fig. 10).

An extortion crime is over once the demand is expressed. The abduction crime is started (Fig. 11). We now show a tree-like visualization of an arbitrary MMDT that can represent a crime scenario as well as a legal behavior one (Fig. 12). This is an example of an MMDT where discourse units are data elements such as phone calls, ANPR records, financial transactions, and texts.

3.2 Multimodal data sources and references between them

Various data sources are not only connected via a DT but are also linked with each other directly. It is hard to form a meaning from a single source, but once we can correspond event parameters from multiple sources and build a whole picture, the constructed event becomes meaningful.

Realizing their joint criminal intent aimed at committing extortion, acting in accordance with distributed roles and a pre-developed plan, the acting group of persons by prior conspiracy drove up and were in the immediate vicinity of the crime scene, watched the environment, waiting for a signal from the gang leader

```
same-unit
 background (RightToLeft)
  elaboration
   TEXT:Realizing their joint criminal intent
   TEXT:aimed at committing extortion ,
  enablement                                              enablement
   TEXT:acting in accordance with distributed roles and a pre-developed plan , the acting group of
persons by prior conspiracy drove up
   TEXT:and were in the immediate vicinity of the crime scene ,
 elaboration
  TEXT:watched the environment ,
  TEXT:waiting for a signal from the gang leader .
```

FIG. 8

A multimodal discourse tree (MMDT) for a preparation for a crime. The data record for driving is shown by a pictogram connected with the textual DT by *Enablement.*

The victim, unaware of the impending crime against him, at about 5pm, arrived at the house number 162. He was awaited by Tavridova, acting by a group of persons in a prior conspiracy with Magomedov and Gereykhanov, who, under the pretext of taking out the garbage, left the house and went out to call Magomedov and Gereykhanov that the victim was now located indoors. Thus Tavridova gave the signal to start committing the crime.

```
elaboration
 TEXT:The victim , unaware of the impending crime against him , at about 5pm, arrived at the house
number 162 .
 elaboration                                              enablement
  cause
   TEXT:He was awaited by Tavridova ,
   elaboration
    TEXT:acting by a group of persons in a prior conspiracy with Magomedov and Gereykhanov ,
    same-unit
     attribution
      TEXT:who , under the pretext
      TEXT:of taking out the garbage ,
     joint
      TEXT:left the house                                  means
      attribution (RightToLeft)
       TEXT:and went out to call and inform Magomedov and Gereykhanov
       TEXT:that the victim was now located indoors .
  enablement
   TEXT:Thus Tavridova gave the signal
   TEXT:to start committing the crime .
```

FIG. 9

A multimodal discourse tree (MMDT) for initiation of the crime.

For example, if two cars follow each other with a short interval (as determined from the ANPR system), it means that their movement is coordinated. In our examples in Fig. 13A, two attackers were in one car and the gang leader was in the other car. In their explanation of the event, they were driving independently and arrived at the house at different times. However, the ANPR system defeats the accused claim that they arrived with different purposes to repair the house rather than to commit extortion.

In the continuation of her joint criminal intent aimed at committing extortion, Tavridova returned to the house. She did not lock the front door with a key, in order for the gang to enter the house. Magomedov and Gereykhanov acted with her jointly and in agreement. Then they entered the house through the unlocked front door, yelling at the victim.

elaboration
elaboration
temporal_sequence
cause
TEXT:In the continuation of her joint criminal intent
TEXT:aimed at committing extortion ,
TEXT:Tavridova returned to the house .
enablement
TEXT:She did not lock the front door with a key ,
TEXT:in order for the gang to enter the house .
elaboration
TEXT:Magomedov and Gereykhanov acted with her jointly and in agreement .
elaboration
TEXT:Then they entered the house through the unlocked front door ,
TEXT:yelling at the victim with verbal threats of physical harm .

FIG. 10

A multimodal discourse tree (MMDT) for the start of the crime.

Magomedov pointed the knife to the victim's elbow and Gereyhanov pointed the handgun to the victim's back, threatening the victim with the murder, unless he does a money wire from his Chase account to Tavridova's Sberbank account. As the attackers needed more time to have the wire completed, they decided to move the victim to another house to continue money transfer. Tavridova made a call, making sure certain arrangement were made. Then the attackers pulled the victim out of the house and lead him to the car to drive 35 miles north.

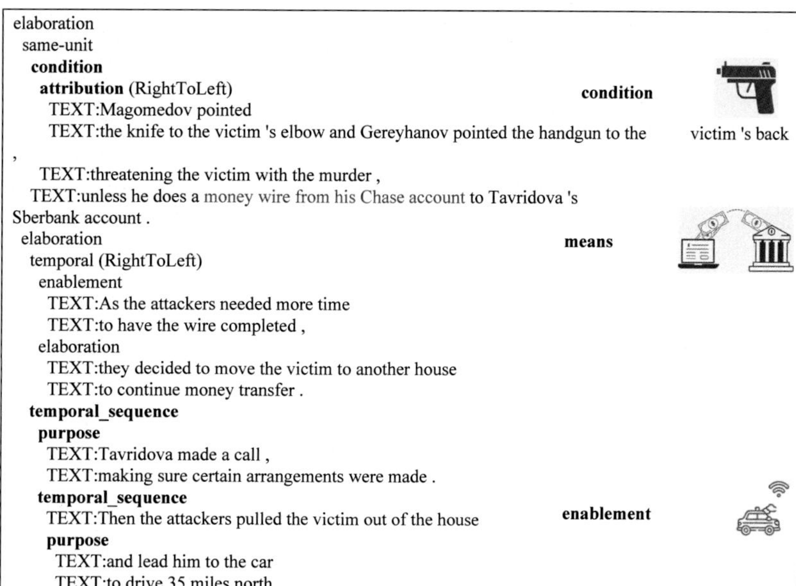

FIG. 11

A multimodal discourse tree (MMDT) for the main stage of the crime.

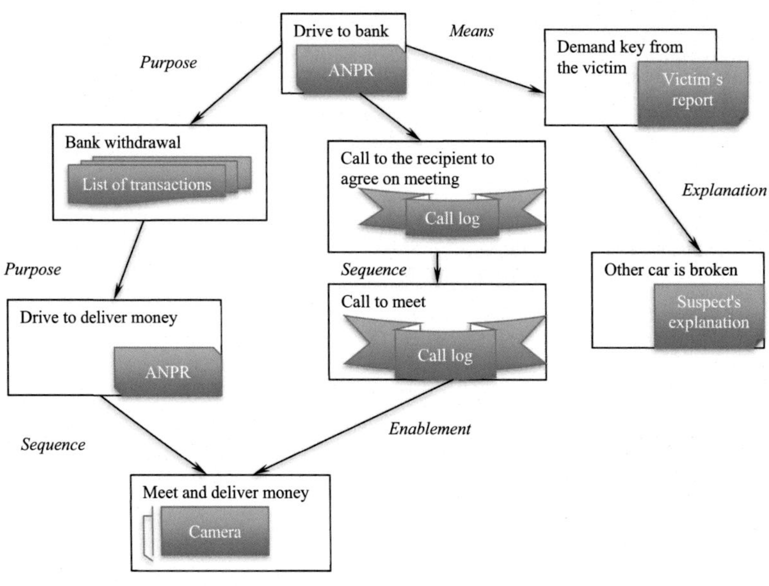

FIG. 12

A multimodal discourse tree (MMDT).

Once the detective establishes that the gang members drove through a certain point one after another, they would look for confirmation from other sources. If people in one car can see another car, they do not need to call with the purpose of coordination or orientation; if they do make calls then they can have another communication purpose (Figs. 13A and B).

It is hard to prove that extortion occurs, as the victim could possibly meet the demands of the attackers voluntarily, or the demands did not occur. Sources like calling logs, banking transfers, and web logs can indicate whether extortion actually occurred or not.

Once the extortion process starts, one would expect the victim to be deprived of communication means including phones and the Internet to keep them from calling for help. The call log can easily confirm or reject this expectation. If the frequency of calls of the victim is zero or much lower than that of the gang members, this is a confirmation of an extortion process. The web log can confirm the activity of the victim directly by showing how the victim logged into different accounts and made transfers. Corresponding weblog activities of the attackers who check the receipt of money would be informative as well. Moreover, the victim's calls to the banker to perform a transaction that cannot be completed online can also be tracked and matched against the transactions themselves. IP addresses of bank requests can be matched against IP addresses of weblogs. Bank branch locations can be matched with ANPR locations (not used in this particular case).

When a financial transaction occurs, a sender and a recipient need to call each other. In addition, they likely drove together or met at some location, as determined by ANRP and call logs. Hence for two sources and events in each of them, there are frequently causal links between these events (Fig. 13B, arrows).

Fig. 13B shows the discovered causal links.

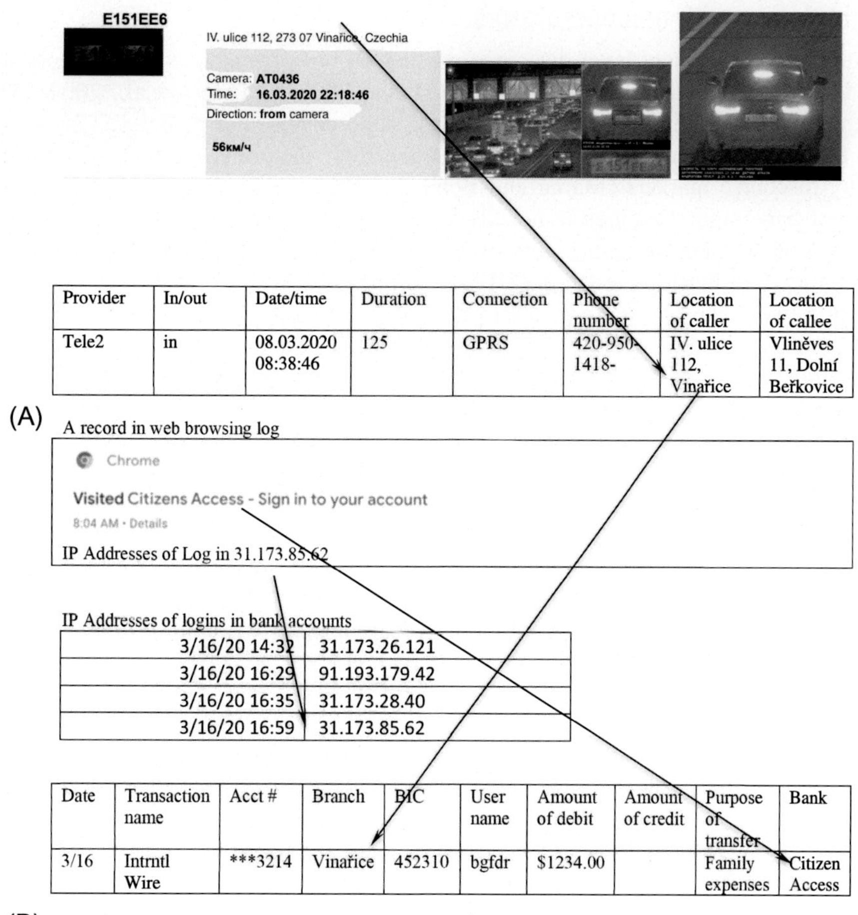

Provider	In/out	Date/time	Duration	Connection	Phone number	Location of caller	Location of callee
Tele2	in	08.03.2020 08:38:46	125	GPRS	420-950-1418-	IV. ulice 112, Vinařice	Vliněves 11, Dolní Beřkovice

A record in web browsing log

Chrome

Visited Citizens Access - Sign in to your account

8:04 AM • Details

IP Addresses of Log in 31.173.85.62

IP Addresses of logins in bank accounts

3/16/20 14:32	31.173.26.121
3/16/20 16:29	91.193.179.42
3/16/20 16:35	31.173.28.40
3/16/20 16:59	31.173.85.62

Date	Transaction name	Acct #	Branch	BIC	User name	Amount of debit	Amount of credit	Purpose of transfer	Bank
3/16	Intrntl Wire	***3214	Vinařice	452310	bgfdr	$1234.00		Family expenses	Citizen Access

FIG. 13

(A) A data record in the driving log (ANPR) and (B) Data records in a call log, web browsing, IP addresses of financial logins, and banking transactions.

We now can enumerate MMDT-based questions that can be formalized and asked against an MMDT:

- *For a given individual, find people who visited at one point any location visited by a given person and transferred money to him or back*
- *Find all pairs of people who drove in different cars following each other within a kilometer of each other*
- *Find people who call each other and then meet*
- *Find people who call each other and then transfer money*
- *Find all people who were once in a location where a given person stayed/visited*
- *If A calls B who is in a branch in location L to check on account B?*

3.3 Manipulation with discourse trees

The idea of staging document-level discourse parsing on top of sentence-level discourse parsing has been developed over the last two decades (Marcu, 2000; LeThanh et al., 2004). These approaches mainly rely on discourse markers and use hand-coded rules to build DTs for sentences first, then for paragraphs, and so on. However, frequently, rhetorical relations are not explicitly indicated by discourse markers (Marcu and Echihabi, 2002), and a mapping between discourse structures and paragraph structures is not always one to one (Sporleder and Lascarides, 2004). Therefore, discourse analysis algorithms proceeded from hand-coded rules based on discourse markers to supervised machine learning (ML) techniques with a large set of informative features. In this section, we make one more generalization step and ascend DTs to the level above documents. This is plausible if we have the means to link these documents via hyperlinks or references or attempt to classify a given rhetorical relation between two occurrences of the same entity in distinct documents.

EDT is an application area of manipulating DTs and combining them. We follow (Grasso, 1999) and provide several formal definitions for how these manipulations can be conducted in terms of the syntax of DTs. The purpose of this formalism is to modify DTs without altering the logic of discourse. One option of DT modification is an exchange of text fragments between trees.

Definition 1 A DT is a tree with nodes <*Identifier, Type, TextFragment*>;

Type = {*root, nucleus, satellite*},

Identifier is either a rhetorical relation holding among the node's children (if the node is intermediate), or the informative unit (IU) associated with the node (if it is a leaf).

The leaves of a DT correspond to contiguous EDUs. Adjacent EDUs are connected by rhetorical relations (e.g., *Elaboration*, *Contrast*), forming larger discourse units (represented by internal nodes), which in turn are also subject to this relation linking. Discourse units linked by a rhetorical relation are further distinguished based on their relative importance in the text; the nucleus is the central part, whereas the satellite is the peripheral one. No constraints are introduced on several nucleus and satellite children of a DT node. Each node has at least two children, with at least one nucleus.

Definition 2 Given two sets of nodes $N = \{n_1, \ldots, n_j\}$ and $M = \{m_1, \ldots, m_k\}$ of T, then N precedes M in DT ($N <_{DT} M$) if each node in N is considered *before* every node in M when exploring T in a depth-first, left-to-right navigation mode.

Definition 3 Given a DT, $L = \{l_1, \ldots, l_n\}$ a set of (not necessarily adjacent) leaves of DT, and n a node (not leaf) of DT, then:

- n *generates* L if L is contained in the set of leaves that n spans.
- The lowest generator of L (γ_L) is the unique node of DT such that:
  (1) γ_L generates L
  (2) for all n_i, nodes of DT generating L, γ_L is a descendant of n_i.
- The context of L (γ_L) is the set of all leaves generated by γ_L.
- L is a *span* if $\gamma_L = L$.

Definition 4 Two set of leaves L_1 and L_2 of a discourse tree are *independent* if their contexts do not overlap ($\chi_{L1} \cap \chi_{L2} = \emptyset$).

Definition 5 Given a DT, the *most nuclear part* of T (Nuc_L) is the set of DT leaves recursively defined as:

(i) if DT consists of a single node, then Nuc_L is DT itself
(ii) otherwise, if R_T is the root of DT, Nuc_L is the union of the most nuclear parts of all R_T's children having a nucleus role.

We define the most nuclear part of a node n as Nuc_{Tn}, where T_n is the sub-tree whose root is n, and the most nuclear part of a span S as $Nuc_{\gamma S}$.

Definition 6 Given a DT, its nuclear structure of N_T is the set of the most nuclear part of all nodes ($N_T = \{N | N = \underline{Nuc_n},\ n \in \mathrm{DT}\}$).

Assumption 1. A rhetorical relation (RR) holding between two spans S_l and S_l also holds between Nuc_{S1} and Nuc_{S2}. It is referred to as RR *projects* a deep-RR between the two most nuclear parts.

Assumption 2. Two DTs having the same set of leaves, the same nuclear structure, and the same set of deep RRs occurring between the elements of their nuclear structures, are equivalent.

Definition 7 DT manipulation operation is *meaning preserving* if the resulting DT is equivalent to the original one.

Task 1. Given a DT, and two independent sets $L_1 = \{l_j, \ldots, l_n\}$ and $L_2 = \{l_k, \ldots, l_m\}$ of DT leaves such that

$L_1 <_{DT} L_2$, generate DT1 equivalent to DT, such that $L_2 <_{\mathrm{DT1}} \mathrm{L}_1$.

We present two basic operations on the DT and then the main algorithm:

Operation 1: Inversion of siblings. Let n be a node of DT, and $N_i = \{n_{i1}, \ldots, n_{ik}\}$ and $N_j = \{n_{j1}, \ldots, n_{jh}\}$, two non-overlapping subsets of n's children such that $N_i <_T N_j$. Then *Inv(n, N_i, N_j)* re-orders n's children in a way so that $N_j < T\ N_i$.

Operation 2: Exchange of satellite children. Let $<n_1,Role_1,RR_1>$ and $<n_2;Role_2;RR_2>$ be two nodes of a DT. Let S_{a1} and S_{a2} be the respective sets of the sub-trees yielded by the children of n_1 and n_2 having a satellite role.

An exchange of satellites between n_1 and n_2, *ExcSat(n_1,n_2)*, consists of:

(1) replacing $<n_1,Role_1,RR_1>$ with $<n_1,Role_1,RR_2>$
(2) replacing $<n_2,Role_2,RR_2>$ with $<n_2,Role_2,RR_1>$
(3) substituting the set S_{a1} with the set S_{a2} in n_1
(4) substituting the set S_{a2} with the set S_{a1} in n_2

Notice that *Inv(n, N_i, N_j)* is always meaning preserving and *ExcSat(n_1, n_2)* is meaning preserving only if $Nuc_{n1} = Nuc_{n2}$.

Algorithm of exchanging two text fragments:

Let χ_1 and χ_2 be the contexts of L_1 and L_2, respectively, and $L_{12} = \chi_1 \cup \chi_2$ and γL_{12} be the lowest generator of L_{12}. Two cases may occur:

(1) $\gamma \mathrm{L}_{12}$ has at least one satellite child. Let γ_{Nuc12} be the lowest generator of $Nuc_\gamma L_{12}$, the most nuclear part of $\gamma \mathrm{L}_{12}$, and $LNuc_{12}$ the set of leaves generated by the nucleus children of γNuc_{12}. Two cases may occur:
  (a) L_{Nuc12} has an empty intersection with L_{12}. Let γ_1 be the lowest generator of $\chi_1 \cup L_{Nuc12}$ and γ_2 be the lowest generator of $\chi_2 \cup L_{Nuc12}$. Naturally, $Nuc_{\gamma 1} = Nuc_{\gamma 2} = Nuc_{\gamma 12}$. Apply *ExcSat($\gamma_1$, γ_2)*. See Fig. 14 (left).
  (b) L_{Nuc12} has a non-empty intersection with L_{12}. Because of the definition of context and the hypothesis of independence, it will have a non-empty intersection with either χ_1 or χ_2 but not both. Then, if N_1 and N_2 are the sets of children of γL_{12} generating χ_1 and χ_2 respectively, apply *Inv(L_{12},N_1,N_2)*.

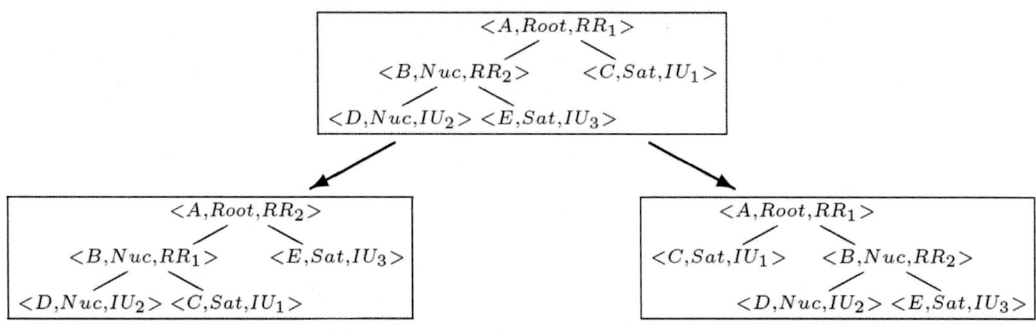

FIG. 14

An example of the exchanging sub-trees in discourse trees (DTs).

(2) γL_{12} has no satellite children: treat as the above case 1(b).

Note that the algorithm can be applied only to two independent sets of leaves. If the independence hypothesis is relaxed, a purely syntactic exchange cannot be performed, and semantics must be taken into account.

Fig. 14 shows an example of the exchanging sub-trees in DTs. An original DT is shown on the top. $\{C\}$ and $\{E\}$ are exchanged on the bottom left and $\{C\}$ and $\{D\}$ on the bottom right.

3.4 Extended discourse tree

An EDT is a combination of DTs of individual textual units (e.g., paragraphs, sentences, phrases, etc.) from multiple documents (Fig. 15). Aspects use EDTs to not only allow zooming in based on keywords but also navigating in or out or back based on how documents are interconnected, thereby providing content navigation such as guided search. An EDT includes multiple groups of DTs. Each group includes a document and a DT generated from the document. Rhetorical relations act inside a regular DT as well as in between DTs. To build rhetoric links between text fragments in different paragraphs, sentences, phrases, words, or documents, we identify a relationship between entities by using a fictitious text fragment or a temporary paragraph/sentence/phrase/word/document from the respective text fragments of the original paragraph and perform co-reference analysis and discourse parsing on the paragraph. Chapter 2 provides further details on EDTs.

4. Mobile location data and COVID-19

Mobile apps related to the novel coronavirus COVID-19 have been found to benefit citizens, health professionals, and decision-makers in facing the pandemic. Mobile apps can help in solving several COVID-19-related challenges by increasing the reach of quality information to both patients and health professionals, reducing misinformation and confusion, assessing symptoms, home monitoring and isolation, optimizing healthcare resource allocation, and reducing the burden on hospitals (Rutledge and Wood, 2020). An exploration of COVID-19 Coach mobile app usage among the general population

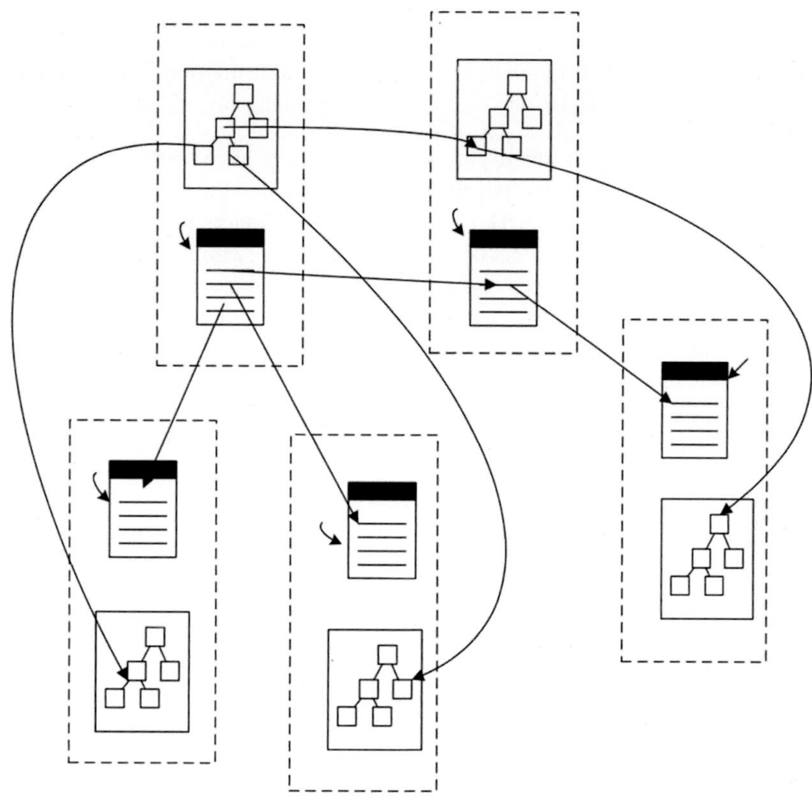

FIG. 15

An illustration for the idea of an extended discourse tree (EDT).

suggests that it may have the reach and accessibility necessary to be a useful medium for disseminating mental health information and resources to individuals experiencing stress related to the COVID-19 pandemic (Jaworski et al., 2021).

Governments and the private sector are increasingly relying on data-driven technologies to help reduce COVID-19. While some see technological solutions as a critical tool for contact tracing, quarantine enforcement, tracking the spread of the virus, and allocating medical resources, these practices raise significant human rights concerns. Human Rights Watch is particularly worried about projects for the use of mobile location data in the COVID-19 response because the data usually contains sensitive and revealing insights about people's identity, location, behavior, associations, and activities.

Mobile location data includes geolocation and proximity information from mobile phones and other devices. Mobile location data is viewed as a key component of measures to contain the spread of COVID-19. They are presenting individualized tracking as a reliable way to track the movement of people who are infected and identify individuals with whom they came into contact during the period in which they were contagious. Individualized tracking can also be used to ascertain whether people are complying with social distancing and quarantine measures. An analysis of aggregated location data, on the other hand, might provide insight into the effectiveness of social distancing measures, model the potential for transmission, and identify possible "hot spots" of transmission. The following technologies are used to respond to COVID-19.

(1) Contact tracing is the method of identifying people who may have come into contact with an infected person. It aims at preventing transmission by quickly identifying people who have been in proximity of someone who has COVID-19, defined by the Centers for Disease Control and Prevention (CDC) as within two meters of someone for about 12 min. The purpose is to convince such people to keep away from others and undergo testing and treatment. Because COVID-19 is mainly transmitted through person-to-person contact by means of respiratory droplets when an infected person coughs, sneezes, or talks, mobile location data is expected to assist in the identification of potentially exposed people.

(2) Maintain quarantine and social distancing orders. Governments are imposing quarantines and other restrictions on relocation, visits, and travel, including broad lockdowns, closures of commercial and public areas, enforced isolations of infected individuals, and demands for voluntary social distancing. Mobile location data is leveraged to monitor compliance with these restrictions by encouraging people to use an app that relies on location data to identify people attempting to break these restrictions.

(3) Big data analytics. Tech companies are utilizing location data in an aggregate form to better understand general patterns and structures of people's movements and behaviors and how these evolve over time. It is important to forecast how COVID-19 might be spreading and the effectiveness of government-ordered interventions such as social distancing measures and identify ways to better allocate testing and medical resources.

(4) Hot spot mapping. This is a subfield of big data analysis that involves the use of location data to link together the movement log of patients who have tested positive for COVID-19 to deliver health warnings about particular locations or to reduce access to or disinfect particular locations.

Mobile location data comes from a variety of sources, including cellphone towers, Global Positioning System (GPS) signals, and Bluetooth beacons. Mobile phones connect their users to telecommunications and Internet networks through cell towers. As a mobile phone moves with its user, the phone pings nearby cell towers (or "cell sites"). This process generates location information stored by the telecommunication operators about the cell towers to which the phone has sent a signal. With proximity information from multiple cell towers, a technique called "triangulation" is used to estimate the location of a cell phone with greater precision.

For COVID-19 prevention and control, Wang et al. (2020) developed a WeChat mini-program called Geo. WeChat is the most popular multifunctional social media app in China covering more than 80% of the population. WeChat is the obvious platform for collecting personal spatiotemporal logs and social behavior data, especially during the COVID-19 pandemic. A key component is the technology of powerful applets within the WeChat ecosystem. It collects data from users' voluntary WeChat activities, including time and location labels, volunteered cell phone-assisted real-world activities history over the previous 2 weeks, and the current maximum incubation period for COVID-19, to generate an updated space-time Quick Response code for identification.

The app (Fig. 16) enables accurate location and tracking of COVID-19 sources in populated areas and offers protection for the most susceptible individuals. The app includes:

(1) a strategy relying on patient-focused biomedical data that centers on the source of infection but cannot identify untraceable mild and asymptomatic patients
(2) a web-like individual tracking network constructed for patients who are infected and for the rest of healthy population
(3) detailed, unique, permanent, and traceable spatiotemporal evolution logs for each individual via social media and GPS-enabled devices using real-time artificial intelligence (AI) algorithms

A mobile phone's GPS capabilities allow it to track its location to within 3 m. Phone apps such as maps and social media retain this location data, which can then be obtained by governments and data brokers. There has been a spectrum of apps for contact tracing and quarantine enforcement that rely on GPS data to track people's movements. Additionally, anonymized GPS data is used to track patterns of movement of populations in the past and in real time.

As systematic management of the COVID-19 pandemic requires big data analysis of multiple sources of various nature and actions on the analysis results, one would expect a uniform way to represent and reason about scenarios of inter-human interactions described in various modalities. If these scenarios are represented in text only, such discipline as *discourse analysis* comes into play. We need to abstract away from text to cover other kinds of information and signals to incorporate all these sources into an actionable plan. To do this, we extend the conventional text-grounded discourse analysis towards *multimodal* discourse representation, where text and structured numerical data is linked by the same rhetorical relations as are usually applied to text.

4.1 Call detail records and COVID-19

A call detail record (CDR) contains transactions between a cell phone and the wireless phone network. These transactions are automatically collected by the equipment at the wireless phone company and stored for a period of time, anywhere from a few months to years, depending on the wireless company's policies (Fig. 17, bottom).

The fact that CDRs are created as the result of the customer's phone (using the wireless phone company's network) provides a legal proof that the service (voice, data, and text) is being provided. Each CDR contains technical details about each transaction a phone has with the wireless phone company's network, such as the date and time of the phone call or text message. Each record may also contain the starting and ending cell tower used for a phone call and in some cases, text messages and data sessions.

The COVID-19 pandemic has highlighted the value of high-frequency, localized data in inferring the economic impact of shocks to inform decision-making. This includes the use of aggregated location data. Since tracking mobility is crucial during a pandemic, researchers have worked with governments and mobile network operators to leverage CDR data, as well as aggregated and anonymized cellphone data. CDR data is used to understand migration patterns and estimate economic characteristics of households. CDR data requires strict protocols restricting access and ensuring confidentiality. In developing countries, the lack of capacity and data access policies can constrain the creation of durable data pipelines linking data availability, analysis, and policymaking. CDR data allows us to track when unique cellphone users travel across administrative boundaries, quantifying mobility as the inflow and outflow.

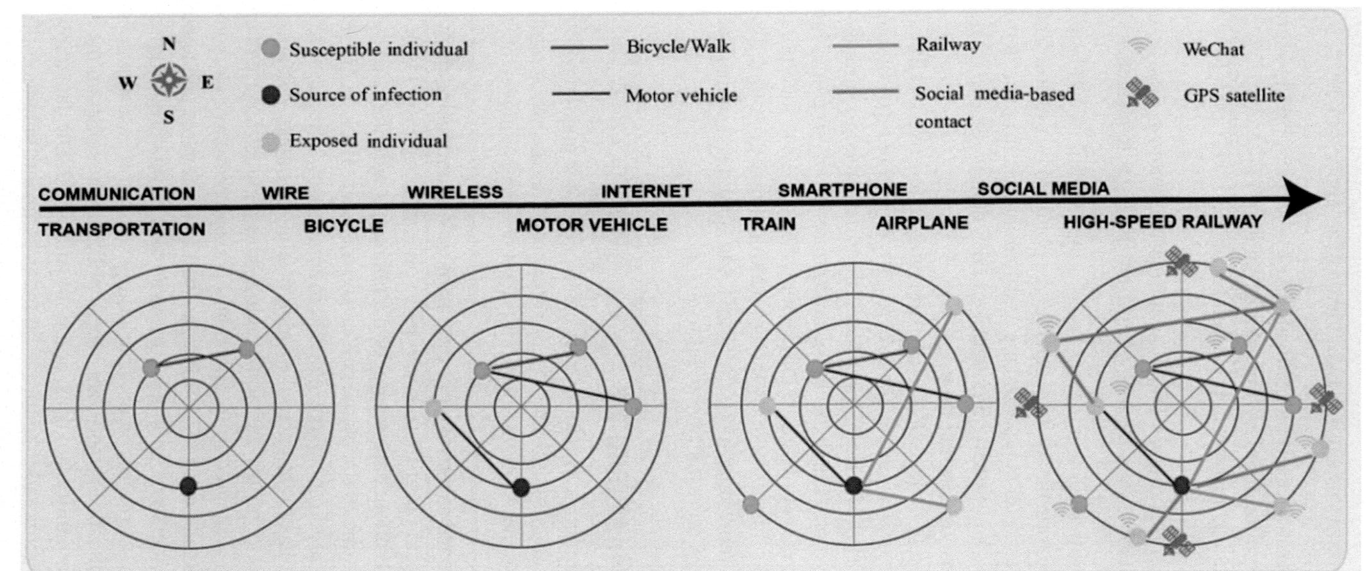

FIG. 16

The evolution of communication and transportation technology, resulting in the era of the Internet of Things in high-speed dynamicity and high-dimensional complexity.

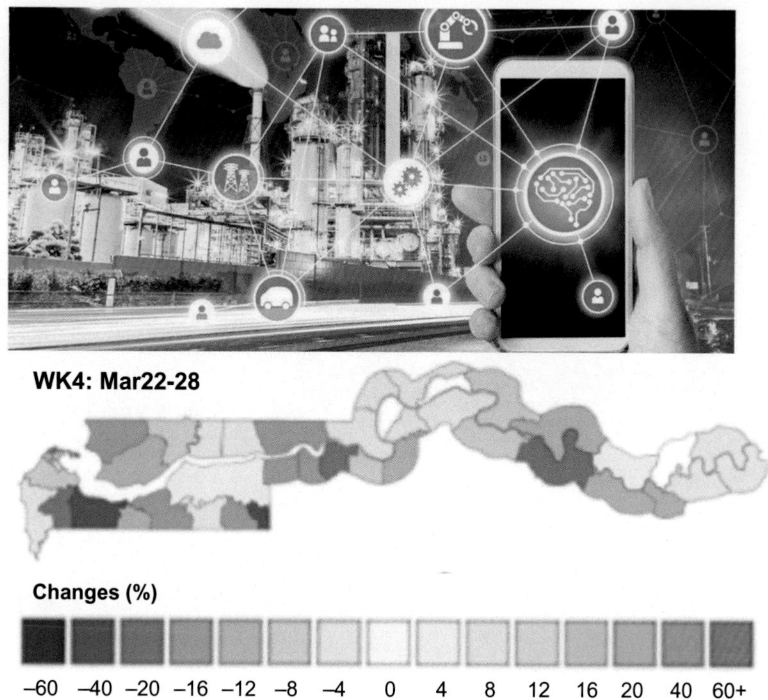

FIG. 17

Linked data sources including call detail records (top). A visualization of call detail records (CDRs) data (bottom).

The World Health Organization (WHO) developed guidelines for large-scale containment and contact tracing. There is a risk of a catastrophic pandemic if isolation, containment, quarantine, and contact-tracing mechanisms are not implemented.

Over a year, an average cellphone user makes 10,000 phone calls (including via apps like Skype and WhatsApp) and 5000 SMS texts representing communication flow; additionally, these users made 2 million Bluetooth interactions representing physical proximity movements. In the case of an infection, these three cases can initiate an exponential number of contacts through these interactions, as shown in Fig. 17. The registered quarantine address can be visualized on the map and a movement of quarantine subjects can be monitored with notifications enabled (Fig. 18).

Fig. 18 (top) shows the movement paths of confirmed cases and possible contact locations. Fig. 18 (bottom) shows that there is a deviation between the confirmed location for registered quarantine and the current location.

Phones that have the app installed exchange short-distance Bluetooth signals when their users are near one another. Records of those encounters, including their duration, are stored in the respective phones for a month, including the location data. If a user is diagnosed with COVID-19, they could allow officials to access their app data to identify people with whom they had close contact with. When a person is contacted, they are required by law to assist the officials in accurately mapping out their movements and interactions to minimize the risk of widespread infection. This includes providing location timelines and physical or digital logs that may be collected by apps (Choudhury, 2020).

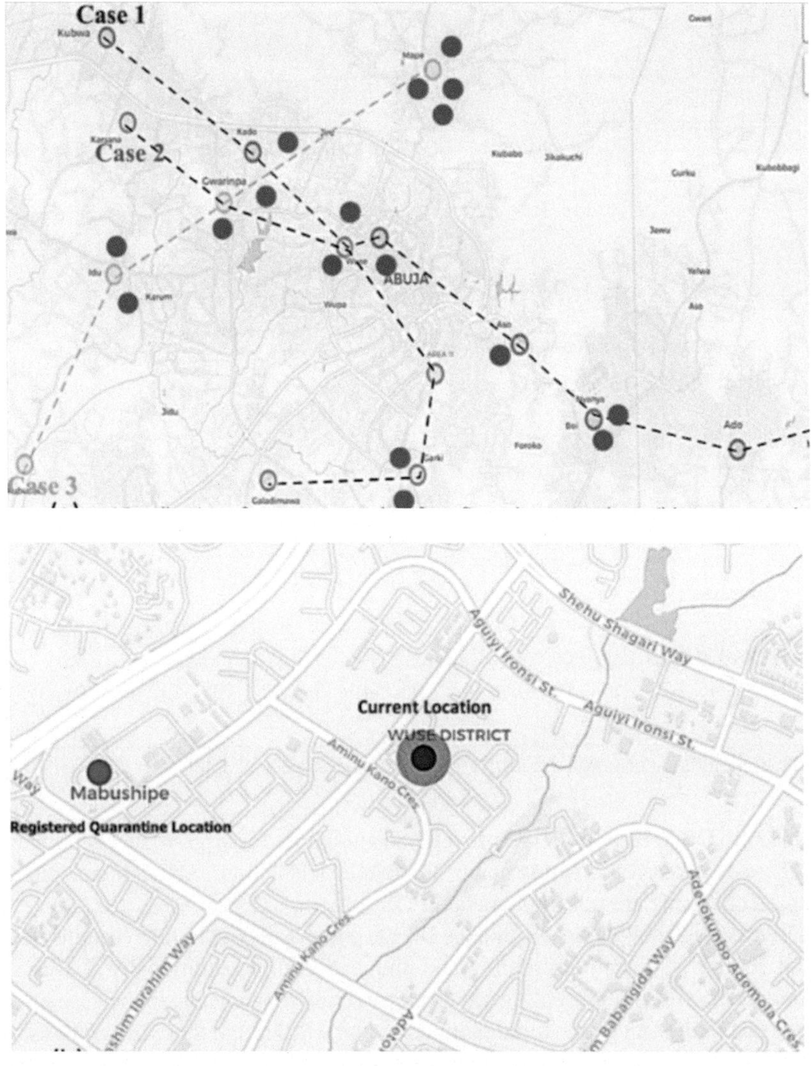

FIG. 18

Visualization of movement paths of cases and quarantine location.

Apple and Google announced a partnership in which the two companies work together to provide tools that help track the spread of coronavirus. Both companies launched APIs that enabled interoperability between Android and iOS devices using apps from public health authorities.

Privacy-safe contact tracing app using Bluetooth Low Energy (Google Blog, 2020) requires explicit user consent to use. The list of people an individual has been in contact with never leaves their phone and the people who test positive are not identified to other users. This app is only intended for contact tracing by public health authorities for COVID-19 pandemic management (Fig. 19).

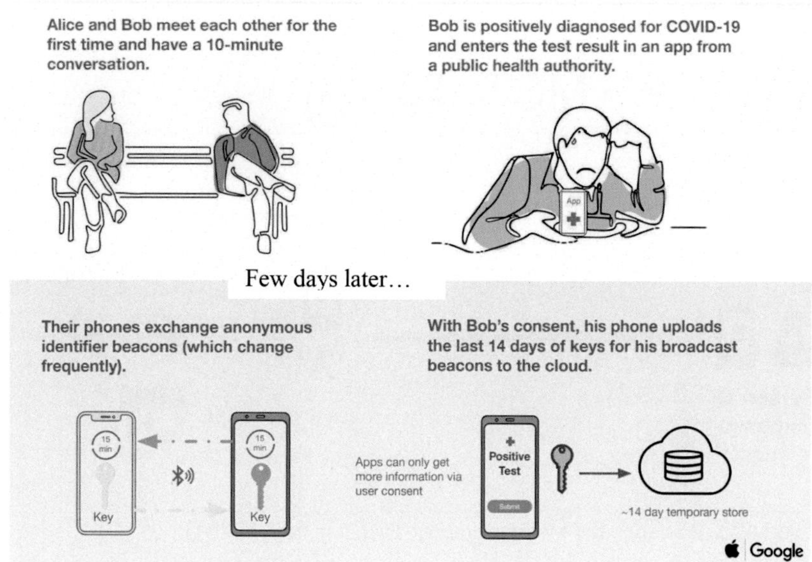

FIG. 19

Illustration for the self-contact tracing app.

A novel approach to proximity tracing is based on peer-to-peer tracking, such as through Bluetooth low-energy beacons (Ferretti et al., 2020). In this approach, apps send out signals that include a user-specific identification number, which are then received by smartphones within a certain radius (Sattler et al. 2020). The signal strength correlates with proximity (the stronger the signal, the closer the sending device), which can be leveraged to determine proximity contacts that occurred within a distance that potentially enables COVID-19 transmission. If one of the proximity contacts tests positive for COVID-19, all other app users with relevant proximity within the window of infectivity are warned by the app. While the accuracy is not perfect, it turns out to work for digital proximity tracking (DPT).

Fig. 20 shows steps in the notification scenario of DPT. Let us imagine an infected person *A* tests positive for COVID-19 (red test tube). She is referred for manual contact tracing (MCT) and receives and uploads a COVID Code to warn other app users (von Wyl et al., 2020). A person *B* was in close proximity and may have been infected. This person receives the app notification, upon which he has several options:

(1) calling an information line (the recommended option)
(2) doing a COVID test
(3) staying home voluntarily

MCT is a foundation of many countries' public health responses to COVID-19, and DPT is designed as a complement to MCT because it has distinct advantages. DPT can notify exposed contacts much faster, warn multiple contacts simultaneously, and reach contacts not personally known to the index case. Conversely, MCT identifies index case contacts through interviews, which is a labor-intensive process. Given that exposed contacts enter quarantine upon app notification, the speed advantage of DPT should

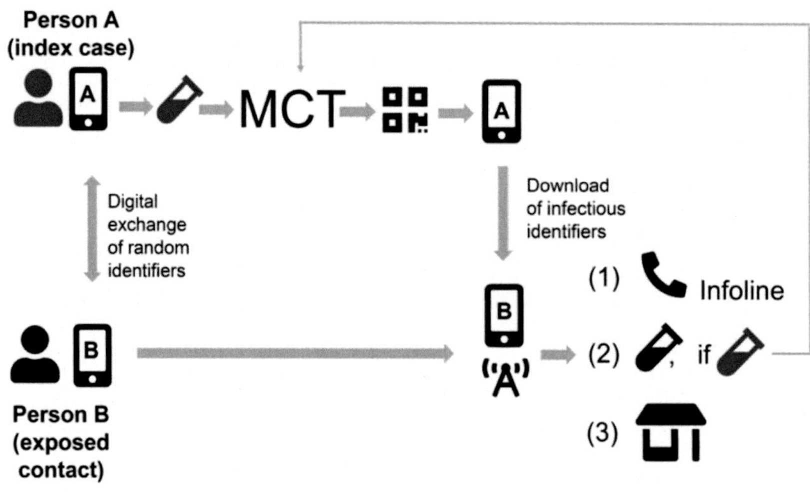

FIG. 20

Scenarios of disease spread supported by a multimodal discourse tree (MMDT).

also lead to a faster interruption of transmission chains. However, to achieve the desired goals, DPT needs adequate integration with an overall test-trace-isolate-quarantine response against the pandemic (von Wyl et al., 2020). Furthermore, MCT is still needed because it enables better identification of transmission chains (e.g., by including persons who do not use a DPT app) to assert prevention compliance with mandatory isolation or quarantine and obtain vital information about the time and setting of transmissions, thus providing valuable epidemiological data.

4.2 Automatic number plate recognition

ANPR is a highly accurate system capable of reading vehicle number plates without human intervention through the use of high-speed image capture with supporting illumination, detection of characters within the images provided, verification of the character sequences as being those from a vehicle license plate, and character recognition to convert image to text. ANPR results in a set of metadata that identifies an image containing a vehicle license plate and the associated decoded text of that plate.

ANPR is a technology used to photograph license plates, scan them using optical character recognition software, identify the vehicle, and reference it against criminal and auto registration databases to catch vehicles reported stolen and motorists with outstanding warrants or expired registration. It is also used by tow truck drivers who roam the streets and parking lots in search of cars with loans that are in default. The adoption of ANPR by a department means that every time a police cruiser, tow truck, traffic camera, overpass, or mobile trailer equipped with ANPR technology captures a license plate, the plate number is logged together with the GPS coordinates, date/time, photos of the vehicles, and even photos of the driver and passengers. An official with access to the system can look up where a given car was at a given time.

ANPR data can build detailed files on individuals or groups of people including where they work, their political affiliations, their religion, whether they attend gun shows or visit gun stores or army

FIG. 21

A sample data obtained from Automatic Number Plate Recognition (ANPR).

surplus stores, what doctors they see or which healthcare clinics they visit, the routes they travel, and other sensitive data (Fig. 21).

New data acquisition methods make it possible to collect complete information about car movements. Data from mobile phones, probe vehicles (e.g., equipped with GPS devices), ANPR cameras, Bluetooth scanners, data from tolling stations, and video recordings from high altitude (e.g., drones) give information to derive vehicle dynamics. For urban areas the methods to obtain dynamic matrices are more limited than for freeway networks. Mobile phone and Bluetooth data are less suitable in urban road networks and tolling stations are rarely present in urban areas. ANPR cameras can give very accurate data about traffic flows through an urban network (Rao et al., 2018).

5. Reasoning about a cause and effect of data records

In this section, we attempt to establish a causal link between two data records based on a connection between certain values in these data records. Usually, multiple data records are interconnected and represent correlated events; some of them cause other ones.

For example, if *A* calls *B* and then *A* transfers money to *B*, we consider that the former event causes the latter. The assumption is that there is no random coincidence between the values in data records; if they share the value, the earlier event causes the later event. A data record can be a cause of an event described in text, and the other way around.

5.1 Representing causal links by R-C framework

We first define an argument representation algorithm following Apothéloz et al. (1993) and Amgoud et al. (2015). The formalism is built upon a propositional language L with the connectives $\neg$, $\vee$, $\wedge$, $\rightarrow$, $\leftrightarrow$. There are also two operators $R(.)$ and $C(.)$ and an additional negation $-$. Thus, two negation operators are needed: $\neg$ for denying propositional formulas ($\neg x$ denotes that x is false), and $-$ for denying $R(.)$ and $C(.)$.

An argument is a formula of the form $R(y)$: $(-)C(x)$. An argument is a reason for concluding a claim. It has two main parts: premises (the reason) and a conclusion. The functions R and C respectively play the roles of giving reason and concluding. Indeed, an argument is interpreted as follows: its conclusion holds because it follows, according to a given notion, from the premises. The notion refers to the nature of the link between them (e.g., the premises imply the conclusion), formally identified by the colon in the definition. However, the conclusion may be true while the functions do not hold and vice versa. The intuitive reading is as follows:

$R(y)$: $C(x)$ means that "y is a reason for concluding x".
$R(y)$: $-C(x)$ means that "y is a reason for not concluding x".

Handling of a nested argument is important for finding a defeating answer since it is insufficient to handle only the object-level or only the meta-level layer of argumentation separately. Nested arguments are central to tackling texts and dialogues; a support for nested arguments and rejections has to be provided. To illustrate some of the expressive richness of our approach, Table 1 shows various forms of arguments and rejections allowed by our definitions (x, y, z, t are propositional formulas to simplify matters). This table is not exhaustive.

It is not shown here how to build a good argument (or a good rejection of an argument). Instead, a representation of arguments (and their rejections) is specified. If an argument or rejection occurs in a text or dialogue, then we want to extract this argument from text and represent it in L. A list of arguments in Table 1 shows that a diversity of logical forms can be used as a target for a natural language (NL) representation. It indicates how to use our language, rather than suggesting that there is a canonical translation of text into the formal target language. Table 2 shows translating a sentence into DTs first and then into R-C logic L.

Our example arguments concern the functionality of a credit card. By default, a credit card works (*is operational*), especially if there is a *positive account balance*. However, there are exceptions; for whatever reason a bank may *decline a transaction*. These examples illustrate that the inner and outer reason R, as well as claim C, can be potentially identified using argument mining techniques. Furthermore, by recursion, the inner reasons and claims can be identified by argument mining techniques. Thus, the nested structure appears to be better suited as a target language for arguments as they arise in NL dialogues and texts.

The templates in Table 2 can be used to extract logical atoms from EDUs, translate rhetorical relations into R-C operators, and form a logical representation of arguments. To do that, we first build a semantic representation for the expressions of interest related to banking $ch(g)$. Then we build DTs and attach these semantic representations to EDUs. The determined structure of the DT then forms R-C representations in L, which are subject to argumentation analysis in downstream components.

Table 1 Discourse representation or arguments and their rejections.

Basic arguments	My credit card is operational $o(c)$. It is not blocked $\neg b(c)$	$R\ (\neg b(c)): C(o(c))$
	My credit card has been compromised $m(c)$. It is blocked	$R\ (b(c)): C(m(c))$
	Credit card is operational. Thus, it is not possible to conclude that a charge can be declined ($d(c)$)	$R(o(c)): -C(d(c))$
Single-embedding meta-arguments in reason R	That debit card can be used $u(c)$ because it is operational, is a reason to conclude that the balance is positive ($p(b)$)	$R(R(u(c)): C(o(c))): C(p(b))$
	That card is not declined because it has a positive balance is a reason to conclude that it has not been compromised ($m(c)$)	$R(R(\neg d(c)): C(p(b))): C(\neg m(c))$
	Card is operational because its balance is positive, so we cannot conclude that it was blocked	$R(R(p(b)): C(o(c))): -C(b(c))$
Single-embedding meta-arguments in conclusion C	The balance on the card is negative. Thus the charge/use attempt will lead to non-sufficient fund fee ($nsf(c)$)	$R(\neg b(c)): C(u(c): C(nsf(c)))$
	The fact that a card has been declined in the past is a reason to conclude that having a positive balance is not a sufficient reason for a credit card to always be operational	$R(d(c)): C(-R(p(b)): C(o(c)))$
	The fact that all credit cards of team members are operational is a reason for not concluding that a decline charge of a particular high-cost transaction $h(c)$ is a reason for team credit cards to be compromised	$R(o(c)): -C(R(h(c)): C(m(c)))$
Double embedding of meta-arguments	Bad credit history ($ch(b)$) leads to a decline of a credit card application ($d(a(c))$). Once a user is unable to use credit card ($u(c)$) it is hard to get a loan ($l(u)$)	$R(R(ch(b)): C(d(a(c)))): C(R(u(c)): C(l(u)))$
	Good credit history ($ch(g)$) usually tells us that a credit card application is not declined ($d(a(c))$). However, we cannot imply that successful credit card application leads to a loan approval (other factors play the role as well)	$R(R(ch(g)): C(d(a(c)))): -C(R(d(a(c))): C(l(u)))$

5.2 Reasoning with arguments extracted from text

In this section, we follow Amgoud et al. (2015) in describing a reasoning system that takes two causal chains and verifies that the latter implied or the former. If this verification succeeds, these chains can be concatenated. We treat a set of arguments and their rejections as a set of formulas that is a subject of a reasoning system application. A consequence operator |— is the least closure of a set of inference rules extended with one meta-rule.

Table 2 Discourse trees (DTs) for selected examples.

<table>
<tr><td>My credit card is operational $o(c)$. It is not blocked $\neg b(c)$</td><td></td><td>$R\ (\neg b(c)): C(o(c))$</td></tr>
<tr><td>My credit card has been compromised $m(c)$. It is blocked</td><td></td><td>$R\ (b(c)): C(m(c))$</td></tr>
<tr><td>Credit card is operational. Thus, it is not possible to conclude that a charge can be declined ($d(c)$)</td><td></td><td>$R(o(c)): -C(d(c))$</td></tr>
<tr><td>That debit card can be used $u(c)$ because it is operational, is a reason to conclude that the balance is positive ($p(b)$)</td><td>**cause**
explanation
TEXT:That debit card can be used,
TEXT:because it is operational,
cause
TEXT:is a reason
attribution (RightToLeft)
TEXT:to conclude
TEXT:that the balance is positive</td><td>$R(R(u(c)): C(o(c))): C(p(b))$</td></tr>
<tr><td>That card is not declined because it has a positive balance. It is a reason to conclude that it has not been compromised ($m(c)$)</td><td></td><td>$R(R(\neg d(c)): C(p(b))): C(\neg m(c))$</td></tr>
<tr><td>Card is operational because its balance is positive, so we cannot conclude that it was blocked</td><td>**conclusion**
cause
TEXT:Card is operational
TEXT:because its balance is positive,
attribution (RightToLeft)
TEXT:so we can not conclude
TEXT:that it was blocked</td><td>$R(R(p(b)): C(o(c))): -C(b(c))$</td></tr>
<tr><td>The balance on the card is negative. Thus the charge or use attempt will lead to non-sufficient fund fee ($nsf(c)$)</td><td>elaboration
cause
TEXT:The balance on the card is negative
cause
TEXT:Thus the charge / use attempt will lead to
TEXT non-sufficient fund fee</td><td>$R(\neg b(c)): C(u(c): C(nsf(c)))$</td></tr>
<tr><td>The fact that a card has been declined in the past is a reason to conclude that having a positive balance is not a sufficient reason for a credit card to always be operational</td><td>**reason**
elaboration
TEXT:The fact
TEXT:that a card has been declined in the past is a reason
conclusion(RightToLeft)
TEXT:to conclude
cause
TEXT:that having a positive balance is not a sufficient reason
TEXT: for a credit card to always be operational</td><td>$R(d(c)): C(-R(p(b)): C(o(c)))$</td></tr>
</table>

Table 2 Discourse trees (DTs) for selected examples—cont'd

The fact that all credit cards of team members are operational is a reason for not concluding that a decline charge of a particular high-cost transaction *h(c)* is a reason for team credit cards to be compromised	elaboration TEXT:The fact **reason** TEXT:that all credit cards of team members are operational is a reason **conclusion**(RightToLeft) TEXT:for not concluding **cause** TEXT:that a decline charge of a particular high cost transaction is a reason for team credit cards TEXT:to be compromised	$R(o(c))$: $-C(R(h(c))$: $C(m(c)))$
Bad credit history (*ch(b)*) leads to a decline of a credit card application (*d(a(c))*). Thus once a user is unable to use credit card (*u(c)*) it is hard to get a loan (*l(u)*)	**cause** **cause** TEXT:Bad credit history TEXT:leads to a decline of a credit card application. **cause** TEXT: Thus once a user is unable to use credit card TEXT:it is hard to get a loan,	$R(R(ch(b))$: $C(d(a(c))))$: $C(R(u(c))$: $C(l(u)))$
Good credit history (*ch(g)*) usually tells us that a credit card application is not declined (*d(a(c))*). However, we cannot imply that successful credit card application leads to a loan approval (other factors play the role as well)	**explanation** (RightToLeft) **cause** (RightToLeft) TEXT:Good credit history usually tells us TEXT:that a credit card application is not declined. **cause** TEXT:However, we can not imply that successful credit card application TEXT: leads to a loan approval	$R(R(ch(g))$: $C(d(a(c))))$: $-C(R(d(a(c)))$: $C(l(u)))$

A meta-rule expresses that one can reverse any inference rule

$$\frac{R(y):F}{-R(y):G}\text{into}\frac{R(y):G}{-R(y):F}$$

This inference rule reversing process occurs whenever negation occurs in front of a leftmost "*R*" so that, in the general case, an inference rule 1 where $i, j \in \{0,1\}$.

As to the regular inference rules, we start from consistency:

$$\frac{R(y):C(x)}{-R(y):-C(x)}\ \frac{R(y):C(x)}{R(y):-C(-x)}$$

Reasons are interchangeable. This rule is referred to as mutual support:

$$\frac{R(y):C(x)\ R(x):C(y)\ R(y):C(z)}{R(x):C(z)}$$

The next rule gathers different reasons for the same conclusion within a single argument:

$$\frac{R(y):C(x)\ R(z):C(x)}{R(y \vee z):C(z)}$$

Cautious monotonicity means that the reason of an argument can be expanded with any premise it justifies. Cut expresses a form of minimality of the reason of an argument:

$$\frac{R(y):C(z)R(y):C(x)}{R(y \wedge z):C(x)} \quad \frac{R(y \wedge z):C(x)R(y):C(z)}{R(y):C(x)}$$

The two next rules describe nesting of $R(.)$ and $C(.)$. Exportation shows how to simplify meta-arguments and permutation shows that for some forms of meta-arguments, permutations of reasons are possible:

$$\frac{R(y):C(R(z):C(x))}{R(y \wedge z):C(x)} \quad \frac{R(y):C(R(z):C(x))}{R(z):C(R(y):C(x))}$$

When is the smallest inference relation obeying the rules above, reflexivity, monotonicity and cut hold, meaning that with the consequence relation, manipulation of arguments by the inference rules is well founded (Tarski, 1956). Indeed, let Δ be a set of (rejections of) arguments, and let α and β be arguments.

$\Delta\,\alpha$ if $\alpha \in \Delta$ (reflexivity).

$\Delta \cup \{\alpha\}\beta$ if $\Delta\,\beta$ (monotonicity).

$\Delta\,\beta$ if $\Delta \cup \{\alpha\}\beta$ and $\Delta\,\alpha$ (cut).

In addition, the consequence relation is paraconsistent in the sense that it is not trivialized by contradiction; not all formulae in language L follow from contradiction.

A domain ontology is required for this reasoning component. It can be constructed manually or mined from a corpus of documents or from the Web (Gomez et al., 2010; Galitsky et al., 2011; Galitsky, 2013).

6. System architecture

We build a conventional CDT from text, convert it into an MMDT using available structured sources, and then put it into the index for classification and search (Fig. 22).

The steps of converting a DT into an MMDT are:

(1) Once we build an individual CDT for each portion of text, we build a single EDT for the whole corpus.

(2) As the EDT is available, we start preparing accompanying data to incorporate it into the EDT to form the MMDT. Each data source is converted into a unified, canonical form with normalized named entities: time, date, location, person name, phone number, account number (if available).

(3) Iterate through each EDU of EDT, identifying candidate phrases that can potentially be associated with accompanying data. Extract name entities with their types. Form a list of candidate EDUs for linking with data record.

(4) For each candidate EDU, attempt to match entity values against those in data records.

(5) In data records taken separately from EDT, match records with each other and establish causal links, employing the R-C reasoning framework (Section 5).

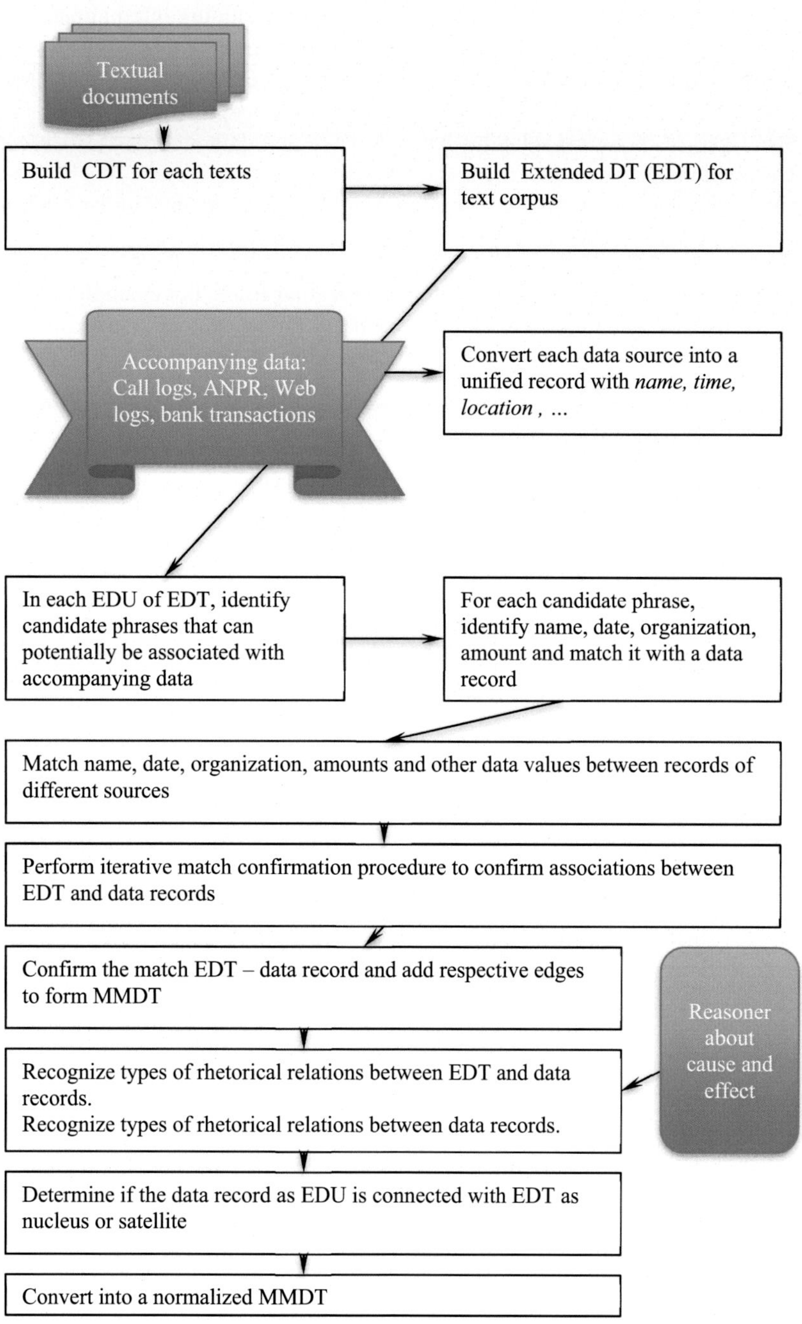

FIG. 22

The architecture of CDT-EDT-MMDT construction procedure.

(6) Iterating through all causal links (and other link types), including internal data records and external (EDT) data records links, and confirm or reject each.
(7) For confirmed causal links, insert respective edges in the EDT to obtain the MMDT without relation labels.
(8) Recognize types of rhetorical relations between EDT and data records. Also, recognize rhetorical relations between data records.
(9) Determine if the data record as EDU is connected with EDT as nucleus or satellite.
(10) Convert obtained labeled MMDT into a normalized MMDT.

The normalization procedure turns the data record into a regular EDU. For example, if a data record is linked to a pair of text EDUs connected with *Elaboration*, then *Cause* is inserted to strengthen the nucleus.

```
elaboration - cause - [12 ... nick ... 12:30 ...]
 TEXT: nucleus
 TEXT: satellite
```

```
elaboration
 cause
  DATA_RECORD: [12 ... nick ... 12:30 ...]
  TEXT: nucleus
 TEXT: satellite
```

7. Evaluation

To evaluate the contribution of MMDT relative to DT for recognizing scenarios such as criminal cases, we classify them with respect to the felony category such as *robbery*, *theft*, *abduction*, and *extortion*. Usually, using keywords is insufficient, as the crime descriptions in court decisions are written in the same or similar keywords for all these crimes: *property, car, guns, threats, violence*. Discourse-level considerations are required, and the more accurate and rich the representation is, the greater the expected recognition accuracy.

We form a dataset of criminal court decisions and attempt to automatically classify with respect to felony class. We mine the case site for criminal cases based on statute number and retain the description of corpus delicti to automatically relate it to the statute number. Case descriptions are mined from www.sudrf.ru and translated from Russian into English via Bing Translation API.

Due to a lack of complete data on criminal cases other than anonymized textual decision documents, evaluation of the contribution of the MMDT is difficult. We build a hybrid dataset of genuine anonymized textual descriptions and attach the same randomized multi-source set of data records. We form a generic dataset of data records (GDDR) of phone calls, ANPR, weblog, and bank transactions available for the crime related to the authors. Having the names, dates, locations, and other entities

Table 3 Recognition accuracy for felony classes.

Recognition method	Keyword-based	DT	CDT	MMDT—brief description	MMDT—structured
Extortion vs robbery	58.2	65.0	66.8	70.3	74.3
Robbery vs theft	61.9	66.8	68.2	71.2	73.7
Extortion vs theft	66.3	70.4	71.6	73.4	75.4
Abduction vs extortion	69.1	74.2	76.0	78.5	80.3
Abduction vs robbery	66.7	72.2	73.6	75.1	81.3
Average	64.4	69.7	71.2	73.7	77.0
Improvement		5.3	1.5	2.5	3.3

anonymized in both GDDR by the authors and in the public criminal dataset by the court authorities, we insert random entity value to associate actual criminal cases with randomized, hypothetical data records to obtain the complete criminal case data.

We use tree kernel learning to classify discourse representations (Galitsky, 2021a). Table 3 shows the recognition accuracy for various classification settings and a variety of classes. We recognize one felony category against another, where there is a high similarity in how a crime in a given category is described.

Our baseline is keyword-based recognition and regular DTs (columns two and three). In the fourth column we include the phone, driving, and money transfer data as a brief description rather than a complete data record and there are no inter-data record rhetorical relations. Finally, in the fifth column, more complete, structured multimodal information is included with built *internal data record-data record* rhetorical relations.

Once can observe that DTs yield more than 5% recognition accuracy compared to keywords, and as we proceed to CDT, we gain just 1.5%. The next step of enhancement towards the "light" MMDT delivers 2.5%, while the "complete" MMDT gives further 3.3%. The recognition rate does not vary significantly across GDDR with the felony class. The contribution of MMDT to an accurate representation of a criminal case turns out to be significant and we expect this representation to not depend significantly on the ML method.

8. Discussions and conclusions

In this chapter, we took the discourse representation via trees to the next level of abstraction, going beyond textual data and enforcing rhetorical relations between arbitrary components of data items. This allowed us to treat computationally complex scenarios of inter-human interactions described in text and as numerical and string vectors, once a causal relationship between the latter is identified. Complex scenarios of interactions such as GDDR appear in such domains as security and health management, where textual descriptions need to be merged with numerical values and the logical structure of these data sources must be analyzed together.

FIG. 23

An illustration for multimodal information sources stored in a human body.

We computationally evaluated that complex scenarios of inter-human interactions described in plain words and in data records can be adequately represented via MMDTs in the forensic analysis domain. Therefore, one can naturally assume that a health management domain such as tracking COVID-19 contacts can be successfully tackled as well. Other domains include complex interactions between people or complex correlation between parameters such as customer and patient complaints, prediction of patients' behavior at pandemic times, control of a military unit, and prediction of market behavior (Fig. 23). These domains are hybrid in the sense that textual information is combined with numerical data and needs to be organized in a uniform way that is invariant with respect to the nature of features used in problem-solving.

Statistical learning including deep learning (DL) families of approaches encodes all information numerically and certain meanings expressed in text are always lost. Even with a high recognition accuracy of statistical methods, explainability is lost because numerical representation cannot always be converted back into an interpretable form. Conversely, MMDTs attempt to encode all available information with the focus on high-level logical flow irrespectively of the learning machine that would be applied. Therefore, the MMDT-based approach fully supports explainability and avoids information loss under knowledge representation. An MMDT can be naturally combined with additional characteristics of numerical data as well as syntactic and semantic representations.

FIG. 24

A complex relation between two people.

MMDTs can express complex relationships between people, and we can expect an important role of MMDT for learning human behavior. An MMDT would successfully extend concept-based models (Galitsky and de la Rosa, 2011) where human behavior is expressed in text as well as in data records. MMDT are also good at expressing complex forms of relations between people (Fig. 24).

The MMDT follows the Greek philosophical concept of Chimera. The Chimera, according to Greek mythology, was a monstrous fire-breathing hybrid creature composed of the parts of more than one animal. It is usually depicted as a lion, with the head of a goat protruding from its back, and a tail that might end with a snake's head (Fig. 25).

A specific example of data records accompanying data for MMDT is electronic health records (EHRs). They contain valuable temporal information for prediction of a disease. However, irregular time intervals between neighboring events are typically neglected. Besides, a lack of transparency and interpretability of DL models with increasing complexity has become a barrier to the models' clinical adoption.

Zhang et al. (2021) proposed an interpretable DL model that better captures time information and achieves promising performance on sepsis prediction in the emergency department. For sepsis-onset prediction, the proposed DL model achieved an average area under the receiver-operating characteristic curve score of 0.89 by incorporating event embeddings, time encodings, and global max pooling. Time encodings help to handle irregular time intervals. The global pooling operation enables the model to associate the contribution of each medical event with the final clinical outcome, assuring interpretable clinical risk predictions (Fig. 26). Systematic use of MMDTs can support similar models in a broad spectrum of hospital scenarios and EHR interpretations.

FIG. 25

The Chimera on a red-figure plate.

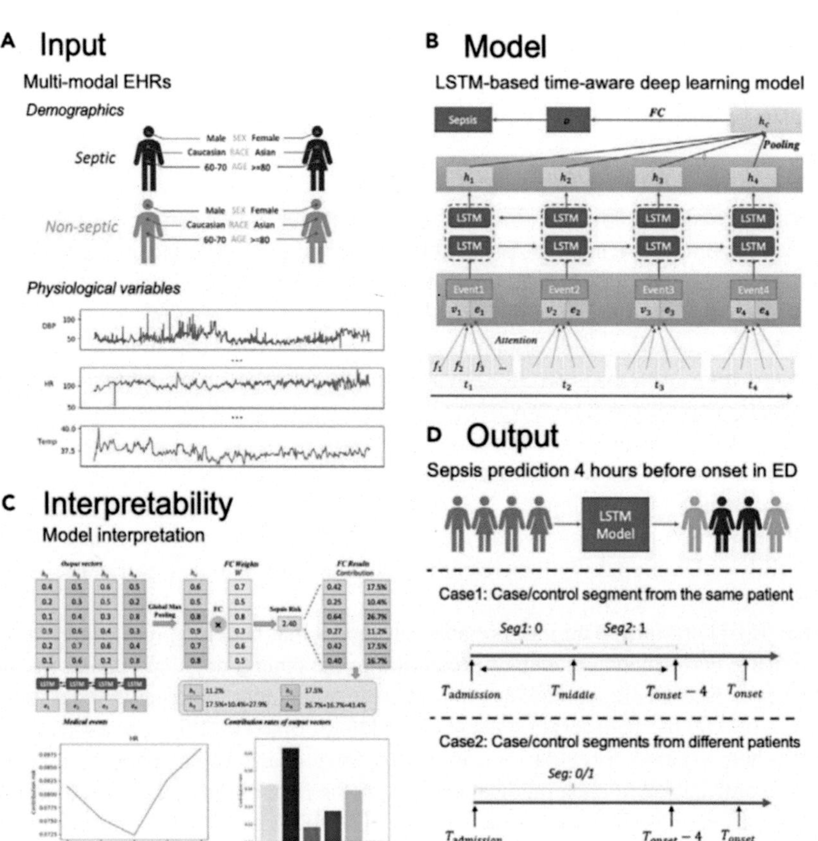

FIG. 26

A high-level view of sepsis prediction based on electronic health records (EHRs) (Zhang et al., 2021).

Zhu et al. (2021) proposed a challenging Q/A dataset called TAT-QA, which was built upon real-world hybrid contexts where the table contains numbers and has comprehensive dependencies on text. To answer questions in TAT-QA, the close interconnection between table and paragraphs and numerical reasoning needs to be established. The authors developed a baseline model based on TAT-QA, merging information from hybrid contexts and conducting numerical reasoning over TAT-QA with pre-defined operators to come to the final answer. Experiments show that the TAT-QA dataset is very challenging and more effort is demanded for tackling Q/A tasks over hybrid data.

MMDTs are expected to be leveraged in a decision support environment with explainability, where a complete explainable chain of facts and clauses for a case is beneficial. Goldberg et al. (2021) presented an approach to creating a bi-directional decision support system as an intermediary between an expert and a ML system for choosing an optimal solution. As a first step, the system analyzes the stability of expert decision and looks for critical values in data that support such a decision. If the expert's decision and that of a ML system continue to be different, the system makes an attempt to explain such a discrepancy, in particular, by navigating the MMDT.

Supplementary data sets

Please visit https://github.com/bgalitsky/relevance-based-on-parse-trees to access all supplementary data sets.

References

Aboul-Enein, H., 1999. Discourse Analysis of Legal Discourse with Reference to Dickens, Cozzens, Kafka, Lee, and Melville. (Ph.D. thesis).

Amgoud, L., Besnard, P., Hunter, A., 2015. Representing and reasoning about arguments mined from texts and dialogues. In: 13th European Conference, ECSQARU 2015, Jul 2015, Compiègne, France, pp. 60–71.

Apothéloz, D., Brandt, P.-Y., Quiroz, G., 1993. The function of negation in argumentation. J. Pragmat. 19, 23–38.

Butters, R.R., 2012. Forensic linguistics: linguistic analysis of disputed meanings: trademarks. In: Chapelle, C. (Ed.), The Encyclopedia of Applied Linguistics. Wiley-Blackwell, Oxford.

Choudhury, S.R., 2020. Singapore Says it Will Make its Contact Tracing Tech Freely Available to Developers. CNBC. Mar 25 URL https://www.cnbc.com/2020/03/25/coronavirus-singapore-to-make-contact-tracing-tech-open-source.html.

Coulthard, M., 2010. Forensic Linguistics: The Application of Language Description in Legal Contexts. https://www.cairn.info/revue-langage-et-societe-2010-2-page-15.htm.

Coulthard, M., Sousa-Silva, R., 2016. Forensic linguistics. In: Dinis-Oliveira, R.J., Magalhães, T. (Eds.), What Are Forensic Sciences?—Concepts, Scope and Future Perspectives. Pactor, Lisbon.

Coulthard, M., Johnson, A., Wright, D., 2017. An Introduction to Forensic Linguistics: Language in Evidence. Routledge, London and New York.

Ferretti, L., Wymant, C., Kendall, M., Zhao, L., Nurtay, A., Abeler-Dörner, L., 2020. Quantifying SARS-CoV-2 transmission suggests epidemic control with digital contact tracing. Science 368 (6491).

Gales, T., 2015. Threatening Stances: a corpus analysis of realized vs. non-realized threats. Lang. Law 2 (2), 1–25.

Galitsky, B., 2013. Transfer learning of syntactic structures for building taxonomies for search engines. Eng. Appl. Artif. Intel. 26 (10), 2504–2515.

Galitsky, B., 2017. Matching parse thickets for open domain question answering. Data Knowl. Eng. 107, 24–50.

Galitsky, B., 2019. Discourse-level dialogue management. In: Developing Enterprise Chatbots: Learning Linguistic Structures. Springer, Cham, Switzerland.

Galitsky, B., 2020. Identifying distributed incompetence in an organization. In: Lawless, B., Mittu, R., Sofge, D.A. (Eds.), Shared Context. Academic Press, pp. 315–340.

Galitsky, B., 2021a. Recognizing abstract classes of text based on discourse. In: Artificial Intelligence for Customer Relationship Management: Keeping Customers Informed. Springer, Cham, Switzerland, pp. 379–414.

Galitsky, B., 2021b. Chatbots for CRM and dialogue management. In: Artificial Intelligence for Customer Relationship Management: Solving Customer Problems. Springer, Cham, Switzerland, pp. 1–62.

Galitsky, B., de la Rosa, J.L., 2011. Concept-based learning of human behavior for customer relationship management. Special issue on information engineering applications based on lattices. Inform. Sci. 181 (10), 2016–2035.

Galitsky, B., Ilvovsky, D., 2017. Chatbot with a Discourse Structure-Driven Dialogue Management. EACL Demo Program.

Galitsky, B., Ilvovsky, D., 2019. Validating correctness of textual explanation with complete discourse trees. In: FCA4AI—Proceedings of the 7th International Workshop "What can FCA do for Artificial Intelligence"? Co-Located with IJCAI 2019.

Galitsky, B., Kovalerchuk, B., 2014. Improving web search relevance with learning structure of domain concepts. In: Clusters, Orders, and Trees: Methods and Applications. vol. 92. Springer, New York, Heidelberg, Dordrecht, London, pp. 341–376.

Galitsky, B., Kuznetsov, S.O., 2008. Learning communicative actions of conflicting human agents. J. Exp. Theor. Artif. Intell. 20 (4), 277–317.

Galitsky, B., González, M.P., Chesñevar, C.I., 2009. A novel approach for classifying customer complaints through graphs similarities in argumentative dialogue. Decis. Support. Syst. 46–3, 717–729.

Galitsky, B., Dobrocsi, G., de la Rosa, J.L., Kuznetsov, S.O., 2011. Using Generalization of Syntactic Parse Trees for Taxonomy Capture on the Web. ICCS, pp. 104–117.

Goldberg, S., Pinsky, E., Galitsky, B., 2021. A bi-directional adversarial explainability for decision support. Hum. Intell. Syst. Integr. 3, 1–14.

Gomez, S.A., Chesñevar, C.I., Simari, G.R., 2010. Reasoning with inconsistent ontologies through argumentation. Appl. Artif. Intell. 24 (1 & 2), 102–148.

Google Blog, 2020. Privacy-safe contact tracing using Bluetooth Low Energy. https://blog.google/documents/57/Overview_of_COVID-19_Contact_Tracing_Using_BLE.pdf.

Grant, T., MacLeod, N., 2018. Resources and constraints in linguistic identity performance—a theory of authorship. Lang. Law 5 (1), 80–96.

Grasso, F., 1999. Playing with RST: two algorithms for the automated manipulation of discourse trees. In: Matousek, V., Mautner, P., Ocelíková, J., Sojka, P. (Eds.), Text, Speech and Dialogue. TSD 1999. Lecture Notes in Computer Science. vol. 1692. Springer, Berlin, Heidelberg.

Hodge, J., Allen, 2018. Can You Sue The Police if They Fail to Investigate a Serious Crime? https://www.hja.net/can-you-sue-the-police-if-they-fail-to-investigate-a-serious-crime/.

Ilvovsky, D., Galitsky, B., 2019. Dialogue management using extended discourse trees. In: Dialogue—Russian Conference on Computational Linguistics, pp. 361–371.

Ilvovsky, D., Kirillovich, A., Galitsky, B., 2019. Controlling chatbot multi-document navigation with the extended discourse trees. In: 4th International Conference on Computational Linguistics in Bulgaria (CLIB 2020).

Jaworski, B.K., Taylor, K., Ramsey, K.M., Heinz, A., Steinmetz, S., Pagano, I., Moraja, G., Owen, J.E., 2021. Exploring usage of COVID coach, a public mental health app designed for the COVID-19 pandemic: evaluation of analytics data. J. Med. Internet Res. 23 (3), e26559.

Joty, S., Carenini, G., Ng, R.T., 2015. CODRA: a novel discriminative framework for rhetorical analysis. Comput. Linguist. 41 (3), 385–435.

Joty, S.R., Carenini, G., Ng, R.T., Mehdad, Y., 2013. Combining intra-and multi-sentential rhetorical parsing for document-level discourse analysis. In: Proceedings of the 51st Annual Meeting of the Association for Computational Linguistics. vol. 1. ACL, pp. 486–496.

Joty, S., Carenini, G., Ng, R.T., Murray, G., 2019. Discourse analysis and its applications. In: ACL Tutorial Abstracts, Florence, Italy, pp. 12–17.

Kredens, K., 2016. Conflict or convergence?: interpreters' and police officers' perceptions of the role of the public service interpreter. Lang. Law 3 (2), 65–77.

LeThanh, H., Abeysinghe, G., Huyck, C., 2004. Generating discourse structures for written texts. In: Proceedings of the 20th International Conference on Computational Linguistics, COLING '04. Association for Computational Linguistics, Geneva, Switzerland.

Marcu, D., 2000. The rhetorical parsing of unrestricted texts: a surface-based approach. Comput. Linguist. 26, 395–448.

Marcu, D., Echihabi, A., 2002. An unsupervised approach to recognizing discourse relations. In: Proceedings of the 40th Annual Meeting on Association for Computational Linguistics, ACL '02, pp. 368–375.

McKimmie, B., Antrobus, E., Baguley, C., 2014. Objective and subjective comprehension of jury instructions in criminal trials. New Crim. Law Rev. 17, 163–183.

Rao, W., Wu, Y.-J., Ou, J., Kluger, R., 2018. Origin-destination pattern estimation based on trajectory reconstruction using automatic license plate recognition data. Transp. Res. C 95, 29–46.

Rutledge, G.W., Wood, J.C., 2020. Virtual health and artificial intelligence: using technology to improve healthcare delivery. In: Lawless, W.F., Mittu, R., Sofge, D.A. (Eds.), Human-Machine Shared Contexts. Academic Press, pp. 169–175.

Sattler, F., Ma, J., Wagner, P., Neumann, D., Wenzel, M., Schäfer, R., 2020. Risk estimation of SARS-CoV-2 transmission from bluetooth low energy measurements. NPJ Digit. Med. 3 (1), 129. Oct 06.

Sporleder, C., Lascarides, A., 2004. Combining hierarchical clustering and machine learning to predict high-level discourse structure. In: Proceedings of the 20th International Conference on Computational Linguistics, COLING '04, Geneva, Switzerland.

Svartvik, J., 1968. The Evans Statements: A Case for Forensic Linguistics. University of Göteborg Publishing.

Tarski, A., 1956. Logic, Semantics, Metamathematics. Oxford University Press.

von Wyl, V., Bonhoeffer, S., Bugnion, E., Puhan, M.A., Salathé, M., Stadler, T., 2020. A research agenda for digital proximity tracing apps. Swiss Med. Wkly. 150, w20324.

Wang, W., Wang, Y., Zhang, X., Jia, X., Li, Y., Dang, S., 2020. Using WeChat, a Chinese Social Media App, for early detection of the COVID-19 outbreak in December 2019: retrospective study. JMIR Mhealth Uhealth 8 (10).

Zhang, D., Yin, C., Buck, K.H., Jiang, X., Caterino, J., Zhang, P., 2021. An interpretable deep learning model for early prediction of sepsis in the emergency department. Patterns 2 (2), 100196.

Zhu, F., Lei, W., Huang, Y., Wang, C., Zhang, S., Jiancheng, L., Feng, F., Chua, T.-S., 2021. TAT-QA: A Question Answering Benchmark on a Hybrid of Tabular and Textual Content in Finance. arXiv:2105.07624.

CHAPTER 15

Improving open domain content generation by text mining and alignment

Boris Galitsky
Oracle Corporation, Redwood City, CA, United States

1. Introduction

E-health services are playing an increasingly important role in healthcare management by providing relevant and timely information to patients about their medical care. An important factor in the fast expansion of online health services is the trend in health management towards patient-centric health care, which aims to involve the patient directly in the medical decision-making process by providing better access to the relevant information that patients need to understand their medical conditions and enabling them to make more informed decisions about their prescribed treatment (Dash et al., 2019). Modern physicians are using emerging technologies such as content generation to advance the limits of medical possibilities with new treatments and insights that were once just a dream. At the same time, health systems have never been under such pressure to improve performance, reduce costs, and meet key challenges to safeguard their future (Thimbleby, 2013; Oracle Healthcare, 2021). Content generation in health care allows for the opportunity to provide a personalized, original recommendation to an individual.

Traditional approaches for natural language generation (NLG; McKeown, 1992) rely on three components:

(1) a content planner that selects the data to be expressed
(2) a sentence planner that decides the structure of sentences or paragraphs based on the content plan
(3) a surface realizer that generates the final output based on the sentence plan

Recent studies proposed end-to-end models based on the encoder-decoder framework (Bahdanau et al., 2015) for structured data-to-text generation. Wiseman et al. (2017) employed the encoder-decoder to generate sports game summaries. Mei et al. (2016) proposed an aligner model that integrates the content selection mechanism into the encoder-decoder for generating weather forecasts from a set of database records. Lebret et al. (2016) described a conditional language model for biography summarization. The follow-up studies on biography summarization employed the encoder-decoder framework. These end-to-end models produce fluent text on an ordered input with a fixed structure but have an inferior performance on disordered input. A major problem in open-domain content generation is a distortion of facts and the truth in a content obtained by sequence-to-sequence models.

Puduppully et al. (2019) proposed Neural Content Planning, which is a two-stage model that includes content planning to handle disordered input. First, the planning uses pointer networks to generate a

Artificial Intelligence for Healthcare Applications and Management. https://doi.org/10.1016/B978-0-12-824521-7.00011-9

content plan. Then, the generated content plan is used as the input of the encoder-decoder model such as text generator to generate a description. However, this two-stage model suffers from error propagation between the content planner and the text generator. The generated content plan may contain errors, missing one or more attributes that should be mentioned in the description. As a result, the text generator produces an incomplete description. In an open-domain setting, the encoder-decoder model significantly distorts facts as well, averaging from multiple sources of training data. In this study, we borrow the content planning results from a neural system but improve the truthfulness of generated content by substituting values and phrases from the available content proven to be truthful.

In this chapter, we improve end-to-end content generation with fact-checking and correct fact substitution, to make the content sound and trusted. We refer to the results of neural text generation as **raw** and apply fact-checking to it to identify entities and phrases that are untrue. We then form queries from these untrue phrases and search available sources for sentences to align with the raw ones to retain the syntactic and logical structure and update the values to turn the raw text into the one with correct facts.

1.1 Content generation in health care

Good communication is vital in health care, both among healthcare professionals, and between healthcare professionals and their patients. And well-written documents, describing and/or explaining the information in structured databases, may be easier to comprehend, more edifying, and even more convincing than the structured data, even when presented in tabular or graphic form. Documents may be automatically generated from structured data, using techniques from the field of NLG. These techniques are concerned with how the content, organization, and language used in a document can be dynamically selected, depending on the audience and context. They have been used to generate health education materials, explanations, and critiques in decision support systems (DSS), and medical reports and progress notes (Cawsey et al., 1999).

Creating good content is hard in any vertical, and creating solid content focused around healthcare and medical topics is among the toughest nut to crack. From getting client buy-in to meeting regulatory issues and navigating algorithm updates, top-notch medical content writing brings its own unique sets of challenges and frustrations (Verblio, 2020).

Different categories of people involved in the healthcare process include consultants, nurses, general practitioners, medical researchers, patients, their relatives, and even accountants and administrators. These people must all be able to obtain and communicate relevant information on patients and their treatment, leveraging the produced content (Rosen et al., 2018). However, there are many obstacles in the way of effective communication; participants may use different terms to describe the same thing. In addition, there is a particular difficulty for patients who do not understand medical terminology. Different participants frequently have distinct information needs and little time to filter information so that no single report is truly adequate for all. As different participants may rarely have time to meet, the care of a patient is shared and passed between them. Hence personalized and thorough quality content is a must.

Writing health-centric hospital content is a headache for many content creators. Creating medical content has a few fundamental challenges, including:

(1) Identifying the expertise required to obtain meaningful expert input.
(2) Conducting all the research and still getting it wrong. In a regulated industry there is a high demand for content correctness.
(3) Supporting the scale. The more challenging the subject matter and scarcity of expertise, the harder the scaling up can be.

1.2 Content generation for personalization

Personalization, that is, adapting to the individual, is becoming an essential component of any computer-based system. In e-health systems, personalization of health information is emerging as a key factor in the trend to patient-centric care. Patient-centric health care aims to engage patients in their treatment to promote greater compliance and satisfaction with their medical treatment, resulting in both better patient outcomes and reduced healthcare costs.

DiMarco et al. (2007) developed a web-based NLG system for the authoring and subsequent personalization of patient education materials. The initial domain is reconstructive breast surgery, but the proposed natural language (NL) software tools and authoring methodologies are generally applicable to all health-related activities and interventions.

Patient educators now support the notion that personalization can:

(1) enhance the uptake of information
(2) bring about increased receptivity to behavioral change
(3) involve patients in their own healthcare decision-making

However, very little is yet known about exactly how to customize language to gain these potential benefits.

Even systems that are designed to provide targeted health information generally do not provide truly personalized content (Galitsky and Kuznetsov, 2013). In a typical case, a patient may have their own "patient portal," which will record their medications, treatments, appointments, and so on; however, the actual content the patient receives will still be generic. In the worst case, the patient might click on a link to gain information about their diagnosed cancer and will receive a pop-up PDF document consisting of a lengthy brochure of "boilerplate" text from a national cancer agency.

Di Marco et al. (2007) combined pre-authoring of input with sophisticated NLG techniques that can automatically edit a text to further refine it. The authors developed a novel paradigm based on generation of new documents from pre-existing text through a process of reuse and revision. The system starts from an existing "Master Document" that contains all the pieces of text that might be needed to tailor the document for any audience. Selections from the Master Document are made according to an individual patient profile, and then are automatically post-edited for personalized data, form, style, and coherence (Fig. 1).

Recent approaches to NLG based on external knowledge bases provide good results (Freitag and Roy, 2018). At the same time, most research considers only superficial descriptions of simple pieces of structured data such as attribute-value pairs of fixed or very limited schema, like E2E and WikiBio (Lebret et al., 2016). For real-world, complex databases, it is often more desirable to provide descriptions involving an abstraction and a logical inference of higher generality about database tables and records. For instance, readers should get a kind of a summary over a structured, relational, or NoSQL database.

It should be mentioned that utilizing only data from the table as input for the neural generation model is not sufficient to generate high-quality volume texts. This is triggered by two factors:

(1) Low fidelity and potential diversity. Existing deep learning (DL) approaches, which use only the table as input, have difficulties producing such logically correct generations involving reasoning and symbolic calculations, such as *max*, *min*, *aggregation*, *grouping*, *counting*, and *averaging*.

Creation of corpora of content variants written in language that will engage the patient and address individual concerns	Doctor's Authoring Tool that assists in mapping from the various options at each stage of a medical intervention to corresponding content variations
Natural Language Generation Engine that automatically select, assemble, and revise content from a library of reusable texts to produce a customized version for an individual patient.	A Web-based framework for delivery of tailored health education, a 'personal patient portal'

FIG. 1

A high-level view of a personalized content management system for e-health.

(2) Uncontrollable content selection. There are various ways to get logically entailed descriptions based on the given table due to a huge number of operations over its values, such as count, comparison, and so forth. A DL model itself cannot reliably select necessary connections due to the difficulty of maintaining high-level semantic constraints in the compositional generation process.

1.3 Natural language generation in intensive care

An implicit assumption of most NLG techniques is that the non-linguistic input information comes from knowledge bases (KBs) with well-defined semantics. In practice, however, in most application domains where automatic textual descriptions are desperately required, such knowledge bases do not exist. The data-intensive clinical environments described in the previous section generate large amounts of clinical data that are not structured into logical forms in a KB. Data-to-text NLG is a recent extension to traditional NLG to allow such naturally occurring data to be described linguistically (Hüske-Kraus, 2003b).

Hallett and Scott (2005) generated summaries of multiple text-based health reports. Cawsey et al. (2000) described a system that dynamically generates hypertext pages that explain treatments, diseases, and more related to the patient's condition using information in the patient's medical record as the basis for the tailoring. Suregen-2 (Hüske-Kraus, 2003a) turned out to be most successful medical data-to-text application that automates the process of writing routine documents, which is regularly used by physicians to create surgical reports. However, the complete summarization of ICU data is a more complex task, involving the processing of time series, discrete events, and short free texts, which has not been accomplished yet.

The system of (Hunter et al., 2008) creates a summary of the clinical data period in four main stages (Fig. 2). All the terms used to describe the discrete events are related to the ontology (Chapter 11). To enable future sharing of this valuable knowledge source, the authors synchronized their ontology with UMLS, a meta-thesaurus that brings together several popular medical ontologies such as SNOMED-CT. The first stage of the processing is *Signal Analysis* component, which extracts the main features of the physiological time series (artifacts, patterns, and trends) using modeling based on a baby's physiological values, auto-regressive filtering, and adaptive bottom-up segmentation techniques.

The *Data Interpretation* component performs some temporal and logical reasoning to infer higher medical abstractions and relations ("re-intubation," "A causes B," etc.) from the signal features and the clinical observations using an expert system (Chapter 2) linked to the ontology. From the large number

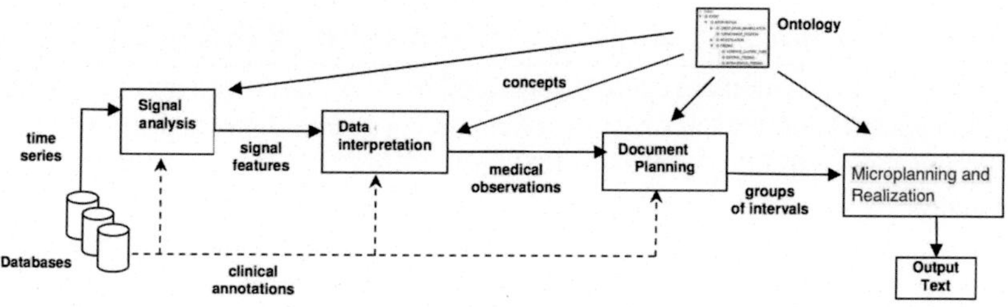

FIG. 2

Content generation in the health domain.

of events generated, the *Document Planning* component selects the most important events based on an importance factor either determined by experts (a surgery must always be included) or computed from the signals (an importance of certain patterns depends on their outcome). The most important events are then structured into a tree. Finally, the *Microplanning* and *Realization* component translates this tree into a text of acceptable readability.

We conclude that in most cases, end-to-end learning can create a high volume of fake, counterfeit content that either needs to be repaired or rejected (Fig. 3).

FIG. 3

Content counterfeiter.

2. Processing raw natural language generation results

The major problem in an open-domain content generated by a DL-based system is its meaninglessness. Although overall syntactic and logical structure, obtained via averaging texts from the training dataset, looks plausible, and some individual phrases might make sense, almost every sentence is meaningless. The main advantage of such raw content is that it is **original**.

Our intent is to take this meaningless raw content and crossbreed it with the one taken piece by piece from various sources so that each sentence is **not original but truthful**. We borrow the structure and content flow from the raw text, and factoids are taken from true texts mined from the Web to correspond to the raw sentences.

Our first example is from the 19th century literature domain. The seed to GPT-3 content generation is shown in bold on the top of Fig. 4. '*then*' part of the first sentence seems plausible. Then the reader proceeds to the invented person *Krafft, and a random, implausible text starts.* To continue to impress the reader with a smooth flow of text, we need to find a real person like *Krafft* related to *Pushkin* via *translation*.

A good candidate multi-sentence text to further extend the idea generated in raw text (but not instantiated properly) is to continue the theme of Nabokov (a well-known Russian American writer):

> Nabokov believed that there were three routes a translator of poetry could choose from: a loose translation with paraphrasing and additions added according to the whim of the translator; a basic translation, with the words in the same order as the original – much like what you get with today's online translator apps; or, rendering, as closely as the syntactical capacities as another language allow, the exact contextual meaning of the original.

Having considered this example, we are now ready to decide what kind of linguistic data should be taken from the raw text, and which should be taken from the true text (Table 1). Sources such as syntax and discourse we attempt to borrow from the **raw** text, and once we determine that this is not possible, we obtain the entities and values from the **true** text. Once we perform a substitution of a phrase from true to raw, we know which linguistic sources can be retained in the raw text.

Each feature from the **raw** sources can be retained if confirmed by the true sentence obtained one way or another. We attempt to retain as many raw features as possible as long as they are confirmed by the mined true sentences.

We define a non-symmetric operation of alignment between raw and true text. This alignment occurs at the level of the whole text, paragraphs, sentences, and phrases. To assess a similarity between texts, paragraphs, sentences, and phrases, we apply a symmetric operation of generalization (Galitsky et al., 2012; Galitsky, 2017). However, to obtain a proper text aligning raw and true texts, the operation is not symmetric since we use distinct sources depending on the source type. An entity from a true sentence kills an entity from a raw sentence, but the rest of the phrase is taken from raw sentence to retain the logical structure, discourse, and coreference. Further details on generalization operation and alignment are available in Chapter 2 and Galitsky et al. (2013).

Exploring the ways to identify a piece of true content to repair a flawed raw content, we observe that it is a complex multi-step process requiring conventional linguistic analysis at multiple layers and a special substitution technique operating at various levels of abstraction.

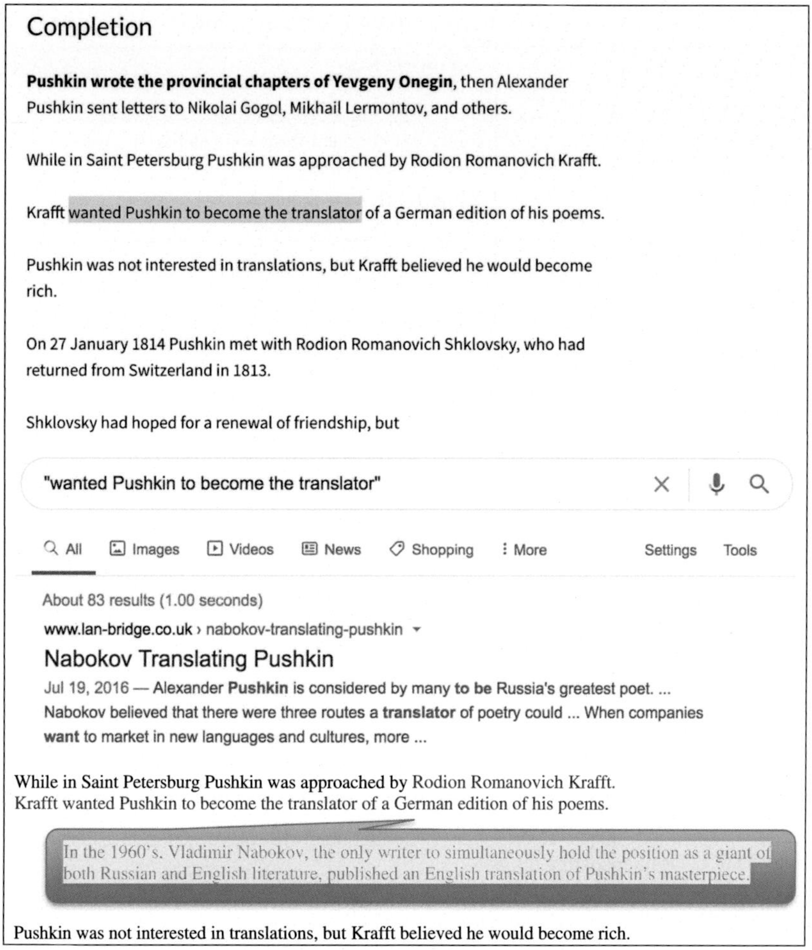

Completion

Pushkin wrote the provincial chapters of Yevgeny Onegin, then Alexander Pushkin sent letters to Nikolai Gogol, Mikhail Lermontov, and others.

While in Saint Petersburg Pushkin was approached by Rodion Romanovich Krafft.

Krafft wanted Pushkin to become the translator of a German edition of his poems.

Pushkin was not interested in translations, but Krafft believed he would become rich.

On 27 January 1814 Pushkin met with Rodion Romanovich Shklovsky, who had returned from Switzerland in 1813.

Shklovsky had hoped for a renewal of friendship, but

"wanted Pushkin to become the translator"

All Images Videos News Shopping More Settings Tools

About 83 results (1.00 seconds)

www.lan-bridge.co.uk › nabokov-translating-pushkin

Nabokov Translating Pushkin

Jul 19, 2016 — Alexander **Pushkin** is considered by many **to be** Russia's greatest poet. ... Nabokov believed that there were three routes a **translator** of poetry could ... When companies **want** to market in new languages and cultures, more ...

While in Saint Petersburg Pushkin was approached by Rodion Romanovich Krafft.
Krafft wanted Pushkin to become the translator of a German edition of his poems.

In the 1960's, Vladimir Nabokov, the only writer to simultaneously hold the position as a giant of both Russian and English literature, published an English translation of Pushkin's masterpiece.

Pushkin was not interested in translations, but Krafft believed he would become rich.

FIG. 4

A raw text and its correction steps: raw text (top), web search to fact-check the phrase (middle), and a fragment of text with embedded mined phrase (*yellow*, bottom).

2.1 Alignment of raw and true content

Let us consider an example of a raw and a true decision for a patient with Liddle's syndrome (Aronson, 2009). This genetic disorder is characterized by early, and frequently severe, high blood pressure associated with low plasma renin activity, metabolic alkalosis, low blood potassium, and normal-to-low levels of aldosterone.

Table 1 Type of linguistic and fact-based data taken from each source.

Raw **sentences**	True **sentences**
Seed is used to generate raw content	
Generated Text by DL	Real Text obtained from sources like the web or intranet, or specific web domains
Syntactic flow, if possible	Syntactic flow, if required
Discourse flow, if possible	Discourse flow, if required
Coreference structure, if possible	Coreference structure, if required
Logical flow, if possible	
Original "idea"	Existing idea if the original idea is too distant from the topic
Entities are most likely wrong and need to be substituted	Entities
Actions can be retained, if confirmed by →	Phrases

A woman with Liddle's syndrome presented with severe symptomatic hypokalemia. Her doctor reasoned as follows [raw text]:

- she has potassium depletion;
- spironolactone is a potassium-sparing drug;
- spironolactone will cause her to retain potassium;
- her serum potassium concentration will normalize.

She took a full dose of spironolactone for several days, based on this logical reasoning, but still had severe hypokalemia.

Her doctor should have reasoned as follows [true text]:

- she has potassium depletion due to Liddle's syndrome, a channelopathy that affects epithelial sodium channels;
- there is a choice of potassium-sparing drugs;
- spironolactone acts via aldosterone receptors, amiloride and triamterene via sodium channels;
- in Liddle's syndrome an action via sodium channels is required.

When she was given *amiloride* instead of *spironolactone,* her serum potassium concentration rapidly increased to within the reference range. This stresses the importance of understanding the relationship between the pathophysiology of the problem and the mechanism of action of the drug. Channelopathies are diseases caused by a broken function of ion channel subunits or the proteins that regulate them. These diseases may be either congenital (often resulting from a mutation or mutations in the encoding genes) or acquired (often resulting from autoimmune attack on an ion channel).

Now let us try to apply generalization/alignment for raw and true texts. Alignment of a graph against a graph is a mapping retaining the labels on arcs between the source and target nodes of these two graphs. We coordinate an alignment between two semantic graphs and respective syntactic trees accordingly; semantic and syntactic relations between the source and target graphs are honored. Further details on alignment of linguistic structures are available in Chapter 3 and Galitsky et al. (2014).

The alignment maps *potassium depletion* into *potassium depletion*, *potassium-sparing* into *potassium-sparing*, and [true] *sodium channel* into [raw] *retain potassium*, and [true] mental action *cause* into raw mental action *chose*. Mapping into the same or synonymous entity is shown in green arrows, and the substitution of **raw** with **true** is shown with red arrows (Fig. 5).

We noticed that a sophisticated algorithm is required to correct a sentence with random facts to become a proper, responsible, and trusted piece of content. A combination of linguistic alignment and fact-checking techniques is worth exploring; anything other than a fine-tuned architecture would be prone to multiple errors (Fig. 6).

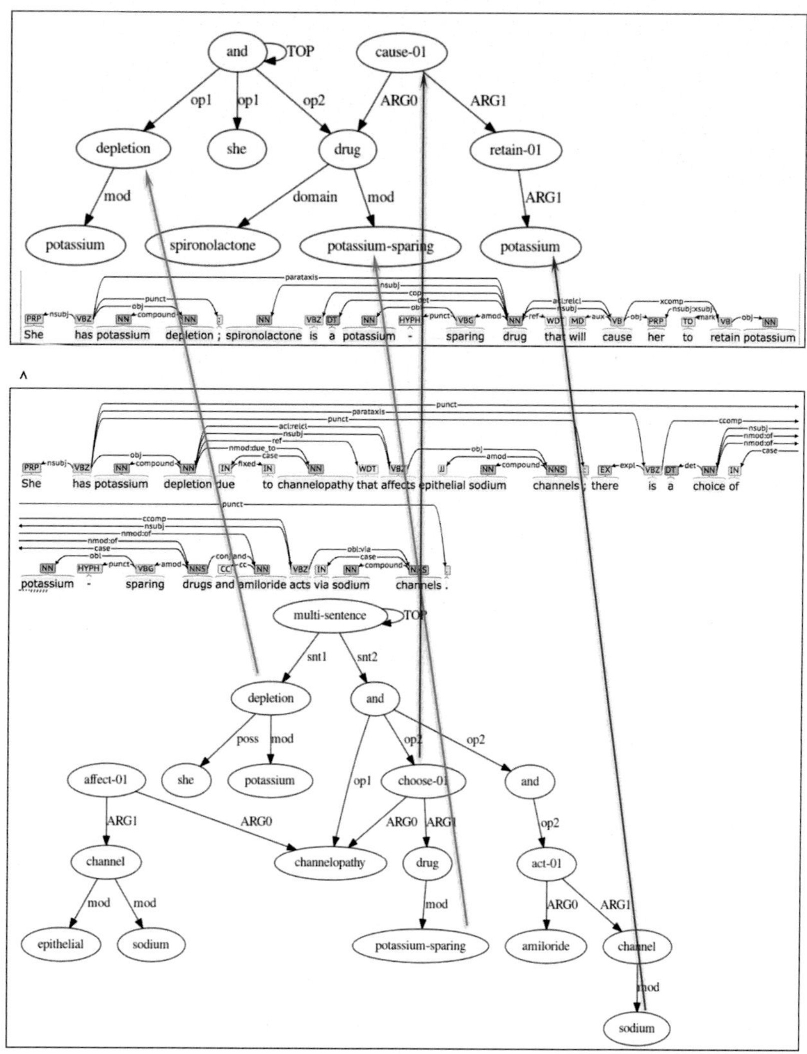

FIG. 5

A map between semantic and syntactic representations for raw (incorrect, on the top) and true (correct, on the bottom) treatment of a disease.

FIG. 6

Sometimes, it is a long and dangerous way to a necessary piece of content.

3. Fact-checking of deep learning generation

We start with another example of a raw text and its correction (Fig. 7).

Neither sentence can pass a fact-checking procedure. Some sentences need entity substitutions and some needs total rewrite by finding the closest available sentence from the source inheriting the syntactic structure. We can see that there are many internal inconsistencies (red arrows) all of which need to be repaired (Fig. 8).

We show the raw sentence and corresponding true sentence. *Incorrect* values (the ones deviating from the correct ones) are shown in *red* in raw sentences. True sentences are highlighted in yellow, and

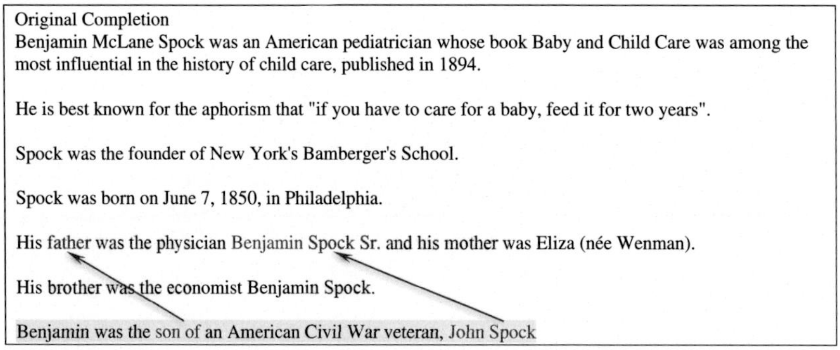

Original Completion

Benjamin McLane Spock was an American pediatrician whose book Baby and Child Care was among the most influential in the history of child care, published in 1894.

He is best known for the aphorism that "if you have to care for a baby, feed it for two years".

Spock was the founder of New York's Bamberger's School.

Spock was born on June 7, 1850, in Philadelphia.

His father was the physician Benjamin Spock Sr. and his mother was Eliza (née Wenman).

His brother was the economist Benjamin Spock.

Benjamin was the son of an American Civil War veteran, John Spock

FIG. 7

Substituting raw entities with true entities. True sentences are highlighted in *yellow*.

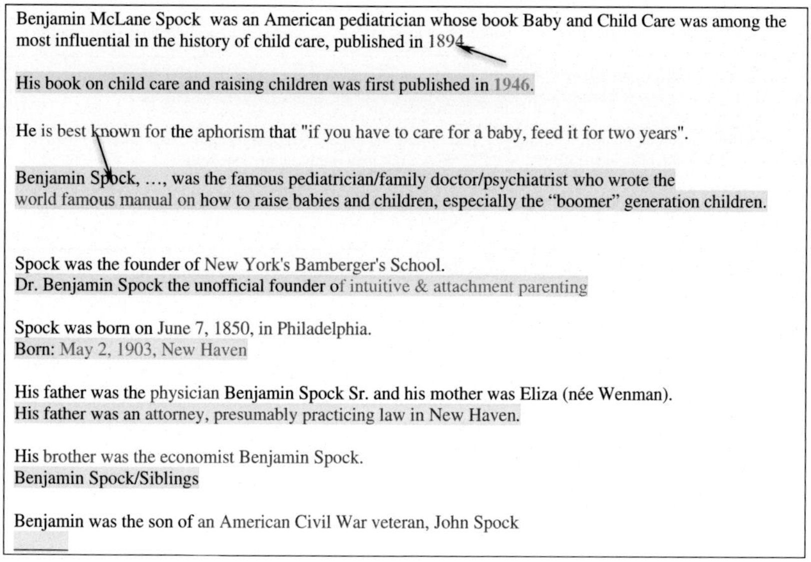

Benjamin McLane Spock was an American pediatrician whose book Baby and Child Care was among the most influential in the history of child care, published in 1894

His book on child care and raising children was first published in 1946.

He is best known for the aphorism that "if you have to care for a baby, feed it for two years".

Benjamin Spock, …, was the famous pediatrician/family doctor/psychiatrist who wrote the world famous manual on how to raise babies and children, especially the "boomer" generation children.

Spock was the founder of New York's Bamberger's School.
Dr. Benjamin Spock the unofficial founder of intuitive & attachment parenting

Spock was born on June 7, 1850, in Philadelphia.
Born: May 2, 1903, New Haven

His father was the physician Benjamin Spock Sr. and his mother was Eliza (née Wenman).
His father was an attorney, presumably practicing law in New Haven.

His brother was the economist Benjamin Spock.
Benjamin Spock/Siblings

Benjamin was the son of an American Civil War veteran, John Spock

FIG. 8

Fact-checking correction and extension of the raw content.

the values that update the ones in raw sentences are shown in *blue*. The relations and attribute names in raw sentences, which are confirmed by true sentences, are also shown in *blue*.

The top six sentences can be successfully corrected. In these sentences, relations and attribute types can be retained, and the values should be taken from true sentences. On the bottom, two raw sentences do not yield meaningful factoid sentences and need to be ignored.

Hence from what we observed, we can formulate the following correction rules:

(1) If an individual value can be updated, the sentence is retained.

(2) If no associated fact can be identified, the sentence is removed, and instead the closest sentence found in an available source is used. We need to update the syntactic structure of the mined sentence to match with the raw one. To do that, we form the syntactic skeleton of the raw sentence and generalize it with the sentence obtained from the source. As we do that, some phrases are removed.

We also need to maintain discourse structure and coreference structure.

3.1 Personalized drug recommendation

We take an example of text generated about the drug *lamotrigine* and attempt to repair it (Fig. 9).

To fact-check that lamotrigine is appropriate to treat *mania* and *depression*, we form the respective queries (Fig. 10, bottom.) We confirm *depression* and substitute *mania* with the whole mined sentence "*Lamotrigine has shown…*" The confirming expression is shown in a *green oval*, and the rejecting expression is shown in a *red oval*.

For many women with bipolar disorder, lamotrigine is an effective mood stabilizer for treating both mania and depression.
Lamotrigine has shown no efficacy in treating acute mania, which makes it less desirable than lithium, quetiapine, or cariprazine in that there will be no coverage for the manic/hypomanic phases

Lamotrigine is an atypical anticonvulsant, that targets the benzodiazepine receptor more potently than do other TCAs. Its side effects are similar to other TCAs, but they are typically less severe.

Lamotrigine, sold as the brand name Lamictal among others, is an anticonvulsant medication used to treat epilepsy

Nortriptyline and desipramine appear to have better tolerated side effects than other tricyclic antidepressants do

Probabilistic additivity models of effect prediction have been used to determine which dose of lamotrigine for which condition may be the most effective.

Is the proposed dose conversion from the lamotrigine IR to the LAMICTAL XR ... intense sampling) using non-linear mixed effects modeling, showed that at ... A proportional error and a constant additive error models were evaluated for the ... logit of the probability of response was a function of a baseline, ..

Because of the unusual characteristics of lamotrigine, no study has assessed the effect

For many women with bipolar disorder, lamotrigine is an effective mood stabilizer for treating depression.
Lamotrigine has shown no efficacy in treating acute mania, which makes it less desirable than lithium, quetiapine, or cariprazine in that there will be no coverage for the manic/hypomanic phases.
Lamotrigine is an atypical anticonvulsant.
Lamotrigine, sold as the brand name Lamictal among others, is an anticonvulsant medication used to treat epilepsy.
Its side effects are similar to other TCAs, but they are typically less severe.
Nortriptyline and desipramine appear to have better tolerated side effects than other tricyclic antidepressants do.

FIG. 9

The log of the correction procedure (top) and the resultant text (bottom) on the drug to treat depression in a pregnant patient. The texts highlighted in *yellow* shows the true sentences obtained from web search snippets.

The generated claim that "*Lamotrigine targets the benzodiazepine receptor*" turns out to be totally wrong, so it needs to be removed. The *Query formation* algorithm (given a sentence) is described in (Galitsky and Kovalerchuk, 2014); we remove the most specific keywords until the current search results match this query well.

3.2 Discourse structure deviation of the corrected content

We compare the original communicative discourse tree (CDT) for the raw content and the resultant CDT for the corrected content (Fig. 11). Most non-trivial rhetorical relations from the raw text must be retained (addressed) in the corrected text; then, the correction properly retains the discourse structure. Indeed, there are four mappings shown in red arcs between the rhetorical relations of the raw text and that of the corrected text. The bottom *Comparison* relation is obtained from web mining and is expected not to break the original discourse structure. However, if the corrected text contains different nontrivial relations, or they are in a totally different order, or it lacks relations, we would confirm that the correction procedure broke the discourse structure.

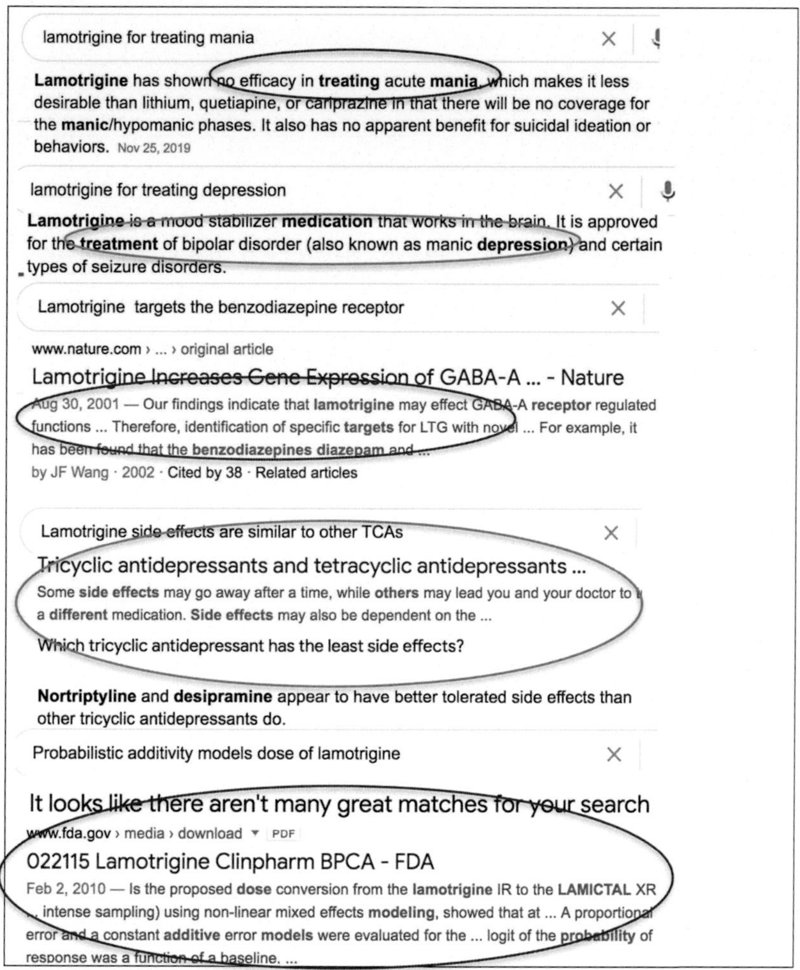

FIG. 10

Fact-checking and entity substitution for a drug recommendation for a pregnant patient.

4. System architecture

We first describe a DL subsystem by Trisedya et al. (2020) that generates text from a structured dataset, as it fits the health domain of personalized recommendations such as drug intake. An arbitrary DL content-generation system such as GPT that inputs a seed sentence and generates a few paragraphs of text can be used to obtain a raw text. After that, we describe our raw text correction system architecture.

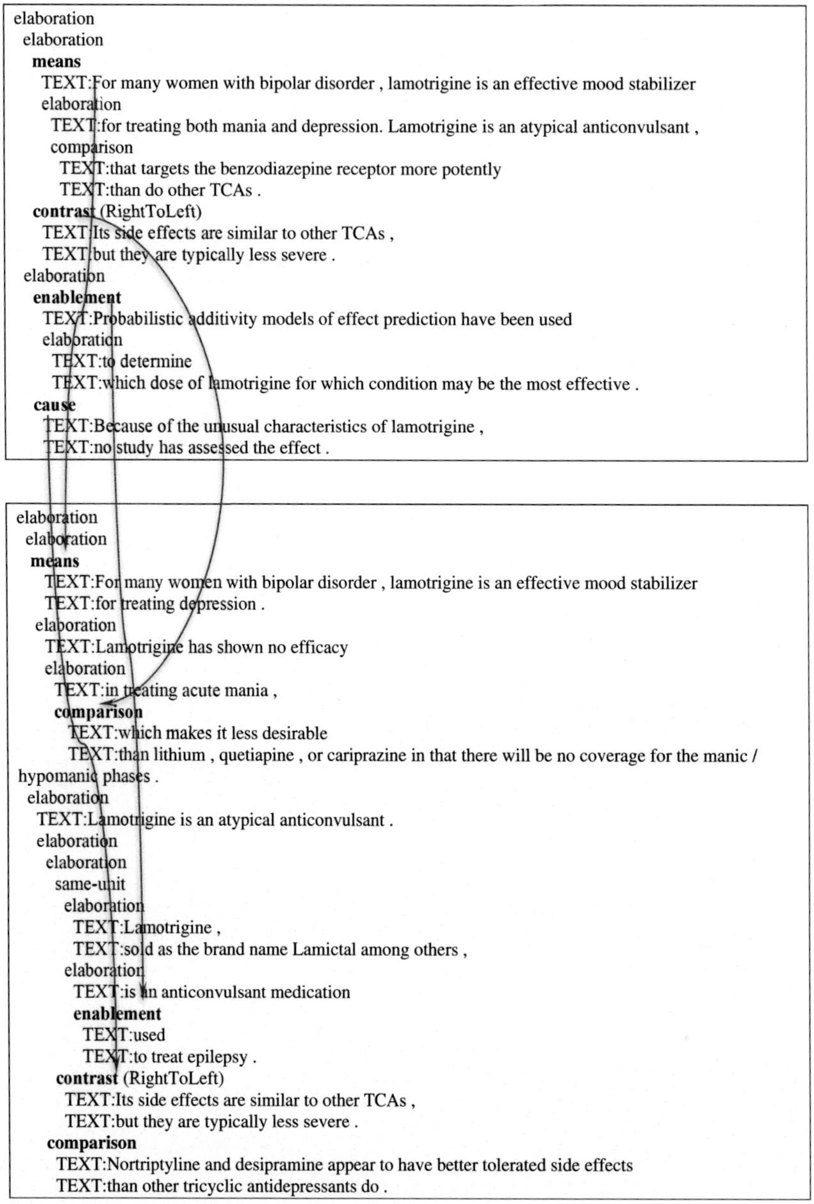

elaboration
elaboration
means
TEXT:For many women with bipolar disorder , lamotrigine is an effective mood stabilizer
elaboration
TEXT:for treating both mania and depression. Lamotrigine is an atypical anticonvulsant ,
comparison
TEXT:that targets the benzodiazepine receptor more potently
TEXT:than do other TCAs .
contrast (RightToLeft)
TEXT:Its side effects are similar to other TCAs ,
TEXT:but they are typically less severe .
elaboration
enablement
TEXT:Probabilistic additivity models of effect prediction have been used
elaboration
TEXT:to determine
TEXT:which dose of lamotrigine for which condition may be the most effective .
cause
TEXT:Because of the unusual characteristics of lamotrigine ,
TEXT:no study has assessed the effect .

elaboration
elaboration
means
TEXT:For many women with bipolar disorder , lamotrigine is an effective mood stabilizer
TEXT:for treating depression .
elaboration
TEXT:Lamotrigine has shown no efficacy
elaboration
TEXT:in treating acute mania ,
comparison
TEXT:which makes it less desirable
TEXT:than lithium , quetiapine , or cariprazine in that there will be no coverage for the manic / hypomanic phases .
elaboration
TEXT:Lamotrigine is an atypical anticonvulsant .
elaboration
elaboration
same-unit
elaboration
TEXT:Lamotrigine ,
TEXT:sold as the brand name Lamictal among others ,
elaboration
TEXT:is an anticonvulsant medication
enablement
TEXT:used
TEXT:to treat epilepsy .
contrast (RightToLeft)
TEXT:Its side effects are similar to other TCAs ,
TEXT:but they are typically less severe .
comparison
TEXT:Nortriptyline and desipramine appear to have better tolerated side effects
TEXT:than other tricyclic antidepressants do .

FIG. 11

Comparison of the communicative discourse trees (CDTs) for raw and corrected texts.

4.1 Deep learning subsystem

Fig. 12 depicts the DL subsystem architecture. The DL subsystem consists of three components:

(1) data collection module
(2) content plan generation module
(3) description generation module

In the data collection module, (Trisedya et al., 2020) collect a dataset in the form of triples of attributes, a content plan, and an entity description. The attributes are extracted by querying Wikidata for Resource Description Framework (RDF) triples that contain the target entity as the subject (RDF is one of the three foundational Semantic Web technologies). The description is obtained from Wikipedia by extracting the first sentence of the Wikipedia page of the target entity. The content plan is extracted by finding the order of attributes in the description using string matching. In the content plan generation module, the pointer network learns a content plan that helps the attention model of the description generation module to form the attributes in the proper order. This module consists of four components:

(1) attribute encoder that encodes a set of attributes into a vector by computing the average of the linear transformation of each token embeddings of the attributes
(2) pointer generator that generates a sequence of indexes (pointers) that represents the order of attributes in the description

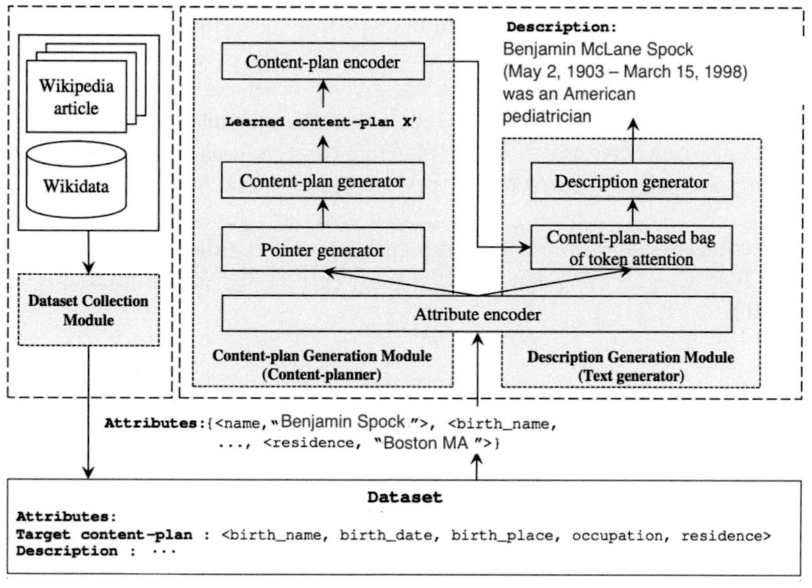

FIG. 12

DL subsystem architecture.

(3) content plan generator that generates the content plan based on the learned pointers
(4) content plan encoder that encodes the learned content plan to be used in the description generation module

In the description generation module, Trisedya et al. (2020) integrated the content plan into the attention mechanism of the encoder-decoder model (Bahdanau et al., 2015). The same encoder is used as in the content plan generation module that treats the input including attributes as a bag of keywords to ensure that the same set of attributes with different orders have the same representation. A long short-term memory (LSTM) system for the content plan encoder is leveraged to encode the obtained content plan that maintains the proper sequence of attributes to capture the links between them. To incorporate the obtained content plan into the attention mechanism of the encoder-decoder model, the content plan-based bag-of-tokens attention model is employed by adapting the coverage mechanism (Tu et al., 2016) to track the order of attributes in a content plan for computing the attention of the attributes. This way, the attention model selects the salient attributes conditioned by the content plan and hence provides a better context for each decoding time step.

4.2 Raw content correction

For each sentence in the raw text, we perform a deterministic fact-checking. We iterate through each sentence in the raw text and try to correct it if necessary, modifying its syntactic structure to an as little degree as possible. Fig. 13 shows the correction procedure for a sentence. We first take a sentence and apply syntactic criteria to determine if it is worth retaining in the corrected content. We then proceed to fact-checking, forming a family of queries from this sentence to obtain the candidate true ones.

Candidate true sentences are extracted from search results snippets and identified documents. The true sentences are extracted and matched against the given raw sentence to determine what is the optimal (minimal change) substitution. Syntactic and semantic alignments are built and the entities and phrases to be substituted are determined. The architecture chart shows major decisions on whether this raw sentence can potentially be corrected; if *yes*, should it be an *entity substitution* or a *phrase substitution*?

For multiple sentences, substitutions should be propagated according to the structure of coreferences in the raw text. Overall discourse structure must be assessed in comparison with that of the raw text as well (Galitsky, 2019b).

5. Probabilistic text merging

Having described our deterministic text alignment approach, we proceed to a probabilistic one that can potentially be used instead.

The probability of output text y conditioned on identifies real text z and input raw text r is modeled as:

$$p(y|r, z) = \prod_{t=1}^{|y|} p(y_t|y_{<t}, z, r)$$

where $y_{<t} = y_1 \ldots y_{t-1}$. To calculate $p(y|r, z)$, an encoder-decoder architecture with attention mechanism can be used.

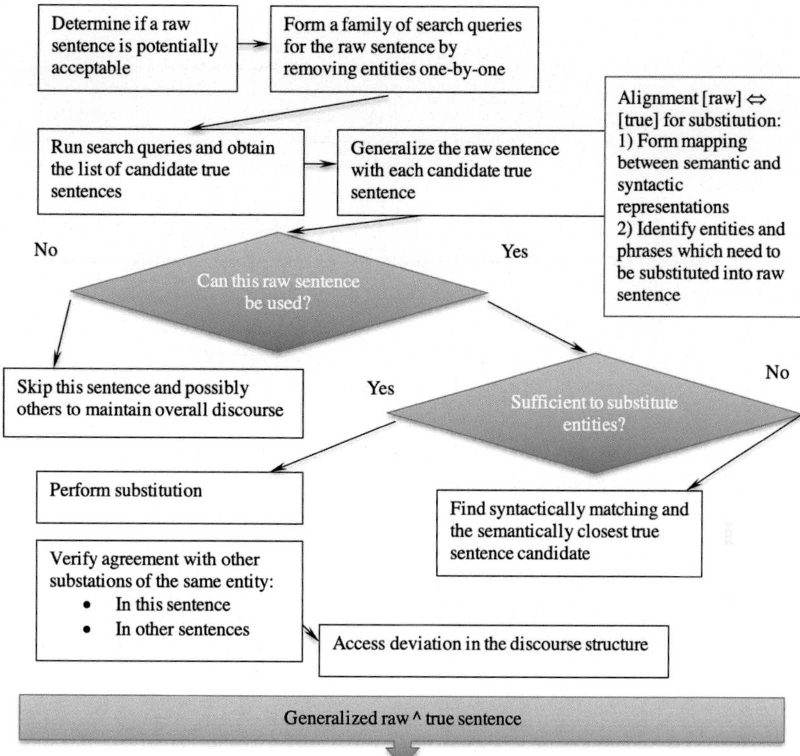

FIG. 13

Raw sentence correction architecture.

In the generation task of (Puduppully et al., 2019), the output text is long but obeys a certain structure. Summaries about certain entities like patients usually begin by discussing the treatment plan, followed by various hospital statistics. It is natural to believe that generation would benefit from an explicit plan specifying both what to say and in which order. The authors' model learns such content plans from training data.

Most data-to-text datasets do not naturally contain content plans. These plans can be derived following an information extraction approach, by mapping the text in the summaries onto entities in the structured data, their values, relations, and types. A plan is a sequence of pointers with each entry pointing to an input record $\{r_j\}^{|r|}_{j=1}$. Table 2 shows a snippet of a plan.

The order in the plan corresponds to the sequence in which entities appear in the game summary. Let $z = z_1 \ldots z_n$ be the content planning sequence. Each z_k points to an input record $\left(\text{i.e.}, z_k \in \{r_j\}^{|r|}_{j=1}\right)$. Given the input records, the probability $p(z|r)$ is decomposed as

$$p(z|r) = \prod_{k=1}^{|z|} p(z_k | z_{<k}, r)$$

Table 2 A snippet of a content generation plan.

Value	Entity	Semantic type	Entity class
Methohexital	Drug	Anesthetic	Painkiller
…	…	…	…

Since the output tokens of the content planning stage correspond to positions in the input sequence, (Puduppully et al., 2019) leverage pointer networks. Perez-Beltrachini and Lapata (2018) consider loosely coupled data and text pairs where the data component is a set P of property values $\{p_1{:}v_1,\cdots,p_{|P|}{:}v_{|P|}\}$ and the related text T is a sequence of sentences $(s_1,\cdots,s_{|T|})$. A mention span τ is defined as a (possibly discontinuous) subsequence of T containing one or several words that verbalize one or more property-value from P. For instance, in Fig. 14, the mention span "*had two children: Michael and John*" verbalizes the property value {*Children*: *Michael and John*'}.

In traditional supervised data-to-text generation tasks, data units (e.g., p_1: v_1, in our particular setting) are either covered by some mention span τ_j or do not have any mention span at all in T. The latter is a case of content selection where the generator will learn which properties to ignore when generating text from such data. Perez-Beltrachini and Lapata (2018) considered text components that are independently edited and will ultimately contain unaligned spans (text fragments that do not correspond to any property value in P). The phrase "*written in 1946*" in the text in Fig. 14 is such an example. Similarly, the sentence about "*opinion of other pediatricians*" is not supported by the available entity properties.

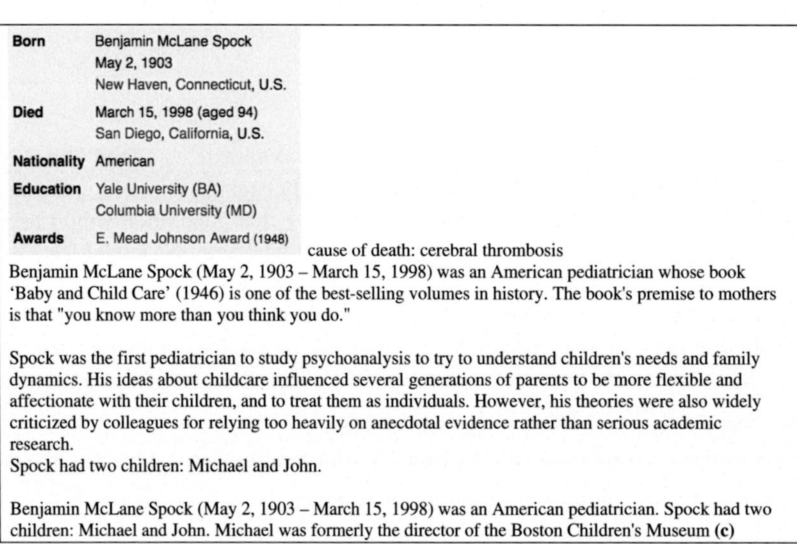

FIG. 14

Property value pairs (a), related biographic abstract (b) for the Wikipedia entity Robert Flaherty, and model verbalization in italics (c).

The model checks the content in both directions; it identifies which properties have a corresponding text span (data selection) and foregrounds (un)aligned text spans (text selection). This knowledge is then used to discourage the generator from producing text not supported by facts in the property set P. The property set P and its loosely coupled text T is viewed as a coarse-level, imperfect alignment. From this alignment signal, a set of finer-grained alignments is being discovered, indicating which mention spans in T align to which properties in P. For each pair (P, T), an alignment set $A(P,T)$ is formed, which contains property-value word pairs. For example, for the properties *children* and *director* in Fig. 14, we would like to derive the alignments.

The task of discovering finer-grained word alignments is posed as a multi-instance learning problem. Words from the text are assigned positive labels for some property values, but it is not known which ones. For each data-text pair (P,T), $|T|$ pairs of the form (P, s) are derived, where $|T|$ is the number of sentences in T. The property sets P and sentences s are encoded into a common multimodal h-dimensional embedding space. While doing this, finer-grained alignments are obtained between words and property values. The intuition is that by learning a high similarity score for a property set P and sentence pair s, it is possible to learn the contribution of individual elements (i.e., words and property values) to the overall similarity score.

As there is no fixed order among the property-value pairs $p{:}v$ in P, we individually encode each one of them. Furthermore, both properties p and values v may consist of short phrases. For instance, the attribute *cause of death* and value *cerebral thrombosis* in Fig. 14. Property-value pairs are considered as concatenated sequences pv and use a bidirectional LSTM network for their encoding. Note that the same network is used for all pairs. Each property-value pair is encoded into a vector representation:

$$\mathbf{p}_i = \mathbf{biLSTM}_{denc}(\boldsymbol{pv}_i)$$

The alignment objective seeks to maximize the similarity score between property set P and a sentence s (Karpathy and Fei-Fei, 2015). This similarity score is in turn defined on top of the similarity scores among property values in P and words in s. This equation defines this similarity function using the dot product. The function attempts to align each word to the best scoring property value:

$$S_{Ps} = \sum_{t=1}^{|s|} \max_{i \in} \{1, \ldots, |P|\} \mathbf{p}_i \cdot \mathbf{w}_t$$

6. Graph-based fact-checking

Given a knowledge graph and a fact (a triple statement), a fact-checking operation decides whether the fact belongs to the existing part of the graph (confirmation) or a missing part of the graph (rejection as a fact).

Fig. 15 shows how to use Wikipedia to fact-check statements. To populate the knowledge graph with facts, we use structured information contained in the "infoboxes" of Wikipedia articles (left, infobox of the article about Dr. Benjamin Spock). Using the Wikipedia Knowledge Graph (WKG), computing the truth value of a subject-predicate-object statement is implemented as finding a path between *subject* and *object* entities. The shortest path is shown returned by the method for the query "*Dr Spock*

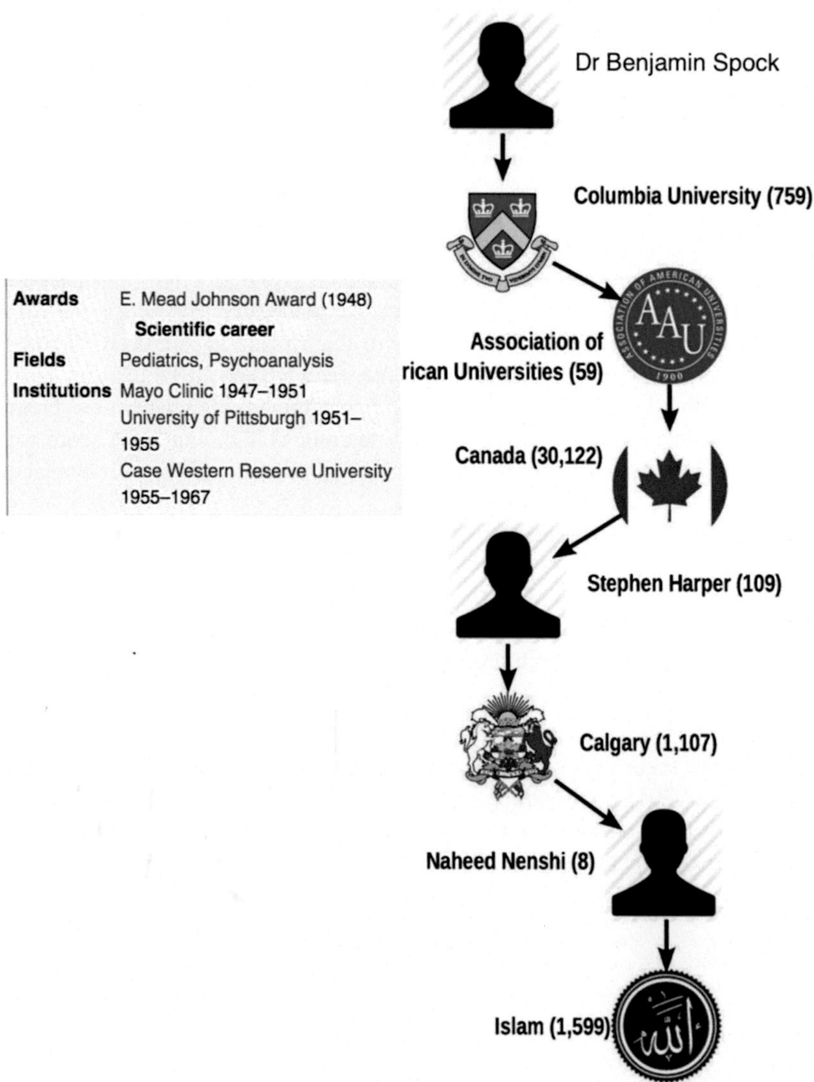

FIG. 15

Fact-checking based on Wikipedia.

related to islam." The numbers in parentheses indicate the degree of the nodes. The path traverses high-degree nodes representing generic entities, such as *Canada*, and is assigned a low truth value.

Ciampaglia et al. (2015) showed that we can leverage any collection of factual human knowledge, such as Wikipedia, for automatic fact-checking (Cohen et al., 2011). Loosely inspired by the principle of epistemic closure, the authors computationally build a support for statements by mining the connectivity patterns on a knowledge graph (Luper, 2012). The initial focus is on computing the support of simple statements of fact using a large-scale knowledge graph obtained from Wikipedia. In general, fact-checking can be seen as a special case of link prediction in knowledge graphs (Nickel et al., 2015).

Let the WKG be an undirected graph $G=(V, E)$ where V is a set of concept nodes and E is a set of predicate edges. Two nodes $v, w \in V$ are said to be *adjacent* if there is an edge between them $(v, w) \in E$. They are said to be *connected* if there a sequence of $n \geq 2$ nodes $v = v_1, v_2, \ldots v_n = w$, such that, for $i = 1, \ldots, n-1$ the nodes v_i and v_{i+1} are adjacent. The transitive closure of G is $G^* = (V, E^*)$ where the set of edges is closed under adjacency, that is, two nodes are adjacent in G if they are connected in G via at least one path. This standard notion of closure has been extended to weighted graphs, allowing adjacency to be generalized by measures of path length, such as the semantic proximity for the WKG we introduce next.

The truth value $\tau(e) \in [0,1]$ of a new statement $e = (s, p, o)$ is derived from a transitive closure of the WKG. More specifically, the truth value is obtained via a path evaluation function: $\tau(e) = \max W(P_{s,o})$. This function maps the set of possible paths connecting s and o to a truth value τ. A path has the form $P_{s,o} = v_1, v_2, \ldots v_n$, where v_i is an entity node, (v_i, v_{i+1}) is an edge, n is the path length measured by the number of its constituent nodes, $v_i = s$, and $v_n = o$. Various characteristics of a path can be taken as evidence in support of the truth value of e. Here we use the generality of the entities along a path as a measure of its length, which is in turn aggregated to define a semantic proximity:

$$W(P_{s,o}) = W(v_1 \ldots v_n) = \left[1 + \sum_{i=2}^{n-1} \log k(v_i)\right]^{-1}$$

where $k(v)$ is the degree of entity v (i.e., the number of WKG statements in which it participates); it, therefore, measures the generality of an entity. If e is already present in the WKG (i.e., there is an edge between s and o), it should obviously be assigned the maximum truth. In fact, $W = 1$ when $n = 2$ because there are no intermediate nodes. Otherwise, an indirect path of length $n > 2$ may be found via other nodes. The truth value $\tau(e)$ maximizes the semantic proximity defined by the preceding equation, which is equivalent to finding the shortest path between s and o (Simas and Rocha, 2013).

We illustrate the graph-based fact-checking method on the *bad cold* vs *flu* example (Fig. 16). The fact-checking method requires defining a measure of path semantic proximity by selecting a transitive closure algorithm such as the shortest paths and a directed WKG representation (Ciampaglia et al., 2015).

The schematic plot shows a subset of the WKG constituted by paths between the node for symptoms of a bad cold (*blue*) and flu (*red*). The position of the nodes is computed using a force-directed layout (Kamada and Kawai, 1989) that minimizes the distance between nodes connected by an edge that is weighted by a higher truth value. For clarity, only the most significant paths, whose values rank in the top 1% of truth values, are shown. This plot is shown for illustration of the WKG semantic similarity idea and should not be used to interpret the features.

Facts in knowledge graphs are often associated with nontrivial regularities that are jointly described by imposing both topological constraints and ontological closeness. Such regularities can be captured by subgraphs associated with the facts (Lin et al., 2018a).

Graph G_1 in Fig. 17 illustrates a fraction of DBpedia that depicts the facts about philosophers such as *Plato*. The ontology O_1 depicts semantic relationships among the entities that are referred by the

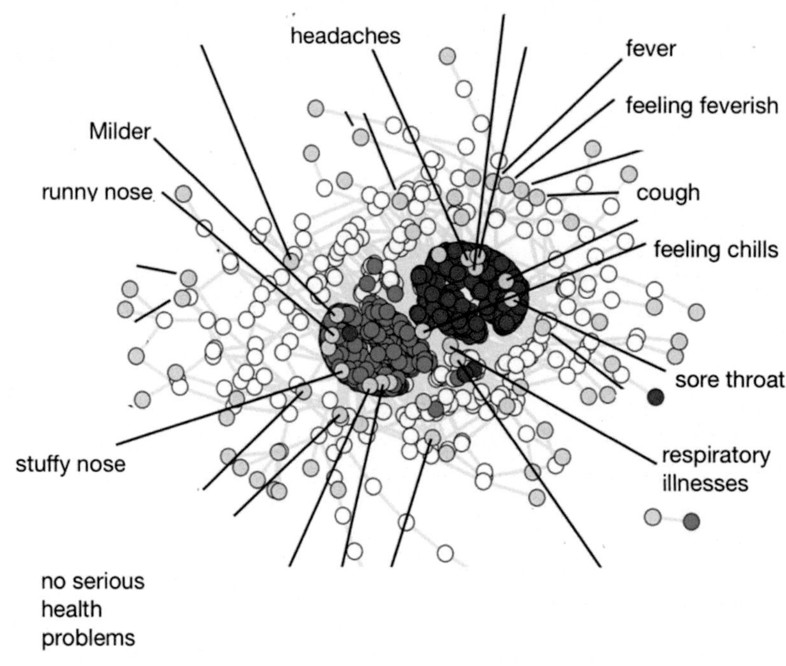

FIG. 16

A schematic plot for *bad cold* vs *flu* obtained from Wikipedia articles on the symptoms of these diseases.

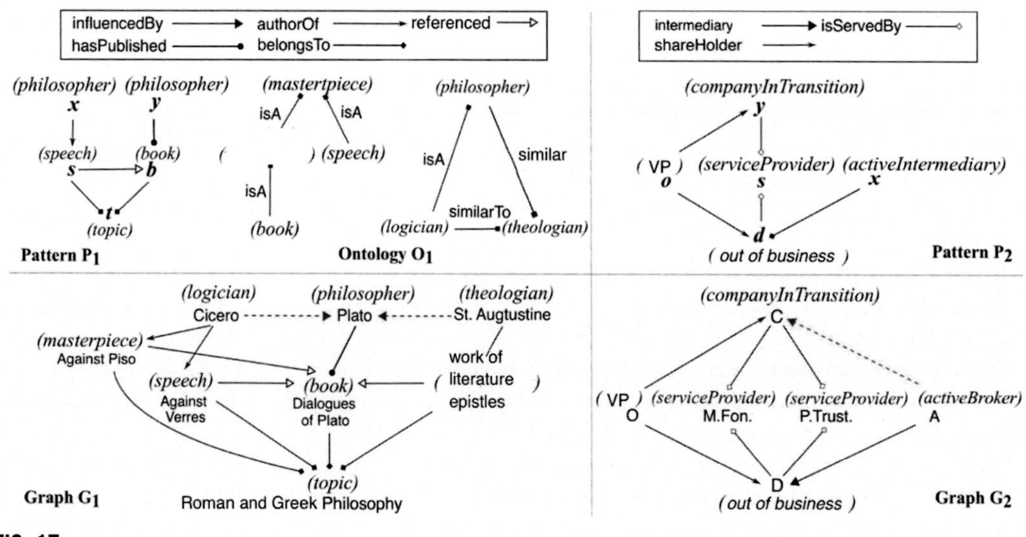

FIG. 17

A graph-based ontology for a fragment of DBpedia.

entity type in G_1. A query can be formulated about a person *Cicero* categorized as a logician or a theologian. *St. Augustine* is influenced by philosopher *Plato*. The graph patterns help to explain the existence of certain entities and relationships in KBs (Lin et al., 2018b).

The graph patterns can be easily interpreted as rules, and the matches of the graph patterns readily provide instance-level evidence to explain the associations between facts. These matches also indicate more accurate predictive models for various facts. We conclude that useful patterns with subgraphs and ontologies can be jointly characterized, discovered, and used in fact-checking in large knowledge graphs.

7. Entity substitution

Lexical substitution consists of finding the most probable alternatives (substitutes) of a target word given its context (McCarthy, 2002). It is well known and understood that entities that occur in similar contexts belong to the same concept(s). This can be seen as a special case of the distributional hypothesis, that is, terms that occur in the same contexts tend to have similar meanings (Harris, 1954).

Given an instance in different contexts, one can substitute it with another of the same ontological type (i.e., of the same category) and probably generate true statements. In fact, most of the predicates that can be asserted for an instance of a particular category can also be asserted for other instances of the same category. For instance, the sentence "*Dr Benjamin Spock is a legendary pediatrician*" preserves its truthfulness when *Dr Benjamin Spock* is replaced with *Dr. Leila Denmark*, while it is false when *Dr. Benjamin Spock* is replaced with the *Prof. Ralf Buhl* who is world-famous *neurosurgeon* and world top neurologist with more than 20 years of experience.

The Web provides a simple and effective solution to the problem of determining whether a statement is true or false. Due to the high redundancy of the Web, the high frequency of a statement generated by a substitution usually provides sufficient evidence for its truth, allowing us to easily implement an automatic method for fine-grained entity classification. Following this intuition, we develop an ontology population technique adopting pre-classified entities as training data (i.e., a partially populated ontology) to classify new ones.

When a new instance must be classified, we first collect snippets containing it from the Web. Then, for each snippet, we substitute the new instance with each of the training instances. The snippets play a crucial role in our approach because we expect that they provide the features that characterize the category to which the entity belongs. Thus, it is important to collect a sufficiently large number of snippets to capture the features that allow a fine-grained classification.

To estimate the correctness of each substitution, (Giuliano and Gliozzo, 2008) calculate a plausibility score using a modified version of the lexical substitution algorithm introduced in Giuliano et al. (2007) that assigns higher scores to the substitutions that generate highly frequent sentences on the Web. In particular, this technique ranks a given list of synonyms according to a similarity metric based on the occurrences in the Web 1T 5-gram corpus, which specify n-grams frequencies in a large Web sample. This approach demonstrated superior performance on the English Lexical Substitution task at SemEval 2007 (McCarthy and Navigli, 2007).

Web mining instance classification algorithm is as follows:

Step 1. For each candidate instance *i*, we collect via search engine API the first *N* snippets containing *i*.

Step 2. For each retrieved snippet q_k ($k< N$), a list of hypothesis phrases is obtained by replacing *i* with each training instance *j* from the available ontology. For instance, from the snippet "*about pediatrician legend Dr Benjamin Spock,*" we derive "*about pediatrician legend Dr. Leila Denmark*" and "about legend neurosurgeon *Ralf Buhl,*" assuming to have the former classified as a *pediatrician* and the latter as a *surgeon.*

Step 3. For each hypothesis phrase h_j, the plausibility score s_j is calculated using the sum of the point-wise mutual information (PMI) of all the n-grams ($1 < n < 6$) that contain *j* divided by the self-information of the right and left contexts. Dividing by the self-information allows us to assign a lower weight to the hypotheses that have contexts with a low information content, such as sequences of stop words. The frequency of the n-grams is estimated from the Web 1T 5-gram corpus. For instance, from the hypothesis phrase "*about pediatrician legend Dr. Benjamin Spock,*" we generate and score the following n-grams: "*according to pediatrician Dr. Benjamin Spock,*" "*as has been said by Benjamin Spock,*" and "*in the classical book for parents, Dr. Benjamin Spock.*"

Step 4. To obtain an overall score s_c for the category *c*, we sum the scores obtained from each training instance of category *c* for all snippets

$$s_c = \sum_{k=1}^{N}\sum_{l=1}^{M} s_l$$

where *M* is the number of training instances for the category *c*.

Step 5. Finally, the instance *i* is categorized with that concept having the maximum

$$\text{score}: c^* = \begin{cases} \underset{c}{\text{argmax}}\, s_c & \text{if}\, s_c \geq \theta; \\ \phi & \text{otherwise} \end{cases}$$

Here a higher value of the parameter θ improves the precision but drops the recall.

Any possible instance in WordNet has been identified by looking for all those synsets containing at least one word starting with a capital letter. The result is a set of instances *I*. All the remaining synsets are considered as concepts, collected in the set *C*. Then, *is_a* relations between synsets are converted into one of the following:

- X subclass-of Y if X is-a Y and $X \in C$ and $Y \in C$
- X instance-of Y if X is a Y and $X \in I$ and $Y \in C$

The formal semantics of both *subclass-of* and *instance-of* is formally defined in OWL-DL (W3C, 2012). *subclass_of* is a transitive relation (i.e., *X subclass-of Y* and *Y subclass-of Z* implies *X subclass-of Z*) and the instance of relation has the following property: *X instance-of Y* and *Y subclass-of Z* implies *X instance- of Z*. To define the ontology of human agents, a sub-hierarchy of WordNet representing people is used, identifying the corresponding top-level synset $X = \{$*person, individual, someone, somebody, mortal, soul*$\}$, and collecting all the classes *Y* such that *Y* is a subclass of *X* and all the instances *I* such that *I* is an instance of *Y*.

Fig. 18 shows the resultant taxonomy to substitute people. The node related to health professionals and the specialty of *Dr. Spock* is shown in red. A taxonomy can be automatically obtained via web mining (Galitsky et al., 2011).

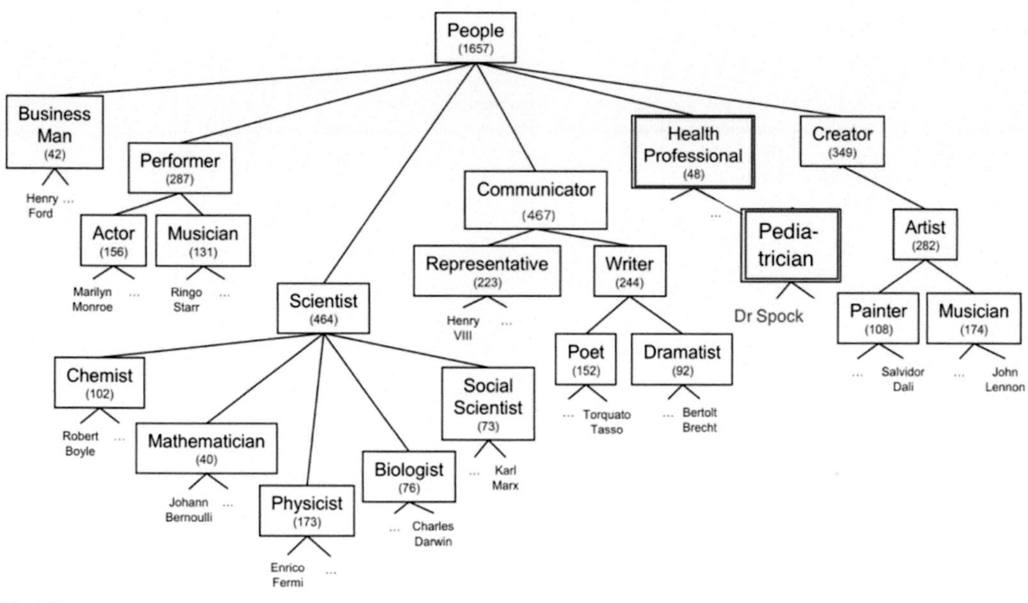

FIG. 18

Ontology of human agents.

8. Evaluation

We generate personalized drug intake recommendations given a patient's set conditions. We obtained the list of drugs from www.rxlist.com and selected 3000 drugs names. The list of medical conditions is available at www.medicinenet.com, from which we selected 500 conditions.

Firstly, we form the pairs of drug-condition (disease) where the relationships are *drug-treats-disease* as well as *side-effect-of-drug-under-condition*, *drug-cause-side-effect-under-condition*. We refer to this data as D-C pair set. In most cases, D is not intended to treat C; instead, we are concerned whether D *has a side-effect* on C, D *might-affect* C, D *might-cause-complication-of* C. Our choice of D-C association is connected with a *personalized recommendation* for a patient with C to take drug D.

These pairs are formed through exhaustive iteration through all drug-condition pairs and retaining these with an explicit relation. These relations were identified in texts about drugs and illnesses at www.rxlist.com/ and illnesses at www.medicinenet.com. As a result, we compile a list of 4600 pairs where we can experiment with writing a personalized content for drug D and a patient with condition C.

Table 3 Correction characteristics.

The class of common symptoms	#/% of corrected sentences (by substituting entities)		#/% of corrected sentences (by substituting phrases)		#/% of rejected sentences		#/% of sentences accepted as they are		Total # of raw sentences	Total # of true sentences used
Bloating	3.6	39.56	1.8	19.78	2.4	26.37	1.3	14.29	9.1	17.1
Cough	2.7	32.14	2.1	25.00	1.9	22.62	1.7	20.24	8.4	16.3
Diarrhea	3.0	33.71	2.1	23.60	2.3	25.84	1.5	16.85	8.9	19.0
Dizziness	2.7	30.68	2.3	26.14	2.5	28.41	1.3	14.77	8.8	18.7
Fatigue	2.9	35.80	1.9	23.46	2.0	24.69	1.3	16.05	8.1	20.4
Fever	3.5	36.84	2.0	21.05	2.4	25.26	1.6	16.84	9.5	19.3
Headache	3.0	36.59	1.7	20.73	2.1	25.61	1.4	17.07	8.2	17.5
Muscle cramp	2.8	32.94	2.2	25.88	2.0	23.53	1.5	17.65	8.5	19.0
Nausea	3.2	36.78	2.0	22.99	2.3	26.44	1.2	13.79	8.7	17.9
Throat irritation	3.1	37.35	1.7	20.48	1.9	22.89	1.6	19.28	8.3	16.4
Average	**3.05**	**35.24**	**1.98**	**22.91**	**2.18**	**25.17**	**1.44**	**16.68**	**8.65**	**18.16**

We show the correction characteristics in Table 3. In the leftmost column, the class of column symptoms is shown for each assessment group. In columns two to four, we show the averaged relative number and the absolute number of sentences subject to the certain operation:

(1) substitution of the entity
(2) substitution of the whole phrase
(3) rejection of the whole sentence

The relative number is computed as a portion of all sentences in raw text.

The right three columns show:

(1) the number and percentage of sentences accepted without modification
(2) the total number of raw sentences
(3) the total number of true sentences mined and used

We observe that in a short, personalized drug recommendation text, there are typically nine sentences in raw text. On average, three of them are corrected by substituting entities, two are corrected by substituting phrases, and more than two are rejected as non-correctable. To correct an average raw text, 18 sentences mined from the Web are needed.

To automatically assess the error rate of corrected content, we subject it to correction again, using a different web source. We count the number of sentences that failed fact-checking. Being automated, this assessment is not 100% accurate with false positives and false negatives, similar in nature with the original correction procedure. On the positive side, this automated assessment is applied to the full evaluation dataset.

We show the overall content generation and correction quality in Table 4. We measure the discourse distortion as a significant deviation of CDTs of original and corrected content (Section 2).

Table 4 The error rate of repaired generated content (%).

The class of common symptoms	Rate of wrong facts per text for **raw** content	Rate of wrong facts per text for **corrected** content	Rate of wrong facts per sentence for **raw** content	Rate of wrong facts per sentence for **corrected** content	Rate of **discourse** distortion per sentence
Bloating	89.6	15.3	68.4	6.4	23.1
Cough	93.5	16.4	70.2	7.1	21.8
Diarrhea	96.1	16.0	69.9	5.8	18.4
Dizziness	94.0	16.8	69.0	6.2	23.6
Fatigue	94.3	15.2	71.4	7.0	17.9
Fever	95.0	13.8	67.7	5.9	20.2
Headache	96.7	17.1	73.8	7.3	19.0
Muscle cramp	94.2	15.6	68.2	6.7	17.3
Nausea	97.1	17.0	67.3	7.2	21.0
Throat irritation	95.3	15.9	69.0	6.4	19.8
Average	94.58	15.91	69.49	6.60	20.21

We observe that only 6% of raw texts can be accepted without repair, according to the automated fact-checking. After correction, 84% of texts do not contain wrong facts. Almost 70% of wrong facts are in raw text, which is reduced to less than 7% by the correction procedure, according to the automated fact-checking. Each fifth text, being factually correct, has a distorted discourse structure, in comparison with the raw text, but we nevertheless accept them.

To automatically verify the truthfulness of the repaired generated content, we repeat the repair procedure and measure the frequency the repaired sentence or repaired phrase is not confirmed by a true sentence or phrase.

Finally, we perform a more accurate hybrid assessment of the resultant quality of content correction (Table 5). It combines automated fact-checking on the Web with manual assessment of meaningfulness. We show the assessment result in the second raw and verify that a deviation between auto and manual assessments do not exceed 10%.

9. Discussions

Natural Language Processing (NLP) techniques can be used to make inferences about peoples' mental states from what they write on Facebook, Twitter, and other social media. These inferences can then be used to create online pathways to direct people to health information and assistance and to generate personalized interventions. Regrettably, the computational methods used to collect, process, and utilize online writing data, as well as the evaluations of these techniques, are still dispersed in the literature. Calvo et al. (2017) proposed a taxonomy of data sources and techniques that have been used for mental health support and intervention. Specifically, the authors survey how social media and other data sources have been used to detect emotions and identify patients who may need psychological assistance; the computational techniques used in labeling and diagnosis. Also, the ways to generate and personalize mental health interventions are analyzed. This review enumerates areas of research where

Table 5 A manual assessment of error rate and ablation study (%).

<table>
<tr><th>System architecture</th><th>Rate of wrong facts per text for raw content</th><th>Rate of wrong facts per text for corrected content</th><th>Rate of wrong facts per sentence for raw content</th><th>Rate of wrong facts per sentence for corrected content</th><th>Rate of discourse distortion per sentence</th></tr>
<tr><td>Complete system – auto assessment</td><td rowspan="6">94.6</td><td>15.9</td><td rowspan="6">69.5</td><td>6.6</td><td>20.2</td></tr>
<tr><td>Complete system – hybrid/manual assessment</td><td>17.5</td><td>7.2</td><td>22.0</td></tr>
<tr><td>Reduced web mining to a number of medical domains</td><td>17.1</td><td>11.3</td><td>26.3</td></tr>
<tr><td>Keyword-based generalization</td><td>23.4</td><td>10.7</td><td>25.6</td></tr>
<tr><td>Always do phrase substitution</td><td>18.7</td><td>9.5</td><td>25.4</td></tr>
<tr><td>Always do entity substitution</td><td>17.0</td><td>8.3</td><td>27.9</td></tr>
</table>

NLP has been applied in the mental health literature. In addition, it develops a common language that draws together the fields of mental health, human-computer interaction, and NLP.

One of the key advancements helping medical systems to improve outcomes is the ability to consolidate and analyze clinical, quality, and operational/cost content and data. In this chapter, we proposed an efficient and high-quality content creation tool for providing personalized on-demand content to patients. The data and content enable clinicians and researchers to better understand specific health risks within a population based on the clinical history and genetic disposition (Oracle Healthcare, 2020).

Many unsuccessful applications of fact-checking cause plenty of sarcasm (Fig. 19). Facebook is an example of a spectacular failure of doing fact-checking at scale. A review (Bengani and Karbal, 2020) of the fact-checking labels on Facebook found that the company failed to consistently label content flagged by its own third-party partners. Facebook's 10 US fact-checking partners debunked more than 70 claims. The authors identified more than 1100 posts across Facebook and Instagram containing the debunked falsehoods; less than 50% have fact-checking labels, even in cases where there were minor deviations from the original vetted posts.

Facebook continues to cite its use of artificial intelligence (AI) to automate fact-checking across thousands or millions of copies of similar posts spreading the same piece of information, thereby enabling their fact-checkers to focus on new instances of misinformation rather than near-identical variations of content they have already seen. Facebook still struggles to recognize similar content at scale. For example, the authors found more than 20 instances of a meme that attributed the murder of a Black Chicago teenager to "other Black kids." At the same time, a fact-check by the Associated Press found that the cited murder investigation was still open. Facebook was unable to detect other iterations of the meme using NLP-based similarity-matching algorithms. On the bottom of Fig. 19, Facebook rejects a post of a book on AI in the "AI & Data Science" group. Fig. 20 illustrates the idea of careful treatment of content.

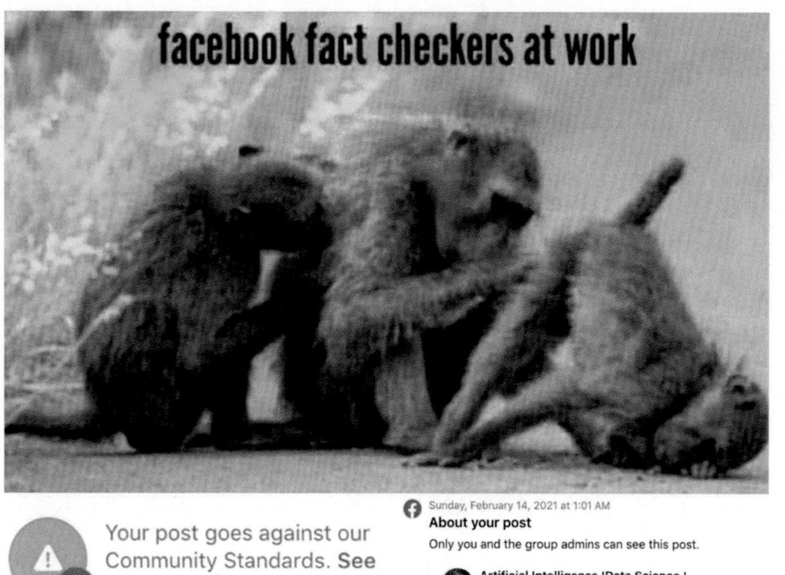

FIG. 19

An audience of users is making fun of Facebook fact-checking.

FIG. 20

It is important to protect certain essential pieces of content from distortion.

FIG. 21

The extra-knowledgeable fact-checking engine can embarrass its users.

We comment on why raw text generated by DL has significant flaws. In general, it is impractical to use machine learning (ML) to generate stuff rather than classify it. By the nature of texts obtained with DL learning, we observe that it is essentially averaging through multiple texts on the topic. What we need to do is to **de-average** by fact-checking, making the content crisp and truthful. Whereas averaging helps to implement some writing ideas, introduced factual noise need to be filtered (Fig. 21).

Content correcting is just one operation intended to automatically process content. A broad spectrum of content genres can be subject to correction, from news to technical description to opinionated content to manage public opinion. Other automated content processing operations are domain-specific; for example, a content inversion operation is needed to transform opinionated content from author-centric to topic-centric form to aggregate opinion (Galitsky, 2019c). Converting content from a document to a dialogue format is beneficial for several educational applications (Galitsky et al., 2019). Automated content compilation from various sources is another essential operation for textual data aggregation (Galitsky, 2016b). Forming utterances on the fly found its application in social promotion on Facebook and other platforms (Galitsky, 2015). Content can be noisy not because it is generated by a DL system but because it is user-generated; discourse-level analysis then helps to process it (Galitsky, 2020).

10. Conclusions

We observed that raw content produced by a DL system like GPT can be substantially improved for factual correctness and meaningfulness in several domains including health. Content generation is especially valuable for personalized medical recommendations where the content such as a description of treatment needs to be tailored to certain conditions.

In our previous studies, we proposed several approaches to the generation of a high volume of content without the use of DL (Galitsky, 2019a). As expected, a hybrid technique of correcting raw DL content instead of taking true content from various sources and modifying it turns out to be fruitful. Over the last decade, the value of generating original content for search engine optimization has been understood and confirmed. A hybrid approach to content generation, retaining the syntactic structure of raw content and relying on true sources to assure a high resultant quality of content, is badly needed by a number of applications, such as in health education (Galitsky, 2016a).

Moreover, chatbots rely on content generated on the fly and tailored to user utterances and preferences. In the study of Galitsky (2021), we address the issue of how to conclude a customer relationship management session in a comprehensive manner, to satisfy a user with the detailed extended answer with exhaustive information. For a question-answering session, the goal is to enable a user with thorough knowledge related to the user's initial question, from a simple fact to a comprehensive explanation. In many cases, a lengthy answer text, including multimedia content compiled from multiple sources, is the best. Whereas a comprehensive, detailed answer is useful most of the time, in some cases, an answer needs to defeat a patient claim or demand when it is unreasonable, unfair, or is originated from a bad mood.

Supplementary data sets

Please visit https://github.com/bgalitsky/relevance-based-on-parse-trees to access all supplementary data sets.

References

Aronson, J., 2009. Medication errors: what they are, how they happen, and how to avoid them. QJM 102, 513–521.

Bahdanau, D., Cho, K., Bengio, Y., 2015. Neural machine translation by jointly learning to align and translate. In: ICLR.

Bengani, P., Karbal, I., 2020. Five Days of Facebook Fact-Checking. The Media Today. https://www.cjr.org/analysis/five-days-of-facebook-fact-checking.php.

Calvo, R., Milne, D., Hussain, M.S., Christensen, H., 2017. Natural language processing in mental health applications using non-clinical texts. Nat. Lang. Eng. 23 (2017), 649–685.

Cawsey, A., Webber, B., Jones, R., 1999. Natural language generation in health care. J. Am. Med. Inform. Assoc. 4, 473–482. https://doi.org/10.1136/jamia.1997.0040473.

Cawsey, A., Jones, R., Pearson, J., 2000. The evaluation of a personalised information system for patients with cancer. UMUAI 10, 47–72.

Ciampaglia, G.L., Shiralkar, P., Rocha, L.M., Bollen, J., Menczer, F., Flammini, A., 2015. Computational fact checking from knowledge networks. PLoS One 10, e0128193.

Cohen, S., Hamilton, J.T., Turner, F., 2011. Computational journalism. Commun. ACM 54 (10), 66–71.

Dash, S., Shakyawar, S.K., Sharma, M., 2019. Big data in healthcare: management, analysis and future prospects. J. Big Data 6, 54.

DiMarco, C., Covvey, D., Bray, P., Cowan, D., Diciccio, V., Lipa, J., Mulholland, D., Cheriton, D., 2007. The development of a natural language generation system for personalized e-health information. J Inf. Technol. Healthcare, 195–199. Optimum Publisher.

Freitag, M., Roy, S., 2018. Unsupervised natural language generation with denoising autoencoders. In: EMNLP. pp. 3922–3929.

Galitsky, B., 2015. Recognizing intent and trust of a facebook friend to facilitate autonomous conversation. In: Workshops at the Twenty-Ninth AAAI Conference on Artificial Intelligence.

Galitsky, B., 2016a. Rehabilitating autistic reasoning. In: Computational Autism. Springer, Cham, Switzerland.

Galitsky, B., 2016b. A tool for efficient content compilation. In: Proceedings of COLING.

Galitsky, B., 2017. Improving relevance in a content pipeline via syntactic generalization. Eng. Appl. Artif. Intel. 58, 1–26.

Galitsky, B., 2019a. Assuring chatbot relevance at syntactic level. In: Developing Enterprise Chatbots: Learning Linguistic Structures. Springer, Cham, Switzerland, pp. 121–162.

Galitsky, B., 2019b. Learning discourse-level structures for question answering. In: Developing Enterprise Chatbots: Learning Linguistic Structures. Springer, Cham, Switzerland, pp. 177–220.

Galitsky, B., 2019c. Content Inversion for User Searches and Product Recommendations Systems and Methods. US Patent 10,402,411.

Galitsky, B., 2020. Utilizing Discourse Structure of Noisy User-Generated Content for Chatbot Learning. US Patent 10,599,885.

Galitsky, B., 2021. Concluding a CRM session. In: Artificial Intelligence for Customer Relationship Management: Solving Customer Problems. Springer, Cham, Switzerland.

Galitsky, B., Kovalerchuk, B., 2014. Improving web search relevance with learning structure of domain concepts. In: Aleskerov, F.T., et al. (Eds.), Clusters, Orders, and Trees: Methods and Applications. Springer, pp. 341–376.

Galitsky, B., Kuznetsov, S.O., 2013. A web mining tool for assistance with creative writing. In: European Conference on Information Retrieval, pp. 828–831.

Galitsky, B., Dobrocsi, G., de la Rosa, J.L., Kuznetsov, S.O., 2011. Using generalization of syntactic parse trees for taxonomy capture on the web. In: ICCS, pp. 104–117.

Galitsky, B., Dobrocsi, G., de la Rosa, J.L., 2012. Inferring semantic properties of sentences mining syntactic parse trees. Data Knowl. Eng. 81, 21–45.

Galitsky, B., Kuznetsov, S.O., Usikov, D., 2013. Parse thicket representation for multi-sentence search. In: International Conference on Conceptual Structures, pp. 153–172.

Galitsky, B., Ilvovsky, D., Kuznetsov, S.O., Strok, F., 2014. Finding maximal common sub-parse thickets for multi-sentence search. In: Croitoru, M., Rudolph, S., Woltran, S., Gonzales, C., (Eds.), Graph Structures for Knowledge Representation and Reasoning. Lecture Notes in Computer Science, Springer, Cham. 8323, pp. 39–57.

Galitsky, B., Ilvovsky, D., Goncharova, E., 2019. On a chatbot conducting dialogue-in-dialogue. In: Proceedings of the 20th Annual SIGdial Meeting on Discourse and Dialogue.

Giuliano, C., Gliozzo, A., 2008. Instance-based ontology population exploiting named-entity substitution. In: COLING, pp. 265–272.

Giuliano, C., Gliozzo, A., Strapparava, C., 2007. FBK-IRST: Lexical substitution task exploiting domain and syntagmatic coherence. In: Proceedings of the Fourth International Workshop on Semantic Evaluations (SemEval-2007), Prague, Czech Republic, June, pp. 145–148.

Hallett, C., Scott, D., 2005. Structural variation in generated health reports. In: 3rd International Workshop on Paraphrasing.

Harris, Z., 1954. Distributional structure. WORD 10, 146–162.

Hunter, J., Gatt, A., Portet, F., Reiter, E., Sripada, S., 2008. Using natural language generation technology to improve information flows in intensive care units. In: 18th European Conference on Artificial Intelligence, Patras, Greece, July 21-25, pp. 678–682.

Hüske-Kraus, 2003a. Suregen-2: A Shell System for the Generation of Clinical Documents. In: Proceedings of EACL-2003 (Demo Session).

Hüske-Kraus, 2003b. Text generation in clinical medicine—a review. Methods Inf. Med. 42, 51–60.

Kamada, T., Kawai, S., 1989. An algorithm for drawing general undirected graphs. Inf. Process. Lett. 31, 7–15.

Karpathy, A., Fei-Fei, L., 2015. Deep visual-semantic alignments for generating image descriptions. In: Proceedings of CVPR, Boston, Massachusetts, pp. 3128–3137.

Lebret, R., Grangier, D., Auli, M., 2016. Neural text generation from structured data with application to the biography domain. In: EMNLP, pp. 1203–1213.

Lin, P., Qi, S., Wu, Y., 2018a. Fact checking in knowledge graphs with ontological subgraph patterns. Data Sci. Eng. 3, 341–358.

Lin, P., Song, Q., Shen, J., Wu, Y., 2018b. Discovering graph patterns for fact checking in knowledge graphs. In: DASFAA.

Luper, S., 2012. The epistemic closure principle. In: Zalta, E.N. (Ed.), The Stanford Encyclopedia of Philosophy, fall ed. The Metaphysics Research Lab, Stanford University.

McCarthy, D., 2002. Lexical substitution as a task for WSD evaluation. In: Proceedings of the ACL02 Workshop on Word Sense Disambiguation, Morristown, NJ, USA, pp. 109–115.

McCarthy, D., Navigli, R., 2007. Semeval2007 task 10: English lexical substitution task. In: Proceedings of the Fourth International Workshop on Semantic Evaluations (SemEval-2007), Prague, Czech Republic, June, pp. 48–53.

McKeown, K.R., 1992. Text Generation. Cambridge University Press.

Mei, H., Bansal, M., Walter, M.R., 2016. What to talk about and how? Selective generation using LSTMs with coarse-to-fine alignment. In: NAACL-HLT, pp. 720–730.

Nickel, M., Murphy, K., Tresp, V., Gabrilovich, E., 2015. A review of relational machine learning for knowledge graphs: from multi-relational link prediction to automated knowledge graph construction. arXiv. preprint arXiv:150300759.

Oracle Healthcare, 2020. Forces of Change. https://www.oracle.com/webfolder/assets/ebook/health-science-industry-viewpoints/index.html#0.

Oracle Healthcare, 2021. Healthcare Industry Viewpoints. https://www.oracle.com/webfolder/assets/ebook/health-science-industry-viewpoints/index.html#0.

Perez-Beltrachini, L., Lapata, M., 2018. Bootstrapping generators from noisy data. In: Proceedings of the 2018 Conference of the North American Chapter of the Association for Computational Linguistics: Human Language Technologies, Volume 1 (Long Papers), New Orleans, Louisiana, pp. 1516–1527.

Puduppully, R., Dong, L., Lapata, M., 2019. Data-to-text generation with content selection and planning. AAAI 33 (01), 6908–6915.

Rosen, M.A., Diaz Granados, D., Dietz, A.S., Benishek, L.E., Thompson, D., Pronovost, P.J., Weaver, S.J., 2018. Teamwork in healthcare: key discoveries enabling safer, high-quality care. Am. Psychol. 73 (4), 433–450.

Simas, T., Rocha, L., 2013. Distance closures on complex networks. Network Sci. 3, 227–268.

Thimbleby, H., 2013. Technology and the future of healthcare. J. Public Health Res. 2 (3). https://doi.org/10.4081/jphr.2013.e28, e28.

Trisedya, B.D., Qi, J., Zhang, R., 2020. Sentence generation for entity description with content-plan attention. AAAI 34 (05), 9057–9064.

Tu, Z., Lu, Z., Liu, Y., Liu, X., Li, H., 2016. Modeling coverage for neural machine translation. In: ACL, pp. 76–85.

Verblio, 2020. Taking the Pulse of Medical Content Writing Challenges in Healthcare. https://www.verblio.com/blog/challenges-of-medical-content-writing.

W3C, 2012. OWL 2 Web Ontology Language Document Overview. https://www.w3.org/TR/owl2-overview/.

Wiseman, S., Shieber, S., Rush, A., 2017. Challenges in data-to-document generation. In: Palmer, M. (Ed.), EMNLP. ACL, pp. 2253–2263.

Index

Note: Page numbers followed by *f* indicate figures, *t* indicate tables, and *b* indicate boxes.

D

E

F

G

H

N

R

S

T

U

Printed in the United States
by Baker & Taylor Publisher Services

ARTIFICIAL INTELLIGENCE FOR HEALTHCARE APPLICATIONS AND MANAGEMENT

Boris Galitsky and Saveli Goldberg

Artificial Intelligence for Healthcare Applications and Management introduces application domains of various AI algorithms across healthcare management. Instead of discussing AI first and then exploring its applications in healthcare afterward, the authors attack the problems in context directly, in order to accelerate the path of an interested reader toward building industrial-strength healthcare applications. Readers will be introduced to a wide spectrum of AI applications supporting all stages of patient flow in a healthcare facility. The authors explain how AI supports patients throughout a healthcare facility, including diagnosis and treatment recommendations needed to get patients from the point of admission to the point of discharge while maintaining quality, patient safety, and patient/provider satisfaction.

AI methods are expected to decrease the burden on physicians, improve the quality of patient care, and decrease overall treatment costs. Current conditions affected by COVID-19 pose new challenges for healthcare management and learning how to apply AI will be important for a broad spectrum of students and mature professionals working in medical informatics. This book focuses on predictive analytics, health text processing, data aggregation, management of patients, and other fields which have all turned out to be bottlenecks for the efficient management of coronavirus patients.

Key Features

- Presents an in-depth exploration of how AI algorithms embedded in scheduling, prediction, automated support, personalization, and diagnostics can improve the efficiency of patient treatment
- Investigates explainable AI, including explainable decision support and machine learning, from limited data to back-up clinical decisions, and data analysis
- Offers hands-on skills to computer science and medical informatics students to aid them in designing intelligent systems for healthcare
- Informs a broad, multidisciplinary audience about a multitude of applications of machine learning and linguistics across various healthcare fields
- Introduces medical discourse analysis for a high-level representation of health texts

About the Authors

Dr. Boris Galitsky has contributed linguistic and machine learning technologies to Silicon Valley startups for the last 25 years, as well as eBay and Oracle, where he is currently an architect of a digital assistant project. An author of 5 computer science books, 300 publications and 50 patents, he is now researching how discourse analysis improves search relevance and supports dialogue management in health applications. In his previous books, Dr. Galitsky presented a foundation of autistic reasoning which shed light on how chatbots should facilitate conversations. He also wrote a two-volume monograph, titled *AI for Customer Relationship Management*, with a focus on discourse analysis for a deep understanding of customer needs.

Dr. Saveli Goldberg has contributed biostatistics and machine learning technologies to research at Harvard Medical School and Massachusetts General Hospital for the last 20 years, where he is currently a biostatistician and data analyst. The author of more than 80 publications and 2 patents, he is currently researching several projects in the field of radiation oncology and endocrinology. The main areas of his research include (a) optimal strategies in cancer radiation therapy, (b) optimal targets and strategies in the treatment of diabetes and hypertension, (c) the optimal combination of expert and artificial intelligence to get the right solution, (d) explanation of the machine learning solution, and (e) the relationship of electronic documentation to patient outcomes.

ISBN 978-0-12-824521-7